Some other books by John McIlwaine

Writings on African Archives
(Hans Zell Publishers, published for the
Standing Conference on Library Materials on Africa/SCOLMA, 1996)

Maps and Mapping of Africa: A Resource Guide
(Hans Zell Publishers, 1997)

Africa: A Guide to Reference Material

2nd revised and expanded edition

John McIlwaine

*Professor Emeritus of the Bibliography of Asia and Africa, School of Library,
Archive and Information Studies, University College London*

Hans Zell Publishing
Lochcarron ◆ Ross-shire ◆ Scotland

First edition 1993
Second revised and expanded edition 2007

British Library Cataloguing in Publication Data

McIlwaine, John
  Africa : a guide to reference material. – 2nd rev. ed.
  1. Africa – Bibliography
  I. Title
  016.9'6

  ISBN-13: 9780954102937

ISBN-10: 0-9541029-3-2   ISBN-13: 978-0-9541029-3-7

Published by Hans Zell Publishing (T/A Hans Zell Publishing Consultants)
Glais Bheinn • Lochcarron • Ross-shire IV54 8YB • Scotland • UK
Telephone: +44-(0)1520-722951 Fax: +44-(0)1520-722953
Email: hanszell@hanszell.co.uk or hzell@btopenworld.com
Web: www.hanszell.co.uk

Cover design by Michael Stuart Green, Lochcarron, Scotland.

Printed on acid-free paper.

Printed and bound in the United Kingdom by Antony Rowe Ltd., Chippenham, Wiltshire.

Contents

SOUTHERN AFRICA

Note: further subdivisions for regions and countries, where the volume of material requires, follow the pattern indicated above under AFRICA IN GENERAL

Preface to the 2ⁿᵈ edition

This is a new edition of the work originally published in 1993. In addition to including material published since 1992, the cut-off date for the first edition, the whole has been extensively revised, new categories of material have been included, and some older publications have been excluded. Detail on these changes follows.

CHANGES FROM THE 1ˢᵗ EDITION (AGRM1, 1993)

- The major change is that in order to save space, coverage is only of works **published in and since the year 1938** (this includes works whose original publication date was earlier, but which had a later edition or supplement published in or after 1938; also continuing sources which commenced publication before 1938, but continued to be issued after that year). This decision has been taken simply to make room for more recent material, and for new coverage of sources relating to the earth sciences and the biological sciences (*see* below). It in no way affects my view that older sources retain their value for their coverage of data contemporary with publication, and that older editions of a single source are potentially as valuable as later editions. Additionally, older sources may never have been succeeded by more modern titles covering the same field, and may remain the only convenient source of reference. AGRM1 included a substantial number of older imprints, some from the 19ᵗʰ century, and also a 30 page appendix, 'Annual reports on the British possessions in Africa' by Ia McIlwaine, and I hope this edition will be retained by libraries as continuing to be of value to researchers and as a companion to the present volume, AGRM2. I also hope that the pre-1938 imprints omitted from this edition may in future be mounted on a freely available Web site.

Why 1938? Principally because this year saw the publication of the first edition of Lord Hailey's **An African survey** whose pre-eminence as a reference source for the Africa of its time is noted below. "One has only to realize how often historians return to Hailey's 1938 *African survey*, to appreciate how rapidly information which appears to be common currency slips into an oblivion whence it is hard to retrieve" (David Birmingham, *JAH*, 21, 1980, 139). Also published this year was another product of the African Research Survey, namely E.B. Worthington's **Science in Africa: a review of scientific research relating to tropical and**

Southern Africa. (London, Oxford University Press, 1938). It was also the year of publication of the last German and last translated English edition of the very significant Martens & Karstedt's, **Afrika: ein Handbuch für Wirtschaft und Reisen**. 4th ed. (Berlin, Reimer, 1938) and **The African handbook: a guide to West, South and East Africa**. 2nd ed. (London, Allen & Unwin, 1938), and of regional works it was the year of publication of the immensely detailed Touring Club Italiano's **Africa orientale italiana**. (Milan, 1938). Choosing such a starting date also allows the inclusion of works such as the **Encyclopédie coloniale et maritime/ Encyclopédie de l'Afrique française**. (Paris, Éditions de l'empire français, 1940-1951. 7 vols. in 10) and the British Admiralty Naval Intelligence Division Geographical Handbook series volumes for **French West Africa**. (London, 1943-1944); **French Equatorial Africa and Cameroons**. (London, 1942); **The Belgian Congo**. (London, 1944). A number of large scale reference sources were produced by the colonial powers in the years immediately preceding and during World War II and between the end of the War and the securing of independence by the majority of African countries, and these continue to provide major sources for these countries in the generation before independence, and ones on which later reference sources have built.

- Because of the chronological limitation now imposed, *entries are arranged alphabetically by title or author*, rather than by date of publication as in the original edition (AGRM1). Entries for works that have appeared in more than one edition now list the latest edition first, and continuing works are listed under their most recent title.

- Subject coverage has been extended to cover works in the **earth sciences** and in the **biological sciences**, so that the overall work now more nearly approaches the coverage of Duignan and Gann (1971, 1973 *see* below). For details on the type of reference sources included for these subject fields, *see* the Introduction under 'Major categories included'.

- Greater emphasis has been placed on tracing reviews of the works listed. For more details *see* Introduction under 'Citation of reviews, etc.'

- The single index of the first edition has been divided into an Author/title index and a Subject index, with expanded coverage in the latter to accommodate the increased subject coverage of this edition.

Needless to say all entries carried over from AGRM1 have been re-checked in order to incorporate any corrections, new editions, supplements, translations and the like. Numerous items published earlier than 1992 (the cut-off date for AGRM1) are newly included.

An attempt has been made to include items published up to and including the Spring of 2006. A note has also been included of a few significant items and new editions recorded by publishers' Web sites as scheduled to appear later in 2006 and in 2007. All URLs have been checked up to July 2006, and information given about copies of latest issues in libraries is based upon catalogues searched in July/August 2006.

I estimate that some 80% of the titles listed in the present work have been personally inspected (*see* note below on libraries used). This proportion is probably less than for AGRM1 since there is a noticeable, increasing and very regrettable reluctance on the part of U.K. libraries to purchase copies of material published in Africa, and material, wherever published, in languages other than English. The other side of the coin is that once a potentially useful source has been identified from a secondary source, there are now many electronic sources in which its bibliographical details can be cross-checked. For individual items not seen, a note of the source of information is normally added (especially if secondary sources give conflicting data). A list of the sources most frequently cited is provided in the section for *Abbreviations*. It has not of course been possible to see every volume of continuing publications such as yearbooks, directories and statistical bulletins, since few libraries hold complete collections, and this category has presented the most severe problems. Details of change of title, frequency, coverage, relationships with other titles, and dates of publication have been conflated from a number of sources including partial holdings in more than one library, and entries in bibliographies and catalogues. With such continuing works details of all copies and/or of the latest copy actually traced are normally included, citing specific library holdings. Information for several items remains lacking, and although hopefully some errors and "ghosts" present in existing lists have been exorcised, I have no doubt at all but that others have been perpetuated or perpetrated. This is one area in particular where I hope that publication will stimulate users to provide corrections and additional information for a future edition. As indeed I hope they will for a work as a whole.

ACKNOWLEDGEMENTS

I am grateful to the staff of all the libraries noted in the Introduction, but particularly to those of the Afrika Studiecentrum Leiden, and especially to Marlene van Doorn, Katrien Polman and Ella Verkaik for their unfailing hospitality and ready welcome for the U.K. visitor. I should also like to acknowledge the use for the first edition of the Ministry of Defence Library where Michael Chambers checked the Library's entire holdings of War Office reports on Africa, made them accessible to me and supplied information about the War Office and Admiralty series numbering systems; and of the Foreign

& Commonwealth Office Library where the late Margaret Cousins gathered together large quantities of material from the further reaches of the Library which was in the throes of being drastically weeded, and made them available to me in her own office.

For much material present in both editions I am most grateful to the late Donald Simpson for access to the collections of the Royal Commonwealth Society when they were still in the Society's London home, and to his successor Terry Barringer for allowing me privileged access both to the collections in London and in the early years after their move to Cambridge, and for constantly bringing material to my attention during our long association on *African research & documentation*. I should like to acknowledge the assistance, often unconscious on their part, provided over the years by my colleagues on the committee of SCOLMA. I am also particularly grateful to Ana da Cunha of the Arquivo Histórico Ultramarino in Lisbon for checking Portuguese references, and I should like to acknowledge those who responded to my appeal for comments on the series of articles on "Flora and fauna of Africa" in *African research & documentation* especially David Ambrose, David Frodin, Diana Rosenberg.

Finally, inevitably and rightly, acknowledgements to spouse and publisher. To my wife for support, criticism, and help with the indexes, and for patiently coping with my unsystematic approach. Also for the compilation of the entries for the U.K. Colonial Reports series, listed in summary under the appropriate country in AGRM2 and in extenso, with each year's issue identified in the appendix to AGRM1. To Hans Zell for asking me to produce a new edition, and for his patience and encouragement while I was compiling it.

JHM
Norfolk & London, September 2006

Introduction

The intention behind the compilation of this work is to provide a guide to the major reference sources, other than bibliographies, which relate to Africa south of the Sahara.

Bibliographies of Africa are comparatively well covered. J.D. Pearson's **World bibliography of African bibliographies** (Oxford, Blackwell, 1975) provides a detailed listing to its date, although without annotation, and the magisterial works of Yvette Scheven, **Bibliographies for African studies, 1970-1985** (Oxford, Hans Zell, 1988) and **Bibliographies for African studies, 1987-1993** (London, Hans Zell, 1994) are comprehensive and annotated. More specific regional coverage is available from L. Porgès, **Sources d'information sur l'Afrique noire Francophone** (Paris, ORSTOM, 1988). However, coverage of *other* categories of reference work is much less readily available. The most substantial work in existence before the first edition of the present work was the **Guide to research and reference works on Sub-Saharan Africa**, comp. by Peter Duignan and Helen Conover and edited by Peter Duignan (Stanford, Hoover Institution, 1971) which in 1,102pp. has over 3,000 numbered and annotated references (*see* p. xlvii below for fuller details). This includes bibliographies, reference works of the quick-reference nature, and major secondary works in the shape of standard works (both monographs and journals) on history, geography, anthropology, politics, etc. The argument in its preface was that since works of a 'quick-reference' nature were comparatively few for Africa, and those that existed left obvious gaps, it was necessary to supplement these by listing 'standard' monographs as well. The resulting work remains extremely useful, but to attempt to provide an up-dated version with the same scope would now be trying to do much at once.

The present work covers only one of Duignan's three categories, namely 'reference material', in the narrower sense of the term, leaving bibliographies to be covered by the sources noted above, and standard works on individual topics to be covered by appropriate subject or regional guides. The question that then needs to be asked is: what is meant by 'reference material'? With bibliographies, the question is perhaps simpler: a bibliography is a bibliography (when it is not an index, a union list, a library catalogue, an on-line database etc.!). 'Reference material', even when one has specifically excluded bibliographies, is a much vaguer term. Two main characteristics of the majority of titles that will be found in AGRM2 are firstly that they are concerned primarily with providing **factual** data, rather than interpretation, and secondly, that their arrangement is intended to facilitate **rapid** consultation, rather than requiring the whole text to be scanned to locate facts. Such tidy guidelines are of course easy to draw and impossible to maintain. For example, perhaps the first 'reference work' for Africa that would come into many minds would be Lord Hailey's **An African survey**, a volume that accompanies its extensive factual data by equally extensive comment and interpretation, and that is arranged as a straightforward monograph with chapters, rather than having a quick-reference structure. It is of course also wrong to suggest that collections of factual information imply no interpretation: the very process of selection of what data to include and what to exclude, and how they should be presented obviously involves interpretation. The decision on what to include and exclude in this guide is therefore ultimately a very personal one, and must inevitably reflect what Humpty-Dumpty might have said, "a reference book is what I have chosen to call a reference book".

It is hoped that the present work can function at different levels. It should be able to provide reasonably rapid access to a specific source for an enquirer seeking a particular piece of information, but it is also intended to provide additional information on the sources listed for both librarians and researchers who are interested to know the circumstances of compilation and the strengths and weaknesses of the resulting title. Hence the attempt to include a range of reviews, and, for some of the more major sources, references to articles and reports about their compilation. It should of course be noted that inclusion does not imply recommendation. A number of works are included about whose value both I and reviewers have considerable doubts which are indicated in the annotations. They are works that researchers will find on library shelves or on the Web and it is appropriate to voice warnings about their use. For discussion of annotations and reviews see below.

GEOGRAPHICAL COVERAGE

Coverage is of Africa south of the Sahara - that is of Africa other than the countries of the Mediterranean littoral: Morocco, Algeria, Tunisia, Libya and Egypt. The islands and island groups of Cape Verde, the Comoros, Madagascar, Mauritius, Mayotte, Réunion, São Tome e Príncipe, St. Helena and the Seychelles are included. Christopher Fyfe has argued that Sub-Saharan Africa is a "sloppy, lazy-minded" division which "presents the Sahara as a barrier rather than the bridge it has always been" (*JAH*, 20, 1969, 311), but in the context of the present work the division does make sense, since many reference sources take either the 'Middle East and North Africa' or 'Sub-Saharan Africa' as their concern. Western Sahara remains a disputed territory and continues to be included in this edition as a separate entity, although now claimed by a North African country, Morocco, which is not included.

In this edition, material on the earth and biological sciences is included for the first time. The major biogeographical regions within which Africa lies, the Palaearctic Region and the Afrotropical Region, correspond more or less neatly to the North Africa/Sub-Saharan Africa divide. Many sources take the dividing line as following the latitude of 21° N. from the Atlantic coast across the Sahara, swinging northward to about 22°50′ N. at the Red Sea. This means that works concerned with the Palaearctic will often include Cape Verde and Western Sahara, the northern half of Mauritania, and small portions of the northern parts of Niger, Chad and the Sudan. In AGRM2 definition of Francophone West Africa is broadened in the sciences to include works on the Sahara and the Sahel. Note too that the term Afrotropical Region is a relatively new one and that until at least the late 1970s, in biological terms the whole of Sub-Saharan Africa was normally referred to as the Ethiopian Region, and this will be reflected in titles included. (*See* R. Crosskey & G.B. White, 'The Afrotropical Region: a recommended term in zoogeography', *Journal of natural history*, 11, 1977, 541-544 and 'Afrotropical Region: a substitute name for Sclater's Ethiopian Region', *Ibis*, 121, 1979, 518). Additionally, some works on the Afrotropical Region see the Malagasy Region with its very distinct flora and fauna, as a separate entity and do not include it. A further point is that the zoogeographical definition of Southern Africa differs from the normal political definition as used in the contents list of AGRM2 and covers the land lying south of a line between the Kunene (Cunene) and Zambesi rivers, or approximately south of 17° S. Latitude, and including therefore Botswana, Lesotho, Namibia, South Africa, Swaziland and southern Mozambique (i.e. omitting northern Mozambique and Angola).

SOURCES *EXCLUDED*

It may be useful at this stage to provide a list of some categories of material which have been deliberately **excluded**, with indications of other bibliographical sources in which they may be sought:

Bibliographies, indexes, abstracts, etc. Although this exclusion is emphasised in the second paragraph of the Preface above, it is repeated here. Some reviewers of AGRM1 expressed surprise that it did not include guides to archival collections. No source is included whose primary purpose, whatever its label, is to list or describe publications or unpublished documents. The *only exception* is to list **bibliographies of reference works** or of particular categories of reference works (e.g. of biographical sources, statistical sources, etc.). Obviously a number of the other sources listed may contain extensive bibliographical support for their primary focus (e.g. the Scarecrow Press **Historical dictionaries**). Those seeking guidance to bibliographies on African topics should consult Pearson and Scheven (*see* above) and also the continuing 'Africana reference works' in *African book publishing record* (*ABPR*) noted below.

Monolingual African language dictionaries and interlingual dictionaries. These are covered in detail by M.K. Hendrix, **An international bibliography of African lexicons** (Metuchen, NJ, Scarecrow Press, 1982) which records over 2,600 dictionaries and phrase books. David Westley, 'WorldCat and African lexicography since 1980', pp. 169-197 in **Africanist librarianship in an era of change**, ed. Vicki Evalds & David Henige. (Lanham, MD, Scarecrow Press, 2005) lists some 240 titles published 1980-2003 as a supplement to Hendrix. Dictionaries can also be traced in the ongoing African linguistic bibliographies series (Hamburg, Buske Verlag), with volumes published to date for Yoruba (1987); Mande languages (1988); Nubian languages (1993); Hausa & Chadic languages (1996) and the languages of Uganda (1999). The annual listings of reference works in *ABPR* are also very conscientious in listing interlingual dictionaries. The Bisharat Web site http://www.bisharat.net (*see* ASC4, 166) contains a wide range of data on African languages, together with links to over 200 other Web sites including some online dictionaries. *See* also yourDictionary.com:language dictionaries http://www.yourdictionary.com/languages.html#table (*see* ASC4, 169) which provides links to online glossaries, wordlists, and full scale dictionaries, also a few direct translation programmes. Numerous African languages are represented.

Collections of printed texts of laws, treaties, constitutions and other documents, although of course some of the more general compendious sources that are included may contain sections which cover such material. This is a category of source, with originals augmented by microform editions and digital libraries that could usefully form the topic of a separate bibliographical compilation.

Handbooks & guides whose focus is narrowed by the specific group for whom they were intended. Examples would include those for the immigrant, for those in business (with emphasis on trade and financial information), and for the tourist. Exceptions have of course been made and materials included from all these categories, where the works concerned were significantly more detailed or up-to-date than their fellows or where there was a noticeable absence of any other reference source for the region and period covered (examples include the Hachette **Guides bleus**, and works produced by the Touring Club Italiano and the Office du Tourisme du Congo Belge). In general more exceptions have been made for older publications in this category. For contemporary travel guides, the reader is referred to Louis Taussig, **Resource guide to travel in Sub-Saharan Africa**. Oxford, Hans Zell, 1993-1997. 2 vols. (Vol. 1, East and West Africa; vol.2, Central and Southern Africa (and Western Indian Ocean Islands). Reviews, *ARD*, 69, 1995, 53-54; 77, 1998, 47-48) again supplemented by the annual listings in *ABPR*.

General reference sources, covering the whole world, or the Third or "Developing" world. These have been included only sparingly. Where a general source has a specific and readily identifiable section, usually a separate volume, devoted to Africa, for example Gale's **Cities of the world, vol. 1 Africa** this is of course included. Again exceptions are made in cases where little or no specific or regularly revised African coverage is available, and general works on topics such as the European colonial empires and slavery where African content often dominates, are usually included.

More specific categories of *exclusion* are noted below under 'major categories included'.

SELECTIVITY

The selection process has been modified by the varying degrees of availability of material for differing regions of Africa. I have for example been much more selective in listing sources for South Africa (although hopefully covering most significant titles) than for some of the less well recorded countries of North-East, West and Central Africa and the Indian Ocean Islands, e.g. Djibouti, Equatorial Guinea, Réunion.

ARRANGEMENT

Following a general section on Africa as a whole, material is **arranged under the broad regions** of North-East Africa, East Africa, Central Africa, West Africa and Southern Africa, and then by individual sub-regions and countries. Allocation of countries to regions is reasonably conventional, and can be traced from the *Table of Contents*. For Central, West and Southern Africa, countries are initially arranged in groups corresponding to their major European language and former colonial affiliation: for West Africa for example, there are sections for Anglophone, Francophone, Lusophone and former Spanish-speaking areas. This corresponds to the coverage of many of the sources listed, especially of the older literature. Reference works confined to smaller administrative divisions within countries: states, provinces, etc., are only included sparingly, and where there is strong historical warrant (e.g. Katanga, Zanzibar).

Under each geographical unit (whether West Africa, Anglophone West Africa or Ghana for example) material is arranged **according to eight broad categories**: *Handbooks, Yearbooks, Statistics, Directories of organizations, Biographical sources, Atlases & Gazetteers, Earth sciences* and *Biological sciences*. There are notes below on the type of sources which one may expect to find under each of these headings. For regions or countries with a substantial number of references under any one heading, there will be further subdivisions. Cross references are provided to related material.

MAJOR CATEGORIES INCLUDED

Handbooks

This is the section with the most diverse contents. It includes compendious works (which may be entitled handbooks, dictionaries, encyclopaedias, companions, guides, surveys and similar terms) which are concerned with presenting information in a readily accessible format about a region, country, or subject. These include multi-volume encyclopaedias, subject dictionaries, individual works which nevertheless conform to a pattern, such as the guides produced by colonial administrators, a classic example being W.N. Brelsford's **Handbook to the Federation of Rhodesia and Nyasaland**, official works produced by Ministries of Information and more commercially oriented titles produced by various local concerns such as newspapers, railway companies or airlines, and chambers of commerce. Also included are more general works such as Lord Hailey's **African survey**, and scholarly compilations like the International African Institute's **Ethnographic survey of Africa** and **Handbook of African languages** and the Cambridge and UNESCO multi-volume histories of Africa.

Many of the volumes listed in this section come from one of several extensive series each with a range of titles relevant to Africa. Rather than annotate each and every example, general comments on some of the major series follow.

African historical dictionaries, a series from Scarecrow Press, commenced in 1974 providing a separate volume for each country. The basic layout of each volume comprises a note on place-names, and a chronology of major events followed by the dictionary proper, with entries for events, individuals, political parties, etc. There is usually a substantial bibliographical section without annotations. Criticisms of this series in the Africanist journals have been fierce (*see* pp. xlii-xliii for details) noting in particular inaccuracies in detail and lack of overall editorial control. Perhaps their most valuable contribution is in providing guidance for the English-speaking reader for some of the less well known countries of Francophone, Lusophone and former Spanish Africa.

Area handbooks/Country studies. A series originally designed to provide compilations of basic facts for use by United States military and diplomatic personnel in their relationships with the rest of the world. Compilation and editing was for many years undertaken by the Foreign Area Studies Division of the American University in Washington, under contract for the U.S. Department of the Army. A largely standardised format has a brief country profile followed by 'historical setting', 'political system', 'physical and social setting', 'the economy' and 'national security'. Each section usually has an extensive bibliography, there are numerous statistical tables, a glossary of terms and an index. In 1978 the name of the series was changed to **Country studies**. This was applied to new volumes, to new editions of existing volumes, and in one or two cases to unchanged reprints of existing volumes. The intention of the change was to make the series have appeal to a wider audience, which often led to a significant reduction in the amount of detail in later editions. Earlier editions therefore remain valuable not just for their contemporary relevance but because they cover topics that are omitted from later editions. The Library of Congress Federal Research Division took over responsibility for the series in 1987, and the texts of all the volumes produced since then are also freely available online (*see* **9**). In 2005 the Library of Congress commenced a parallel series of very brief overviews entitled **Country profiles**, available as both printed pamphlets and online (*see* **34**).

British War Office series: military reports, handbooks etc. and **British Admiralty series**. A large number of titles produced by the Intelligence Divisions of these two Ministries were included in AGRM1, the majority published in the nineteenth century and the early twentieth. Initially prepared for internal confidential use, they later became more widely available. Several volumes were produced during World War 2 and are listed in the present volume, the most notable being the B.R. (Books of Reference) series produced by the Admiralty from 1942 (*see* **1460, 1610, 2105**).

Landenreeks series compiled under the auspices of the Koninklijk Instituut voor de Tropen in Amsterdam and published in a standard and accessible format usually of 74/80pp. covering peoples, politics, the economy and cultural life in over 20 Sub-Saharan African countries from 1994 to 2005.

Die Länder Afrikas series published by the Deutsche Afrika-Gesellschaft during the late 1950s and 1960s provides individual volumes compiled by specialists for most African countries, with much factual data in compact form, and an emphasis on statistics. A number of volumes went into significantly expanded 2nd editions.

Notes et études documentaires. Issued by the French government's Direction de la Documention. These provide brief (usually 40/60pp) background surveys for individual countries of Francophone Africa emphasising the administration, the economy, and statistics at the time of compilation. Most countries were covered by volumes issued in the late 1950s and early 1960s giving data contemporary with the coming of independence. Some were also later covered by revised editions in the late 1960s and early 1970s. The commercial series **Encyclopédie politique et constitutionnelle. Série Afrique** of the 1970s offers very similar coverage for the Francophone countries and a similar and more recent successor for the same range of countries is the **Collection guide d'information** produced by the French Ministère de la coopération in the 1990s.

Terres lointaines and **Pays africains**. These two related series were issued by the Société d'éditions géographiques, maritimes et coloniales in Paris. Volumes in the "Terres lointaines" series give encyclopedic treatment to groups of countries, mostly French colonies but also to other regions. The "Pays africains" series provides shorter handbooks, concentrating on the contemporary scene, for individual countries, all Francophone.

A series of individual volumes, lacking an overall title but providing standardised surveys of history, politics and economics for most African countries was compiled by the Afrika Institut, Akademiia Nauk in Moscow in the 1970s, 1980s and 1990s.

Yearbooks

A mixed category containing works variously entitled Yearbook/Annual/ Annuaire/Anuário/Almanac(k)/Directory. In a sense, these are compendious sources, like many of those in the **Handbooks** category above, that are updated and re-issued on a regular basis and normally emphasize the recording of current information. Many yearbooks and annuals of course appear much more infrequently than annually, and indeed a number of the sources noted here never proceeded beyond their first issue. Two major categories will be found. **Official sources** will usually emphasize the current structure of the administration and its activities during the preceding year, often with extensive statistics. The general "annual reports" issued by the colonial powers, and exemplified by the long series produced by the British Colonial Office are listed here with a brief summary of the bibliographic history of each report. Fuller details of the Colonial Office reports including individual Command numbers can be found in Ia McIlwaine's Appendix to AGRM1. **Commercial sources** will often concentrate on providing economic, industrial and financial information and some will be largely confined to providing lists of organizations in these spheres. Works which are solely concerned with giving names and addresses of commercial firms, and which proliferate in South Africa for example, have been listed only sparingly, with the major examples for any country cited. Among categories **excluded** from this section are telephone directories and 'yellow books', annual reports of individual ministries (as opposed to those of the national or colonial government as a whole) and annuals, often produced by local journals, which contain articles rather than structured factual data, e.g. *Annuaire des pays de l'Océan indien*. Some titles which call themselves 'Handbooks' are nevertheless listed in this section, since their emphasis is on regular production of new issues with data such as civil lists and commercial directories.

Statistics

Coverage is of substantial 'one-off' statistical compilations, and of the principal **general statistical series** (bulletins and yearbooks) for each region or country as issued by the regional or national statistical agency, or by the appropriate colonial power or international agency. No attempt is made to cover more specialized statistical series, e.g. for trade or agricultural production, for which reference may be made to the bibliographies listed at the beginning of the section for **Statistics: Africa**. Similarly, individual **population census reports** are not listed, but details are provided of the major sources which will give information on these. Important series covering most Sub-Saharan African countries are those produced by the Economist Intelligence Unit (EIU) in the U.K., by the International Monetary Fund (IMF) and by the Statistisches Bundesamt in Germany in their series *Länderberichte*.

Directories of organizations

This somewhat clumsy title is chosen to emphasize that these are not general directories in the sense of titles which are included with almanacks and annuals under **Yearbooks**. Rather these are guides that are largely concerned with listing organizations: lists of societies, research institutions, libraries, museums, universities, commercial and industrial institutions. Also included are directories of individual specialists (scientists, researchers) which offer an alternative guide to the names of the institutions to which they are attached. Many of the titles listed in the **Handbooks** and **Yearbooks** category above will of course also have sections devoted to listing organizations.

Biographical sources

Listed here are works of collective biography of the 'who's who' (the notable living) or 'dictionary of national biography' (the notable dead) nature. Coverage is usually limited to works covering a whole region or country, or substantial and significant groups within these (political leaders, members of a particular ethnic or social group) and does not include biographical works confined to a particular profession (e.g. lawyers). Lists of current government officials (civil lists) are not included. Many of the works in the categories *Handbooks* and *Yearbooks* will of course include biographical sections and the annotations endeavour to draw attention to this. Also included are works on genealogy. Works on onomastics will be found under *Handbooks*.

Atlases & gazetteers

This section is normally subdivided according to these two categories of source. Under **atlases**, in addition to specialist titles, some fairly popular works are included for certain countries, where little else in atlas form provides specific coverage. Historical atlases will be found in the *Handbooks* section. Collections of facsimiles of early maps are treated as atlases and entered here. In the annotations, indications are given where possible and appropriate of the major scales of the maps provided, providing some indication of the depth of coverage available. Under **gazetteers** are also entered guides to place-names, and a selection of works that discuss the characteristic features or problems of local place-names and can be useful in interpreting gazetteers. Also included (and not covered by AGRM1) are **pilots** (sailing directions). More detailed coverage of such materials, including for example much greater coverage of school atlases, will be found in J.H. McIlwaine. **Maps and mapping of Africa: a resource guide**. London, Hans Zell, 1997.

Earth sciences and *Biological sciences*. Coverage of these is new for this edition. I decided soon after the publication of AGRM1, basically concerned with the human and social sciences, that it would be useful for a new edition to extend the subject coverage to include what I have called the Earth sciences, by which I mean fields such as Physical Geography, Geology, Geomorphology, Stratigraphy, Pedology, Mineralogy, Hydrology, Limnology, Oceanography, Climatology and Meteorology, and the Biological sciences, including Zoology, Botany and Ecology. These are very much the fields covered by E.B. Worthington's. **Science in Africa** (London, Oxford, 1938, *see* **664**) and by UNESCO's **A review of the natural resources of the African continent**. (Paris, 1963, *see* **642**).

Reference sources in these two broad collections of disciplines are taken to mean those which provide **factual** data on the topics studied within the disciplines: geological strata, minerals, soils, lake and river systems, weather statistics, vegetation, plant and animal species. In the biological sciences these can readily be identified as including taxonomic checklists concerned with establishing the particular species to be found within a given area;

handbooks/manuals/floras with detailed treatment of species; field/ identification guides with emphasis on illustration, and atlases and distribution guides mapping the distribution of species.

It is **not** intended to cover technologies. However there are certain technologies which are very closely associated with the earth and biological sciences, relating to the exploitation of resources and phenomena such as minerals (mining), soils, weather and vegetation (agriculture, forestry) and of animal species (animal husbandry, fishing), and reference sources often cover both the natural phenomenon and its use by man. The rule of thumb has been to include works in agriculture, forestry, mining, animal husbandry and fishing only where the emphasis is on the crops, trees, minerals, and animal species rather than on the management and marketing aspects of the disciplines. Works on **agriculture** which could logically have been included under either the earth or the biological sciences have been placed under the former. Again, although sources relating to medicine in general are not covered, works relating to plants used by man for medical purposes are included.

The sequence of sub-divisions followed, where appropriate, for these two categories is **Earth sciences**: Agriculture; Climate & meteorology; Geology & minerals; Hydrology, limnology & oceanography; **Biological sciences**: Zoology (Birds; Mammals; Reptiles & Amphibians; Fishes; Invertebrates) Botany. For further subdivisions *see* Contents list for 'Africa in General'. There are several important series within these sections. In the earth sciences, the **Lexique stratigraphique international** series for Africa, published by the CNRS in France, has volumes for many African countries. The Wissenschaftliche Länderkunden published by the Wissenschaftliche Buchgesellschaft in Darmstadt provides substantial regional geographies for a dozen countries, described as a "monumental undertaking" in a lengthy review in *Geographical journal*, 148, 1982, 69-71. In the biological sciences the Agence de coopération culturelle et technique (ACCT) in Paris has published a series of large scale studies in its series *Contribution aux études ethnobotaniques et floristiques* covering eleven countries, mostly in Francophone Africa. The Southern African Biological Diversity Network (SABONET) a project of the National Botanical Institute (later National Biodiversity Institute) at Kirstenbosch, South Africa from 1996 to 2005 published over twenty volumes of guides to botanical resources in the region.

The series of articles I published in *African research & documentation* under the overall title of 'African flora & fauna' should also be noted: Part 1, Birds, *ARD*, 75, 1997, 12-38; part 2, Mammals, 77, 1998, 20-38; part 3, Flora, 81, 1999,

23-52; part 4. Reptiles, Amphibians and Fishes, 82, 2000, 13-30; part 5. Invertebrates, 85, 2001, 25-46 and Supplement 1, 86, 2001, 27-38. Although many of the entries originally published in these have been updated and included in AGRM2, the articles will provide additional information. The introduction to each contains a full discussion about the type of reference sources selected, pre 1938 sources and the countries of North Africa are included, and coverage of the literature is more extensive than in AGRM2, especially in the article on invertebrates. Site guides to national parks are also included. Note that Louis Taussig, **Resource guide to travel in Sub-Saharan Africa**. Oxford, Hans Zell, 1993-1997, noted above in the discussion of travel literature, includes extensive sections on 'Natural history field guides' under each region and country.

ENTRIES

Where a work has a title in English and another language, the English form is chosen for entry. The English form of places of publication is used. Many reference works published in South Africa are issued in both English and Afrikaans editions and the Afrikaans version is not normally noted unless it is known to differ substantially from the English. Where an entry for a later edition of a title records only place of publication and date, this indicates that the author and publisher are the same as in the earlier edition. An attempt has been made to list all editions of monographs. Where there have been many editions, or where the full extent of editions is unclear, the entry refers simply to "earlier eds."

The annotations provide information on the scope of the work recorded, particularly in terms of matters such as the number of entries in a directory, gazetteer, or biographical source, the number and major scales of maps provided by an atlas, the range of topics covered by a handbook or yearbook, the number of species covered by a natural history guide. The bibliographical relationship of the work to others is noted, as also (so far as possible) are changes in title and frequency in serially published titles. No attempt has been made to record all changes in name of issuing bodies for the latter. Another major intent of the annotations is to provide some qualitative judgements, and to relate the work to others in the field – for discussion of this *see* below under 'Publishing and reviewing of reference works'.

Most sources receive only a single entry. If a source covers more than one country within the broad region in which it is included, it is entered under the first named in the title with a cross reference from other countries. Exceptions are made for works that cover countries located in different broad regions: for example the **Encyclopedia Africana dictionary of African biography. Vol. 1.**

Ethiopia and Ghana, is entered twice, once under each country. Cross references are employed liberally throughout AGRM2.

PUBLISHING & REVIEWING OF REFERENCE WORKS

There have been some interesting and detailed recent studies of the nature and use of reference works in the Africanist field, and of their publishing and their reviewing. Deborah LaFond and Gretchen Walsh co-edited **Research, reference service and resources for the study of Africa**. Binghamton, NY, Haworth Press, 2004 (pub. simultaneously as *Reference librarian*, 87/88, 2004) in which Gretchen Walsh's own paper, pp.5-96, 'Can we get there from here? Negotiating the washouts, cave-ins, dead ends and other hazards on the road to research on Africa' is a masterly exposition. It looks at the whole matter of the reference query: the approaches that researchers take to find their information, and the problems that are raised for them by variously the publishers, the reviewers, the cataloguers, the indexers and reference librarians, and IT and the Internet. It distils her observations, frustrations and triumphs as Head of the African Studies Library at Boston University for some thirty years, and is trenchant, witty, wide-ranging, vastly informed, and unsparing of any thoughtlessness and carelessness by any of those concerned.

While the nature of many quick reference sources, being large quantities of very specific information rapidly outdated, would seem to make online publishing an obvious answer, a change from print to online for existing sources has not been as marked between the two eds. of AGRM as I had expected. Only a few continuing sources have abandoned print form: the Country studies guides now produced by the Library of Congress (*see* **9**) and the Gazetteers originally produced by the U.S. Board on Geographic Names (*see* **631**) are two examples. Hans Zell's paper, 'The perilous business of reference publishing in African studies', pp. 199-226 in **Africanist librarianship in an age of change**, ed. Victoria K. Evalds & David Henige. Lanham, MD, Scarecrow Press, 2005 is based largely on his 30 years experience running his own imprint. On pp. 203-207 he considers particularly the question of print or online in this field, and notes the absence in either form of new editions or successors to many key works of African reference of the 1980s and 1990s. He does record the appearance in the last decade of a number of large scale handbooks & encyclopaedias in print form, borne out by the entries in the Handbooks sections of AGRM2, and feels that titles with a potential appeal beyond the academic specialist to general and public libraries still attract publishers. His own **African studies companion** (*see* **391**) has in its last two editions of 2003 and 2006 appeared both in print and as a continuously updated online source.

Many statistical sources continue to appear in print, although increasingly the data are also available on a Web site. In AGRM2 I have listed all the URLs I have traced for the *official* Web sites of individual African countries. These will often have general historical, administrative and social data, and links to other data collections. I have also noted websites for national statistical offices and national mapping agencies in the appropriate sections. As regards reference information on the internet in general, Walsh (*see* above) refers, pp. 83-87 to "Surfing the tangled Web: a mixed metaphor for a mixed blessing". An ever increasing number of guides help to provide information on Web sites of potential African interest (*see* p. l below) and Hans Zell in the 4th ed. of his **African studies companion** (2006, *see* **391**) has the latest version of his advice for those who wish to seek African related information on the Internet, 'Using Google for African studies research: a guide to effective Web searching', a condensed and updated version of a pilot edition previously published at http://ww.hanszell.co.uk/google/.

Reviews

Reference works of the sort listed in this volume comparatively rarely feature in detailed reviews in the specialist Africanist journals. If treated at all, they will often be only in the 'shorter review' section with comments limited to little more than: "researchers will be glad to note the appearance of a new edition of ... ". No doubt such summary treatment also discourages publishers of reference works, often expensive titles in small editions, from wide provision of review copies. The result is that there is often little real analysis of the merits, demerits and significance in relation to existing works of new publications, or re-assessments of continuing sources and new editions.

A notable exception to this lack of interest has been the attention awarded to the series of "African historical dictionaries" published since 1974 by Scarecrow Press. Even here, over a dozen volumes had been published before the first really detailed critique appeared, that by Dennis Cordell of the volume for Chad (1977) in the *International journal of African historical studies*, 11, 1978, 376-379. This was followed rapidly by two major assessments, one by David Henige, 'African historical dictionaries: through the looking glass', *Africana journal*, 10, 1979, 120-128, where he considered eight volumes in the series and the second by David Tambo, 'African historical dictionaries in perspective', *ASA review of books*, 6, 1980, 199-209 which discussed four volumes. These two reviews were critical of the publisher's choice of authors for the series, of the chosen format and presentation, and of the inaccuracy and lack of balance of the contents.

They also make a number of interesting points about reference works in general. Henige is severe about the use of a monographic series as a publisher's device to increase sales by persuading libraries to place a standing order without waiting to assess each individual volume as it appears. Tambo is unhappy about what he sees as the largely uncritical acceptance of the series in reviews appearing in professional library journals, e.g. *Choice* and *Library journal* as opposed to the specialist Africanist journals. He feels the volumes themselves are trying to be too many things at once: "encyclopedias, area handbooks, current biographies, handbooks of source materials". Henige justifies severe criticism of errors because "the compilers of reference tools cannot be satisfied merely to aspire to being reasonably accurate, or even almost accurate. Rather they must attempt perfection, knowing that most users will be unable to distinguish what happens to be correct from that which happens not to be".

Probably stimulated by these detailed analyses, book review editors in the Africanist journals have made a point of featuring later volumes in the Historical dictionaries series. Criticisms could be fierce: the volume for Tanzania, already considered by both Henige and Tambo, was "a volume to be avoided" (Norman Bennett, *IJAHS*, 12, 1979, 321) and "this type of book could bring African studies into disrepute" (Alison Redmayne, *Africa*, 50, 1980, 101). In the *Journal of African history* there have been interesting group reviews by Q.N. Parsons, *JAH*, 20, 1979, 146-147, and by Andrew Roberts, *JAH* 23, 1982, 139-140. *African research & documentation* has regularly made a point of publishing detailed reviews of volumes in the series, often comparing several volumes at a time. *See* 'African historical dictionaries revisited', by John McIlwaine, *ARD*, 75, 1997, 50-57 and block reviews of 8 volumes, *ARD* 84, 2000, 83-90 and of 5 volumes, *ARD*, 99, 2005, 51-54.

Some of the criticisms may well have been noted by the publishers in commissioning later volumes in the series. As early as 1981, reviewing the volume for Niger, Anthony Kirk-Greene was wondering if some of his colleagues were being unnecessarily harsh: "has not the series given many not-too-specialist users a lot of useful data on a lot of countries about which many Africanists know too little?" (*Africa*, 51, 1981, 788-789). Adam Jones however, looking back over more than forty volumes in his review of the example for the Ivory Coast (*IJAHS*, 22, 1989, 347-348) felt that although "some volumes merit revision ... we would be better served by a completely fresh attempt undertaken by a team of recognized historians". David Henige, one of the earliest and severest critics, was eventually able to welcome the second edition of the dictionary for Zimbabwe "as the best reference on Zimbabwean history, as well as a challenge for most other volumes in the series" (*ARBA*, 23, 1992, 40). Considerable credit is due to Henige for his efforts over the past 30 years and more to raise both the standards of reference book compilation and of reference book reviewing. In addition to the articles cited above, references will be found below to his 'African chronology', *African affairs*, 75, 1976, 104-108, reviewing Freeman-Grenville's **Chronology of African history** (1973, *see* **139**) and his 'One-eyed man in the kingdom of the blind', *History in Africa*, 28, 2001, 395-404, discussing J.D. Stewart **African states & rulers** (1999, *see* **233**). He has also contributed astringent reviews to the wider library professional press, notably in *American reference books annual (ARBA)*. Note also his 'Reviewing reviewing', *Journal of scholarly publishing*, 33, 2001, 23-36 (and on this theme *see* Terry Barringer, 'Reviewing reviews' forthcoming in *ARD*, 102, 2006).

CITATION OF REVIEWS, AWARDS & OTHER COMMENT

Reviews in general can not only provide potential users of the work reviewed with a critical assessment, but will often offer comparisons with works of similar scope, and be of value to those interested in the whole topic of the problems of compiling reference works on the subject in question and indeed in general. An attempt has therefore been made to provide bibliographical references to all reviews of substance in the following Africanist journals:

Africa: journal of the International African Institute; Africa today; African affairs: the journal of the Royal Africa Society; African book publishing record; African historical studies later *International journal of African historical studies; African research & documentation; ASA* (African Studies Association) *review of books; African studies review; Africana library journal; Canadian journal of African studies; Journal of African history; Journal of modern African studies*

Of professional library journals, *Choice*, published monthly by the American Library Association, is by far the most conscientious in regularly covering reference sources relating to Africa, its reviewers in the 1990s and early 2000s including such well known names as David Easterbrook, Al Kagan, Nancy Schmidt and Gretchen Walsh. Hans Zell's inclusion of reviews from *Choice* in his ASC3 and ASC4 has encouraged me to cite reviews in *Choice* over the last 20 years or so. These are also online from 1988 at http://www.choicereviews.org (but require a subscription/license). Recent reviews are also cited from the professional journals *American reference books annual* published in the U.S. and from *Reference reviews*, published in the U.K. Reviews in more specialised subject journals are noted as appropriate. For entries in the new sections covering the Earth & Biological sciences, the *Geographical journal* (Royal Geographical Society) for many years provided a wide-ranging reviewing policy on a broad range of topics. An attempt has been made to note reviews in appropriate specialist journals, e.g. *Journal of mammalogy* (American Society of Mammalogists); *Ibis* (British Ornithologists' Union); *Copeia* (American Society of Ichthyologists and Herpetologists) and so forth with an increasing number of specialist titles appearing in Africa itself from the 1990s onwards. Brief quotations are included from reviews if they were either particularly enthusiastic or particularly critical. In view of the strictures passed on the 'African historical dictionaries' above, a special effort has been made to cite a range of reviews for this series. In all over 700 reviews are noted from over 80 journals. Note that all references to reviews cite *pages*, not item numbers which are used by some of the sources (e.g. *Choice*, ASC4).

The African historical dictionaries discussed above were graded by the American Library Association's *Guide to reference books*. 11th ed. Chicago, 1996 (*see* p. xlix below), and these grades are noted. Titles selected by *Choice* as "outstanding academic title" (formerly "outstanding academic book") of the year are indicated, as are those volumes selected as winners/joint winners of the Africana Librarian's Council's Conover-Porter Award, given biennially for "outstanding achievement in Africana bibliography and reference works".

Several large scale reference sources are the result of major projects, often lasting several years, and may be the subject of articles and conference papers discussing the problems and process of their compilation. Where traced, such articles and papers have been cited, hoping that they can throw light on the coverage and limitations of the sources discussed and of the problems associated with creating reference sources in the relevant subject field.

SOURCES USED

The original basis for the compilation of AGRM1, was the series of indexes to sources covering all countries of the Third World which I accumulated over 35 years of teaching courses related to area studies bibliography. These were taken from a very wide scan of bibliographies, journals, databases and library holdings, and the same range has been used to check references and gather further detail for the present work.

Libraries & catalogues

The two library collections most frequently used in person for compiling this second edition were those of the School of Oriental and African Studies (SOAS), University of London and of the Afrika Studiecentrum (ASC), Leiden. Other U.K. libraries used were the Bodleian Library, Oxford, especially the Social Sciences Library, the Map Library and the Library of Commonwealth and African Studies at Rhodes House (still better known to the outside world as Rhodes House Library), the British Library, Cambridge University Library, especially the Royal Commonwealth Society Collections, the Institute of

Commonwealth Studies and the Senate House Library of the University of London, University College London and the Library of the Royal Botanic Gardens, Kew. Overseas libraries in which I had relatively brief opportunities to inspect material since the publication of AGRM1 include the Library of Congress, the Smithsonian Institution, the Melville Herskovits Library at Northwestern University, the Bibliothèque nationale de France, the Biblioteca Nacional, Lisbon, the Koninglijk Bibliotheek in the Hague and the Cape Town branch of the National Library of South Africa.

Since AGRM1, the opportunity to consult library catalogues on the Internet has opened up immense bibliographic resources (and numerous examples of conflicting data). All those noted above have at least part of their catalogues available on the Web. Particularly useful for checking data were the following:

Catalogue collective de France (CCFR) http://www.ccfr.bnf.fr/ rnbcd_visu/acc1.htm, representing the holdings of the Bibliothèque nationale de France and numerous other French collections

COPAC, http://copac.ac.uk/, representing the holdings of 27 members of CURL the Consortium of Research Libraries (in the U.K.) to which the holdings of SOAS were added in 2005

Library of Congress (LC), http://catalog.loc.gov

Northwestern University Library (NuCAT)
http://nucat.library. northwestern.edu

PORBASE: Base Nacional de Dados bibliográficos o Catálogo Colectivo em linha das Bibliotecas Portuguesas. http://opac.porbase.org/

South African Places of Legal Deposit WebPAC http://natlib1.sabinet.co.za/ including the holdings of the National Library of South Africa, Cape Town and Pretoria branches

Stanford University Library http://jenson.stanford.edu/uhtbin/cgisirsi/ including the holdings of the Hoover Institution

Additionally the following were especially helpful for tracing or checking entries for the new sections on the Earth and Biological sciences:
Natural History Museum, London, U.K.
http://library.nhm.ac.uk/uhtbin/cgisirs/

Royal Botanic Gardens, Kew, U.K., Library
http://www.kew.org/data/ index.html

Smithsonian Institution Libraries, Washington D.C., Smithsonian Institution Research Information System (SIRIS) http://siris-libraries.si.edu/ipac

Complementary sources

The following titles have been used in the compilation of this work, but **should also be consulted** by enquirers as offering alternative approaches to tracing reference material. They will contain some of the same references that are in AGRM2 but with different arrangements, collocations and comments, and they will of course have entries for sources not included in AGRM2.

General guides to Africa/Sub-Saharan Africa

Guide to research and reference works on Sub-Saharan Africa, comp. Peter Duignan & Helen Conover, ed. Peter Duignan. Stanford, Hoover Institution, 1971. 1,102pp. Over 3,000 numbered and annotated references. Also pub. as P. Duignan & L.H. Gann, **Colonialism in Africa, 1870-1960: vol. 5. A bibliographic guide to colonialism in sub-Saharan Africa**. Cambridge, Cambridge University Press, 1973 with some small amendments, and an Addenda, pp. 463-474. Includes bibliographies, quick-reference sources and standard works on history, geography, anthropology, politics and the like for Africa in general and for regions and individual countries. The resulting work, particularly its generous annotations, remains extremely useful for reference material published in the period before the independence of many African countries. (*See* p. xxix above)

Kagan, Alfred. **Reference guide to Africa: a bibliography of sources**. 2nd ed. Lanham, Md, Scarecrow Press, 2005. ix, 223pp. (Reviews, *ABPR*, 32, 2006, 10; *Ref. revs.* 20(4) 2006, 61-62. ASC4, 85-86) - - Orig. pub. as **Reference guide to Africa**, comp. Alfred Kagan & Yvette Scheven. Lanham, MD, 1999. (Reviews, *ARD*, 81, 1999, 81-8; *Choice*, 36, 1999, 1754). The 2nd ed. contains 793 numbered entries, but a number of sources receive multiple entry. Part I, General sources. Chap. 1, Bibliographies & indexes; 2, Guides, handbooks, directories & encyclopedias; 3, Biography; 4, Primary sources; 5, Government publications; 6, Statistics. Part II, Subject sources covering seventeen different topics including Agriculture; Development; Environment; Folklore; Geography & maps; History; Languages; Literature; Politics & government; Religion and Women. Chapters are further broken down by headings, e.g. Surveys, Directories. Brief annotations for all sources. A valuable source because of its compactness and subject approach. The major difference from AGRM2 is that there is no coverage of regions or countries, and that bibliographical history of works cited is kept to a minimum).

The African studies companion: a guide to information sources, comp. Hans Zell. 4th ed. Lochcarron, Scotland, Hans Zell Publishing, 2006. Online updated version available at http://www.africanstudiescompanion.com/ for registered purchasers of the hardcopy. One of the key Africana reference sources. *See* main entry for the work at **391** for full details of coverage, earlier eds. etc. As with Kagan the focus is on Sub-Saharan Africa as a whole and virtually no sources limited to regions and countries are included. Of the 25 sections, the principal overlap with AGRM2 is with section 1, General online resources on Africa and African studies; section 2, The major general reference tools (includes e.g. sections for 'Annuals and yearbooks', 'Handbooks and encyclopaedias' & directories of various kinds); section 4, Major biographical resources; section 6, Guides to statistical sources & section 7, Cartographic sources. Most of the entries have extensive critical reviews. Entries in AGRM2 make cross references to treatment of items in ASC4.

Regional guides

Musiker, Reuben & Musiker, Naomi. **Guide to South African reference books**. 6th ed. London, Mansell, 1997.vii, 240pp. (Includes 1,139 entries, some duplicated under different headings. Review, *Choice*, 35, 1998, 1343). *See* full entry at **2675**. Thanks to the dedication of Musiker over more than fifty years, South Africa is better served with guidance than any other region of Sub-Saharan Africa and this has allowed AGRM2 to be selective in its listing of South African sources. Older eds. of Musiker's titles remain valuable for listing contemporary material, not always repeated in later editions.

Skreslet, Paula Youngman. **Northern Africa: a guide to reference and information sources**. Englewood, CO, Libraries Unlimited, 2000. xv, 405pp. 1,483 numbered & annotated items for both bibliographies and non-bibliographical reference works. "Emphasizes works published … in the 1980s and 1990s", pref. A very clear and detailed source, which can be seen as a complement to AGRM2 for Africa north of the Sahara. In her Part 3, 'Reference sources by country & region', in addition to the countries of Africa bordering the Mediterranean, Skreslet also has sections for 'The Sahel Region: Sahara' including Chad, Mali, Mauritania, Niger, Sudan & Western Sahara; and for 'The Horn of Africa', including Djibouti, Eritrea, Ethiopia & Somalia. For these ten countries therefore there is direct overlap with AGRM2 and Skreslet's Part 1, General reference works and Part 2, Area studies references by subject also contain a number of sources relating to Africa as a whole. Reviews, *ARD*, 87, 2001, 102-103; *Choice*, 38, 2001, 1251, "model reference work"; H-Africa, http://www.h-net.org/reviews/. ASC4, 92.

General guides

Two major regularly revised **general** guides to reference works (all subjects, worldwide coverage) which can be used to trace not only materials specifically on Sub-Saharan Africa but also more general sources that possess some African coverage are:

American Library Association (ALA). **Guide to reference books**, 11th ed., ed. Robert Balay. Chicago, 1996. xxvii, 2,020pp. Worldwide coverage of all subject fields. Note pp. 1,318-1,346, Section D, History & area studies: DD Africa, comp. Alfred Kagan, Phyllis P. Bischof & Regina Kammer. The volumes in the Scarecrow Press African historical dictionaries series are each graded as E = excellent, G = good, F = fair or P = poor and these grades are noted in the entries in AGRM2. First published as **Guide to the study and use of reference books** in 1902 and known over the years by the names of its successive editors, Kroeger, Mudge, Winchell, Sheehy and now Balay. A 12th electronic edition has been announced for 2007 by the ALA. Selective updates are published twice a year in the journal *College & research libraries*, issued by the College & Research Libraries Section of the ALA.

The new Walford: guide to reference resources, ed.-in-chief, Ray Lester. London, Facet Publishing, 2005- . 3 vols. "Succeeds **Walford's guide to reference material**, published in eight editions between 1959 and 2000 by Library Association Publishing", pref. Vol. 1, 2005. Science, technology and medicine. Until the new ed. is complete, use can continue to be made of **Walford's guide to reference material**. 8th ed. Vol. 2, 2000. xiv, 794pp. Social and historical sciences, philosophy and religion; vol. 3, 2001. Generalia, language and literature, the arts. Worldwide coverage of all subject fields, the U.K. equivalent of Balay. *The new Walford* departs quite radically from its predecessor in both selection and arrangement: *see* review in *Ref.revs* 20(2) 2006, 6-9. New eds. are planned every 5/7 years.

Continuing sources

'Africana reference works'. This invaluable and wide-ranging listing has been compiled for the last 25 years by members of the Africana Librarians Council of the African Studies Association. The list for 1980 & 1981 appeared in *ASA news*, 15, 1982, 41-46; for 1982, in *ASA news*, 16, 1983, 19-24; for 1983, in *ASA news*, 18, 1985, 36-42; for 1984/85 in *ASA news*, 19, 1986, 18-28 and an expanded version in the *African book publishing record (ABPR)*, 12, 1986, 81-92. Since 1986, it has appeared annually in *ABPR*. The editors have been Phyllis Bischof et al (1980/81-1984/85 in *ASA news*); Joseph Lauer et al. (1984/85-1988); Yvette Scheven et al (1989 to 1992); Phyllis Bischof et al (1993-1996); Mette Shayne et al (1997-1998) and Jill Young-Coelho et al (1999-2005). Entries in the issues for 1980/81 and 1982 are alphabetical by author; entries for 1983-1987 are arranged under broad categories: bibliographies (general, subject, regional), biographical sources, directories, handbooks and manuals, etc; entries in issues since 1988 are arranged under specific headings, including individual countries. All entries since *ABPR* took over publication have been annotated. An essential updating service for AGRM2.

Guides to African sources on the Internet

Africa south of the Sahara – selected Internet resources. http://www-sul.stanford.edu/depts/ssrg/africa/guide.html. Created, developed and maintained by Karen Fung at Stanford University Libraries. "One of the very best sites for Internet Resources on Africa" (ASC4, 24). Frequent updates and easy to use. Searchable by countries or by topic headings which include: 'Reference' and also numerous others directly relevant to sections in AGRM2 such as 'African studies', 'Birds', 'Environment', 'Maps', 'Statistics' etc.

Columbia University Libraries – African studies Internet resources http://www.columbia.edu/cu/lweb/indiv/africa/cuvl/. Compiled and maintained by Joe Caruso, Africana Librarian at Columbia University. "Enormously rich resource" (ASC4, 29). Searchable sections include 'African studies programs, research centers and universities', 'Libraries, bibliographies, book dealers and publishers' & 'African studies resources – by region and country' '… by organization' & '… by topic' This last section includes headings for 'African biography', 'Business and economic information', 'History and cultures' and 'Maps'.

An A-Z of African studies on the Internet – "A directory of Africa & African studies" http://www.lib.msu.edu/limb/a-z/az.html. Created by Peter Limb, Africana Librarian at Michigan State University and maintained by Limb and Ibra Sene of the University's History Department. One of the longest running guides (since 1995) to online resources for African studies, covering "Internet sites, discussion lists and any other e-resources of relevance to Africa or African studies". Arranged under A/Z topic headings including individual countries and themes such as 'Language', 'Literature', 'Maps'. Frequently updated. "High quality annotated guide" (ASC4, 27)

These are probably the three most useful portals for accessing reference material on the Internet. Numerous others are identified and discussed by Hans Zell in ASC4 (*see* **391**) in the section 'General online resources … Academic and scholarly resources on African studies' pp. 21-35.

ABBREVIATIONS & ACRONYMS

Of countries, institutions, libraries, organizations, databases

ACCT	Agence de coopération culturelle et technique, Paris
ACP	African, Caribbean & Pacific Group of States
AEF	Afrique équatoriale française
AETFAT	Association pour l'étude taxonomique de la flore de l'Afrique tropicale
AOF	Afrique occidentale française
ASA	African Studies Association (U.S.A.)
AU	African Union (*formerly* OAU)
AUPELF	Association des universités partiellement ou entièrement du langue français
BL	British Library
BnF	Bibliothèque nationale de France
CAR/RCA	Central African Republic /République Centrafricaine
CARDAN	Centre d'analyse et de recherche pour l'Afrique noire
CCFR	Catalogue collective de France
CCTA	Commission for Technical Cooperation in Africa
CIRAD	Centre de coopération internationale en recherche agronomique pour le développement
CNRS	Centre national de recherche scientifique (France)
CODESRIA	Council for the Development of Economic & Social Research in Africa
CSA	Scientific Council for Africa south of the Sahara
CUL	Cambridge University Library
FAO	Food & Agricultural Organization (of the United Nations)
GB	Great Britain
HMSO	His/Her Majesty's Stationery Office (*later* The Stationery Office)
IAI	International African Institute
ICS	Institute of Commonwealth Studies, Universty of London
IEMVT	Institut d'élevage et de médicine véterinaire des pays tropicaux
IFAN	Institut Français (*later* Fondamental) pour l'Afrique noire
IFLA	International Federation of Library Associations & Instititions
IMF	International Monetary Fund
IRD	Institut de recherche pour le développement
IUCN	International Union for Conservation of Nature & Natural Resources
LC	Library of Congress
NGO	Non Government Organization

NLSA	National Library of South Africa
NWU	Northwestern University
OAU	Organization of African Unity (*later* AU)
OECD	Organization for European Co-operation & Development
ORSTOM	Office de recherche scientifique et technique d'outre-mer (*later* IRD)
PORBASE	Base Nacional de Dados bibliográficos (Portugal)
RCA	*see* CAR
RCS	Royal Commonwealth Society
RHL	Rhodes House Library (i.e. Library of Commonwealth & African Studies at Rhodes House)
SABONET	Southern African Botanical Diversity Network
SADC	Southern African Development Community
SCOLMA	Standing Conference on Library Materials on Africa
SIDA	Swedish International Development Cooperation Agency
SSL	Social Sciences Library, Oxford University Library Service
SOAS	School of Oriental & African Studies, University of London
Stanford	Stanford University Libraries
SWA	South-West Africa (*now* Namibia)
UK	United Kingdom
UN	United Nations
UNDP	United Nations Development Programme
UNECA	United Nations Economic Commission for Africa
UNEP	United Nations Environment Programme
UNICEF	United Nations Children's Fund
US	United States
USBGN	United States Board on Geographic Names

Of bibliographical sources cited

ABAS-EAIO	Africana Bibliographical Alert Service - East Africa & Western Indian Ocean Region (Library of Congress) http://www.loc.gov/rr/amed/afs/abas-eaio/abas.html.
AGRM1	**Africa: a guide to reference material**, comp J.H. McIlwaine. London, Hans Zell, 1993. (1st ed. of the present work).
AGRM2	**Africa: a guide to reference material**. 2nd ed. comp J.H. McIlwaine. Lochcarron, Scotland, Hans Zell Publishing, 2007. (The present work).

ALA   American Library Association, Government Documents Round Table. **Guide to official publications of foreign countries**. 2nd ed., ed. G. Westfall. Chicago, IL, 1997.

ASC3   **African studies companion**, comp. Hans Zell. 3rd ed. Lochcarron, Scotland, Hans Zell Publishing, 2003.

ASC4   **African studies companion**, comp. Hans Zell. 4th ed. Lochcarron, Scotland, Hans Zell Publishing, 2006.

Balay   **Guide to reference works**, 11th ed. ed. Robert Balay. Chicago, American Library Association, 1996.

Duignan   P. Duignan, *ed.* **Guide to research & reference works on Sub-Saharan Africa**, comp. H.F. Conover & P. Duignan. Stanford, CA, Hoover Institution, 1971.

Frodin   D.G. Frodin **Guide to standard floras of the world**. Rev. ed. Cambridge, Cambridge University Press, 2001.

Westfall   G. Westfall. **Bibliography of official statistical yearbooks and bulletins**. Cambridge, Chadwyck-Healey, 1986.

Of reviewing journals

Note that the titles of all journals from which articles are cited as main entries are given in full. Abbreviations are only used in annotations and in citing reviews.

ABPR   *African book publishing record*
AHS   *African historical studies* later *International journal of African historical studies*
ARBA   *American reference books annual*
ARD   *African research & documentation*
ASQ   *African studies quarterly* (http://web.africa.ufl.edu/asq)
ASR   *African studies review*
AZ   *African Zoology* formerly *South African journal of zoology*
BABC   *Bulletin of the African Bird Club*
CJAS   *Canadian journal of African studies*
GJ   *Geographical journal*
IJAHS   *International journal of African historical studies* formerly *African historical studies*
JAH   *Journal of African history*
JALL   *Journal of African languages & linguistics*

JMAS	*Journal of modern African studies*
QBSAL/NLSA	*Quarterly bulletin of the South African Library/... of the National Library of South Africa*
Ref. revs	*Reference reviews*
RREO	*Reference reviews Europe online* (http://rre.casalini.it/)
SAGJ	*South African geographical journal*
SAHJ	*South African historical journal*
SAJZ	*South African journal of zoology* later *African zoology*

In bibliographical entries & annotations

A/Z	alphabetical
b. & w.	black & white (of illustrations & maps)
c.	circa (about, approximately)
chap.	chapter
col.	coloured (of illustrations and maps)
comp.	compiled/compiler
ed.	edition/editor/edited
et al.	and others (of authors/editors/contributors)
fasc.	fascicle
ff.	following (of pages)
illus.	illustrations
irreg.	irregular (in frequency of publication)
M	million (as in map scale: 1:1M = 1:1 million)
n.d.	no date
n.p.	no place (of publication)/no publisher
n.s.	new series
orig.	originally
p.a.	per annum (frequency of publication)
pref.	preface
pt.	part
pub.	publisher/published/publication
rev.	revised/revision
sp(p).	species (singular and plural)
suppl.	supplement
t.p.	title page
trans.	translation/translator/translated
var.	various (usually of paging)
vol.	volume

AFRICA IN GENERAL

HANDBOOKS

General

Published 1938 to 1989

1 **Les 50 Afriques**, comp. Hervé Bourges & Claude Wauthier. Paris, Éditions du Seuil, 1979. 2 vols. (678pp; 677pp.) Vol. 1. Maghreb, Afrique du nord-est, Corne de l'Afrique, Afrique sahélo-soudanienne, Golfe du Bénin; vol. 2, Afrique centrale, Afrique des grands lacs, Afrique australe, Océan indien. (Individual entries for 54 countries with map, basic factual details, and a narrative account of history, topography, resources, politics, culture)

2 **Les 56 Afriques: guide politique**, ed. Frank Tenaille. Paris, Maspero, 1979. (Petite collection Maspero, 231, 232). 2 vols. maps. (Small format work arranged A/Z by country; vol. 1, A- L, vol. 2, M-Z. 225 maps. "Ce livre s'addresse délibérément à un public français ... [avec] l'accent ... sur le rôle joué par l'imperialisme française", pref.)

3 **Africa factbook: basic data on and for the continent**, comp. Frank Barton & Kul Bhushan. Nairobi, Newspread International & International Press Institute, 1989. 136pp. illus. maps. (Africa-wide data on population, agriculture, minerals, communications etc., with economic and population statistics for individual countries)

4 **Africa internazionale**, comp. Sergio Luigi Sergiacomi de' Aicardi. Milan, Istituto Internazionale per l'Africa, 1971. 391pp. map. (Pt. 1, international organizations and Africa; pt. 2, country by country surveys with brief topographical and historical details, and population and economic statistics for 43 Sub-Saharan African states)

5 **Africa south of the Sahara**: an assessment of human and material resources, prepared by a study group of the South African Institute of International Affairs under the chairmanship of Sir Francis de Guingand; ed. Anne Welsh. Cape Town, Oxford University Press, 1951. xxiv, 271pp. illus. maps. (Effectively a mini-Hailey. Main sections for the 'Physical background', including climate and vegetation; 'Population and the political framework'; 'Agricultural production'; 'Economic development' and 'Communications' (i.e. the media). Among the appendices is an interesting table 'Constitutional structures of the territories south of the Sahara'. Most contributors are from South African universities. Review, *African affairs*, 52, 1953, 73-74 notes "over-concentration on South Africa")

6   **African encyclopedia**, ed. W. Senteza Kajubi et al. London, Oxford University Press, 1973. 544pp. (Over 1,800 short articles by a wide range of British, African and American contributors. African emphasis, but also general articles, e.g. on space exploration. Some 500 photos, 200 maps and diagrams. Popular level. Review, *IJAHS*, 8, 1975, 477-478)

7   **Afrika: entsiklopedicheskii spravochnik**. Rev. ed., ed.-in-chief A.A. Gromyko. Moscow, Akademiia nauk, Institut Afriki, 1986-1987. 2 vols. illus. maps. (General articles on natural resources, peoples, and the economy, followed by regional surveys. Numerous col. illus.). - - Orig. ed., ed.-in-chief Ivan I. Potekhin. Moscow, Sovetskaya entsiklopediia, 1963. 2 vols. illus. maps. *See also* **27**

8   **Cambridge encyclopedia of Africa**, ed. Roland Oliver & Michael Crowder. Cambridge, Cambridge University Press, 1981. 492pp. illus., maps. (Over 90 contributors. Four sections: 'Africa past' with treatment of pre-colonial history, European occupation and rule to 1939; 'Struggle for independence'; 'Contemporary Africa' with brief profiles of each country and general chapters on government, natural resources, politics, economics, society, religion, arts and recreation; 'Africa and the world'. Numerous illus. and 46 maps. Lacks an introduction explaining the policy of coverage. Favourable review in *JAH* 24, 1983, 545, although coverage of the pre-colonial era is seen as giving undue emphasis to North Africa and to activities by Europeans. The standard one vol. source for its time, and without any real successor)

9   **Country studies**. Washington, DC., Library of Congress. Federal Research Division. The Library took over responsibility for the series of volumes entitled Area Handbooks (later Country Studies) produced under the Program sponsored by the U.S. Department of Army. Vols. published post 1987 for Angola, Chad, Comoros, Congo (Democratic Republic), Côte d'Ivoire, Ethiopia, Ghana, Indian Ocean: five island territories, Madagascar, Mauritania, Nigeria, Seychelles, Somalia, South Africa, Sudan and Uganda are available in hard copy as well as online at http://lcweb2.loc.gov/frd/cs/. Vols. in the series published before 1987 and available in hard copy only are Burundi, Cameroon, Congo, Guinea, Kenya, Liberia, Mozambique, Rwanda, Senegal, Sierra Leone, Tanzania, Malawi, Zambia and Zimbabwe. *See* full entries for each vol. under the appropriate country/region. (Review of Web site, *ARBA*, 35, 2004, 37. ASC4, 31-32). *See also* **30, 34**.

10   Dictionary of black African civilization, comp. Georges Balandier & Jacques Maquet. New York, Leon Amiel, 1974. ix, 350pp. illus. - - Orig. pub. as **Dictionnaire des civilisations africaines**. Paris, F. Hazon, 1968. 448pp. illus. (Note to English ed. "we have attempted to up-date the original French ed. on a limited basis", mostly by amending political articles to reflect recent events. Numerous brief entries with many illus.)

11   Encyclopaedia Africana. A project with editorial headquarters in Accra since 1963, but with origins going back to the concept of W.E. DuBois (1868-1963) for an Encyclopaedia of the Negro first voiced in 1909: "in celebration of the 50th anniversary of the emancipation of the American Negros, I am proposing to bring out an encyclopaedia covering the chief points in the history and condition of the Negro race" (letter to Edward Blyden, **Correspondence of W.E. DuBois**, ed. H. Aptheker, vol. 1. Amherst, 1973). DuBois and various collaborators returned periodically to this proposal and in 1945 the **Encyclopaedia of the Negro: preparatory volume with reference lists and reports** was published in New York by the Phelps-Stokes Fund. The larger part of this was occupied by a list of potential topics to be covered in the main work itself. Failing to make further progress in the U.S., DuBois moved to Ghana in 1961, where the project, now named Encyclopaedia Africana, was given support by Nkrumah. "I propose an encyclopaedia edited mainly by African scholars, but I am anxious to have this encyclopaedia a scientific production and not a matter of propaganda, and to have included among its writers the best students of Africa in the world. I want, however, to have the encyclopaedia written mainly from the African point of view, from people who know and understand the history and culture of Africans". (DuBois to Charles Julien, 17 April 1961, quoted by Julien in his **Les Africains**, vol. 1, 1977, p.14. *See* **300**). Following the death of DuBois in 1963, the Editorial Committee met for the first time in 1964 with representatives from 24 African countries and formally declared its aim to "compile and publish a scientific and authentically African compendium of the known facts of African life, history and culture", (**Proposed plan for the Encyclopedia Africana**. Accra, Secretariat for an Encyclopedia Africana, 1964. 62pp.) Work on planning the encyclopaedia can be followed through the pages of its newsletter, *For co-operation towards an Encyclopaedia Africana*, Accra, issues 1-18, 1962-1979. Proposals included the production of English, French and Arabic versions, and abridged one volume editions for use in schools. Lists of topics to be covered and proposed contributors provide an interesting insight into the attempt to construct the most ambitious reference work on Africa ever conceived. To date no volume as originally devised by the Editorial Office has appeared. An agreement was reached with an American publisher, Scholarly Press of Algonac, Michigan, to publish the biographical content as a separate series, the **Encyclopaedia Africana dictionary of biography** (*see* **545**) commencing in 1971. This series too has run into difficulties, with only three vols. having so far appeared out of the proposed 20, *see* **889, 1652, 2842**. For an account of the historical origins of the project *see* C.G. Contee, 'The *Encyclopaedia Africana* project of W.E. Du Bois', *AHS*, 4, 1971, 77-91; for some indication of the problems that the Editorial Board faced after its creation in 1964, *see* 'Interview with Professor L.H. Ofusu-Appiah, Director *Encyclopaedia Africana* project', *ABPR*, 1, 1975, 289-291 and M. Afrani, 'An African dream come true', *African concord*, 9 July 1987, 12-14. The Web site of the Encyclopaedia Africana Project http://www.endarkenment.com/eap/ contains the text of a number of mission statements and other documents issued over the years, including that by Grace Bansa, Acting Director of the Project, disassociating it from the **Microsoft Encarta Africana** (*see* **32**).

12   Grande encyclopédie du monde, l'épopée des hommes, la géographie, la culture, l'histoire de tous les pays. Vol. 11, Afrique: Afrique de l'Ouest, Afrique centrale, Afrique équatoriale, Afrique australe, Madagascar, île Maurice, les Comores, les Seychelles, la Réunion. Paris, Atlas/Mezzovico, Finabuch Ed. Transalpines, 1988. Pp. 4630-5115. (Originally issued as a part work)

13   Hailey, W.M. 1st baron Hailey. **An African survey: a study of problems arising in Africa south of the Sahara**. London, Oxford University Press for Royal Institute of International Affairs, 1938. xxviii, 1837pp. illus. maps. (This classic compilation of data for its time originated from a series of conferences on 'African problems' held in Oxford in 1929. The initial proposal was for the establishment of Institute of African studies at Rhodes House, Oxford. When funding for this failed to materialise, it was decided to initiate a preliminary survey of African research, and the Committee of the African Research Survey was set up by the Royal Institute of International Affairs in 1931. For a detailed account of the transition from the idea of an Institute to that of the survey, *see* chapter 2 of Helen Tilley, 'Africa as a 'living laboratory' – the African Research Survey'. D.Phil, Oxford University, 2001. Preliminary collection of data began in 1933, and Hailey became involved in 1935. The survey resulted in three large-scale volumes, all issued by Oxford University Press in 1938: Hailey's **Survey**; E.B. Worthington's **Science in Africa** (*see* **644**) and S.H. Frankel's **Capital investment in Africa; its causes and effects**. Helen Tilley makes the point that "while Worthington's and Hailey's volumes were issued under their names alone, they were in truth the product of an extensive network of hundreds of experts", (p. 257 in her 'Ambiguities of racial science in colonial Africa; the African Research Survey …', in *Science across the European empires, 1800-1950*, ed. Benedikt Stuchtey. Oxford, Oxford University Press, 2005). Contents: 1, Physical background; 2, Peoples; 3, Languages; 4, Population records; 5, Political and social objectives in government; 6, Systems of government; 7, Law and justice; 8, Non-European immigrant communities; 9, Native administration; 10, Taxation; 11, Labour; 12, The state and the land; 13,

Agriculture; 14, Forests; 15, Water supply; 16, Soil erosion; 17, Health; 18, Education; 19 & 20, External and internal aspects of economic development; 21, Co-operatives; 22, Minerals; 23, Transport; 24, The future of African studies; 25, Conclusions. For contemporary discussions of the work *see* **Lord Hailey's African survey, surveyed for the Royal African Society by the Rt. Hon. Lord Harlech** [etc.], ed. F.H. Melland. London, Macmillan, 1938. 70pp. (Issued as a suppl. to the *Journal* of the Society) and R. Coupland, 'The Hailey survey', *Africa*, 15, 1939, 1-11.

14 Hailey, W.M. 1st baron Hailey. **An African survey: a study of problems arising in Africa south of the Sahara: revised 1956**. London, Oxford University Press for Royal Institute of International Affairs, 1957. xxvi, 1,676pp. maps. ("The present volume, though similar in its objectives and in the arrangement of its material ... is, in many respects, a new work", pref. Compilation commenced in 1952, and the revision attempts to cover developments to the end of 1955. Contains an additional 5 maps. Reviews, *Africa*, 28, 1958, 168-170; *African affairs*, 56, 1957, 325-327, "no book of reference on Africa has made so continuous or so widespread an impact"; *GJ*, 124, 1958, 380-384. Later assessments of the whole enterprise are provided by John W. Cell, 'Lord Hailey and the making of the African survey', *African affairs*, 88, 1989, 481-506 and **Hailey: a study in British imperialism, 1872-1969**. Cambridge, Cambridge University Press, 1992. *See* chapter 15, 'Surveyor of Africa' for the original ed. and pp. 299-302 for the 2nd ed.)

15 Junod, Violaine I. ed. **The handbook of Africa**. New York, New York University Press, 1963. xiv, 472pp. (Arranged alphabetically by country in the form of summarised data, based on the format of the U.K. Colonial Office *Fact sheets*. Data up to December 1961. Notes on sources. Lengthy appendices on colonial policies in Africa, regional groupings of African countries, and foreign aid)

16 Kitchen, Helen, ed. **A handbook of African affairs**. London, Pall Mall Press/New York, Praeger for African-American Institute, 1964. vii, 311pp. 9 maps. (Reprints material originally published in *Africa report*. Pt. 1, country by country surveys with basic data; pt. 2, armies of Africa; pt. 3, OAU; pt. 4, contemporary African poetry and prose. Review, *African affairs*, 64, 1965, 239)

17 **Klett Handbuch für Reise und Wirtschaft in Afrika**. 3rd ed. comp. Peter Colburg et al. Stuttgart, Klett, 1971-1975. 3 vols. illus. maps. Vol. 1, West & central Africa; vol. 2, North and north-east Africa; vol. 3, Southern Africa. (Describes itself as a **Martens/Kardstedt** (*see* **20**) for a new generation. Introductory sections on geography, history, peoples and languages, then wide-ranging basic data for each country. Includes list of major African organizations and index to place-names. Maps include street plans). - - Orig.

pub. as **Afrika-Handbuch für Wirtschaft und Reise** Hamburg, Übersee Verlag for Afrika-Verein Hamburg-Bremen, 1967-1968. 2 vols. 430pp; 456pp. Vol.1, North, West and Central Africa; vol. 2, North-east, East and Southern Africa. - - 2nd ed. **Klett Handbuch für Reise und Wirtschaft in Afrika**. Stuttgart, Klett, 1967-1968. 2 vols.

18   Legum, Colin, ed. **Africa: a handbook to the continent**. Rev ed. Harmondsworth, Penguin, 1969. 682pp. ("Something that lies between Lord Hailey's invaluable **African survey** (written by experts for experts) and John Gunther's **Inside Africa** (written by a non-expert for non-experts)", pref. Pt. 1 covers Africa by region, pt. 2 is a series of essays on themes: economics, art, literature etc.). - - Orig. pub. London, Anthony Blond, 1961/New York, Praeger, 1962. xiv, 553pp. maps. (Review, *African affairs*, 61, 1962, 260, "enormously useful reference book"). - - 2nd ed. rev. and enlarged. London, 1965/New York, Praeger, 1966. xii, 558pp. (Adds essay coverage of the press and trade unions. Review, *GJ*, 134, 1968, 419-420, "recommended to anyone ... requiring a well-informed understanding of African affairs". For the completely revised version issued as **Handbooks to the modern world: Africa** (1989) *see* **23**)

19   **Macdonald's encyclopedia of Africa**. London, Macdonald Educational, 1976. 224pp. U.S. ed. pub. as **The encyclopedia of Africa**. New York, F. Watts, 1976. (Popular, multi-illus. approach with thematic sections on e.g. 'Economy', 'The land', 'The arts'. Includes gazetteer with long entries for each country and major cities, and 'Guide to peoples and languages' comp. J.D. Pearson of SOAS and based on the card index of the International African Institute)

20   Martens, Otto & Karstedt, Oskar. **Afrika: ein Handbuch für Wirtschaft und Reisen**. 4th ed. Berlin, D. Reimer, 1938. 2 vols. xii, 525pp; xvi, 693pp. - - Orig. pub. Berlin, 1930. xv, 940pp. illus. Maps; - - 2nd ed. Berlin, 1931. xv, 988pp; - - 3rd ed. Berlin, 1936. 2 vols. xii, 532pp; xvi, 642pp.
- - English trans. **The African handbook: a guide to West, South and East Africa**. 2nd ed. London, Allen & Unwin, 1938. xv, 726pp. illus. maps. (Includes considerably less factual data and statistics than the 1st ed. with more emphasis on information for tourism, and an additional 25 town plans). - - Orig. pub. as **The African handbook and traveller's guide**. London, Allen & Unwin, 1932. xvi, 948pp. illus. 23 maps. ("On the one hand ... a dependable guide to the geographical, climatic and economic conditions of ... African countries, and on the other, to be of assistance to persons travelling", pref. An immensely detailed guide-book arranged by region. Includes 17 city plans)

21   **Meyers Handbuch über Afrika**. Mannheim, Bibliographisches Institut, [1962]. 779pp. illus. maps. (Pt. 1, thematic treatment of Africa as a whole with sections for natural resources, peoples, history, industry, communications etc;

pt. 2, country by country accounts in a standardized format. Includes biographies for 63 African leaders)

22   Meyers Kontinente und Meere; Daten, Bilder, Karten: Afrika, ed. Werner Jopp. Mannheim, Bibliographisches Institut, Geographisch-Kartographisches Institut Meyer, 1968. (Meyers Kontinente und Meere, 1). 380pp. illus. maps. (First section covers the continent as a whole: geology, topography, climate, vegetation, history, peoples, including a tribal map showing 985 groups, and then the major sub-regions. Second section gives coverage of each individual country with a wide range of data)

23   Moroney, Sean, ed. Handbooks to the modern world: Africa. New York & Oxford, Facts on File, 1989. 2 vols. (Extensively rev. version of Colin Legum, **Africa: a handbook to the continent** (*see* **18**) with over 30 contributors. Vol. 1 contains factual information A/Z by country, covering topography, recent political and constitutional history, the economy, social services, education, and mass media. Includes biographical sketches and comparative statistics (pp. 625-665). Vol. 2 contains thematic essays covering Africa as a whole)

24   Morrison, Donald G. et al. Black Africa: a comparative handbook. 2nd ed. New York, Irvington Publications/London, Macmillan, 1989. xxii, 716pp. (A substantial compendium of data and a major revision of the 1st ed. while retaining the same basic structure. Coverage is expanded to 41 countries with new data for Angola, Djibouti, Equatorial Guinea, Guinea-Bissau, Madagascar, Mozambique, Namibia, Swaziland and Zimbabwe. Pt. 1 gives comparative profiles under topics such as demography, social and economic development, political development, and urban and ethnic patterns. Pt. 2 gives individual country profiles. Much of the information is in tabular form. For the sections in Pt. 1, 'Demography, ecology and pluralism', 'Economic development and social mobilization', 'Political development', 'International relations', an attempt is made to provide comparative data for each of the years 1955, 1961, 1966, 1972 and 1977. For the country surveys in pt. 2, data goes up to 1982. Contains 187 separate tables. For the companion vol. **Understanding black Africa**, *see* **25**. The text of the **Comparative handbook** formed one component in a Black Africa database marketed separately on disk by the publishers). - - Orig. pub. New York, Free Press, 1972. xxviii, 483pp.

25   Morrison, Donald G. Understanding Black Africa: data and analysis of social change and nation building. New York, Paragon House & Irvington Publications, 1989. xvii, 237pp. ("[It was] apparent at the time we were preparing **Black Africa** (*see* **24**) that there was also a need for a relatively inexpensive comparative handbook for students of Africa ... this book is the result", pref. Basically an abbreviated version of **Black Africa** with some 85 tables. Pts. 1 to 4, pp. 1-134, cover themes such as population, languages, education, urbanization, communications, religion, politics, development, economics, and foreign relations in relation to Africa as a whole; pt. 5, pp. 135-229, provides individual country profiles)

26   Mveng, P. Engelbert. **Dossier culturel Pan-Africain**. Paris, *Présence africaine*, 1965. 236pp. maps. (Sees itself as complementing the largely political and economic emphasis of other contemporary reference works on Africa. Initial data on population distribution is followed by a series of 25 maps of 'les foyers culturels', e.g. use of symbols in house decoration, and features on religion with statistics and distribution maps, languages, writers, universities, research institutes, and relationships of African countries with UNESCO)

27   **Strany Afriki: politiko-ekonomicheskii spravochnik**. [Rev. ed.] ed. A.A. Gromyko et al. Moscow, Akademiia nauk, Institut Afriki, 1988. 334pp. map. - - Orig. pub. Moscow, 1969. 218pp. (General handbook). *See also* **7**

Published 1990 onwards

28   **Africa A-Z: continental and country profiles**, ed. Pieter Esterhuysen. Pretoria, Africa Institute of South Africa, 1998. vi, 393pp. (Part of a trilogy from the Institute, a companion to **Africa at a glance** (*see* **29**) and *Africa wall map and Africa fact sheet* (1995-). Large format. Section 1, Profile of the continent: geography, demography, ethnography, history, economics; section 2, Country profiles, A/Z: each includes map plus text. ASC3, 235)

29   **Africa at a glance: facts and figures**. Sandton, South African Freedom Foundation/Pretoria, Africa Institute of South Africa, 1967- . Irreg. (normally every 2/3 years. Not pub. 1971-1972, 1974-1977, 1979-1981, 1983-1984, 1986-1987, 1989-1991). 11th ed. 2001/02. 104pp. (Issue for 1982 pub. as *Africa insight*, 11(3) 1981; for 1985 *ibid.* 15(3) 1985; for 1988 *ibid.* 17(4) 1987. Presents basic factual statistical data in an accessible form, tables, statistics, diagrams, drawn from some 40 named sources Review, *ABPR*, 28, 2002, 205. ASC4, 121.)

30   **Africa on CD-ROM**: Angola, Chad, Egypt, Ethiopia, Ghana, Ivory Coast, Libya, Madagascar, Mauritania, Nigeria, Somalia, South Africa, Sudan, Uganda, Zaire; comp. and index Richard Seltzer. West Roxbury, MA, B & R Samizdat Express, 2003. 1 CD-ROM. ("This CD contains the full text of [the] Country Studies published as printed books by the Federal Research Division of the Library of Congress between 1987 and 1995 under a program sponsored by the U.S. Department of Army. Also contains the 2002 edition of the CIA *World fact book*". Texts of these country studies are also available online from the LC Web site, *see* **9**. ASC4, 117)

31   **Africa today**, ed. Raph Uwechue. 3rd ed. London, Africa Books Ltd., 1996. xix, 1,669pp. illus. maps. (Based on the pattern of **Africa yearbook and who's who**, *see* **278,** and a companion vol. to **533** and **548**. Sections on Africa in general (topography, languages etc.), and regional organizations, followed by country surveys covering the whole continent, other than Mayotte. Entry under Sahrawi Arab Democratic Republic for Western Sahara. Atlas of 21 col. thematic maps using the Peters projection. A major source of contemporary reference. ASC4, 118). - - Orig. pub. London, *Africa journal*, 1981. (Know Africa series). xx, 1506pp; - - 2nd ed. London, Africa Books, 1991. xx, 2056pp.

32   **Africana: the encyclopedia of the African and African American experience**. 2nd ed., ed. Kwame Anthony Appiah & Henry Louis Gates, Jr. New York, Oxford University Press, 2005. 5 vols. (Vol. 5 includes a list of some 250 contributors and a bibliography; also a 'Topical outline of selected entries' listed under 14 broad headings, and a general index, both new to this ed. The introduction claims that an additional 1,200 entries have been included since the first ed. and that over 1,000 entries have been updated. ASC4, 117). - - Orig. pub. as a one vol. work, New York, Basic Civitas Books, 1999. xxxvii, 2,095pp. (The early publicity for this work spoke of it having been "inspired by the dream of the late African American scholar W.E.B. Du Bois" which associated it with the proposed Encyclopaedia Africana (*see* **11**) and indeed the title was originally announced as the *Encyclopaedia Africana*, but had eventually to be changed since that was already pre-empted. *See* ASC3, 74-75 for more details. Reviews, *African affairs*, 99, 2000, 478-480, "a scholarly delight"; *JAHS*, 34, 2001, 147-148)

- - Also available as **Microsoft Encarta Africana**. Redmond, WA, Microsoft, 1993-. CD-ROM. 2 disks. Regularly revised. (Review of electronic version, *Choice*, 37, 1999, 120, sees the work as "essential". *Choice* "outstanding academic title", 1999. For a different critical reaction *see* H-Africa, http://www.h-net.org/~africa/reviews/, Feb. 1999, "has numerous inaccuracies and incomplete articles ... ostensibly claims to be about African culture and history but is really the projection of Europe on and in Africa ... it is useful, perhaps, that Encarta was done; it is bad certainly that it was done badly". ASC4, 125)

33   Bute, Evangeline L. & Harmer, Harry J.P. eds. **The black handbook: the people, history and politics of Africa and the African diaspora**. London, Cassell, 1997. viii, 392pp. (A collection of miscellaneous information, with no sources given, covering Africa, the Caribbean and African Americans. Includes sections for 'People' with some 300 brief biographies of the living and the dead; 'Places and events' with entries for e.g. 'Scramble for Africa'; a chronology, brief details on the individual countries of Africa and the diaspora, and on their political parties. A work that needs to be read through to discover information rather than referred to. Review, *Choice*, 35, 1998, 976, "no criteria for selection ... not recommended". ASC3, 229)

34   Country profiles. Washington, DC., Library of Congress. Federal Research Division, 2005- . A parallel series to the **Country studies** *see* **9**, of very brief overviews. "The profiles offer reasonably current country information independent of the existence of a recently published Country Study". As of August 2006, published vols. for countries of Sub-Saharan Africa comprise Eritrea, Ethiopia, Kenya, Mali, Nigeria and Sudan. These are available in hard copy and also online at http://lcweb2.loc.gov/frd/cs/profiles.html. *See* entries for each vol. under the appropriate country.

35   *The Economist* pocket Africa, ed. Roland Dallas. London, The Economist in association with Hamish Hamilton, 1995. 245pp. (Covers all Africa. Small format compilation of basic contemporary political and economic data. Includes tables of 'country rankings' for area, population, literacy, GDP etc.)

36   Encyclopedia of African nations and civilizations, comp. Keith Lye & the Diagram Group. New York, Facts on File, 2002. (Facts on file library of world history). 400pp. (A companion volume to **Encyclopedia of African peoples**, *see* **83**, and employing some of the same text. Section 1, 'Africa today'; 2, 'Development of the continent', broadly chronological chapters on history; 3, 'Nations and civilizations', A/Z entries for countries and personalities. Aimed at school and college libraries and the general reader. Reviews, *Choice*, 39, 2002, 194; H-Africa, http://www.h-net.org/~africa/reviews/. ASC4, 124-125)

37   Encyclopedia of the developing world, ed. Thomas M. Leonard. New York, Routledge, 2006. 3 vols. (Topics treated A/Z. Emphasis on post 1945 period. Includes some 800 entries for countries, regions, e.g. East Africa, for peoples and for organizations, e.g. ADB. Index entries for 'Africa', 'African' provide 50+ references)

38   Encyclopedia of the Third World, ed.-in-chief, George Thomas Kurian. 4th ed. New York, Facts on File, 1992. 3 vols. (Single A/Z sequence of entries for individual countries. For each, there is a standardized presentation of topographic, political, social and economic information). - - Orig. pub. New York, Facts on File/London, Mansell, 1979. 2 vols; - - 2nd ed. New York, 1982. 3 vols; - - 3rd ed. New York, 1987. 3 vols.

39   Gbotokuma, Zekui S. A Pan-African encyclopedia. Lewiston, NY, Edwin Mellon Press, 2003. 2 vols. xi, 800pp. (Most unusual work with all entries commencing with one of only four letters: A, for Africa(n), Africain,

Afro; B for Bantu, Black; C for Color(ed), Colour (ed) and N for Negro, Nègre, Noir. The majority of entries are reprinted from existing sources, some published as long ago as 1907. Review, *ARD*, 93, 2003, 79-80, "a curiosity rather than a genuine reference work")

40 Grace, John & Laffin, John. **Fontana dictionary of Africa since 1960**: **events, movements, personalities**. London, Fontana Press, 1991. xix, 395pp. (Small format work for the popular market with entries for countries, individuals, principally in political life and political groupings)

41 **Handbuch Afrika**, ed. Walter Schicho. Frankfurt-am-Main, Brandes & Apsel, 1999-2004. 3 vols. Vol. 1. 1999. Zentralafrika, Südliches Afrika und die Staaten im Indischen Ozean. 351ppp; vol. 2. 2001. Westafrika und die Inseln im Atlantik. 384pp; vol. 3. 2004. Nord- und Ostafrika. 400pp. (Each country entry has a brief statistical summary, followed by 15 to 25pp. account of political history emphasizing the post-colonial period)

42 **Handbuch der Dritten Welt**, ed. Dieter Nohlen & Franz Nuscheler. 3rd ed. Bonn, Dietz, 1992-1994. 8 vols. Vol. 4. 1991. Westafrika und Zentralafrika. 500pp; vol. 5. 1993. Ostafrika und Südafrika. 578pp; vol. 6. 1994. Nordafrika und Naher Osten. 576pp. (Vol. 5 includes Burundi and Rwanda, also St. Helena. Covers history, demography, economy and social development). - - Orig. pub. Hamburg, Hoffmann & Campe, 1974-78. Vol. 2 , Afrika. 2pts; - - 2nd ed. Hamburg, 1982-1983. 8 vols. Vol. 4. Westafrika und Zentralafrika; vol. 5. Ostafrika und Südafrika

43 **International dictionary of historic places. Vol. 4, Middle East and Africa**, ed. K.A. Berney & Trudy Ring. Chicago, IL, Fitzroy Dearborn, 1996. 766pp. illus. maps. (Includes 94 lengthy entries for locations in 17 African countries, with list of sites by country and extensive index. ASC4, 94)

44 Mabe, Jacob E. & Harding, Leonhard. **Das kleine Afrika-Lexikon: Politik, Gesellschaft, Wirtschaft**. Bonn, Bundeszentrale für Politische Bildung, 2003. vi, 224pp.

45 Middleton, John, ed.-in-chief. **The Encyclopedia of Africa south of the Sahara**. New York, Charles Scribner's Sons, 1999. 4 vols. 2,466pp. (Conceived in 1991 "to be the standard four volume encyclopedia" on the region. Some 8,900 signed articles, many by African contributors. Lengthy review article, 'Knowing Africa, or what Africa knows' by David Schoenbrun, *ASR*, 44 (1) 2001, 97-112. Reviews, *ARBA*, 30, 1999, 43-44, "will be … a major reference source for decades"; *Choice*, 36, 1998, 98, "essential … no really similar work". *Choice* "outstanding academic title", 1998; Conover-Porter Award, 2000. ASC4, 125-126)

- - **Africa: an encyclopedia for students**, ed. John Middleton. New York, Charles Scribner's Sons, 2002. 900pp. (Abridged and updated version of the above, intended for high school and undergraduate students. Review, H-Africa, http://www.h-net.org/~africa/reviews/)

46 Nantet, Bernard. **Afrique, les mots clés**. Paris, Bordas, 1992. (Compacts, 29). 254pp. illus. maps. (Pocket sized general summary of political, social and economic information aimed at the popular market)

47 U.S. Central Intelligence Agency (CIA). World factbook. Washington, DC. Available at: http://www.odci.gov/cia/publications/factbook/index.html. Annual. (Basic political, social and economic facts for each country of the world under 8 headings: Geography, People, Government, Economy, Communications, Transportation, Military, Transnational Issues. A source widely used by compilers of more specific regional reference works)

48 U.S. Department of State. Background notes on Africa. http://www.state.gov/p/af/ci/. (Brief summary of information for each country under standardized headings: geography, people, history, government, political conditions, economy, defense, international relations, U.S. relations, travel/business. Regularly updated. Where appropriate provides links to the LC Country studies, *see* 9)

49 Vogel, Joseph O. & Vogel, Jean, eds. **Encyclopedia of precolonial Africa: archaeology, history, languages, cultures and environments**. Walnut Creek, CA, AltaMira Press, 1997. 605pp. 70 illus. (Concerned principally with Sub-Saharan Africa. Contains 94 essays from 81 authors in sections for 'African environments'; 'Histories of research'; 'Technology'; 'People and culture' and 'Prehistory of Africa'. Reviews, *African affairs*, 98, 1999, 130-132, "the material cries out for rationalisation"; *ASQ*, 2, 1998, http://web.africa.ufl.edu/asq/v2/v2i1a7.htm; *ASR*, 42 (1) 1999, 141-143; *Choice*, 35, 1998, 964, "no comparable work"; *IJAHS*, 31, 1998, 378-379; *JAH*, 40, 1999, 127-128. *Choice* "outstanding academic title", 1998. ASC4, 130)

50 **Worldmark encyclopedia of the nations. Vol. 2: Africa**. 11th ed. Detroit, Gale, 2004. - - Orig. pub. New York, Worldmark Press, 1960. - - 2nd ed. New York, 1963; - - 3rd ed. New York, 1967; - - 4th ed. New York, 1971; - - 5th ed. New York, 1976; - - 6th ed. New York, 1984; - - 7th ed. New York, 1988; - - 8th ed. Detroit, Gale, 1995; - - 9th ed. Detroit, 1998; - - 10th ed. Detroit, 2001. (1st ed. 1960, treated all countries of the world in a single alphabetical sequence; 2nd and subsequent eds. present the information by continent, covering "the geographical, historical, political, social and economic status of all nations", pref. 12th ed. announced for 2006)

Francophone Africa

51 **L'Afrique noire de A à Z**. 2nd ed. Paris, Ediafric-La documentation africaine, 1975. [394pp.]. (Pub. as special issue of *Bulletin de l'Afrique noire*. Covers Francophone countries of West and Central Africa and for each contains assorted information arranged under A/Z headings from 'Aerodromes' to 'Universités', 'Villes'). - - Orig. pub. Paris 1971. [317pp].

52 **Dictionnaire universel francophone**: noms communs: 110,000 définitions; grammaire-conjugaison; noms propres: 13,000 articles; 53 dossiers encyclopédiques: les états d'Afrique et de l'océan indien, ed. Michel Guillou & March Moingeon. 4th ed. Paris, Hachette/Edicef & AUPELF/UREF, 1997. xii, 1507pp. illus. maps. (Standard dictionary including proper names based on the **Dictionnaire Hachette**, with notes identifying particular usage in Francophone countries. Appendix has entries for 53 Francophone countries with map, brief economic, historical and statistical data). - - Orig. pub. Paris, 1995. 1503pp; - - 2nd ed. Paris, 1997. xii, 1554pp.

53 **Encyclopédie africaine et malgache**. Paris, Larousse, 1964. (Issued in two formats (a) as 7 fascs with general coverage: 'Géographie', 'Histoire du monde', 'Histoire de l'Afrique', 'Littérature et grammaire français', 'Arithmétique et géométrie', 'L'homme, anatomie et santé' plus a further 19 fascs. covering the individual countries of Francophone Africa, including all former French colonies other than Djibouti, also Congo (Kinshasa), Burundi and Rwanda. Those for Sub-Saharan Africa are all of 32pp. each, except for fasc. 19, Madagascar et térritoires de l'Océan indien, with 64pp ; (b) As 19 separate country vols. each with the same 463pp. of the general articles plus the appropriate section for each country)

54 **Encyclopédie coloniale et maritime** [etc.]. Paris, Éditions de l'empire français, 1940-1951. 7 vols. in 10. (Comp. 'sous la direction d'Eugène Guernier'. A very detailed work with a complex publishing history on which none of the standard bibliographical sources agree. A preliminary ed. was issued in fascs. of 24 to 40 pp. each, 1936-?1940. The publishing plan as set out in each fasc. was for 150 (later amended to 132) fascs. to be issued, eventually comprising 9 vols. of c.400pp each; however fasc. 23 (1940) is the last traced. Published vols. in the 1940-51 ed. are: **Le Maroc** (1st ed. 1940; 2nd ed. 1948); **Tunisie** (1942); **Algérie-Sahara** (1946) 2 vols; **Madagascar-Réunion** (1947) 2 vols; **Afrique occidentale française** (1949) 2 vols.; **Afrique équatoriale française** (1950); **Cameroun-Togo** (1951). The last four titles are discussed below under the appropriate region (*see* **1459, 2102, 2216, 3232**). In all vols. published up to 1950, the introduction refers to the plan for a complete *Encyclopédie* of 15 vols., with individual vols. proposed for Indochina, French Pacific territories, French

North American and Caribbean territories, and a general survey of the French empire. The whole work is referred to variously as the *Encyclopédie de l'empire français* and the *Encyclopédie de l'union française*. By the **Cameroun-Togo** vol. of 1951, the introduction refers to the whole work as the *Encyclopédie de l'Afrique française* in 10 vols. Early titles claimed that coverage of the Côte française des Somalis would be included in the vol. for Afrique occidentale française. This was not the case, and later titles promised inclusion of Somaliland with the vol. for Indochina which was never published.

- - **Encyclopédie coloniale et maritime: revue encyclopédique des pays d'outre-mer**, Paris, 1950-1958. Monthly. Title varies: **Encyclopédie mensuelle d'outre-mer** (1951-58); **Encyclopédie mensuelle de l'Afrique** (1958). (Early issues claimed this to be not only a review of current events but 'en même temps compléter et développer les volumes de *l'Encyclopédie de l'Afrique française*'. Every 24 issues were to form a complete vol. of suppl. By 1953 it was claiming only to be a current affairs monthly)

55 **États africains d'expression française et République malgache**. 2nd ed. Paris, René Julliard, 1964. 344pp. (Individual surveys of 14 countries, omitting Comoros, Djibouti, Réunion, with sections on major regional organizations, French agencies for technical assistance, and international aid organizations). - - Orig. pub. Paris, 1962. 342pp.

56 **Guide pratique sur les républiques**: ... à l'usage des agents de la coopération. Paris, Ministère de la coopération, Direction de la coopération culturelle et technique, 1964. 222pp. illus. maps. (Covers 15 Francophone countries including Madagascar. Geographical, economic, social, political and administrative information)

57 Martin, Jean. **Lexique de la colonisation française**. Paris, Dalloz, 1988. xiii, 395pp. (Approximately 1,000 A/Z entries for countries, cities, persons, organizations, treaties, wars, trading companies, concepts, e.g. 'esclavage')

Former German Africa

58 **Das Buch der deutschen Kolonien**. 6th ed. Leipzig, Goldmann, 1942. 446pp. illus. - - Orig. pub. Leipzig, Goldmann, 1933. 352pp; - - 2nd ed. Berlin, R. Gobbing, 1936. 327pp; - - 3rd ed. Leipzig, Goldmann, 1937. 367pp; - - 4th ed. Leipzig, Goldmann, 1938. 446pp; - - 5thed. Leipzig, Goldmann, 1940. 446pp. (Eds Paul Julia Vahl (1st to 4th eds.), Alex Haenicke (5th & 6th eds); "under the direction of the former Governors of the German colonies". Heavily illustrated general overview of former German Africa)

Lusophone Africa

59   Abshire, David M. & Samuels, Michael A. **Portuguese Africa: a handbook**. London, Pall Mall Press, 1969. xiii, 480pp. 25 maps. (Pt. 1, Background: topography, history, peoples; pt. 2, Government and society; pt. 3, Economy; pt. 4, Political and international issues. Reviews, *African affairs*, 70, 1971, 182; *AHS*, 4, 1971, 186-189 which is critical of the emphasis on the interests of Portugal, with little attention to African activities)

60   Albuquerque, Luís de & Domingues, Francisco C. **Dicionário de história dos descobrimentos portugueses**. Lisbon, Caminho, 1994. 2 vols. 1,120pp. illus. maps. (Detailed scholarly work with signed and referenced entries for territories, e.g. Cabo Verde; for topographical entities, e.g. Cabo Bojador; for individual sailors, explorers, cartographers and local rulers and for ships, navigational instruments, etc.)

61   Almeida, Pedro Ramos de. **Historia do colonialismo português em Africa: cronologia**. Lisbon, Estampa, 1978-79. 3 vols. (Vol. 1 covers 15th to 18th centuries; vol. 2, 19th century; vol. 3, 1900-1961. Extensive bibliography in vol. 3, pp. 393-476. No index. For each year covers events in general, in Africa, and in each colony)

62   Correia, António Augusto Mendes. **Síntese da Africa**. Lisbon, Agência Geral das Colónias, Divisão de Publicações e Biblioteca, 1949. (Ultramar Português, I). 436pp. illus. maps. (Broad overview which emphasizes Portuguese territories but in fact covers the whole continent with sections on geography, climate, vegetation, fauna, peoples, languages and education, health, politics and administration, economics. English and French abstracts of each section are included. Over 100 illus)

63   Galvão, Henrique & Selvagem, Carlos. **Império ultramarino Português (Monografia do Império)**. Lisbon, Empresa Nacional, 1950-1953. 4 vols. illus. maps. (Vol. 1, pp. 69-358, Cape Verde; pp. 359-402, Guinea; vol. 2, pp. 11-180, Guinea (contd.); pp. 181-416, São Tomé e Príncipe; vol. 3, pp. 1-474, Angola; vol. 4, pp. 8-272, Mozambique. Encyclopaedic work with sections for each country on its exploration and history, peoples, politics and administration, the economy, communications and finance)

64   Nunez, Benjamin. **Dictionary of Portuguese-African civilization**. Oxford, Hans Zell, 1995-1996. 2 vols. Vol. 1, 1995. From discovery to independence. xxvi, 532pp. (Includes some 3,000 terms relating to topography, history, politics and flora and fauna of former Portuguese Africa, and background data on individual states. Reviews, *African affairs*, 96, 1997, 124-

125, "potentially useful compendium, cannot be relied on unquestionably"; *ARD*, 70, 1996, 75, "inordinately large number of errors"; *Choice*, 33, 1995, 442, "important addition to the literature"; vol. 2, 1996. From ancient kings to presidents. xix, 478pp. (Biographical articles, including individuals concerned not only with the five former Portuguese colonies but also with Ethiopia, Kenya, Madeira, the Azores and North Africa. Reviews, *African affairs*, 96, 1997, 125-126, "worrying number of errors"; *Choice*, 34, 1996, 256. ASC4, 92)

65   Portugal. Agência Geral do Ultramar. **Political and administrative structures of the Portuguese overseas provinces**. Lisbon, 1974. 446pp.

66   Portugal. Agência Geral do Ultramar. **Portugal overseas provinces: facts and figures**. Lisbon, 1965. 179pp. illus. (African provinces are covered on pp. 5-112 with data on topography, climate, population, administration and history)

See also **231**

For general works on **former Belgian Africa** see under **CENTRAL AFRICA**; for **former Italian Africa** see under **NORTH-EAST AFRICA**; for **former Spanish Africa** see under **WEST AFRICA**

Special subjects

Art & Architecture

67   Faïk-Nzuji, Clémentine M. **Tracing memory: a glossary of graphic signs and symbols in African art and culture**. Hull, Québec, Canadian Museum of Civilization & International Centre for African Language, Literature & Tradition, 1996. (Canadian Centre for Folk Culture Studies; Paper, 70). 217pp. illus. maps. (Also pub. simultaneously in French)

68   Oliver, Paul, ed. **Encyclopedia of the vernacular architecture of the world. Vol. 3, Cultures and habitats (Latin America, North America, Sub-Saharan Africa)**. Cambridge, Cambridge University Press, 1997. xi, pp. 1,617-2,384.   illus. maps. (Pp. 1969-2170, 2311-2322, Sub-Saharan Africa. Includes some 200 brief entries, mostly for the architecture of particular cultures, under 11 regional/cultural sections. Detailed index, e.g. 15 items for Mali. Note also Vol. 1, Theories and principles)

69   Schädler, Karl-Ferdinand. **Lexikon afrikanische Kunst und Kultur**. Munich, Klinkhardt & Biermann, 1994. 447pp. (Includes c. 600 illus in b & w. & col.)

Economics

70 Arnold, Guy. **A guide to African political and economic development**. Chicago, Fitzroy Dearborn, 2001. 246pp. Illus. (Primarily concerned with the period post 1960. Emphasis on economic data. Arranged under broad topics, e.g. Resources, Development, each sub-divided by 7 broad regions. No sources indicated. Reviews, *ARBA*, 33, 2002, 47; *Ref. revs.*, 15(6) 2001, 46-48) *See also* **216**

71 Ben Hammouda, Hakim & Farhat, Magdi. **L'Afrique et l'OMC, les 100 mots clés**. Paris, Maisonneuve, 2005. 119pp. (Africa in relation to the World Trade Organization/Organisation mondiale du Commerce)

72 Hodd, Michael. **African economic handbook**. London, Euromonitor, 1986. 335pp. illus. (Emphasizes period 1973 to 1984. Includes regional overviews of the economic structures of East, West, Central and Southern Africa with detailed treatment of Nigeria and South Africa, followed by general surveys of each region in terms of recent political record and economic performance, with more detailed accounts of selected countries. 'Statistical fact-file', pp. 211-331 covering 34 countries with a population in excess of 1M. Reviews *African affairs*, 86, 1987, 588-589; *Choice*, 24, 1986, 384, "major contribution")

73 Hodd, Michael. **The economies of Africa**: geography, population, history, stability, structure, performance, forecasts. Aldershot, Dartmouth, 1991. viii, 363pp. (Bulk of the work comprises individual surveys for 48 sub-Saharan countries, with brief information on their topography, historical and economic background followed by tables and charts of economic statistics)

74 Walsh, Brian W.W. & Butorin, Pavel. **Dictionary of development: Third World economy, environment, society**. New York, Garland, 1990 (Garland reference library of social science, 487). 2 vols. (Brief country by country statistical profiles; dictionary of terms in their development context; list of development agencies. Useful for the situation in the 1980s)

75 **Worldmark encyclopedia of national economies. Vol. 1. Africa**, ed. Sara Pendergast & Tom Pendergast. Detroit, Gale Group/Thomson Learning, 2002. Also pub. on CD-ROM. (Country by country account emphasising recent economic history and current economic indicators, with statistics. Credits the IMF, UN and World Bank as principal sources. Review, *Ref. revs.* 16(8) 2002, 24-25)

Education

76   Teferra, Damtew & Altbach, Philip G. eds. **African higher education: an international reference handbook**. Bloomington, IN, Indiana University Press, 2003. ix, 714pp. (13 chaps. on themes, then individual surveys of the educational structure and institutions in every African country. Can helpfully be used with **427** and **436**. Conover-Porter Award, 2006)

Ethnography

77   **African ethnonyms: index to art-producing peoples of Africa**, comp. Daniel P. Biebuyck et al. New York, G.K. Hall/London, Prentice Hall, 1996. 378pp. ("A reference work for librarians, visual resources catalogers, museum scholars and researchers", pref. Lists some 4,500 names representing over 2,000 African peoples, clustering all variants under a single recommended entry form, with information on geographical location, language affiliation, and the name form used in Library of Congress Subject Headings (LCSH) and in the Getty Art & Architecture Thesaurus (AAT). Review, *Choice*, 34, 1997, 1634, "standard reference resource". *Choice* "outstanding academic title", 1997. ASC4, 118-119)

78   American Museum of Natural History. **Tribal map of negro Africa: map N and tribal key**. New York, American Museum of Natural History, 1956. 56pp. folded map. ('Research and preparation' by C.B. Hunter. Lists 1,016 tribes giving for each a map location and a reference to one of the items in the bibliography of 49 items. No cross references from alternative names)

79   **Atlas vorkolonialer Gesellschaften/Atlas of precolonial societies**: Kulturelles Erbe und Sozialstrukturen der Staaten Afrikas, Asiens und Melanesiens. Ein ethnologisches Kartenwerk für 95 Länder mit digitalem Buch, Datenbanken und Dokumentationen auf CD-ROM, ed. Hans-Peter Müller. Zurich, Ethnologisches Institut der Universität Zurich/Berlin, Reimer, 1999. Übersicht und English abstracts. 15pp. + 21 maps + 1 CD-ROM in slipcase. (8 thematic maps of the world show language families, subsistence modes, family typology etc. 5 maps for Africa show distribution of ethnic units and the population of each.)

80   Baumann, Herman ed. **Die Völker Afrikas und ihre tradionellen Kulturen**. Wiesbaden, Franz Steiner, 1975-1979. 2 vols. Vol. 1, 1975. ix, 815pp. 41 maps. (Covers 8 'cultural provinces' in Southern Africa, together with a general introduction); vol. 2, 1979. ix, 734pp. 25 maps. (Covers 14 'cultural provinces' in East, West and North Africa. An extensively revised version of **Völkerkunde von Afrika** (*see* **81**). Baumann himself had died in 1972. D. McCall in a review in *IJAHS*, 13, 1980, 753-757 concludes that "the only thing in English that can be compared is the **Ethnographic survey of Africa"** (*see* **86**) but that this had the disadvantage of being a series of individual local volumes appearing over a number of years)

81 Baumann, Herman, et al. **Völkerkunde von Afrika: mit besonderer Berücksichtigung der kolonialen Aufgabe**. Essen, Essener Verlagsanstalt, 1940. xv, 665pp. 461 illus. 23 maps in pocket. (Pt. 1, 'Völker und Kulturen Afrikas' by Baumann; pt. 2, 'Sprache und Erziehung' by Diedrich Westermann. Pt. 3 by Richard Thurnwald looks at various aspects of European contact. For the extensively revised **Die Völker Afrikas** (1975-79) *see* **80**. - - French trans. **Les peuples et les civilisations de l'Afrique, suivi de les langues et l'éducation**. Paris, Payot, 1948. (Bibliothèque scientifique). 605pp. (Reprint, Paris, 1967). Trans. by L. Homburger. (Omits pt. 3 of German original)

82 Bernatzik, Hugo Adolph, ed. **Afrika: Handbuch der angewandten Völkerkunde**. Innsbruck, Schlüsselverlag, 1947. 2 vols. xxi, 1429pp. Vol. 1, North Africa, Sudan, West Africa; vol. 2, Congo, Eastern Africa, Southern Africa. Each vol. has general introductory chapters, then country by country surveys, e.g. Kenia pp. 888-925, including 3pp. bibliography, with detailed accounts of each ethnic group. 33 contributors. A work in planning since 1937)

83 **Encyclopedia of African peoples**. New York, Facts on File, 2000. (Facts on file library of world history). 400pp. illus. maps. (A companion volume to **36**, and employing some of the same text. Four sections: 'Peoples of Africa', A/Z list of the larger ethnic groups; 'Culture and history'; 'Nations', covering 53 countries including Western Sahara; 'Biographies', with some 300 entries. For general readers and school and college libraries. Review, *Choice*, 38, 2001, 104. ASC4, 119. Although unacknowledged, this work is essentially a new ed. of **Peoples of Africa**. New York, Facts on File, 1997. 6 vols. 672pp (ASC4, 120) which had separate vols. for each of the broad regions of Africa, while vol. 6 treated the continent as a whole, and was also issued separately as **Nations of Africa**. New York, 1997. 112pp. Reviews, *ARBA*, 29, 1998, 141; *IJAHS*, 31, 1998, 647-648)

84 **Encyclopedia of world cultures. Vol. 9, Africa and the Middle East**, ed. John Middleton & Amal Rassam. New York, G.K. Hall, 1994. xv, 447pp. (Compiled in association with Human Relations Area Files. Articles on some 100 African groups by a range of specialists. Appendix, 'Additional African cultures' lists some 500, with an index of variant names. Review, *Choice*, 34, 1996, 428. *Choice* "outstanding academic title", 1996. ASC). - - **Supplement**. New York, 2002. (To the complete work, but contains considerable coverage of Africa)

85   **Encyclopedia of world popular cultures. Vol. 5, Sub-Saharan Africa**. Westport, CT, Greenwood Press. Announced as forthcoming 2006/07 by publisher. Text completed Dec 2005. *See* http://www.h-net.org/announce/show.cgi?ID=142605.

86   **Ethnographic survey of Africa**. London, IAI, 1950-1977. 60 vols. French series pub. for IAI by Presses Universitaires, Paris as 'Monographies ethnologiques africaines'. (The most extensive collection of ethnographic data on Africa, based on the literature and on field studies. A series of monographs on individual peoples, but with a largely consistent structure of presenting information on geographical distribution, size of population, social and political organization, religious beliefs, and economic and cultural activities. Issued in 7 sub-series: **North-Eastern Africa**, 3 vols (*see* **794**); **East Central Africa**, 18 vols (*see* **1006**); **West Central Africa**, 4 vols (*see* **1255**); **Belgian Congo** later **Congo** later **Zaire**, 5 vols. (also published as 'Monographies ethnographiques' by Musée Royal du Congo Belge/de l'Afrique Centrale; *see* **1609**); **Western Africa**, English series, 15 vols; French series, 10 vols. (*see* **1738**); **Southern Africa**, 4 vols. (*see* **2704**); **Madagascar**, 1 vol. (*see* **3286**).

87   Froelich, Jean-Claud. **Carte des populations de l'Afrique noire**. Paris, La documentation française, 1955. (Carte 71). col. map. 76 x 111 cm. - - **Notice et catalogue**. Paris, 1955. xxx, 113pp. Map at 1:5M. (The accompanying text lists 1,540 tribal groups with map locations. Coverage is of West and Central Africa)

88   Haskins, Jim & Biondi, Joann. **From Afar to Zulu: a dictionary of African cultures**. New York, Walker & Co., 1995. 212pp. (Popular level coverage of 32 major groups)

89   Hrbek, Ivan. 'A list of African ethnonyms', pp. 141-186 *in* **African ethnonyms & toponyms**: report and papers of the meeting of experts organized by UNESCO, Paris, 3-7 July, 1978. Paris, UNESCO, 1984. (General History of Africa: studies and documents, 6). 198pp. (Over 1,500 names of African peoples, giving alternative forms, relationships, and geographical location)

90   **International thesaurus of cultural development: Sub-Saharan Africa**, comp. African Cultural Institute, Regional Research & Documentation Centre for Cultural Development. Paris, UNESCO, 1985. x, 609pp. (Includes c. 2,700 relevant terms from the general **International thesaurus of cultural development**. Paris, UNESCO, 1980 with some 500 African terms added. Uses Greenberg, **157**, as source of terms for languages)

91   Johannesburg Public Library. **African native tribes**: rules for the classification of works on African ethnology in the Strange Collection of Africana with an index of tribal names and their variants. Johannesburg, 1956. a-f, xxvii, 142pp. (A classification schedule, being an expanded version of the Dewey Decimal Classification's class 572, which basically arranges tribes by geographical region, followed by an alphabetical index of names)

92   **Karta narodov Afriki**, ed. Boris Vasilevich Andrianov. Moscow, Institut Etnografii N.N. Mikluho-Maklaja, 1960. 79pp. (2 ethnic and population density maps at 1:8M plus text)

93   Levinson, David. **Ethnic groups worldwide: a ready reference handbook**. Phoenix, AZ, Oryx Press, 1998. 436pp. (Section for Africa, pp. 101-182 covers 53 countries. Aimed at the general reader)

94   Moss, Joyce & Wilson, George. **Peoples of the world: Africans south of the Sahara**: the culture, geographical setting, and historical background of 34 African peoples. Detroit, MI, Gale, 1991. 443pp. (Part of a series aimed at the popular market)

95   Murdock, George P. **Africa: its peoples and their culture history**. New York, McGraw-Hill, 1959. xii, 456pp. illus. maps. (General introduction, followed by systematic surveys by cultural area. Index of c.5,000 names of ethnic groups, and folding map of culture areas. A major and much quoted source. Reviews, *Africa*, 30, 1960, 277-278; *JAH* 2, 1961, 299-309 where J.D. Fage ultimately compares the work unfavourably with Baumann (*see* **80**) which he sees as the "standard handbook to the peoples of Africa")

96   Ol'derogge, Dmitri A. & Potekhin, Ivan I. **Die Völker Afrikas: ihre Vergangenheit und Gegenwart**. Berlin, Deutscher Verlag der Wissenschaften, 1961. 2 vols. (Rev. and updated trans. of **Narody Afriki**. Moscow, Akademiia nauk, Institut Etnografii, 1954. (Narody Mira; etnograficheski-ocherki). 731pp.)

97   Olson, James S. **The peoples of Africa: an ethnohistorical dictionary**. Westport, CT, Greenwood Press, 1996. 681pp. (Entries of varying detail for some 1,800 separate groups. References are largely to sources such as the **African historical dictionaries** and the **Country studies** series. Reviews, *Choice*, 34, 1996, 593, "hard to imagine a more complete dictionary"; *IJAHS*, 30, 1997, 671-672, concludes that the author has "no glimmer of awareness" of central historical issues in African studies. Gretchen Walsh comments on this total mismatch of reviewer reactions in **Research, reference service and resources for the study of Africa**. New York, Haworth Press, 2004, p.60. ASC4, 94)

98 **Peoples, nations and cultures; an A-Z of the peoples of the world, past and present**; general ed. John M. Mackenzie. London, Weidenfeld & Nicolson, 2005. 672pp. maps. (Africa, pp. 158-280. A work by specialists for a general readership with no sources or bibliography. "A three-fold focus on prehistorical, historical, as well as current peoples and cultures", pref., produces a useful combination of entries for the same region: e.g. entries for 'Great Zimbabwe culture', 'Zimbabweans', 'Shona' and 'Ndebele')

99 **Peoples of Africa**. New York, Marshall Cavendish, 2001. 11 vols. (Vol. 1. Algeria-Botswana; vol. 2. Burkina Faso-Comoros; vol. 3. Congo-Eritrea; vol. 4. Ethiopia-Guinea; vol. 5. Guinea-Bissau-Libya; vol. 6. Madagascar-Mayotte; vol. 7. Morocco-Nigeria; vol. 8. Réunion-Somalia; vol. 9. South Africa-Tanzania; vol. 10. Togo-Zimbabwe; vol. 11. Index. Series of brief regional volumes aimed at the school and college market)

100 Weekes, Richard V. ed. **Muslim peoples: a world ethnographic survey**. 2nd ed. Westport, CT, Greenwood Press, 1984. 2 vols. (A/Z by ethnic group, with some 4 to 6pp. on each. 78 entries for African peoples out of some 200 in the work as a whole. Entries for specific groups, e.g. Akan, Yoruba, and for categories, e.g. Asians of East Africa). - - Orig. pub. Westport, CT, 1978. xli, 546pp.

101 **Worldmark encyclopedia of cultures and daily life. Vol. 1. Africa**, ed. Timothy L. Gall. Detroit, Gale, 1998. xxii, 550pp. (Contains entries for 93 ethnic groups with treatment under a standardized list of topic headings: 'Location and homeland', 'Language', 'Religion', 'Family life', 'Food', 'Education' etc. Review, *Choice*, 35, 1998, 1692)

102 Yakan, Mohamad Z. **Almanac of African peoples & nations**. New Brunswick NJ, Transaction Publishers, 1999, vii, 847pp. (Pt. 2, African language families; pt. 3, African languages by country (very summary list); pt.4, African peoples & nations by country; pt. 5, African peoples and nations A/Z, with very small scale sketch maps showing approximate distribution. Few refs. are given for comments made. Reviews, *ARD*, 82, 2000, 86-87; *ASR* 43(3) 1999, 94-96; *ABPR*, 26, 2000, 95; *Choice*, 37, 2000, 1087, "impossible to recommend". ASC4, 130)

Folklore & Mythology

103 Bonnefoy, Yves, ed. **American, African and Old European mythologies**. Chicago, University of Chicago Press, 1993. xxi, 274pp. illus. maps. ('Africa', pp. 111-176. Lengthy signed articles on topics such as masks, graphic signs, kinship etc. Trans. of selections from **Dictionnaire des**

mythologies et des religions des sociétés traditionelles et du monde antique. Rev. ed. Paris, Flammarion, 1981)

104 **The Greenwood encyclopedia of world folklore and folklife. Vol. 1, Topics and themes, Africa, Australia and Oceania,** ed. William M. Clements. Westport, CT, Greenwood Press, 2006. illus. maps. (For students and general readers. Noted on publisher's Web site)

105 Knappert, Jan. **The Aquarian guide to African mythology**. Wellingborough, Aquarian Press, 1990. 272pp. illus. (Reprinted as **African mythology: an encyclopedia of myth and legend**. London, Diamond Books, 1995. ("This modest guide ... does not pretend to give more than an anthology of myths and mythological figures", pref. A/Z sequence: general entries for e.g. astrology, gods, sorcery, specific entries for peoples, animals and objects. Seen as "relatively superficial" in review of Scheub in H-Africa, *see* **108**)

106 Lynch, Patricia Ann. **African mythology A to Z**. New York, Facts on File, 2004. 160pp. illus. (Popular work with entries for deities, events, beliefs etc. Includes list of African countries with their tribal regions)

107 Peek, Philip M. & Yankah, Kwesi, eds. **African folklore: an encyclopedia**. London & New York, Routledge, 2004. xxxii, 593pp. (Some 300 A/Z signed entries, and index. Includes entries for myths, epics, riddles, songs and also ornaments. Appendices include a list of 'African study centers and libraries in the USA and Africa', 'Field and broadcast sound recording collections at the Indiana University Archives of Traditional Music' and a filmography. The first source to attempt standardized treatment of the topic throughout the continent. Reviews, *ABPR*, 30, 2004, 13-14; *ARBA*, 36, 2005, 545, "exceptionally well researched and well written volume"; *Choice*, 41, 2004, 1861-1862. ASC4, 127-128)

108 Scheub, Harold A. **A dictionary of African mythology: the mythmaker as storyteller**. Oxford, Oxford University Press, 2002. 384pp. Also available on subscription from Oxford Reference Online at http://www.oxfordreference.com/pages/Subjects_Titles_2E_MF01. (Contains some 400 entries for specific myths and folk tales, summarizing the story and discussing the belief system from which it originates, its cultural contexts and main characters. Review, *Choice*, 37, 2000, 1799; H-Africa, http://www.h-net.org/reviews/. *Choice* "outstanding academic title", 2000. ASC4, 95)

History

109   **African historical dictionaries**, gen. ed. Jon Woronoff. Metuchen, NJ/ Lanham, MD, Scarecrow Press, 1974- . (Voluminous continuing series, now covering every independent African country, often with several eds. *See* p. xlii for comments on the series in general. Entries are made below under the appropriate country. ASC4, 93)

110   Collins, Robert O. **Historical dictionary of pre-colonial Africa.** Lanham, MD, Scarecrow, 2001. (Historical dictionaries of ancient civilizations and historical eras, 3). iv, 615pp. (Bibliography, pp. 451-615. Attempts to cover the continent from c. 500 B.C. to the mid 19th century. Includes chronology, and c. 2,000 short entries for events, persons, ethnic groups, places etc. Reviews, *Choice*, 39, 2001, 664; *IJAHS*, 35, 2002, 199-200. ASC4, 93-94)

111   Falola, Toyin. **Key events in African history: a reference guide.** Westport, CT, Greenwood Press, Oryx Books/Oxford, Harcourt Education. 2002. 376pp. ("Directed toward high school and college libraries". In 36 topic chapters, each arranged chronologically. Review, *ABPR*, 29, 2003, 111; *Choice*, 40, 2003, 1799-1800. ASC4, 121)

112   Nantet, Bernard. **Dictionnaire de l'Afrique, histoire, civilisation, actualité.** [Rev. ed.]. Paris, Larousse, 2006. (Collection in extenso) viii, 303pp. illus. maps. (Small format work aimed at the general reader, an historical companion to **46**). - - Orig. pub. as **Dictionnaire d'histoire et civilisations africaines.** Paris, 1999. (Les referents). 228pp.

113   Page, Melvin E. & Sonnenburg, Penny M. eds. **Colonialism: an international, social, cultural and political encyclopedia.** Santa Barbara, CA, ABC-Clio, 2003. 3 vols. xxii, 1,208pp. illus. maps. (Aimed at undergraduates and the general reader. Some 600 entries A/Z in vols. 1 and 2 covering individual countries, major empires, ethnic groups, e.g. Zulus, and persons, e.g. Achebe, Kenyatta, Livingstone. Vol. 3 contains reprints of documents. Review, *Choice*, 41, 2004, 1276. *Choice* "outstanding academic title", 2004. ASC4, 127)

114   Page, Willie F. **Encyclopedia of African history and culture.** Rev. ed., ed. R. Hunt Davis Jr. New York, Facts on File, 2005. 5 vols. illus. maps. (Comprises rev. versions of vols. 1 to 3 of 1st ed. plus two additional vols. ed. R. Hunt Davis Jr. continuing the chronological coverage: vol. 4, The colonial era (1850-1960); vol. 5, Independent Africa (1960-present). - - Orig. pub. New York, Facts on File, 2001. 3 vols. illus. maps. Vol. 1, Ancient Africa (Prehistory to 500 CE); vol. 2, African Kingdoms (500 to 1500); vol. 3, From conquest to colonization (1500 to 1850). ("Intended for students and general readers", pref. Reviews, *ARBA*, 33, 2002, "a brave effort ... published ... apparently without any editorial assistance or standards"; *Choice*, 39, 2002, 1404, "seriously flawed ... not recommended"; H-Africa, http://www.h-net.org/~africa/reviews/. ASC4, 127)

115 Peregrine, Peter N. & Ember, Melvyn. **Encyclopedia of prehistory. Vol. 1, Africa**. Dordrecht, Kluwer Academic/New York, Plenum Publishers, 2001. xxxii, 376pp. (Published in association with Human Relations Area Files. Entries for 30 major cultures with details under each of sub-traditions and individual sites. 12 maps showing the continent from 2 million B.C. to 1,000 B.C. No illus. ASC4, 128)

116 Shillington, Kevin, ed. **Encyclopedia of African history**. New York, Fitzroy Dearborn, 2005. 3 vols. 1,824pp. illus. maps. (Covers the whole continent, and all surrounding islands in both the Atlantic and Indian Oceans: "it is an indispensable feature of this work that students can find African history presented with a view to the continent in its entirety". Over 1,000 entries by 330 contributors, approximately 130 of them African. About one third of the entries cover history before the 19th century. Most articles are c. 1,000 words in length on specific topics and states, with some longer essays up to 5,000 words on broader topics, e.g. the African diaspora. Alphabetical list of all entries at the start of each volume; thematic list of entries at the start of vol. 1, arranged under 15 broad, basically chronological headings; detailed index at end of vol. 3. Reviews, *Choice*, 42, 2005, 1564; *Ref.revs.*, 20(1) 2006, 61-62, "essential one-stop gateway to all periods of African history". ASC4, 129)

117 Zeleza, Paul Tiyambe & Eyoh, Dickson, eds. **Encyclopedia of twentieth century African history**. London/New York, Routledge, 2003. 672pp. (Includes some 250 signed entries, many by African scholars, presenting "critical interpretation ... in the context of the pertinent historiographical debates" for African peoples, societies, states and politics. Longer entries, c. 4,000 words, for key issues; shorter entries of c. 2,000 words for specific topics, themes and events; and 'area surveys' of 600 to 1,500 words for geographical, environmental and linguistic entities. Detailed cross-referencing, index, thematic entry list and suggestions for further reading. Reviews, *ABPR*, 29, 2003, 10; *ARBA*, 35, 2004, 211-212; *Choice*, 40, 2003, 1346; *Ref. revs.*, 17(5) 2003, 61-62, "authoritative, balanced and scholarly". *Choice* "outstanding academic title", 2003. ASC4, 131)

Atlases

118 **African history on file**. Rev. ed. New York, Facts on File for the Diagram Group, 2003. Loose-leaf. (Series of over 500 standardized b. & w. maps of 53 countries, arranged in 7 geographic regions. *See also* **Africa on file** (**584**). Review, *ARBA*, 35, 2004, 211). - - Orig. pub. New York, 1994.

119 Ajayi, J.F.A. & Crowder, Michael, eds. **Historical atlas of Africa**. Longman, 1985. 168pp. col. maps. (Over 50 contributors and ten years in preparation. Includes 72 'map-sets', altogether comprising over 300 individual maps. 5,000 entry index provides a "unique guide to name changes over 3,000 years of African history", pref. Reviews, *African affairs*, 85, 1986, 301-302, "invaluable and accurate source"; *Choice*, 23, 1986, 1196; *JAH* 28, 1987, 151-152, "difficult to find anything negative to say ... unlikely to be surpassed as the standard work for years to come")
- - **Atlas historique de l'Afrique**: adaptation française publiée sous la direction de Catherine Coquery-Vidovitch et al. Paris, Jaguar, 1988. 174pp.

120 Animated atlas of African history 1879-2002, comp. Nancy Jacobs et al. http://www.brown.edu/Research/AAAH/. Originally designed for a Brown University Summer Institute in 2004, refined 2004 to 2006 with continuous revision anticipated. Available on the Web or as download for individual computers. Constructed using Macromedia Flash. Displays a base map of Africa which can be viewed year by year from 1879 to 2002, or can be made to move forward or backward at varying speeds. 'Color-coding of territories reflects political changes; symbols show conflicts as isolated events; bar graphs give demographic and economic data, and labels show country names'. These elements can each be displayed or suppressed. 'Designed to be an instructional tool at the secondary and college levels, and also for the general learner'.

121 Bayly, Christopher Alan, ed. **Atlas of the British empire**. London, Hamlyn, 1989. 256pp illus. 38 col. maps. (Text written by scholars for a general readership. Includes some 10 sections specifically on Africa, with many others relevant. Review, *Choice*, 27, 1990, 1294. *Choice* "outstanding academic book", 1991)

122 Clark, J. Desmond. **Atlas of African prehistory**. Chicago, IL, University of Chicago, 1967. 62pp. maps. (Comp. under the auspices of the Pan African Congress on Prehistory and Quaternary Studies. 12 base maps, 38 transparent overlays (25 at 1:20M, 13 at 1:38M). Includes maps showing rainfall, vegetation, soils etc. of modern Africa, together with maps showing similar hypothetical data for prehistoric times, accompanied by transparent 'cultural overlays' for various periods of prehistory from the Earlier Stone Age to the Neolithic. 62pp handbook section of explanatory notes includes a gazetteer of prehistoric sites. Reviews, *AHS*, 1, 1968, 111-112; *GJ*, 137, 1971, 592-593. *See* J.D. Clark, 'The *Atlas ...*', pp. 311-328 in **Actes du IVe Congrès panafricain de préhistoire et de l'étude du quarternaire, Léopoldville, 1959**. Tervuren, 1962)

123 Fage, John D. **An atlas of African history**. 2nd ed. London, Arnold, 1978. 72pp. Maps by M. Verity. 71 maps. (Uses two tones of brown shading to improve clarity. Covers 410 to 1957A.D. Maps new to 2nd ed. are for pre 19th century. Detailed legends. Reviews, *GJ* 144, 1978, 521-522; *JAH* 20, 1979, 377). - - Orig. pub. London, 1958. 64pp. 62 maps. (Review, *Africa*, 29, 1959, 98-100)

124 Freeman-Grenville, Greville S.P. & Munro-Hay, Christopher. **Historical atlas of Islam**. Rev. ed. London, Continuum, 2002. xvii, 416pp. illus. maps. ("Portions of this vol. have been previously pub. as ... the *New atlas of African history*", t.p. verso, *see* **125**. Part 5, The further spread of Islam; sect, iii, Eastern Africa; sect, iv, Western Africa. Greater African emphasis than the more scholarly atlases such as the **Historical atlas of Islam**, 2nd ed. Leiden, Brill, 2002). - - Orig. pub. as **Historical atlas of the Middle East**. New York, Simon & Schuster, 1993. 144pp.

125 Freeman-Grenville, Greville S.P. **The new atlas of African history**. London/New York, Simon & Schuster, 1991. 144pp. maps. (103 b. & w. & red maps accompanied by 64pp. text. Reviews, *Choice*, 29, 1991, 58, "idio-syncratic ... contentious rather than informative text"; *Meridian*, 6, 1991, 50-52. Extensively rev. & updated version of his **A modern atlas of African history.** London, Rex Collings, 1976. 63 pp. maps. (Includes 70 two-col. maps, about half concerned with Africa pre 1500. Reviews, *Choice*, 13, 1977, 1416; *IJAHS*, 11, 1978, 134-135)

126 Gailey, Harry A. **The history of Africa in maps**. Chicago, IL, Denoyer-Gappert, 1967. 96pp. maps. (47 hand-drawn and lettered b. & w. maps with accompanying text. For schools and colleges)

127 Gray, Richard. 'Eclipse maps', *Journal of African history*, 6, 1965, 251-262; 'Annular eclipse maps', *ibid.*, 9, 1968, 147-157. (Together the two articles reproduce 9 maps (which were also advertised as being available in enlarged size 1:10M on plastic from the journal) showing the actual paths taken across the continent by 164 total solar eclipses visible in Africa between post 1000 A.D. The intention is to aid in linking oral traditions with particular eclipses and dates. Much of the data are drawn from that originally published in T. von Oppolzer, **Canon der Firslinissi**. Vienna, 1887; English trans. by O. Gingerich. New York, Door, 1902).

128   Jolly, Jean. **L'Afrique et son environnement européen et asiatique.** Paris, Editions Paris-Méditerranée, 2002. 118pp. maps. (Cover title adds 'Atlas historique'. Using a single base map for each theme attempts to place Africa within the wider context of western Eurasia, Europe, the Middle East and Central Asia and the Indian subcontinent)

129   Kasule, Samuel. **The Macmillan history atlas of Africa**. New York, Macmillan, 1998. 160pp. illus. maps. (Sections for Early humans; Kingdoms and empires; Europe in Africa; the African diaspora; Imperialism to independence. For schools and colleges. ASC3, 243)

130   Kwamena-Poh, M. et al. **African history in maps**. Harlow, Longmans, 1982. 80pp. 36 col. maps.

131   Lemarchand, Phillipe. **L'Afrique et l'Europe: atlas du XXe siècle**. Brussels, Editions Complexe, 1994. 251pp. illus. maps.
- - Spanish trans. **Atlas de Africa**. Madrid, Acento Ed., 2000. 254pp. (Review, *Estudios africanos*, 15, 2001, 284-285)

132   Lugan, Bernard. **Atlas historique de l'Afrique des origines à nos jours**. [Monaco], Rocher, 2001. 268pp. illus. maps. (Detailed coverage in a small format, with some 150 b. & w. maps and accompanying text on a wide range of topics, from pre-history to date. Some emphasis on Francophone Africa, but coverage of the whole continent. Notes on sources. Catherine Coquery-Vidrovitch, H-NET List for African History and Culture <H-AFRICA@H-NET.MSU.EDU>, 16 April 2006, comments on what she sees as the racist nature of the text. ASC4, 124)

133   McEvedy, Colin. **Penguin atlas of African history**. New ed. London, Penguin, 1995. 144pp. (Outline schematic b. & w. maps as in the author's series of world history atlases. Excludes Mauritius, Seychelles and Réunion).
- - Orig. pub. Harmondsworth, Penguin, 1980, 142pp. 59 plates. (Highly critical review, *African affairs*, 79, 1980, 602-603)

134   Porter, Adrian N. **Atlas of British overseas expansion**. London, Routledge, 1991. x, 279pp. (Includes 32 maps specifically treating Africa and many more which are relevant. Review, *Choice*, 29, 1991, 715)

135   Sellier, Jean. **Atlas des peuples d'Afrique**. Paris, La Découverte, 2003. 207pp. 18 x 24cm. (Summary historical text for each region or country, with col. maps showing political, linguistic and ethnic data. Sections for the Nile valley, Ethiopia and neighbouring countries, the Maghreb, Ancient West Africa, West Africa from the 19th century, Ancient Bantu Africa, Bantu Africa from the 19th century, Madagascar)

- - Portuguese trans. **Atlas dos povos de África**, trans. Isabel Gentil. Lisbon, Campo da Comunicação, 2004. 175pp. illus.

Cambridge & UNESCO histories

Although not "reference works" in the sense normally used in AGRM2, these two major compilations are included, since use of their contents lists and individual vol. indexes (sadly neither set has provided an overall index vol.) can give access to specific data. The Cambridge history contains between 9 and 15 chapters per volume with 72 contributors, almost all from Europe and North America, and the great majority from Britain and the U.S.A. The UNESCO history contains from 27 to 30 chapters per volume with almost 350 contributors, the great majority from Africa. For an overview of the two series at the planning stage, *see* J.D. Fage, one of the general editors of the Cambridge history, 'Cooperative multi-volume histories of Africa', *ARD*, 7, 1975, 1-3, and for a review of the first two vols. of the UNESCO series by Roland Oliver, the other general editor of the Cambridge series, in which he makes comparisons between the two series, *see Times literary supplement*, 4068, 20 March 1961, 299)

136   Cambridge history of Africa. Cambridge, Cambridge University Press, 1975-1986. 8 vols. illus. maps. Vol. 1. 1982. From the earliest times to c. 500 B.C., ed. J. Desmond Clark. xxiii, 1157pp; vol. 2. 1978. From c.500 B.C. to A.D. 1050, ed. John D. Fage. xvii, 840pp; vol. 3. 1977. From c.1050 to c.1600, ed. Roland Oliver. xiii, 803pp; vol. 4. 1975, From c.1600 to c.1790, ed. Richard Gray. xiv, 738pp; vol. 5. 1977. From c.1790 to c.1870, ed. John Flint. xv, 617pp; vol. 6. 1985. From 1870 to 1905, ed. Roland Oliver & G. Neville Sanderson. xiv, 942pp;   vol. 7. 1986. From 1905 to 1940, ed. Andrew D. Roberts. xx, 1063pp; vol. 8. 1984. From c.1940 to c.1975, ed. Michael Crowder. xvi, 1011pp. (Reviews range from "comprehensive, meticulous, definitive", *IJAHS*, 12, 1979, 306-311 on vol. 4, to "lacks balance ... doubt whether it deserves the praise accorded to some earlier volumes", *JAH*, 21, 1980, 547-550 on vol. 2, but are in general agreement that the vols. contain useful collections of data, and significant individual chapters, but do not provide coherent syntheses)

137   UNESCO general history of Africa. London, Heinemann/Berkeley, CA, University of California Press, 1981-1993. 8 vols. Vol. 1. 1981. Methodology and African prehistory, ed. Joseph Ki-Zerbo. xxvii, 819pp; vol. 2. 1981. Ancient civilisations of Africa, ed. G. Mokhtar. xvii, 804pp; vol. 3. 1988. Africa from the seventh to the eleventh century, ed. M. Elfasi. xxv, 869pp;   vol. 4. 1984. Africa from the twelfth to the sixteenth century, ed. Joseph Ki-Zerbo & D.T. Niane. xxvii, 751pp; vol. 5. 1992. Africa from the sixteenth to the eighteenth century, ed. B.A. Ogot. xxxi, 1045pp; vol. 6. 1985. Africa in the nineteenth century until the 1880's, ed. J.F.Ade Ajayi. 865pp; vol. 7. 1989. Africa under colonial domination 1880-1935, ed. A. Adu Boahen. xxxi, 861pp; vol. 8. 1993. Africa since 1935, ed. Ali A. Mazrui. xxviii, 1025pp.

(Comp. under the direction of a 39 man UNESCO International Scientific Committee for the Drafting of a General History of Africa, established in 1970 and holding its final meeting in 1999, with two-thirds of the members being from Africa. The Committee also published a series of working documents between 1978 and 1985 as UNESCO. **General history of Africa: studies and documents,** *see* **89** for one of these).

- - Abridged ed. in English. Oxford, James Currey, 1990-1999. 8 vols.

- - Abridged ed. in French. Paris, UNESCO/Edicef/Présence Africaine, 1989-1998. 8 vols. (Note that in each ed. vol. 8 is in fact unabridged. Complete trans. of the 8 vols. are available in Arabic. Vol. 1 is available in full in Chinese, Italian, Japanese, Portuguese, and Spanish, and abridged in Fulani, Hausa and Kiswahili; vol. 2 in full in Italian, Portuguese, Spanish and abridged in Fulani, and Hausa; vol. 3 in full in Spanish; vol. 4 in full in Chinese, Japanese, Portuguese, and Spanish; vol. 7 in full in Chinese, Japanese, Portuguese, and Spanish. "Africa is considered in this work as a totality. The aim is to show the historical relationships between the various parts of the continent, too frequently subdivided in works published to date. Africa's historical connections with the other continents receive due attention ... bringing out, in its appropriate light, Africa's contribution to the history of mankind. The **General History of Africa** is, in particular, a history of ideas and civilizations, societies and institutions. It is based on a wide variety of sources, including oral tradition and art forms. The *History* is viewed essentially from the inside. Although a scholarly work, it is also, in large measure, a faithful reflection of the way in which African authors view their own civilization". (Taken from Web site http://www.unesco.org/culture/africa/html_eng/index_en.htm. in March 2006, but site no longer active in September 2006). Reviews vary from the dismissive: "very doubtful utility" on vol. 1, and "cannot be welcomed without serious reservations" on vol. 2, both in *JAH,* 23, 1982, 115-116, to "impressively successful", *IJAHS,* 18, 1985, 551-552 on vol. 4 and "by far the best guide to the colonial impact on Africa", *JAH* 27, 1986, 178-180 on vol. 7. The consensus is that the far larger number of individual authors compared with the Cambridge History makes for an even greater absence of coherence, and lack of currency in the contributions)

Chronologies

138   African timelines, http://web.cocc.edu/cagatucci/classes/hum211/timelines/htimelinetoc.htm. Arranged in 5 broad sections, e.g. Pt. I, Ancient Africa, pt. V, Post-independence Africa, then year by year with list of events. Numerous links provided for each event. Detailed list of sources used. Compiled to support a U.S. college course and many of the links are to other U.S. college course sites.

139 Freeman-Grenville, Greville S.P. **Chronology of African history**. London, Oxford University Press, 1973. xxii, 312pp. (Columns for different regions of Africa, together with one for other continents, listing events year by year. Four principal sections, 1300 B.C.-600 A.D.; 600-1300; 1300-1800; 1800 to date, with headings for regions varying in each section. Reviews *Africa*, 44, 1974, 212-213; *GJ*, 140, 1974, 497; *JAH*, 15, 1974, 489-490. Detailed critical review article, 'African chronology', by David Henige, *African affairs*, 75, 1976, 104-108, "the work is, to put it bluntly, quite unusable")

140 Jenkins, Everett. **Pan-African chronology: a comprehensive reference to the Black quest for freedom in Africa, the Americas, Europe and Asia**. Jefferson, NC, McFarland, 1990-1999. 3 vols. (Vol. 1. 1990. 1400-1865. 448pp; vol. 2. 1998, 1865-1905. 572pp; vol. 3. 1999. 1905-1929. 628pp. Immensely detailed work, with events in each year divided by region: U.S., The Americas, Europe, Australia, Asia and Africa, the last further divided by sub-regions. Detailed indexes. No refs to sources used. Reviews of vol. 2, *ARD*, 77, 1998, 54, "at times eccentric and of limited value"; *Choice*, 36, 1998, 99; of vol. 3, *Choice*, 39, 2001, 1956. ASC4, 123)

141 Lea, David et al, eds. **A political chronology of Africa**. London, Europa Publications/Taylor & Francis Group, 2001. 508pp. (Fourth vol. in a six vol. set covering the world. A/Z by country. Attempts to begin "at least as early as the emergence of an entity resembling the modern nation", pref., but emphasises more recent events, especially elections, wars and treaties. No list of sources. Review, *ABPR*, 28, 2002, 307. ASC4, 124)

142 **Worldmark chronology of the nations. Vol. 1, Chronology of Africa**. Detroit, Gale, 1999. vii, 691pp. (Broad historical introduction followed by A/Z country entries, with key dates followed by some narrative about the event. Western Sahara subsumed under Morocco)

Slavery

143 Drescher, Seymour & Engermann, Stanley L. eds. **A historical guide to world slavery**. Oxford, Oxford University Press, 1998. xxiv, 429pp. (Arranged under broad subjects, e.g. Abolition and anti-slavery; Capitalism and slavery; Slave trade: trans-Saharan. Main entry on Africa, pp. 27-50. Articles by over 100 contributors. Very broad scope from Biblical times to the present militates against detailed coverage of any one topic)

144 Klein, Martin A. **A historical dictionary of slavery and abolition**. Lanham, MD, Scarecrow Press, 2002. (Historical dictionaries of religions, philosophies and movements, 40). xxiii, 348pp. (Review, *Choice*, 40, 2002, 80.

Also issued in paperback as **The A to Z of slavery and abolition**. Lanham, MD, Scarecrow Press, 2002. xxiii, 312pp.)

145   Macmillan encyclopedia of world slavery, ed. Paul Finkelman & Joseph C. Miller. New York, Macmillan Reference USA & Simon & Schuster/London, Simon & Schuster & Prentice Hall International, 1998. 2 vols. 1,065pp. (Main entry for Africa, pp. 26-45; also entries for regions of Africa, and specific sub-headings for Africa and regions under longer topical entries, e.g. for Slave trade. General index has two columns of refs. for Africa. Review, *Choice*, 40, 1999, 80. ASC4, 121)

146   Rodriguez, Junius P. **Chronology of world slavery**. Santa Barbara, CA, ABC-Clio, 1999. 580pp. (Companion to **147**. Principal African coverage pp. 119-146 with numerous other relevant entries traceable via detailed index. Review, *Ref. revs.*, 14(1)2000, 10-11)

147   Rodriguez, Junius P. **Historical encyclopedia of world slavery**. Santa Barbara, CA, ABC-Clio, 1997. 2 vols. 805pp. (Some 60 articles out of 650 have significant African content. Review, *Choice*, 35, 1998, 1520. *Choice* "outstanding academic title", 1998)

Human rights

148   Lawrence, James T. ed. **Human rights in Africa**. New York, Nova Science Pubs., 2004. vii, 252pp. (A/Z list of countries, each with a 2 to 3pp. summary of its human rights record and a bibliography)

Information retrieval

149   African studies thesaurus: subject headings for library users. New York, Greenwood Press, 1992. (Bibliographies and indexes in Afro-American and African studies, 29). 435pp. (From the Library of Congress Subject Headings (LCSH). Lists some 4,000 subject headings including 600 names of ethnic groups and nearly 600 languages. LC classification numbers also added).

150   International Council of Museums (ICOM). **Manuel des normes: documentation des collections africaines/Handbook of standards: documenting African collections**, ed. Chédlia Annabi. Paris, 1996. 65pp. illus. Also available on the ICOM Web site at http://icom.museum/afridoc/

Language

151   Bender, M. Lionel. 'Classification génétique des langues Nilo-Sahariennes', *Linguistique africaine*, 9, 1992, 15-39

152 Bendor-Samuel, John & Hartell, Rhonda L. eds. **The Niger-Congo languages: a classification and description of Africa's largest language family**. Lanham, MD, University Press of America, 1989. 518pp. (Various specialist authors contribute chapters on each of 20 main sub-families)

153 Campbell, George L. **Compendium of the world's languages**. 2nd ed. London, Routledge, 2000. 2 vols. (Review, *Choice*, 38, 2001, 1051, "most easily accessible and up-to-date guide to the world's languages"). - - Orig. pub. London, 1991. 2 vols.

154 Dalby, David. **Language map of Africa and the adjacent islands**. Provisional ed. London, International African Institute, 1977. 63pp. (Map at 1:5M on 4 sheets, with inset enlargements. Text includes discussion of principles of compilation, and a checklist of all languages shown on the map in both a structured and an A/Z sequence. Later used as the basis for his **Thesaurus of African languages**, *see* **165**)

155 **Ethnologue: languages of the world**, 15th ed., ed. Raymond G. Gordon Jr. Dallas, TX, SIL International, 2005. 1,272pp. (Also available at: http://www.ethnologue.com/. "The Ethnologue database has been an active research project for more than fifty years. Once every four years we take a snapshot of the contents of the database and publish it along with language maps for many of the countries of the world", pref. Database searchable under continent, country, language name and language family tree. Details for each language include alternative names, areas in which spoken, number of speakers. ASC4, 162)

156 Fivaz, Derek & Scott, Patricia E. **African languages: a genetic and decimalised classification for bibliographic and general reference**. Boston, MA, G.K. Hall, 1977. xxxiv, 332pp. (Compilation by a linguist, Fivaz and a librarian, Scott. "In general terms ... we have followed the most widely accepted genetic framework for Africa, that of Joseph H. Greenberg", pref; *see* **157**. Includes a classified schedule (pp. 3-82) of languages according to their perceived relationships; alphabetical list of preferred names for languages and dialects (pp. 83-256) with references from all traced alternative names and spellings; list of sources (pp. 257-304); language family charts and distribution maps (pp. 305-321). Gives comparative tables of the basic approach to classifying African languages offered by Greenberg (*see* **157**) and the Bliss, Library of Congress, Universal Decimal Classification and Dewey Decimal library classification schemes)

157 Greenberg, Joseph H. **The languages of Africa**. 3rd. ed. Bloomington, IN, Indiana University, 1966. (Research Center for the Language Sciences, 25). 180pp. 5 maps. ("A complete genetic classification of the languages of Africa", pref. Lists 730 languages classified into Niger-Congo, Afroasiatic, Khoisan, Chari-Nile, Nilo-Saharan and Niger-Kordofanian groups). - - Orig. pub. as 'Studies in African linguistic classification', *Southwestern journal of anthropology*, 5, 1949, 79-100; 190-198; 309-317; 6, 1950, 47-63, 143-160, 223-237; 388-398; 10, 1954, 405-415. These articles were then reprinted as **Studies in African linguistic classification**. Branford, CN, Compass Publishing for Language & Communication Research Center, Columbia University & Program of African Studies, Northwestern University, 1955. 116pp. maps. - - 2nd ed. **The languages of Africa**. Bloomington, IN, Indiana University, 1963. (*International journal of American linguistics*, 29(1) part 2). 179pp. ("Expanded and extensively revised version of the author's *Studies in African linguistic classification*", pref. Greenberg's work remains one of the most widely followed, if much debated and disputed, systems of arranging African languages. For discussion contemporary with the earlier versions *see* Diedrich Westermann, 'African linguistic classification', *Africa*, 22, 1952, 250-256, and reviews in *Word*, 19, 1963, 407-417; *African language studies*, 7, 1966, 160-170 and critical review by Malcolm Guthrie of SOAS, *JAH*, 5, 1964, 135-136 which "looks in vain for an admission that in respect to most of the problems discussed, more than one conclusion might be drawn". For later comments, including discussion of the controversies, *see* Colin Flight, 'Trees and traps: strategies for the classification of African languages and their historical significance', *History in Africa*, 8, 1981, 43-74, which reviews especially the differing receptions of Greenberg by British anthropologists and by British historians. *See also* 'Criticism of Greenberg's methodology', pp. 120-124 in Meritt Ruhlen. **A guide to the world's languages**. Vol. 1, Classification, London, 1987, **169**)

158   Handbook of African languages. London, Oxford University Press for IAI, 1952-1959. 4 vols. (Vol. 1. 1952. La langue berbère, by A. Bassett. v, 72pp; vol. 2. 1952. Languages of West Africa by D. Westermann & M.A. Bryan. 215pp. (*see* **1741**); vol. 3. 1956. The non-Bantu languages of North Eastern Africa by A.N. Tucker & M.A. Bryan. xvi, 228pp. (*see* **796**); vol. 4. 1959. The Bantu languages of Africa by M.A. Bryan. xi, 170pp. Although several additional studies are listed in bibliographies, library catalogues, and the IAI's own lists of publications as parts of the **Handbook**, these 4 vols. in fact represent the Institute's complete original concept of a four vol. general survey covering all the languages of Africa, recording language groups, and estimates of numbers of speakers and their topographical distribution (*see* foreword by Darryl Forde, Director of the IAI, to vol. 4 *above*). Among the various other volumes issued by the Institute 'in connection with the **Handbook**' note especially **The classification of the Bantu languages** by Malcolm Guthrie. London, Oxford University Press, 1948. 91pp. (Review, *African affairs*, 48, 1949, 164-165) a standard work of one school of thought on African language classification. A slightly modified outline appears as 'Key list of Bantu languages', pp. 11-15 in vol. 2 of Malcolm Guthrie **Comparative Bantu**. Farnborough, Gregg, 1970. For discussion of the classification of Guthrie, comparison with that of Greenberg, and comments on the **Handbook**, *see* the two papers by Colin Flight, 'Malcolm Guthrie and the reconstruction of Bantu prehistory', *History in Africa*, 7, 1980, 81-118; 'The Bantu expansion and the SOAS network', *ibid.* 15, 1988, 261-301)

159 Heine, Bernd & Nurse, Derek. **African languages: an introduction**. Cambridge, Cambridge University Press, 2000. xx, 396pp. maps. (Includes chapters on the major groups Niger-Congo, Nilo-Saharan, Afroasiatic, Khoisan, each with a discussion of their major sub-groups and the history of their classification)

160 Heine, Bernd. **Status and use of African lingua francas**. Munich, Weltforum Verlag, 1970. (Afrika-Studien, 49). 206pp. maps. (Covers some 40 languages. Review, *African affairs*, 71, 1972, 342, "its wealth of statistics and secondary material makes it a useful work of reference")

161 Heine, Bernd. **A typology of African languages based on the order of meaningful elements**. Berlin, Reimer, 1976. (Kölner Beiträge zur Afrikanistik, Bd. 4). 89pp. illus. maps. (Samples the word order in some 300 languages to devise the typology. Review, *JALL*, 1, 1979, 199-224)

162 Jungraithmayr, Hermann & Moehlig, Wilhelm J.G. eds. **Lexikon der Afrikanistik: afrikanische Sprachen und ihre Erforschung**. Berlin, Reimer, 1983. 351pp. illus. maps. (Entries for language terms and names of languages, with maps)

163 Maho, Jouni Filip. **African languages country by country: a reference guide**. 3rd ed. Gothenburg, Department of Oriental & African languages, Göteborg University, 1998. (Göteborg Africana informal series, 1). 188pp. (Pt. 1, pp. 9-21, Historical maps; pt. 2, pp. 23-35, Continental language maps; pt. 3, pp. 37-157, African languages country by country. Each country has a very brief political/administrative history, a list of current administrative sub-divisions, and a map with a very broad brush indication of language distribution). - - Orig. pub. Gothenburg, 1997; - - 2nd ed. Gothenburg, 1997.

164 Malherbe, Michel. **Répertoire simplifié des langues africaines**. Paris, Harmattan, 2000. 95pp. maps. (Arranged A/Z by country, with A/Z index of languages and a brief account of the major language groups)

165 Mann, Michael & Dalby, David. **A thesaurus of African languages: a classified and annotated inventory of the spoken languages of Africa, with an appendix on their written representation**. Oxford, Hans Zell for IAI, 1988.

336pp. (Lists 2,550 languages classified into 315 sets and sub-sets, with a language index of some 12,000 entries. Follows system of Dalby, **Language map of Africa** (*see* **154**). Sees many features of the classifications of Greenberg (*see* **157**) and Fivaz and Scott (*see* **156**) as "open to debate or already discredited", pref. Notes language use in education and the media in each African country. Detailed bibliography, and index of 12,000 entries. Reproduces names of each language in phonetic script, the 'African reference alphabet' as agreed at the UNESCO Meeting of Experts on the Transcription and Harmonization of African Languages, Niamey, 17-21 July 1978 (*see* **Final report**. Paris, UNESCO, 1978 and **176** below). Typeset entirely in lower-case. The transcription and typesetting are among aspects singled out for comment in long critical reviews in *IJAHS*, 21, 1988, 747-750 and in *JALL*, 11, 1989, 175-182 where Paul Newman concludes "since the book as it now stands absolutely cannot serve as the reference work for which it was intended, I would suggest that the publisher withdraw [it] from the market")

166 Moseley, Christopher & Asher, Ron. E. **Atlas of the world's languages**. London, Routledge, 1993. viii, 372pp. (Pp. 263-286, maps 74-78, Middle East, North Africa and Ethiopia by Arthur K. Irvine; pp. 287-346, maps 79-113, Sub-Saharan Africa by Benji Wald. Review, *Choice*, 32, 1994, 63. ASC4, 163)

167 Nurse, Derek & Philippson, Gérard, eds. **The Bantu languages**. London, Routledge, 2003. xvii, 708pp. (Surveys some 500 Bantu languages, spoken by 240 million in 27 sub-Saharan countries. Review, *BSOAS*, 68, 2005, 500-502)

168 The Rosetta Project. http://www.rosettaproject.org/live. 'A global collaboration of language specialists and native speakers building a publicly accessible online archive of all documented human languages', first screen of Web site. A National Science Digital Library since 2004. Searchable by continent, by country, by language family and by individual language. Uses codes from **Ethnologue** (*see* **155**). A developing site which will eventually bring together data from existing sources including classification studies, orthographies, word lists, etc. ASC4, 167.

169 Ruhlen, Merritt. **A guide to the world's languages. Vol. 1, Classification**. London, Edward Arnold, 1987. xxv, 463pp. (Re-issued, London, 1991, "with a postscript on recent developments". Pp. 76-124, Africa. Discusses various proposed classifications for the major language families, especially that of Greenberg, *see* **157**)

170 UNESCO. Regional Bureau for Education in Africa. **Les langues communautaires africaines et leur utilisation dans l'enseignement et l'alphabétisation: une enquête régionale**. Dakar, [1984]. 94pp. (Statistical data on the 23 most widely spoken African languages. Includes list of relevant research centres and journals)

171 Voegelin, Charles Frederick & F.M. **Classification and index of the world's languages**. New York, Elsevier, 1977. viii, 658pp. (All languages are treated in one alphabetical sequence. For African languages, the authors' earlier article in *Anthropological linguistics*, 1964, *see* **172**, is probably more convenient to use)

172 Voegelin, Charles Frederick & F.M. 'Languages of the world: Africa, fasc. one', *Anthropological linguistics*, 6(5) 1964, 1-339. (General discussion of the problems of African language classification, followed by a structured list arranging individual languages under 47 families and five main groups (Niger-Congo, Nilo-Saharan, Nilo-Hamitic, Afro-Asiatic, Khoisan). Maps and detailed notes on topographic distribution and numbers of speakers. Data later revised and incorporated into the authors' **Classification and index of the world's languages** (1977) *see* **171**, where however all languages and language groups are arranged alphabetically rather than by continent)

173 Webbook of African Language Resources. http://www.isp.msu.edu/ AfrLang/hiermenu.html/. Hosted by African Studies Center, Michigan State University. (Provides a profile for each of the 82 'high priority' languages (designated as such by a 1979 Conference held at Michigan State) giving its language group, geographical distribution, number of speakers, orthography, and materials such as textbooks and dictionaries, and institutions around the world with relevant expertise and sources. ASC4, 168)

174 Welmers, William Everett. 'Checklist of African language and dialect names', pp. 759-900 in **Linguistics in Sub-Saharan Africa**, ed. Thomas A. Sebeok. The Hague, Mouton, 1971. (*Current trends in linguistics*, 7). (Useful quick-reference list, largely following Greenberg, **157**: includes language, country where spoken, number of speakers and numerous alternative names)

Etymology

175 Dalgish, Gerard M. **A dictionary of Africanisms: contributions of sub-Saharan Africa to the English language**. Westport, CT, Greenwood Press, 1982. xviii, 203pp. ("Terms from African languages that have entered into the general vocabulary of the English-speaking world", pref. Long critical review in *JALL*, 8, 1986, 210-218)

Orthography

176   African reference alphabet. http://www.bisharat.net/Documents/ Niamey78annex.htm.   Reproduced   on   the   Bisharat   Web   site, http://www/bisharat.net.   Originally pub. as an annex to **African languages: proceedings of the meeting of experts on the transcription and harmonization of African languages, Niamey, 17-21 July, 1978**. Paris, UNESCO, 1978. A revision of this alphabet was carried out by Michael Mann & David Dalby (*see* **165** above) and is reproduced in Peter Constable. The   international   Niamey   keyboard   layout,   http://scripts.sil.org/ IntlNiameyKybd. The attempt to standardize the orthography of African languages was a major initial activity of the International Institute for African Languages & Cultures (AAALC) later IAI. Their **Practical orthography of African languages**. 2nd ed. London, 1930 (Orig. pub. London, 1927) came to be known as the original 'Africa' alphabet and is still used today in developing new systems.

177   African writing systems. http://www.library.cornell.edu/africana/ Writing_Systems/. Web site created at Cornell University by Prof. Ayele Bekerie in 1996. Has sections for alphabetic, chromatographic, petrographic, philosophical, pictographic, and syllagraphic systems, also an approach by African region. Reproduces the characters in each system.

178   Alphabets de langues africaines, ed. Rhonda L. Hartell. Dakar, UNESCO-Bureau régional de Dakar, 1993. x, 311pp. (Sees itself as continuing Tucker, *see* **179**. Chapters for the languages of Benin, Burkina Faso, Cameroon, CAR, Chad, Congo (Brazzaville), Côte d'Ivoire, Ghana, Guinea, Kenya, Liberia, Mali, Niger, Nigeria, Senegal, Sierra Leone, Sudan, Togo, Uganda, Zaire)

179   Tucker, Archibald N. 'Orthographic systems and conventions in Sub-Saharan Africa', pp. 618-653 in **Linguistics in Sub-Saharan Africa**, ed. Thomas A. Sebeok. The Hague, Mouton, 1971. (*Current trends in linguistics*, 7). (Historical account of systems developed using the roman alphabet. Includes comparative list of alphabets from four systems, including that of IAI)

Law

180   Allott, Antony N. ed. **Judicial and legal systems in Africa**. 2nd ed. London, Butterworth, 1962. (African law series, 4). x, 314pp. (Covers British territories, excluding South Africa, and Liberia. Sections for West, East and Central Africa and the High Commission territories. For each country lists types of court, and outlines their constitution and powers). - - Orig. pub. London, 1962. xiii, 226pp.

181 Encyclopédie juridique de l'Afrique. Abidjan/Dakar/Lomé, Les Nouvelles éditions africains, 1982. 10 vols. Vol. 1, L'État et le droit; vol. 2, Droit international et relations internationales; vol. 3, Systèmes budgétaires etc.; vol. 4, Organisations judicaires; vol. 5, Droit des biens; vol. 6, Droit des personnes; vol. 7, Droit des entreprises; vol. 8, Droit des relations professionnelles; vol. 9, Droit des contrats; vol. 10, Droit pénal etc.; index thématique. (A massive compilation of comparative data on African law and legal systems with over 100 French and African contributors)

182 Modern legal systems cyclopedia. Vols. 6, 6a: Africa. 2nd ed. Buffalo, NY, William S. Hein, 1990. Loose-leaf in folders. (Intended for professional and academic use. Arranged A/Z by country: for each provides an introductory section on geography, the economy and the peoples, followed by sections on the constitution, governmental system, judicial system, law enforcement, penal system, legal education and the legal profession. Includes an entry for Bophutatswana, one for the other "homelands" treated together, and an entry for Diego Garcia). - - Orig. pub. Buffalo, 1985.

Literature

183 Benson, Eugene & Conolly, L.W. eds. **Encyclopedia of post-colonial literatures in English**. 2nd ed. London, Routledge, 2005. 3 vols. (Ed. for East and West Africa sections, G. Douglas Killam; eds. for South Africa, Jeremy Fogg & Craig Mackenzie. Includes entries for individual authors and for African countries, and subdivisions as appropriate for East, West and South Africa under topics such as forms of literature: drama, essays, memoirs, novels, poetry etc., and other themes such as awards, censorship and publishing. Index entries under Africa do not lead to these subdivisions, necessitating use of the contents list. Review, *Ref. revs.*, 19(7) 2005, 41-42). - - Orig. pub. London, 1994. 2 vols. 1,874pp

184 Boddaert, Nadine. **Anonymous classics: African literature: epics and assimilated**. (Draft. Version of 10 August 2005). [The Hague], IFLA Division of Bibliographic Control, Cataloguing Section, 2005. 15pp. Available at: http://www.ifla.org/VII/s13/pubs/AnonymousClassics_Africa_Draft.pdf (Some 130 titles with numerous references from variant forms of name. Non-Arabic titles only)

185 Cabakulu, Mwamba. **Dictionnaire des proverbes africains**. Paris, ACCT & Harmattan, 1992. 303pp. (Lists 2,739 proverbs with brief comments on meaning. Listed by theme with notes on country and ethnic group of origin)

186 Cox, Brian, ed. **African writers**. New York, Charles Scribner's Sons, 1997. 2 vols. 936pp. (Detailed accounts of 65 African literary figures by 53 scholars. Index by country. Chronology of the political and social events within which the authors were writing. Reviews, *ASR*, 44(2) 2001, 215-217; *Choice*, 34, 1997, 1775. *Choice* "outstanding academic title", 1997)

187 Gikandi, Simon, ed. **Encyclopedia of African literature**. London, Routledge, 2004. xv, 629pp. map. ("Intended to be a starting point", pref. 114 contributors. A/Z sequence of authors, forms of writing, themes, literatures in particular languages. General index but no structured list of contents. Reviews, *ARBA*, 35, 2004, 501; *CJAS*, 39, 2005, 160-162, "indispensable contribution"; *Ref. revs.*, 17(4) 2003, 27-28)

188 Herdeck, Donald E. **African authors: a companion to Black African writing. Vol. 1**. Washington, DC, Black Orpheus Press, 1973. xi, 605pp. No more pub. (Intended originally to have supplements at two-yearly intervals with new eds. "about every six years", pref. Entries for 594 authors, writing in 37 vernacular and European languages. Indexes by genre, date, country, language, gender. Also lists of relevant publishers, journals and booksellers and a bibliography)

189 Jahn, Janheinz et al. **Who's who in African literature: biographies, works, commentaries**. Tübingen, Horst Erdman, 1972. 412pp. (Over 400 entries for Sub-Saharan African writers)

190 Killam, G. Douglas & Rowe, Ruth. **The companion to African literatures**. Oxford, James Currey/Bloomington, IN, Indiana University Press, 2000. xiii, 322pp. maps. (Entries for themes, 'Selected list of topics and themes' p. vii, e.g. biography and autobiography, censorship, poetry, and some 350 entries for individual authors. Strong emphasis on writing in English, "or widely available in [English] translation". Reviews *African affairs*, 100, 2001, 167-168; *ARD*, 85, 2001, 76-77; *ASR*, 43 (3) 2000, 152-153; *ibid.*, 44 (3) 2001, 215-217; *Choice*, 38, 2001, 90, "highly recommended"; *IJAHS*, 33, 2000, 702-703)

191 Klein, Leonard S. **African literatures in the 20th century: a guide**. New York, Ungar, 1986/Harpenden, Oldcastle, 1988. x, 245pp. (Reprints articles on African countries and individual writers originally published in **Encyclopedia of world literature in the twentieth century,** rev. ed. New York, Ungar, 1981-1984. 5 vols. Entries for 38 national literatures and 42 individual authors)

192 Page, James A. & Jae Min Roh. **Selected Black American, African and Caribbean authors: a bio-bibliography**. Littleton, CO, Libraries Unlimited, 1985. xiii, 388pp. Earlier version pub. as **Selected black American authors**.

Boston, MA, G.K. Hall, 1977. Expanded version includes 48 African authors out of a total of 632, a number of them political, e.g. Kenyatta, Nkrumah)

193 Parekh, Pushpu Naidu & Jagne, Siga Fatima. **Postcolonial African writers: a bio-bibliographical critical sourcebook**. London, Fitzroy Dearborn/ Westport, CT, Greenwood Press, 1998. 525pp. (Profiles of some 60 authors by fifty scholars. Review, H-Africa, http://www.h-net.org/~africa/reviews/, "despite minor flaws ... excellent in scope and organization")

194 Poddar, Prem & Johnson, David. **A historical companion to postcolonial literatures in English**. Edinburgh, Edinburgh University Press, 2005. xxiii, 574pp. (220 entries. No main entry for Africa, but sub-headings for regions of Africa under topics such as 'Anti-colonialism and resistance', 'Languages and ethnicities' etc. Entries for individual authors and political figures: Amin, Banda, Kaunda, etc. Review, *Ref. revs.*, 20(1) 2006, 37-38)

195 Rouch, Alain & Clavreuil, Gérard. **Littératures nationales d'écriture française: Afrique noire, Caraïbes, Océan indien**. Paris, Bordas, 1986. 512pp. illus. (By country. Each entry has a brief note on the historical and political background, an 'histoire littéraire' and a selection of biographical entries. 17 African countries have 126 biographies)

196 Skurjat, Ernestyna. **Afryka w twórczósci jej pisarzy**. Warsaw, University of Warsaw, 1973. (Kura szkolenia ekspertów-Studium Afrykanistygne Universytetu Warszawskiego, 14). 153pp. (Bio-bibliography of African authors)

197 Lindfors, Berndth & Sander, Reinhard, eds. **Twentieth-century Caribbean and Black African writers**. Detroit, Gale, 1992-1996. (Dictionary of literary biography, 117, 125, 157). 3 vols. First series, 1992. xi, 406pp. (Includes 19 African writers); Second series, 1993. xiv, 443pp. (Includes 21 African writers); Third series, 1996. xiii, 461pp. (Includes 24 African writers. Lengthy articles by specialists, with bibliographies of writings by and about each author)

198 The wisdom of African proverbs: collections, studies, bibliographies, ed. Stan Nussbaum. Version 1.2 June 1998. Colorado Springs, CO, Global Mapping International, 1998. CD-ROM. (Includes texts of over 27,000 proverbs, 42 maps, full texts of many earlier publications on proverbs, etc. For more information *see* http://www.gmi.org/ products/proverbs.htm. ASC4, 104-105)

199 Zell, Hans M. et al. **A new reader's guide to African literature**. 2nd ed. London, Heinemann, 1983. xvi, 553pp. (In addition to bibliographical sections, includes biographies, pp. 343-506, of 95 authors, 50 new to the 2nd ed. Both eds. include lists of booksellers and publishers and 2nd ed. also lists libraries with Africana collections. Conover-Porter Award, 1984.). - - Orig. pub. as **A reader's guide to African literature**, comp. Hans Zell & Helene Silver. London, Heinemann, 1971. xxi, 218pp. (Includes biographies of 51 authors. Review, *Africana J.*, 14, 1983, 84-85; *ARD*, 34, 1984, 48-49, "nothing to compete with it")

Onomastics

200 Asante, Molefi Kete. **The book of African names**. Trenton, NJ, Africa World Press, 1991, 64pp. (Lists some 1,200 personal names, giving their geographical rather than ethnic and linguistic origins. Review, *Choice*, 30, 1992, 71 which finds Chuks-Orji (*see* **201**) a more useful source. ASC4, 104)

201 Chuks-Orji, Ogonna. **Names from Africa: their origin, meaning and pronunciation**. Chicago, IL, Johnson Publishing Co., 1972. 91pp. (Separate lists of male and female African personal names identifying their language and country of origin, and their meaning)

202 Madubuike, Ihechukwu. **A handbook of African names**. 2nd ed. Colorado Springs, CO, Three Continents Press, 1994. 158pp. - - Orig. pub. Washington, DC, Three Continents Press, 1976. v, 233pp. (General discussion of names, followed by sections on those of various African peoples. Emphasis on Nigerian names)

203 Musere, Jonathan & Odhiambo, Christopher. **African ethnics and personal names**. Los Angeles, CA, Ariko Publications, 1998. 281pp. (Naming practices of some 49 ethnic groups and list of over 4,000 names)

204 Musere, Jonathan. **Traditional African names**. Lanham, MD, Scarecrow Press, 2000. 403pp. (Some 6,000 primarily personal names, emphasising those used in ten countries of eastern, central and southern Africa, but omitting West Africa. Discusses origins, usage and connotations of each name. Reviews, *ARD*, 85, 2001, 73-74; *IJAHS*, 34, 2001, 458-460; *Ref. revs.* 14(5), 2000, 30. ASC4, 104)

205 Stewart, Julia. **1,001 African names: first and last names from the African continent**. New York, Carol Publishing Group, 1996. 214pp. (Listed A/Z and by gender. ASC4, 105. An expansion of her **African names**. New York, 1994. 171pp.)

See also **618**

Performing arts

Cinema

206   Les cinémas d'Afrique: dictionnaire. Paris, Karthala, 2000. 592pp. (List of film-makers with details of their flms, and title and country indexes of films. Sponsored by organizers of the Fespaco Festival of Film and TV)

Music

207   Africa: folk music atlas, ed. Leonardo d'Amico & Francesco Mizzau. Florence, Amharsi, 1996. 85pp. text + CD-ROMS. (Review, *IJAHS*, 32, 1999, 569-571)

208   African music encyclopedia. http://africanmusic.org Reviews, *Choice*, 38, 2001, 1054, "well designed ... but seems to have been abandoned"; *Ref. revs.*, 17(5) 2003, 45, notes many sections not updated since 1998)

209   Dictionary of African composers, ed. Alexander Johnson & Chris Walton. http://sacomposers.up.ac.za/. A research project of the Music Department of the University of Pretoria, funded jointly by the University, the Mmino South Africa and Norwegian Education & Music Programme, and the National Research Foundation of South Africa. 142 name entries in August 2006 of which 76 provided links to biographies with lists of compositions, discographies etc. The majority of entries on the database at this date were for South Africans.

210   Garland encyclopedia of world music. Vol. 1, Africa. New York, Garland Publishing, 1998. 851pp.+ 1 CD (Part of a 10 vol. set, 1998-2002. Includes 39 sections by 35 authors. CD contains 21 recordings. Section 1, Overview; 2, Issues and processes in the music; 3, Regional case studies. Review, *Choice*, 35, 1998, 1347-1348)

211   The Garland handbook of African music, ed. Ruth M. Stone. New York, Garland Press, 2000. xiv, 397pp. + 1 CD. (Includes articles previously pub. in *Garland encyclopedia of world music*, vol. 1. New York, 1998, *see* **210**)

212   Graham, Ronnie. **The world of African music**. London, Pluto Books, 1992. (Stern's guide to contemporary African music, vol. 2). viii, 235pp. (Entries for 35 African countries, with for each a section on traditional and modern music, further subdivided by style as appropriate with brief biographies and discographies for specific performers)

213   Norborg, Åke. **Musical instruments from Africa south of the Sahara**.
Copenhagen, Musikhistorisk Museum, 1982. 91pp. illus.

Theatre

214   The Cambridge guide to African and Caribbean theatre, ed. Martin
Banham et al. Cambridge, Cambridge University Press, 1994. vii, 261pp.
(Part 1, Africa, provides entries for individuals, genres, festivals etc. in 26
African countries. Advisory editor for Africa, Olu Obafemi. Review, *ARBA*,
26, 1995, 615)

215   The world encyclopedia of contemporary theatre, ed. Don Rubin.
London, Routledge, 1994-2000. 6 vols. Vol. 4. 1997. Africa. x, 426pp. (Articles
on general aspects, followed by overviews for 32 Sub-Saharan countries,
covering history of performance, details of companies and buildings.
Reviews, *ARBA*, 33, 2002, "invaluable"; *Choice*, 36, 1998, 293-294, "highly
recommended"); vol. 5. 1999. The Arab World. x, 311pp. (Includes entries for
the Comoros, Djibouti, Mauritania, Somalia and Sudan); vol. 6. 2000.
Bibliography/cumulative index. x, 531pp.

Politics

216   Arnold, Guy. **Political and economic encyclopedia of Africa. Harlow,
Longman Current Affairs, 1993. x, 342pp. map. (Entries for 56 African
countries, and for organizations, political parties, individuals and broad
themes. Review, *ARD*, 64, 1994, 63-65) *See also* **70**

217   Cook, Chris & Killingray, David. **African political facts since 1945. 2nd
ed. London, 1991. vii, 280pp. (Chronology of main events, lists of governors,
heads of state, and major ministerial appointments, parliaments, political
parties, trade unions, major conflicts and coups, demographic statistics, basic
economic statistics, biographies of some 150 figures. Very few sources quoted.
2nd ed. brings coverage up to the independence of Namibia in 1990). - - Orig.
pub. London, Macmillan, 1983. vii, 263pp. (Review, *African affairs*, 84, 1985,
296-297. Similar but much briefer coverage of Commonwealth African
countries with a wider time span, is in the companion vol., **Commonwealth
political facts, 1900-1977**, comp. Chris Cook and John Paxton. London,
Macmillan, 1979)

218   Phillips, Claude S. **The African political dictionary. Santa Barbara, CA,
Clio Press, 1984. (Clio Dictionaries in Political Science). xxviii, 245pp. maps.
(Comp. originally for U.S. political science students. Arranged in broad
sections, e.g. Land and people, Governmental institutions and processes, with

discursive A/Z entries in each section. Tables with comparative data. Country and general indexes. Review, *Choice*, 21, 1984, 1449)

219   Politisches Lexikon Schwarzafrika. 4th ed. comp. Rolf Hofmeier & Mathias Schönborn. Munich, C.H. Beck, 1988. (Beck'sche Reihe, 810). 530pp. (Covers Africa south of the Sahara. 1st ed. omits South Africa and includes Sudan. Subsequent eds. include South Africa and omit Sudan (covered in the publisher's companion volume **Politisches Lexikon Nahost**). 2nd and subsequent eds. include a chapter on African international organizations. Detailed and compact country accounts by individual authors with statistics). - - Orig. pub. as **Politisches Lexikon Afrika**. Munich, 1978 (Beck'sche schwarze Reihe, 166). 540pp; - - 2nd ed. Munich, 1985. (Beck'sche schwarze Reihe, 281). 510pp; - - 3rd ed. Munich, 1987. (Beck'sche Reihe, 810). 530pp.

220   Seddon, David. **Political and economic dictionary of Africa**. London, Routledge, 2005. (Europa political & economic dictionaries). ix, 519pp. (Covers the whole continent with 2 to 4pp. entries for countries, political figures, political parties, economic groupings. No index, no discussion of criteria for selecting entries. ASC4, 94)

221   Shavit, David. **The United States in Africa: a historical dictionary**. New York, Greenwood Press, 1989. xxii, 298pp. ("Information about the persons, institutions and events that affected the relations between the U.S. and Africa, persons who have actually been in Africa ... organizations ... that functioned in Africa itself and events that occurred in that area", pref. Brief entries, some four to a page. Includes references to sources. Index of individuals by profession and occupation. Review, *IJAHS*, 23, 1990, 733)

See also **70**

Elections & parliaments

222   African elections database: a database of election results in African countries. http://africanelections.tripod.com/, chronology of elections, and voting details in Africa since 1990, section results of recent elections, calendar of forthcoming elections

223   Derbyshire, J. Denis & Derbyshire, Ian. **Political systems of the world**. 3rd ed. Oxford, Helicon, 1999. 2 vols. (Vol. 2, pp. 464-573, Central and South Africa; Pp. 828-829, Réunion; p. 830; Mayotte, pp. 838-839; Western Sahara. Entries for each country, with brief details of political structures, latest election, etc.). - - Orig. pub. Edinburgh, Chambers, 1989. xii, 932pp; - - 2nd ed. Oxford, Helicon, 1996. xii, 684pp.

224   Elections in Africa: a data handbook, ed. Dieter Nohlen et al. Oxford, Oxford University Press, 1999. xvi, 984pp. ("Systematic documentation of electoral data of African countries since independence", pref. A product of ongoing work on elections around the world being undertaken at the Institute of Political Science, University of Heidelberg. For each country has dates of national elections, referendums, coups d'état, statistics of voters registered and votes cast in every election from the colonial period up to 1989. Detailed list of sources. Review, *Choice*, 37, 2000, 2046. *Choice* "outstanding academic title", 1999. ASC4, 126)

225   Kurian, George, T., ed. World encyclopedia of parliaments and legislatures. Chicago, Fitzroy Dearborn, 1998. 2 vols., 878, 38pp. (Sponsored by the Research Committee of Legislative Specialists, International Political Science Association and the Commonwealth Parliamentary Association. Includes entries for 48 African countries, with details on historical background, electoral eligibility, legislative procedures)

Flags

226   Flags of the world. http://fotw.vexillum.com/flags/index.html. (Site originally created by Guiseppe Bottasini, currently hosted by Yahoo Groupos.com. Searchable by country. For each provides colour images and descriptions of current and previous national (and if appropriate, state and provincial) flags, and coats of arms and where appropriate flags of the armed forces, police and other official bodies. Also illustrated and described are flags of political parties, freedom and liberation movements, and those of a wide variety of miscellaneous organizations. A very detailed site)

Office holders

227   Bidwell, Robin L. Guide to African ministers. London, Rex Collings, 1978. (Bidwell's guide to government ministers, 4). 79pp. (Basically covers the period post 1st Jan. 1950. Information on Ethiopia and Liberia pre-1950 is given in a note at the back of the vol. South Africa and Southern Rhodesia pre-1950 are covered in the companion **Bidwell's guide to government ministers. vol. 3: the British Empire and successor states, 1900-1974**, London, Cass, 1974. The coverage of Gambia, Ghana, Kenya, Nigeria, Sierra Leone, Tanzania and Uganda in the 1974 volume is superseded by the 1978 vol., as is the coverage of the Sudan in **vol. 2: the Arab World**, London, 1973. States are arranged in eight groupings largely corresponding to colonial empires; for each state there is a chronological list, with actual day of appointment of heads of state, prime ministers, and ministers for foreign affairs, defence, internal affairs and finance or their equivalents. No index of names)

228   Bosworth, Clifford Edmund. **The new Islamic dynasties: a chronological and genealogical manual**. Rev. ed. Edinburgh, Edinburgh University Press, 1996. xxvi, 389pp. (Coverage of Africa is more extensive than in previous ed. Chap. 7, pp. 122-134. West Africa; chap. 8, pp.132-139, East Africa and the Horn of Africa). - - Orig. pub., Edinburgh, 1967, xviii, 245pp. (reissued Edinburgh, 1980).

229   Da Graça, John V. **Heads of state and government**. 2nd ed. Basingstoke, Macmillan, 2000. 1,222pp. (Section A, Major international organizations, includes e.g. OAU; section B, Countries. Includes contemporary office-holders for provinces and other sub-national administrative areas; also for 'rival governments', 'secessionist movements' and the like. No specific sources cited). - - Orig. pub. as **Heads of state and government**: lists of rulers of international organizations, today's states, territories and their autonomous regions. London, 1985. 265pp.

230   Henige, David. **Colonial governors from the fifteenth century to the present: a comprehensive list**. Madison, WI, University of Wisconsin Press, 1970. 461pp. (Lists of governors or other colonial administrators arranged by empire or 'imperial system' then by colony. Historical notes on each empire, each colonial unit, and on sources used. Index of some 10,000 personal names. 81 out of the 412 listings provided refer to Africa. An essential source. Review, *AHS*, 6, 1973, 128-130)

231   [Portugal. Agência-Geral do Ultramar]. **Lista cronológica dos governadores de Cabo Verde e datas da posse**; Lista cronológica dos governadores da província da Guiné e datas de posse; Lista cronológica dos governadores da província de S. Tomé e Príncipe e datas de posse; Lista cronológica dos governadores gerais da província de Angola e datas de posse; Lista cronológica dos capitães mores, governadores, capitães-generais, conselhos governativos e governadores gerais de Moçambique ... Lisbon, Agência Geral do Ultramar, [195-]. Var. pag. (Typed list produced for use in government agencies. Copies in Archivo Histórico Ultramarino & Biblioteca Nacional, Lisbon)

232   Sainty, John Christopher. **Colonial Office officials**. London, University of London, Institute of Historical Research, 1976. (Office-holders in modern Britain, 6). x, 52pp. (Officials of the Secretary of State for War, 1794-1801, of the Secretary of State for War and Colonies, 1801-1854 and of the Secretary of State for Colonies, 1854-1870. 25 listings ranging from Secretaries of State down to Assistant Junior Clerks)

233   Stewart, John D. **African states and rulers**. 2nd ed. Jefferson, NC, McFarland & Co., 1999. xii, 420pp. (Major change from 1st ed. is that all information relating to earlier incarnations or parts of a state is gathered together under a main entry for that state, rather than receiving separate entries. Chronology, pp. 241-296. Index of Colonial power's holdings. Detailed critical review article by David Henige, 'One-eyed man in the kingdom of the blind', *History in Africa*, 28, 2001, 395-404, which dissects the work and concludes "two thumbs down ...index might best be described as a disaster". Henige's own **The chronology of oral tradition**. Oxford, Clarendon Press, 1974, warns against the uncritical acceptance of African dynastic lists. ASC4, 129-130). - - Orig. pub. as **African states & rulers: an encyclopedia of native, colonial & independent states & rulers, past & present**. Jefferson, NC, McFarland, 1989. xx, 395pp. (Entries for 1,139 separate administrative units with references to earlier, later, and related titles. List of names and dates of office of principal officials, kings, governors, presidents, prime ministers etc. provided for each entry. Index of 10,500 personal names. Reviews, *Choice*, 27, 1989, 294, "not recommended for any library"; *ABPR* 16, 1990, 89, "not recommended"; *JAH*, 31, 1990, 339, sees the work, with some reservations, as useful. Gretchen Walsh comments on the author's reaction to her unfavourable *Choice* review and also discusses Henige's review of the 2nd ed. in **Research, reference service and resources for the study of Africa**. New York, Haworth Press, 2004, 58-59. A 3rd ed. has been announced by the publishers for summer 2006. Their Web site notes that the text has been updated to summer 2005, that it now contains over 11,000 names and, unexpectedly, given the principal focus of the work, that "a new table details AIDS in the African states")

234   Truhart, Peter. **Regents of nations: systematic chronology of states and their political representatives in past & present: a biographical reference book. Part 2, America & Africa**. 2nd ed. Munich, Saur, 2002. xvi, 1,079pp. (Africa, pp. 587-1079. Attempts extensive coverage of "all states and all state-like communities ... going back to the dawn of history", pref. Arranged by broad region/country. Cites some 250 sources for the data on Africa, but not Bidwell, **227** or Henige, **230**. For e.g. Ghana, contains lists for 32 African kingdoms, Dutch governors, Danish governors, governors of the British Company of Merchants Trading to Africa, governors of the Gold Coast, and heads of state, chiefs of government and foreign ministers since independence). - - Orig. pub. Munich, Saur, 1984. xxx, 980pp. Africa, pp. 1-465.

235   U.S. Central Intelligence Agency (CIA). Chiefs of state and Cabinet members of foreign governments. https://www.cia.gov/cia/publications/chiefs/index.html (Includes heads of Central Bank, Ambassadors to U.S., Permanent Representative to U.N. Updated weekly)

236   World rulers: Heads of State and Prime Ministers. http://www.info-regenten.de/regent/regent-e/index.htm. Maintained by Enno Schulz. Data for each country since independence. Includes portraits and links to other country related Web sites.

Political parties & groupings

237   Balancie, Jean-Marc & La Grange, Arnaud de. **Les nouveaux mondes rebelles, conflits, terrorisme et contestations**. Paris, Michalon, 2005- . illus. maps. (Detailed coverage of guerrilla movements, ethnic militias, other paramilitary groups). - - Orig. pub. as **Mondes rebelles, acteurs, conflits et violences politiques**. Paris, Michalon, 1996. 2 vols. (Vol. 1, Amériques, Afrique); - - 2nd ed. pub. as **Mondes rebelles, guerres civiles et violences politiques**. Paris, Michalon, 1999. 1,561pp. (Africa, pp. 229-652); - - 3rd ed. pub. as **Mondes rebelles, guérillas, milices, groupes terroristes**. Paris, Michalon, 2001. 1677pp

238   Bustin, Edouard. **Guide des partis politiques africains: inventaire de 300 partis recensés dans 45 pays africains**. Léopoldville, Éditions CRISP-IPC, 1962. 80pp. (First published in *Études congolaises*, 7, 1962. Brief descriptions of history and policies of each party. Country of origin index)

239   Decraene, Phillipe. **Tableau des partis politiques de l'Afrique au sud du Sahara**. Paris, Fondation nationale des sciences politiques, Centre d'étude des relations internationales, 1963. (Série C, recherches, 8). 137pp. (Includes country by country lists of parties with information on their history, objectives, and leaders)

240   East, Roger & Joseph, Tanya. **Political parties of Africa and the Middle East**. Harlow, Longman, 1993. ix, 354pp. (Covers 51 African countries with Western Sahara under Morocco. Brief details on major parties and a note on the existence of minor ones, with information on their performance in the most recent elections where appropriate)

241   Janke, Richard & Sim, Richard. **Guerrilla and terrorist organizations: a world directory and bibliography**. Brighton, Harvester Press, 1983. xxviii, 531pp. (Africa, pp. 117-213, with entries for 74 movements under 18 Sub-Saharan African countries)

242   Marques da Costa, Fernando & Falé, Natália. **Guia político dos PALOP**. Lisbon, Fragmentos, 1992. 209pp. illus. (Guide to political parties in Lusophone Africa. PALOP = Países Africanos de Língua Oficial Portuguesa)

243   Minahan, James. **Encyclopedia of the stateless nations: ethnic and national groups around the world**. Westport, CT, Greenwood Press, 2002. 4 vols. (Extensively rev. and expanded version of his **Nations without states,**

244 below. Arranged A/Z by ethnic or national group, differently from **244**, with sketch map, population estimate, brief history. Discusses 53 Sub-Saharan Africa groups, such as Afars, Ibos, Ruwenzoris. Also lists political parties and groupings for each group)

244 Minahan, James. **Nations without states: a historical dictionary of contemporary national movements**. Westport, CT, Greenwood Press, 1996. xxiv, 692pp. (Arranged A/Z by 'national entity'. Appendix B lists entries by continent and country, listing 36 Sub-Saharan Africa entities, such as Biafra, Bioko, Darfur, Katanga. Also lists political parties and groupings for each entity)

245 Ray, Donald I. **Dictionary of the African left: parties, movements and groups**. Aldershot, Dartmouth, 1989. vi, 273pp. (Introduction followed by chronology of Left states in Africa 1952-1988 and dictionary of the left parties, movements and groups. Lists almost 300 parties with dates of activity, details of organization, membership, statutes, publications, history and leadership. Indexes by acronym and by country)

246 Szajkowski, Bogdan. **Political parties of the world**. 6th ed. London, John Harper, 2005. x, 710pp. (Arranged A/Z by country: covers 51 sub-Saharan African countries incl. Western Sahara. Because of its frequent revisions useful to complement the other Africa-specific sources listed). - - Orig. pub. ed. Harlow, Longman, 1980; - - 2nd ed. Harlow, 1984; - - 3rd ed. Harlow, 1988; - - 4th ed. Harlow, 1996; - - 5th ed. Harlow, 2002.

247 Szajkowski, Bogdan. **Revolutionary and dissident movements of the world**. 4th ed. London, John Harper, 2004. xiv, 562pp. (Companion to **246** above. Includes entries for parties in 48 African countries. Similar, but briefer and more diffuse coverage is offered by the **Encyclopedia of modern separatist movements**, comp. Christopher Hewitt & Tom Cheetham. Santa Barbara, ABC-Clio, 2000. ix, 366pp). - - Orig. pub. as **Political dissent**. Harlow, Longman, 1983; - - 2nd ed. comp. H.W. Degenhardt. Harlow, 1987; - - 3rd ed. comp. Guy Arnold & H.W. Degenhardt. Harlow, 1991. xvii, 401pp.

See also **559**

Wars & borders

248 Anderson, Ewan W. **Global geopolitical flashpoints: an atlas of conflict**. London, The Stationery Office, 2000. xvi, 391pp. (Entries arranged A/Z for countries, e.g. Angola, Zimbabwe and for specific regions, e.g. Caprivi strip, Lake Nyasa, Ogaden. 26 entries for Africa, each with map and discussion. Review, *Choice*, 38, 2001, 1248, "highly recommended"). - - Orig.

pub. as **An atlas of world political flashpoints : a sourcebook of geopolitical crisis**. London, Pinter, 1993. xiv, 243pp.

249 Arnold, Guy. **Historical dictionary of civil wars in Africa**. Lanham, MD, Scarecrow Press, 1999. (Historical dictionaries of war, revolution and civil unrest, 11). xxi, 377pp. (Covers post 1945, with 20 main entries for wars plus other entries for liberation movements and similar bodies. Bibliography but no index. Reviews, *African affairs*, 99, 2000, 142-143; *ARD*, 84, 2000, 77-78; *Choice*, 37, 2000, 1083. ASC4, 93)

250 Arnold, Guy. **Wars in the Third World since 1945**. London, Cassell, 1991. xxv, 579pp. (Pp. 7-68, Colonial liberation wars in Africa; pp.120-126, Big power intervention wars, Africa; pp. 171-226, Border wars, Africa; pp.332-426, Civil wars, Africa)

251 Brownlie, Ian. **African boundaries: a legal and diplomatic encyclopedia**. London, C. Hurst for Royal Institute of International Affairs, 1979. xxxvi, 1355pp. maps. (A study of 105 separate boundary alignments involving 48 African states. For each provides an historical account of its development and detailed documentation of the currently agreed location, often reprinting the text of the appropriate documents. Each boundary is shown on a sketch-map. Review, *African affairs*, 78, 1979, 565-566. Standard guide to its date. For more recent boundary agreements *see* Gideon Biger. **The encyclopedia of international boundaries**. New York, Facts on File, 1995. 544pp. which has entries for 97 African boundaries; & Ewan W. Anderson. **International boundaries: a geopolitical atlas**. London, The Stationery Office, 2003. xiv, 941pp., arranged A/Z by country. For maritime aspects *see* John R.V. Prescott & Clive Schofield. **The maritime political boundaries of the world**. 2nd ed. Leiden, Martinus Nijhoff, 2005. xiv, 665pp. illus. maps. (Chap. 13, The Atlantic Ocean; chap. 19, The Indian Ocean; chap. 20, The Red Sea). - - Orig. pub. London, Methuen, 1985. xv, 377pp.)

252 Calvert, Peter, ed. **Border and territorial disputes of the world**. 4th ed. London, John Harper, 2004. x, 533pp. (Pp. 3-75, Africa, covering 21 disputes, including, pp. 66-74, The Western Sahara question. Review, *Ref. revs.*, 19(2) 2005, 21-22). - - Orig. pub. ed. Alan J. Day. Harlow, Longman, 1982, x, 406pp; - - 2nd ed. Harlow, Longman, 1987. x, 462pp; - - 3rd ed. rev. John Allcock. Harlow, Longman, 1992. 630pp.

253 **Encyclopedia of conflicts since World War II**, ed. James Ciment. New York, M.E. Sharpe, 1999. 4 vols. (A/Z entries for conflicts with map and brief chronology). 2nd ed. announced for 2006 will have text re-arranged by continent with entries for 49 African conflicts (Publisher's Web site)

Religion

254 **Encyclopedia of African and African-American religions**, ed. Stephen D. Glazier. New York, Routledge, 2001. (Religion and society: a Berkshire reference work). xx, 452pp. (Arranged A/Z, with preliminary list of entries. 70 contributors, mostly from the U.S. Includes entries for Islam in East and West Africa, and for countries, sub-heading 'African-derived religions'. Also entry for 'Cyberspace, African and African-derived religions, in' with recommended Web sites. Review, *Choice*, 38, 2001, 1932-1933, "lacks the breadth and specificity required from an encyclopedia")

255 **Encyclopedia of Islam**. New ed. Leiden, Brill, 1960-2004. 11 vols. + Suppl. Also available on CD-ROM and as a subscription online service, *see* www.encislam.brill.nl. (With the new ed. finally completed, articles relevant to the African continent can now be readily traced through **Index volume, fasc.1, Index of subjects**, comp. P.J. Bearman. Leiden, Brill, 2005. This contains a general heading for Africa, with subdivisions for Central, East, North, Southern and West, indicating main headings in the Encyclopedia for 20 Sub-Saharan African countries, together with numerous other refs.)

256 Jenkins, Everett. **The Muslim diaspora: a comprehensive reference to the spread of Islam in Asia, Africa, Europe and the Americas**. Jefferson, NC, McFarland, 1999- .Vol. 1. 1999. 570-1500. 437pp. (Review, *Ref. revs.*, 14(4) 2000, 10-11); vol. 2. 2000. 1500-1799. 432pp; vol. 3. 2006. 1800-1824. 432pp. (Companion to his **Pan-African chronology**, *see* **140**)

257 **Oxford encyclopedia of the modern Islamic world**, ed. John L. Espositas. Oxford, Oxford University Press, 1995. 4 vols. ('Synoptic table of contents' in vol. 4 indicates main entries for 17 Sub-Saharan African countries, also African entries under 'Institutions, organizations and movements', individual biographies, etc.)

258 **Petit atlas des églises africaines**, pour comprendre l'enjeu du Christianisme en Afrique, ed. Luc Terras & Gwendoline Cazier. Lyon, Éditions Golias, 1994. 280pp. (Despite title, not an atlas, but country surveys of the presence of the Roman Catholic church, with statistics of adherents and clergy, and a brief chronology. Introductory chapters include 10 pages on Protestantism and 6 on Islam)

259 Shaikh, Farzana. **Islam and Islamic groups: a worldwide reference guide**. Harlow, Longman, 1992. 316pp. (Data on Islamic political parties, popular fronts, governmental bodies, associations etc. Includes 30 African countries)

260 **World Christian encyclopedia: a comparative survey of churches and religions in the modern world**. 2nd ed. comp. David B. Barrett, et al. Oxford, Oxford University Press, 2001. 2 vols. Vol. 1. The world by countries: religionists, churches, ministries. xii, 876pp; vol. 2. The world by segments: religions, peoples, languages, cities, topics. v, 823pp. (Includes a detailed account and statistics of the situation of the church in each African country). - - Orig. pub. Oxford, 1982. xv, 1,010pp.
- - World Christian database. http://worldchristiandatabase.org/wcd/, represents the databases associated with the encyclopedia which are being continually developed by the Center for the Study of Global Christianity, Gordon-Conwell Theological Seminary, South Hamilton, MA, US. "The World Christian Database provides comprehensive statistical information on world religions, Christian denominations, and people groups. Extensive data are available on 9,000 Christian denominations, 13,000 ethnolinguistic peoples, as well as data on 5,000 cities, 3,000 provinces and 238 countries". (Web site, June 2006)

Sociology

261 **Encyclopedia of the world's minorities**, ed. Carl Skutsch et al. London, Routledge, 2005. 3 vols. xxxi, 1,413pp. (562 entries relating to cultural, ethnic, gender and sexual minorities. Includes general entries for Africa, also for Africans in Europe, for countries, for cultural groups, e.g. Afar, Yoruba, and biographies, e.g. for Achebe, Saro Wiwa, Senghor)

262 **The Greenwood encyclopedia of women's issues worldwide. Vol. 6, Sub-Saharan Africa**, ed. Aili Mari Tripp. Westport, CT, Greenwood Press, 2003. xvi, 649pp. illus. (Part of 6 vol. set. An overview essay discusses women in terms of education, employment and economics, inheritance, property, and land rights, social and government programmes, health, politics and law, religion and spirituality. These themes are then examined for 22 African countries: Botswana, Burundi, Cameroon, Eritrea, Ethiopia, Ghana, Guinea, Kenya, Mali, Mozambique, Namibia, Niger, Nigeria, Rwanda, Senegal, Somalia, South Africa, Sudan, Tanzania, Togo, Uganda and Zimbabwe. Each entry includes a list of national organizations and Web sites. Review, *Choice*, 41, 2004, 1644; *Ref. revs.*, 18(4) 2004, 21-22. ASC4, 122)

263 Kinnear, Karen L. **Women in the Third World: a reference handbook**. Santa Barbara, CA, ABC-Clio, 1997. 348pp. (Includes biographical entries for leading figures, directory of organizations, statistics, chronology and references. Extensive coverage of African women and useful for comparative approach)

264 Roni, Nelly. **Atlas des migrations ouest-africaines vers l'Europe, 1985-1993**. Paris, ORSTOM, 1996. 109pp. col. maps (Maps and statistics which often relate to the whole of Africa on the origins of African populations in Europe)

265 Segal, Aaron. **An atlas of international migration**. London, Hans Zell, 1993. ix, 233pp. (Numerous b. & w. maps. Author was former ed. of *Africa report*. Sections for 'Voluntary migrations', 'Involuntary migrations', 'World's major diasporas', 'World migration characteristics'. Africa features widely. Review, *Choice*, 31, 1994, 921)

266 Sheldon, Kathleen, E. **Historical dictionary of women in Sub-Saharan Africa**. Lanham, MD, Scarecrow Press, 2005. (Historical dictionaries of women in the world, 1). xli, 405pp. (Some 1,000 entries, mostly for persons but also for women's organizations. Chronology. Reviews, *ABPR*, 31, 2005, 193, "excellent resource"; *ARD*, 100, 2006, "truly comprehensive, well thought-out"; *Choice*, 43, 2005, 82-83, "good companion to the Greenwood encyclopedia [**262**]". ASC4, 157)

267 **World directory of minorities**. [Rev. ed.] London, Minority Rights International, 1997. xvi, 840pp. (Pp. 388-465, North, West and the Horn of Africa by Julia Maxted & Abebe Zegeye; pp. 466-533, Central and Southern Africa by Chris Dammers & David Sogge. Articles for each group arranged under country. Saharawis treated under Morocco). - - Orig. pub. London, Longman, 1990. xvi, 427pp; - - [2nd ed.] London, Cartmell, 1995. xv, 427pp.

Transport

268 Guttery, Ben R. **Encyclopedia of African airlines**. Jefferson, NC, McFarland & Co., 1998. xiii, 291pp. (Arranged by country, and lists 723 airlines current and defunct, including those with only a single aircraft, from 53 African countries. Appendix lists major airports. No sources given. Reviews, *ARBA*, 30, 1999, 654; *Choice*, 36, 1999, 862)

YEARBOOKS

General

269 **Advertising & press annual of Africa**. Cape Town, National Publishing Co. Ltd., 1949- Annual. Title varies: **South African advertising annual & press guide** (1949); **African press & advertising annual** (1950-1954/55). (Includes periodicals and newspapers arranged A/Z by country, commercial radio and television stations, cinemas, and advertising agencies.

Countries covered by the 1970s were Angola, Kenya, Malawi, South Africa, Tanzania, Uganda, Zimbabwe (with all categories of data); Burundi, Congo, Gabon, Ghana, Lesotho, Madagascar, Mauritius, Mozambique, Namibia, Nigeria, Réunion, St. Helena, Seychelles, Swaziland, Zaire, Zambia, with basically press only)

270   Africa, 1966 [etc.]. Harpers Ferry, WV, Stryker-Post, 1966- . Annual. (Issue for 2005. viii, 324pp. illus. Articles on Africa in general, followed by country articles under 8 regions, including North Africa)

271   Africa, 2001 [etc.]. Washington, DC, Corporate Council on Africa & Business Books International, 2002- . Annual. (Issue for 2005. 400pp. "Comprehensive guide for American individuals and businesses seeking to learn more about doing business with the nations of Africa", pref. General overview sections followed by country studies of topography, demography and economic and financial structures of 53 African countries. ASC4, 119)

272   Africa annual, ed. E.M. Crossley. London, Foreign Correspondents Ltd., 1958-1968. Annual (irreg.) 9 issues. (Basic information with an emphasis on agriculture, mining, industry and trade. 140/160pp per issue. Up to 1966 arranged alphabetically by country, 1967 and 1968 arranged first by region)

273   Africa annual review, 1972 [-1974/75] ed. Raph Uwechue. London, *Africa journal*, 1972-1974. 3 issues. (General articles on economics and industry, followed by a country by country survey. Includes loose wall map of Africa at 1:10M)

274   Africa contemporary record: annual survey & documents, 1968/69 [etc.]. New York, Holmes & Meier [etc.], 1969- . Annual/Bi-annual (irreg.). (Vol. 27 for 1998-2000 pub. 2003 in an increasingly delayed pub. schedule. Ed. Colin Legum & J. Drysdale (to 1988), Marion E. Doro (1989-1991); Colin Legum (1992-). Detailed reviews of the political, economic and social developments in each country for the year(s) covered, including statistics. Also prints texts of significant documents issued during the year by international and regional organizations such as the UN and OAU. Review of vol. 1, *African affairs*, 69, 1970, 299; of vol. 6, 1973/74, *ASA review of books*, 2, 1976, 8-9 which is critical of variation in nature of coverage from year to year, and of the lack of good maps and historical background; of vol. 9, 1976/77, *IJAHS*, 11, 1978, 728-730, "single best annual reference work on African affairs"; of vol. 10, 1977/78, *JAH*, 21, 1980, 139, "the highest standards of both scholarship and journalism", of vol. 12, 1979/80, *Africana J.*, 12, 1981, 254-255. ASC4, 75)

275   Africa review: the economic and business report. London, Kogan Page Business Books (*formerly* Saffron Walden, World of Information), 1977- Annual. As **Africa guide**, 1977-1984. (Annual economic and business survey of 55 African countries. General articles followed by country surveys with map, overview of recent events, key facts, business directory, tourist information. Review of 25th ed. 2003/04, *Ref.revs*. 18(5) 2004, 55. ASC4, 75)

276   Africa south of the Sahara. London, Europa Publications, 1971-. Annual.   Also   available   as   a   paid   for   online   service   at http://www.europaworld.com. (Part 1, Background to the continent, includes general surveys, list of African regional organizations, who's who. Part 2 provides country by country surveys of 52 African countries, with background essays, economic, demographic and statistical data, directories of political cultural and commercial institutions. A standard work since its inception. Reviews of 10th ed., 1980, *Africana, J.*, 12, 1981, 74-75; of 13th ed., 1984, *African affairs*, 83, 1984, 427, "by far the most detailed and the most authoritative of the African yearbooks"; of 25th ed. 1995, *GJ*, 163, 1997, 226, "a very static and dated view of … geography"; *IJAHS*, 31, 1998, 182-183; of 29th ed. 2000, 30th ed. 2001, 31st ed. 2002, *Ref. revs.*, 14(3) 2000, 54-55; 15(8) 2001, 47-48; 16(3) 2002, 49-50. ASC4, 75-76. For coverage of Chad, Ethiopia, French Somaliland, Mali, Mauritania, Niger, Somalia and Sudan from 1964 to 1970 *see* **Middle East and North Africa, 289** below)

277   Africa yearbook 2004 [etc.]: **politics, economy and society of the Sahara**. Leiden, Brill for Africa-Europe Group for Interdisciplinary Studies (AEGIS), 2005- . Annual. (Comp. Africa Studiecentrum, Leiden, Institut für Afrika-Kunde, Hamburg & Nordiska Afrikainstitutet, Uppsala. Provides general and regional surveys of developments and trends in the year covered. "While based on scholarly work, it is oriented towards a wider readership", pref. to vol. 1). Review, *ABPR*, 32, 2006, 10. ASC4, 76. *Continues* **Afrika Jahrbuch 1988** [etc.]: **Politik, Wirtschaft und Gesellschaft in Afrika südlich   der   Sahara**, comp. Institut für Afrika-Kunde, Hamburg. Opladen/Wiesbaden, VS Verlag für Sozialwissenschaft, 1989-2004. Annual.

278   Africa yearbook and who's who, ed. Raph Uwechue. London, *Africa journal*, 1977. xlvii, 1,364pp. No more pub. (Comprises: diary of important events, 1975 & 1976; pt. 1, general: topography, peoples, economy etc.; pt. 2, regional organizations; pt. 3 (pp. 207-932) country by country surveys; pt. 4, Africa and international organizations; pt. 5, sport; pt. 6, who's who. A greatly expanded successor to **273** and one of the most detailed works of its kind. Although no further eds. followed, it formed the model for the Know Africa series from the same publishers, whose first editions were pub. in 1981 (*see* **Africa today (31)** ; **Africa who's who, (533); Makers of modern Africa, (548)**

279 **African freedom annual**. Sandton, S.A., Southern African Freedom Foundation, 1977,1979. 2 issues. (Includes 'Africa in brief' with summary details of each country's politics, chronology of events during preceding year, and articles on themes, e.g. Soviet involvement in Africa)

280 **African trade directory, 1987** [etc.]. Addis Ababa, UNECA/Abidjan, International Business Centre, 1987-?1993. (Issue for 1987 covers Malawi, Tanzania and Zambia; Issue for 1989 covers Cameroon, Egypt, Ethiopia, Gabon, Ghana, Kenya, Mauritius, Morocco, Nigeria, and Zimbabwe. Issue for 1993 in multiple parts with v. 1 covering West Africa and Ethiopia)

281 **Afrique 1968 [-1982]**. Paris, *Jeune Afrique*, 1968-1982. Annual. Pub. as special issues of *Jeune Afrique*. Title and coverage vary: **Afrique 1968-Afrique '71/72**, thematic surveys, general articles, country surveys; **Afrique '73** contains no country surveys; **Afrique et Moyen-Orient '75-1976/77** expands coverage to include Middle East, and restores country surveys; **Annuaire de l'Afrique et du Moyen-Orient 1979; Annuaire ... 1980: les armées et la défence; Annuaire ... 1981/82: économie et développement**. Succeeded by **L'annuaire *Jeune afrique*** from 1991 (*see* **286**).
 - - English language ed. **Africa 1968-[1974/5]**. New York, Africana Publishing, 1969-1970. 6 vols. Issues for 1968, 1969/70, 1971, 1972, 1973, 1974/75.

282 **Almanach africain**. Paris, ACCT, 1974-1984. Irreg. 6 vols. Issues for 1974, 1976/77, 1979, 1980, 1983, 1984. (A general survey of African history, economics, communications, social services, literature, and religion)

283 **Année africaine 1963-[1992/93]**. Paris, Pedone, 1965-1993. Annual. (Initially a joint compilation by CHEAM (Centre des hautes études administratives sur l'Afrique et l'Asie moderne), CERI (Centre d'étude des relations internationales de la Fondation des sciences politiques) and CEAN (Centre d'études d'Afrique noire de l'Université de Bordeaux); from 1970 issued by CEAN alone. Until issue for 1976 contains sections on Africa and the world, on inter-African relations and country surveys of all Africa south of the Sahara, with a narrative overview followed by a detailed chronology of events of the year. After 1976 changes format to emphasize general feature articles, and is no longer of the same value for quick reference purposes. *Continued by* **Afrique politique**. Paris, Karthala for CEAN, 1994- . Annual, which continues to contain feature articles rather than factual summaries)

284 **L'année politique africaine**. Dakar, Société africaine d'édition, 1966-1979. Annual. 14 issues. (Issued in cyclostyled format, 1966-1970; from 1971 issued as Supplément to *Revue française d'études politiques africaines*. Country by country surveys for all Africa within five regions, covering major political events of the previous year. Merged in **L'année politique et économique africaine** (*see* **285**).

285 **L'année politique et économique africaine**. Dakar, Société africaine d'édition, 1981-1985. Annual. (A merger of the former **Année politique africaine** (*see* **284**) and **Économie africaine** (*see* **375**). Economic and political data for the preceding year for 26 African states in Anglophone and Francophone West Africa and Francophone Central Africa)

286 **L'annuaire *Jeune afrique* 1991 [-1994.]: rapport annuel sur l'état de l'Afrique**. Paris, *Jeune afrique*, 1991-1994. Annual. 4 issues. (Initiated to mark 30th anniversary of the Groupe *Jeune Afrique*. Resumes the coverage previously provided by the same publishers in **Afrique 1968 [-1982]** *see* **281**. Provides "informations historiques, politiques, sociales, économiques et financières les plus récentes" with general sections, followed by country by country surveys of 52 African countries)

287 **Commercial directory of Africa, 1950/51**. Nairobi, International Marketing Service Corporation, 1950. xxxv, 279pp. ("Believed to be the first commercial directory to cover Africa as a whole", pref. Arranged under 487 headings for professions and industries)

288 **Invest Africa**, comp. African Business Round Table & NEPAD Business Group. London, The Stationery Office, 2003- . Annual.

289 **Middle East and North Africa**. London, Europa Publications, 11th ed. 1964- . Annual. (Commenced publication 1948 as **The Middle East**. Initial coverage of the Asian Middle East was extended to cover North Africa in 1964, including Chad, Ethiopia, French Somaliland, Mali, Mauritania, Niger, Somalia, Sudan. From 1971, all these countries are also covered by the same publisher's **Africa south of the Sahara**, *see* **276**. ASC4, 76-77)

290 **New African yearbook**. London, IC Publications Ltd., 1978-?2001. Annual (irreg.). ("Africa's politics, economics, history, statistics, organisation, population, essential dates, facts and figures." 1st ed. 1978 covers all Africa; 2nd to 7th eds., 1979 to 1986/87 cover Africa south of the Sahara only; after 7th ed. 1987/88 coverage reverts to whole continent. 5th and 6th eds. each issued in 2 vols. **West and Central Africa**, 1983/84, 1985/86 (*see* **1742**); **East and Southern Africa**, 1984/85, 1986/87 (*see* **1014**). 13th ed. 2001. Basic facts and statistics for 53 African countries. ASC3, 113)

291 **Owen's Africa business directory**. London, Owen's Commerce and Travel (*later* Oxford, Owen's Worldwide Trade), 1953-?1988. Annual. Title varies extensively: **Owen's African and Middle East commerce and travel**

and international register/Owen's commerce & travel & international register: Africa, Middle & Far East/Owens's trade directory and business travel guide: Middle East & Africa/Owen's business directory & travel guide/Owen's world trade Africa & Asia business directory, etc. Present title from 34th (? & last) ed. 1988. (Coverage of Africa south of the Sahara varies: 1971 ed. includes Angola, Cameroon, Central African Republic, Côte d'Ivoire, Dahomey, Djibouti, Ethiopia, Gabon, Gambia, Ghana, Kenya, Liberia, Malawi, Mauritania, Mauritius, Mozambique, Nigeria, Rhodesia, Senegal, Sierra Leone, Somalia, Sudan, Tanzania, Togo, Uganda, Zambia; 1985 ed. covers only Cameroon, Côte d'Ivoire, Ethiopia, Gabon, Kenya, Malawi, Nigeria, Senegal, Seychelles, Somalia, Sudan, Tanzania, Togo. General data on geography, population, communications, industry plus classified commercial directories)

292   The state of Africa, 2003/04: a thematic and factual review, ed. P. Hugo & E. Maloka. Pretoria, Africa Institute of South Africa, 2004 - . Annual. illus. maps. (2003/04 ed. 180pp. Organized in 4 sections: 'Politics and governance'; 'Meeting the Millenium development goals'; 'Peace and conflict'; 'Regional developments'. Includes statistics. Review, *ABPR*, 32, 2006, 126. ASC4, 77).

Francophone Africa

293   Africascope: guide économique de la francophonie. Paris, Éditions Mermon, 1984-1989/90. 7 issues. (Sub-title varies: **... guide économique des pays francophones**. Includes organizations in Francophone Europe (Belgium, France, etc.) with African interests. Sections for West Africa, Central Africa, and the Indian Ocean: within each, country surveys with standardised text on the economy, resources, and communications, and a commercial directory)

294   L'Afrique d'expression française et Madagascar. Paris, Éditions France d'outremer, 1961- ?1983. Annual. 22nd ed. for 1983 last noted in CCFR. (Pub. as special issues of *Europe d'outremer*. Preceded by a single vol. **Communauté zone franc d'Afrique et Marché commun** (1959) produced by the same publishers and giving identical coverage, but not counted by them in issue numbering. Country surveys with political, economic and statistical information. Includes Mauritius and Seychelles)

295   Afrique noire: politique et économique. Paris, Ediafric-La documentation africaine, 1977-?1987. Annual. 6th issue 1987 last recorded in CCFR. (Special issues of *Bulletin de l'Afrique noire*. Covers Francophone countries of West and Central Africa in standardised format: politics, economics, agriculture, industry, finance, communications. Essentially a continuation of **La politique africaine ...** *see* **301**).

296 Annuaire des entreprises d'outre-mer, des organismes officiels et professionnels d'outre-mer, etc. Paris, R. Moreux, 1912-1989. Annual. 79th ed. 1989/90. Initially pub. as **Annuaire des entreprises coloniales, commerce, industrie, agriculture** (to 1957). Cover titles: **Annuaire des entreprises coloniales/Annuaire des entreprises et organismes d'outre-mer**. (Includes 20 Francophone countries south of the Sahara, with administrative and commercial directories for each, together with information on general commercial organizations of Francophone Africa)

297 Annuaire Noria: Afrique noire: guide économique. Limoges, 1950-1964. Title varies: **Annuaire Noria: Afrique noire et Océan indien** (1963-64) following the incorporation of the vol. for **Océan indien** (*see* **3235**) previously published separately. Merged with **Annuaire économique des états d'Afrique noire** from 1965 (*see* **300**).

298 L'Annuaire vert: annuaire économique des territoires français d'Afrique noire et de l'Océan indien: administratif, juridique, agricole, commercial, industriel, financier. Casablanca, 1951-?1955. Sub-title & coverage vary : initially AOF, Togo, Cameroon, with other French territories added from 2nd issue. BnF has issues for 1951, 1953, 1955.

299 Bottin de l'Afrique centrale et de Madagascar. Paris, Société Didot-Bottin, 1946-1973. Annual. Title varies : **Bottin de la France d'outre-Mer** (1946-1950); **Bottin. France d'outre-Mer** (1951-1952); **Bottin de l'Union française (Etats associés et territoires d'outre-Mer)** (1953-1956); **Bottin d'outre-Mer** (1957-1963); **Bottin. Afrique centrale. Algérie. Maroc. Tunisie. Antilles, etc.** (1964-1972). (At its maximum extent covered 21 countries, excluding Burundi, Mauritius, Rwanda, Seychelles and Zaire. Administrative and commercial directories for principal towns in each country. Street plans of Abidjan, Brazzaville, Dakar, Antananarivo)

300 France Afrique, annuaire des sociétés et fournisseurs: les fournisseurs français, les sociétés d'Afrique noire, les sociétés d'Afrique du Nord. Paris, Ediafric-La documentation africaine [etc.], 1962- ?1993. Annual. Issue for 1993 last noted in CCFR. Title varies: **Annuaire économique des états d'Afrique noire** (1962); **Sociétés et représentations industrielles et commerciales: Afrique noire, Madagascar** (1963); **Sociétés et fournisseurs d'Afrique noire et Madagascar** (1964); from 1965 amalgamated with **Annuaire Noria** (*see* **297**) as **Sociétés et fournisseurs ... : guide économique Noria** (1965-1987)

301 La politique africaine en 1968 [-1969]. Paris, Ediafric-La documentation africaine, 1968-1969. 2 issues. (Covers 13 countries of Francophone West and

Central Africa, omitting Guinea. Special issues of *Bulletin de l'Afrique noire*. Lists government officials, and political events of the year)

Lusophone Africa

302   Anuário comercial de Portugal. Vol. 2 (later **vol. 3**), **Ilhas e Ultramar**. Lisbon, Anuário Comercial de Portugal, ?1901 - . ?Annual. 101st ed. 1983 last traced. (For each territory includes details on the civil and religious administration, and a directory of agricultural, commercial, industrial and professional enterprises)

303   Portugal. Agência Geral das Colónias. **Anuário do Ultramar Português**. Lisbon, 1935-1964. 34 vols. Annual. Title varies: **Anuário do Império Colonial Português** (1935-1950)

STATISTICS

General accounts & directories

304   Chander, Ramesh. **Information systems and basic statistics in sub-Saharan Africa: a review and strategy for improvement**. Washington, DC, World Bank, 1990. (World Bank discussion papers, 73). v, 47pp.

305   G.B. Department of Trade & Industry. **National statistical offices of the world**. London, 1997. 72pp. (Earlier eds. London, DTI, 1975, 1976, 1979, 1980, 1985, 1988, 1991) Title varies ... **of overseas countries**

306   World Bank. Statistics in Africa. Partners and related resources. http://www4.worldbank.org/afr/poverty/partners/ Includes addresses of national African statistical agencies, links to statistical data on the Web sites of international organizations including the UN and its agencies.

Bibliographies

Demographic statistics

307   Domschke, Elaine M. & Goyer, Doreen S. **The handbook of national population censuses: Africa & Asia**. New York, Greenwood Press, 1987. xiii, 1,032pp. (A detailed analysis of the various methods of conducting censuses, the varieties of data included and details of all post 1945 censuses for each country. Africa covered on pp.35-545. Review, *Africana J.*, 16, 1994, 462-463)

308   Evalds, Victoria K. **Union list of African censuses, development plans and statistical abstracts**. Oxford, Hans Zell, 1985. 180pp. (Covers material published 1945-1983 held in 12 U.S. collections. Review, *ARD*, 40, 1986, 28-29)

309   France. Institut national de la statistique et des études économiques (INSEE). **Recensements et enquêtes démographiques dans les états africains et malgaches**. Paris, 1978. 88pp.

310   Northwestern University Library. **Censuses in the Melville J. Herskovits Library of African Studies**. Rev. ed. comp. Mette Shayne. Evanston, IL, 1999. 92pp. - - Earlier ed. comp. J.L. McAfee. Evanston, IL, 1975. 19pp - - rev ed. to 1978, comp. Maidel K. Cason. Evanston, IL, 1978. 34pp; - - rev. ed. comp. Mette Shayne. Evanston, IL, 1995. 84pp.

311   Pinfold, John R. **African population census reports: a bibliography and checklist**. Oxford, Hans Zell, 1984. 120pp. (Compiled for SCOLMA. Some 600 entries, with holdings in the U.K. (25 collections), Sweden (9 collections), France, Belgium, the Netherlands, and West Germany)

312   UNECA.   Population   Information   Africa   (POPIA). http://www.uneca.org/popia/. Developed as an element of the U.N. Population Information Network (POPIN). (Provides links to a wide range of sites of national and international sites with population data)

313   U.S. Census Bureau. Census dates of countries and areas of Africa, 1945 to   2014.   http://www.census.gov/ipc/www/cendates/cenafric.html (Includes proposed dates for censuses to be held 2006-2014)

314   U.S. Library of Congress. Census Library Project. **Population censuses and other official demographic statistics of Africa (not including British Africa): an annotated bibliography**. Washington, 1950. 53pp. (Lists 198 censuses)

315   U.S. Library of Congress. Census Library Project. **Population censuses & other official demographic statistics of British Africa: an annotated bibliography**. Washington, 1950. 78pp. (Lists 285 censuses)

316   University of Texas. Population Research Center. **International population census bibliography**. Austin, 1965-68. 7 vols. Vol. 2. 1965. Africa; vol. 7. 1968. Suppl. (Africa, pp. 25-52). - - Goyer, Doreen S. **International population census bibliography, revision and update, 1945-1977**. New York, Academic Press, 1980. (Texas bibliography 2). 576pp. (Revises entries for post 1945 censuses in the original volumes, and extends coverage to 1977. Arranged A/Z by country. These bibliographies have been used as the basis for an extensive microform publishing programme of the original censuses: *see* http://microformguides.gale.com/ Data/Introductions/ 10100FM.htm)

317   Wilson, Angela S. Locating international census data. Washington, DC, Library of Congress, Business Reference Services. Science, Technology, & Business Division, 20 June 2005.   http://www.loc.gov/rr/business/ census/intlcensus.html

Economic statistics

318   Ball, Joyce & Gardella, Roberta. **Foreign statistical documents**. Stanford, Hoover Institution for War, Revolution & Peace, 1967. 173pp. (A listing limited to the holdings of the Hoover Institution, but with good coverage of African material to its date)

319   Batiste, Angel D. 'African business and economic resource index: selected Internet resources', pp. 109-149 *in* **Research, reference service and resources for the study of Africa**, ed. Deborah M. L. Fond & Gretchen Walsh. Binghampton, NY, Haworth Press, 2004. (Lists a wide range of resources based in Africa and overseas arranged by category. Numerous entries, despite the title, lack specific URLs. ASC4, 170-171)

320   Blake, David. 'From paper to PDF? The publications of Africa-related international organizations, past, present and future', *African research & documentation*, 89, 2002, 57-67 (Looks at publishing activities of major African organizations, many of them relating to statistics and assesses their Web sites. Includes UNECA, African Development Bank, African Union, Economic Community of West African States (ECOOWAS) and Southern African Development Community (SADEC). ASC4, 171)

321   Blauvelt, Euan & Durlacher, Jennifer. **Sources of African and Middle Eastern economic information**. Aldershot, Gower, 1982. 2 vols. (Africa is included in vol. 2 with a country by country list of the principal contemporary statistical series)

322   Harvey, Joan. **Statistics-Africa: sources for market research**. 2nd ed. Beckenham, CBD Research, 1978. 374pp. (For each country records the central statistical office and other official sources of government statistics; any non-official sources; libraries with statistical collections and bibliographies. Then lists major statistical series. Over 1,400 titles in 2nd ed., compared with 675 in 1st. The fullest source to its date, but limited almost entirely to series issued post independence). - - Orig. pub. Beckenham, 1970. xii, 175pp.

323 Hjortsäter, Katarina. 'Statistics', pp. 39-57 in Studying Africa: a guide to sources, ed. Kristina Rylander, trans. Linda Linnarsson & Andrew Byerley. Uppsala, Nordiska Afrikainstitutet, 2005. http://www.nai.uu.se/publications/download.html/91-7106-546-6.pdf?id=25112 (One of the most useful chapters in this study guide. Provides links to significant statistical organizations with summary details of their principal publications)

324 Institute of Developing Economies (Ajia Keizai Kenkyujo Toshokan-zo). Tokyo. **Bibliography** [later **Catalogue**] **of statistical materials of developing countries**. Tokyo, 1968 etc. Regularly revised. 14th ed. Tokyo, 1992. xxxiv, 653pp; 15th ed. Tokyo, 1994. xx, 157pp. Since 1998 pub. every two years on CD-ROM

325 Kpedekpo, G.M.K. & Arya, P.L. **Social and economic statistics for Africa: their sources, collection, uses and reliability**. London, Allen & Unwin, 1981. x, 259pp.

326 Pinfold, John. 'Africa', pp. 319-342 in **Information sources in official publications**, ed. Valerie J. Nurcombe. London, Bowker Saur, 1997. (The best general overview of its kind with sections for statistics and censuses)

327 UNECA. **Bibliography of African statistical publications, 1950-1965**. Addis Ababa, 1966. 256pp. (Preceded by **Preliminary draft**. Addis Ababa, 1962) *Supplemented by* **Bibliography ..., 1966-1973**. Addis Ababa, 1973. 45pp; - - **Bibliography ..., 1969-1975**. Addis Ababa, 1975. 85pp; - - **Bibliography ..., 1982-1985**. Addis Ababa, 1985. 63pp; - - **Bibliography ..., 1985-1987**. Addis Ababa, 1987.

328 Westfall, Gloria. **Bibliography of official statistical yearbooks and bulletins**. Cambridge, Chadwyck-Healey, 1986. 247pp. (World-wide survey of the major general statistical bulletins and annuals for each country, not including specialist series for specific topics, e.g. trade. For African countries, concentrates on post independence series with only brief mention of the colonial series. Cited in AGRM2 as Westfall)

329 Westfall, Gloria, ed. **Guide to official publications of foreign countries**. 2nd ed. Chicago, American Library Association, Government Documents Round Table, 1997. xxii, 494pp. (Arranged A/Z by country, with a section on statistics, listing current statistical series, both general and special. Most references are for titles current in the 1980s and 1990s. Indicates latest copies received by North American libraries. Review, *Choice*, 35, 1998, 1172. ASC4, 107. Cited in AGRM2 as ALA). - - Orig. pub. Chicago, IL, 1990. xxi, 359pp.

See also **308**.

General

330 African population database documentation. Version 4. http://grid2.cr.usgs.gov/globalpop/africa/. Supported by UNEP. Comp. Andy Nelson, University of Leeds, U.K. (Contains population figures for some 109,000 administrative units in Africa (83,000 in South Africa). Includes decennial population estimates for each from 1960. ASC4, 174)

331 Afrika; statisticheskiia sbornik, comp. G.R. Ushakova et al. Moscow, Akademiia nauk, Institut Afriki, 1969. 277pp.

332 Afrika-Vademecum, 1972: Grunddaten zur Wirtschaftsstruktur und Wirtschafts-entwicklung Afrikas. 2nd ed. comp. Fritz H. Betz. Munich, Weltforum Verlag for Afrika-Studienstelle, IFO Institut für Wirtschafts-forschung, 1972. 207pp. illus. maps. ("Statistical survey of the most important economical [sic] facts about Africa", pref. Sections for Africa in the world, population, natural resources, agriculture, mining and manufacture, communications, trade, public finance, and development aid. 81 separate tables. Introductory sections also in English and French). - - Orig. pub. Munich, 1968. 164pp. illus.

333 Cross-cultural statistical encyclopedia of the world, ed. Philip M. Parker. Westport, CT, Greenwood Press, 1997. 4 vols. (Vol. 1, Religious cultures; vol. 2, Linguistic cultures; vol. 3, Ethnic cultures; vol. 4, National cultures. Assignment of African cultures to each vol. is problematical, and the many statistical tables are difficult to read)

334 International Monetary Fund (IMF). For its various publications and databases *see* 'Country information' http://www.imf.org/external/country/index.htm which lists all IMF reports and publications by country and provides links to online versions where these are available. Individual IMF 'Country reports' which are largely statistical, i.e. those entitled 'Statistical appendix/annex' are listed below under each country. All published since Report 97/101, 1997 are also available online at http://www.imf.org/external/pubind.htm

335 IMF. **Surveys of African economies**. Washington, DC, 1968-1977. 7 vols. (Vol. 1. 1968. Cameroon, CAR, Chad, Congo (Brazzaville), Gabon. xxiv, 365pp.; vol. 2. 1969. Kenya, Tanzania, Uganda, Somalia. xxiv, 448pp; vol. 3. 1970. Dahomey, Ivory Coast, Mauritania, Niger, Senegal, Togo, Upper Volta. xxv, 480pp; vol. 4. 1971. Congo (Zaire), Malagasay Republic, Malawi, Mauritius, Zambia. xxv, 471pp; vol. 5. 1973. Botswana, Lesotho, Swaziland, Burundi, Equatorial Guinea, Rwanda. xxiii, 471pp; vol. 6. 1975. Gambia, Ghana, Liberia,

Nigeria, Sierra Leone. xxv, 480pp; vol. 7. 1977. Algeria, Mali, Morocco, Tunisia. xxi, 374pp.(Collections of statistics with commentary)

336 Johnson, Marion. **Anglo-African trade in the eighteenth century: English statistics on Africa trade, 1699-1808**, ed. J. Thomas Lindblad & Robert Ross. Leiden, Centre for the History of Overseas Expansion, 1990. iv, 96pp.

337 Mitchell, Brian R. **International historical statistics. Vol. 1, Africa, Asia & Oceania, 1750-2000**. 4th ed. Basingstoke, Macmillan, 2003. 1,113pp. (Review, *Choice*, 41, 2004, 1445). - - Orig. pub. London, 1982. xx, 761pp. (Reviews, *IJAHS*, 17, 1984, 127; *JAH*, 24, 1983, 411-413 which praises the wide range of data assembled and the care taken to help users in assessing their reliability and comparability; "a mine of well-ordered information"); - - 2nd ed. Basingstoke, 1995; - - 3rd ed. Basingstoke, 1998. (Review, *Choice*, 36, 1999, 1441)

338 U.N. **Statistics and indicators on women in Africa, 1986**. New York, United Nations, 1989. xi, 255pp. (Extracted from the UN's **Compendium of statistics and indicators on the condition of women**, 1986, and covers the period 1970-1986)

339 UNECA. http://www.uneca.org. One of the most active organizations collecting & producing statistics on Africa

340 UNECA. **Country economic profiles**. Addis Ababa, 1989. 109pp. (Useful summary of the economic situation in the mid 1980s)

341 UNECA. **Status of women in Africa**. Addis Ababa, 2005. 1 CD-ROM *See* http://www.uneca.org/eca_resources/cdroms/ status_of_african_women/pages/foreword.htm

Bulletins & yearbooks

342 **Africa in figures**. Vienna, United Nations Industrial Development Organization, Statistics & Survey Unit, Division for Industrial Studies. 1985-?1988. Annual. Vols. for 1985, 1986, 1988. (Vol. for 1988. 125pp)

343 **Africa in figures**. Cairo, African Export-Import Bank, 1998- . Every 2 yrs. ?No more pub. (1998 ed. 119pp)

344 African Development Bank (ADB). **ADB statistics pocketbook/Livre de poche des statistiques le la BAD**. Abidjan, African Development Bank, 1999- . Annual. (40 tables in two sections: data on the Bank Group and selected socio-economic data on regional member countries. Also available at http://www.adb.org/pls/portal/docs. ASC4, 173.

345 African Development Bank (ADB). **African development report.**, Oxford, Oxford University Press, 1996- . Annual. 1st issue, published Abidjan. (Part 1, Africa in the world economy; part 2, articles on the annual theme; part 3, economic and social statistics. ASC4, 170. Contents lists available at http://www.afdb.org/pls/portal/docs)

346 African Development Bank (ADB). **Selected statistics on African countries/Statistiques choisies sur les pays africains**. Abidjan, 1998- Annual. (Vol. 25, 2006. 296pp. ASC4, 173. Also available at http://www.adb.org/pls/portal/docs. *Continues* **Selected statistics on regional member countries**. Abidjan, 1981-1997).

347 Economist Intelligence Unit. London. http://www.eiu/. Offers a variety of economic surveys and statistics on a subscription basis. Currently (2006) 47 African countries are covered by both *Country profiles* (updated annually) and by *Country reports* (updated monthly). For details *see* http://www.eiu.com/site_info.asp?info_name=ps_electronicServicesNpubs &entry1=psNav&page=noads. Printed versions commenced 1985, with *Quarterly economic reviews* (later *Country reports*) and annual suppls. called *Country profiles*. The groupings of countries actually covered by each issue changed almost annually. ASC4, 477 discusses the online service. Individual entries are made in AGRM2 for the *Country profiles.*

348 Global Coalition for Africa. **African social and economic trends: annual report of the Global Coalition for Africa**. Washington, DC, 1992- . Annual. (Vol. for 2004. Pt. 1, Review of trends; pt. 2, Africa and international trade. Pp. 52-88, Sub-Saharan development indicators)

349 OECD/African Development Bank. **African economic outlook, 2001/02-** . Paris, 2002- . Annual. 2005/06 (2006). Available also as an e-book. (Pt. 1, general overviews, pt. 2, country reviews of 30 countries (2005/06 ed); pt. 3, Statistical annex. ASC4, 176)

350 **Statistik des Auslandes: Länderberichte**. Wiesbaden, Statistisches Bundesamt, 1961- . Irreg. Title varies: **Länderberichte** (1989-). Booklets (earlier issues 20/40pp. on average, expanding to 80pp. for many countries by late 1980s) issued separately and regularly revised for many countries of the world. *See* entries under individual countries below)

351   U.N. Conference on Trade & Development (UNCTAD). **The least developed countries report**. New York, 1984- . Annual. 2004 ed. xxxii, 362pp. (Includes essays on themes with numerous comparative tables and charts, and c. 50pp. 'Statistical annex: basic data on the least developed countries'. As of 2004, the UN designated 50 countries in this category of which 34 were African. ASC4, 178)

352   UNECA. **Africa in figures**. Addis Ababa, 1994- . Annual. (Pocket-book format "to disseminate important basic facts of Africa". Vol. for 1996. iii, 83pp. with one page of statistics for each country)

353   UNECA. **African socio-economic indicators, 1972-1994**. Addis Ababa, 1972-1994. Annual. Not published, 1974, 1976-1977? (LC cat). (Includes 35 datasets)

354   UNECA. **African statistical yearbook**. Addis Ababa, 1970- . Irreg. Title varies: **Statistical yearbook** (1970-1989). 1st ed., 1970; 2nd-4th eds, 1972-1974; 5th ed. 1976; 6th ed. 1980; from 7th, 1983, annual. (1st ed. comprises 7 vols., each devoted to a particular theme; subsequent eds. comprise a varying number of vols. each devoted to countries in a particular region. Issue for 2002 (2004) 2 vols. Vol. 1, part 1, North Africa; part. 2, West Africa; vol. 2, part 3, Central Africa; part 4, East Africa; part 5, Southern Africa. From 1997 also available online from UNECA Web site. A key source. ASC4, 178)

355   UNECA. **Demographic handbook for Africa**. Addis Ababa, ?1966- . Irreg. Issues for 1968, 1971, 1975, 1980, 1982, 1988, 1992. ("Major objective is to present in a consolidated form, demographic data and analysis from various sources pertaining to the principal demographic indicators of member states", pref.)

356   UNECA. **Economic and social survey of Africa, 1994/95-** . Addis Ababa, UNECA, 1994- . *Continues* **Survey of economic and social conditions in Africa, 1976 [- 1991/92]**. New York, United Nations, 1976-1993. Annual

357   UNECA. **Economic report on Africa**. Addis Ababa, 1997- . Annual. (Each report focuses on a particular theme and is also available online: for URLs *see* UNECA Web site. http://www.uneca.org. ASC4, 179)

358   UNECA. **Statistical information bulletin for Africa**. Addis Ababa, 1969-1988. Annual. Title varies: **Quarterly statistical bulletin for Africa** (1969-71); **Statistical & economic information bulletin for Africa** (1972-1977). *Continues* **Statistical bulletin for Africa**. Addis Ababa, 1965-67. 2 issues. Issue 1, Nov. 1965. 2 pts; issue 2, Mar. 1967. 3 pts. ("Replaces the statistical annexes to *Economic bulletin for Africa* issued 1962-1964", pref.)

359 World Bank. **African development indicators**. Washington, DC, World Bank, 1992- . Annual. Prepared by the Economics & Finance Division, African Technical Department, International Bank for Reconstruction & Development. (Vols for 1992 (pub. 1992); 1994/95(1995); 1996 (1996); 1997 (1997); 1998/99 (1998); 2000 (1999); 2001 (2002); 2002 (2003); 2005 (2005). Reviews of 1996, *Choice*, 34, 1997, 765; of 2001, *ARBA*, 33, 2002, 47; *Choice*, 40, 2002, 614. Also available on CD-ROM. Contains over 500 macroeconomic, sectoral and social indicators covering over 50 African countries with comparative data from 1970 onwards). *Continues* **African economic and financial data**. Washington, DC, 1989. Selected sections also available as **World Bank Africa database** at http://www4.worldbank.org/ afr/stats/default.cfm (*see* **361**)

360 World Bank. Statistics in Africa. http://www4.worldbank.org/ afr/stats/default.cfm. ("This site brings together information and resources related to statistics in Africa, both from within the World Bank and from many other sources identified by World Bank staff ... inclusion of information on this site does not necessarily imply endorsement by the World Bank. Nor does the absence of information imply deliberate exclusion. We are aware that the information is incomplete. We hope to build on it. If an organization working in relation to statistics in Africa is missing it is because we had insufficient or no information on it". Includes **African Development indicators**, *see* **359** *above* for print and CD-ROM versions)

361 World Bank. **World Bank Africa database 2005**. Washington, DC, World Bank, 2005. CD-ROM. (Over 1,200 indicators of economic and social data for all African countries and 20 regional groups, much of the data going back to 1970. Includes 'Country-at-a-glance' tables for all countries. Drawn from database at http://www4.worldbank.org/afr/stats/default.cfm. ASC4, 180)

Anglophone Africa

362 Kuczynski, Robert René. **Demographic survey of the British colonial empire**. London, Oxford University Press for Royal Institute of International Affairs, 1948. 4 vols. Vol.1, West Africa; vol. 2, High Commission Territories, Central and East Africa, Mauritius and Seychelles. (Compilation commenced in 1939 at the request of the Population Investigation Committee. For each country discusses methods of census taking, then provides a chronological account of demographic estimates, censuses, and provisions for registration of births and deaths with comments on fertility, mortality, and population growth together with extensive statistics. "Monuments of scholarly erudition", A.D. Roberts, *History in Africa*, 5, 1978, 160. Reviews, *African affairs* 48, 1949, 162-163; 49, 1950, 76-77)

363   G.B. Board of Trade. **Statistical abstract for the several colonial and other possessions of the U.K., 1851/1863 [-1939/45]**. London, Board of Trade, 1865-1948. Irreg. Vols. 1-72. Title varies: **Statistical abstract for the British self-governing Dominions, Possessions and Protectorates** (1917-1925); ... **for the several British overseas Dominions and Protectorates** (1929-1938); ... **for the British Commonwealth** (1946-48). *Continued by* G.B. Colonial Office. **The Commonwealth & the Sterling Area: statistical abstract, 1949/52 [-1967]**. London, HMSO, 1953-1968. Vols. 73-87.

364   G.B. Colonial Office. **An economic survey of the colonial territories**. London, HMSO, 1932-1951. Irreg. Issues for 1932-33, 1935-37, 1951. (Presents a systematic account and statistics of each colony's economy with background data on topography, the administration, communications, etc. 1932-1937 issued in single vols.; 1951 issued in 7 vols :Vol. 1, The Central African and High Commission territories Northern Rhodesia, Nyasaland, Basutoland, Bechuanaland and Swaziland; vol. 2, The East African Territories: Kenya, Tanganyika, Uganda, Zanzibar and the Somaliland Protectorate with Aden, Mauritius and Seychelles; vol. 3, The West African territories: The Gambia, The Gold Coast, Nigeria and Sierra Leone and St. Helena; vol. 7, The products of the Colonial Territories)

365   G.B. Colonial Office. **Digest of colonial statistics**. London, HMSO, 1952-1964. Quarterly/annual. Annual 1963-64.

Francophone Africa

366   Afristat: Observatoire économique et statistique de l'Afrique subsaharienne. http://www.afristat.org/. (Headquarters in Bamako, Mali. Members, as of April 2006 : Benin, Burkina Faso, Cameroon, Côte d'Ivoire, Guinea, Mali, Mauritania, Senegal, Togo ; Central African Republic, Chad, Congo, Gabon ; Comoros: also Cape Verde, Equatorial Guinea and Guinea-Bissau from non-Francophone Africa. Includes general comparative statistics from 1996, together with country pages for members with national statistics. ASC4, 174)

367   **L'économie des pays d'Afrique noire de la zone franc**. 2nd ed. Paris, Ediafric-La documentation africaine, 1979. 209pp. (Covers Francophone West and Central Africa). - - Orig. pub. Paris, 1973. ('Constitute en fait un mise à jour de la 7ième ed. (1972) de **Mémento ...** ', *see* **379**)

368   **Etats africains et malgaches de la Communauté, principales données statistiques. Décembre 1959**. Paris, P. Dupont, 1959. 88pp.

369 France. Institut national de la statistique et des études économiques (INSEE)/ Service de coopération, Institut national d'études démographiques. **Afrique noire, Madagascar, Comores: démographie comparée**, comp. Jean-Marc Cohen et al. Paris, Délégation générale à la recherche scientifique et technique, 1966-67. 10 vols.

370 France. Ministère de la France d'outre-mer. Service de statistiques. **Inventaire social et économique des territoires d'outre-mer, 1950-1955**. Paris, 1957. 467pp. (Data on politics and administration, geography and climate, population, health, scientific organizations, justice, agriculture, forestry, mining, industry, communications, trade, and public finance)

371 France. Ministère de la France d'outre-mer. Service de statistiques. **Outre-mer 1958: tableau économique et social des états et territoires d'outre-mer à la veille de la mise en place des nouvelles institutions**. Paris, 1959. 862pp. maps. (Another collection of statistical data, updating the **Inventaire ...** *see* **370**).

372 Groupe de Démographie Africaine. **L'évaluation des effectifs de la population des pays africains**. Paris, 1982-1984. 2 vols. (Country-by-country survey of the characteristics of the population of African countries)

373 Organisation commune africaine, malgache et maurice (OCAM). **Annuaire statistique**, réalisé par le Service statistique de l'OCAM avec la collaboration du Département de la coopération de l'Institut national de la statistique et des études économiques, France. Yaoundé, 1970. 917pp. illus. (Despite the title, this is simply a 'one-off' large scale compilation of statistics, intended as a continuation of **Outre-mer 1958 ...** *see* **371**)

374 **La zone franc et l'Afrique**. 3rd ed. Paris, Ediafric-La documentation africaine, 1981. 299pp. (All eds. pub. as special issues of *Bulletin de l'Afrique noire*. Statistics, especially on trade between France and the Francophone countries of West and Central Africa). - - Orig. pub. Paris, 1977. 376, xivpp. - - 2nd ed. 1979. 370pp.

Bulletins & yearbooks

375 **L'économie africaine, 1971** [etc.]. Dakar, Société africaine d'éditions, 1971-1979. Annual. (Pub. as special issues of *Moniteur africain*. Covers Francophone West and Central Africa with statistical country by country surveys. Merged with **L'année politique et économique africaine**, *see* **285**)

376 France. Institut national de la statistique et des études économiques (INSEE). **Bulletin des statistiques des départements et territoires d'outre-mer**.

Paris, 1960- . Quarterly. *Continues* France. Ministère des Colonies. **Bulletin mensuel des statistiques coloniales**. Paris, 1936-1939. Monthly; France. Institut national de la statistique et des études économiques (INSEE). **Bulletin mensuel de statistique d'outre-mer**. Paris, 1945-1959. Vols. 1-16. Monthly.

377   France. Institut national de la statistique et des études économiques (INSEE). **Données statistiques: africains et malgaches**. Paris, 1961-1972. Quarterly.

378   France. Institut national des territoires d'outre-mer. **Annuaire statistique des territoires d'outre-mer**. Paris, 1959- . Annual (irreg). Issues for 1959 (1961); 1961 (1963) ; 1962-1965 (1967); 1965-1966 (1968) ; 1967-1968 (1969) ; 1969-1971 (1973). *Continues* France. Institut national de la statistique et des études économiques (INSEE) & Ministère de la France d'outre-mer, Service des statistiques. **Annuaire statistique des possessions françaises**. éd. provisoire. Paris, 1944-46. Originally issued in fascs. - - 2nd ed. **Annuaire statistique de l'Union française d'outre-mer, 1939/46**. Paris, 1949. 930pp. (Includes some data up to and including 1948/49); - - 3rd ed. **Annuaire statistique ... 1939/49**. Paris, 1951. 2 vols. 453, 613pp. *Continued by* **Annuaire statistique de l'Union française, 1949/54**. Paris, 1956. 2 vols. 138, 138pp. *Continued by* **Annuaire statistique de la Zone Franc, 1949/55**. Paris, 1957-1958. 2 vols. 239pp.

379   **Mémento statistique de l'économie et de la planification africaines**. Paris, Ediafric-La documentation africaine. 1964- ?1980. Irreg. 10th issue 1980. Title varies: **Mémento de l'économie africaine** (1965-). (Pub. as special issues of *Bulletin de l'Afrique noire*. Covers 13 countries of Francophone West and Central Africa)

380   OECD. Office statistique des Communautés Européennes. **Annuaire statistique des E.A.M.M. (États africaines et malgache associés)**. Luxembourg, 1969- . Annual.

381   Organisation commune africaine, malgache et maurice (OCAM). **Études et statistiques**. Yaoundé, 1971- . Quarterly. *Continues* OCAM. **Bulletin statistique**. Yaoundé, 1970-1971. (Covers Cameroon, Central African Republic, Chad, Gabon, Rwanda, Madagascar, Mauritius. Each issue discusses a particular theme)

Lusophone Africa

382   Gonçalves, José Júlio. **Portugueses dispersos pelo mundo: síntese estatística**. Lisbon, Agência-Geral do Ultramar, 1971. 301pp. + 28 plates.

383   Portugal. Instituto Nacional de Estatística. **Anuário estatístico do ultramar/Annuaire statistique d'outre-mer. 1943 [-1960]**. Lisbon, 1945-1962. Annual. Title varies: **Anuário estatístico do Império colonial/Annuaire statistique de l'empire colonial**, (1945-1949).

384   Portugal. Instituto Nacional de Estatística. **Anuário estatístico. Vol. 2 : Ultramar**. Lisbon, 1962-1974. Annual. Title varies : ... **Vol. 2 : Territórios Ultramarinos**. (Following the cessation of **Anuário estatístico do Império colonial** (*see* **383**) this general national Portuguese statistical annual added a second vol. covering colonial territories. Last pub. vol. covers statistics of 1972)

DIRECTORIES OF ORGANIZATIONS

Guides to abbreviations & acronyms

385   **Abbreviations in the African press**. [Rev. ed.] Arlington, VA, Joint Publications Research Service (JPRS), 1975. ii, 163pp. (Some 2,000 abbreviations and acronyms for organizations of all types. Covers all African countries, also entries for organizations in Belgium, France, Italy, Portugal, Spain, Vatican, West Germany). - - Orig. pub. New York, CCM Information, 1972. ix, 108pp. (Earlier version pub. as **Glossary of abbreviations relating to African affairs**. Washington, DC, JPRS, 1966. 91pp.)

386   Deutsche Afrika-Gesellschaft. **Abbreviations in Africa**. Bonn, 1969. ix, 260pp. (Some 4,000 abbreviations used by African organizations, research institutes, government agencies etc. Emphasis on Francophone Africa)

387   Hall, David E. **African acronyms and abbreviations: a handbook**. London, Mansell, 1996. 364pp. (Includes over 12,000 entries for both current and defunct organizations. In addition to specifically African entities includes entries for e.g. international organizations which are frequently cited in Africanist publications. Based upon the authority files developed by the compiler while editing the *International African bibliography*. Reviews, *ARD*, 72, 1996, 69-70; *Choice*, 34, 1996, 252. ASC4, 122. For a much briefer but up-to-date list *see* 'Abbreviations and acronyms in African studies' pp. 708-716 in Hans Zell. ASC4 (2006). *See also* ROAPE (Review of African political economy) African acronym demystifier at http://www.roape.org/acronym1.html)

388   Sokoll, Alfred H. **Afrika: Abkürzungen und Acronyme**. Munich, Alkos-Verlag Sokoll, 1995. viii, 951pp. (Review, *RREO*, http://rre.casalini.it/1998/AM-98-34.html compares with Hall, **387** and notes "the number of

entries in Sokoll is much greater [but]… Hall has taken greater care with his work and provided more detail … perhaps the best solution is to use both works in tandem")

Bibliographies

389 Anderson, Ian Gibson. **Current African directories**, incorporating African companies - a guide to sources of information, a guide to directories published in or relating to Africa, and to sources of information on business enterprises in Africa. Beckenham, CBD Research, 1972. xii, 187pp. (Very detailed for sources published in the 1960s)

390 **Guide to directories on science and technology in Africa**. Dakar, African Regional Centre for Technology in collaboration with the African Academy of Sciences and the American Association for the Advancement of Science, 1993. 135pp. (Lists 242 directories, including international directories with African coverage. Includes entries for many general sources such as the Clio Press country bibliographies and the **Country studies** series)

General

391 **The African studies companion: a guide to information sources**. 4th ed. comp. Hans Zell. Lochcarron, Scotland, Hans Zell Publishing, 2006. xxx, 833pp. Online updated version available at http://www.africanstudies companion.com/ for registered purchasers of the hardcopy. (One of the key Africana reference sources, combining a very wide range of detailed bibliographical and directory information. Sections 1 to 23 contain 2,908 numbered items, covering general online sources, major reference tools, with separate sections for current bibliographies, biographical, statistical and cartographic sources; directories of African studies periodicals and of the African press; directories of African studies collections around the world, of major libraries and archives in Africa, and of centres of African studies worldwide; directories of publishers with African studies list and dealers of African studies materials; directories of major African and international organizations, of foundations and donor agencies, of African studies associations, of online forums and mailing lists and of awards and prizes in African studies. Section 23 is a guide to Web sites and resources on ICT in Africa; section 24 is a list of abbreviations and acronyms in African studies, section 25 is 'Using Google for African studies research', a condensed and updated version of a pilot version originally published at http://www.hanszell.co.uk/google/ in Sept. 2004. All items are provided with critical annotations. Clear and detailed preface and introduction draw attention to features new to this ed. especially the directories of the African press (section 11) and the directory of centres of African studies (section 14).

Review, *ARD* 101, 2006, forthcoming. New ed. announced for 2009. Cited as ASC4 in the present work, where cross references are made). - - Orig. pub. as **The African studies companion: a resource guide and directory**, comp. Hans Zell. Oxford, Hans Zell, 1989. x, 165pp. (Reviews, *Choice*, 27, 1990, 1812. *Choice* "outstanding academic title", 1991); - - 2nd ed. comp. Hans Zell & Cecile Lomer. London, Hans Zell, 1997. xvi, 276pp. (Reviews, *ARD*, 78, 1998, 58-59; *Choice*, 35, 1997, 612. *Choice* "outstanding academic title", 1997); - - 3rd ed. **The African studies companion: a guide to information sources**. Lochcarron, 2003. xiii, 545pp. (Reviews, *ARBA*, 35, 2004, 42, "one of the most essential tools in African studies"; *ARD*, 93, 2003, 95-96; *Choice*, 41, 2004, 1049; *Journal of Southern African studies*, 30, 2004, 713-714.).

392 IAI. **International directory of African studies research**. 3rd ed. comp. Philip Baker. London, Hans Zell, 1994. 319pp. (1,815 entries for institutions throughout the world, with details of courses offered, staff specialization, library resources and publications. Indexes by name of organization and scholar, and subjects and regions of specialization. Reviews, *ARD*, 70, 1996, 75-76; *Choice*, 32, 1995, 1574. ASC4, 103. - - Orig. pub. as **International guide to African studies research**. London, IAI, 1975. x, 185pp. (Pp. 1-66, an enlarged and revised ed. of **International register ...** , *see* **393**. A total of 446 institutions from 41 African countries, and 26 others. Pp. 67-185 comprise the 4th issue in the series of guides to *Current Africanist research*); - - 2nd ed. comp. Philip Baker. London, Hans Zell, 1987. 276pp. (Covers over 1,100 institutions. Review, *ARD*, 46, 1988, 53-55)

393 IAI. **International register of organizations undertaking Africanist research in the social sciences and humanities, 1970**. London, IAI Research Information Liaison Unit, 1971. v, 64pp. (Based on a questionnaire. Pp. 1-20, African countries, listing 174 institutions from 43 countries; pp. 21-58, other countries, listing 332 institutions from 28 countries. In addition to Europe and North America includes Brazil, India, Israel, Japan, Taiwan. Review, *Africa*, 43, 1973, 159-161)

394 The International directory of African studies scholars (IDASS) http://www.columbia.edu/cu/lweb/indiv/africa/cuvl/directory.html Maintained by Joe Caruso at Columbia University Library. Scholars submit their own entries. "The Directory is fully indexed, allowing readers to conduct a search by name or keyword,e.g. subject of interest, city or country, university or affiliation, etc.". ASC4, 64. Essentially supersedes **International directory of scholars and specialists in African studies**. Waltham, MA, African Studies Association (ASA), 1978. viii, 355pp. (Some 2,700 entries, based upon a questionnaire)

Organizations in Africa

Some sources also include coverage of organizations located **outside** Africa.

General

395   Africa's NGOs. Geneva, International Council of Voluntary Agencies, 1968. 299pp. (Lists 1,839 non-governmental organizations arranged by country. Includes religious bodies, social welfare organizations, and a few research institutes. Detail varies, with often only name and address provided. Index by nature of activity and by affiliation to international organizations)

396   African Union directory, 2002. Port Louis, Mauritius, Millennium Africa Communications for African Union, 2002. 210pp. (Large format glossy official publication to mark the 2002 summit with the transition from the OAU to the African Union (AU). Includes country profiles with basic economic, social and political data for all African countries, including Western Sahara but not Morocco. Pp. 181-206, directory of 'government bodies and associated central groups')

397 Contemporary African database (CAD): Institutions. http://institutions.africadatabase.org/ London, Africa Centre, 2001- . ("A directory of African institutions including governments, pan-African bodies, non-governmental organisations, and significant businesses. For inclusion in *Institutions*, the organisation must be active, must have a physical address in Africa and must not be a subsidiary of a non-African organisation". As of August 2006 the file contained entries for just under 2,400 institutions. The prinicpal search possibilities are by name of institution, by country and by category: Arts, Business, Education, Academia and research, Media, Religion, Society, Politics and governance and Sports, each with sub-categories. For the majority of institutions included there is little more than contact details and the database has a long way yet to go) *See also* **540**

International organizations

398   Adotevi, Adovi John-Bosco, ed. **ROCIA: répertoire des organisations de coopération interafricaine**. Yaoundé, Inter Media, 1984. 155pp. (Eight sections: politics, finance, development, agriculture, medicine, culture, and sport. Detailed accounts of the history and activities of some 50 organisations)

399 African international organization directory and African participation in other international organizations, 1984/85. Munich & New

York, K.G. Saur, 1984. (Guides to International Organizations, 1). 604pp. (Compiled by the Union of International Associations, and based upon their **Yearbook of international organizations**. Principal sections comprise a list of 817 individual organizations arranged under five categories, e.g. Intercontinental membership, Regional membership. Indexes to countries, subjects, acronyms and former names of organizations)

400 Belaouane-Gherari, Sylvie & Gherari, Habib. **Les organisations régionales africaines: recueil de textes et documents** [etc.]. Paris, Ministère de la coopération, La documentation française, 1988. 472pp. (Lists regional organizations, and reproduces their charters and other significant documents). *See also* **403**

401 DeLancey, Mark W. & Mays, Terry M. **Historical dictionary of international organizations in Sub-Saharan Africa**. 2nd ed. Lanham, MD, Scarecrow Press, 2002. (Historical dictionaries of international organizations, 21). li, 356pp. (Entries for international, intergovernmental, and NGOs with descriptions of their activities; also for individuals. Covers both active and defunct organizations. Chronology, list of acronyms and abbreviations. Detailed bibliography. ASC4, 99). - - Orig. pub. Metuchen, NJ, 1994. (Historical dictionaries of international organizations, 3). lviii, 517pp (Reviews, *Choice*, 32, 1994, 746-748; *IJAHS*, 28, 1995, 657-65. ASC4, 99)

402 Fredland, Richard. **A guide to African international organizations**. London, Hans Zell, 1990. vii, 316pp. (Wide variety of information including detailed treatment of eight major organizations, e.g. ECOWAS; A/Z list of some 500 organizations, current and defunct; biographical data on some 120 miscellaneous individuals (including Africanus Horton, Nkrumah, Ali Mazrui); a chronology of significant dates in the founding and activities of organizations. Appendices include list of acronyms, list of organizations by date of foundation, individual country membership of organizations. Reviews, *ARD*, 4, 1990, 43-44; *Choice*, 29, 1991, 258)

403 Kalonji, M.T. Zezeze, ed. **Dictionnaire des organisations interafricaines: lexiques et textes**. Paris, Agence de la francophonie/Editions Giraf, 1997. 1,166pp. (Lists some 1,200 inter-African organizations with information on membership and purpose, followed by texts of their charters, and of byelaws and treaties. Essentially an updated version of **400**)

404 Kalonji, M.T. Zezeze ed. **Dictionnaire francophone des organisations panafricaines (DIFOP)**. Paris, Conseil international de la langue française, 1992. 291pp.

405 Söderbaum, Frederik. **Handbook of regional organizations in Africa**. Uppsala, Nordiska Afrikainstitutet, 1996. 161pp. (Based on available published data, mostly from 1995. Covers organizations which represent 3 or more African countries, and were thought to be currently active. Part 1 covers the 15 major regional organizations in some detail, part 2 covers some 250 other organizations much more briefly. Includes list of acronyms. No bibliographical references or subject index. Review, *Choice*, 34, 1997, 1786)

406 UNECA. **Directory of intergovernmental co-operation organizations in Africa**. 2nd ed. Addis Ababa, 1976. viii, 170pp. - - Orig. pub. Addis Ababa, 1972. vii, 94pp.

Administration

407 **African administration: directory of public life, administration and justice for the African states. Vol. 1**, comp. W.Z. Duic. Munich, K.G. Saur, 1978. 1,285pp. No more pub. (Includes Benin, Cameroon, Gabon, Gambia, Ghana, Guinea, Guinea-Bissau, Ivory Coast, Liberia, Nigeria, Senegal, Sierra Leone, Togo, Upper Volta, Zaire, Zambia. Detailed lists of major government departments and business, financial, judicial, labour, social and religious organizations. Text in English, French, Dutch, German, Italian, Spanish and Serbo-Croat. Numerous maps including city plans)

408 African governments on the WWW, comp. Gunnar Anzinger. http://www.gksoft.com/govt/en/africa.html. A section of the author's Governments on the WWW, created 1995. Lists "parliaments, ministries, offices, law courts, embassies, city councils, public broadcasting corporations, central banks, multi-governmental institutions etc. Includes also political parties". Few details about these, other than a link to their Web site. As of July 2006, no country site had been updated since 2002 and many links no longer work. Also provides links from each country to general sources such as the **World factbook (47)** & **Ethnologue (155)**. ASC4, 8.

409 **Guide permanent de l'administration africaine: institutions de l'Afrique noire**. Paris, Ediafric-La documentation africaine, 1980- ? Semi-monthly. NWU & CCFR record issues to 1988. *Continues* **Institutions d'Afrique noire**. Paris, Ediafric, 1964-1979. 6 p.a. (Each issue consists of revised and updated looseleaf inserts)

410 IFLA. International Office for Universal Bibliographic Control. **African legislative and ministerial bodies: list of uniform headings for higher legislative and ministerial bodies in African countries**. London, 1980. viii, 37pp. (Produced in association with African Standing Conference on Bibliographic Control (ASCOBIC). Covers Benin, Botswana, Burundi, Côte d'Ivoire, Gabon, Gambia, Ghana, Kenya, Madagascar, Nigeria, Rwanda, Senegal, Sierra Leone, Tanzania, Togo. Lists headings used during the period 1970-1979. *See* Barbara Jover. 'The compilation of **African legislative and ministerial bodies'**, *ARD*, 26, 1981, 5-7)

411 **Répertoire des pouvoirs publics africains**: Cameroun, RCA, Congo, Côte d'Ivoire, Dahomey, Gabon, Haute-Volta, Mali, Mauritanie, Niger, Sénégal, Tchad, Togo. 2nd ed. Paris, Ediafric-La documentation africaine, 1975. 342pp. - - Orig. pub. as **Répertoire de l'administration africaine**. Paris, 1969. (Issued as special numbers of *Bulletin de l'Afrique noire*. Lists government ministers, members of national assemblies, and senior government officials).

Development

412 ACCT. **Informations pour le développement**. Paris, IBISCUS, 1995-1997. 3 vols. Vol. 1, Environment. 1995. 286pp ; vol. 2, Agriculture, 1995. 271pp ; vol. 3, Education, 1997. 277pp. (Covers Francophone countries around the world. Vol. for education has addresses and contacts for universities and departments, ministries of education, national commissions for UNESCO etc.)

413 ACCT. **Recherche scientifique et développement 1980: répertoire des institutions francophones**. Paris, 1980. 2 vols. (A directory of institutions and scholars in Francophone countries involved in research into the Third World. Vol. 1 includes Africa)

414 **African development sourcebook**. Paris, UNESCO, 1991. 157pp. (Directory of institutions and NGOs involved in a wide range of development activities. Review, *Choice*, 30, 1992, 267)

415 **Directory of activities of international voluntary agencies in rural development in rural Africa**. 3rd ed. Addis Ababa, UNECA, 1977. 173pp. - - Orig. pub. Addis Ababa, 1973; - - 2nd ed. Addis Ababa, 1975.

416 **Directory of African development institutions, 1991**. Addis Ababa, UNECA. Pan African Development Information System (PADIS), 1991. 112pp. (Lists 115 institutions. Country and subject indexes)

417 **Directory of co-operative organizations: Africa south of the Sahara**. Geneva, International Labour Office (ILO), 1975. (*Cooperative information*, Suppl. 3). 273pp. (For each country gives a brief chronological outline of the development of such bodies, then a directory of existing organizations and statistics on their operation)

418 Directory of development organizations: resource guide to development organizations and the Internet. Africa. 2006 ed. Comp. Bert Wesselink, 2000-. http://www.devdir.org/africa.htm. Pdf files downloadable by country or in two parts for the entire African region. For each country covers: (1) international organizations; (2) government institutions; (3) private sector support organizations; (4) finance institutions; (5) training and research centres; (6) civil society organizations; (7) development consulting firms; (8) information providers (development newsletters/journals); (9) grantmakers. Minimal contact information provided for each. "This site is highly recommended for its comprehensiveness, its maintenance and its ease of use", *ABPR*, 31, 2005, 202. ASC4, 58-59.

419 **Directory of development research and training institutes in Africa**. [4th rev. ed.]. Paris, OECD Development Centre & CODESRIA, 1992. 248pp. (Lists some 640 institutions. Based upon a computerised database, from which the compiling agencies offer specific subject searches and printouts. Uses U.N. Macrothesaurus keywords). - - Orig. pub. Paris, 1972. (*Liaison bulletin*, 1972, 1). 80pp. Prepared in co-operation with CODESRIA. (Covers 26 institutions in 15 African countries); - - [2nd rev. ed]. Paris, 1982. (*Liaison bulletin*, n.s. 8, 1982). xvi, 156pp. (*also pub.* Dakar, CODESRIA, 1983); . - - [3rd rev. ed.]. Paris, OECD Development Centre & CODESRIA, 1986. xxviii, 262pp. (Lists 497 institutions in 46 African countries)

420 **Directory of development resources: Africa**, comp. Dennis Culkin, ed. Sabra Breslin. Mt. Rainier, MD, Volunteers in Technical Assistance (VITA), 1979. [207]pp. (Lists 187 African organizations by country with name and subject of interest indexes)

421 **Directory of social development institutions in Africa**, comp. A. Guerma. Tripoli, African Centre for Applied Research and Training in Social Development (ACARTSOD), 1983. 167pp. (Includes international, regional and national institutions)

422 **The INASP directory of organizations and networks in rural development: Africa**. Pilot ed. Oxford, International Network for the Availability for Scientific Publications (INASP), 1998. xiii, 229pp. (Main arrangement by topic: Agriculture, Animal production, Forestry, Natural resources, Environment, Energy, etc. Indexes by name and country)

423 **Institutions engaged in social and economic planning in Africa**. Paris, UNESCO, 1967. 155pp. (Prepared by the International Committee for Social Science Documentation and CARDAN)

424 **Inventaire des sources africaines de conseil et d'assistance technique: répertoire.** Levallois-Perret, Cités unies développement, 1990. 245pp. (Lists government and research organizations concerned with technical support)

425 **Pays lusophones d'Afrique: sources d'information pour le développement,** comp. Christiane Lalonde. Paris, Ibiscus, 2000. 221pp. (Comp. for the Ministère français des affaires étrangères. Includes sections for international organizations, and for organizations in Angola, Cape Verde, Guinea-Bissau, Mozambique, São Tomé e Principe and South Africa. Also lists libraries and information centres)

426 **Répertoire d'organismes francophones d'appui au développement: Afrique, Canada, Europe.** Paris, Ministère des affaires étrangères & IBISCUS, 1999. (Réseaux documentaires pour le développement). 288pp. (Lists 197 government agencies and NGOs which support development in the Francophone world)

See also **455**

Education

427 African higher education resource directory. http://africa.msu.edu/ AUP/. (Collaborative project between the Association of African Universities (AAU), the African Studies Association (ASA) and the African Studies Center, Michigan State University. Searchable by country, by institution name, and by field of study. The site also contains the text of documents, conferences etc, relating to higher education. ASC4, 57-58)

428 Association of African Universities. **Handbook.** Accra, 1993- ?Annual (*Continues* **Directory of African universities,** *see* **429** below. 1993 ed. xviii, 240pp. Gives details on universities in 34 African countries)

429 Association of African Universities. **Directory of African universities.** 5th ed. Accra, 1988. 495pp. - - Orig. pub. Accra, 1974.192, 94pp. - - 2nd ed Accra, 1976. 2 vols. Vol. 1, Anglophone Universities. vi, 278, 9pp; vol. 2, Universités francophones. vi, 111, 9pp; - - 3rd ed. Accra, 198?; - - 4th ed. Accra, 1986. x, 508pp. (All eds. maintain separate sequences for Anglophone and Francophone Africa)

430 AUPELF. **Répertoire des enseignants et chercheurs Africains, universités d'Afrique membres de l'AUPELF.** Dakar & Montreal, AUPELF, 1984. 374pp.

431 AUPELF. **Enseignants et chercheurs des institutions membres de l'AUPELF-UREF; Afrique, Caraïbe, Océan indien** [etc.]. Montreal, AUPELF, 1991-1998/99. Irreg. (Title varies. A broader based continuation of **430**)

432 AUPELF. **Répertoire des établissements d'enseignement supérieur membres de l'AUPELF-UREF**. Montreal, 1966- . Annual (irreg.). Recent issues for 1976, 1986, 1991, 1992, 1993/94, 1994/95, 1996/97, 1998/99. (Includes Francophone Africa. Companion to **431**)

433 Commonwealth universities yearbook. London, Association of Commonwealth Universities [etc.], 1914- . Annual. Title varies : **Yearbook of the universities of the empire** (1914-1948). (Regularly rev. and the best source for both current and historical activity of universities in Commonwealth Africa)

434 Directory of adult education centres in Africa. Dakar, UNESCO Regional Office for Education in Africa, 1974. iv, 130pp. (108 institutions, arranged by country. Covers Sub-Saharan Africa but excludes Republic of South Africa)

435 A directory of selected African training institutions, comp. Richard L. Betz et al. Gaborone, Directorate of Public Service Management, 1990. ix, 192pp. ("With the support of the U.S. Agency for International Development").

436 Guide to higher education in Africa. 3rd ed. Basingstoke, Macmillan for Association of African Universities, International Association of Universities, UNESCO Information Centre on Higher Education, 2004. xvi, 584pp. (Reviews, *ARD*, 96, 2004, 87; *Choice*, 42, 2004, 640). - - Orig. pub. Basingstoke, 1999. xix, 420 p. - - 2nd ed. Basingstoke, 2002. xvi, 530pp. (ASC4, 99)

437 A panafrican directory of African universities. Nashville, TN, Panafrica, 1995- . ("To be pub. every three years". Also called **Directory of African universities and colleges**)

Finance & commerce

438 Les 500 (cinq cents) premières entreprises d'Afrique noire. 3rd ed. Paris, Ediafric-La documentation africaine, 1976. 287pp. (Covers Francophone West and Central Africa. Special issue of *Bulletin de l'Afrique noire*). - - Orig. pub. 1969. 348pp.

439 African Economic Digest (AED). **The AED African financial directory, 1986**. London, Middle East Economic Digest Ltd., 1987. 289pp. (Based on data acquired during compilation of weekly *African economic digest* since 1980. Covers 52 member states of OAU. General information on banking and currencies, directory of banks and other financial institutions by country)

440 The Commonwealth Africa investment almanac. London, Commonwealth Secretariat & Commonwealth Business Council, 1998- . Annual. (The Commonwealth Business Council was founded at the Commonwealth Heads of Government Meeting (CHOGM), Edinburgh, 1997. The almanac is an attempt to attract greater private investment. Pt. 1, general information and advice; pt. 2 has sectoral surveys for banking, mining, etc.; pt. 3 is a survey of 19 countries, including Nigeria, at the time suspended from the Commonwealth. Review, *African affairs*, 98, 1999, 125-126)

441 L'industrie africain en 1973. 4th ed. Paris, Ediafric, 1973. 425pp. (Covers the countries of Francophone West and Central Africa). - - Orig. pub. as **Mémento de l'industrie africaine, 1966**. Paris, 1966. 447ppp. - - 2nd ed. Paris, 1969. 300pp; - - 3rd ed. Paris, 1970. 306pp. (Special issues of *Bulletin de l'Afrique noire*)

442 Investor's guide to the African stock markets, 1998 ed., comp. Joe Appiah-Kusi & Antonios Antoniou. London, Emerging Markets Global Research, 1998. xxv, 284pp. ("Arose as a result of the need by academics and practitioners for more information about the African emerging markets". Comparative overview followed by specific sections for Botswana, Côte d'Ivoire, Egypt, Ghana, Kenya, Mauritius, Morocco, Namibia, Nigeria, South Africa, Swaziland, Tunisia, Uganda, Zambia and Zimbabwe, each with statistics and brief directory of stock markets, banks, brokers, etc.)

443 McGregor's who owns whom in Sub-Saharan Africa, excluding South Africa. Rustenberg, S.A., Purdey Publishing, 1980- Annual. (16th ed. 1996, ed. Robin & Anne McGregor. 1,701pp. Includes profiles of 1,000 listed companies and of 430 major South African unlisted companies. Full South African coverage is in the companion **2822**)

444 Major companies of Africa south of the Sahara. London, Graham & Whiteside/Ermington Hills, MI, Gale, 1996- . Annual. (2004 ed. 1,103pp. Includes over 6,000 of the largest companies arranged by country with company name and 'index of business activities' indexes. Review of 1st ed. *ARBA*, 28, 1997, 105)

445   **L'usine africaine, 1972**. 2nd ed. Paris, Ediafric, 1972. 407, vipp. (Covers countries of Francophone West and Central Africa). - - Orig. pub. Paris, 1971. 2 vols. 512pp. (Special issues of *Bulletin de l'Afrique noire*)

446   **World investment directory: foreign direct investment, legal framework and corporate data. Vol. 5, Africa**. New York, United Nations, 1997. lxxvi, 462pp.

Human rights

447   **African directory: human rights organizations**. [Rev.ed.]. Ottawa, Human Rights Internet (HRI)/Utrecht, Netherlands Institute of Human Rights (SIM), 1996. (*Human rights internet reporter*, 16/1). 276pp. (Lists 750+ organizations in 53 African countries). - - Orig. pub. Ottawa, 1989. (*Human rights internet reporter*, 12/4). 308pp.

448   Saha, Santosh C. **Dictionary of human rights advocacy organizations in Africa**. Westport, CT, Greenwood Press, 1999. 290pp. (Lists some 300 African based and 10 international organizations A/Z by title. No addresses or other contact details. Review, *Choice*, 37, 1999, 704)

449   **The status of human rights organizations in sub-Saharan Africa**. Stockholm, Swedish NGO Foundation for Human Rights/Washington, DC, International Human Rights Internship Program, Institute of International Education, 1994. ii, 230pp. (Arranged by region and country. Comments on the activities of an organization are based on interviews. Appendix supplies contact data)

Libraries, Archives, Museums & the Book Trade

450   **The African book world and press: a directory**. 4th ed., ed. Hans Zell. Oxford, 1989. xxi, 306pp. (Includes sequences listing university, college and public libraries, special libraries, booksellers, commercial and institutional publishers, periodicals and newspapers, book industry associations and literary societies, commercial and government printers (from 2nd ed.). Appendices list book-trade events, prizes, book clubs, news agencies (from 4th ed.), dealers in African studies material. Lists 2,347 organizations in 1st ed., over 4,400 in 4th. Review, *ARD*, 49, 1989, 18-19). - - Orig. pub. Oxford, Hans Zell, 1977. xxvi, 299pp. (Review, *ARD* 15, 1977, 24-25); - -2nd ed. Oxford, 1980. xxiv, 244pp; - - 3rd ed. Oxford, 1983. xx, 285pp. (Review, *ARD* 34, 1984, 50-51)

Libraries & archives

451 Directory of administrative information services in Africa. Tangiers, Centre africain de formation et de recherche administratives pour le développement (CAFRAD), 1977. 123pp.

452 Directory of documentation, libraries and archives services in Africa. 2nd ed. comp. Dominique Zidouemba, rev. Eric de Grolier. Paris, UNESCO, 1977. 311pp. (Based on questionnaire circulated 1974/75 with some up-dating. Only minimal information on archives, with users referred to the **International directory of archives** (Paris, 1975). - - Orig. pub. as **Directory of archives, libraries & schools of librarianship in Africa**, comp. E.W. Dadzie & J.T. Strickland. Paris, UNESCO, 1965. 112pp. (Covers Sub-Saharan countries other than the Republic of South Africa)

453 Directory of scientific and technical libraries in Africa South of the Sahara. Kikwyu, CSA, 1953. (CSA publication, 10). 61pp. (Lists 240 collections)

454 Edoka, B. Eziukwu. Guide to national and university libraries in Africa. Lagos, Libriservice, [1992]. 174pp. (Based on questionnaire of 1987/88. Lists 76 libraries in 31 countries, each with a page of general description, followed by details of stock etc. according to the 21 sections of the questionnaire. Not complete even for countries covered, e.g. only 2 libraries in South Africa)

455 Répertoire des sources d'information francophones pour le développement. Paris, ACCT, 1987. xi, 557pp. (Covers libraries and documentation centres in Francophone African countries including Mauritius but excluding Madagascar; also relevant institutions in France, Belgium, Canada)

Museums

456 Aircraft museums and collections of the world. Vol. 11, Africa and Australasia. 2nd ed. comp. Bob Ogden. Woodley, author, 2000. 136pp. illus. maps. - - Orig. pub. Woodley, 1997.

457 Directory of museums in Africa. Rev. ed. comp. Susanne Peters et al. London, Kegan Paul for UNESCO & International Council of Museums (ICOM), 1990. 211pp. (Lists 503 museums in 48 countries, including North Africa but excluding the Republic of South Africa. More than half the entries give name and address only, without further details. Review in *Africa*, 61, 1991, 130-131 is very critical of obvious omissions: "this volume ... approaches the useless category"). - - Orig. pub. as **Directory of African museums**. Paris, UNESCO, 1981. iv, 219pp.

458   International Council on Museums (ICOM). African museums and related organisations on the Internet. http://icom.museum/ africom/africa1m.htm. (As of summer 2006 last revised 1997 when only 13 African countries were represented)

459   Museums in Africa: a directory. Bonn, Deutsche Afrika Gesellschaft, 1970. xi, 594pp. (Lists 506 museums by country. Index by broad type of museum, e.g. Art museums and galleries, Botanical and zoological gardens. Based on questionnaire, but detailed references given to other sources used)

> *Book trade*

460   African publishers networking directory, 1999/2000. 3rd ed. Oxford, African Books Collective, 1999. vi, 66pp. - - Orig. pub. Oxford, 1993. iii, 60pp; - - 2nd ed. Oxford, 1997. v, 54pp. (Review, *Choice*, 35, 1997, 95)

461   The African publishing companion: a resource guide, comp. Hans M. Zell. Lochcarron, Scotland, Hans Zell Publishing, 2002. 356pp. (Includes directory of e-mail addresses of some 700 African publishers, directory of 500+ book trade organizations of all types, publishing statistics, extensive bibliography. Reviews, *Choice*, 40, 2002, 440; H-Africa, http://www.h-net.org/ ~africa/reviews/, "this work is so useful to such a broad spectrum of readers that it should be on the shelf of every library and every research institute". ASC4, 97 notes that "no new eds. are planned at this time")

462   APNET consultants register, 1998/99. Harare, African Publishers Network (APNET), 1998. 94pp. (66 entries)

463   The book trade of the world. Vol. 4, Africa, ed. Sigfred Taubert & Peter Weidhaas. Munich, Saur, 1984. 391pp. (Introduction, pp. 15-56 by Hans Zell with overview of the history and organization of the book trade. Chapters on each country. Review, *ARD*, 36, 1984, 37-38. To some extent, a revised version of **Africa book trade directory, 1971**, ed. Sigfred Taubert. Munich, Verlag Dokumentation/New York, Bowker, 1971. 319pp.)

464   Development directory of indigenous publishing, 1995, comp. Carol Priestley. Harare, African Publishers Network (APNET), 1995. xii, 199pp.

465   Directory of government printers and prominent bookshops in the African region. Addis Ababa, UNECA, 1970. 48pp.

466   Gibbs, James L. & Mapanje, Jack, eds. **The African writers' handbook**. Oxford, African Books Collective (ABC), 1999. xvii, 432pp. (Part, 2, 'Getting started' includes various directories of prizes, awards and contests; writers' organizations; publishers; agents and book fairs)

467   Stringer, Roger. **The book chain in Anglophone Africa: a survey and directory**. Oxford, International Network for the Availability of Scientific Publications (INASP), 2002. 274pp. Also available at http://www.inasp.info/ pubs/bookchain/index.html. (Individual surveys of library & book development in 18 countries. Includes 170pp. 'Directory of selected organizations' listing publishers, professional associations, booksellers, libraries, etc. ASC4, 98, suggests "probably the most up-to-date and most comprehensive source to the library world in English-speaking Africa")

Religion

468   **Christian communication directory: Africa**, ed. Franz-Josef Eilers et al. Paderborn, Verlag Ferdinand Schöningh, 1980. 544pp. (Compiled jointly by the Catholic Media Council, Aachen, World Association for Christian Communication, London and Lutheran World Federation, Geneva. Lists Christian publishers, periodicals, printers, radio and television production studios)

469   **Directory of theological institutions, associations, lay training centres in Africa**. Geneva, Lutheran World Federation, 1984. 219pp. (Covers theological seminaries, university departments, Bible schools)

Research centres

470   **Dimitra guidebook rural women and development 2001: a directory of NGOs, research institutes and information centres in Africa and the near East**. Brussels, FAO Dimitra Project, 2001. 2 vols.

471   **Directory of African experts, 1982**, comp. UNECA. Pan African Documentation & Information System (PADIS). New York, UN, 1983. xviii, 457pp. - - **Suppls**. 1 to 4, New York, 1984. (Information on 3,600 experts from 46 African countries. Indexed by field of specialization and country of origin). - - [Rev. & abbreviated ed]. Addis Ababa, UNECA, 1989. 160pp. (Lists 400 specialists)

472   **Directory of African institutions. Vol. 1. ECA sponsored institutions**. Addis Ababa, UNECA. Pan African Documentation & Information System (PADIS). 1988 - . ?No more pub.

473 **Directory of African technology institutions**, comp. Jean-Claude Woilet & Moise Allal. Geneva, International Labour Office (ILO), 1985. 2 vols. 623; 577pp. (Describes 711 organizations including university departments, research centres, and technical departments of government ministries principally in the agricultural and building sectors)

474 **Directory of science and technology institutions, consulting organizations and experts in Africa**. Dakar, African Regional Centre for Technology, 1986. 357pp. (Lists over 1,400 institutions by country)

475 **Directory of scientific and engineering societies in Sub-Saharan Africa**. 2nd ed. Washington, DC, American Association for the Advancement of Science/Dakar, African Regional Centre for Technology, 1987. x, 146pp. - - Orig. pub. Washington, DC,. 1985. 156pp. (1st ed. lists 245 societies, 2nd ed., 267 by region and country with subject index)

476 **Directory of scientific institutes, organizations and services in Africa south of the Sahara**. London, CSA, 1955. 255pp. (Arranged by country with subject index). - - Orig. pub. London, 1954. (CSA publication, 14). xiv, 133pp.

477 **Directory of scientists and institutions working in social sciences and health in Africa**. 2nd ed. Nairobi, Social Science & Medicine Africa Network (SOMA-Net), 1996, vii, 124pp. (Based on questionnaire administered 1992-1994. Lists 593 individuals from 166 institutions in 24 African countries, Belgium, Canada, India, Israel, UK, USA, with brief biographical and contact details and notes on research interests). - - Orig. pub. Nairobi, 1992.

478 **Directory of social science research and training units in Africa**. Paris, OECD, 1975. (*Liaison bulletin*, 1975, 2). xxiv, 170pp. (Covers 162 institutes in 37 African countries, including South Africa). - - *Continued by* CODESRIA. **Inventaire des chercheurs africains en sciences sociales**. Dakar, 1978- ? 3rd ed. 1983 includes 1,090 researchers from 305 institutions in 38 countries. 4th ed. 1986. Currently maintained as database by CODICE, CODESRIA Documentation and Information Centre, *see* http://www.codesria.org/ Documentation.htm, *and by* CODESRIA. **Instituts de recherche en sciences sociales**. Dakar, 1983- ? Every 2/3 years.

479 International Conference on the Organization of Research & Training in Africa in Relation to the Study, Conservation and Utilization of Natural Resources. **Scientific research in Africa: national policies, research institutions**. Paris, UNESCO, 1966. 214pp. (Basically a directory of research organizations)

480   Profiles of African scientific institutions, 1992. Nairobi, African Academy of Sciences, 1992. xiii, 282pp. (Based on questionnaire. Discusses 186 institutions from 36 African countries. Review, *ARD*, 63, 1993, 53-54)

481   Profiles of African scientists. 3rd ed. Nairobi, African Academy of Sciences, 1996. 284pp. (1st ed. includes some 400 from 32 countries; 2nd ed., over 600 from 40 countries; 3rd ed. some 350. ASC4, 155) - - Orig. pub. Nairobi, 1990. x, 362pp; - - 2nd ed. Nairobi, 1991. xi, 661pp.

482   Survey on the scientific and technical potential of the countries of Africa, comp. UNESCO. Field Science Office for Africa, Nairobi. Paris, UNESCO, 1970. 296pp. (Principally an 'Inventory of the scientific and research institutions in Africa' presented as an updated version of the list in **Scientific research in Africa ...** (*see* **479**). Includes details of over 600 institutions in 40 African countries including North Africa)

483   Wissenschaft in Afrika: Ein Verzeichnis der Institutionen. Bonn, Deutsche Afrika Gesellschaft, 1962. (Beiheft zu *Afrika-heute Jahrbuch*, 1961). 168pp. (Lists principal research centres and scientific organizations arranged by country)

See also **517**. For directories relating to the EARTH SCIENCES and BIOLOGICAL SCIENCES *see* under those sections below

Trade Unions

484   Directory of labor organizations: Africa. Rev. ed. Washington, DC, Department of Labor, Bureau of International Labor Affairs, 1966. 2 vols. - - Orig. pub. Washington, DC, 1958. 1 vol. var. paging. - - 2nd ed. Washington, 1962. 2 vols. (Arranged by country listing trade unions and trade union federations)

Women's Organizations

485   Directory of African women's organizations. Addis Ababa, UNECA. African Training & Research Centre for Women 1978. iii, 120pp.

486   Roster of African women experts. [Rev. ed.] Addis Ababa, UNECA. African Training & Research Centre for Women, 1991. iii, 87pp. - - Orig. pub. Addis Ababa, 1988. 58pp.

African-related organizations outside Africa

Some sources also include coverage of organizations located **within** Africa

General and international

487 'Collections of Africana' , *UNESCO bulletin for libraries*, 15, 1961, 277-287; 16, 1962, 47-48; 17, 1963, 98-102; 18, 1964, 193. (An early attempt to bring together information on some 90 collections located in Europe in Belgium, France, West Germany, Italy, Netherlands, Poland, Portugal, U.K.; in the U.S.A., Japan, and Africa itself, Cameroon, Congo (Brazzaville), Congo (Léopoldville), Kenya, Rhodesia and Nyasaland, Portuguese possessions in Africa, Senegal, South Africa. Remains of historical interest)

488 Dikomfu, L. et al **Répertoire des institutions africanistes situées hors de l'Afrique sub-saharienne**. Kinshasa, Centre de co-ordination des recherches et de la documentation en sciences sociales en Afrique sub-saharienne (CERDAS), 1989. 109pp. (Lists 184 institutions indicating activities and publications. Includes 19 European countries, Canada, USA, India, Israel, Jamaica, Japan. Korea, Turkey ; also Egypt, South Africa and the Sudan. Index by country and subject)

489 Fenton, Thomas P. & Heffron, Mary J. **Africa: a directory of resources**. Maryknoll, NY, Orbis Books, 1987. 144pp. (Updated and expanded version of the appropriate sections of the authors' **Third World resource directory** (Maryknoll, NY, 1984; later pub, rev. eds. 1995, 1996). Includes lists of organizations focussing on Sub-Saharan Africa. Emphasis in selection is on the "alternative" and "radical", and on North American institutions)

490 **Non-Governmental organizations and Sub-Saharan Africa:** profiles of non-governmental organizations based in Western Europe, Australia and New Zealand, and their work for the development of Sub-Saharan Africa. Geneva, U.N. Non-Governmental Liaison Service, 1988. 284pp. (Lists by country)

491 **Répertoire des principales institutions s'intéressant à l'Afrique noire**. Geneva, Institut africain de Genève & Centre de documentation de l'Institut universitaire de hautes études internationales, 1963. loose leaf. (Covers some 180 European and North American universities, research institutes, libraries, archives and museums with details of their activities and publications. Records the situation contemporary with independence for African countries)

492   UNESCO. **Social scientists specializing in African studies.** Paris, 1963. 375pp. (Lists 2,072 individuals. Index by subject or region of specialization. Based on questionnaire circulated 1959/61)

Australasia

493   African Studies Association of Australia and the Pacific. **Directory of Africanists in Australia, New Zealand and Papua.** 6th ed. Parkville, 2005. 117pp. (Includes some 300 entries. ASC4, 101-102). - - Orig. pub. Geelong, 1979; - - 2nd ed. Geelong, 1984. 39pp; - - 3rd ed. Geelong, 1986. 51pp; - - 4th ed. Geelong, Deakin University, 1991. 72pp. *See also* African Studies Association of Australia and the Pacific: membership list. http:// www.ssn.flinders.edu.au/ global/afsaap. ASC4, 63.

Europe

494   ACCT. **Études africaines en Europe: bilan et inventaire.** Paris, Karthala, 1981. 2 vols. 655, 714pp. (Vol. 1 includes Belgium, Denmark, Finland, West Germany, Italy, Netherlands, Norway, Portugal, Sweden, U.K. and essays on studies in France; vol. 2 is a directory of French organizations. Indexes by subject and country of interest)

495   European Economic Community. Commisson. **Répertoire d'organisations ayant leur siège dans un des états membres de la C.E.E. et dont l'activité s'étend à l'Afrique et Madagascar.** 2nd ed. Luxembourg, 1963. 137pp. - - Orig. pub. Luxembourg, 1961. 131pp.

496   **The SCOLMA directory of libraries and special collections on Africa in the United Kingdom and in Europe.** 5th ed. comp. Tom French. London, Hans Zell, 1993. viii, 355pp. (Broadens scope of 4th ed. to cover the whole of Europe. Includes entries for 392 collections in 24 countries. Based on a questionnaire and secondary sources. Reviews, *African affairs*, 93, 1994, 462-463; *ARD*, 65, 1994, 38-39; *Choice*, 31, 1994, 1554. ASC4, 115. 6th ed. announced as forthcoming in both hard copy and online in 2007); - - 4th ed. as **The SCOLMA directory of libraries and special collections on Africa in the U.K. and Western Europe,** comp. Harry Hannam. Oxford, Hans Zell, 1983. 183pp. (Includes 275 entries of which 142 are for the U.K. Other countries covered are Austria, Belgium, Denmark, Finland, France, Germany, Iceland, Ireland, Italy, Netherlands, Norway, Portugal, Spain, Sweden, Switzerland). - - For 1st to 3rd eds. of the directory which covered U.K. only *see* **524**).

Belgium

497 Afrika-studies in België, Sociale en Humane Wetenschappen. http://home.pi.be/~hv980630/afrika-studies_in_Belgie.htm. (Provides links to principal Belgian teaching institutions with African interests. ASC4, 63)

498 De Belgische Afrika-expertise: inventaris van de middelen en voorstal tot herorganisatie. Brussels, Afrika Institut, Afrika Studie-en Dokumentation, 1997. 64pp.

499 Dauphin, J.C. 'Belgian centers of documentation and research on Africa', *African studies bulletin* 8, 1965, 21-39. (Includes some 50 organizations.)

500 Inventaire des études africaines en Belgique. [Rev.ed.] comp. E. Simons. Brussels, Centre d'études et de documentation africaine (CEDAF), 1993. (*Cahiers africains*, 1993,1/2) ii, 341pp. (Details on 155 institutions arranged by city with indexes by discipline and region of study). - - Orig. pub. Brussels, 1985. (*Cahiers du CEDAF*, 1985, 7/8). 303pp

501 Inventaris van de wetenschappenijke expertise in België met betrekking tot Midden-Afrika, comp. Karel Arnaut. Tervuren, Koninklijk Museum voor Midden-afrika, 2005 (i.e. 2006). ii, 102ff. (Includes details on 25 'Centre voor documentatie')

502 Liste des sociétés, entreprises, associations et institutions d'activité coloniale ayant un siège en Belgique. Brussels, Centre d'information et de documentation du Congo Belge et du Ruanda-Urundi., 1952. 74pp.

France

503 Dauphin, J.C. 'French provincial centers of documention and research on Africa', *African studies bulletin*, 9, 1966, 48-65. (Checklist of some 40 organizations outside Paris)

504 Dauphin, J.C. et al. **Inventaire des resources documentaires africanistes à Paris**. Paris, CARDAN, 1969. (*Recherche, enseignement, documentation africanistes francophones, bulletin d'information et de liaison* 1(1) 1969). [102pp.]. (Lists 129 libraries and research institutes. Indexes by acronym, subject and region of coverage, and by title of publications issued by each body)

505 France-Afrique subsaharienne: organisations culturelles et sociales: annuaire 1989. Paris, Harmattan, 1988- . ?No more pub. (1989 issue. ed. Jean-Médard M'Foumouangana & Aubert Macaire Passy is a directory of institutions in France with African interests, containing some 375 entries, A/Z by title, including publishers and broadcasting services)

506 Guide de bibliothèques à Paris et en régions dont les fonds présentent un intérêt pour la recherche sur l'Afrique. Paris, Centre d'études africaines (CEAf), École pratique des hautes études, 2006. (Also available at http://ceaf.ehess.fr/docannexe.php?id=261. Some 70 libraries listed)

507 Lombard, Raphaële. **Guide des études africaines.** Paris, Harmattan, 2004. 136pp. (Brief guide to resources in France for graduate students with lists of research centres, major libraries in Paris, associations, internet sites and embassies of African countries in France)

508 Rupp, B. et al. **Études africaines: inventaire des enseignements dispensées dans les pays francophones, 1971-72: enquête avec l'appui de l'AUPELF.** Paris, CARDAN, 1972. (*Bulletin d'information et liaison CARDAN,* 4(1/2) 1972). ix, 273pp. (Covers institutions in 21 Francophone African countries, including North Africa, also in Belgium, Canada, France, Haiti, Switzerland. Bulk of coverage is for France, pp. 123-229)

See also **494**

Germany

509 Deutsches Institut für Afrika-Forschung. **Afrika-bezogene Literatur-sammlungen in der Bundesrepublik und Berlin (West),** comp. Heidrum Henze. Hamburg, 1972. (Dokumentationsdienst Afrika, 2). xi, 214pp. (Lists 142 libraries)

510 Deutsches Institut für Afrika-Forschung. **Institutionen der Afrika-Arbeit in der Bundesrepublik und Berlin (West),** comp. Ursula Gerlach & Ties Möller. Hamburg, 1971. (Dokumentationsdienst Afrika, 1). iv, 189pp. (206 entries in sections for university and non-university institutes. Indexes by title, and subject and regional interest)

511 Deutsches Übersee-Institut, Übersee-Dokumentation, Referat Afrika. **Institutionen der Afrika-Forschung und Afrika-Information in der Bundesrepublik Deutschland und Berlin (West),** comp. Marion Gebhardt. Hamburg, 1990. (Dokumentationsdienst Afrika, Reihe B, 5). xi, 285pp. (A revised version of **509** and **510**. In three sections for research institutes, libraries, and documentation centres and archives. Lists 210 institutions in total with indexes of acronyms, and areas of subject and regional interest)

The Netherlands

512 Afrika-Studiecentrum. **Africa in the Netherlands: African organizations, artists and businesses: directory 2002,** comp. Mindenda Mohugu. Leiden, 2002. 213pp. (Under broad topic headings with name and country of interest indexes). Also available at http://www.africaserver.nl/africadirectory/index.html. - - Orig. pub. comp. Yohannes Habtom. Leiden, 1999. 170pp.

513 Afrika-Studiecentrum. **Gids van Afrika-Collecties in Nederlandse bibliotheken en documentatiecentra,** comp. Bouwe Hijma. Leiden, 1986. 153pp. (Details of 123 collections).

514 **COHESA directory: Co-operation in Higher Education between the Netherlands and Southern Africa (COHESA);** including Netherlands expertise on Southern Africa, ed. Ingeborg Krukkert et al. The Hague, Netherlands Organization for International Co-operation in Higher Education (NUFFIC), 1997. ("Joint publication of the Netherlands Institute for Southern Africa (NiZA) and the Nuffic Centre for International Research & Advisory Networks (CIRAN)". Section 3, Register of programmes of co-operation. Includes South Africa; Botswana, Lesotho, Swaziland; Namibia; Angola, Mozambique; Tanzania; Malawi, Zambia, Zimbabwe)

515 **Directory of Africanists in the Netherlands,** ed. Freek Schiphorst et al. Leiden, Werkgemeenschap Afrika, 1996. 115pp. (Lists 276 scholars)

516 **Information on developing countries: inventory of libraries and documentation centres in the Netherlands,** ed. Annemarie Gerbrandy. The Hague, Netherlands Organization for International Cooperation in Higher Education (NUFFIC), 1990. ix, 279pp. (Geographic index allows indentification of institutions with interest in Africa)

Portugal

517 Portugal. Junta de Investigações do Ultramar. Centro de Documentação Científica Ultramarina. **Istituições portuguesas de interesse ultramarino.** Lisbon, 1964. 138pp. (Arranged by the Universal Decimal Classification (UDC). Name of institution, address, brief details of its publications. Lists 147 institutions in Portugal, 165 in Angola, 138 in Mozambique, 47 in Portuguese Guinea, 38 in Cape Verde Islands, 35 in São Tomé e Principe). - - Prov. ed. Lisbon, 1960. 109pp.

518 Portugal. Junta de Investigações do Ultramar. Centro de Documentação Científica Ultramarina. **Siglas de interesse ultramarino.** Lisbon, 1964. 135pp.

(A list of abbreviations and acronyms for official, academic and political organizations concerned with activities in Portugal's overseas possessions) - - Orig. pub. as **Contribução para um dicionário de siglas de interesse ultramarino**. Lisbon, 1961. 70pp. + **1° Aditamento**. Lisbon, 1961. 10pp.

Scandinavia

519 Africanists in the Nordic countries. http://www.nai.uu.se/research/africanists/ Maintained by Nordiska Afrikainstitutet, Uppsala. (Searchable by name, institution, with links to university departments, and by topics or countries of specialization. ASC4, 63)

Switzerland

520 **Who's who: Die Afrika-Forschung in der Schweiz/Les recherches africaines en Suisse**. Rev. ed. comp. Charlotte von Graffenried & Emil Schreyger. Berne, Schweizerische Afrika-Gesellschaft/Société suisse d'études africaines, 1991. 188pp. (Covers 158 individual scholars and 27 institutions). - - Orig. pub. as **Die Afrika-Forschung in der Schweiz**, comp. H. Huber. Berne, 1976. 171pp. (Covers some 100 scholars with a brief narrative account of major institutions); - - Rev. ed. Berne, 1985. 165pp. (Information on 125 individual scholars and directory of 29 institutions)

United Kingdom

521 Bradbury, R.E. 'Directory of African studies in United Kingdom universities'. Rev. ed., *African research & documentation*, 16/17, 1978, 39-87; 18, 1978, 37-59; 19, 1979, 8-15; 20, 1979, 22-24; 21, 1979, 35-44; 22, 1980, 31. (55 separate entries for universities and colleges, 11 for polytechnics, and section on Inter-University Council supported links between British and African universities). - - Orig. pub. Birmingham, African Studies Association of the U.K., 1969. iv, 73pp. (38 universities and colleges listing relevant courses and staff, also 10 non-university institutions)

522 **Directory of Africanists in Britain**, 3rd ed. comp. Anne Merriman. Bristol, University of Bristol for Royal African Society, 1996. viii, 157pp. (Contains 448 entries. Africanists are defined as "all those contributing either through active research or through teaching in the tertiary sector, to the study of Africa", pref. Review, *ARD*, 70, 1996, 74-75. ASC4, 102). - - Orig. pub. comp. Richard Hodder-Williams. Bristol, 1986. 85pp; (443 entries); - - 2nd ed. Bristol, 1990. 141pp. (512 entries)

523 Mapping Asia in U.K. libraries. http://www.asiamap.ac.uk/index.php. (Online directory maintained by SOAS on behalf of the National

Council on Orientalist Library Resources (NCOLR). Original data collection completed 2002, file to be updated by participating institutions. Collection descriptions provide links to library and archival collections for North African countries and also for Djibouti (5 records); Eritrea (8 records); Ethiopia (17 records); Somalia (10 records); Sudan (18 records). The choice of name for the directory often leads to it being overlooked since it is wrongly assumed to be concerned only with cartographic material. ASC4, 186-187)

524 The SCOLMA directory of libraries and special collections on Africa. 3rd ed. comp. Robert L. Collison, rev. John Roe. St. Albans, Crosby Lockwood, Staples, 1973. vii, 118pp. - - Orig. pub. London, SCOLMA, 1963. iii, 101pp; - - 2nd ed. comp. Robert L. Collison. London, Crosby Lockwood, 1967. vii, 92pp. (1st ed. covers 142 institutions, 2nd ed., 157, 3rd ed., 141. The 4th and subsequent eds. expanded coverage to include Europe and are listed above at **496**)

North America

Canada

525 Bullock, Ronald A. & Killam, G. Douglas. **Resources for African studies in Canada**. Ottawa, Canadian Association of African Studies, 1976. vi, 139pp. (Lists both institutions and individual researchers. *See also* Canadian Association of African Studies: list of members. http://caas.concordia.ca/ htm/list.htm. (2005/2006 ed. lists 130 scholars. ASC4, 63)

USA

526 African Studies Association (ASA). Research Liaison Committee. **Directory of African and African-American studies in the United States**. 8th ed. Atlanta, GA, ASA, 1993. v, 170pp. (Lists 326 programmes by state). - - Orig. pub. as **Directory of African studies in the United States, Feb. 1971**. Waltham, MA, 1971. [143pp]. (Covers 80 institutions); - - [2nd ed.] Waltham, MA, 1972. 158pp; - - [3rd ed.] Waltham, MA, 1973. 201pp. + Suppl., 1973. iv, 28pp. (Main vol. lists 238 institutions; suppl. adds corrections and details of a further 38); - - 4th ed. ... **1974/75**. Waltham, MA, ASA, 1975. iii, 204pp. (268 full entries, with briefer details on 59 which did not answer questionnaire); - - 5th ed. **Directory of African and Afro-American studies in the United States**. Waltham, MA, ASA, 1976. v, 329pp. (908 entries); - - 6th ed. Waltham, MA, Crossroads Press for ASA, 1979. v, 306pp. (900+ entries); - - 7th ed. Los Angeles, ASA, 1987. vi, 273pp. (388 entries. Pref. explains that reduction in entries since earlier eds. is partly explained by decision to omit institutions not replying to questionnaire)

527 Africana Librarians Council (ALC).   ALC   directory. http://www.loc.gov/rr/amed/afs/alc/alcdir10202004.html.   (Latest   ed.

October 20, 2004 lists the names and contact details of 85 librarians. The ALC is a section of the African Studies Association (ASA). ASC4, 95)

528 Bhatt, Purnima Mehta. **Scholars' guide to Washington D.C. for African studies**. Washington, D.C., Smithsonian Institution, 1980. (Scholars' guide, 4). xiv, 347pp. (Comp. Woodrow Wilson International Center for Scholars. Lists libraries, archives, museums, galleries, research centres, government agencies, etc. Review, *Africana J.*, 12, 1981, 237-238. Sudan is covered by **Scholars' guide to Washington, D.C. for Middle Eastern studies**. Washington, DC, 1981.)

529 Contact Africa: Africa 2001. **A directory of U.S. organizations working on Africa**. 4th ed. comp. Kim Olson. Washington, DC, African-American Institute, 2001. 400pp. (Lists U.S. government agencies, NGOs, major international agencies based in the U.S., African diplomatic representation in the U.S. and U.S. representation in Africa. Review, *ABPR*, 28, 2002, 206. ASC4, 100). - - Orig. pub as **Contact Africa: a directory of organizations in Washington, D.C. involved in African affairs**. Washington, DC, 1992. 69pp.; - - 2nd ed. Washington, DC, 1994; - - 3rd ed. Washington, DC, 1999.

530 Duignan, Peter. **Handbook of American resources for African studies**. Stanford, Hoover Institution, 1966. (Hoover Institution on War, Revolution and Peace, Bibliographical series, 29). 234pp. (Describes 95 library and manuscript collections, 108 church and missionary libraries and archives, 95 art and ethnographic collections and 4 business archives. A major resource in its time and still historically valuable for its level of detail)

531 Gosebrink, Jean E. Meeh. **African studies information resources directory**. Oxford, Hans Zell for African Studies Association, 1986. 572pp. (Entries for 437 U.S. institutions including libraries, archives, museums, documentation centres and learned societies. Sections for 86 church and mission organizations, 43 booksellers and distributors, 48 publishers. Conceived as a partial revision of **530**. The standard guide to U.S. institutional interest in Africa in the mid 1980s. Review, *ARD*, 43, 1987, 31-33. Conover-Porter Award (joint winner) 1988. ASC4, 110)

532 Mithun, Jacqueline S. **African programs of U.S. organizations**. [3rd ed]. Washington, DC, U.S. Dept. of State, Bureau of Intelligence & Research, External Research Division, 1965. iv, 132pp. ("A selective directory". Details on 724 programmes, arranged under categories such as universities, business organizations, and private institutions). - - Orig. pub. Washington, DC, 1958; - - 2nd ed. Washington, DC, 1961.

BIOGRAPHICAL SOURCES

General

533   Africa who's who, ed.-in-chief, Raph Uwechue. 3rd ed. London, Africa Books, 1996. 1,507pp. (Includes c.14,000 brief biographies of living figures, restricted to dates, official positions and activities. A major biographical resource. ASC4, 152-153). - - Orig. pub. London, *Africa journal*, 1981. (Know Africa series). vii, 1169 pp. - - 2nd ed. London, Africa Books, 1991. viii, 1863pp. (1st ed. includes entries for c.7,000, 2nd ed. for c.12,000). Developed from **Africa yearbook and who's who**, *see* **278**. Companion to **31** and **548**)

534   Les africains, ed. in chief, Charles-André Julien. Paris, *Jeune afrique*, 1977-1978. 12 vols. (Detailed biographies of 120 figures 'qui ont marqué de leur empreinte l'histoire du continent', pref. Portraits, illus., reproductions of texts of contemporary documents, references to sources. Covers all periods with entries for figures from Hannibal to Lumumba. Emphasis on areas of Africa of French interest, with over half the entries coming from North Africa)

535   African biographical archive. Munich, K.G. Saur, 1994-1997. 457 microfiche. (Reproduces the text of 233 separate biographical works pub. between 1807 and 1993, but only some 60 titles pub. pre 1960. ASC4, 152)

536   African biographical index. Munich, K.G. Saur, 1999. 3 vols. (Index to *African biographical archive* microfiche collection (**535**) of some 88,000 names, with one line information: dates, occupation, country of origin, and a reference to entries in the microfiche ed. ASC4, 152)

537   African biography. New York, UXL Publishing, 1998. 3 vols. 602pp. (Articles on 75 current and historical African leaders, major writers and other significant figures, with portraits. Aimed at schools and colleges. Review, *ARBA*, 30, 1999, 149-150)

538   Brockman, Norbert C. An African biographical dictionary. Santa Barbara, CA, ABC-Clio, 1994. viii, 440pp. (Entries for 549 prominent persons active in Sub-Saharan Africa at all periods of history, but with emphasis on the post-colonial and contemporary period. Indexes by country, and by 'fields of significance' e.g. colonial personalities, novelists and writers, Christian missionaries. Review, *ARD*, 75, 1997, 56-57; *Choice*, 32, 1995, 1426, "excellent source for information not easily available elsewhere". ASC4, 153)

539   Burke's royal families of the world. Vol. 2, Africa and the Middle East, comp. David Williamson. London, Burke's Peerage, 1980. xvi, 320pp.

(Genealogical information on families reigning 'in comparatively recent times', i.e. since c. 1920. In addition to lists, contains brief essays on various North African dynasties, also on Ethiopia, Zanzibar and Zululand. Admits that Sub-Saharan Africa "presented severe problems which compilers ... have been unable to solve", pref. Appendix contains much briefer notes on Pre-colonial African states. Review, *JAH*, 22, 1981, 419-420)

540 Contemporary African database (CAD): People. http://people.africa database.org/. London, Africa Centre, 2001- . ("The Contemporary Africa Database is a continuously growing, participatory online project, designed to provide easily accessible and current information concerning prominent Africans, African organisations, and dates in the African calendar" (Introductory screen). The People database provides a "Who's who of prominent Africans now living, or who have died since 1950, in all fields of expertise". They must have been born in Africa or have acquired the nationality of an African country. As of mid 2006, the file contained some 11,500 entries, of whom 591 had so far been provided with 'profiles', i.e. specially commissioned accounts of their life. Other entries are brief, with dates and positions held and hyperlinks to Web sites for countries, political parties, etc.; also articles in Wikipedia. It is possible to search by category, e.g. 'Society, politics and governance' which has some 30 searchable sub-categories, and in total contains well over 5,000 entries or about half the database, by country, by gender, and by special lists, e.g. Nobel Prize winners. A source that will grow in significance as its coverage and detail develop. ASC4, 159-160) *See also* **397**

541 Deutsche Afrika-Gesellschaft. **Afrikanische Köpfe**. Bonn, Deutscher Wirtschaftsdienst, 1962. 2 vols. loose-leaf. (Biographies and portraits of contemporary African leaders. Updated sheets issued until at least 1983)

542 Dickie, John & Rake, Alan. **Who's who in Africa: the political, military and business leaders of Africa**. London, *African development*, 1973. 602pp. (610 entries grouped by country, with some countries, e.g. Burundi, CAR, having only a single entry. *See also* **556-558**)

543 **Dictionary of African biography**, ed. Ernest Kay. London, Melrose Press, 1970-1971. 2 issues. (Some 2,500 entries in each issue for living figures in 'free Africa', i.e. excluding South Africa, Southern Rhodesia, and Portuguese colonies)

544 **Dictionnaire des personnalités célèbres du monde négro-africain**, comp. Tharcisse Gatwa & Georgina Tsala-Clemençon. Yaoundé, Editions CLE, 2004. 273pp. (Brief unsigned entries for Africans and African-Americans notable in all fields of activity)

545 **Encyclopaedia Africana dictionary of African biography**. Algonac, MI, Reference Publications, 1977- . To be published in 20 vols. Vol. 1, Ethiopia and Ghana (1977) *see* **889, 1859**; vol. 2, Sierra Leone and Zaire (1979) *see* **1652, 2034**; vol. 3, South Africa, Botswana, Lesotho and Swaziland (1995) *see* **2842**. (The only products to date of the long established **Encyclopaedia Africana** project, *see* **11**. Each vol. is announced as covering two to three countries, with a very wide range of contributors. The Web site of the Encyclopaedia Africana Secretariat http://www.endarkment.com/eap/index.html lists coverage of proposed vols and claims (July 2006) that the vols. for Egypt and Nigeria are "well advanced". ASC4, 153)

546 Friedrich-Ebert-Stiftung. Forschungsinstitut. **Afrika Biographien**. Hanover, Verlag für Literatur und Zeitgeschichte, 1967-1970. 4 vols. loose-leaf. - - English trans. **African biographies**. Bad Godesberg, Verlag Neue Gesellschaft, [1971-1979]. 7 vols. loose-leaf. Originally issued in 46 parts with suppl. pages. (The English trans. is revised and updated. Coverage is of contemporary figures, mostly political)

547 Lipschutz, Mark R. & Rasmussen, R. Kent. **Dictionary of African historical biography**. 2nd ed. expanded & updated. Berkeley, CA, University of California Press, 1986. xi, 328pp. (Reprint of 1st ed with some 750 entries for figures, both living and dead, of significance in the history of Sub-Saharan Africa before 1960, plus a Suppl. with entries for 57 post-1960 political leaders. Includes lists of rulers and office-holders, subject index, and detailed bibliography. Lists some 120 non-Africans. Review, *Choice*, 24, 1987, 1201-1202, "essential for all academic libraries". ASC4, 421). - - Orig. pub. Berkeley, CA, 1978. 304pp. (Reviews, *ASA review of books*, 5, 1979, 97-98, which notes relatively sparser coverage of Francophone Africa; *JAH*, 20, 1979, 311-312).

548 **Makers of modern Africa: profiles in history**, ed.-in-chief, Raph Uwechue. 3rd ed. London, Africa Books, 1996. xii, 733pp. (Published as a companion to **Africa today (31)** and **Africa who's who (533)** Covers some 650 prominent figures both living and dead, often with portraits. Robert Mugabe gets 1½ pp. as opposed to 28 lines in **Africa who's who**. "Written by African historians", pref., but these are not listed, and critical comments are fairly anodyne. Sources given have only minimum bibliographical detail. ASC4, 154. - - Orig. pub. London, *Africa journal*, 1981. (Know Africa series). 591pp. (Some 500 entries); - - 2nd ed. London, Africa Books, 1991. xvii, 797pp. (680 entries)

549 Taylor, Sidney, ed. **The new Africans: a guide to the contemporary history of emergent Africa and its leaders**. New York, Putnam, 1967. 504pp. (Written by some 50 Reuters News Agency correspondents. Includes c. 600 entries for living figures in Africa south of the Sahara, excluding the Republic of South Africa)

Special subjects

Note that biographical sources for **literature** are listed under HANDBOOKS: Literature

Cinema & Music

550   Seck, Nago & Clerfeuille, Sylvie. **Musiciens africains des années 80: guide**. Paris, Harmattan, 1986. 167pp. (Biographies and discographies)

551   Shiri, Keith. **Directory of African film-makers and films**. Trowbridge, Flicks Books, 1992. 194pp. (Biographies and filmographies of 259 film-makers)

552   Southern, Eileen. **Biographical dictionary of Afro-American and African musicians**. Westport, CT, Greenwood Press, 1982. (Greenwood encyclopedia of black music). 478pp. (Includes entries for some 40 African musicians who can be traced via Appendix 2, 'Place of birth'.)

Politics

553   Adi, Hakim & Sherwood, Marika. **Pan-African history: political figures from Africa and the diaspora since 1787**. London, Routledge, 2003. 203pp. (Biographies of 40 figures of African descent, about half principally active in Africa. Reviews, *Choice*, 41, 2003, 686, "highly recommended"; *ASR*, 48 (1) 2005, 214-217 indicates errors, but concludes "a timely addition to the African biographical literature". ASC4, 151)

554   Glickman, Harvey, ed. **Political leaders of contemporary Africa south of the Sahara: a biographical dictionary**. Westport, CT, Greenwood Press, 1992. xxii, 362pp. (Covers 54 persons prominent in the period from 1945, Reviews, *Choice*, 30, 1993, 943-944, "important reference work"; *IJAHS*, 23, 1973, 427-428. ASC4, 154)

555   Lentz, Harris M. **Encyclopedia of heads of state and government, 1900 through 1945**. Jefferson, NC, McFarland, 1999. xii, 508pp; - - **Heads of state and government, a worldwide encyclopedia of over 2,300 leaders, 1945 through 1992**. London, Fitzroy Dearborn, 1995. xi, 912pp. (Arranged by country, with biographies of each leader named. Reviews, *ARBA*, 26, 1995, 312; *Choice*, 37, 1995, 1086)

556   Rake, Alan. **100 great Africans**. Metuchen, NJ, Scarecrow Press, 1994. 431pp. maps. (Covers the living and the dead in 11 topical chapters. "Book is essentially journalistic, not based on profound academic research", pref. ASC4, 155)

557 Rake, Alan. **African leaders: guiding the new millennium**. Lanham, MD, Scarecrow Press, 2001. 261pp. (Provides profiles of some 60 leading political leaders and military rulers as of late 2000. Only five countries have more than one profile. Few sources noted other than the Scarecrow Press *Historical dictionaries*. Reviews, *ABPR*, 28, 2002, 206; *ARBA*, 33, 2002, 339, "does not visibly fill any discernable gap"; *ARD*, 88, 2002, 90-91. ASC4, 155)

558 Rake, Alan. **Who's who in Africa: leaders for the 1990s**. Metuchen, NJ, Scarecrow Press, 1992. vii, 448pp. (324 entries arranged under the countries of Sub-Saharan Africa. Similar treatment to **Who's who in Africa**, comp. J. Dickie & A. Rake (*see* **542**) but only 25% of entries are common. "Does not cover prominent personalities in cultural, artistic, religious or business fields", pref. Review, *Choice*, 30, 1992, 280)

559 Segal, Ronald, ed. **Political Africa: a who's who of political personalities and parties**. London, Stevens/New York, Praeger, 1961. xi, 475pp. (Pt. 1 includes c. 400 living figures. Pref. notes that data are comparatively more complete for Kenya, Nigeria and South Africa. Pt. 2, pp. 291-475, discusses contemporary political parties country by country). - - Rev. & abridged ed. **African profiles**. Harmondsworth, Penguin, 1962. 351pp.

560 Wiseman, John A. **Political leaders in Black Africa: a biographical dictionary of the major politicians since independence**. Aldershot, Edward Elgar, 1991. xxiii, 248pp. (485 brief biographies with a country index. No sources listed. Reviews, *Choice*, 29, 1992, 1378; *IJAHS*, 23, 1993, 427-428)

Religion

561 Dictionary of African Christian biography. New Haven, CT, Overseas Ministries Study Center 2003- Available at: http://www.dacb.org. *See also DACB newsletter* http://www.dacb.org/newsletterframe.html. (c.1,200 entries by August 2006, a number of them reprinted from existing published sources. On the genesis and execution of the project as a whole *see* Jonathan J. Bonk, 'Ecclesiastical cartography and the problem of Africa', *History in Africa*, 32, 2005, 117-132. ASC4, 160)

Women

562 Schwarz-Bart, Simone & Schwarz-Bart André. **In praise of Black women**. Madison, WI, University of Wisconsin Press, 2001- 4 vols. illus. Trans. of **Hommage à la femme noire**. Paris, Éditions Consulaires, 1988-89. 6 vols. 1,479pp. illus. (Vol. 1, 2001. Ancient African queens. 456pp. col. illus. Trans of vols. 1 & 2 of the French ed.; vol. 2. 2002. Heroines of the slavery era. 250pp. Trans. of vol. 3 of the French ed.; vol. 3. 2003. Modern African women.

250pp. Trans. of vol. 4 of the French ed. with new material. Vol. 4, Modern African women of the diaspora, trans. of vols. 5 & 6 of the French ed. with new material, announced for 2006. ASC4, 156)

Anglophone Africa

563   Kirk-Greene, Anthony H.M. **A biographical dictionary of the British colonial governor. Vol. 1, Africa**. Brighton, Harvester Press, 1980. 256pp. (Some 200 entries for the period 1875 to 1980. Includes strictly factual data on birth, education, career, and publications with reference to sources. Reviews, *African affairs*, 81, 1982, 587-588; *JAH*, 23, 1982, 430-431)

564   Kirk-Greene, Anthony H.M. **A biographical dictionary of the British Colonial Service, 1939-1966**. London, Hans Zell Publishers, 1991. xvii, 401pp. (Some 15,000 entries "being a cumulative and composite reproduction of all the biographical entries as they appeared in the *Colonial Office lists*", pref. Includes detailed and valuable introduction covering the history of the British Colonial Service and the history and development of the *List* with lengthy notes on the ten major categories of information that each biographical entry comprises, and an indication of other biographical sources for the same officers in departmental service lists, Blue books etc. Kirk-Greene has written of his work in compiling these lists and of sources for colonial officers in general in 'The British colonial governor in the literature', *ARD*, 12, 1977, 10-13; and 'Colonial service biographical data: the published sources', *ARD*, 46, 1988, 2-16. Reviews, *African affairs*, 91, 1992, 304-305; *ARD*, 57, 1991, 31-33; *ASR*, 36, 1993, 155-156; *Choice*, 29, 1991, 575. ASC4, 154)

565   Simpson, Donald H. 'Biographical sources for colonial history in Africa', *African research & documentation*, 29, 1982, 19-21. (Brief but a good starting point. Based on holdings of the RCS)

Francophone Africa

566   **Annuaire des états d'Afrique noire: gouvernements et cabinets ministériels, partis politiques**. 2nd ed. Paris, Ediafric-La documentation africaine, 1962. 443pp. (Brief biographies of leading political officials in the 14 countries of Francophone West and Central Africa, and in regional and international African organizations). - - Orig. pub. as **Annuaire parlementaire des états d'Afrique noire**. Paris, *Annuaire afrique*, 1961. 332pp. (1,100 brief biographies)

567   Broc, Numa. **Dictionnaire illustré des explorateurs et grands voyageurs français du XIXe siècle. 1, Afrique**. Paris, Comité des travaux historiques et scientifiques, Ministère de l'éducation nationale, 1988. xxxi,

346pp. illus. 5 maps (389 biographies with refs. to sources. Numerous illus. from the photographic collections of the Société de géographie. Note that vol. **4, Océanie**. Paris, 2003, contains a *Supplément* to the whole work. Review, *JAH*, 32, 1991, 169, "an erudite and judicious compilation")

568   Dictionnaire biographique des anciens élèves de l'École nationale de la France d'outre-mer, promotions de 1889 à 1958. Paris, Association des anciens élèves de l'ENFOM, 2003. 2 vols. 2,034pp.

569   Les élites africaines 1970/71 [etc.]. Paris, Ediafric-La documentation africaine, 1971- ?1979. Published as special issues of *Bulletin de l'Afrique noire*. Issues for 1970/71, 1972, 1974, 1977, 1979. (Brief biographies of political leaders of Francophone West and Central Africa. Over 5,000 entries per issue)

570   Hommes et destins (Dictionnaire biographique d'outre-mer), ed. Robert Cornevin et al. Paris, Académie des sciences d'outre-mer, 1975-1989. 10 vols. in 11. Vol. 3, 1979. Madagascar. 543pp; vol. 7, 1986. Maghreb-Machrek. 536pp; vol. 8, 1988. Gouverneurs, administrateurs, magistrates. 488pp; vol. 9, 1989. Afrique noire. 539pp. (Each vol. contains an individual A/Z sequence, and a cumulative index to earlier vols. with some 250 detailed signed entries for individuals of significance in French colonial history, each provided with a bibliography. A large scale project originally founded in 1971, which acknowledges example of the **Biographie belge d'outre-mer**, *see* **1650**)

571   Présidents, administrateurs et directeurs généraux des sociétés publiques et privées d'Afrique noire. Paris, Ediafric-La documentation africaine, 1969. 471pp. (Running title: **PDG afrique**. Special issue of *Bulletin de l'Afrique noire*. Includes some 1,500 biographies of key officials in the economic sphere in Francophone West and Central Africa)

Lusophone Africa

572   Colecção pelo império. Lisbon, Agência Geral do Ultramar, Divisão de Publicações e Biblioteca, 1935-61. Fascs. 1-131. (A collection of biographies of those active in the Portuguese colonies: governors, administrators, missionaries, military leaders)

573   Gomes, Aldónio & Cavacas, Fernanda. Dicionário de autores de literaturas africanas de língua portuguesa. Lisbon, Caminho, 1997. 454pp. (Contains c.1,700 entries in a main sequence and an appendix with shorter entries for writers born in Africa but with a literary life elsewhere. Structured directory type entries)

See also **64**

ATLASES & GAZETTEERS

Atlases

Bibliographies & portals

574 Dahlberg, Richard E. & Thomas, Benjamin E. 'An analysis and bibliography of recent African atlases', *African studies bulletin*, 5, 1962, 22-32. - - Suppl. 1, *ibid.*, 6, 1963, 6-9. (Original article lists 92 items, suppl. adds 25. Covers material published since 1945)

575 Dahlberg, Richard E. 'A preliminary bibliography of African atlases', *Bulletin of the Geography & Map Division of the Special Libraries Association*, 59, 1965, 3-9, 32-37. (Lists 175 items, incorporating the majority of entries from **574** and adding 62 new items, most published before 1945. Includes refs. to entries in LC **List of geographical atlases,** *see* **576**. Covers a wide range including school atlases and some world atlases with good African coverage)

576 Library of Congress (LC). **List of geographical atlases in the Library of Congress**. Washington, DC, 1909-1974. 8 vols. (Vols. 1-4 cover material published before 1920 (Africa, vol. 1, pp. 1189-1192; vol. 2, pp. 686-691); vols. 5-8 cover material published 1920-1960 (Africa, vol. 6, pp. 426-475; *see also* sections under European countries, e.g. 'France: colonies', pp. 159-161. Detailed source that often lists topic of every plate)

577 Map History/History of Cartography. Images of early maps on the Web, 5. Africa and the islands. http://www.maphistory.info/imageafrica.html. (Ed. Tony Campbell, former Map Librarian, British Library. Links to 25 sites (as of June 2006) with comments on the content of each, the quality of resolution of the images, whether enlargeable etc.)

578 Perry-Castaneda Map Collection, University of Texas at Austin. Historical maps of Africa. http://www.lib.utexas.edu/maps/historical /history_africa.html . (Includes as of June 2006 links to images of 44 maps pub. 1808 to 1986. Also includes Africa: historical maps on other Web sites http://www.lib.utexas.edu/maps/map_sites/ hist_sites.html#africa)

579 Stams, W. **National and regional atlases: a bibliographic survey, up to and including 1978**. Enschede, International Cartographic Association, 1984. 249pp. (Africa, pp. 149-164 and 225-227. No annotations)

General

Note that **ethnographic, linguistic** & **historical** atlases are listed under HANDBOOKS

580   AFIM Africa interactive maps. Version 1. Odenton, MD, AFIM, 1998. 1 CD-ROM. (Developed by W. Bediako Lamousé-Smith & Joseph School at the Department of Africana Studies & Department of Geography & Environmental Systems, University of Maryland. 'A learning and teaching tool to communicate basic geographic information about Africa'. Some 700 maps with associated text, statistics, etc. Aimed at schools and colleges. *See* http://www.africamaps.com/. ASC4, 183)

581   Africa adventure atlas: Africa, the Indian Ocean Islands, the Atlantic Ocean Islands, ed. Sean Fraser. Evergreen, CO, National Geographic, 2003. 336pp. (The main section, pp. 40-160 comprises touring maps at scales of 1:3,500,000 for Northern, Western and Central Africa, 1:1M for Eastern and Southern Africa and 1:4,635,000 for Madagascar. Very clear maps emphasising routes from 'major connecting routes' down to hiking tracks. Pp. 164-207 provide 68 town plans for African cities with street indexes. Other sections provide maps of national parks and of adventure activities. A valuable source for any purpose despite popular appearance)

582   Africa in maps, ed. Geoffrey J. Martin. Dubuque, IA, W.C. Brown, 1962. 124pp. (58 b. & w. thematic maps covering climate, political history, population, ethnography, agriculture, communications, and industry)

583   Africa: maps and statistics/Kaarte en statistic Afrika. Pretoria, Africa Institute, 1962-65. 10pts. 194pp. 87 maps. 74 tables. 6 figs. 32x35 cm. (Originally announced as to appear in 12 pts. and so referred to in pts. 1-9. Pt. 10 notes change of policy. Parallel English/Afrikaans text, with statistical tables and col. maps. Scales 1:30M and 1:60M. Pt. 1, Population; pt. 2, Vital and medical aspects; pt. 3, Cultural and educational aspects; pt. 4, Transport and communication; pt. 5, Energy resources, production and consumption; pt. 6, Agriculture and forestry; pt. 7, Livestock, farming and fishing; pt. 8, Mining, industry and labour; pt. 9, Trade, income and aid; pt. 10, Political development)

584   Africa on file. New York, Facts on File, 1995. 2 vols. 384pp. looseleaf. Vol. 1, East, Southern and North Africa; vol. 2, West and Central Africa; regional issues. (Over 1,000 loose leaf maps charts and diagrams of topography and natural resources for each of 52 Sub-Saharan African countries, with extra detail on six: Kenya, Nigeria, South Africa, Sudan, Tanzania, Uganda. Review, *Choice*, 33, 1996, 1445. ASC4, 181)

585   **Africa: testo-atlante**, comp. Salvatore Foderaro et al. Rome, Istituto Italiano per l'Africa, 1961. 127pp. col. maps.

586   **Africa today: a reproducible atlas**. Rev. ed. Wellesley, MA, "World Eagle", 1990. Loose leaf. 252pp. maps. (Includes numerous thematic maps with accompanying statistical data, and 53 maps of individual countries reprinted from those issued by the U.S. Central Intelligence Agency and Department of State). - - Orig. pub. as **Africa today: an atlas of reproducible pages**. Wellesley, MA, 1983. 153pp. (Review, *Choice*, 21, 1984, 945)

587   **Afrika**, ed. Hans Kramer et al. Gotha, VEB Hermann Haack, Geographisch-Kartographische Anstalt, 1989. 432pp. (Added title-page: **Haack Kartenbuch: Afrika**)

588   **Afrika-Atlas**, ed. F. Pfrommer. Karlsruhe, Kunstdruckerei Künsterbund, [194?]. 8pp. incl. col. maps. 32 x 24cm. (Comp. Reichskolonialbund Bundesführung. Covers topography, vegetation, agriculture, communications, natural resources, population, ethnography. Emphasizes former German colonies)

589   Auger, Alain, et al. **L'Afrique historique et géographique**. St. Germain-en-Laye, Editions M.D.I., 1977. 32pp. 30 x 35cm. Cover-title: **Atlas de l'Afrique**. (30 thematic maps at 1:30M, showing relief, geology, soils, climate, vegetation, farming, mining, demography, education, health, communications, etc. Includes 8 historical maps)

590   **Atlas Afriki/Atlas of Africa**. Moscow, Glavnoe Upravienie Geodezii i Kartographie, 1968. 118pp. 32 x 27cm. (Text in Russian with separate 39pp. pamphlet containing English trans. of map titles, legends and reference data. Includes thematic maps of Africa as a whole covering history, climate, geology, vegetation, fauna, peoples, language, agriculture, industry, communications. Regional maps, pp. 20-45. *See* 'The Africa Atlas', pp. 284-286 *in* U.N. **2nd UN Regional Cartographic Conference for Africa, Nairobi, 1966. Vol. 2, Proceedings**. New York, 1967)

591   **Atlas de l'Afrique**, ed. Renaud de Rochebrune & Anne Lerebours Pigeonnière. Paris, Editons du Jaguar, 2001. 207pp. illus. maps. - - Orig. pub. as **Atlas *Jeune Afrique* du continent africain**, comp. Danielle Ben Yahmed & Pierre Vennetier. Paris, Editions du Jaguar, 1993. 175pp. 29cm. col. maps.

592   **Atlas de l'Afrique: un continent jeune, révolté, marginalizé**, comp. Stephen Smith. Paris, Autrement, 2005. 80pp. (Popular thematic atlas with double page spread of maps and text on each topic. Coverage mostly

political and economic, and emphasis on the period post 1960. Author is a journalist for *Libération* and *Le monde*)

593 **An atlas of African affairs**, comp. Andrew Boyd & Patrick van Rensburg. 2nd ed. London, Methuen/New York, Praeger, 1965. 133pp. (37 b. & w. sketch maps of contemporary Africa, with supporting text). - - Orig. pub. London/ New York, 1962. 133pp.

594 **An atlas of African affairs**, comp. Ieuan Ll. Griffiths. 2nd ed. London, Routledge, 1993. ix, 233pp. (Text discusses 55 themes, broadly divided into environmental, historical, political, economic, and the South, with a total of 121 b. & w. maps. Appendices give a chronology of African independence, with notes on major administrative changes and political leaders post independence. Reviews, *ARD*, 63, 1993, 54-55; *IJAHS*, 28, 1995, 194-195). - - Orig. pub. London. Methuen, 1984. vii, 200pp. (Reviews, *African affairs*, 83, 1984, 426-427; *Choice*, 22, 1985, 964)

595 **Atlas mira: Africa**. Moscow, Glavnoe Upravienie Geodezii i Kartographie, 1985. iv, 17pp.

596 **Atlas podziałów administracyjnych krajów Afryki**. Warsaw, Centralny Instytut Informacji Naukowo-Technicznej i Ekonomieznej Ośrodek Informacji o Afryce, 1964. 63pp.

597 Davies, Harold R.J. **Tropical Africa: an atlas for rural development**. Cardiff, University of Wales Press, 1973. xiv, 81pp. 40pp. of maps. 41 x 24 cm. (Basically West, Central and East Africa from Senegal east to Somalia, south to Zaire and Tanzania. 40 thematic maps at 1:20M and 1:40M. Compiled by Department of Geography, University College of Swansea for UNESCO Agricultural Education and Science Division. Covers climate, population, communications, subsistence agriculture and cash crops)

598 **Feizhou Dituji**. Beijing, Ditu Chubanche, 1985. 250pp. 37 x 53cm. (Large scale general atlas of Africa. 41 plates with 72 thematic maps, the majority at 1:40M or 1:60M; 55 plates with 94 topographic regional maps. Contents list in English, index arranged by Chinese characters, but with romanized equivalents added. All other information in Chinese)

599 **Grand atlas du continent africain**, ed. Regine Nguyen Van Chi-Bonnardel. Paris, *Jeune Afrique*, 1973. 336pp. 140 maps. Also pub. in English as **Atlas of the African continent**. New York, Free Press, 1973. 336pp. 140 maps. (Comp. jointly by publishers of *Jeune Afrique* and *Africa magazine*. Maps prepared by L'Institut géographique national in Paris. Col. maps at scales of 1:1M to 1:10M. Each country covered on 2 maps with accompanying text and statistics. Index-gazetteer of 6,000 entries. *See* S.J.K. Baker, 'An atlas of African emergence', *Bulletin of the Society of University Cartographers*, 9(1), 1975, 13-17. Remains the standard large-scale topographic atlas of Africa to its date with no obvious successor. **591** from the same publisher is a much slighter work)

600 Google Earth. http://earth.google.com/index.html for details. (Available in a free version and in two priced versions: Google Earth Plus, and Google Earth Professional. Reproduces photographs taken by satellites and aircraft since 2002. "The whole world is covered with medium resolution imagery and terrain data. This resolution allows you to see major geographic features and man-made development such as towns, but not detail of individual buildings. Additional high-resolution imagery which reveals detail for individual buildings is available" – but not yet for Africa (July 2006). *See* ASC4, 768-769 for a detailed account)

601 Horrabin, James Francis. **An atlas of Africa**. London, Gollancz/New York, Praeger, 1960. 162pp. (50 small b. & w. sketch-maps each with a facing page of interpretation. "For the intelligent newspaper reader", pref. Emphasis on historical maps)

602 **Maps of the world's nations. Vol. 2, Africa**. Washington, DC, U.S. Central Intelligence Agency (CIA), 1977. 53pp. (One page map for each country showing only major cities, road and rail routes and airports)

603 Murray, Jocelyn, ed. **Cultural atlas of Africa**. 2nd ed. New York, Checkered Books, 1998. 240pp. col. maps. illus. (85 maps with accompanying text and over 300 photos. Pt.1, physical background; pt.2, cultural; pt. 3, nations of Africa, arranged by 8 regions and then by country. Bibliography and gazetteer. Only minimal updating from 1st ed., e.g. adding entry for Eritrea, revising plate of national flags and bibliography. Very critical review *Choice*, 36, 1999, 144. ASC4, 126). - - Orig. pub. Oxford, Phaidon/New York, Facts on File, 1981. (Review, *Africa*, 52, 1982, 90-92)

604 **Oxford regional economic atlas: Africa**. Oxford, Clarendon Press, 1965. 64, 164pp. incl. 112 pp. col. maps. (45pp. topographical maps, later revised and issued as **Shorter atlas of Africa**, *see* **605**, remainder thematic. Critical review, *GJ*, 131, 1965, 400-401. Other reviews, *East African geographical review*, 4, 1986, 87-88; *Rivista geografica italiana*, 1966(1), 81-82)

605 **Shorter Oxford atlas of Africa**. Oxford, Clarendon Press, 1966. 96pp. incl. 48pp. topographic maps. (Derived from topographic section of **Oxford regional economic atlas: Africa** (*see* **604**). Index of 18,000 names)

606   The Times atlas of the world, mid-century edition. Vol. 4, Southern Europe and Africa. London, Times Publishing, 1956. 96 plates. (Plates 85-95 cover Africa, mostly at 1:5m. Later rev. eds. of this atlas as The Times atlas of the world: comprehensive edition are issued as a single vol. The 1956 ed. remains convenient and useful for coverage of Africa towards the end of the colonial period)

607   U.N. United Nations Cartographic Section. Maps and geographic information resources. http://www.un.org/Depts/Cartographic/english/ htmain.htm. (The Africa pages contain a variety of general, regional and country maps, mostly very current. Also provides access to large scale maps of UN peacekeeping activities. ASC4, 187)

See also 31, 629, 648. For atlases of agriculture, climatology, geology, oceanography, soils, etc. see under EARTH SCIENCES below; for atlases of animals and plants see under BIOLOGICAL SCIENCES below

Facsimiles

608   Klemp, Egon. Africa on maps dating from the twelfth to the eighteenth century. Leipzig, Edition Leipzig, 1968. 77 maps. 60pp. booklet in pocket. (High quality coloured facsimiles, reproducing originals located in 14 libraries and archives. The booklet provides a description of each plate)

609   Norwich, Oscar I. Norwich's maps of Africa: an illustrated and annotated carto-bibliography. 2nd ed. rev. & ed. Jeffrey C. Stone. Norwich, VT, Terra Nova Press, 1997. 443pp. illus. (Rev. of original ed. based upon "probably the finest private collection of early maps of Africa", adding for the 2nd ed. reproductions of additional maps from the editor's own collection. Lists and describes over 350 maps of Africa dating from 1486 to 1886, arranged by region. Each map is reproduced in b. & w., with ten also being reproduced in col. ASC4, 183). - - Orig. pub. as Maps of Africa: an illustrated and annotated carto-bibliography. Johannesburg, Donker, 1983. 444pp. Bibliographical descriptions by P. Kolbe)

610   Tooley, Ronald Vere. Collectors' guide to maps of the African continent and Southern Africa. London, Carta Press, 1969. xvi, 132, 100pp. (Includes reproductions of some 120 maps dating from 1540 to 1872 in b. & w., with 6 in col.)

611   Yusuf Kamal, Prince. Monumenta cartographica Africae et Aegypti. Cairo, author, 1926-51. 5 vols. in 16. (Privately printed in the Netherlands in an edition of 75 copies. Much of the work on assembling the plates was undertaken by F.C. Wieder and J.H. Kramers in the Netherlands. Pts. 1-14 pub.

1926-1939; pts. 15-16 pub. 1951, delayed by the war and the death of Wieder. A complete set is claimed to weigh over 500lbs. Comprises 1,652 high quality collotype reproductions of maps from earliest times to the 19th century. Also reproduces many relevant texts in their original language with accompanying French translation. Vol. 1. 1926, Époque avant Ptolémée; vol. 2. 1928-1933, Ptolémée et époque gréco-romain; vol. 3. 1930-1935, Époque arabe; vol. 4. 1936-1939, Époque des portulans, suivie par l'époque des découvertes; vol. 5. 1951, Additamenta (naissance et évolution de la cartographie moderne). Use of this vast and valuable collection of material is facilitated by the author's **Quelques éclaircissements épars sur mes** *Monumenta* ... , Cairo, author, 1935. 216pp. **A list of geographical atlases in the Library of Congress,** (*see* **576**) vol.6, pp. 426-458 lists the subject of every plate. Reviews in *GJ*, 73, 1929, 549-550; 79, 1932, 143-144; 91, 1938, 558-559; *Geographical review*, 24, 1934, 175-176; 27, 1937, 686-687; 41, 1951, 670; *Imago mundi*, 2, 1937, 100; *Petermanns Mitteilungen*, 82, 1936, 373-374. Reprinted in reduced size in 6 vols. Frankfurt, Institut für Geschichte der Arabischen-Islamischen Wissenschaften an der Wolfgang Goethe Universität, 1987)

Francophone Africa

612 **Atlas de la zone franc en Afrique subsaharienne: monnaie, économie, société.** Paris, Ministère de la coopération, La documentation française, 1995. 112pp. (Thematic atlas covering Francophone West and Central Africa and Equatorial Guinea. 2 page spread for each with map and text on facing page, covering climate, demography, land use, industry, communications, health, finance. The Comores are listed as being covered, but only appear in some of the statistical tables, not on the maps)

613 **Atlas économique permanent**. Paris, Ministère de la coopération, 1965. 15 fascs. (Pt. 1, Divers (i.e. Rwanda, Guinée); pts. 2 to 14 each cover a Francophone country)

Former German Africa

614 Deutsche Kolonialgesellschaft. **Deutscher Kolonialatlas mit Jahrbuch**. Berlin, D. Reimer, 1905-1941. Irreg. 22 issues. (Each issue contains 8 (later 9) maps, of which sheets 2 to 6 (later 2 to 7) cover Africa). *Continues* Deutsche Kolonialgesellschaft. **Kleiner deutscher Kolonialatlas**. Berlin, D. Reimer, 1896. 4pp. 7 col. maps. 32 x 16 cm. - - 2nd to 6th eds. pub. Berlin, 1898-1904.

Lusophone Africa

615 **Atlas missionário português**, comp. António da Silva Rego & Eduardo dos Santos. 2nd ed. Lisbon, Centro de Estudos Históricos Ultramarinos, Junta de Investigações do Ultramar, 1964. vii, 198pp. (High quality col. production.

Covers Roman Catholic and Protestant missions and activities in the Portuguese Empire. 2nd ed. includes additional maps on non-missionary activities such as administrative divisions, ethnography, languages, and demography). - - Orig. pub. Lisbon, Missão para o Estudo da Missionologia Africana, Centro de Estudos Políticos e Socias, 1962. 177pp.

616 Portugal. Ministério das Colónias. Junta das Missões Geográficas e de Investigações do Ultramar. **Atlas de Portugal ultramarino e das grandes viagens Portuguesas de descobrimento e expansão.** Lisbon, 1948. viiipp. 110 colour maps on 118pp. 49 x 37cm. - - **[Index]**, *Garcia de Orta* 2, 1954, 257-261. (Rev. ed. of **Atlas colonial Português**. Lisbon, Ministério das Colónias, 1914. Maps 2 and 8 show voyages and travels exploring Africa, 15th-19th centuries; maps 12-86, Africa. Thematic maps for Cape Verde, Guinea, São Tomé and Príncipe, Angola and Mozambique, covering ethnography, linguistics, geology, the economy, and communications)

617 Silveira, Luis. **Ensaio de iconografia dos cidades portuguesas do ultramar.** Lisbon, Junta de Investigações do Ultramar, [1952]. 4 vols. illus. maps. (Vol. 2, pp.125-301, África Ocidental e África Oriental. Reproductions and descriptions of maps, drawings, city plans, fortifications, etc. P. 301: English summary, 'Portuguese towns in Africa')

For atlases **of former Spanish Africa** *see* **2624**

Gazetteers

Bibliographies & manuals

618 Batoma, Atoma. African ethnonyms and toponyms: an annotated bibliography. (Electronic journal of Africana bibliography, 10, 2006). http://sdrc.lib.uiowa.edu/ejab/10/index.html (106 references by region)

619 Meynen, Emil. **Gazetteers and glossaries of geographical names of the member-countries of the United Nations: ... bibliography, 1946-1976.** Wiesbaden, Steiner, 1984. xiv, 518pp. (Arranged by country. The fullest available listing for its period of coverage)

620 Raper, Peter E. **United Nations documents on geographical names: prepared for the United Nations Group of Experts on Geographical Names.** Pretoria, Names Research Institute, 1996. 150, 32pp. ("Guideline...to any persons or agencies dealing with geographical names". Includes script conversion tables)

See also **621**.

African toponymy in general

621   **African ethnonyms and toponyms**: report and papers of the meeting of experts organized by UNESCO, Paris, 3-7 July, 1978. Paris, UNESCO, 1984. (General History of Africa: studies and documents, 6). 168pp. (Includes 8 papers on problems of choice of appropriate forms and spelling of names of African peoples and places (*see* Hrbek, **89**). Pp. 187-196, 'African toponymy: a bibliography': footnote indicates that this was originally prepared by C.V. Taylor in 1967, and had not been updated)

622   Aurousseau, Marcel. **The spelling of African place names**. London, Royal Geographical Society, Permanent Committee on Geographic Names, 1950-1953. (PCGN leaflets 6, 6a, 6c).

623   Groom, Nigel. **A dictionary of Arabic topography and place names**: a transliterated Arabic-English dictionary with an Arabic glossary of topographical words and placenames. Beirut, Librairie du Liban/Longman, 1983. 369pp. (Valuable especially for the countries of North-East and West Africa)

624   Room, Adrian. **African placenames: origins and meanings of the names for over 2,000 natural features, towns, cities, provinces and countries**. Jefferson, NC, McFarland, 1994. x, 235pp. (Includes glossary of place-name elements, principally Arabic. Aimed at the general reader. Reviews, *ARD*, 70, 1996, 74-75, "rather variable work"; *Choice*, 32, 1994, 76, "not recommended". ASC4, 105)

625   Tucker, Archibald N. 'Towards place name gazetteers in Africa; some problems of standardization', **Sixth International Congress of Onomastic Sciences, Munich 24-28 Aug., 1958, Report**. Munich, Bayerische Akademie der Wissenchaften, 1961. Vol.3, Paper 92, pp. 744-749. (Discusses problems relating to the colonial presence, the multi-lingual nature of many countries, and whether standardization should be on a political, linguistic or regional basis. Among earlier articles by Tucker, *see* especially 'The spelling of African place-names on maps', *Bulletin of the School of Oriental & African Studies*, 12, 1948, 824-830 and 'Conflicting principles in the spelling of African place-names', *Onoma*, 7, 1956/57, 215-228)

General (including place-name directories)

World

626   **Columbia gazetteer of the world**. [3rd ed.], ed. Saul B. Cohen. New York, Columbia University Press, 1998. 3 vols. 3,578pp. (The major descriptive gazetteer covering the world, with coverage of Africa expanded since the 1962 ed. Also available on CD-ROM and as a paid on-line sevice. Review, *Choice*, 36, 1998, 283-284; of online version, *Ref. revs.* 15(6) 2001, 39-40). - - Orig. pub. as **Lippincott's new gazetteer of the world**. Philadelphia, PA, J.B. Lippincott, 1906. (A revision of **Lippincott's gazetteer of the world**. Philadelphia, 1855); - - [2nd ed.]. **Columbia-Lippincott gazetteer of the world**, ed. Leon E. Seltzer. New York, 1952. x, 2,148pp. (Reprinted with 1961 Suppl., New York, 1962)

627 GEONET Names Server (GNS). http://earth-info.nga.mil/gns/html/index.html. ("Provides access to the National Geospatial-Intelligence Agency's (NGA) and the U.S. Board on Geographic Names (USBGN) database of foreign geographic feature names. The database is the official repository of foreign place-name decisions approved by the USBGN". Specific country files can be downloaded. ASC4, 186)

628 Getty thesaurus of geographic names online (TGN). http://www.getty.edu/research/conducting_research/vocabularies/tgn/. (Worldwide coverage of geographic names, including vernacular forms and historic names. Functions as an index gazetteer with geographical co-ordinates. ASC4, 41)

629 Law, Gwillim. **Administrative subdivisions of countries: a comprehensive world reference 1900 through 1998**. Jefferson, NC. McFarland, 1999. (Kept up to date by the Web site 'Statoids', http://www.statoids.com/statoids.html. For each country provides lists of the various primary and secondary administrative sub-divisions with a history of changes, and population details from the latest censuses. The Web site provides links to up to 6 on-line maps for each country. A major source with much fascinating detail. Review, *ARD*, 94, 2004. ASC4, 172-173)

630 Truhart, Peter. **Historical dictionary of states and state-like communities from their origins to the present**. Munich, K.G. Saur, 1995. xxxiv, 872pp. (By state, past and present, with notes on dependencies, dates of existence, political constitution, major events in history)

631 U.S. Board on Geographic Names. **Gazetteers**. Washington, DC, 1955- . (Most countries in Africa are covered individually by a vol. in this series of index-gazetteers which give geographical co-ordinates for each feature listed, but no descriptive text, and these vols. have entries below as appropriate. Responsibility for compilation is now with the U.S. National Geospatial-Intelligence Agency (NGA), formerly National Imagery and Mapping Agency (NIMA), formerly Defense Mapping Agency). Contents of all the gazetteers are available on GEONET Names Server, *see* **627**. For a general account of the work of the USBGN *see* 'The USBGN, 1890-1990', *Meridian*, 8, 1992, 1-74)

Africa

632 Automobile Association of South Africa. **Trans-African highways: a route book of the main trunk roads in Africa**. 5th ed. Johannesburg, 1963. 352pp. (Sketch maps, descriptions of routes, index of placenames). - - Orig. pub. Johannesburg, 1929; - - 2nd ed. Johannesburg, 1949. 408pp; - - 3rd ed. Johannesburg, 1956. 548pp; - - 4th ed. Johannesburg, 1958. 539pp.

633 Broadley, Donald G. & Minshull, John L. 'A gazetteer of African countries, their constituent parts, and their synonyms', *Arnoldia Zimbabwe*, 9(26)1986, 333-342. (Pub. by Natural History Museum of Zimbabwe, Bulawayo. Summary list intended initially for use in zoogeographical work)

634 **Cities of the world:** a compilation of current information on cultural, geographical, and political conditions ..., based on the Department of State's Post reports. **Vol. 1, Africa**. 6th ed. Detroit, MI, Gale Research, 2002. ix, 596pp. - - Orig. pub. Detroit, 1982; - - 2nd ed. Detroit, 1986; - - 3rd ed. Detroit, 1987; - - 4th ed. Detroit, 1993. - - 5th ed. Detroit, MI, 1999, ix, 596pp. (Only includes countries with which the US had diplomatic relations at the time of compilation, e.g. eds. 1 to 3 omit Angola. Arranged by country with general country profile, followed by long entries for major cities, 75 in 1st and 2nd eds., 84 in 3rd; 85 in 5th, and very brief comments on some 600 others)

635 G.B. Army. G.H.Q. Middle East. Survey Directorate. **Africa: index gazetteer showing place-names on 1:2M map series**. Fayid, 1947. iv, 501pp. (Over 50,000 names derived from 37 sheets comp. by various mapping agencies. References to sheet and degree square together with abbreviated indication of the feature named. Lists of meanings of terms in local languages)

636 Kirchherr, Eugene C. **Abyssinia to Zimbabwe: a guide to the political units of Africa in the period 1947-1978**. 3rd ed. Athens, OH, Ohio University, Center of International Studies, 1979. (Papers in International Studies, Africa series, 25). 1979. x, 80pp. (Guide to name changes of African states. Each ed. is considerably expanded in depth of coverage). - - Orig. pub. as **Abyssinia to Zona Al Sur Del Draa: an index to the political units of Africa in the period, 1950-1974**. Kalamazoo, MI, Western Michigan University, Institute of International & Area Studies & School of Graduate Studies, 1968. (Monographic Series on Cultural Changes, 2). 32pp. maps; - - 2nd ed. Athens, OH, Ohio University, Center of International Studies, 1975. x, 40pp. maps Later completely rev. and pub. as **Place names of Africa, 1935-1986** (*see* **637**)

637 Kirchherr, Eugene C. **Place names of Africa, 1935-1986: a political gazetteer**. Metuchen, NJ, Scarecrow Press, 1987. viii, 136pp. "Completely revised, updated and enlarged ed." of **636**. (Alphabetical list of current and past names of African states, with detailed notes on name and boundary changes, illus. by 23 maps. Detailed supplementary notes on mandates and trusteeships, French colonial federations in West and Central Africa, former Italian colonies, North-west Africa, former British territories of Central and Southern Africa, African islands, secessionist states, independent homelands. Reviews, *Choice*, 26, 1988, 82, "tremendous amount of information and scholarship"; *GJ*, 155, 1989, 253; *IJAHS*, 21, 1988, 759-760. ASC4, 104)

638   Lieux et peuples d'Afrique. Paris, Éditions Nathan for Radio France internationale service coopération, 1987. 276pp. (Originally prepared by Jaqueline Sorel and Baba Ibrahim Kaké for broadcast 'Mémoire d'un continent'. A/Z list of 740 place and a few ethnic names, notes on their origins, and references to sources. Index by country). - - Orig. pub. Paris, 1985. 275pp.

639   U.S. Board on Geographic Names. **Africa and South West Asia: official standard names approved by the USBGN: gazetteer supplement, Aug. 1972**. Washington, DC, 1972. 182pp.   (Contains supplementary lists to vols. for individual countries issued by the USBGN)

Pilots (Sailing directions)

640   **African harbour pilot**. 3rd ed. comp. Helge Nagel. Copenhagen, Hans Gade's Harbour Pilots, 1981. 550pp. maps. - - 2nd ed., comp. A.H. Kok. Copenhagen, Hans Gade's Harbour Pilots, 1969. 394pp. maps.

For pilots relating to the **Red Sea**, *see* below under **North-East Africa**; for those relating to the **Indian Ocean** *see* below under **Southern Africa: Indian Ocean islands**; for those relating to the **Northern Atlantic** *see* below under **West Africa**; for the **Southern Atlantic** *see* below under **Southern Africa**.

EARTH & BIOLOGICAL SCIENCES

641   **IUCN directory of Afrotropical protected areas**. Gland, IUCN, 1987. xviii, 1,014pp.illus. maps. (By country. Each has a map, general information on parks and reserves and legislation, and detailed information on each park or reserve)

642   UNESCO. **A review of the natural resources of the African continent**. Paris, 1963. 437pp. illus. maps. (Comprehensive survey with sections on Topographic mapping; Geology and minerals; Seismicity; Climate and meteorology; Hydrology; Soils; Flora; Fauna; Conservation)

643   World Conservation Monitoring Centre. **Ecologically sensitive sites in Africa**. Washington, DC, World Bank, 1993. 6 vols. (Vol. 1, Occidental and Central Africa; vol. 2, Eastern Africa; vol. 3, South-Central Africa and Indian Ocean; vol. 4, West Africa; vol. 5, Sahel; vol. 6, Southern Africa. Each vol. contains the same 64pp introductory text discussing ecological considerations in general followed by a directory of local sites, both officially designated and unprotected)

644   Worthington, Edgar Barton. **Science in Africa: a review of scientific research relating to tropical and Southern Africa**. London, Oxford University Press for Committee of the African Research Survey under the auspices of the Royal Institute of International Affairs, 1938. xv, 746pp. (A major survey prepared to accompany and complement Hailey's **African survey**. For comments on the African Research Survey, *see* **13**. Chapters on the various disciplines, geology, meteorology, forestry, zoology etc. A major reference source for the state of research and institutions involved before World War II. Review, *Africa*, 12, 1939, 233-238)

645   Worthington, Edgar Barton. **Science in the development of Africa: a review of the contribution of physical and biological knowledge South of the Sahara**. London, CCTA & CSA, 1958. xix, 462pp. (A post-war revision of **644**, once again related to Hailey's *African survey revised* (1957, *see* **14**) Since the 1938 work Worthington had become the first Secretary-General of the Commission for Scientific Co-operation in African South of the Sahara (CCTA) and the Scientific Council for Africa South of the Sahara (CSA). Topics covered in three broad groups: physical background, biology and man. Review, *African affairs*, 58, 1959, 180-182)

EARTH SCIENCES

646   Adams, William Mansfield, et al, eds. **The physical geography of Africa**. 2nd ed. Oxford, Oxford University Press, 1999. xxii, 429pp. illus. ("To provide a reasonably durable statement of physical conditions ... environmental facts, climate, tectonic history, soil types ... [&] the main types of environment". Numerous specialist contributors). - - Orig. pub Oxford, 1996. xxii, 429pp. (Review, *GJ*, 163, 1997, 95. The work is dedicated to Alfred T. Grove with an introductory essay on his contribution to African geography, and is intended as an updated version of Grove's **Africa**. 3rd ed. Oxford, Oxford University Press, 1978. xii, 338pp. - - Orig. pub. as **Africa south of the Sahara**. Oxford, 1967. xiv, 275pp; - - 2nd ed.. Oxford, 1970. xiv, 280pp. and of his **The changing geography of Africa**. 2nd ed. Oxford, Oxford University Press, 1993. x, 241pp. - - Orig. pub. Oxford, 1989. x, 241pp. Review *SAGJ*, 74, 1992, 78)

647 **Africa and the Middle East: a continental overview of environmental issues**, comp. Kevin Hillstrom & Laurie Collier Hillstrom. Santa Barbara, CA, ABC-CLIO, 2003. xxvi, 277pp. illus. maps. (Sections for Biodiversity; Parks, preserves, and protected areas; Forests, agriculture and freshwater; Oceans and coastal areas; Energy and transportation; Air quality and the atmosphere; Environmental activism)

648 **Africa data sampler**: a geo-referenced database for all African countries (AEO-1). Washington DC, World Resources Institute, 1995. 1 CD-ROM + Users guide. 148pp. (A set of internationally comparable digital maps at a scale of 1:1M for every country, based on the Digital Chart of the World. Data on topography, infrastructure, sub-national administrative boundaries, demography, and environmentally protected or sensitive areas, forests, mangroves, wetlands, drainage, etc. Users with the appropriate software (ArcView 1 for Windows) can view, query, print, and distribute maps. ASC4, 183)

649 **Africa environment outlook: past present and future perspectives**. Stevenage, Earthprint for UNEP, 2002. xxii, 422pp. Also available at http://www.unep.org/dewa/Africa/publications/AEO-1/ (*See* especially chap. 2, 'The state of Africa's environment and policy analysis' which takes as themes the atmosphere, biodiversity, coastal and marine environments, forests, freshwater, land, urban areas and discusses each under regional headings for Northern Africa, Eastern Africa, Western Indian Ocean Islands, Southern Africa, Central Africa and Western Africa. Numerous statistics. Complemented by **Africa environment outlook: case studies: human vulnerability to environmental change**. Stevenage, 2004. ix, 182pp)

650 **African compendium of environment statistics, 1991-** . Addis Ababa, UNECA, 1992- . (SOAS holds issues for 1991-1995 only)

651 **Directory of African environmental experts and list of institutions on environmental matters in Africa, 1984/86** [etc.]. Addis Ababa, UNECA, 1987- . Irreg. Issues for 1984/86, 1996.

652 **Encyclopedia of world geography**. 2nd ed., gen. ed. Peter Haggett. New York, Marshall Cavendish, 2002. 24 vols. (Vol. 16. North Africa; vol. 17. West Africa/Central Africa/East Africa; vol. 18. Southern Africa. Aimed at schools and public libraries). - - Orig. pub. New York, 1994. 24 vols.

653 **Encyclopédie géographique universelle Marco Polo**. Genève, Édito-service/Paris, La Grange Batelière, 1969-1974. Vol. 17, 1974. Pp. 181-352. Tunisie II, Libye, Egypte, Soudan, Ethiopie I; vol. 18, 1974. Pp. 353-512; Ethiopie II, Territoire français des Afars et des Issas, Somalie, Mauritanie,

Province du Sahara, Sénégal, Gambie, Mali, Haute-Volta ; vol. 19, 1974, Pp. 1-152 ; Niger, Tchad, Guinée portugaise, Îles du Cap-Vert, Guinée, Sierra Leone, Liberia, Côte d'Ivoire, Ghana, Togo, Dahomey I; vol. 20, 1974, Pp. 153-300; Dahomey II, Nigeria, Cameroun, République centrafricaine, Guinée équatoriale, Gabon, République populaire du Congo, Zaïre, Angola I; vol. 21, 1974, Pp. 301-428; Angola II, Sao Tomé et Principe, Sainte-Hélène, Ascension, Tristan da Cunha, Rwanda, Burundi, Ouganda, Kenya, Tanzanie, Mozambique, Malawi, Zambie I; vol. 22, 1974. Pp. 429-552. Zambie II, Rhodésie, Botswana, Namibie, République Sud-africaine, Lesotho, Ngwane, Les Comores, Madagascar, Les Seychelles, La Réunion, Ile Maurice.

654 Hance, William Adams. **The geography of modern Africa**. 2nd ed. New York, Columbia University Press, 1975. xvii, 657pp. (Economic geography: general overview followed by regional surveys, covering physical features, population, agriculture, industry, transport etc. 119 maps. Review, *SAGJ*, 59, 1977, 65-69 which includes detailed comparison of the two eds.). - - Orig. pub. New York, 1964. xiv, 653pp. (Review, *GJ*, 131, 1965, 398-399, "deserves to remain a standard work of reference for many years to come")

655 Harrison-Church, Ronald J. et al. **Africa and the islands**. 4th ed. New York, Wiley, 1977. xviii, 542pp. illus. maps. - - Orig. pub. London, Longmans, 1964. xiv, 494pp. (Review, *GJ*, 131, 1965, 116); - - 2nd ed. London, 1969. xiv, 494pp; - - 3rd ed. London, 1971. xviii, 542pp. (Classic study of African physical and human geography)

656 Kimble, George H.T. ed. **Tropical Africa**. New York, Twentieth Century Fund, 1960. 2 vols. (Vol. 1. 'Land and livelihood' covers physical and economic geography; vol. 2. 'Society and polity' covers social and political geography. Most statistics date from the mid 1950s. 46 contributors). - - Abridged ed. New York, Doubleday, 1962. 2 vols.

657 Migliorini, Elio. **L'Africa**. Turin, Unione Tipografico-Editrice Torinese, 1955. (Geografia universale illustrata, 5). 821pp. illus. maps. (Provides coverage of physical, social, economic and political geography, lavishly illus.)

658 Stamp, Sir Dudley. **Africa: a study in tropical development**. 3rd ed. rev. William T.W. Morgan. Chichester, Wiley, 1972. xiii, 520pp. illus. maps. (In its time a classic work and a forerunner to modern ecological studies of Africa). - - Orig. pub. London, Chapman & Hall, 1953. vii, 568pp. (Review, *GJ*, 120, 1954, 97-98); - - 2nd ed. New York, Wiley, 1964. xx, 534pp. (Review, *Africa*, 35, 1965, 446, "outmoded approach ... serious gaps in information")

659   **World geographical encyclopedia. Vol. 1, Africa**. New York, McGraw-Hill, 1995. vi, 350pp. 5 vol. work is English trans. of **Enciclopedia geografica universale**, 1994. Country articles arranged under 6 regions, and with sections on topography, political, economic and social geography. Numerous col. illus. 5 historical maps showing travellers's routes. Review, *Choice*, 33, 1996, 770-772. Whole encyclopedia, *Choice* "outstanding academic title", 1996)

See also **412**

Agriculture

660   **Africa: statistical basebook for food and agriculture**. Rome, FAO, 1986. vi, 254pp. illus. maps.

661   **African agriculture: the next twenty five years. Annex 5: Atlas of African agriculture**, comp. R. Clarke et al. Rome, FAO, 1986. 72pp. 22 x 32cm. (Maps on production, population and the economy. Text includes numerous statistical tables and diagrams)

662   **Agricultural information resource centers: a world directory**. 3rd ed., comp. Rita C. Fisher et al. Twin Falls, ID, International Association of Agricultural Librarians & Documentalists (IAALD), 2000. xxxiv, 718pp. (Arranged by country. Some 600 entries for African countries). - - Orig. pub. Urbana, IL, IAALD, 1990. 641pp; - - 2nd ed. Twin Falls, ID, IAALD, 1995. 860pp.

663   **Répertoire des institutions et stations de recherche agricole en Afrique**. Rome, FAO, 1966. 218pp.

664   **World atlas of agriculture. Vol. 4, Africa**. Novara, Istituto Geografico de Agostini for Committee for the World Atlas, 1976. xi, 761pp. (Small b. & w. maps, mostly in text, with comment and statistics. Arrangement is A/Z country, with subdivisions for physical environment and communication; population; exploitation of resources, ownership and local tenure; land utilization, crops and communal husbandry and agricultural economy)

Climate & meteorology

665   **Agroclimatological data for Africa**. Rome, FAO, 1984. (FAO plant production & protection series, 22). 2 vols. (Vol. 1, Countries north of the Equator; vol. 2, Countries south of the Equator. Arranged by country and reporting station. Monthly average data for temperature, precipitation, wind, sunshine etc.)

666   Atlas des régimes pluviométriques de l'Afrique, comp. René Emsalem. Limoges, Presses de l'Université de Limoges et du Limousin, 1990. 25pp. 20 maps. 34 x 40 cm.

667   Atlas of the climate of Africa, comp. Basil W. Thompson. London, Oxford University Press, 1965. 15pp. 132 maps. 46 x 52cm. b. & w. maps (1:22M to 1:30M) based on 1956-60 data. (Review, *GJ*, 132, 1966, 291-292, "A most valuable store of information ... not readily available from any other source")

668   Aubréville, André. **Climats, forêts et desertification de l'Afrique tropicale**. Paris, Société d'éditions géographiques, maritimes et coloniales. 1949. 352pp. illus. maps. (Includes systematic classification of climatic regions and forest formations)

669   **Climatological atlas of Africa**, comp. & ed. Stanley P. Jackson. Lagos & Nairobi, CCTA & CSA, 1961/New York, International Publishers' Service, 1963. viii, 110pp. (Compiled at the African Climatology Unit, University of the Witwatersrand, Johannesburg. Text in English, French and Portuguese. 55 double page maps, mostly at 1:5M. General and regional maps showing annual and monthly data for rainfall, temperature and humidity)

670   G.B. Meteorological Office. **Tables of temperature, relative humidity, precipitation and sunshine for the world. Part 4, Africa**, the Atlantic Ocean south of 35° N. and the Indian Ocean, comp. World Climatology Branch of the Meteorological Office. 3rd ed. London, HMSO, 1983. xiv, 229pp. - - Orig. pub. London, 1958. xii, 258pp; - - 2nd ed. London, 1967. xiii, 208pp.

671   Griffiths, John Frederick. **Climates of Africa**. Amsterdam, Elsevier, 1972. (World survey of climatology, 10). xv, 604pp. illus. maps. (Major source of comparative data)

672   **Klimadiagramm-Karte von Afrika**, ed. Heinrich Walter. Bonn, Deutsche Afrika Gesellschaft, 1958. (Dag Schriftenreihe, 4). 32pp. 46 figs. map.

673   **Klimaticheskii atlas Afriki**, ed. A.N. Lebedev. Leningrad, Gidrometeoizdat, 1978. 2 vols. 30 x 40cm. (166 maps in total, most at 1 :30M. Vol. 1. Solnechnaia radiatsiia, temperatura vozdukha, otnositel'naia vlazhnost' vozdukha; vol. 2. Oblachnost', atmosfernye osadki, veter. Preface and table of contents in English. Based on data in **The climate of Africa**. Jerusalem, 1970, *see* **674** *below*.)

674   Lebedev, A.N. **The climate of Africa**. Jerusalem, Israel Program for Scientific Translations, 1970. 2 vols. (Trans. of **Klimaticheskii spravochnik Afriki**. Leningrad, Gidrometeoizdat, 1967).

675   Leroux, Marcel. **The meteorology and climate of tropical Africa**. London, Praxis, 2001. xxxiv, 548pp. illus. maps. + 1 CD-ROM. Rev. ed. of **Le climat de l'Afrique tropicale**. Paris, Éditions Champion, 1983. 2 vols. maps. (Vol. 1, Text. 633pp; vol. 2, Maps. 24pp. 247 plates including maps and diagrams. Parallel French and English text)

676   **Solar radiation atlas of Africa** ... derived from imaging data of the geostationary satellite METEOSAT 2, ed. Ehrhard Raschke et al. Rotterdam, Balkema, 1991. (Euratom publications - EUR 13129). 172pp.

677   **Topographic and climatic database for Africa**. Version 1.0., ed. M.F. Hutchinson. Canberra, Centre for Resource & Environmental Studies, Australian National University, 1995. CD-ROM. See http:// cres.anu.edu.au/outputs/africa.php for details of contents. See also M.F. Hutchinson, et al. 'The development of a topographic and climatic database for Africa', http://www.ncgia.ucsb.edu/conf/SANTA_FE_CD-ROM/ sf_papers/hutchinson_michael_africa/africa.html

678   **World atlas of desertification**. 2nd ed., ed. Nick Middleton & D.S.G. Thomas. London, Arnold, 1997. x, 182pp. (Section 2, Africa, pp. 55-75. maps, statistical tables. Review, *GJ*, 165, 1999, 325-326). - - Orig. pub. London, Arnold for United Nations Environment Programme (UNEP), 1993. ix, 69pp. (Reviews, *Choice*, 30, 1993, 1302; *GJ*, 160, 1994, 210-211. 1st ed. produced to coincide with the U.N. Rio Earth Summit, 2nd following the ratification of the U.N. Convention to Combat Desertification, 1996)

Geology & minerals

679   Cahen, Lucien et al. **The geochronology and evolution of Africa**. Oxford, Clarendon Press, 1984. xiii, 512pp. illus. maps. (Arranged by broad regions. Standard work produced to synthesise the many specific regional studies produced post 1945)

680   De Kun, Nicolas A. **The mineral resources of Africa**. Amsterdam, Elsevier, 1965. xxvi, 740pp. illus. maps. (Pt. 1 deals with mineral economics in general, pt. 2 treats mineral groups individually)

681   Furon, Raymond. **Géologie de l'Afrique**. 3rd ed. Paris, Payot, 1968. 374pp. illus. maps. - - Orig. pub. Paris, 1950. 350pp; - - 2nd ed. Paris, 1960. 440pp. - - **Geology of Africa**; trans. from the 2nd French ed. Edinburgh,

Oliver & Boyd, 1963. xii, 377pp. illus. maps. (A classic study in its time, but review, *GJ*, 129, 1963, 524-525 is critical of poor trans. and out-of-date text)

682 Furon, Raymond. **Lexique stratigraphique international, 4, Afrique, fasc. 12: Introduction à la stratigraphie générale de l'Afrique.** Paris, CNRS, 1966. 109pp. - - **fasc. 13: Introduction à la géochronologie de l'Afrique.** Paris, CNRS, 1969. 112pp.

683 Furon, Raymond. **Les ressources minérales de l'Afrique**: géologie et mines, la production africaine dans le monde, la production régionale, les nouveaux problèmes. 2ⁿᵈ ed. Paris, Payot, 1961. 284pp. illus. 34 maps. - - Orig. pub as **Les ressources minérales de l'Afrique**: leur découverte, leur exploitation, les nouveaux problèmes. Paris, 1944. 275pp. 65 maps.

684 **Geological map of Africa**. Rev. [2ⁿᵈ] ed. Notice explicative, comp. Raymond Furon & Jean Lombard. Paris, UNESCO & Association for African Geological Surveys, 1964. 39pp. (Map issued on 9 sheets, 59 cm x 62 cm at 1:5M). - - Maps alone orig. pub. Paris, International Geographical Congress, 1939. - - 3ʳᵈ ed. of maps alone without explanatory text. Paris, Commission for Geological Map of the World (CGMW) and UNESCO, 1985-1990. 6 sheets. 96 cm x 92 cm.

685 Haughton, Sidney Henry. **Lexicon de stratigraphie. Vol. 1 Africa**. London, Thomas Munby, 1938. vi, 432pp. (Part of a series set up by the International Commission on the Lexicon de stratigraphie, following the 15th International Geological Congress in South Africa, 1929)

686 Haughton, Sidney Henry. **The stratigraphic history of Africa south of the Sahara**. Edinburgh, Oliver & Boyd, 1963. xii, 365pp. (Review, *GJ*, 129, 1963, 530)

687 Krenkel, Erich. **Geologie und Bodenschätze Afrikas**. 2ⁿᵈ ed. Leipzig, Geest & Portig, 1957. xv, 597pp. - - Orig. pub. as **Geologie Afrikas**. Berlin, Borntraeger, 1925-38. (Geologie der Erde). 3 vols.

688 Petters, Sunday W. **Regional geology of Africa**. Berlin, Springer-Verlag, 1991. 722pp. 50 figs. 25 tables. (An overview of geology, tectonics, and mineral resources)

689 Schlüter, Thomas. **Geological atlas of Africa: with notes on stratigraphy, tectonics, economic ecology, geohazards and geosites of each country**. Berlin, Springer-Verlag, 2006. 272pp. ("First attempt to summarize the geology of Africa by presenting it in an atlas ...aims to contribute to capacity building in African Earth Sciences and to initiate research and economic opportunities by providing a database of basic geological background information", pref.)

690   Selley, Richard C. ed. **African basins**. Amsterdam, Elsevier, 1997. (Sedimentary basins of the world, 3). xvii, 394pp. illus. maps. (Sections for North Africa, Central Africa including Sudan, West Africa and East Africa, Southern Africa)

691   **Soils map of Africa**, ed. J.L. d'Hoore. Lagos, CCTA, 1964. (Joint project, 11; Publication, 93). 2 vols. Vol. 1, Maps (7 sheets at 1:5,000,000); vol. 2, Explanatory monograph. 205pp. (Uses the soil classification developed by the CCTA)

692   **Tectonique de l'Afrique/Tectonics of Africa**. Paris, UNESCO, 1971. 602pp. illus. maps. (Review, *GJ*, 139, 1973, 119-121, "standard work of reference")

693   **Terroirs africaines et malgaches**, comp. École pratique des hautes études, Section des sciences économiques et sociales. Paris, Mouton, 1970. 555pp. illus. maps. (African soils. Special issue of *Études rurales*, 37/39, 1970)

694   Woolley, Alan R. **Alkaline rocks and carbonates of the world. Part 3, Africa**. London, Geological Society, 2001. 372pp. illus. maps. (A catalogue of their occurrence in the continent of Africa arranged by country. All Sub-Saharan countries are represented apart from CAR, Congo (Brazzaville), Gambia, Lesotho, Liberia and Swaziland which lack such formations)

Hydrology, limnology, oceanography

695   Beadle, Leonard Clayton. **The inland waters of tropical Africa: an introduction to tropical limnology**. 2nd ed. London, Longman, 1981. x, 475pp. illus. maps. - - Orig. pub. London, 1974. viii, 365pp. illus. maps. (Review, *GJ*, 141, 1975, 480-481)

696   Burgis, Mary J. & Symoens, Jean-Jacques. **Zones humides et lacs peu profonds d'Afrique: répertoire/African wetlands and shallow water bodies: directory**. Paris, ORSTOM, 1987. (Travaux et documents, Institut français de recherche scientifique pour le développement en coopération, 211). 650pp. illus. maps

697   Hughes, R.H. & Hughes, J.S. **A directory of African wetlands**. Gland, IUCN, 1992. xxxiv, 820pp. illus. maps. (With a chapter on Madagascar by G.

Bernacsek. Sponsored by UNEP & World Conservation Monitoring Center (WCMC), Nairobi)

698 Shahin, Mamdouth M.A., ed. **Hydrology and water resources of Africa**. Dordrecht, Kluwer, 2002. xxii, 659pp. + 1 CD-ROM. (Describes the hydrologic characteristics of 16 rivers and wadi basins, also sundry lakes, wetlands and reservoirs and the principal groundwater aquifers)

699 U.N. Department of Economic & Social Affairs. **Ground water in Africa**. New York, 1973. vi, 170pp. map in pocket. (An overview followed by a country by country survey. Map of aquifers. The U.N. later produced a map *Africa: ground water resources*. New York, 1988, at the scale of 1:12M)

700 **Wetlands of the world: inventory, ecology and management. Vol. 1, Africa, Australia, Canada and Greenland, etc**. Dordrecht, Kluwer, 1993. (Handbook of vegetation science, 15/2). xx, 768pp. illus maps.

701 **World ocean atlas. Vol. 2, Atlantic and Indian oceans**, ed. Sergei G. Gorshkov; with introductory text and gazetteer trans. into English, key for non-Russian-speaking users. Oxford Pergamon Press, 1978. xxii, 116pp. illus. col. maps. (Trans. of **Atlas okeanov: Atlanticheskii i Indiiskii okeany**. Moscow, Gl. upr. navigatsii i okeanografii, 1978. Comp. by Central Cartographic Production Department of the Russian Navy. Scales range from 1:12M for ocean charts to 1:50,000 for port charts)

BIOLOGICAL SCIENCES

702 **Freshwater ecoregions of Africa and Madagascar**, comp. Michele L. Thieme et al. Washington, DC, Island Press, 2005. xxi, 431pp. illus. (Comp. under the aegis of the World Wildlfe Fund. Companion vol. to **705**, below. Includes detailed descriptions of each of Africa's 83 freshwater ecoregions and 6 appendices of statistical data)

703 Monod, Théodore. **Les grandes divisions chorologiques de l'Afrique**: rapport presenté à la réunion de spécialistes sur la phytogéographie, Yangambi, 29 juillet – 8 août 1956. London, CSA/CCTA, 1957. 146pp. illus. map. (Defines and describes the major botanical regions of the continent and compares them with those established by zoologists)

704 **Nomenclatures de la faune et de la flore Afrique au sud du Sahara, Madagascar, Mascareignes, latin, français, anglais**, comp. ACCT & Conseil international de la langue française. Paris, Hachette, 1977. iv, 186pp. (Spine title: **Faune et flore d'Afrique continentale, tropicale et équatoriale**)

705 Terrestrial ecoregions of Africa and Madagascar: a conservation assessment, comp. Neil Burgess et al. Washington, DC, Island Press, 2004. 644pp. illus. maps. (Compiled under the aegis of the World Wildlife Fund. "A comprehensive examination of African biodiversity across all biomes and multiple taxonomic groups". Includes, pp. 219-446, a detailed description of each of Africa's 119 terrestrial ecoregions, with 9 detailed appendices of statistical data. *See* companion volume for **Freshwater ecoregions 702**)

706 Zones humides d'Afrique. Paris, Conseil international de la chasse et de la conservation du gibier, Secrétariat de la faune et de la flore, Muséum national d'histoire naturelle, 1986. (Inventaire de faunes et de flores, 34,35). 2 vols. Vol.1, Bibliographie; vol. 2, Inventaire préliminaire et méthodologie, comp. François de Beaufort & Alexandre-Michel Czajkowski.

Zoology

Birds

Checklists

707 African Bird Club. African Bird Club List of African Birds, Rev. ed. June 2005. http://www.africanbirdclub.org/resources/checklist.html. Basically follows names used in **Birds of Africa** (*see* **711**) supplemented by Dowsett & Forbes-Watson (*see* **708**) for birds of the Indian Ocean islands.

708 Dowsett, Robert J. & Forbes-Watson, A.D. **Checklist of birds of the Afrotropical and Malagasy regions**. Liège, Tauraco Press, 1993. 2 vols. Vol. 1, Species limits and distribution; vol. 2, A contribution to the distribution and taxonomy of Afrotropical and Malagasy birds. (Vol. 1 includes spp. and subspp. and a gazetteer of avian type-localities. Intended to replace White (*see* **709**) and update W.L. Sclater. **Systema avium Aethiopicarun** (London, British Ornithologists' Union, 1924-1930) for the Malagasy sub-region. Acknowledges the new Sibley & Monroe system (C.G. Sibley & B.L. Monroe. **Distribution and taxonomy of birds of the world**. New Haven, CN, 1990) but provides sequence and nomenclature close to that of **Birds of Africa** (*see* **711**). Follows political rather than zoogeographical boundaries in delineating area covered, i.e. all countries other than Western Sahara, Morocco, Algeria, Libya, Egypt. Includes Yemen, Socotra. Lists 2,176 spp. with cross references for each to their treatment in **Birds of Africa (711)**, Mackworth-Praed & Grant **(713)** and Roberts **(2975)** and to 11 other more local avifaunas, including page refs. to any col. illus; also to 12 collections of bird-song recordings. Provides notes on each sp. distribution country by country. Vol. 2 rearranges material to provide individual checklists for each of 53 African countries. The current major starting point for taxonomy and distribution. Reviews, *Auk*, 112, 1995, 1081-

1083; *BABC*, 2, 1995, 56-57, *Ibis*, 136, 1994, 501-502; *Ostrich*, 65, 1994, 349-350; *Scopus*, 17, 1994, 144)

709   White, Charles M.N. **A revised checklist of African birds**. Lusaka, Government Printer, 1961-65. 4 vols. Pts. 1-3, 1961-1963, Passerines; pt. 4, 1965. Non-passerines. (Includes mainland Africa only. Review, *Ibis*, 105, 1963, 125. The first major taxonomic revision post World War II)

Handbooks

710   Birdlife's   Africa   Programme.   http://www.birdlife.org/regional/ africa/ index.html. (Based in Kenya, part of Birdlife International. Includes 'Data Zone' with access to the World Bird Database (WDBD). Searchable by spp. on scientific or common name with possibility of combining country name, giving access to basic taxonomic and distribution information. ASC4, 11-12)

711   **Birds of Africa**. London, Academic Press, 1982-2004. 7 vols. (Detailed discussion and numerous illus. of variant plumages of every breeding sp. with briefer treatment for visiting spp. One of the world's major regional avifaunas, the starting point for all research on African birds. Reviews, *Auk*, 100, 1983, 1005; 115, 1998, 809-811; *BABC*, 5, 1998, 60-64; 8, 2001, 142-143; *Ibis*, 125, 1983, 214-215; 143, 2001, 334; *Malimbus*, 21, 1999, 124-125; 23, 2001, 70-71; *Ostrich*, 68, 1997, 85; 76, 2005, 95. One vol. ed. announced for pub. 2006)

712   Bouet, Georges. **Oiseaux de l'Afrique tropicale**. Paris, ORSTOM, 1955-1961. (Faune de l'Union française, 16; Faune tropicale, 17). 2 vols. illus. (Emphasis on West and Central Africa)

713   Mackworth-Praed, Cyril W. & Grant, Claude H.B. **African handbook of birds: Series I, Birds of Eastern and North Eastern Africa**. London, Longmans, 1952-55. 2 vols. - - 2nd ed. London, 1957-60. 2 vols; **Series II, Birds of the southern third of Africa**. London, Longmans, 1962-63. 2 vols; **Series III, Birds of West Central and Western Africa**. London, Longmans, 1970-73. (The first large-scale post 1945 attempt to describe all the spp. of the Afro-tropical region. *See* **816, 1256, 1775, 2974**)

Field guide

714   Sinclair, Ian & Ryan, Peter. **Birds of Africa south of the Sahara: a comprehensive illustrated field guide**. Cape Town, Struik, 2003. 760pp. 359 plates. (Includes whole of Afrotropical region with Socotra, Pemba and the islands of the Gulf of Guinea, but omits Madagascar and other Indian Ocean Islands. Lists 2,105 spp. plus 70 vagrants, and illustrates over 2,000 with distribution maps. The first field guide to attempt to cover the whole region. Reviews, *Honeyguide*, 50, 2004, 116-117; *Malimbus*, 26, 2004, 43-44)

Mammals

Checklists

715 Allen, Glover M. 'A checklist of African mammals', *Bulletin of the Museum of Comparative Zoology, Harvard*, 83, 1939, 1-763. (Includes the whole of the African continent and Madagascar. The major starting point for all later work. Review, *Journal of mammalogy*, 20, 1939, 388-389. Desmond Morris, **The mammals: a guide to the living species**. London, Hodder & Stoughton/Zoological Society of London, 1965, pp. 26-27 sees "Allen's African check list [as] ... full of meaningless splitting. He has listed every named form with little attempt at a critical evaluation". Morris recommends use of Ellermann (**2981**) for Southern Africa, resorting to Allen only for West and Central Africa and Madagascar: "this region would amply repay a ruthless taxonomic reassessment". P. Grubb. 'Controversial scientific names of African mammals', *African zoology*, 39, 2004, 91-109, discusses the revision of a number of names in Allen in the light of the **International code of zoological nomenclature**. 4th ed. London, 1999)

716 Ansell, William F.H. **African mammals, 1938-1988**. Zennor, Trendrine Press, 1989. 77pp. (Supplements Allen, *see* **715** with references to recent taxa, plus 35 older taxa omitted from Allen. Review, *Mammal review*, 20, 1990, 196)

Handbooks

717 **A databank for the conservation and management of the African mammals**, ed. Luigi Boitani et al. Rome, Istituto di ecologia applicata, 1999. 1,149pp. col. illus. Also available as African mammals databank (AMD) at: http://www.gisbau.uniroma1.it/amd/. (Includes 281 species belonging to 28 families of medium and large mammals seen as in special need of conservation. Includes distribution maps for each)

718 Dekeyser, Pierre Louis. **Les mammifères de l'Afrique noire française**. 2nd ed. Dakar, IFAN, 1955. (Initiations africaines, 1). 426pp. illus. - - Orig. pub. Dakar, 1948. 63pp.

719 Meester, Jurgens A.J. & Setzer, Henry Wilfred eds. **The mammals of Africa: an identification manual**. Washington, DC, Smithsonian Institution, 1966-77. Issued in 29 parts covering individual families, with accompanying file binder. ("A U.S./South African contribution to the International Biological Programme". Standard work used as a basis by many later authors)

720   Smith, Stephen J. **Atlas of Africa's principal mammals**. Fourways, S.A., Natural History Books, 1985. 241pp. (Maps at scale of c. 1:4M)

Field guides

721   Alden, Peter C. **National Audubon Society field guide to African wildlife**. New York, Knopf, 1995. 988pp. illus, maps. (Covers 850 spp. throughout the whole continent. 577 col. photos, 470 maps)

722   Dorst, Jean & Dandelot, Pierre. **A field guide to the larger mammals of Africa**. 2nd ed. London, Collins, 1972. 287pp. + 44 plates. (Describes, maps and illus. 233 spp. found south of 23° N. latitude, i.e. omits North Africa, also the Malagasay Region. Covers spp. "which a watcher can identify in the field". Includes Sirenia, but not Pinnipedia or Cetacea). - - Orig. pub. London, Collins, 1970. 287pp. 44 plates.
- - Also pub. in French as **Guide des grands mammifères d'Afrique**. Neuchâtel, Delachaux et Niestlé, 1972; - - 2nd ed. Neuchâtel, 1976. (Reprinted 1997); - - in German as **Säugetiere Afrikas: ein Taschenbuch für Zoologen und Naturfreunde**. Hamburg. Parey, 1973; - - in Spanish as **Guia de Campo de los Mamíferos Salvajes de Africa**. Barcelona, Omega, 1973.

723   Estes, Richard D. **The behavior guide to African mammals, including hoofed mammals, carnivores and primates**. Berkeley, CA, University of California Press, 1991. xxii, 611. 426 illus. maps. (To complement existing field guides which emphasize visual appearance. Covers 91 spp. Reviews, *Choice*, 29, 1991, 573; *Journal of mammalogy*, 73, 1992, 223-224. - - **The safari companion: a guide to watching African mammals, including hoofed mammals, carnivores and primates**. Rev. ed. White River Junction, VT, Chelsea Green, 1993. xx, 458pp. (Popularized version of his 1991 work). - - Orig. pub. Post Mills, VT, Chelsea Green, 1993. xii, 463pp.

724   Haltenorth, Theodor & Diller, Helmut. **A field guide to the mammals of Africa including Madagascar**. London, Collins, 1980. 400pp. 350 col. illus. 245 distribution maps. (Covers 324 "large and medium sized spp. only"; i.e. omits bats and many rodents and insectivores. Includes Sirenia and Pinnipedia but not Cetacea. Covers all African mainland, Madagascar, Fernando Poo, Comoros, Pemba, Socotra, but omits Mauritius, Réunion. Bases taxonomy on Meester & Setzer, **719**). - - Orig. pub. in German as **Saügetiere Afrikas und Madaskars**. Munich, BLV Verlagsgesellschaft, 1977. 403pp. - - Also pub. in French as **Mammifères d'Afrique et de Madagascar**. Lausanne, Delachaux & Niestlé, 1985. 397pp.

725   Kingdon, Jonathan. **The Kingdon field guide to African mammals**. San Diego, CA, Academic Press, 1997. xvii, 462pp. (Covers all mainland

Africa, excludes Madagascar and other islands. Limited to land mammals, omits Pinnipedia, Sirenia, Cetacea. Lists some 1,150 spp. but only provides individual descriptions, maps and illus. for some 450 larger spp. with a description and representative illus. of genera only for the bats, insectivores and rodents. Reviews, *Journal of mammalogy*, 80, 1999, 692-693; *SAJZ*, 33, 1998. 257). - - **Kingdon pocket guide to African mammals**. London, Christopher Helm, 2004. 240pp. 106 col. plates. 400 maps. (Abbreviated version of the 1997 publication)
- - Kingdon e-guide to African mammals. Craighall, PDA Solutions, 2005. 1 PDA card. (Requires a PDA running Microsoft Pocket PC 2003 or later. Search by common name or scientific name using complex or simple categories, or by country/region giving access only to animals found therein. Program updates are promised free of charge)

726   Stuart, Chris & Stuart, Tilde. **Field guide to the larger mammals of Africa**. 2nd ed. Cape Town, Struik, 2000. 319pp. 400+ col. photos. - - Orig. pub. Cape Town, Struik/London, New Holland, 1997. 318pp.

Reptiles & Amphibians

727   **Checklist for African snakes**, comp. Rupert Wilkey. London, Richard Terrell Society, 2002- . 7 vols. Vol. 1. 2002. The family Viperidae (adders and vipers). 72pp. (Checklist of 52 species, with 14 subspecies and 1 fossil form); vol. 2. 2002. The family Elapidae (cobras, mambas and allied species) and the family Hydrophidae (seasnakes). viii, 78pp. (Checklist of 35 species, with 35 subspecies and 1 fossil form. For each entry provides scientific name, synonyms, distribution, type locality and comments); vol. 3. The family Atractaspididae, "in preparation".

728   Isemonger, Richard M. **Snakes of Africa; southern, central and east**. Johannesburg, Nelson, 1962. viii, 236pp. illus. (Reprint, Cape Town, Books of Africa, 1983)

729   Meirte, D. **Clés de détermination des serpents d'Afrique**. Tervuren, Musée royal de l'Afrique centrale, 1992. (Annales. Sciences zoologiques, 267). 152pp. illus.

730   Schiøtz, Arne. **Treefrogs of Africa**, Frankfurt-am-Main, Chimaira, 1999. 350pp. illus. maps.

731   Spawls, Stephen & Branch, Bill. **The dangerous snakes of Africa: natural history, species directory, venoms and snakebite**. London, Blandford, 1995. 192pp. (Review, *Copeia*, 1996, 754-755)

732   Turtles of the world, Volume 1: Africa, Europe and Western Asia, comp. Holger Vetter. Frankfurt-am-Main, Chimaira, 2003. (Terralog: herpetological reference of the world). 97 pages, 450 col photos. (Photos and decriptions of turtles and tortoises. Review *Copeia*, 2004, 440, "aimed primarily at the zoo and terrarium-keeper market".)

733   Welch, Kenneth R.G. **Herpetology of Africa: a checklist and bibliography of the orders Amphisbaenia, Sauria and Serpentes**. Malabar, FL, Krieger, 1982. x, 293pp. (Despite title does not include amphibians. Review, *Copeia*, 1983, 574-575)

Fishes

734   **African cichlids: an abridged classified modern taxonomic listing of over 1,000 species as recorded on the Calypso Ichthyological Database**, ed. Gerald H. Jennings. London, Calypso, 2001. 256pp. (Companion to **736**)

735   **African freshwater fishes**. (Fishes of the world: modular regional database (taxonomic classification, vol. 7). London, Calypso, 2000. 2 x 3½ inch computer disks. Based on Calpyso Ichthyological Database

736   **African freshwater fishes: Calypso database numbers for all CLOFFA listed species (excluding cichlidae)**, ed. Gerald H. Jennings. London, Calypso, 1999. 256pp.

737   **Atlas démographique des populations de poissons d'eau douce d'Afrique**, ed. Jacques Moreau, et al. Paris, ACCT, 1995. 140pp. illus. maps.

738   Checklist for fishes of Africa. Fish-Bol (Fish Barcode of Life Initiative). Guelph, Canada. http://www.fishbol.org/ checklists.php?region=2

739   **Check-list of the freshwater fishes of Africa (CLOFFA)/Catalogue des poissons d'eau douce d'Afrique**, ed. Jacques Daget et al. Paris, ORSTOM/ Tervuren, Musée royal de l'Afrique centrale, 1984-91. 4 vols. (Text in English and French. Covers whole continent and islands of the Indian Ocean, and includes extensive bibliography. Review, *Copeia*, 1987, 1082-1083)

740   Lévêque, Christian & Paugy, Didier. **Les poissons des eaux continentales africaines**: diversité, écologie, utilisation par l'homme. Paris, IRD, 1999. 521pp. illus. maps.

741   Poll, Max & Gosse, Jean-Pierre. **Genera des poissons d'eau douce de l'Afrique**. Brussels, Académie royale de Belgique, Classe des sciences, 1995. (*Mémoire*, 3e sér., 9). 324pp. illus. - - Orig. pub. as **Les genres des poissons**

d'eau douce de l'Afrique, comp. Max Poll. Tervuren, Musée royal de Congo belge, 1957. 191pp.

Invertebrates

Butterflies

742   Carcasson, Robert Herbert. **Carcasson's African butterflies: an annotated catalogue of the Papilionoidea and Hesperioidea of the Afrotropical Region**, ed. Philip Ronald Ackery et al. East Melbourne, CSIRO/London, Natural History Museum, 1995. xi, 803pp. (Covers 3,593 spp. "Includes all sub-Saharan Africa, the Malagasay subregion and southern Arabia. In terms of political rather than biogeographical entities, we ... include Mauritania, Mali, Niger, Chad, Sudan and Ethiopia")

743   Carcasson, Robert Herbert. **Collins handguide to the butterflies of Africa**. London, Collins, 1981. xix, 188pp. illus. (Pp. 110-188, 'Simplified provisional check-list of the butterflies of the Afrotropical region')

744   D'Abrera, Bernard. **Butterflies of the Afrotropical region**. New & rev ed. Melbourne, Hill House, 1997- . (Butterflies of the world, 2). Pt. 1, 1997. Papilionidae, Pieridae, Acraeidae, Danaidae, Satyridae. 263pp; pt.2, 2004, Nymphalidae, Libytheidae. 336pp. ("Based on Synonymic catalogue of the butterflies of the Ethiopian region by R.H. Carcasson" (**742**). To be complete in 3 vols. Pt. 3 announced for 2006). - - Orig. pub. Melbourne, Lansdown in association with E.W. Classey, 1980. xx, 593pp.

745   Darge, Phillipe H. ed. **Catalogue commenté et illustré des Lépidoptères Saturniidae de l'Afrique du Centre et de l'Ouest**, avec des renseignements sur les espèces des autres régions de l'Afrique continentale. Clenay, author, 1995- . To be pub. in 8 vols. Vol. 1, 1995. 165pp; vol. 2, 2003. pp. 166-273.

746   Villiers, André, et al.   **Lépidoptères de l'Afrique noire française**. Dakar, IFAN, 1957-1962. 4 vols. Vol. 1. Introduction: structure, moeurs, récolte, conservation, classification, comp. A. Villiers; vol. 2. Papilionidés, comp. A. Villiers; vol. 3. Lucaenidés, comp. H. Stempffer; vol. 4. Arracidés (Saturniidés), comp. P. C. Rougeot.

747   Williams, John G. **A field guide to the butterflies of Africa**. London, Collins, 1969/Boston, Houghton Mifflin, 1971. 238pp. illus. (Omits Madagascar. Describes 430 most commonly found spp.)

Other groups

748 Betbeder-Matibet, M. **Insect pests of food crops in Africa and the Indian Ocean region.** Montpellier, Institut de recherches agronomiques tropicales et des cultures vivrères (IRAT), 1990. 122pp. illus. maps.

749 Crosskey, Roger W. **Catalogue of the Diptera of the Afrotropical Region.** London, British Museum (Natural History), 1980. 1,437pp. (Bibliog. pp. 891-1,196)

750 Daget, Jacques. **Catalogue raisonné des mollusques bivalves d'eau douce africains.** Leiden, Backhuys/Paris, ORSTOM, 1998. 329pp.

751 Delvare, Gérard & Aberlanc, H.-P **Les insectes d'Afrique et d'Amérique tropicale: clés pour la reconnaissance des familles.** Montpellier, Laboratoire de faunistique, for CIRAD, 1989. 302pp. illus.

752 Dippenaar-Schoeman, Anna Sophia & Jocqué, R. **African spiders: an identification manual.** Pretoria, Agricultural Research Council, Plant Protection Research Institute, 1997. 392pp.

753 Dirsh, Vitaly Michailovich. **The African genera of Acridoidea.** Cambridge, Cambridge University Press for the Anti-Locust Research Centre, 1965. xiii, 578pp. (Study of Locusts published as a companion to Johnston, 1956, **754** below)

754 Johnston, Henry Bennett. **Annotated catalogue of African grasshoppers.** Cambridge, Cambridge University Press for the Anti-Locust Research Centre, 1956. xxii, 833p. - - **Supplement.** Cambridge, 1968. xiv, 447pp.

755 **Mosquitoes of the Ethiopian region.** 2nd ed. comp. George H.E. Hopkins & Peter Frederick Mattingley. London, British Museum (Natural History), 1952- . Vol. 1, 1952. Larval bionomics of mosquitoes and taxonomy of Culicine larvae. viii, 355pp. ?Vols. 2 & 3 not pub. - - Orig. pub. comp. George H.E. Hopkins, et al. London, 1936-1941. 3 vols.)

756 Oldroyd, Harold. **The horse-flies (Diptera: Tabanidae) of the Ethiopian Region.** London, British Museum (Natural History), 1952-1957. 3 vols. Vol. 1. Haematopota and Hippocentru; vol. 2. Tabanus and related genera; vol. 3. Subfamilies: Chrysopinae, Scepsidinae and Pangonünae and a revised classification.

757   Pinhey, Elliot C.G. **A descriptive catalogue of the Odonata of the African continent (up to December 1959***)*. Lisbon, Companhia de Diamentes de Angola, 1962. (Publicações culturais, 59). 2 pts. 320pp.

Botany

758   Database of the flowering plants of Africa south of the Sahara. http://www.ville-ge.ch/cjb/bd/africa/index.php. Joint project by South African National Biodiversity Institute (SANBI), *see* **3022,** and Conservatoire et Jardin botaniques de la Ville de Genève. Based on Lebrun & Stork, 1991-1997 (*see* **775**) for Tropical Africa, and on Germishuizen & Meyer, 2003 (*see* **3024**) for Southern Africa. When completed will be the major starting point for a complete checklist.

759   **Forest resources of tropical Africa**. Rome, FAO, 1981. 2 vols. (Vol. 1, Regional synthesis; vol. 2, Country briefs. Report prepared with UNEP)

760   Knapp, Rüdiger. **Die Vegetation von Afrika: unter Berücksichtigung von Umwelt, Entwicklung, Wirtschaft, Agrar- und Forstgeographie**. Stuttgart, Fischer, 1973. (Vegetationsmonographien der einzelnen Grossräume, 3). xliii, 626pp. illus. maps. (Includes over 8,700 plates)

761   Lebrun, Jean-Pierre. **Les bases floristiques des grandes divisions chorologiques de l'Afrique sèche**. Maisons-Alfort, IEMVT, 1981. (Étude botanique, 7). iii, 483pp. (Floral plants characteristic of the major biological divisions of tropical Africa)

762   Letouzey, René. **Manual of forest botany: tropical Africa**. English ed. rev. & updated by R. Huggett. Nogent-sur-Marne, Centre technique forestier tropical, 1986. 2 vols. in 3. 194, 451pp. Vol. 1, General botany; vol. 2, A & B, Families. - - Orig. pub. as **Manuel de forestière: Afrique tropicale**. Nogent-sur-Marne, 1969-72.

763   Rattray, James McFarlane. **The grass cover of Africa**. Rome, FAO, 1960. (Agricultural studies, 49). 168pp. + map in pocket, scale 1:10M. 88 x 78 cm. (Text in English, French & Spanish).

764   Schnell, Raymond. **Flore et végétation de l'Afrique tropicale**. Paris, Gauthier-Villars, 1976-1977. 2 vols. x, 459pp; 378pp. - - Orig. pub. as vols. 3 & 4 of **Introduction à la phytographie des pays tropicaux**. Paris, 1970-1976. (Review, *GJ*, 144, 1978, 495-496, "remarkably clear synthesis")

765   White, Frank. **The vegetation of Africa: a descriptive memoir to accompany the UNESCO/AETFAT/UNSO vegetation map of Africa**. Paris,

UNESCO, 1983. 356pp. illus. (Map published in 3 sheets at 1:5M, covering Northwestern Africa, Northeastern Africa and Southern Africa. Memoir is a major discussion which proposes a revised classification for African vegetation with 18 main phytochoria (vegetation zones based on floristic distinctiveness), and examines the geological, soil and climatological factors of each. The work has been widely used as a basis by later researchers. Bibliography of c. 1,200 titles, pp. 275-324. Review, *GJ*, 151, 1985, 108-109, 132-134, "will be an enduring and essential source of reference". *See also*, F. White, 'The vegetation map of Africa: the history of a completed project', *Boissiera*, 24, 1976, 659-666)

Atlases

766   Distributiones plantarum africanarum. Brussels, etc., Jardin botanique nationale de Belgique. 1969- . (Major continuing source, covering vascular plants. 1 or 2 fascs. of 30 maps each normally pub. each year. Pt. 44, 1999 latest pub. at mid 2006)

767   Keay, Ronald W.J. **Vegetation map of Africa south of the Tropic of Cancer: explanatory notes**. London, Oxford University Press, 1959. 24pp. (Pub. for AETFAT & UNESCO. Map issued at scale of 1:10M, 73 x 83 cm)

768   Lebrun, Jean-Pierre. **Éléments pour un atlas des plantes vasculaires de l'Afrique sèche**. Maisons Alfort, IEMVT, 1977-79. (Étude botanique, 4, 6). 2 vols. maps.

769   Lebrun, Jean-Pierre & Stork, Adelaide L. **Index des cartes de répartition, plantes vasculaires d'Afrique (1935-1976)/Index of distribution maps, vascular plants of Africa**. Geneva, Conservatoire et jardin botaniques de la ville de Genève, 1977. x, 138pp. - - **Supplément, 1977-1981; avec addendum A-Z**. Maisons Alfort, IEMVT, 1981. (Étude botanique, 8). 98pp. - - **Supplément II , 1982-1985; avec contribution à une histoire des cartes de répartition**. Maisons Alfort, 1988. lxvii, 128pp. maps.

770   Sayer, Jeffrey A. et al. eds. **The conservation atlas of tropical forests. [2]: Africa**. London, Macmillan for World Conservation Union/New York, Simon & Schuster, 1992. 288pp. illus. maps. (Review, *GJ*, 159, 1993, 339-340)

Floras

Bibliographies

771   Frodin, David G. **Guide to standard floras of the world**. Rev. ed. Cambridge, Cambridge University Press, 2001. 1,124pp. (A major revision of this magisterial work, which is the essential starting point for information on published floras. *See* especially Africa, pp. 434-516, also Madagascar and associated islands, pp. 419-430; and Islands of the Atlantic Ocean, pp. 115-120, which includes Cape Verde, Ascension, St. Helena and Tristan da Cunha. Detailed annotations and discussion, histories of local botanical activities etc. Available also over the Internet on subscription basis from ebrary, Palo Alto, CA). - - Orig. pub. Cambridge, 1984. xx, 619pp.

772   Lebrun, Jean-Pierre. **Introduction à la flore d'Afrique**. Paris, CIRAD, 2001. 156pp. illus. (Includes discussion of using published floras, catalogues and herbaria and a history of botanical exploration. Note also his: **Introduction à la flore d'Afrique, faits et chiffres**. Maisons-Alfort, IEMVT, 1982. 80pp.)

General

773   African Plants Initiative (API). A digital library that will be available from   2007   on   the   Web   site   of   Aluka,   *see* http://www.aluka.org/page/content/plants.jsp. ("A collaboration among more than 50 institutions in Africa, Europe, and the United States ... API's long-term goal is to build a comprehensive online research tool aggregating and linking presently scattered scholarly resources about African plants, thereby improving access for students, scholars, and scientists around the globe. When complete, the digital library will include images of more than 250,000 type specimens drawn from the estimated 60,000 plant species in Africa, Madagascar, and the other islands surrounding the African continent. A wide range of related images and data, including photographs, drawings, botanical art, field notes, and reference works, is also included". Will include for example **The Useful Plants of West Tropical Africa** (*see* **1793**), **La Flore du Cameroun** (*see* **2277**) and **Flora of Southern Africa** (*see* **3029**); also 2,500 images of African plants from *Curtis's Botanical Magazine* (1797 to date). The Aluka digital library's mission is "to create a sustainable digital library of scholarly resources from and about the developing world, beginning in Africa,   as   an   aid   for   research   and   teaching   worldwide". http://www.aluka.org/page/about/historyMission.jsp.   Aluka   is   a programme within Ithaca (*see* www.ithaka.org)

774   Hedberg, Olov. **Afroalpine vascular plants: a taxonomic revision**. Uppsala, Lundequiststka bokhandeln, i distribution, 1957. (Symbolae botanicae Upsalienses, 15). 411pp.

775   Lebrun, Jean-Pierre & Stork, Adelaide L. **Tropical African flowering plants: ecology and distribution**. Geneva, Conservatoire et jardin botaniques de la ville de Genève, 2003- . 6 vols. Vol. 1, 2003. 797pp. illus.

maps. (Includes 4,481 distribution maps). Vol. 2 announced for 2006. (Substantially rev. and updated English language version of the original. Provides ecological notes summarized from floras and catalogues, species descriptions, and simple distribution maps). - - Orig. pub. in French as **Énumération des plantes à fleurs d'afrique tropicale**. Geneva, Conservatoire et jardin botaniques de la ville de Genève, 1991-1997. (*Boissiera*, pub. Hors série, 7a-d). 4 vols. (Annotated checklist of c. 35,000 spp.)

776   Lock, J. Michael. **Legumes of Africa: a check-list**. Kew, Royal Botanic Gardens, 1989. 619pp. (Covers 5,825 taxa found in mainland Africa, Zanzibar, Pemba, the Cape Verde Islands and the islands of the Gulf of Guinea)

Plants used by or affecting man

777   **Aflora catalog of useful plants of tropical Africa**, ed. Hideaki Terashima et al. Kyoto, Center for African Area Studies, Kyoto University, 1991. (African study monographs, Suppl. issue, 16). 195pp.

778   AFlora on the Web: the database of traditional plant utilization in Africa. http://130.54.103.36/aflora.nsf. (Created in 1998, based on the Study on the Traditional Use of Plants in Africa project at the Center for African Area Studies, Kyoto University. Each record comprises a set of data about a particular plant species, with a total of 27 fields, including usage categories for food, medicinal purposes, as a narcotic, for ritual and magic, etc.)

779   Bolza, Eleanor & Keating, W.G. **African timbers: the properties, uses and characteristics of 700 specimens**. Melbourne, Commonwealth Scientific & Industrial Research Organization (CSIRO), 1972. 700pp.

780   Iwu, Maurice M. **Handbook of African medicinal plants**. Boca Raton, FL, CRC Press, 1993. 435pp. illus. (Describes some 250 plants. Review, *ARBA*, 26, 1995, 674-675)

781   **Lost crops of Africa**. Washington, DC, National Research Council, Board on Science and Technology for International Development, 1996-   . Vol. 1, 1996. Grains. xix, 383pp. Vols. 2, Cultivated fruits & 3, Wild fruits in preparation. (Describes and discusses over 2,000 native food plants as an overlooked food resource in sub-Saharan Africa. Also available at http://www.nap.edu/books/0309049903/html/)

782   Neuwinger, Hans Dieter. **African ethnobotany: poisons and drugs; chemistry, pharmacology, toxicology**. Stuttgart, Medpharm Scientific, 1995. 941pp. illus. (Handbook which covers the use of plants for the preparation of hunting poisons and traditional medicine. Describes 240 plants with names in various African languages and dialects; the use of the plant as a poison and in traditional medicine; the chemistry of the plant's active principles; pharmacology and toxicology of the plant preparations)

783   Neuwinger, Hans Dieter. **African traditional medicines: a dictionary of plant use and applications with supplement: search system for diseases.** Stuttgart, Medpharm Scientific, 2000. x, 589pp. illus.

784   Peters, Charles R. et al. **Edible wild plants of Sub-Saharan Africa:** an annotated checklist emphasizing the woodland and savanna floras of eastern and southern Africa, including the plants utilized for food by chimpanzees and baboons. Kew, Royal Botanic Gardens, 1992. 239pp.

785   Phongphaew, Peter. **The commercial woods of Africa.** Fresno, CA, Linden Publishing, 2003. 206pp. illus. (Guide to 90 African woods. Gives scientific name, common trade name, vernacular names, range, and trade applications. Col. photo of each wood and tables of its physical properties)

786   **Plant resources of tropical Africa (PROTA).** Wageningen, PROTA/Leiden, Backhuys, 2004- . Vol.1. 2006. Cereals and pulses, ed. M. Brink & G. Belay. 298pp. + 1 CD-ROM; Vol. 2. 2004. Vegetables, ed. G.J.H. Grubben, et al. 667pp.+ 1 CD-ROM; vol. 3. 2005. Dyes and tannins, ed. Paulos C.M. Jansen & D. Cardon. 216pp. + 1 CD-ROM. To be complete by 2012 in 16 vols. (Will cover details of some 7,000 plant spp. used by man in Africa. The PROTA project was established in 2000 by Wageningen University which hosts the Network Office Europe. Network Office Africa is hosted by the World Agroforestry Centre (ICRAF), Nairobi. For details *see* http://www.prota.org)

787   **Plantas úteis da África Portuguesa.** 2nd ed. Comp. F. de Melho de Ficalho, ed. Ruy Telles Palhinha. Lisbon, Agência Geral das Colónias, 1947. 301pp. - - Orig. pub. comp. de Ficalho. Lisbon, 1884. (Indexed by Portuguese, vernacular , including creoles, and botanical names)

788   Schippers, Rudy R. **Légumes africaines indigènes: presentation des espèces cultivées.** Leiden, Backhuys, 2004. 482pp. illus. (381 col. figs.). Also available as **African indigenous vegetables: an overview of the cultivated species.** Aylesford, Natural Resources International Ltd, 2002. 1 CD-ROM

789   Sofowora, Abayomi. **Plantes médicinales et médecine traditionnelle d'Afrique.** Berne, Académie suisse des sciences naturelles/Paris, Karthala, 1996. 378pp. illus.

NORTH-EAST AFRICA

Djibouti
Eritrea
Ethiopia
Somalia
Sudan

HANDBOOKS

790   Africa orientale italiana. Milan, Touring Club Italiano (TCI), 1938. (Guida d'Italia, 24). 640pp. 15 maps. 16 city plans. (Covers Ethiopia, Eritrea, Italian Somaliland. Pp. 33-174 contain general information on geography, natural resources, history, peoples and communications; pp. 175-623 treat each district individually; pp. 623-640, index-gazetteer. Col. folding maps at 1:6M; regional maps at 1:1M. "Excellent work ... much more than a mere guide" (Duignan). *See also* P. Dagradi. 'Turismo e ambiente nella Guida del Touring dell'Africa Orientale Italiana (1938)', *Terra d'Africa*, 10, 2001, 183-192, an examination of the famous TCI guide fifty years on to see how far it anticipated current interest in environmental issues)

791   Burgess, Michael. **The Eastern Orthodox Churches: concise histories with chronological checklists of their primates**. Jefferson, NC, McFarland, 2005. viii, 324pp. (Includes sect. 30, Church of Eritrea; sect. 32, Church of Ethiopia and other entries for churches active in the region)

792   Coptic encyclopedia, ed. Aziz S. Atiya. London, Macmillan, 1991. 8 vols. lxxiii, 2,372, 371pp. (Substantial signed articles on persons, places, events and concepts relating to the history of Coptic Christianity in Egypt, Ethiopia and ancient Nubia, arranged A/Z in vols. 1-7. Vol. 8 contains maps, index and appendices including a lengthy treatment of the Coptic language)

793   Encyclopaedia Aethiopica: a reference work on the Horn of Africa (EAE) ed. Siegbert Uhlig. Wiesbaden, Harrassowitz, 2003- . 5 vols. projected for completion by 2009. illus. maps. Vol. 1. 2003. A to C. xxxii, 846pp.; vol. 2. 2005. D to Ha. xxxix, 1,082pp. Vol. 5 will be an index. (Major scholarly reference work. Each vol. contains some 1,000 articles by 250 contributors. For details of the project *see*: http://www.rrz.uni-hamburg.de/EAE/ which also contains addenda and corrigenda. "EAE will be the only existing lexicon to contain such a wide range of information on the whole Horn of Africa including historical, religious, linguistic, literary, cultural aspects, basic data (geography, flora, fauna) and anthropological research", Web site.

Lengthy review of vol. 1 by Joseph Tubiana, *Aethiopica*, 7, 2004, 194-211 analyses the work's purpose, and comments on a wide range of sample entries for persons, places, and topics)

794   Ethnographic survey of Africa: North-Eastern Africa. London, IAI, 1955-1974. 4 vols. illus. maps. Sub-series of the **Ethnographic survey**, *see* **86**. Vol. 1, Peoples of the Horn of Africa; Somali, Afar and Saho, by I.M. Lewis. 1955. 199pp; vol. 2, The Galla of Ethiopia; the kingdoms of Kafa and Janjero, by G.W.B. Huntingford. 1955. 156pp; vol. 3, Peoples of South-west Ethiopia and its borderland, by E. Cerulli. 1956. 148pp; vol. 4, The central Ethiopians: Amhara, Tigrina and related peoples, by W.A. Shack. 1974. 152pp. Rev. ed. of vol. 1, London, IAI, 1969. 204pp. (A reprint of the 1955 ed. with additional bibliography); - - new ed. London, HAAN Associates, 1994. 228pp; - - 4th ed. London, 1998. 228pp.

795   G.B. War Office. A gazetteer of Abyssinia (including Eritrea, Italian, British and French Somaliland), comp. Capt. Guy C. Shortridge. Khartoum, Directorate of Army Printing, 1940. [137pp.] (Despite the title, this is basically a general handbook. Pt. 1, pp. 1-38, geographical; pt. 2, pp. 1-45, political; pt. 3, pp. 1-54, diplomatic and military history)

796   Tucker, Archibald N. & Bryan, Margaret A. The non-Bantu languages of North Eastern Africa; with a supplement on the non-Bantu languages of southern Africa by E.O.J. Westphal. London, Oxford University Press for IAI, 1956. (Handbook of African languages pt. 3). xvi, 228pp. maps. (Systematic survey of languages, speakers and their location. Maps at 1:4,190,080. *See* **158** for note on the **Handbook**. Review, *Africa*, 27, 1957, 297-300)

YEARBOOKS

797   Annuario dell'Africa italiana. Rome, Istituto Fascista dell'Africa Italiana [etc.], 1926-1940. Annual. 14 issues (1938/39 issued as 1 vol.) Title varies: **Annuario delle colonie italiane [e dei paesi vicini]** (1926-1936); **Annuario dell'Impero** (1937). (Ed. for 1938/39 includes list of events of 1937 and other general political and administrative information; pt. 3. Africa Orientale Italiana, pp. 443-814, covers historical, geographical, administrative and economic data. Detailed index)

798   Italy. Ministero della Cultura Popolare. Guida amministrativa e delle attività economiche dell'impero Africa orientale italiana, 1938/39. Turin, Briscioli, 1938. 612pp. illus. (Covers administrative districts of Addis Ababa, Asmara, Eritrea, Galla-Sudan, Harar, Somalia. Essays on the empire in general, and data on major relevant societies, libraries etc. in Italy, followed by details of the administration, judiciary, military, communications, trade, finance, and professional and commercial directories for each district)

799 **State of the Horn: yearbook of political, economic, strategic and diplomatic developments in the Horn of Africa**. Vasterås, Sweden, NINA Press. 1998- Annual. (Produced jointly by *Eye on Ethiopia and the Horn of Africa* and Horn of Africa Democracy and Development International Lobby (HADAD)

See also **1015**

BIOGRAPHICAL SOURCES

800 Stella, Gian Carlo. **Dizionario biografico degli Italiani d'Africa (Eritrea-Etiopia-Libia-Somalia-Sudan) 1271-1990**. Fusignano, Biblioteca-Archivio "Africana", 1998- . Parte 1A: Civili. 1998. 132pp. (Intended as a multi volume work to cover an estimated 100,000 Italian civilians. Part 1A covers c. 2,500 surnames beginning with A. Details are extremely brief. Very critical review in *Aethiopica*, 4, 2001, 255-257, "scarcely been a work ... which promised so much and offered so little")

ATLASES & GAZETTEERS

Gazetteers

801 G.B. Army. G.H.Q. Middle East. Survey Directorate. **East Africa: index gazetteer showing place names on 1:500,000 map series**. Cairo, 1946-1948. 3 vols. in 4. Vols. 2, 2A (1946-47). vii, 474pp. Abyssinia, Eritrea, British, French and Italian Somaliland and part of the Sudan. (Sudan is included only where it appears on edges of sheets covering other countries). *See also* **1031, 3018**

802 U.S. Board on Geographic Names. **Ethiopia, Eritrea and the Somalilands; official names approved by the USBGN**. Washington, DC, 1950. v, 498pp. (Pp. 1-250, Ethiopia; pp. 251-308, Eritrea; pp. 309-380, British Somaliland; pp. 403-498, Italian Somaliland; pp. 381-401, French Somaliland. For later eds. covering individual countries *see* **841, 896, 935**)

Pilots

803 France. Service hydrographique et océanographique de la marine. **Instructions nautiques, L7: Mer Rouge; Golfe d'Aden**. Brest, 2004. 520pp. *Continues* **Mer Rouge et golfe d'Aden**. Brest, 1997. 520pp. - - Earlier eds. (title varies) 1885, 1895, 1958, 1974, 1987.

804 Germany. Deutsches Hydrographisches Institut. **Handbuch für das Rote Meer und den Persischen Golf**. 6th ed. Hamburg, 1983. (Loose-leaf). - - Earlier eds. (title varies) 1937, 1978.

805 G.B. Admiralty. Hydrographic Department [etc.]. **Admiralty sailing directions: Red Sea and Gulf of Aden pilot**. London, U.K. Hydrographic Office, 2005. 436pp. *Continues* **Red Sea and Gulf of Aden pilot**: Suez Canal, Gulf of Suez and Gulf of 'Aqaba, Red Sea, Gulf of Aden, south-east coast of Arabia from Ras Ba Ghashwah to Ras al Junayz, coast of Africa from Raas Caseyr to Raas Binna, Suqutrá and adjacent islands. 13th ed. Taunton, U.K. Hydrographic Office, 2002. xiv, 455pp. Earlier eds. (sub-title varies) 1873, 1883 1892, 1900, 1909, 1921, 1932, 1944, 1955, 1967, 1980, 1987.

806 Italy. Istituto Idrografico. **Portolano dell'Oceano Indiano: Mar Rossa**. Genoa, 1943. xxviii, 482 p.

807 U.S. Hydrographic Office [etc.] **Sailing directions for the Red Sea and Gulf of Aden:** includes Suez Canal, Gulf of Suez, Africa north of Ras Hafun, Suqutra, and Arabian coast eastward to Ra's al Hadd. 5th ed. 1965. (Rev. ed. 1976). Washington, DC, 1976. Looseleaf in continuation. - - Orig. pub. as **Red Sea and Gulf of Aden pilot**. Washington, DC, 1916. Other eds. 1922, 1943, 1952, 1965.

808 U.S. National Geospatial-Intelligence Agency. **Pilot guide (en route): Red Sea and the Persian Gulf**. 10th ed. Bethesda, MD, 2004. (Pub. 172). 1 CD-ROM. - - Orig. pub. Washington, DC, Defense Mapping Agency, Hydrographic Center, 1978. 1 vol. looseleaf. Other eds. 1990, 1993, 1997, 2001.

EARTH SCIENCES

809 Dainelli, Giotto. **Geologia dell'Africa orientale**. Rome, Reale Accademia d'Italia. Centro Studi per l'Africa Orientale Italiana, 1943. (Pubblicazione, 7). 4 vols. Vol. 1, Progresso delle conoscenze; vol. 2, L'imbasamento cristallino e la serie sedimentaria mesozoica; vol. 3, La successione terziaria dei fenomeni del quaternario; vol. 4, Tavole.

810 Hunt, John et al. **Lexique stratigraphique international, 4, Afrique, fasc. 5a: Somali anglaise; fasc. 5b Somali française; fasc. 5c: Somalia italiana; fasc. 5d: Ethiopie-Erythrée** Paris, CNRS, 1956. 80pp.

811 Merla, Giovanni et al. **A geological map of Ethiopia and Somalia (1973), 1:2,000,000 and comment**. Florence, Centro Stampa, 1979. viii, 95pp. illus.

812   Palaeogeographic-Palaeotectonic   atlas   of   North-Eastern   Africa, **Arabia and adjacent areas**. Rotterdam, Balkema, 1997. 2 vols. [Vol. 1], Explanatory notes, eds. Heinz Schandelmeir & P.-O. Reynolds. xix, 160pp. (Includes a chapter for each map); [vol. 2], Plates. (17 maps)

813   Usoni, Luigi. **Risorse minerarie dell'Africa orientale: Eritrea, Etiopia, Somalia**. Rome, Jandi Sapi for Ministero dell'Africa Orientale, 1952. x, 553pp. illus. maps.

BIOLOGICAL SCIENCES

Zoology

814   **CLOFRES: checklist of the fishes of the Red Sea**, comp. Menahem Dor. Jerusalem, Israel Academy of Sciences & Humanities, 1984. xxii, 437pp. illus. (Review, *Copeia*, 1986, 267-268). - - **An updated checklist of the fishes of the Red Sea, CLOFRES II**. Jerusalem, 1994. xii, 120pp.

815   Grasseau, Jean. **Les oiseaux de l'est africain**. Paris, Boubée, 2003. 960pp. illus. (Descriptions and illus. of 1,187 spp. in Djibouti, Eritrea, Ethiopia, Somalia, Sudan; Kenya, Tanzania, Uganda; Burundi, Congo (Democratic Republic), Rwanda; Malawi, Zambia, Zimbabwe and Mozambique)

816   Mackworth-Praed, Cyril W. & Grant, Claude H.B. **African handbook of birds: Series I: Birds of Eastern and North Eastern Africa**. 2nd ed. London, 1957-60. 2 vols. Vol. 1. 1957. Non-passerines. xxxiv, 836pp; vol. 2. 1960. Passerines. xiii, 1,113pp. - - Orig. pub. London, Longmans, 1952-55. 2 vols.

817   Moltoni, Edgardo & Riscone, G.G. **Gli ucelli dell'Africa Orientale Italiana**. Milan, Museo Civico di Storia Naturale, 1940-1944. 4 vols. illus.

See also **1051, 1052**

Botany

818   Burger, William C. **Families of flowering plants in Ethiopia**: an introduction with keys for the identification of the families of flowering plants and gymnosperms found in Ethiopia and adjacent areas of Eastern Africa. Stillwater, OK, Oklahoma State University Press, 1967. (Haile Sellassie I University College of Agriculture, Experiment Station bulletin, 45). 236pp.

819 Cufodontis, Georg. **Enumeratio plantarum Aethiopiae: Spermato-phyta**. Brussels, Jardin botanique national de belgique, 1975. 2 vols. xxvi, 1,657 pp. (Orig. pub. in 26 parts in *Bulletin du Jardin botanique de l'état/national de Belgique*, 23-42, passim, 1953-1972. Covers Ethiopia, Eritrea, Somalia, Djibouti)

820 **Flora of Ethiopia and Eritrea**, ed. Inga Hedberg et al. Addis Ababa, Addis Ababa University, Biology Department, National Herbarium of Ethiopia & University of Asmara/Uppsala, Uppsala University, Department of Systematic Botany, 1989- . Vol. 2(1). 2000; vol. 2(2). 1995; vol. 3. 1989; vol. 4 (1). 2003; vol. 4(2). 2006; vol. 6. 1997; vol. 7. 1995. Scheduled for completion in 8 vols. (Vol. 1 entitled **Flora of Ethiopia**)

821 Friis, Ib. **Forests and forest trees of northeast tropical Africa**: their natural habitats and distribution patterns in Ethiopia, Djibouti and Somalia. London, HMSO for Royal Botanic Gardens, 1992. (Kew bulletin additional series, 15). iv, 396pp. (250+ spp.)

822 Pichi-Sermolli, R.E.G. et al. **Adumbratio florae aethopicae**. Florence, Istituto Botanico dell'Università, 1953- . *Webbia*, 9-[33], 1953-[78]. 32 pts. to 1978. (None pub. since 1978, when some 5% of the vascular flora had been described *see* Frodin, 2001, 472. Covers Ethiopia, Eritrea, Somalia, Djibouti, Socotra. Based on work done in Erbario Coloniale/Erbario Tropicale di Firenze)

823 Pichi-Sermolli, R.E.G. 'Una carta geobotanica dell'Africa orientale (Eritrea, Etiopia, Somalia)', *Webbia*, 13, 1977, 15-132. illus. map.

DJIBOUTI

Site officielle de la République de Djibouti. http://www.presidence.dj/

HANDBOOKS

824 Africa Orientale Italiana. Governo Generale. **Costa francese dei Somali**, comp. G. Adami. Addis Ababa, 1939. 3 vols. illus. maps. (Vol. 1, 154pp. Topography, climate, flora and fauna, communications; vol. 2, 70pp. Tribes, administration, economics and politics; vol. 3, 21pp. Suppl. to vol. 2 specifically regarding the contemporary military situation)

825 Farah, Gaouad. **La république de Djibouti: naissance d'un état: chronologie**. [Tunis, Imprimerie officielle de la République tunisienne], 1982. 203pp. illus. map.

826 France. Ministère de la coopération. **Djibouti, 1992/93: guide d'information**. Paris, 1993. (Collection guides d'information). 51pp. map.

827 **Guide pratique de la république de Djibouti**. Djibouti, Office de développement du tourisme, 1982. 109pp. illus. maps.

828 **Historical dictionary of Djibouti**, comp. Daoud Aboubakar Alwan & Yohannia Mibrathu. Lanham, MD, Scarecrow Press, 2000. (African historical dictionaries, 82). xxviii, 165pp. (Reviews, *African affairs*, 100, 2001, 668-670; *Choice*, 38, 2001, 1939; *IJAHS*, 34, 2001, 439-440; *JAH*, 42, 2001, 543)

829 Morin, Didier. **Dictionnaire historique Afar (1288-1982)**. Paris, Karthala, 2004. viii, 304pp. (Entries for places, plants, ethnic groups, but especially for persons, with numerous genealogical trees)

830 **Petit guide de Djibouti.** 5th ed. Djibouti, Association démocratique des français de Djibouti, 1991. 118pp. (Practical information aimed at the French-speaking expatriate settling in Djibouti)

831 **Répertoire culturel: Djibouti**. Paris, ACCT, 1985. (Inventaire des activités, etc. des pays membres de l'ACCT). 63pp. illus. maps.

832 Zhuralev, V.L. **Dzhibuti spravochnik**. Moscow, Akademiia nauk, Institut Afriki, 2003. 191pp.

See also **3228**

YEARBOOKS

833 Annuaire de la Côte française des Somalis. Djibouti, Service d'information de la Côte française des Somalis. 1955- ?1959. (Title varies: **Guide-annuaire** ...)

834 Annuaire des entreprises Djibouti/Djibouti business directory. Djibouti, Chambre de commerce de Djibouti, 2003- . ?Annual.

See also **3302**.

STATISTICS

835 Country profile: Djibouti. London, Economist Intelligence Unit, 2004-Annual. *Continues in part* **Country profile: Ethiopia, Somalia, Djibouti**. London, 1986-1992; **Country profile: Ethiopia, Eritrea, Somalia, Djibouti**. London, 1993-1996; **Country profile: Eritrea, Somalia, Djibouti**. London, 1997-2003.

836 Djibouti. Direction nationale de la statistique [etc.]. **Annuaire statistique de Djibouti 1975/78** [etc.]. Djibouti, 1971- . Annual. Last issue in LC is for 2000.

837 Djibouti. Direction nationale de la statistique [etc.]/French Territory of the Afars and Issas. Service de statistique et documentation. **Bulletin semestriel de statistique**. Djibouti, 1970- . Quarterly (irreg.). Title varies: **Bulletin de statistique et de documentation** (issues 1-31); **Bulletin trimestriel de statistique** (issues 32-36). Issue 41, 1987. ALA notes issue for 1991

838 Dossier national: Djibouti, comp. Abdallah Dini. Louvain-le-Neuve, Centre international de formation et de recherche en population et développement (CIDEP), 1995. 48pp. (Contemporary statistics)

839 Germany. Statistisches Bundesamt. **Statistik des Auslandes: Länderberichte: Dschibuti**. Wiesbaden/ Stuttgart, Metzler-Poetschel, 1983.

840 IMF. **Djibouti, statistical appendix**. Washington, DC, 2004. (IMF country report, 04/75). 53pp. - - Earlier issues (title varies) 1996 (Country report, 96/44); 1998 (Country report, 98/70); 1999 (Country report, 99/137). Full text of reports from 1997 also available online, *see* **334**

ATLASES & GAZETTEERS

841 U.S. Board on Geographic Names. **Gazetteer of Djibouti**. Washington, DC, 1983. 151pp. (Rev. version of the appropriate section in **Ethiopia, Eritrea and the Somalilands ...** (*see* 802). Includes 6,750 entries from maps at scale of 1:100,000)

EARTH SCIENCES

842 Boucarut, Marc et al. **Étude stratigraphique de la république de Djibouti**. Bordeaux, Université de Bordeaux III, 1980. 56pp. illus. maps.

843 Vellutin, Pierre & Piguet, Patrick. **Djibouti: itinéraires géologiques**. Djibouti, Imprimerie nationale, 1994. 289pp. illus. maps.

BIOLOGICAL SCIENCES

844 Audru, Jacques et al. **Les plantes vasculaires de la république de Djibouti: flore illustrée**. Djibouti, Mission française de coopération et d'action culturelle de Djibouti, 1994. 2 vols. in 3. 968pp. illus. maps. (Pub. with the co-operation of CIRAD. Covers 783 spp. "A work more of prestige than of real utility", Frodin, 2001, 513)

845 Audru, Jacques, et al. **La végétation et les potentialités pastorales de la république de Djibouti**. Maisons-Alfort, IEMVT, 1987. 384pp. illus. maps.

846 Lebrun, Jean-Pierre et al. **Catalogue des plantes vasculaires de la république de Djibouti**. Maisons-Alfort, IEMVT, 1989. (Études et synthèses, 34). 277pp. illus.

847 Simoneau, Edmond-Louis. **Les animaux du térritoire français des Afars et des Issas**. Djibouti, author, 1973. 153pp. (Describes principal spp., 61 mammals, 100 birds, 13 reptiles, with b. & w. drawings)

ERITREA

Many of the sources noted under Ethiopia will also cover the area of Eritrea

HANDBOOKS

848   Eritrea a country handbook, ed. Dan Connell. Asmara, Ministry of Information, 2002. 131pp. illus. maps.

849   Eritrea at a glance. Rev. ed. comp. Mary Houdek & Leonardo Oriolo. Asmara, International Guidebook Committee, 1996. vi, 209pp. illus. maps. - - Orig. pub. ed. Alli Alamin. Asmara, 1995. 68pp. illus. maps.

850   Eritrea: country profile. Washington, DC, Library of Congress. Federal Research Division, 2005. 16pp. Also available at: http://lcweb2.loc.gov /frd/cs/profiles/Eritrea.pdf.

851   G.B. War Office. General Staff (Intelligence). Headquarters Troops in the Sudan. **Handbook of Eritrea. Vol. 2, Communications**. Khartoum, 1943. iii, 195pp. illus. maps. (Revised version of vol. 2 of the **Handbook of Western Italian East Africa** (*see* **868**), omitting Abyssinia and giving greatly increased detail on each route and more illustrations. Map at 1:1M)

852   Historical dictionary of Eritrea, comp. Tom Killion. Lanham, MD, Scarecrow Press, 1998. (African historical dictionaries, 75). xli, 535pp. (Reviews, *African affairs*, 98, 1999, 253-254; *Africa today*, 47, 2000, 196-198; *ARD*, 84, 2000, 83-90; *ASR*, 42 (3) 1999, 93-94; *CJAS*, 32, 1998, 632-634; *JMAS*, 37, 1999, 361-362. Replaces entries for Eritrea in **Historical dictionary of Ethiopia and Eritrea**. Lanham, MD, 1994. *See* **870** below)

YEARBOOKS

853   Eritrea business directory. Asmara, Eritrean National Chamber of Commerce, 199? Issue for 1999/2000 (1999)

STATISTICS

854   Country profile: Eritrea. London, Economist Intelligence Unit, 2004- . Annual. *Continues in part* **Country profile: Eritrea, Somalia, Djibouti**. London, 1997-2003.

855   Eritrea. National Statistics Office. **Eritrea: demographic and health survey**. Asmara, 1997. xx, 324pp. (Detailed statistical compilation supported by the U.S. Agency for International Development (AID)

856   IMF. **Eritrea: selected issues and statistical appendix**. Washington, DC, 2003. (Country report, 03/166). 120pp. - - Earlier ed. (title varies) 2000 (Country report 00/55). Full text of reports also available online, *see* **334**

BIOGRAPHICAL SOURCES

857   Puglisi, Giuseppe. **Chi é? dell'Eritrea: dizionario biografico: con una cronologia**. Asmara, Agenzia Regina, 1952. xxiii, 304pp. (Basically concerned with resident Italians)

ATLASES & GAZETTEERS

858   Italy. Istituto Geografico Militare. **Indice dei nomi contenuti nella carta demostrativa della colonie Eritrea e regioni adiacenti alla scala di 1:400,000.** [Florence, ?1940] 128pp.

BIOLOGICAL SCIENCES

859   Bein, E. et al. **Useful trees and shrubs in Eritrea: identification, propagation and management for agricultural and pastoral communities**. Nairobi, Regional Soil Conservation Unit (RSCU) & SIDA, 1996. xxxviii, 422pp. illus. maps.

ETHIOPIA

HANDBOOKS

860   Economic handbook of Ethiopia. Rev. ed. Addis Ababa, Ethiopia Ministry of Commerce & Industry, 1958. xii, 171pp. illus. map. - - Orig. pub. Addis Ababa, 1951. 212pp.

861   Ethiopia: a country study. 4ᵗʰ ed. comp. Thomas P. Ofcansky & Laverle Berry Washington, DC, Library of Congress, Federal Research Division. 1993. xxvi, 412pp. Also available at: http://lcweb2.loc.gov/frd/cs/ettoc.html. - - Orig. pub. as **Area handbook for Ethiopia**, comp. George A. Lipsky et al. Washington, DC, U.S. Department of Defense, 1960. xi, 621pp. maps. (Reprinted, 1964); - - 2ⁿᵈ ed. comp. Irving Kaplan et al. Washington, DC, 1971. xiv, 543pp. maps; - - 3ʳᵈ ed. comp. Irving Kaplan & Harold D. Nelson. Washington DC, 1981. xxix, 366pp. illus. maps.

862   Ethiopia: country profile. Washington, DC, Library of Congress. Federal Research Division, 2005. 21pp. Also available at: http://lcweb2.loc.gov/ frd/cs/profiles/Ethiopia.pdf)

863   Ethiopia: the handbook for Ethiopia, incorporating welcome to Ethiopia. Nairobi, University Press of Africa for Ethiopia Ministry of Information, 1969. 328pp. illus. maps. (Topographic, political and economic information. Includes economic statistics and business directory)

864   Ewert, Kurt. Äethiopien. Bonn, K. Schroeder for Deutsche Afrika-Gesellschaft, 1959. (Die Länder Afrikas, 22). 99pp.

865   Facts about Ethiopia. Addis Ababa, Ministry of Information, Press & Audiovisual Department, 2004. 203pp. (Noted in EBAS-AIEO)

866   Gräber, Gerd et al. Äthiopien: ein Reiseführer. Heidelberg, Kasparek, 1997. 225pp. illus. maps. (Information on topography, history, peoples, culture and politics, with only a small section on actual travel advice. City plans)

867   G.B. War Office. General Staff. Intelligence Division. A handbook of Ethiopia, provisional ed. Khartoum, 1941. 150pp.

868   G.B. War Office. General Staff (Intelligence). Headquarters Troops in the Sudan. Handbook of Western Italian East Africa. Khartoum, 1941. (B.1214, B.1214-1). 2 vols. Vol. 1, General. iv, 195pp. maps. (Includes gazetteer of 71 settlements. Covers Abyssinia and Eritrea to the north and west of Addis

Ababa); vol. 2, Communications. ii, 263pp. illus. maps. (Includes itineraries for some 60 road routes with the "greater part of information taken from **Africa orientale italiana**" (*see* **790**). Maps of whole region at 1:6M and of western region at 1:2M)

869 Guide book of Ethiopia. Addis Ababa, Ethiopian Chamber of Commerce, 1954. xxx, 443pp. illus. maps. (Sections on government, people, culture, physiography, climate, geology, agriculture, commerce, industry and finance, together with much general information and statistics and notes on each province. Bibliography, pp. 417-433. Numerous photos and maps)

870 Historical dictionary of Ethiopia. New ed., comp. David H. Shinn & Thomas P. Ofcansky. Lanham, MD, Scarecrow Press, 2004. (African historical dictionaries, 91). lx, 633pp. (Review, *ARD*, 99, 2005, 51-54, "stands head and shoulders above the rest". Rev. of the material on Ethiopia previously published in **Historical dictionary of Ethiopia and Eritrea**, 2nd ed. comp. Chris Prouty & Eugene Rosenfeld. Metuchen, NJ, Scarecrow Press, 1994. (African historical dictionaries, 56). xxvi, 614pp. - - Orig. pub. as **Historical dictionary of Ethiopia**, comp. Chris Prouty & Eugene Rosenfeld. Metuchen, NJ, 1981. (African historical dictionaries, 32). xv, 436pp. (Review, *JAH*, 23, 1983, 425)

871 Leclercq, Claude. **L'empire d'Éthiopie**. Paris, Berger-Levrault, 1969. (Encyclopédie politique et constitutionnelle. Série Afrique). 79pp.

872 Lipsky, George A. et al. **Ethiopia: its people, its society, its culture**. New Haven, CN, Human Relations Area Files, 1962. (Survey of world cultures, 9). xii, 376pp. illus. maps. ("Prepared under the auspices of the American University, Washington". Detailed survey with sections on history, geography, ethnic groups, languages, literature, administration, economy)

873 Petros, Yohannes. **Ethiopia in brief: basic facts**. Addis Ababa, Tesfa Print Press, 1979. 100pp. + 26pp. plates.

874 Rosenfeld, Chris Prouty. **A chronology of Menilek II of Ethiopia, 1844-1913, Emperor of Ethiopia, 1889-1913**. East Lansing, MI, Michigan State University, Committee on Ethiopian Studies, 1976. ix, 282pp.

875 Van Beurden, Jos. **Ethiopië: mensen, politiek, economie, cultuur**. Amsterdam, Koninklijk Instituut voor de Tropen/The Hague, Novib, 2004. (Landenreeks). 80pp.

Date-conversion tables

876   Conti-Rossini, Carlo. **Tabelle comparative del calendario etiopico col calendario romano**. Rome, Istituto per l'Oriente, 1948. 47pp. (Comparative date tables from 1341 to 2000 A.D. More extensive tables for the modern period, converting both the Coptic and the Ethiopic calendars into a further eight calendars including the Julian and Georgian are available in Edward M. Reingold & Nachum Derskowitz. **Calendrical tabulations, 1900-2200**. Cambridge,   Cambridge   University   Press,   2001.   *See   also* http://www.calendarists.com)

877   Hammerschmidt, Ernst. **Äthiopische Kalendertafeln**. Wiesbaden, Franz Steiner, 1977. 21pp. (Reprinted from the author's **Äthiopische Handschriften vom Tanasee**. Vol. 2, Die Handschriften von Dabra Maryam und von Rema. Wiesbaden, F. Steiner Verlag, 1977. Conversion tables from the Ethiopian calendar to the Julian and Gregorian calendars)

YEARBOOKS

878   **Trade directory and guide book to Ethiopia**. Addis Ababa, Ethiopian Chamber of Commerce, 1954- . Irreg. (Title varies: **Ethiopian trade directory**. Issues traced for 1954, 1967, 1971/72, 1976, 1984, 1990, 1994, 1998/9. Includes general geographical and economic information, and a commercial directory)

879   **Trade directory of the Empire of Ethiopia**; including classified trade index. London, Diplomatic Press & Publishing Co., 1965. 64pp. (Announced as an annual but no more pub.)

See also **1015**.

STATISTICS

880   **Country profile: Ethiopia**. London, Economist Intelligence Unit, 1997- Annual. *Continues in part* **Country profile: Ethiopia, Somalia, Djibouti**. London, 1986-1992; **Country profile: Ethiopia, Eritrea, Somalia, Djibouti**. London, 1993-1996.

881   Ethiopia. Central Statistical Office [etc.]. **Statistical abstract**. Addis Ababa, 1963- . Annual (bi-annual, 1980-). Text in English and Amharic. 1967/68 issued as one vol. Not issued for 1973-74. NWU has issue for 2004. - - Abbreviated version issued as **Statistical pocket book** (later **People's Democratic Republic of Ethiopia in facts and figures**) Addis Ababa, 1963- .

882   Ethiopia. Central Statistical Office [etc.]. **Statistical bulletin**. Addis Ababa,   1968- . Irreg. SOAS holds issue 205 for 1999.

883   Germany. Statistisches Bundesamt. **Statistik des Auslandes: Länderberichte: Äthiopien** (later **Länderbericht: Äthiopien**). Wiesbaden/ Stuttgart, Metzler-Poetschel, 1965- . Irreg. Issues for 1965, 1972, 1982, 1990.

884   IMF. **The Federal Democratic Republic of Ethiopia: selected issues and statistical appendix**. Washington, DC, 2006. (Country report 06/122). 64pp. - - Earlier eds. (title varies) 1998 (Staff country report, 98/06); 2005 (Country report, 05/28). Full text of reports also available online, *see* **334**.

DIRECTORIES OF ORGANIZATIONS

885   **Directory of Ethiopian libraries**, comp. Geraldine Odester Amos. Addis Ababa, Ethiopian Library Association, 1968. 76pp. (Lists 94 libraries)

886   **eBizguides Ethiopia**. Dublin, eBiz guides, 2004. 232pp. illus. maps. (Includes general background information and statistics, sections for 'The economy', pp. 41-198, including directory; 'Tourism and leisure', pp. 199-231)

887   **Profile of science and technology professional associations in Ethiopia**. Addis Ababa, Ethiopian Science & Technology Commission, 1998. 57pp.   Also   available   at   http://www.estc.gov.et/Professional%20 Assocations.pdf.   (Directory   of   40   Ethiopian   non-governmental organizations)

See also **1032**

BIOGRAPHICAL SOURCES

888   **Dictionary of Ethiopian biography**, ed. Belaynesh Michael et al. Addis Ababa, Addis Ababa University, Institute of Ethiopian Studies, 1975- . Vol. 1. 1975. From early times to the end of the Zagwé Dynasty c.1270 A. D. 218pp. No more pub. (Review, *IJAHS*, 10, 1977, 517-519)

889   **Encyclopedia Africana dictionary of African biography. Vol. 1, Ethiopia and Ghana**. Algonac, MI, Reference Publications, 1977. 367pp. (Ethiopia, pp. 22-166, ed. R.L. Haas. Historical introduction, pp. 22-41, by Richard Pankhurst. 152 entries, many with portraits, and bibliographies. Includes entries for Europeans, e.g. James Bruce, Orde Wingate. Reviews, *IJAHS*, 11, 1978, 546-550; *JAH*, 20, 1979, 310-312, "solid scholarship ...

unquestionably a work of major importance". For the planned encyclopedia as a whole *see* **11**; for the dictionary of biography *see* **545**)

890 Tekle-Tsadik Mekouria. **Les noms propres, les noms de baptême et l'étude généalogique des rois d'Éthiopie (XIII-XX siècles) à travers leurs noms patronymiques**. Belgrade, author, 1966. ii, 186pp. (Mimeo)

891 Verdier, Isabelle. **Ethiopia: the top 100 people**. Paris, Indigo, 1997. 195pp.

See also **64**

ATLASES & GAZETTEERS

892 **An atlas of Ethiopia**. Rev. ed. comp. M. Wolde-Mariam. Addis Ababa, Ethiopia Ministry of Education, 1969. x, 84pp. (53 b. & w. maps, plus text, diagrams and reproductions of aerial photos. Majority of maps at 1:9M. "The boundaries shown on these maps are not necessarily those recognized by the Imperial Ethiopian Government", pref. Review, *GJ*, 139, 1973, 381). - - Orig. pub. as **Preliminary atlas of Ethiopia**. Addis Ababa, 1962. 47pp.)

893 Ethiopian Mapping Authority. http://www.telecom.net.et/~ema/

894 Italy. Ministero dell'Africa Italiana. Servizio Cartografico. **Indice dei nomi contenuti nella III edizione della carta dell'A.O.I. a 1:200,000**. Bergamo, [?1940]. 79pp.

895 **National atlas of Ethiopia**. 1st ed. Addis Ababa, Ethiopian Mapping Agency, 1988. viii, 156pp. 39 x 39cm. (76 thematic col. maps, including 12 on historical themes, and accompanying text. Principal scale 1:5M). - - Orig. pub. as Prelim. ed. Addis Ababa, 1981. 93pp. 90 b. & w. maps. (*See* B. Winid, 'A national atlas for Ethiopia', *Ethiopian geographical journal*, 4, 1966, 38-41)

896 U.S. Board on Geographic Names. **Gazetteer of Ethiopia**. Washington, DC, 1982. xxii, 663pp. (Rev. version of appropriate section of **Ethiopia, Eritrea and the Somalilands** ... (*see* **802**). Includes 30,500 names from maps at 1:250,000)

EARTH SCIENCES

897 Huffnagel, H. P. **Agriculture in Ethiopia**. Rome, FAO, 1961. xv, 484pp. illus. maps.

898   Italy. Ministero degli Affari Esteri. **Contributo alla climatologia dell'Etiopia**, ed. Amilcare Fàntoli. Rome, 1965. lxxxxv, 558pp. (Massive compilation of climatological readings)

899   Jelenc, Danilo A. **Mineral occurrences of Ethiopia**. Addis Ababa, Ministry of Mines, 1966. 720pp. illus. maps.

900   Kazmin, V. **Explanation of the geological map of Ethiopia**; summarised by A.J. Warden. Addis Ababa, Geological Survey of Ethiopia, 1975. (Bulletin, 1). 14pp. (To accompany 1:2M Geological map of Ethiopia, Addis Ababa, Geological Survey, 1973)

901   Mohr, Paul A. **The geology of Ethiopia**. Addis Ababa, University College of Addis Ababa, 1964. vii, 268pp. illus. maps. Reprinted Addis Ababa, 1971. (Includes discussion of the wider Horn of Africa region)

902   Morton, Bill. **A field guide to Ethiopian minerals, rocks and fossils**. Addis Ababa, Addis Ababa University Press, 1978. vii, 170pp. illus.

BIOLOGICAL SCIENCES

Zoology

903   Hill, Dennis S. **Catalogue of crop pests of Ethiopia**. Alemaya, Alemaya University of Agriculture, Department of Plant Sciences, 1989. iii, 104pp.

904   Largen, M.J. 'Catalogue of the amphibians of Ethiopia, including a key for their identification', *Tropical zoology*, 14, 2001, 307-342

905   Largen, M.J. & Rasmussen, J.B. 'Catalogue of the snakes of Ethiopia (Reptilia: Serpentes), including identification keys', *Tropical zoology*, 6, 1993, 313-434

906   Urban, Emil K. & Brown, Leslie H. **A checklist of the birds of Ethiopia**. Addis Ababa, Haile Selassie I University Press, 1971. 143pp. (Reprinted, Addis Abba, 1994)

907   Yalden, David W. et al. 'Catalogue of the mammals of Ethiopia [& Eritrea], 1. Chiroptera', *Monitore zoologico italiano*, n.s. Suppl. 5(16) 1974, 221-298; '2, Insectivora and Rodentia', *ibid.*, Suppl. 8(1) 1976, 1-118; '3, Primates', *ibid.* Suppl. 9(1) 1977, 1-52; '4, Carnivora', *ibid.* Suppl. 13(8) 1980, 169-272; '5,

Artiodactyla', *ibid*. Suppl. 14(4) 1984, 67-221; '6. Perissodactyla [to] Cetacea', *ibid*. Suppl. 21(4) 1986, 31-103; '7, Revised checklist, zoogeography and conservation', *Tropical zoology*, 9, 1996, 73-164

Botany

908 Bekele-Tesemma, Azene et al. **Useful trees and shrubs for Ethiopia: identification, propagation and management for agricultural and pastoral communities**. Nairobi, Regional Soil Conservation Unit (RSCU) & SIDA, 1993. x, 474pp. illus. maps.

909 Demissew, Sebsebe. **Field guide to Ethiopian orchids**. Kew, Royal Botanic Gardens, 2004. 300pp. illus. (Review, *Journal of East African natural history*, 94, 2005, 371-372)

910 Fröman, Bengt & Persson, Sven. **An illustrated guide to the grasses of Ethiopia**. Asella, Chilalo Agricultural Development Unit (CADU), 1974. 504pp. illus. (In relation particularly to their use as fodder crops. Pp.141-504, b. & w. illus)

911 Thirakul, Souane. **Manual of dendrology for the south, south-east and south-west of Ethiopia**. Addis Ababa, Canadian International Development Agency (CIDA), 1994. iv, 478pp. illus.

912 Von Breitenbach, Friedrich. **The indigenous trees of Ethiopia**. 2nd rev. ed. Addis Ababa, Ethiopian Forestry Association, 1963. 306pp. illus. - - Orig. pub. Addis Ababa, 1960.

913 Wolde, Michael Kalecha. **A glossary of Ethiopian plant names**. 3rd ed. Addis Ababa, author, 1980. xiii, 262pp. - - Orig. pub. comp. Henry Francis Mooney. Dublin, Dublin University Press, 1963. viii, 79pp; - - 2nd ed. Addis Ababa, n.p., 1977. viii, 175pp. illus

SOMALIA

Official Government Web site for Somalia. http://www.somali-gov.info/
(Note also http://www.somalilandgov.com/, the Web site of the Republic of
Somaliland, an unrecognized breakaway state in the north west since 1991)

HANDBOOKS

914   Bader, Christian. **Les noms de personnes chez les Somali**. Paris,
Harmattan, 2004. 288pp.

915   G.B. War Office. General Staff. **Military report on Somaliland, 1940**.
London, 1940. (B. 454). iii, 83pp. map. (Covers history, geography,
ethnography, communications. Map at 1:2M)

916   **Historical dictionary of Somalia**. New ed. comp. Mohamed Haji
Mukhtar. Lanham, MD, Scarecrow Press, 2003. (African historical
dictionaries, 87). xlv, 353pp. (Review, *ARBA*, 35, 2004, 213, "solid
contribution"). - - Orig. pub. comp. Margaret Castagno, Metuchen, NJ, 1975.
(African historical dictionaries, 6). xxviii, 213pp. (Rated "excellent", Balay,
1996)

917   Hunt, John A. **A general survey of the Somaliland Protectorate, 1944-
1950**. Final report on 'An economic survey and reconnaissance of the British
Somaliland Protectorate, 1944-1950', Colonial Development and Welfare
Scheme D. 484. London, Crown Agent for the Colonies, 1951. 203pp. maps.
(Includes information on topography, climate, resources, with accounts of
tribes and genealogies and a gazetteer, pp. 16-39)

918   Johnson, J.W. **Historical atlas of the Horn of Africa**. Mogadishu, 1967.
15 pp. (Author was a U.S. Peace Corps volunteer in Somalia, 1966-69. 15 hand-
drawn, cyclostyled maps showing changing boundaries between Somalia and
its neighbours, 1888-1967)

919   Lewis, Ioan Myrddin. **Understanding Somalia: a guide to culture,
history and social institutions**. 2nd ed. London, HAAN Associates, 1993.
111pp. (Covers anthropology, history, economics. Includes chronology and
glossary). - - Orig. pub. London, 1981.

920   **Socio-economic survey, 2002**. Nairobi, World Bank & UNDP, Somalia
country office, 2003. xiv, 109pp.

921   Somalia. Ministry of Information & National Guidance. **Somalia today: general information**, comp. Ismail Mohamed Ali. Rev. ed. Mogadishu, 1970. vii, 311pp.

922   **Somalia: a country study**. 4th ed., ed. Helen Chapin Metz. Washington, DC, U.S. Government Printing Office, 1993. xxxvii, 282pp. illus., maps. Also available at: http://lcweb2.loc.gov/frd/cs/sotoc.html. (Review, *Northeast African studies*, n.s. 2, 1995, 189-190). - - Orig. pub. as **Area handbook for Somalia**, comp. Irving Kaplan et al. Washington, DC, U.S. Department of Defense, 1969. xiv, 455pp. maps; - - 2nd ed. Washington, DC, 1977. xvi, 392pp. maps; - - 3rd ed. **Somalia: a country study**, comp. Harold D. Nelson. Washington, DC, 1982. 346pp. illus. maps.

923   Zöhrer, Ludwig G.A. **Somaliländer**. Bonn, K. Schroeder for Deutsche Afrika-Gesellschaft, 1959. (Die Länder Afrikas, 17). 194pp. illus. maps.

YEARBOOKS

924   **Chamber of Commerce directory**. Mogadishu, Somali Chamber of Commerce, Industry & Agriculture, 1983- . Issue for 1983/84 in LC. - - Earlier ed. **Trade directory/Guida commerciale.** Mogadishu, Somali Chamber of Commerce, Industry & Agriculture. Issue for 1977/78 in LC

925   G.B. Colonial Office. **[Annual reports]: Somaliland, 1904-1959**. London, 1906-1960. (As **Annual report on Somaliland**, 1904/05-1919/20 (as Command papers); **Colonial Office annual report**, 1920-1958 (not pub. 1938-1947). From 1950/1951-1958/1959 pub. biennially)

926   Italy. Ministero degli Affari Esteri. **Rapport du gouvernement italien à l'assemblée générale des Nations Unies sur l'administration de tutelle de la Somalie, 1951 [-1959]**. Rome, 1952-60. Annual. 9 issues. (Each vol. has a large range of statistics and administrative information)

927   **The Somali business community guide, July 1987**. Mogadishu, Halane Marketing & Advertising, 1987. 41pp. (Alphabetical by company: no index)

STATISTICS

928   **Country profile: Somalia**. London, Economist Intelligence Unit, 2004- Annual. *Continues in part* **Country profile: Ethiopia, Somalia, Djibouti**. London, 1986-1992; **Country profile: Ethiopia, Eritrea, Somalia, Djibouti**.

London, 1993-1996; **Country profile: Eritrea, Somalia, Djibouti**. London, 1997-2003.

929 Germany. Statistisches Bundesamt. **Statistik des Auslandes: Länderberichte: Somalia** (later **Länderbericht: Somalia**). Wiesbaden/ Stuttgart, Metzler-Poetschel, 1966- . Irreg. Issues for 1966, 1967, 1970, 1974, 1984, 1986, 1988, 1991.

930 Somalia. Central Statistical Department [etc.]. **Somalia in figures**. Mogadishu, 1965- . Every 3 years. Latest in LC is 11th ed. 1990.

931 Somalia. Central Statistical Department [etc.]. **Statistical abstract**. Mogadishu, 1964-?1988. Annual. From 1964-1971 had added title **Compendio statistico** with text in English and Italian; from 1972 text in English and Somali, with added title **Koobaha istaatistikada**. Latest issues in NWU are for 1988.

932 Somalia. Ministry of Planning & Co-ordination. **Monthly statistical bulletin**. Mogadishu, 1967-?1989. Title varies: **Somali statistics: monthly bulletin**. (1967-1972). From 1978 also has title **Faafinta istaatistikada bisha**. SOAS has issues for 1972, 1973-74, 1978-83, 1989. NWU also has issue for 1985) *Continues* Somalia. Planning Directorate. Statistical Department. **Bollettino trimestrale di statistica/Quarterly statistical bulletin**. Mogadishu, 1965-1966.

ATLASES & GAZETTEERS

933 **An atlas for Somalis/Atlaska Soomaalida**, prepared & designed by UNDP Data & Information Management Unit in collaboration with UNESCO Programme of Education for Emergencies & Reconstruction (UNESCO PEER). Paris, UNESCO, 2004. 64pp. (Recorded in EBAS-EAIO)

934 Somaliland Protectorate. Survey Department. **Gazetteer of place names, British Somaliland and grazing areas**. Rev. ed. [Hargeisa], 1946. 45pp. - - Orig. pub. Hargeisa, 1945. 45pp.

935 U.S. Board on Geographic Names. **Gazetteer of Somalia**. 2nd ed. Washington, DC, 1987. xviii, 519pp. - - Orig. pub. Washington, 1982. xii, 231pp (Rev. version of the appropriate sections of **Ethiopia, Eritrea and the Somalilands ...** (*see* **802**). 23,000 entries based on maps at 1:200,000)

BIOLOGICAL SCIENCES

Zoology

936   Archer, Sir Geoffrey Francis & Godman, Eva M. **The birds of British Somaliland and the Gulf of Aden: their life histories, breeding habits and eggs**. London, Gurney & Jackson/Edinburgh, Oliver & Boyd, 1937-61. 4 vols. 1,570pp. illus. (Large scale descriptive avifauna: *see also* **1120**)

937   Ash, John S. & Miskell, J.E. **Birds of Somalia**. London, Pica Press, 1998. 304pp. 8 col. plates. (Atlas showing ranges of 650 spp; some 50 spp. illus. Reviews, *BABC*, 7, 2000, 80; *Ibis*, 141, 1999, 152. Rev. ed. of their **Birds of Somalia: their habitat, status and distribution**. Nairobi, East African Natural History Society, 1983. (*Scopus*, special suppl., 1). 95pp. (Covers 639 spp.)

938   Funaioli, Ugo. **Guida breve dei mammiferi della Somalia**. Florence, Istituto Agronomico per l'Oltremare, 1971. 232pp. + 17pp. plates. illus.

939   Funaioli, Ugo & Simonetta, A.M. **Nomi vernacolari degli animali in Somalia e denominazioni corrispondenti in Latino, Inglese ed Italiano: primo elenco**. Florence, Istituto Agronomico per l'Oltremare, 1985. 93pp. maps.

940   Lanza, Benedetto. 'A list of the Somali amphibians and reptiles', *Monitore zoologico italiano*, n.s. suppl. 18(8) 1993, 193-247

941   Parker, Hampton W. **The snakes of Somaliland and the Sokotra Islands**. Leiden, Brill, 1949. (Zoologische verhandelingen, 6). 115pp. illus. map.

942   Sommer, Corinna, et al. **The living marine resources of Somalia**. Rome, FAO, 1996. (FAO species identification guide for fishery purposes). vii, 376pp. + 32pp. plates. illus.

Botany

943   Cope, Thomas A. **Key to Somali grasses**. Mogadishu, National Herbarium, National Range Agency, 1985. 77pp. illus. map.

944   **Flora of Somalia**, ed. Mats Thulin. Kew, Royal Botanic Gardens, 1993-2006. 4 vols. illus. Vol. 1. 1993. 493pp; vol. 2. 1999. 303pp; vol. 3. 2006. 456pp; vol. 4. 1995. 298pp. (Flora of Somalia Project administered by Department of Systematic Botany, Uppsala University)

945 Glover, Phillip Earle. **A provisional check-list of British and Italian Somaliland trees, shrubs and herbs,** including the reserved areas adjacent to Abyssinia. London, Crown Agents, 1947. 446pp. illus. map.

946 Kuchar, Peter. **The plants of Somalia: an overview and checklist.** Mogadishu, Central Rangelands Development Project, National Range Agency & L. Berger International, [1986]. 2 vols. 339pp. (Mimeograph).

947 Mahoney, Desmond. **Trees of Somalia: a fieldguide for development workers.** Oxford, Oxfam in conjunction with Henry Doubleday Research Association, 1990. viii, 196pp. illus. maps.

SUDAN

Government of the Sudan Web site http://www.sudan.gov.sd/

HANDBOOKS

948   Al-Shahi, Ahmed. **La république du Soudan**. Paris, Berger-Levrault, 1979. (Encyclopédie politique et constitutionnelle. Série Afrique). 83pp.

949   G.B. War Office. General Staff (Intelligence). Headquarters Troops in the Sudan. **The Anglo-Egyptian Sudan: handbook of topographical intelligence**. Khartoum, 1940. (B. 1215). vi, 229pp. illus. maps. (Detailed topographic and economic information. Includes descriptive gazetteer of 32 settlements. Plans of Port Sudan, 1:10,000 and Khartoum, 1:20,000)

950   Herzog, Rolf. **Sudan**. 2nd ed. Bonn, K. Schroeder for Deutsche Afrika-Gesellschaft, 1961. (Die Länder Afrikas, 8). 101pp. illus. maps. - - Orig. pub. Bonn, 1958. 85pp.

951   **Historical dictionary of ancient and medieval Nubia**, comp. Richard Andrew Lobban. Lanham, MD, Scarecrow Press, 2004. (Historical dictionaries of ancient civilizations and historical eras, 10). lx, 522pp. (The result of a decision by Scarecrow Press to split the coverage of their historical dictionary of the Sudan into two vols. for the early and modern periods. This vol. covers pre, ancient and medieval history up to the end of the Christian kingdoms in c.1500 A.D. Reviews, *ARD*, 97, 2005, 45-47; *IJAHS*, 38, 2005, 125-126; *JAH*, 46, 2005, 328-330)

952   **Historical dictionary of the Sudan**. 3rd ed. comp. Richard Andrew Lobban et al. Lanham, MD, Scarecrow Press, 2002. (African historical dictionaries, 85). cviii, 396pp. (Covers from the Islamic period to date. For coverage of the pre 1500 period, included in earlier eds., *see* **951**). - - Orig. pub. comp. John O. Voll. Metuchen, NJ, 1978. (African historical dictionaries, 17). xvii, 175pp. (Reviews, *Africana J*, 10, 1979, 120-128; *ASA review of books*, 6, 1980, 199-209; *IJAHS*, 14, 1981, 770-772); - - 2nd ed., comp. Carolyn Fluehr-Lobban et al. Metuchen, NJ, 1992. (African historical dictionaries, 53). cvii, 409pp. (Reviews, *Africa*, 67, 1997, 159-173; *ARD*, 59/60, 1992, 36; *Choice*, 30, 1993, 1600-1601; *IJAHS*, 26, 1993, 651-653; *JAH*, 35, 1994, 171-172. Rated "excellent", Balay, 1996)

953   Sudan. Ministry of Culture & Information. **Sudan facts and figures**. Khartoum, 1974. 62pp.

954 **Sudan: a country study**. 4th ed. comp. Helen C. Metz. Washington, DC, Library of Congress, Federal Research Division, 1992. xxxiii, 336pp. illus. maps. Also available at: http://lcweb2.loc.gov/frd/cs/sdtoc.html. - - Orig. pub. as **Area handbook for the Republic of the Sudan**, comp. John A. Cookson et al. Washington, DC, U.S. Department of Defense, 1960. viii, 473pp. maps; - - 2nd ed. **Area handbook for the Democratic Republic of Sudan**, comp. Harold D. Nelson et al. Washington, DC, 1973. xiv, 351pp; - - 3rd ed. Washington, DC, 1982. 365pp.

955 **Sudan: country profile**. Washington, DC, Library of Congress. Federal Research Division 2004. 16pp. Also available at: http://lcweb2.loc.gov/ frd/cs/profiles/Sudan.pdf

956 **Sudan today**. Nairobi, University Press of Africa for Sudan Ministry of Information & Culture, 1971. iv, 234pp. (Covers topography, history, administration, health, education, the economy, agriculture. Includes statistics)

957 Van Beurden, Jos. **Sudan: mensen, politiek, economie, cultuur**. Amsterdam, Koninklijk Instituut voor de Tropen/The Hague, Novib, 2006. (Landenreeks). 128pp.

958 Willis, Charles Armine. **The Upper Nile Province handbook: a report on peoples and government in the Southern Sudan, 1931**; ed. Douglas H. Johnson. Oxford, Oxford University Press for British Academy, 1995. (Oriental and African archives, 3). xx, 476p. (Compiled by Willis as the retiring Governor of the Province, and submitted to the Civil Secretary's Office, Khartoum, but not pub. at the time. This version uses the text of the original in the National Record Office, Khartoum, Civsec 57/2/8, with detailed critical apparatus added by Johnson. Reviews, *African affairs*, 96, 1997, 460-462; *BSOAS*, 60, 1997, 426-427)

See also **1006**.

YEARBOOKS

959 G.B. Foreign Office. **[Annual reports]: Sudan, 1899-1952.** London, 1899-1956. Annual. (As **Report by HM Agent and Consul General on the finances, administration and condition of Egypt and the Soudan**, 1899-1920, **Report on the finances, administration and condition of the Sudan**, 1921-52 (all as Command papers). 1914-1919 covered in one report, reports for 1939/41 and 1942/44 issued 1950/51)

960   Sudan almanac 1884/85 [etc.]. London, Khartoum etc., 1884-?1971. Annual. Issuing body varies: pre-independence issued by G.B. War Office, Intelligence Department, *later* Egypt. Intelligence Department, *later* Sudan. Intelligence Department; post-independence by Sudan. Public Relations Office, etc. (A long-running title growing from a first issue containing 14pp. of purely calendrical information to issues of 350+ pages by 1960s including detailed historical, administrative and topographical information, statistics, lists of government departments and agencies and other institutions, and a directory of newspapers and periodicals)

961   Sudan directory. Khartoum/Cairo, Sudan Advertising & Publishing Co., 1921-1951/52. Annual. ('Patronized by the Sudan Government'. Substantial work; 1921 ed. 726pp., includes civil list, directory of British residents, texts of ordinances, statistics, and a commercial directory)

962   Sudan guide. Khartoum, Planning & Management Consultancy, 1980- Annual. NWU has issues for 1981 to 1984/85

963   Sudan trade directory. London, Diplomatic Press & Publishing Co., (Diprepu Co.) Ltd., 1958-?1980. Annual (irreg.). Title varies: **Trade directory of the Republic of the Sudan 1957/58 [-1965/66]**. (Includes lists of officials, statistics, commercial directory. 1st to 5th eds., 1957-58 to 1963, include a who's who of some 120 entries. Last issue in NWU is for 1980)

964   Sudan trade directory. Khartoum, Ministry of Foreign Trade, Trade Information Centre, ?2000. LC has issue for 2000 only.

965   Sudan year book, comp. SUDANOW. Khartoum, Sudan Publicity, 1983- . Annual. ?No more pub. ("Partly based on the **Sudan almanac**, last published in 1971", pref. 1983 ed., 332pp. includes history, economics, statistics, directories of organizations)

STATISTICS

966   Country profile: Sudan. London, Economist Intelligence Unit, 1986- . Annual

967 Germany. Statistisches Bundesamt. **Statistik des Auslandes: Länderberichte: Sudan** (later **Länderbericht: Sudan**). Wiesbaden/Stuttgart, Metzler-Poetschel, 1966- . Irreg. Issues for 1966, 1976, 1985, 1987, 1990.

968   IMF. **Sudan: statistical appendix**. Washington, DC, 2000. (IMF country report, 00/80). 40pp. - - earlier ed. 1998 (Staff country report, 98/35). Full text of reports also available online, *see* **334**

969   Sudan. Central Bureau of Statistics & United Nations Population Fund (UNFPA). **Statistical year book**. Khartoum, 1998- ? Annual. NWU has issue for 2000. (?Successor to **971**)

970   Sudan. Ministry of Planning [etc.] Department of Statistics. **Internal statistics**. Khartoum, ?1961- . Annual. NWU has issues for 1960/61 to 1967

971   Sudan. Ministry of Planning [etc.] Department of Statistics. **Statistical yearbook** Khartoum, 1970-?. ?Irreg. Title varies. 6th issue, 1983, **Statistical abstract**.

DIRECTORIES OF ORGANIZATIONS

972   **Directory of research centres, institutes and related bodies engaged in scientific and technical research**, comp. Lufti Abdel Gadir & Adil Hassib. Khartoum, Sudan National Council for Research. Council of Scientific and Technical Research, 1974. 77pp.

973   **eBizguides Sudan**. Dublin, eBiz guides, 2005. 214pp. (Business directory)

See also **1032**

BIOGRAPHICAL SOURCES

974   Daly, Martin W. 'Principal office holders in the Sudan Government, 1895-1955', *International journal of African historical studies*, 17, 1984, 309-316

975   Hill, Richard L. **A biographical dictionary of the Sudan**. 2nd ed. London, Frank Cass, 1967. xvi, 409pp. (1,900 entries for those dead pre 1948. 2nd ed. is a reprint with a new introduction and additional notes). - - Orig. pub. as **A biographical dictionary of the Anglo-Egyptian Sudan**. Oxford, Clarendon Press, 1951. xvi, 392pp. (Review, *African affairs*, 51, 1952, 168)

976   Ibrahim Abu Shouk, Ahmed. 'Governors of Kordofan (1821-1955) with biographical lists', *Sudanic Africa*, 8, 1997, 67-83. (Brief lives of 25 governors during Turco-Egyptian rule, 1821-1855; 3 under the Mahdist regime, 1883-1898; 14 under Anglo-Egyptian rule, 1898-1956. *See also* R.L. Hill. 'Rulers of Sudan, 1820-1885', *Sudan notes and records*, 32(1) 1950, 85-95)

977 Muhammad Shamuq, Ahmed. **Mu'jam al-shakhsiyat al-Sudaniyah al-mu'asirah**. Khartoum, Bayt al-Thaqafah, 1988. 482pp. (Biographical dictionary of the modern Sudan)

978 Qasim, Awn al-Sharif. **Mawsuat al-qabail wa-al-ansab fi al-Sudan wa-ashhar asma al-alam wa-al-amakin**. Khartoum, author, 1966. 6 vols. 2,628pp. (Encyclopedia of clans and lineages)

See also **963**

ATLASES & GAZETTEERS

979 **Atlas Jumhuriyat al-Sudan al-Dimiqiratiyah**. [Rev. ed.]. Khartoum, Ministry of Education, 1973. 49pp. (World atlas with 13pp., 21 maps, devoted to Sudan. All text in Arabic). - - earlier ed. Khartoum, 1967. 49pp.

980 Hinkel, Friedrich W. **The archaeological map of the Sudan (AMS)**. Berlin, Akademie Verlag, 1979-1992. 10 fascs. (Most maps at 1:500,000, some at 1:2M. Sponsored by Akademie der Wissenschaft der Deutsche Demokratische Republik, Zentralinstitut für alte Geschichte und Archäologie. Accompanied by **The archaeological map of the Sudan: a guide to its use and explanation of its principles**. Berlin, 1977. Review, *IJAHS*, 15, 1982, 295-296)

981 **Index gazetteer of the Anglo-Egyptian Sudan showing place names**. Rev. ed. London, HMSO for Sudan Survey Department, 1952. 360pp. (Based on the coverage of the 1:250,000 map series). - - Orig. pub. Khartoum, Sudan Survey Department, 1921. vi, 200pp. maps; - - Rev. ed. Khartoum, 1932. 360pp.

982 Khayr, Abbas Muhammad. **Mujam al-asma al-jughrafiyah al-Sudaniyah/ Sudan gazetteer and geographical generic terms**. Omdurman, Markaz Muhammad Umar Bashir lil-Dirasat al-Sudaniyah, 2002. 417pp. (Claims to be the first gazetteer of the Sudan to give information in Arabic as well as English).

983 U.S. Board on Geographic Names. **Gazetteer of the Sudan**. 2nd ed. Washington, DC, 1989. xxi, 614pp. (28,800 entries from maps at 1:100,000). - - Orig. pub. as **Sudan: official standard names approved by the USBGN**. Washington, DC, 1962. (Gazetteer, 68). xi, 358pp. (Rev. version of **984**).

984 U.S. Department of the Interior. Division of Geography. **Preliminary N.I.S Gazetteer, Anglo-Egyptian Sudan**. Washington, DC, Central Intelligence Agency, 1949. 11, 136pp.

See also **1030**

EARTH SCIENCES

985 Awad, Rushdi Said & Delany, F. **Lexique stratigraphique international, 4, Afrique, fasc. 4b; Egypt and Sudan**. Paris, CNRS, 1966. 105pp. (Sudan covered on pp. 75-105)

986 Barbour, Kenneth M. **The Republic of the Sudan; a regional geography**. London, University of London Press, 1961. 292pp. illus. map. (Review, *African affairs*, 32, 1962, 183-184)

987 Craig, Gillian M. ed. **The agriculture of the Sudan**. Oxford, Oxford University Press, 1991. (Centre for Agricultural Strategy series, 1). xiv, 468pp. illus. maps. (Builds upon **Agriculture in the Sudan: being a handbook of agriculture as practised in the Anglo-Egyptian Sudan**, ed. John Douglas Tothill. London, Oxford University Press, 1948. xviii, 974pp. + 76 plates. maps which it sees as "a classic, and despite its age remains a much quoted and authoritative work of reference ... up to the mid twentieth century", pref.)

988 Lebon, John Harold George. **Land use in Sudan**. Bude, Geographical Publishers, 1965. (World Land Use Survey Monographs, 4). xiii, 191pp. illus. maps. (Accompanies World Land Use Survey map at 1:1M. Review, *GJ*, 132, 1966, 106-107)

989 Vail, J.R. **Geochronology of the Sudan**. London, HMSO, 1990. (Overseas geology and mineral resources, 66). 58pp. maps.

990 Vail, J.R. **Lexicon of geological terms for the Sudan**. Rotterdam, Balkema, 1988. vii, 199pp. maps.

991 Vail, J.R. **Outline of the geology and mineral deposits of the Democratic Republic of the Sudan and adjacent areas**. London, HMSO, 1978. (Overseas geology and mineral resources, 49). iv, 68pp. illus. maps. (Includes two sheet maps at 1:2M)

992 Whiteman, Arthur J. **The geology of the Sudan Republic** Oxford, Clarendon Press, 1971. xiv, 290pp.illus. maps. (Review, *GJ*, 138, 1972, 70-72)

BIOLOGICAL SCIENCES

Zoology

993 Amirthalingam, C. & el Yasaa Khalifa, M. **A guide to the common commercial freshwater fishes in the Sudan**. Khartoum, Game & Fisheries Department, 1965. vii, 197, 24, 11pp. illus. (Text in English and Arabic)

994 Cave, Francis Oswin & MacDonald, James D. **Birds of the Sudan: their identification and distribution**. Edinburgh, Oliver & Boyd, 1955. xxxvii, 444pp. + 24pp. plates. - - *Additions & corrections*. 1955. var. paging. Loose leaf typescript in binder, presented to Natural History Museum by F.O. Cave, 1972. (MSS. Cave.1)

995 Nikolaus, Gerhard. **Birds of South Sudan**. Nairobi, East African Natural History Society, 1989. (*Scopus* special suppl., 3). ii, 124pp. illus. maps.

996 Nikolaus, Gerhard. **Distribution atlas of Sudan's birds with notes on habitat and status**. Bonn, Zoologisches Forschungsinstitut und Museum Alexander Koenig, 1987. 322pp. illus. maps. (Covers 938 spp.)

997 Setzer, Henry Wilfred. 'Mammals of the Anglo-Egyptian Sudan', *Proceedings of the U.S. National Museum, Smithsonian Institution*, 106, 1956, 447-587.

See also **1122**

Botany

998 el-Amin, Hamza Mohamed. **Trees and shrubs of the Sudan**. Exeter, Ithaca Press, 1990. vii, 484pp. illus.

999 Andrews, Frederick William. **The flowering plants of the Anglo-Egyptian Sudan**. Arbroath, T. Buncle for Government of Sudan, 1950-56. 3 vols. (Lays most emphasis on the plants of the central and northern Sudan. For southern Sudan *see* **1001** and **1005**, below). - - Wickens, G.E. 'Some additions and corrections', *Sudan forests bulletin*, n.s. 14, 1969, 1-49
- - **Vernacular names of plants as described in** *Flowering Plants of the Anglo-Egyptian Sudan*. Khartoum, McCorquodale, 1948-1953. 2 pts.

1000 Bebawi, Faiz Faris. **A review of plants of northern Sudan: with special reference to their uses**. Eschborn, Deutsche Gesellschaft für Technische Zusammenarbeit, 1991. 294pp. illus. map.

1001 Friis, Ib & Vollesen, Kaj. **Flora of the Sudan-Uganda border area east of the Nile**. Copenhagen, Munksgaard, for Kongelige Danske Videns-kabernes Selskab, 1998-2005. (Biologische skrifter, 51/1 & 2). 2 vols. Vol. 1, 1998. Catalogue of vascular plants. 398pp. illus. maps; vol. 2. 2005. Vegetation and phytogeography, with a chapter on zoogeography by Jon Fjeldsa, pp. 399-855. illus. maps. (Covers much of the former East Equatoria Province)

1002 el-Ghazali, Gamal et al. eds. **Medicinal plants of the Sudan**. Khartoum, National Centre for Research, Medicinal & Aromatic Plants Research Institute, 1986-1998. 5 vols.

1003 Harrison, M.N. & Jackson, J.K. **Ecological classification of the vegetation of the Sudan**. Khartoum, Ministry of Agriculture, 1948. (Forests bulletin, n.s. 2). 45, ivpp. maps.

1004 Macleay, K.N.G. 'The ferns and fern-allies of the Sudan', *Sudan notes & records*, 34, 1953, 286-298 (To complement Andrews, *see* **999**)

1005 Wickens, Gerald E. **The floral of Jebel Marra (Sudan Republic) and its geographical affinities**. Kew, Royal Botanic Gardens, 1976. ix, 368pp. illus. 208 distribution maps. (Covers 982 spp., and supplements the sketchy coverage of Andrews, *see* **999**, for this region)

EAST AFRICA

Kenya
Tanzania
Uganda

HANDBOOKS

1006 Ethnographic survey of Africa: East Central Africa. London, IAI, 1950-1977. 18 vols. (Sub-series of **Ethnographic survey** (*see* **86**). Vol. 1. 1950. The peoples of the Lake Nyasa Region, by M. Tew. 156pp; vol.2. 1951. Bemba and related peoples of Northern Rhodesia etc., by W. Whiteley & J. Slaski. 100pp; vol.3. 1952. The coastal tribes of the north-eastern Bantu, by A.H.J. Prins. 138pp; vol.4. 1952. The Nilotes of the Anglo-Egyptian Sudan and Uganda, by A.J. Butt. 198pp; vol.5. 1953. The Kikuyu and Kamba of Kenya, by J. Middleton. 107pp; vol. 6. 1953. The northern Nilo-Hamites, by G.W.B. Huntingford. 108pp; vol. 7. 1953. The central Nilo-Hamites, by P. & P.H. Gulliver. 106pp; vol. 8. 1953. The southern Nilo-Hamites, by G.W.B. Huntingford. 152pp; vol. 9. 1953. The Azande and related peoples of the Anglo-Egyptian Sudan and Belgian Congo, by P.T.W. Baxter & A.J. Butt. 152pp; vol.10. 1959. The Gisu of Uganda, by J.S. La Fontaine. 68pp; vol. 11. 1960. The eastern lacustrine Bantu, by M.C. Fallers. 86pp; vol. 12. 1961. The Swahili-speaking peoples of Zanzibar and the East African coast, by A.H.J. Prins. 143pp; vol. 13. 1962. The western lacustrine Bantu, by B.K. Taylor. 159pp; vol. 14. 1962. Les anciens royaumes de la zone interlacustrine méridionale (Rwanda, Burundi, Buha), by M. d'Hertefelt et al. 252pp; vol. 15. 1966. The Fipa and related peoples of South-west Tanzania and North-eastern Zambia, by R.G. Willis. xvi, 82pp; vol. 16. 1967. The matrilineal peoples of Eastern Tanzania, by T.O. Beidelman. 94pp; vol. 17. 1967. The peoples of Greater Unyamwezi, Tanzania, by R.G. Abrahams. 95pp; vol. 18. 1977. The Chagga and Meru of Tanzania, by S.F. Moore & P. Puritt. xiv, 140pp)

1007 Guide to the East African territories of Kenya, Tanganyika, Uganda and Zanzibar, comp. L.S. Levin. Nairobi, East African Airways, 1959. 356pp. illus. map. ("First attempt ever made to publish a comprehensive guide dealing solely with these territories", pref. Based on pattern of the author's guide to Rhodesia and Nyasaland, *see* **1264**. General section followed by country surveys. Historical background and current political, social and economic data with statistics)

1008 Ostafrika: Reisehandbuch Kenya und Tanzania. 3rd ed. comp. Goswin Baumhögger, et al. Frankfurt-am-Main, Otto Lembek, 1981. 796pp. illus. maps.

(Very detailed traveller's guide which includes background essays on history, politics, geography and peoples followed by itineraries). - - Orig. pub. Bonn, Deutsche Afrika-Gesellschaft, 1973. 570pp. illus. maps; - - 2nd ed. Frankfurt-am-Main, Otto Lembek, 1975. 570p. illus. maps.

1009 Roux, Louis. **L'Est africain brittanique: Kenya, Tanganyika, Uganda et Zanzibar**. Paris, Société d'études géographiques, maritimes et coloniales, 1950. (Terres lointaines, 5). 223pp. illus. 4 maps. (Covers topography, peoples, history, politics and administration, resources and communications)

1010 Weigt, Ernst. **Kenya und Uganda**. Bonn, K. Schroeder for Deutsche Afrika-Gesellschaft, 1958. (Die Länder Afrikas, 10). 103pp. illus.

See also 1368.

YEARBOOKS

1011 **British Africa trade directory, 1952/53: East African edition**, ed. S.H. Abid. Nairobi, S.H. Abid, 1952. 266pp. (Kenya has 28pp. of general information and statistics followed by a commercial directory; Tanganyika, Uganda and Zanzibar have only a commercial directory)

1012 **East African business directory**, **1994/95** [etc]. Nairobi, Nation Marketing & Publishing, 1994- . Every 2 years.

1013 G.B. Colonial Office. **[Annual reports]: East Africa High Commission, 1948-68**. London etc., 1949-1969. Annual. (As **Annual report on the East Africa High Commission**, 1948-60; **Annual report on the East African Common Services Organization**, 1961-67; **East African Community annual report**, 1968. 1949-53 pub in Colonial series. Reports for 1956 and 1961-68 pub. in Nairobi)

1014 **New African yearbook: East and Southern Africa, 1984/85 [-1986/87]**. London, IC Magazines Ltd., 1984-1986. 2 issues. (Issued as vol. [2] of 5th and 6th editions of **New African yearbook** (*see* **290** for publishing history)

1015 **The year book and guide to East Africa**. London, Robert Hale, 1950-1965. Annual. 16 issues. (Sponsored by the Union-Castle Mail Steamship Co. Formerly incorporated in **Brown's South Africa** etc. (1893-1949, *see* **2774**). Emphasis on information for traveller and potential settler. First issue covers Belgian Congo, British and French Somaliland, Egypt, Eritrea, Ethiopia, Kenya, Nyasaland (to 1954, thereafter transferred to **Yearbook and guide to Southern Africa** *see* **2777**), Portuguese East Africa, Somalia, Tanganyika,

Uganda, Zanzibar. From 1955 coverage was extended to Madagascar, Mauritius, Réunion, and the Seychelles)

1016 A year book of East Africa 1953/54. Nairobi, English Press Ltd., 1954. 480pp. illus. (Well illus. Includes various signed contributions on special topics. Lacks normal directory structure and index, but contains much miscellaneous information on politics, administration, education and agriculture)

See also **2760, 2762**

STATISTICS

1017 East African Common Services Organization. East African Statistical Department. **Economic and statistical review**. Nairobi, 1961-?1977. Quarterly. *Continues* East Africa High Commission. East Africa Statistical Department. **Economic and statistical bulletin**. Nairobi, 1948-1961. Quarterly. Issues 1-52.

1018 Germany. Statistisches Bundesamt. **Statistik des Auslandes: Länderberichte: Ostafrika**. Wiesbaden, 1971. (There are also volumes for the individual countries of East Africa, *see below*).

1019 IMF. **Survey of African economics, 2, Kenya, Tanzania, Uganda and Somalia**. Washington, DC, 1969. xiv, 448pp.

1020 Netherlands. Ministerie van Landbouw en Visserij. Directoraat-General de Landbouw en de Voedselvoorziening. Afdeling Statistik en Documentatie. **Basesreeksen Kenya, Tanzania, Uganda**. Hague, 1972. 82pp. (Collection of basic demographic and economic statistics.)

DIRECTORIES OF ORGANIZATIONS

1021 A regional directory of African tertiary level environmental training institutions, programmes, and resource persons. Nairobi, UNEP Regional Office for Africa, 1989. 262pp.

1022 Register of social scientists in Eastern and Southern Africa, comp. Taye Assefa. 2nd ed. Addis Ababa, Organization for Social Science Research in Eastern and Southern Africa (OSSREA), 2001. 326pp. (Covers Ethiopia, Sudan; Kenya, Tanzania, Uganda; Malawi, Zambia, Zimbabwe; South Africa, Botswana, Lesotho, Swaziland. Each entry includes contact information, professional activities, publications, research projects. ASC4,

103). - - Orig. pub. Addis Ababa, 1994. 194pp. To be updated regularly on the OSSREA Web site: http://www.ossrea.net/publications/

1023 Research services in East Africa. Nairobi, East African Publishing House for East African Academy, 1966. 239pp. (Based on information gathered by Marco Surveys Ltd. Government, commercial and private research organizations in some thirty subject fields)

BIOGRAPHICAL SOURCES

1024 Dictionary of East African biography (DEAB). Project commenced in 1961 by Donald H. Simpson, Librarian, Royal Commonwealth Society, Sir John Gray & H.B. Thomas, with later participation by A.T. Matson and the History Department, University of Makerere. The data available in the Library's collections consists of lists of names under various categories, e.g. missionaries, doctors, Uganda Railway staff, etc. Coverage is limited to those who had made some public impact on East Africa by 1900. Lists of the names collected to date (a total of 5,370) were published in a number of cyclostyled pamphlets, comp. D.H. Simpson et al. **Dictionary of East African Biography project**. London, 1965. 7 parts. General introduction (6pp); UMCA missionaries (12pp); Roman catholic missionaries (17pp); Other missionaries (15pp); Royal Naval personnel (22pp); Germans (23pp); Miscellaneous (74pp). D.H. Simpson, 'The DEAB project', *Library materials on Africa*, 9, 1971, 98-101 estimated the file at that time as containing 6,000 to 6,500 entries, of whom some 1,500 were missionaries. In 1992, the total number of entries was approaching 10,000. Proposals to publish the files in their entirety have so far proved unsuccessful. A number of published biographical works have used the file as a source. Currently available as GBR/0115/RCMS 155 in the Royal Commonwealth Society Collections, Cambridge University Library. Finding list of files in this collection available at http://janus.lib.cam.ac.uk/

1025 Gillett, Mary. **Tribute to pioneers: Mary Gillett's index of many of the pioneers of East Africa**. Oxford, author, 1986. [250]pp. + 3 suppls. (Biographical dictionary of Europeans reaching East Africa pre 1914. Details often very brief, and no sources given)

1026 North, Stephen J. **Europeans in British administered East Africa: a biographical listing, 1888-1905**. 3rd rev. ed. Wantage, author, 2005. xx, 530pp. (Covers the period from the arrival of the British East Africa Company to the completion of major work on the Uganda Railway. Based on the *DEAB* (*see* **1024**), sources in the National Archives (Public Record Office), gazettes, newspapers, War Office Lists. Detailed introduction discusses the sources). - - Orig. pub. Wantage, 1995. 559pp. (Review, *ARD*,

74, 1997, 88-89); - - rev. ed. with suppl., Wantage, 1997; - - 2nd ed. Wantage, 2000. xii, 367pp. (Review, *ARD*, 86, 2001 62-63)

1027 Who's who in East Africa 1963/64 [-1967/68]. Nairobi, Marco Publishers (Africa) Ltd., 1963-1967. 3 issues. (Separate sequences for Kenya, Uganda, Tanganyika, Zanzibar. c.4,500 entries in 1967/68 issue. Includes portraits)

See also **1273**.

ATLASES & GAZETTEERS

Atlases

1028 Goldthorpe, John E. & Wilson, Fergus B. **Tribal maps of East Africa and Zanzibar**. Kampala, East African Institute of Social Research, 1960. (East Africa Studies, 13). vi, 14pp. 8 maps. (Ethnic maps for East Africa in general, Uganda and Kenya; population maps for Zanzibar and Pemba. Review, *GJ*, 126, 1960, 363)

1029 Oxford atlas for East Africa. London & Nairobi, Oxford University Press, 1966. 65, 11pp. 20 x 26cm. (Comp. by Cartographic Department, Clarendon Press, with advice from F.C.A. McBain. 13 maps cover East Africa, 9 the remainder of Africa, 43 the rest of the world)

1030 U.N. Economic & Social Council. **Maps of the transport networks of the Eastern African region**, comp. UNECA. Paris, 1962. 10pp. 9 maps. (Prepared for UNECA Eastern African Transport Conference, Addis Ababa, Oct/Nov 1962. Shows roads, railways and air routes in Sudan, Ethiopia, French Somaliland, Somalia, Uganda, Kenya, Tanganyika, Ruanda-Urundi, Rhodesia and Nyasaland, Bechuanaland, Mozambique, Madagascar)

See also 1432.

Gazetteers

1031 G.B. Army. G.H.Q. Middle East. Survey Directorate. **East Africa: index gazetteer showing place-names on 1:500,000 map series. Vol. 1, Kenya, Uganda, Tanganyika**. Cairo, 1946. vi, 173pp. (One of 3 vols. in 4, pub. 1946-48). *See also* **801, 3018**

1032 Royal East African Automobile Association. **Road book for 1952**: Kenya Colony and protectorate, Tanganyika territory, the Uganda protectorate, and Zanzibar. Nairobi, 1952. 277pp. ("The 1952 Road Book combines the functions of former publications of the R.E.A.A.A. such as the

1949 *Road Book* and the 1950 *Handbook,* both of which it replaces". Includes city plans and itineraries. **Handbook** orig. pub. Nairobi, 1939 ("Modelled on *Handbook* of the Automobile Association of South Africa", pref.). **Roadbook** orig. pub. Nairobi, 1930)

1033 U.S. Board on Geographic Names. **British East Africa: official standard names approved by the USBGN.** Washington, DC, 1955. (Gazetteer, 1). ii, 601pp. (Pp. 1-170, Kenya; pp. 171-247, Tanganyika; pp. 429-558, Uganda; pp. 559-601, Zanzibar. 24,700 names. Rev. eds. later published for each territory; **Kenya** (*see* **1114**); **Tanzania** (*see* **1182**); **Uganda** (*see* **1238**).

EARTH SCIENCES

1034 Acland, Julian Dyke. **East African crops: an introduction to the production of field and plantation crops in Kenya, Tanzania and Uganda.** London, Longman for FAO, 1971. 272pp. illus. maps.

1035 East Africa livestock survey: regional – Kenya, Tanganyika, Uganda. Vol. 3, Atlas. Rome, FAO, 1967. 9 maps at 1:4M. (Reproduces existing maps for topography, administrative divisions etc., + 5 maps drawn specially for the atlas at 1:4M showing rainfall, vegetation, tsetse distribution and stock routes and cattle distribution)

1036 East African Community. East African Meteorological Department. **Climatological statistics for East Africa.** 3rd ed. Nairobi, 1975. 3 vols. in 1. map. - - Orig. pub. as **Collected climatological statistics for East African states.** Nairobi, 1964. 3 vols.

1037 Hecklau, Hans. **Ostafrika: (Kenya, Tanzania, Uganda).** Darmstadt, Wissenschaftliche Buchgesellschaft, 1989. (Wissenschaftliche Länderkunden, 33) xxi, 572pp. illus. maps. (Physical and economic geography)

1038 Johnson, Thomas C. & Odada, Eric O. **The limnology, climatology and paleoclimatology of the east African lakes.** Amsterdam, Gordon & Breach Science Publishers, 1996. xii, 664pp. illus. maps. (Includes discussion of tectonics, aquatic chemistry, food webs and fisheries)

1039 Kokwaro, John O. **Classification of East African crops.** Nairobi, Kenya Literature Bureau, 1979. xi, 87pp. illus. maps.

1040 Matheson, J.K. & Bovill, Edward W. eds. **East African agriculture: a short survey of the agriculture of Kenya, Uganda, Tanganyika, and**

Zanzibar, and of its principal products. London, Oxford University Press, 1950. xvi, 332pp. illus. maps. (Review, *African affairs*, 49, 1950, 256-257)

1041 Morgan, William T.W. **East Africa**. London, Longman, 1973. (Geography for advanced study). xx, 410pp. (Review, *GJ*, 141, 1975, 112-113)

1042 Morgan, William T.W. ed. **East Africa: its people and resources**. 2nd ed. Nairobi, Oxford University Press, 1972. viii, 312pp. + 16pp. plates. - - Orig. pub. Nairobi, 1969. viii, 312pp. ("A new and completely rev. version" of Edward W. Russell. **The natural resources of East Africa**. Nairobi, East African Publishing House, 1962. 144pp. illus. map. Handbook prepared for 8th Commonwealth Forestry Conference, held in East Africa, June/July 1962. Reviews, *African affairs*, 62, 1963, 175-176; *GJ*, 129, 1963, 352-353, "major landmark in the scientific exploration of East Africa")

1043 Pulfrey, William et al. **Lexique stratigraphique international, 4, Afrique, fasc. 8a: Kenya; fasc. 8b: Ouganda; fasc, 8c: Tanganyika**. Paris, CNRS, 1956. 173pp.

1044 Schlüter, Thomas. **Geology of East Africa**. Berlin, Borntraeger, 1997. (Beiträge zur regionalen Geologie der Erde, 57). xii, 484pp. illus. maps.

BIOLOGICAL SCIENCES

1045 Richmond, Matthew D. **A field guide to the seashores of Eastern Africa and the Western Indian Ocean**. 2nd ed. Stockholm, SIDA/Department for Research Cooperation, SAREC, 2002. 461pp. 154 col. plates. - - Orig. pub. Stockholm, 1997. (Covers 1,600+ spp. of plants and animals from all coastal habitats)

1046 Williams, John G. **A field guide to the national parks of East Africa**. London, Collins, 1967. 352pp. (Pt. 1, The national parks: maps and spp. lists; pt. 2, The mammals of the national parks, pp. 166-228, 13 plates; describes and illustrates 137 spp. with broader descriptions of families and genera; pt. 3, The birds; describes 212 spp.)

Zoology

Birds

1047 Britton, P.L. ed. **Birds of East Africa: their habitat, status and distribution**. Nairobi, East African Natural History Society, 1980. (*Scopus* special suppl., 4). 271pp. (Lists 1,293 spp. Review, *Ibis*, 124, 1982, 362-364)

1048 Guggisberg, G.W. **Birds of East Africa**. Nairobi, Mount Kenya Sundries Ltd., 1986-88. 2 vols. Vol. 1, 1988. Non-passerines. 168pp; vol. 2, 1986. Passerines. 196pp. Reprinted as 1 vol. Nairobi, 1990. 124pp.

1049 Short, Lester L. & Horne, Jennifer F.M. 'Annotated checklist of the birds of East Africa', *Proceedings of the Western Foundation of Vertebrate Zoology*, 4(3) 1990, 61-246. illus. maps. (Lists 1,320 spp. in Kenya, Tanzania and Uganda, following the arrangement of **Birds of Africa** (*see* **711**). No index. Review, *Scopus*, 15, 1992, 139-140)

1050 Stevenson, Terry & Fanshawe, John. **A field guide to the birds of East Africa**. Berkhamsted, Poyser, 2001. 602pp. 286 col. plates. maps. (Covers Kenya, Tanzania, Uganda, Rwanda and Burundi. Describes 1,388 species. Earlier works by Williams (**1052**) & Van Perlo (**1051**), both include Eritrea, Ethiopia and Somalia, but omit Rwanda and Burundi. Williams also covers Central Africa. Reviews, *BABC*, 9, 2002, 155-160; *Ibis*, 144, 2002, 363; *Malimbus*, 27, 2003, 66-68)
- - Finch, B. et al. **Bird sounds of East Africa**. CD. 2001. (Companion to the above)

1051 Van Perlo, Ber. **Collins illustrated checklist: birds of Eastern Africa**. London, Harper Collins, 1995. 224 pp. 96 col. plates. (To replace Williams (**1052**), as far as illustrations are concerned. Includes Eritrea, Ethiopia, Somalia; Kenya, Tanzania, Uganda. Covers 1,487 spp. recorded up to 1992 with illus. of each: all those in Short (**1049**), Urban & Brown (**906**) Ash & Miskell (**937**) and new records carried in *Scopus* until July 1992. Sequence and nomenclature basically follows **Birds of Africa** (**711**) and Short (**1049**). Review, *BABC*, 3, 1996, 57-58)

1052 Williams, John G. **A field guide to the birds of East Africa**. London, Collins, 1980. 415pp. 48 col. plates. (New ed. of Williams's works **1046**, **1053**. Includes Eritrea, Ethiopia, Somalia; Kenya, Tanzania, Uganda; Malawi, Zambia, Zimbabwe; Mozambique. 665 spp. treated in detail and illus. with brief information on an additional 633. Review, *Ibis*, 123, 1981, 564-565)

1053 Williams, John G. **A field guide to the birds of Eastern & Central Africa**. London, Collins, 1963. 288pp. (428 sp. covered in detail and illus. with brief information on a further 324. 212 of this latter group were later described and illustrated in J.G.Williams, **A field guide to the national parks of East Africa**. London, Collins, 1967. *See* **1046**)

See also **815, 816**

Mammals

1054 East African Natural History Society. **Checklist of the mammals of East Africa**. Nairobi, 1994.

1055 Kingdon, Jonathan. **East African mammals: an atlas of evolution in Africa**. New York, Academic Press, 1971-1982. 3 vols. in 7. (Vol. 1, 1971. Primates. 446pp; vol. 2a, 1971. Insectivores and bats. 392pp; vol. 2b, 1971. Hares and rodents. 362pp; vol. 3a, 1977. Carnivores. 491pp; vol. 3b, 1977. Large mammals. 450pp; vol. 3c & d, 1982. Bovids I and II. 394, 358pp. Review, *Journal of mammalogy*, 65, 1984, 361-362)

Reptiles, Amphibians & Fishes

1056 Branch, Bill. **Photographic guide to snakes, other reptiles and amphibians of East Africa**. Cape Town, Struik, 2005. 144pp. (Text and photos describing the 260 most common spp.)

1057 Channing, Alan & Howell, Kim M. **Amphibians of East Africa**. Frankfurt-am-Main, Chimaira, 2006. 360pp. illus. (Detailed accounts of 194 frogs and 9 caecilians, with col. illus., line drawings & maps)

1058 Copley, Hugh. **Common freshwater fishes of East Africa**. London, Witherby, 1958. viii, 172pp. illus.

1059 Loveridge, Arthur. 'Checklist of the reptiles and amphibians of East Africa (Uganda, Kenya, Tanganyika, Zanzibar)', *Bulletin of the Museum of Comparative Zoology, Harvard*, 117, 1957, 151-362, xxxvipp.

1060 Schiøtz, Arne. **The treefrogs of Eastern Africa**. Copenhagen, Steenstrupia, 1975. 232pp. illus.

1061 Spawls, Stephen et al. **Field guide to the reptiles of East Africa**. New York, Academic Press/London, A.& C. Black, 2002. 543pp. (Includes some 500 col. photos and maps for all known spp. in Kenya, Tanzania, Uganda, Rwanda and Burundi. Reprinted with corrections, London, 2004). - - **Pocket**

guide to the reptiles and amphibians of East Africa. New York, Academic Press/London, A. & C. Black, 2006. 144pp. illus. maps. (Covers the most prominent 150 reptiles, drawing on the **Field guide** above and adds coverage of some 80 amphibians, each illus. with a col. photo)

Invertebrates

1062 de Pury, Janine M.S. **Crop pests of East Africa**. Nairobi/London, Oxford University Press, 1968. xii, 227pp. illus.

1063 Pinhey, Elliot C.G. **A survey of the dragonflies (Order Odonata) of eastern Africa**. London, British Museum (Natural History), 1961. vii, 214pp.

Botany

1064 Blundell, Michael. **Collins photoguide to the wild flowers of East Africa**. 2nd ed. London, Harper Collins, 1997. 464pp. illus. (Covers Ethiopia, Kenya, Tanzania, Uganda, Zimbabwe, Mozambique. 1,200 spp. with 864 col. photos). - - Orig. pub London, Harper Collins, 1992. 464pp. - - First issued as **Collins guide to the wild flowers of East Africa**. London, Collins, 1987. 464pp

1065 Dharani, Najma. **Field guide to the common trees and shrubs of East Africa**. Cape Town, Struik, 2002. 320pp. 1,000+ col. photos. (Covers Kenya, Tanzania, Uganda; Burundi, Rwanda; Zambia)

1066 Flora of tropical East Africa, prepared at the Royal Botanic Gardens, Kew, ed. William B. Turrill et al. London, Crown Agents/Lisse, Balkema, 1952- . pub. in fascs., covering individual families. (Vols.1 to 37 (1952-1980) pub. Crown Agents; vols. 38 (1982-) pub. Balkema. Adopted as one of the programmes of the East African Community during the lifetime of that body. Scheduled for publication in 225 parts with some 200 pub. to 2005, completion envisaged as 2006/2007. Most recent volumes prepared in association with the East African Herbarium, the National Herbarium of Tanzania, and the Herbaria of Makerere University and Dar es Salaam University. - - Turrill, William B. *Flora of tropical East Africa*: **foreword and preface**. London, Colonial Office, 1952. 12pp.
- - Polhill, Diana. *Flora of tropical East Africa*: **index of collecting localities**.[Rev. ed.]. Kew, Royal Botanic Gardens, 1998. 398pp. - - Orig. pub. Kew, 1970. 262pp.
- - Beentje, Henk & Cheek, Martin. *Flora of tropical East Africa*: **glossary**. Lisse, Balkema, 2003. 115pp. illus. map.

1067 Heine, Bernd & Legère, Karsten. **Swahili plants: an ethnobotanical survey**. Cologne, R. Koppe, 1995. 376pp.

1068 Johns, Robert J. **Pteridophytes of tropical East Africa: a preliminary check-list of the species**. Kew, Royal Botanic Gardens, 1991. 131pp. illus. maps. (Covers some 510 spp. of ferns and fern allies, "to fill the gap in our knowledge until ... publication ... in the **Flora of tropical East Africa**")

1069 Kokwaro, John O. **Flowering plant families of East Africa: an introduction to plant taxonomy**. Nairobi, East African Educational Publishers, 1994. 292pp. illus.

1070 Kokwaro, John O. **Medicinal plants of East Africa**. Kampala, East African Literature Bureau, 1976. 384pp. illus. *See also* **3058**

1071 Lind, Edna M. & Morrison, Michael E.S. **East African vegetation**. London, Longman, 1974. xvii, 257pp. (Pt. 1, Vegetation types by biome; pt. 2, vegetation and the environment)

KENYA

Government of Kenya. http://www.kenya.go.ke/

HANDBOOKS

1072 G.B. War Office. General Staff. **Kenya: military report**. London, 1939. (B. 433). iv, 140pp. map in pocket. (Covers history, administration, peoples, topography and communications. Detailed accounts of 6 settlements: Eldoret, Kisumu, Kitwe, Mombasa, Nairobi, Nakuru. Map at 1:2M)

1073 Historical dictionary of Kenya, comp. Robert M. Maxon & Thomas P. Ofcansky. 2nd ed. Lanham, MD, Scarecrow Press, 2000. (African historical dictionaries, 77). xxvi, 449pp. (Reviews, *ARD*, 84, 2000, 83-90; *Choice*, 38, 2001, 312). - - Orig. pub. comp. Bethwell A. Ogot. Metuchen, NJ, 1981. (African historical dictionaries, 29). xvii, 279pp. (Critical reviews in *African affairs* , 81, 1982, 444-446; *JAH* 23, 1982, 431. Rated "excellent", Balay, 1996)

1074 Horrut, Claude. **La république du Kenya**. Paris, Berger-Levrault, 1972. (Encyclopédie politique et constitutionnelle; Série Afrique). 76pp.

1075 Katamanga, Musambayi. **National elections data book: Kenya 1963-1997**. Nairobi, Institution for Education in Democracy, 1997. 313pp. (Full results of all elections by party, electoral district. Maps showing voter turnout etc.)

1076 Kenya: a country study. 3rd ed. comp. Harold D. Nelson et al. Washington, DC, U.S. Department of Defense, 1984. 340pp. illus. maps. - - Orig. pub. as **Area handbook for Kenya**, comp. Irving Kaplan et al. Washington, DC, 1967. xii, 707pp. maps; - - 2nd ed. Washington, DC, 1976. xiv, 472pp. maps.

1077 Kenya: an official handbook. Nairobi, Ministry of Information & Broadcasting, 1988. 309pp. illus. (Produced to mark the 25th anniversary of Kenyan independence). - - Orig. pub. Nairobi, East African Publishing House for Government of Kenya, 1973. 208pp. illus. (Col. and b. & w. illus. 5 maps at 1:3M. "First of its kind to be published by our government", pref; - - [2nd ed.] Nairobi, Kenya Literature Bureau, 1983. 336pp. illus. (Issued to mark 20th anniversary of Kenyan independence)

1078 Kenya coast handbook: culture, resources and development in the East African littoral, ed. Jan Hoorweg et al. Hamburg, Lit for Africa-studiecentrum, Leiden, 2000. xxvi, 527pp. (Covers the area approximately

150km inland from the sea. Detailed accounts of the geology, soils, agriculture and other economic resources, the population, religion, health and education. Numerous statistical tables, and 9 thematic maps)

1079 Kenya: country profile. Washington, DC, Library of Congress. Federal Research Division, 2005. 22pp. Also available at: http://lcweb2.loc.gov/frd/ cs/profiles/Kenya.pdf

1080 Language and dialect atlas of Kenya, ed. Bernd Heine & Wilhelm J.G. Moehlig. Berlin, Reimer, 1980-1982. 10 pts. (Review, *JALL*, 3, 1981, 203-204). - - **Supplement**. Berlin, 1982-1986. 6 pts.

1081 Pegushev, A.M. et al. **Respublika Keniia: spravochnik**. Moscow, Akademiia nauk, Institut Afriki, 1991. 222pp.

1082 Pickford, Martin. **Kenya palaeontology gazetteer**. Nairobi, National Museums of Kenya, Department of Sites and Monuments Documentation, 1984- . Vol. 1, 1984. Western Kenya. ?No more pub.

YEARBOOKS

1083 G.B. Colonial Office. **[Annual reports]: Kenya, 1891-1962**. London, 1894-1966. (As **Report ... on the East African Protectorate**, 1891/94, 1895/97-1903/04 (not issued 1898/99, 1902/03), **Report on the East Africa Protectorate**, 1904/05-1917/18, (all as Command papers); **Colonial Office annual report on the East African Protectorate**, 1918-19, **Colonial Office annual report for Kenya Colony and Protectorate,** [title varies], 1919/20-1962 (not issued 1939-45). Prior to 1904/05 issued by the Foreign Office)

1084 Industrial and trade directory. Nairobi, Industrial & Trade Directory Co., 1982- . ?Annual. Last issue in NWU is 5th ed. 1986/87

1085 Kenya business directory. Nairobi, Beaver Marketing Co., 1982- ? annual. Latest issue in NWU is for 1991.

1086 Kenya factbook. Nairobi, Newspread International, 1974- . Annual (irreg.). Title varies: 1st to 9th eds. as **Kenya yearbook: Uhuru 10** [etc.]. 15th ed. 1997/98 last held by NWU. (Magazine style format. Chronology of Kenyan history, sections on peoples, economy, finance, industry, natural resources, communications, medicine, education and a commercial directory)

See also **1269**

STATISTICS

1087 Country profile: Kenya. London, Economist Intelligence Unit, 1986- . Annual

1088 Germany. Statistisches Bundesamt. **Statistik des Auslandes: Länderberichte: Kenia** (later **Länderbericht: Kenia**). Wiesbaden/Stuttgart, Metzler-Poetschel, 1964- . Irreg. Issues for 1964, 1969, 1982, 1983, 1985, 1987, 1989, 1994. *See also* **1118**.

1089 Hoeven, Ralph van der. **Kenya**. Helsinki, World Institute for Development Economics Research, U.N. University, 1987. 75pp. tables. (Largely statistical)

1090 IMF. **Kenya: selected issues and statistical appendix**. Washington, DC, 2003. (Country report, 03/200). 81pp. - - Earlier eds. 1998 (Staff country report, 98/66); 2002 (Country report, 02/84). Full text of reports also available online, *see* **334**.

1091 Kenya. Central Bureau of Statistics. http://www.cbs.go.ke/. On-line statistics and full text documents such as the latest **Economic survey** (*see* below)

1092 Kenya. Central Bureau of Statistics [etc.]. **Economic survey**. Nairobi, 1960- . Annual. Latest issue 2005.

1093 Kenya. Central Bureau of Statistics, [etc.]. **Monthly statistical bulletin**, Nairobi, 1986- . Latest issue in NWU is for 1990. *Continues* **Kenya statistical digest**. Nairobi, 1963-1986. Quarterly.

1094 Kenya. Central Bureau of Statistics [etc.]. **Statistical abstract**. Nairobi, 1961- . Annual. Latest issue in NWU is for 2004. *Continues* East Africa High Commission, East African Statistical Department (Kenya Unit). **Statistical abstract**. Nairobi, 1955-1960. Annual. (1956/57 issued as one vol.)

DIRECTORIES OF ORGANIZATIONS

1095 A directory of non-government (voluntary) organizations in Kenya, comp. C.M. Lekyo & A. Mirikau. Nairobi, National Council of Social Service, [1988]. 485pp. (Lists nearly 300 organizations according to their area of activity)

1096 Directory of non-governmental organizations. Nairobi, Non-Governmental Organizations Coordination Board, 1994- . Irreg.

1097 eBizgides Kenya. Dublin, eBiz guides, 2000. 161pp. (Business directory)

1098 A guide to women's organizations and agencies serving women in Kenya. Nairobi, Mazingira Institute, 1985, 311pp. (Detailed directory of over 150 organizations, grouped by function. Name, subject and geographical indexes)

1099 Mulaha, A.R. **Subject guide to information sources in Kenya**. Nairobi, Kenya Library Association & National Council for Science and Technology, 1984. 207pp. (A guide to Kenyan libraries)

1100 Mwathi. P.G. **Directory of associations in Kenya**. Nairobi, National Academy for Advancement of Arts and Sciences, 1980. 113pp.

1101 NGOs Kenya 2000. Nairobi, Parchment Media Services, 2000. 79pp. (Directory of approximately 1,000 institutions)

BIOGRAPHICAL SOURCES

1102 Kenya elections 2002 and who's who in Kenya politics today. 3rd ed. Nairobi, Parchment Media Services, 2003. 28pp. - - Earlier ed. **Who is who in Kenyan politics today**. Nairobi, Kenya Periodicals, 1992? 96pp

1103 Verdier, Isabelle. **Kenya: the top 100 people**. Paris, Indigo, 1998. 222pp.

1104 Who is who in Kenya, 1982-83, ed. M. Nzoiki & M.B. Dar. Nairobi, African Book Services, 1982. vii, 376pp.

ATLASES & GAZETTEERS

1105 Atlas of ethnic distributions in colonial and post-colonial Kenya, ed. Roderick Charles Fox. Grahamstown, Rhodes University, Department of Geography, 1991. [iv], 80 leaves. 30 cm.

1106 A computer atlas of Kenya, with a bibliography of computer mapping, comp. David R.F. Taylor. Ottawa, Carleton University, Department of Geography, 1971. 121pp. maps. (64 thematic maps. "This atlas has been designed to draw attention to the growing field of computer mapping ... and its application to mapping socio-economic variables in developing countries")

1107 Eastern Africa atlas of coastal resources: Kenya. Nairobi, etc., UNEP/Belgian Administration for Development Co-operation, 1998. 119pp. (Text and statistics + 4 loose sheet maps at 1:250,000 showing topography, resources and recreational facilities)

1108 Kenya from space: an aerial atlas. Nairobi, East African Educational Publisher for Department of Resource Surveys and Remote Sensing and Centre de recherche, d'échanges et de documentation universitaire (CREDU), 1992. 162pp. col. maps. (Result of a decade of Franco-Kenyan co-operation in remote sensing of 36 regions of the country. Topographic and thematic maps covering land use, vegetation etc. Vertical and oblique aerial photographs. Highly critical review in *SAGJ*, 95, 1993, 80-81, "an atlas in need of an editor, some clear themes and direction")

1109 A land system atlas of Western Kenya, comp. Ralph Myles Scott et al. Christchurch, War Office Military Vehicles & Engineering Establishment, 1971. xix, 363pp. 29 x 48cm. (Mapping done by Soil Science Laboratory, Oxford University)

1110 National atlas of Kenya. 5th ed. Nairobi, Survey of Kenya, 2003. xxi, 245pp. maps. (Majority of maps at 1:3M. - - Orig. pub. as **Atlas of Kenya**: a comprehensive series of new and authentic maps prepared from the National Survey and other governmental sources with gazetteer and notes on pronunciation and spelling. Nairobi, Survey of Kenya, 1959. ix, 44pp. 46 x 49cm. (Reviews, *Empire survey review*, 16, 1961, 93, *GJ*, 127, 1961, 554); - - 2nd ed. Nairobi, Survey of Kenya, [1962]. ix, 44pp. (Updated reprint of the 1959 ed. with a few corrections); - - 3rd ed. Nairobi, Survey of Kenya, 1970. iv, 103pp. 43 plates. 38 x 40cm. (Substantially "rearranged, enlarged, recompiled and redrawn" (foreword). Detailed col. topographic and thematic maps. 5 provincial maps at 1:1M. Plans of Nairobi and Mombasa (1:20,000), smaller townships (1:50,000). Six reproductions of maps of 1564, 1596, 1662, 1809, 1850, 1856. Review, *GJ*, 137, 1971, 590-591. *See* A.G. Dalgleish, 'Territorial atlases: the production problem facing survey departments with limited resources', pp. 290-292 *in* U.N. **U.N. Regional Cartographic Conference for Africa, Nairobi, 1963. Vol. 2, Proceedings**. New York, 1966, an account of producing the 2nd ed.); - - 4th ed. Nairobi, Survey of Kenya, 1991. xv, 156pp. illus. maps.

1111 Population atlas of Kenya, ed. Roderick Charles Fox. Grahamstown, Rhodes University, Department of Geography, 1995. 2 computer disks + user's guide (i, 17 leaves)

1112 Population census atlas of Kenya: 1989 census. Nairobi, Ministry of Planning & National Development, 1996. viii, 34pp. (34 maps showing mortality, education, housing, employment, etc.)

1113 **Road atlas of Kenya**, ed. Michael Brett. London, New Holland, 1995. (Globetrotter travel atlas). 64pp. col. maps.

1114 U.S. Board on Geographic Names. **Kenya: official standard names approved by the USBGN**. 2nd ed. Washington, DC, 1978. vii, 470pp. (c.30,000 names from maps at 1:50,000, for south and south-west and at 1:100,000 for rest of the country). - - Orig. pub. Washington, DC, 1964. (Gazetteer, 78). vi, 467pp. (Replaces appropriate section of **British East Africa ...** (*see* **1033**)

EARTH SCIENCES

1115 Du Bois, Charles G.B. **Minerals of Kenya**. 2nd ed. rev. John Walsh. Nairobi, Kenya Mining & Geological Department, 1970. (Bulletin, 11). iv. 182pp. 24 maps. - - Orig. pub. Nairobi, 1966. (Bulletin, 8). iv, 187pp.

1116 Ojany, Francis F. & Ogendo, Reuben B. **Kenya: a study: physical and human geography**. Nairobi, Longman, 1973. viii, 228pp. (Review, *GJ*, 142, 1976, 147, "remarkable and useful range of precise statistics and data")

1117 Pulfrey, William. **The geology and mineral resources of Kenya**. 2nd ed. rev. John Walsh. Nairobi, Geological Survey, 1969. 34pp. (Bulletin, 9). - - Orig. pub. Nairobi, 1954. (Bulletin, 1). 27pp; - - rev ed. Nairobi, 1960. (Bulletin, 2). 41pp.

BIOLOGICAL SCIENCES

Zoology

Birds & Mammals

1118 Aggundey, I.R. & Schlitter, Duane A. 'Annotated checklist of the mammals of Kenya. 1: Chiroptera', *Annals of the Carnegie Museum, Pittsburgh*, 53, 1984, 119-161. ?No more pub.

1119 East African Natural History Society. Ornithological Sub-committee. **Checklist of the birds of Kenya**. Nairobi, 1996.

1120 Jackson, Sir Frederick John & Sclater, William L. **The birds of Kenya Colony and the Uganda Protectorate**. London, Gurney & Jackson, 1938. 3 vols. 1,592pp. + 24plates. illus. map. *See also* **936**.

1121 Lewis, Adrian & Pomeroy, Derek. **Bird atlas of Kenya**. Rotterdam, Balkema, 1989. 620pp. (Maps ranges of 1,065 spp). - - **First updating bulletin for** *A bird atlas of Kenya*. [Nairobi, Adrian Lewis], 1989. 9pp. - - Oyugi, Joseph O. **New records for the** *Bird atlas of Kenya*, **1984-1994**. Nairobi, National Museums of Kenya, 1994. (Research reports:ornithology, 15). 49pp.

1122 Zimmermann, Dale, et al. **Birds of Kenya and Northern Tanzania**. London, Christopher Helm, 1996. 740pp. 124 col. plates. (Covers 1,114 spp. Includes 90% of the 1,040 spp. recorded in Tanzania and 85% of 1004 spp. recorded in Uganda, also "majority of those of southern Ethiopia, Somalia and Sudan". Review, *BABC*, 4, 1997, 48-49). - - **Field guide to the birds of Kenya and Northern Tanzania**. London, Christopher Helm, 1999. 576pp. 124 col. plates. (Portable version of the 1996 vol. Text abbreviated, some maps omitted. Includes new spp., taxonomic changes post 1996. Review, *Ibis*, 142, 2000, 342)

Reptiles, Amphibians & Fishes

1123 Seegers, Lothar, et al. 'Annotated checklist of the freshwater fishes of Kenya (excluding the lacustrin Harochromines from Lake Victoria)', *Journal of East African Natural History*, 92, 2003, 11-47. illus. maps. (Lists 206 spp.)

1124 Spawls, Stephen. 'A checklist of the snakes of Kenya', *Journal of the East African Natural History Society*, 31, 1978, 1-18

1125 Spawls, Stephen & Rotich, D. 'An annotated checklist of the lizards of Kenya', *Journal of East African Natural History*, 86, 1997, 61-83 (Lists 99 spp.)

Invertebrates

1126 Larsen, Torben B. **The butterflies of Kenya and their natural history**. Rev. ed. Oxford, Oxford University Press, 1996. xxii, 500pp. + 64pp. plates. (Describes 871 spp.) - - Orig. pub. Oxford, 1991. xxii, 492pp.

Botany

1127 Agnew, Andrew David Q. 'A field guide to upland Kenya grasses', *Journal of East African natural history*, 95, 2006, 1-86. illus. (Companion to **1128**)

1128 Agnew, Andrew David Q. **Upland Kenya wild flowers: a flora of the ferns and herbaceous flowering plants of upland Kenya**. 2nd ed. Nairobi, East African Natural History Society, 1994. 374pp. 175 plates (Land above 1,000 metres, lying in the southwest of the country. 1st ed. intended to complement Dale & Greenway, **1134**. 2nd ed. intended as a companion to Beentje, **1133** and omits spp. covered in 1st ed, but now in Beentje. Covers some 3,000 spp. with 1,000+ illus.). - - Orig. pub. London, Oxford University Press, 1974. ix, 827pp.

1129 Blundell, Michael. **The wild flowers of Kenya**. London, Collins, 1982. 160pp. + 48pp. plates. (Later developed into his **Collins photoguide to the wild flowers of East Africa** (*see* **1064**)

1130 Ibrahim, Kamal M. & Kabuye, C.H.S. **An illustrated manual of Kenya grasses**. Rome, FAO, 1987. 765pp. illus. map.

1131 Ibrahim, Kamal M. **An illustrated manual of Kenya legumes (herbs and climbers)**. Kitale, FAO/UNDP Forage Plant Development and Extension, National Agriculture Research Centre, 1989. 656pp. illus.

1132 Maundu, Patrick M., et al. **Traditional food plants of Kenya**. Nairobi, Kenya Resource Centre for Indigenous Knowledge, National Museums of Kenya, 1999. x, 270pp. + 8pp. plates. illus. maps.

Trees

1133 Beentje, Henk. **Kenya trees, shrubs and lianas**. Nairobi, National Museum of Kenya, 1994. ix, 722pp. illus. maps. (Covers some 1,850 spp. Indexes in several local languages)

1134 Dale, Ivan R. & Greenway, Percy J. **Kenya trees and shrubs**. Nairobi, Buchanan's Kenya Estates, 1961. xxvii, 654pp. 110 text figs. 31 col. plates.

1135 Noad, Tim & Birnie, Ann. **Trees of Kenya: a fully illustrated field guide**. 3rd ed. Nairobi, authors, 1992. 308pp. 18 col. plates. (Covers c. 300 more common spp.). - - Orig. pub. Nairobi, 1989; - - 2nd ed. 1990. Nairobi, 1990. 308pp.

TANZANIA

Official online gateway of the Republic of Tanzania
http://www.tanzania.go.tz/

HANDBOOKS

1136 Arning, Wilhelm. **Deutsch-Ostafrika: gestern und heute**. 2nd ed. Berlin, D. Reimer, 1942. viii, 425pp. (Sections for former German East Africa in general, Tanganyika and Ruanda-Urundi. Detailed account of topography, history, politics, industry, and agriculture). - - Orig. pub. Berlin, 1936. xii, 388pp. illus.

1137 Historical dictionary of Tanzania. 2nd ed. comp. Thomas P. Ofcansky & Roger Yeager. Lanham, MD, Scarecrow Press, 1997. (African historical dictionaries, 72). xxxi, 291pp. (Review, *IJAHS*, 32, 1999, 566-567). - - Orig. pub. comp. Laura S. Kurtz. Metuchen, NJ, 1978. (African historical dictionaries, 15). xxxi, 331pp. (Reviews, *Africa*, 50, 1980, 101; *Africana J.*, 10, 1979, 120-128; *ASA review of books*, 6, 1980, 199-209, *IJAHS*, 12, 1979, 321; *JAH*, 23, 1982, 139-140. Rated "poor", Balay, 1996)

1138 Katsman, V.I.A. **Obedinennaia Respublika Tanzaniia: Spravochnik**. Moscow, Akademiia nauk, Institut Afriki, 1980. 261pp.

1139 Makaidi, Emmanuel J.E. **A dictionary of historic records of Tanzania (1497-1982)**. Dar es Salaam, Sunrise, 1984. 73pp. (Historical chronology)

1140 Makaidi, Emmanuel J.E. **Emma's encyclopaedia Tanzaniana of national records, 1497-1995**. Dar es Salaam, Sunrise, 1995. iv, 279pp. (1,104 entries arranged chronologically. Many popular entries, e.g. for local football competitions, but some useful political data especially in election years)

1141 Moffett, John Perry, ed. **Handbook of Tanganyika**. 2nd ed. Dar es Salaam, Government of Tanganyika, 1958. xi, 703pp. illus. maps. (A completely recast 2nd ed. of G.F. Sayers, ed. **The handbook of Tanganyika**. London, Macmillan, 1930. "Mainly historical and descriptive ... complementary to **Tanganyika: a review** (*see* **1142**) which was primarily economic", pref. Author was Commissioner for Social Development. Numerous statistics, 12 maps, extensive bibliography, pp. 567-677. The two volumes provide an immense store of information on the country in the final decade of colonial rule)

1142 Moffett, John Perry, ed. **Tanganyika: a review of its resources and their development**. Dar es Salaam, Government of Tanganyika, 1955. xviii, 924pp. maps. (Extremely detailed account devoted largely to the economic situation of the country. Numerous statistics, and 61 tables of data. 12 maps)

1143 Scheel, Julius Otto Walther. **Tanganyika und Sansibar**. Bonn, K. Schroeder for Deutsche Afrika-Gesellschaft, 1959. (Die Länder Afrikas, 20). 136pp.

1144 Tanganyika. Information Services. **Tanganyika data book**. Dar es Salaam, 1961. Issued loose leaf with binder. Maps. No revs. traced. (Sections for administration, agriculture, commerce, local government, social services)

1145 Tanganyika guide. 3rd ed. Letchworth, Garden City Press, 1953, 180pp. illus. map. (Covers history, topography, natural resources, tourism, statistics). Orig. pub. Nairobi, *East African Standard*, 1936. 136pp. illus. map; - - 2nd ed. Letchworth, 1948. 160pp. illus. maps.

1146 Tanzania. Ministry of Information & Tourism. **Tanzania today: a portrait of the United Republic**. Nairobi, University Press of Africa, 1968. vii, 316pp. (Topographical, economic and statistical information)

1147 Tanzania: a country study. 2nd ed. comp. Irving Kaplan et al. Washington, DC, U.S. Department of Defense, 1978. xix, 344pp. illus. maps. - - Orig. pub.as **Area handbook for Tanzania**, comp. Allison B. Herrick et al. Washington, DC, 1968. xvi, 522pp. maps.

1148 Urfer, Sylvain. **La république unie de Tanzanie**. Paris, Berger-Levrault, 1973. (Encyclopédie politique et constitutionnelle; Série Afrique). 91pp.

See also **2755**

Zanzibar

1149 Mohamed, Amir A. **Zanzibar: facts, figures and fiction**. Zanzibar, Alkhayria Press, 1994. 128pp.

1150 Shelswell-White, Geoffrey H. **A guide to Zanzibar**. 4th ed. rev. K.S. Madon. Zanzibar, Government Printer, 1952. x, 146pp. photos, maps. (The standard guide, originally comp. by the private secretary to the Sultan and regularly revised, with historical, topographical, and tourist information). - - Orig. pub. Zanzibar, Government Printer, 1932. 73pp; - - 2nd ed. Zanzibar,

Government Printer, 1939. 74pp; - - 3rd ed. rev. J. O'Brien et al. Zanzibar, Government Printer, 1949. xii, 109pp

YEARBOOKS

1151 G.B. Colonial Office. **[Annual reports]: Tanganyika, 1918-60.** London, 1921-1961. (As **Report to the Council of the League of Nations on the administration of Tanganyika Territory**, 1918/20, 1921, (as Command papers); **Report by H.B.M. Government to the League of Nations**, [title varies], 1922-1938 (not pub. 1939/46), **Report ... to the Trusteeship Council of the UN**, 1947, **Report ... to the General Assembly of the UN**, 1948-60 (in Colonial series)

1152 Tanganyika. Department of Commerce and Industry. **Commerce and industry in Tanganyika.** Dar es Salaam, 1957, 1961. 2 issues. (Information on topography, natural resources, communications and trade with statistics)

1153 Tanzania directory. Dar es Salaam, Government Printer, 1966- . Latest issue in NWU is 1987. *Continues* **Tanganyika directory.** Dar es Salaam, 1961-1966.

1154 Tanzania trade directory. Dar es Salaam, Business Times Ltd., 1999- Annual. *See also* **1266**

Zanzibar

1155 G.B. Colonial Office. **[Annual reports]: Zanzibar, 1913-1960.** London, 1914-1963. (As **Annual report on Zanzibar**, 1913-19, (as Command papers); **Colonial Office annual report** 1920-60, (not pub. 1939-45). Pub. biennially from 1949/50-1959/60. Preceded by four reports issued by the Foreign Office: **Reports on Zanzibar Protectorate**, 1893-94 (C.6955); **Report on the revenue and administration in Zanzibar in 1894** (C.7706); **Report ... on Island of Pemba**, 1896-97 (C.8701); **Despatch from H.M.'s Agent and Consul General furnishing a report on the administration, finance and general condition of the Zanzibar Protectorate**, 1909 (Cd.4816).

STATISTICS

1156 European Communities. Statistical Office. **Reports on ACP countries: Tanzania.** Luxembourg, Office for Official Publications of the European Communities, 1988. 81pp.

1157 IMF. **Tanzania: selected issues and statistical appendix**. Washington, DC, 2004. (Country report 04/284). 78pp. - - Earlier eds. (Title varies) 1996 (Country report, 96/2); 1998 (Staff country report, 98/05); 2000 (Country report, 00/122); 2003 (Country report, 03/02). Full text of reports from 97/101, 1997 also available online, *see* **334**

1158 Tanzania. Bureau of Statistics [etc.] **A bibliography of economic and statistical publications on Tanzania**. 2nd ed. Dar es Salaam, 1975. - - Orig. pub. Dar es Salaam, 1967. 23pp.

1159 Tanzania. Bureau of Statistics [etc.]. **Guide to official statistics**. Dar-es Salaam, 1992. 7pp. - - Earlier eds. **A guide to Tanzania statistics**. Dar es Salaam, 1968. 51pp; - - **A guide to official statistics of Tanzania, January 1985**. Dar es Salaam, 1985. 20pp.

1160 Tanzania. Government of Tanzania & World Bank. **Tanzania at the turn of the century: background papers and statistics**. Washington, DC, World Bank, 2002. xix, 350pp. (Text, pp. 3-247 with figures and tables; statistics, pp. 250-335. Detailed contents list identifies all figures and tables)

1161 Tanzania. National Bureau of Statistics. http://www.nbs.go.tz/

Bulletins & yearbooks

1162 **Country profile: Tanzania**. London, Economist Intelligence Unit, 2003- . Annual. *Continues* **Country profile: Tanzania**. London, 1886-1992; *Continues in part* **Country profile: Tanzania, Comoros**. London, 1993-2002

1163 Germany. Statistisches Bundesamt. **Statistik des Auslandes: Länderberichte: Tansania** (later **Länderbericht: Tansania**). Wiesbaden/ Stuttgart, Metzler-Poetschel, 1965- . Irreg. Issues for 1965, 1987, 1989, 1994. *See also* **1118**.

1164 Tanzania. Maktaba ya Takwimu/Bureau of Statistics [etc.] **Quarterly statistical bulletin**. Dar es Salaam, 1964- . Title varies: **Monthly statistical bulletin** (1964-1970). ALA notes issue for 1992. *Continues* East Africa High Commission. East African Statistical Department (Tanganyika Unit). **Tanganyika monthly statistical bulletin**. Dar es Salaam, 1951-1964

1165 Tanzania. Maktaba ya Takwimu/Bureau of Statistics [etc.] **Selected statistical series, 1951-[1985]**. Dar es Salaam, 1987 – Annual. (Collection of summary statistical tables. Ed for 1951-1991 (1991). 113pp.)

1166 Tanzania. Maktaba ya Takwimu/Bureau of Statistics [etc.]. **Statistical abstract**. Dar es Salaam, 1961- . Annual (irreg.). No issues published for 1967-69, 1974-78. Vols. for 1973/79 (1983); 1979 (1981); 1982 (1983); 1984 (1986); 1987, 1991, 1992-1995, 2002. *Continues* East Africa High Commission. East African Statistical Department (Tanganyika Unit). **Statistical abstract 1938/51** [etc.]. Nairobi, 1953-1960. Irreg. (Issues for 1951-52, 1954-1960);

1167 Tanzania. Maktaba ya Takwimu/Bureau of Statistics [etc.] **Tanzania in figures**. Dar es Salaam, 1980- . Latest issue in NWU is for 2003.

Zanzibar

1168 Zanzibar. Department of Statistics. **Statistical abstract of Zanzibar**. Zanzibar, 1981- . Annual. Latest issue in NWU is for 1997.

1169 Zanzibar. Department of Statistics. **Summary digest of useful statistics**. Zanzibar, 1961.

DIRECTORIES OF ORGANIZATIONS

1170 Directory of training institutions. Dar es Salaam, Tanzania Ministry of Manpower Development, 1977. 130pp. (Lists 132 institutions by ministry responsible, plus 47 Folk Development Colleges and very brief details on another 98 organizations)

1171 eBizguides Tanzania. Dublin, eBiz guides, 2003. 215pp. (Directory of commercial and business institutions)

1172 NGO Directory 2001. Dar es Salaam, Tanzania Association of Non-Governmental Organizations (TANGO), 2001. 54 pp. (Brief details on some 325 organizations. Updating provided at http://www.tango.or.tz/dir.htm)

1173 Tanzania business contacts. Dar es Salaam, Tanzania Chamber of Commerce, Industry & Agriculture, 1995- 2 p.a.

See also **2819**

BIOGRAPHICAL SOURCES

1174 Iliffe, John, ed. **Modern Tanzanians: a volume of biographies**. Nairobi, East African Publishing House for Historical Association of Tanzania, 1973. 258pp. illus.

ATLASES & GAZETTEERS

Atlases

1175 **Atlas of Tanganyika, East Africa**. 3rd ed. Dar es Salaam, Department of Lands & Mines, Survey Division, 1957. iv, 30pp. incl. col. maps. 56 x 59 cm. (Text and tables on verso of most maps. Omits historical maps of earlier eds., adds maps of rainfall, labour distribution, water supply. Maps now at the larger scale of 1:3M. Includes plans of Dar es Salaam at 1:25,000, Tanga at 1:10,000, Dodoma at 1:5,000, Morozoro at 1:2,500). - - Orig. pub. as **Atlas of the Tanganyika Territory**. Dar es Salaam, 1942. 31pp. incl. part col. maps. 46 x 48cm (Maps showing geology, rainfall, temperature, forest resources, game, population, agriculture, minerals, communications, with text ion verso. Maps 19-27 show development of cartographic knowledge of East Africa and routes of explorers. Majority of sheets at 1:4M); - - 2nd ed. Dar es Salaam, 1948. 35pp. incl. part col. maps. (Adds maps for soils, vegetation, drainage basins, mines. Review, *Geographical review*, 41, 1951, 483-484)

1176 **Atlas of Tanzania**. 2nd ed. Dar es Salaam, Ministry of Lands, Housing & Urban Development. Surveys & Mapping Division, 1976. 83pp. (Essentially a rev. ed. of **1175**. Includes 24 map plates at 1:3M and the 4 city plans. Sections for topography, climate, flora and fauna and human geography.). - - Orig. pub. Dar es Salaam, 1967. iii, 61pp. 46 x 55cm. (Reviews, *GJ*, 136, 1970, 311-312; *Tanzania notes & records*, 72, 1973, 81-87);

1177 Berry, Leonard. **Tanzania in maps: graphic perspectives of a developing country**. London, University of London Press, 1971/New York, Africana Publishing Corporation, 1972. 172pp. (Comp. Tanzania Bureau of Resource Development & Land Use Planning and Department of Geography, University of Dar es Salaam. 61 b. & w. thematic maps, with text and statistics. Reviews, *ASA review of books*, 1, 1975, 109-110, "single most valuable reference work available on Tanzania"; *GJ*, 138, 1972, 525)

1178 **Eastern Africa atlas of coastal resources: Tanzania**, comp. UNEP/Belgian Ministry of Foreign Affairs/Institute of Marine Sciences, University of Dar es Salaam. Nairobi, UNEP, 2001. viii, 113pp.

1179 Gerlach, Hans-Henning & Birken, Andreas. **Deutsch-Ostafrika, Zanzibar und Wituland: Atlas, Handbuch, Katalog der postalischen Entwertungen**. [Königsbronn?], Philathek-Verlag, 1999. (Deutschen Kolonien und deutsche Kolonialpolitik, 2). 89pp. col. maps. 39 maps including detailed coverage of German East Africa as of 1905, street plans of

Pangani, Zanzibar, Tanga and Dar es Salaam in the 1990s. Chronology. Catalogue of stamp issues)

1180 Jensen, Søren B. **Regional economic atlas, mainland Tanzania**. Dar es Salaam, University College of Dar es Salaam, Bureau of Resource Assessment and Land Use Planning, 1968. 74pp. (18 b. & w. maps at 1:6,500,000 featuring population, industry, trade, education and natural resources, with accompanying text and statistical tables)

See also **1454, 3241**

Gazetteers

1181 Tanzania. Surveys & Mapping Division. **Tanzania Gazetteer**. Dar es Salaam, 1969. v, 236pp. maps.

1182 U.S. Board on Geographic Names. **Tanzania: official standard names approved by the USBGN**. Washington, DC, 1965. (Gazetteer, 92). v, 236pp. (Pp. 1-199, Tanganyika, 14,150 entries from 1:100,000/1:500,000 series; pp. 201-236, Zanzibar (incorporating separately published **Zanzibar: official standard names ...** , *see* **1184**). Replaces appropriate sections in **British East Africa ...** (*see* **1033**).

Zanzibar

1183 Piggott, P.H. **The gazetteer of Zanzibar Island**. Zanzibar, Government Printer, 1962. ii, 17pp. (Some 650 entries. Based on sheets 1 and 2 of 1:63,360 series produced by 89 Field Survey Squadron, Royal Engineers)

1184 U.S. Board on Geographic Names. **Zanzibar: official standard names approved by the USBGN**. Washington, DC, 1964. (Gazetteer, 76). iii, 36pp. (Some 2,400 names from maps at 1:63,360. Text also incorporated into **Tanzania: official standard names ...** (*see* **1182**).

EARTH SCIENCES

1185 **Directory of agricultural research institutes in Tanzania: with special reference to crop research**. Dar es Salaam, Tanzania Ministry of Agriculture. Research & Disease Control Section, 1974. iv, 73pp.

1186 Hathout, A.S. **Soil atlas of Tanzania**. Dar es Salaam, Tanzania Publishing House, 1983. 56pp. 39 x 39cm. 49 maps. (*See also* his **Soil resources of Tanzania**. Dar es Salaam, Tanzania Publishing House, 1972)

1187 Kent, Sir Percy Edward et al. **The geology and geophysics of coastal Tanzania**. London, HMSO, 1971. (Institute of Geological Sciences. Geophysical paper, 6). vi, 103pp. illus. maps.

1188 Kimambo, R.H.N. **Mining and mineral prospects in Tanzania**. Arusha, Eastern Africa Publications, 1984. v, 250pp. maps.

1189 Quennell, A.M. et al. **Summary of the geology of Tanzania**. Dar es Salaam, Tanzania Mineral Resources Division, 1956-1970. 4 vols. (Vol. 1, Introduction and stratigraphy; vol. 2, Geological map at 1:2M; vol. 3, *not pub.*; vol. 4, Economic geology; vol. 5, Structure and geotectonics of the Pre-Cambrian)

BIOLOGICAL SCIENCES

Zoology

1190 Broadley, Donald G. & Howell, Kim M. **A checklist of the reptiles of Tanzania, with synoptic keys**. Bulawayo, National Museums & Monuments of Zimbabwe, 1991. (*Syntarsus*, 1). 70pp. illus. maps.

1191 Eccles, David H. **Field guide to the freshwater fishes of Tanzania**. Rome, FAO, 1992. (FAO species identification sheets for fishery purposes). v, 145pp. *Companion to* Bianchi, Gabriella. **Field guide to the commercial marine and brackish-water species of Tanzania**. Rome, FAO, 1985. (FAO species identification sheets for fishery purposes). xiii, 199pp. + 32pp.plates.

1192 Kielland, Jan. **Butterflies of Tanzania**. Melbourne/London, Hill House, 1990. 363pp. illus. 68 plates. - - **Supplement**, comp. Colin Congdon & Steve Collins, Nairobi, African Butterfly Research Institute/Tervuren, Union des Entomologistes belges, [1998]. 143, vipp. illus.

1193 Swynnerton, G.H. & Hayman, Robert W. 'A checklist of the land mammals of the Tanganyika Territory and the Zanzibar Protectorate', *Journal of the East African Natural History Society*, 20, 1951, 274-392. - - 'Addenda & corrigenda', *ibid.* 23, 1958, 9-10

Botany

1194 **Check-lists of the forest trees and shrubs of the British Empire. Vol. 5, Tanganyika Territory**. Oxford, Imperial Forestry Institute, 1940-1949. 2 vols.

Vol. 1. 1940, ed. F.Bayard Hora. vi, 312pp; vol. 2. 1949, ed. J.P. Brenan & Percy J. Greenway. xviii, 653pp.

1195 Cribb, Philip J. & Leedal, G.P. **The mountain flowers of southern Tanzania: a field guide to the common flowers**. Rotterdam, Balkema, 1982. ix, 244pp. illus. maps.

1196 **A field key to the savanna genera and species of trees, shrubs and climbing plants of Tanganyika Territory**. Dar es Salaam, Government Printer, 1939-1953. 2 vols. Vol. 1, 1939. Genera and some species, comp B.D. Burtt. xvi, 53pp.; vol. 2, 1953. The species of the more important genera, with general index. xxvi, 53-128pp. Rev. ed. comp. Philip Earle Glover & C.H.N. Jackson. - - Vol. 1, 2nd ed, rev. J.R. Welch. Dar es Salaam, East African Trypanosomiasis Research Organization, 1957.

1197 Mbuya, L.P. et al. **Useful trees and shrubs for Tanzania**: identification, propagation and management for agricultural and pastoral communities. Nairobi, Regional Soil Conservation Unit & SIDA, 1994. xx, 542pp.

1198 Ruffo, Christopher K. **Edible wild plants of Tanzania**. Nairobi, Regional Land Management Unit & SIDA, 2002. x, 765pp. illus.

Zanzibar

1199 Koenders, Ludo. **Flora of Pemba Island: a checklist of plant species**. Dar es Salaam, Wildlife Conservation Society of Tanzania, 1992. 104pp. illus.

1200 Pakenham, R.H.W. **The birds of Zanzibar and Pemba: an annotated checklist**. Tring, British Ornithologists' Union, 1979. 134pp. maps.

1201 Pakenham, R.H.W. **The mammals of Zanzibar and Pemba islands**. Harpenden, author, 1984. 81pp. (Notes 48 spp. on Zanzibar, 23 on Pemba. Review, *Mammal review*, 16, 1986, 205-206)

1202 Pakenham, R.H.W. **The reptiles and amphibians of Zanzibar and Pemba Islands (with a note on the freshwater fishes)**. Nairobi, East African Natural History Society & Museum, 1983. (*Journal*, 177). 40pp.

1203 Williams, Robert Orchard. **The useful and ornamental plants in Zanzibar and Pemba**. Zanzibar, n.p., 1949. ix, 497pp. illus. (Covers the more common native and introduced plants)

UGANDA

State House, Republic of Uganda, Web site http://www.statehouse.go.ug/

HANDBOOKS

1204 Berger, Herfried. **Uganda**. Bonn, K. Schroeder for Deutsche Afrika-Gesellschaft, 1964. (Die Länder Afrikas, 27). 80pp. map. - - Orig. pub as part of **1010**.

1205 Broere, Marc & Vermaas, P. **Uganda: mensen, politiek, economie, cultuur**. Amsterdam, Koninklijk Instituut voor de Tropen/The Hague, Novib, 2005. (Landenreeks). 80pp.

1206 Gakwandi, Arthur, ed. **Uganda pocket facts: a companion guide to the country, its history, culture, economy and politics**. 2nd ed. Kampala, Fountain Publishers, 1999. 125pp. (Data current only to 1996). - - Orig. pub. as **Pocket facts about Uganda**. Kampala, Bow & Arrow Publishers, 1992. 102pp.

1207 G.B. War Office. General Staff. **Uganda military report**. London, 1940. (B. 140). iii, 135pp. maps. (Covers history, administration, topography, ethnography, communications. Detailed treatment for Entebbe, Jinja, Kampala)

1208 Historical dictionary of Uganda, comp. M. Louise Pirouet. Metuchen, NJ, Scarecrow Press, 1995. (African historical dictionaries, 64). xiv, 534pp. (Reviews, *ARD*, 78, 1998, 64-65; *ASR*, 40, 1997, 176-178; *IJAHS*, 30, 1997, 208-209)

1209 King'ei, Kitula G. **Classification of Ugandan languages**. Cape Town, Centre for Advanced Studies of African Society, 2000. (Notes & records, 17). 23pp.

1210 Otiso, Kefo M. **Culture and customs of Uganda**. Westport, CT, Greenwood Press, 2006. 224pp. illus. maps. (Recorded on publisher's Web site)

1211 Pankratev, V.P. **Uganda**. Moscow, Akademiia nauk, Istitut Afriki, 1976. 104p.

1212 Uganda: a country study. 2nd ed., comp. Rita M. Byrnes. Washington, DC, Headquarters, Dept. of the Army, 1992. xxviii, 298pp. illus. maps. Also available at: http://lcweb2.loc.gov/frd/cs/ugtoc.html. - - Orig. pub as **Area handbook for Uganda**, comp. Allison B. Herrick et al. Washington, DC, U.S. Department of Defense, 1969. xvi, 456pp. maps.

1213 Uganda districts information handbook. Expanded ed., comp. Mugisha Odrek Rwabwogo. Kampala, Fountain Publishers, 2005. x, 182pp. (Gives demographic, agricultural, topographic and educational data for each of 56 districts). - - Orig. pub. Kampala, 1992. iii, 113pp; - - 4th ed. Kampala, 1997. 134pp; - - 5th ed. Kampala, 2002. 184pp.

YEARBOOKS

1214 G.B. Colonial Office. **[Annual reports]: Uganda, 1901-1961**. London, 1901-1963. (As **Preliminary report by Her Majesty's special Commissioner on the Protectorate of Uganda**, 1900, (Cd.256) with maps (Cd.361), **Annual report on Uganda**, [title varies], 1902/03-1918/19 (as Command papers); **Colonial Office annual report**, 1919/20, 1920-1961 (not pub. 1939-45). Reports prior to 1904/05 issued by the Foreign Office)

1215 Indigo business directory: Uganda 1997/98- . London, Indigo Publications for Uganda Investment Authority, 1997- . Annual. 1997/98 ed. (1997). 164pp.

1216 Saben's commercial directory and handbook of Uganda. Kampala, Saben, 1947/48-?1960/61 . ?Annual. Last issue in NWU is for 1960/61. (General topographic and economic information, directories of residents and institutions. 1955/56 issue is "the first to include a classified commercial directory", pref.).

1217 Uganda. Ministry of Information, Broadcasting & Tourism. **Uganda 1962/63** [etc.]. Kampala, 1964-1970. 3 issues for 1962/63, 1964, 1967. Running title: **Uganda report**. (A post-independence continuation of **1214**)

1218 Uganda. Ministry of Information & Broadcasting. **Uganda 1983 yearbook**. Kampala, 1983- . ?No more pub. ("First publication of its kind to be issued since ... liberation of 1979", pref. to 1983 ed. Largely economic and statistical data)

1219 Uganda trade directory 1966/67. London, Diplomatic Press & Publishing Co. (Diprepu Co.) Ltd., 1966. ?No more pub.

STATISTICS

1220 Country profile: Uganda. London, Economist Intelligence Unit, 1986- Annual

1221 European Communites. Statistical Office. **Country profile, Uganda, 1991**. Luxembourg, EUROSTAT/Wiesbaden, Statistisches Bundesamt, 1992. 192pp. illus. maps.

1222 Germany. Statistisches Bundesamt. **Statistik des Auslandes: Länderberichte: Uganda** (later **Länderbericht: Uganda**). Wiesbaden/ Stuttgart, Metzler-Poetschel, 1965- . Irreg. Issues for 1965, 1986, 1988, 1991. *See also* **1018**

1223 IMF. **Uganda, selected issues and statistical appendix**. Washington, DC, 2005 (Country report, 05/172). 83pp. - - Earlier eds. (title varies) 1996 (Staff country report, 96/46); 1997 (Staff country report, 97/48); 1998 (Country report, 98/61); 1999 (Country report, 99/116); 2003 (Country report, 03/84). Full text of reports from 97/101, 1997 also available online, *see* **334**.

1224 Uganda. Bureau of Statistics (UBOS). http://www.ubos.org/. (Includes a wide variety of data)

1225 Uganda. Bureau of Statistics. **Uganda facts and figures**. Entebbe. LC has issue for 2003. (Pub. not recorded on Bureau Web site)

1226 Uganda. Statistics Division [etc.] **Quarterly economic and statistical bulletin**. Entebbe, 1969-1974. *Continues* **Quarterly digest of statistics**. Entebbe, 1965-1969.

1227 Uganda. Statistics Division [etc.]. **Statistical abstract**. Entebbe, 1960- . Annual. Not pub. 1972, 1975-1995. Latest issue in NWU is 2005. From 2005 also on CD-ROM. *Continues* East Africa High Commission, East African Statistical Department (Uganda Unit). **Statistical abstract**. Entebbe, 1957-1960.

1228 World Bank. **Uganda: country economic memorandum**. Washington, DC, 1982. xiv, 161pp. (Largely statistical)

DIRECTORIES OF ORGANIZATIONS

1229 Directory of human rights and development organisations in Uganda. Kampala, Human Rights Network (Hurinet) Uganda, 2002. 151pp.

1230 Okech, Anthony. **Directory of adult education agencies in Uganda**. Kampala, Makerere University Centre for Continuing Education & UNESCO, 1984. 123pp.

BIOGRAPHICAL SOURCES

1231 A directory of Uganda's Sixth Parliament, 1996-2001. Kampala, Fountain Publishers, [?1997]. vi, 195pp. (All entries include portraits)

1232 Uganda creative writers directory. Kampala, Alliance française & FEMWRITE (Uganda Women Writers' Association). 2000. (Cahiers, 3). xx, 74pp. (Bio-bibliographical details on some 60 authors with another 30 names having entries for their publications only)

1233 Who's who in Uganda, 1993/94, ed. David Isingoma. 2nd ed. Kampala, Fountain Publishers, 1994. 11, 102pp.illus. (c.1,000 entries, some with portraits). - - Orig. pub as: **Who's who in Uganda, 1988/89**, ed. Catherine Nyindombi. Kampala, 1989. 156pp. illus.

ATLASES & GAZETTEERS

1234 Atlas of population census 1969 for Uganda, comp. Brian W. Langlands. Kampala, Makerere University, Department of Geography, 1974. 184pp. maps. (Includes 60 maps, and 31 tables of data. "Aims to present key findings of the census in the visual form of maps")

1235 Atlas of Uganda. 2nd ed. Entebbe, Department of Lands & Surveys, 1967. 81pp. 49 x 51cm. (37 col. maps and text. Thematic coverage of physical features, climate, flora and fauna, human geography, agriculture, industry, trade, communications and historical themes: archaeological sites, early travels, evolution of borders. Main maps at 1:1,500,000, town plans of Kampala and Jinja at 1:10,000. Gazetteer. 2nd ed. extensively rev. but contains reduced scale coverage of crop distribution. *See* B.B. Whittaker, 'The Atlas of Uganda', *Chartered surveyor*, 99, 1967, 521-528. - - Orig. pub. Entebbe, Department of Lands & Surveys, 1962. 83pp. 49 x 51cm. (Review, *East African geographical review*, 1, 1963, 49-52)

1236 Uganda. Department of Lands & Surveys. **Gazetteer of Uganda**. Kampala, 1971. vi, 203pp. map.

1237 Uganda atlas of disease distribution, ed. Stuart A. Hall & Brian W. Langlands. Nairobi, East African Publishing House, 1975. xvi, 165pp. (Review, *GJ*, 143, 1977, 143)

1238 U.S. Board on Geographic Names. **Uganda: official standard names approved by the USBGN.** Washington, DC, 1964. (Gazetteer, 82). iii, 167pp. (Includes 11,900 names from maps at 1:250,000. Replaces appropriate section in **British East Africa ...** (*see* **1033**).

EARTH SCIENCES

1239 Barnes, John W., et al. **Mineral resources of Uganda**. Entebbe, Geological Survey, 1961. (Bulletin, 4). iii, 89pp. maps.

1240 Mukiibi, Joseph K. **Agriculture in Uganda**. Kampala, Fountain Publishers/ Wageningen, Technical Centre for Agricultural and Rural Cooperation (CTA), 2001. 4 vols. Vol. 1. Geology, climate, soils, water resources, marketing systems, etc. 466pp; vol.2. Crops. 572pp; vol. 3. Forestry. 109pp; vol. 4. Livestock. 380pp. (A massive compilation. Review, *ABPR*, 29, 2003, 233. *See also* J.D. Jameson. **Agriculture in Uganda**. London, Oxford University Press for Uganda Ministry of Agriculture & Forestry, 1970. xvii, 395pp. 40 plates. illus. maps)

1241 Reedman, Anthony J. **Geochemical atlas of Uganda**. Entebbe, Geological Survey & Mines Department, 1973. 10pp. 32 plates maps. (Scales 1:2M & 1:4M)

BIOLOGICAL SCIENCES

Zoology

1242 Carswell, Margaret, et al. **The bird atlas of Uganda**. Tring, British Ornithologists' Club & British Ornithologists' Union, 2005. 553pp. maps. (Provides two-col. maps for 1,000+ spp. Over twenty years in compilation)

1243 Delany, Michael James. **The rodents of Uganda**. London, British Museum (Natural History), 1975. (Publications, 764). viii, 165pp.

1244 Greenwood, Peter Humphrey. **The fishes of Uganda**. 2nd ed. Kampala, Uganda Society, 1966. vii, 131pp. illus. - - Orig. pub. Kampala, 1958. ii, 124pp.

1245 Pitman, Charles R.S. **A guide to the snakes of Uganda**. Rev ed. Codicote, Wheldon & Wesley, 1974. xii, 290pp. - - Orig. pub. Kampala, Uganda Society, 1938. xxi, 362pp. (First pub. *Uganda journal*, vols. 3-5. *See* K. Adler. 'The publishing history of Pitman's **Snakes of Uganda**', *Newsletter & bulletin of the International Society for the History & Bibliography of Herpetology*, 4, 2003, 5-14)

Botany

1246 Adjanohoun, Edouard J. **Contribution to ethnobotanical and floristic studies in Uganda**. Porto-Novo, OAU, 1993. (Traditional medicine and pharmocopoeia series). 433pp. illus.

1247 Eggeling, William Julius. **An annotated list of the grasses of the Uganda Protectorate**. 2nd ed. Entebbe, Government Printer, 1947. vii, 54pp. - - Orig. pub. Entebbe, 1944. 79pp.

1248 Eggeling, William Julius. **The indigenous trees of the Uganda Protectorate**. 2nd ed. rev. & enlarged Ivan R. Dale. Entebbe, Government Printer, 1951. xxx, 491pp. 20 col. plates. 94 text figs. - - Orig. pub. Entebbe, 1940. xxii, 296pp.

1249 Hamilton, Alan Charles. **A field guide to Uganda forest trees**. [?Kampala, Makerere University Printery, 1981]. 279pp. illus. (Covers 447 spp. with keys)

1250 Harker, K.W. & Napper, D. **An illustrated guide to the grasses of Uganda**. Entebbe, Government Printer, 1960. 63pp. illus. map.

1251 Katende, Anthony B. et al. **Useful trees and shrubs for Uganda: identification, propagation and management for agricultural and pastoral communities**. Nairobi, Regional Soil Conservation Unit & SIDA, 1995. xxiv, 710pp. illus. maps.

1252 Lind, Edna M. **Some common flowering plants of Uganda**. Rev. ed. Nairobi, Oxford University Press, 1971. iii, 259pp. illus. - - Orig. pub. London, Oxford University Press, 1962. vi, 257pp. *See also* **1001**

CENTRAL AFRICA

Anglophone Central Africa

> Malawi
> Zambia
> Zimbabwe

Francophone Central Africa

> Former French Equatorial Africa
>> Central African Republic   Congo
>> Chad   Gabon

> Former Belgian Africa
>> Congo (Democratic Republic) Burundi
>> Burundi & Rwanda   Rwanda

HANDBOOKS

1253 Ethnographic survey of Africa: West Central Africa. London, International African Institute, 1951-1953. 4 vols. maps. Sub-series of **Ethnographic survey** (*see* **86**). Vol. 1, The southern Lunda and related peoples (Northern Rhodesia, Angola, Belgian Congo), by M. McCulloch. 1951. 110pp; vol. 2, The Ovimbundu of Angola, by M. McCulloch. 1952. 50pp; vol. 3, The Lozi peoples of North-Western Rhodesia, by V.W. Turner. 1952. 64pp; vol. 4, The Ila-Tonga peoples of North-Western Rhodesia, by M.A. Jaspan. 1953. 72pp. *See also* **1006**

EARTH SCIENCES

1254 Holland, Charles H. **Lower Palaeozoic of north-western and west-central Africa**. Chichester, Wiley, 1985. (Lower Palaeozoic rocks of the world, 4). xii, 512pp. illus. maps.

BIOLOGICAL SCIENCES
Zoology

1255 Channing, Alan. **Amphibians of Central and Southern Africa**. Ithaca, NY, Cornell University Press, 2001. 470pp. 160 col. photos. 200 maps. (Covers 200 spp. of frogs, 3 caecilians in Malawi, Zambia, Zimbabwe; South Africa, Namibia; Botswana, Lesotho, Swaziland; Angola, Mozambique. Identification keys. Includes addresses of museums. Reviews, *African journal of herpetology*, 51, 2002, 155-156, *Copeia*, 2002, 1157-1158)

1256 Mackworth-Praed, Cyril W. & Grant, Claud H.B. **African handbook of birds: Series II: Birds of the southern third of Africa**. London, Longmans, 1962-63. 2 vols. Vol. 1, 1962. xxvii, 688pp; vol. 2, 1963. x, 747pp. (First major post 1945 attempt at a detailed avifauna for the region. *See also* **713, 1775**)

1257 Pinhey, Elliot C.G. **Dragonflies (Odonata) of Central Africa**. Livingstone, Rhodes-Livingstone Museum, 1961. (Occasional papers, n.s. 14). 97, 12pp. illus.

1258 Pinhey, Elliot C.G. **A guide to the butterflies of Central and Southern Africa**. London, Sir Joseph Causton, 1977. 106pp. col. illus. (Covers 135 spp.)

1259 Poynton, John C. & Broadley, Donald G. 'Amphibia Zambesiaca', *Annals of the Natal Museum*, 26, 1985, 503-553; 27, 1985, 115-181; 28, 1967, 161-229; 29, 1988, 447-486; 32, 1991, 221-277. (Covers Malawi, Zambia, Zimbabwe; Botswana, Mozambique)

See also **1773, 1774**

Botany

1260 Talifer, Y. **La fôret dense d'Afrique centrale: identification pratique des principaux arbres**. Wageningen, Centre technique de Coopération agricole et rurale (CTA), 1990. 2 vols. 1,271pp. illus. Vol. 1, Approche forestière et morphologique (includes keys, list of vernacular names and glossary); vol. 2, Approche botanique et systematique (systematic list of trees. Covers the forests from Sierra Leone to the Great Lakes)

1261 Vivien, Jacques & Fauré, J.J. **Arbres des forêts denses d'Afrique centrale**. Paris, ACCT, 1985. viii, 565pp. illus.

ANGLOPHONE CENTRAL AFRICA

Note that many English language sources, particularly those published during the colonial period, whose main emphasis is on **Southern Africa**, and are listed in that section, will often include coverage of the countries of this region. Similarly, many sources in the biological sciences covering Southern Africa and listed there, will also cover this region.

HANDBOOKS

1262 Banda, Felix. **Language across borders: the harmonisation and standardisation of orthographic conventions of Bantu languages within and across the borders of Malawi and Zambia**. Cape Town, Centre for Advanced Study of African Society (CASAS), 2002. 160pp. (*Note also* his **The classification of languages in Zambia and Malawi**. Cape Town, CASAS, 1998. 14pp)

1263 Brelsford, William V. **Handbook to the Federation of Rhodesia and Nyasaland**. London, Cassell for Federation Information Department, 1960. xii, 803pp. 180 photos. maps in text & folding maps. (Brelsford was Director of Information of the Federation. 25 contributors. An immensely detailed work covering all aspects of topography, history, and the social, administrative and economic structure of the region). - - **Index to the** *Handbook* **...** Comp. A.S.C. Hooper, M.S. in Library Science, Catholic University of America, 1969.

1264 **Central African Airways guide to the Federation of Rhodesia and Nyasaland**. 3rd ed. comp. L.S. Levin. Salisbury, A.J. Levin, 1961. 661pp. (Popular layout with photos, but very detailed information, greatly increased in 3rd ed. Covers topography, government, administration, communications, economics, with civil list, descriptive gazetteer of over 120 locations). - - Orig. pub. Salisbury, 1957. 264pp; - - 2nd ed. Salisbury, 1958. 298pp.

1265 Schmidt, Werner. **Föderation von Rhodesien und Nyassaland**. Bonn, Schroeder for Deutsche Afrika-Gesellschaft, 1959. (Die Länder Afrikas, 16). 139pp. illus. maps. (Later expanded to individual vols. in the series for **Malawi** (*see* **1287**), **Rhodesien** (*see* **1396**) and **Zambia** (*see* **1341**)

See also **2688, 2755**

YEARBOOKS

1266 **African trade directory: Malawi, Tanzania and Zambia**. Addis Ababa, UNECA for Federation of African Chambers of Commerce, 1987- . ?No more pub.

1267 **Boldad's commercial directory of Zimbabwe**. Bulawayo, Publications (Central Africa)/Ndola, Directory Publishers of Zambia, 1910- ?. Annual. 78th issue 1989. Title varies: **The Rhodesia directory/Rhodesia-Zambia-Malawi directory/Directory for Zambia, Malawi, Botswana and adjacent territories/Zimbabwe directory including Botswana [and Malawi]/Braby's commercial directory of Zimbabwe**. (Coverage varies: in addition to countries identified in titles above also covers Mozambique. Detailed lists of officials, residents, and commercial directory. Certain sections also published separately, e.g. **Salisbury** (later **Harare**) **directory**, 1962- ; **Bulawayo directory**, 1962- ; *see* **1401**; **Zambia directory**, 1963-)

1268 **Central African classified directory: business and trades**. Salisbury, Morris Publishing Co., 1953-1961. 8 issues. (Principal coverage of Northern and Southern Rhodesia and Nyasaland; more summary coverage of Kenya, Tanganyika and Uganda; Mozambique; Madagascar; Belgian Congo, and in 7th and 8th eds., Ghana and Nigeria. Over 1,000pp. per issue. An exclusively commercial directory, with no information other than names and addresses)

1269 **Directory of Central Africa**. Durban, A.C. Braby/Bulawayo, B. & T. Directories) 1954- . Annual. Title varies: **Central Africa business directory/ Braby's Central and East African directory/Central Africa business directory/Braby's commercial directory of Central Africa/Zimbabwe & Rhodesia business directory**. Current title from 25th ed. 1981. (Coverage varies: Rhodesia/Zimbabwe with details of government and commercial directory; Angola, Botswana, Lesotho, Malawi, Mauritius, Mozambique, Swaziland, Zambia with commercial directory only. From 1981 includes Kenya, Réunion, Seychelles, Namibia, excludes Angola, Mozambique)

1270 **Year book and guide of the Rhodesias and Nyasaland**. Salisbury, Rhodesian Pubns., 1937-?1962. Annual (irreg.). (Issues for 1937, 1938/39, 1940/41, 1942/43, 1943/44, 1944/45, 1946/47, 1948/49, 1950/51, 1962. In addition to topographical, historical and economic information contains a gazetteer with 150/200 locations, and a biography section, 400/600 entries)

See also **1022, 2760, 2762, 2765, 2774 , 2777, 2819**

STATISTICS

1271 Federation of Rhodesia & Nyasaland. Central African Statistical Office. **Monthly digest of statistics of the Federation of Rhodesia and Nyasaland**. Salisbury, 1954-1964.

BIOGRAPHICAL SOURCES

1272 Great Britain. Commonwealth War Graves Commission. **The Register of the names of those who fell in the 1939-1945 War and are buried in Malawi, Zambia, Zimbabwe and Namibia**. Maidenhead, 1992. viii, 50pp.

1273 Who's who of Rhodesia, Mauritius, Central and East Africa. Johannesburg, Combined Publishers [etc.], 1960-?1974. Annual. (Published separately, and also as a section within **Who's who of Southern Africa** (1959- *see* **2850**). (Includes Rhodesia/Zimbabwe, Zambia, Malawi, Botswana, Mauritius, Mozambique). *Continues* **Central and East African who's who for 1953** [etc.]. Salisbury, Central Africa Who's Who Ltd., 1953-56. 3 issues for 1953, 1955, 1956; **Who's who of the Federation of Rhodesia and Nyasaland, Central and East Africa**. Johannesburg, Ken Donaldson, 1957-59. 3 issues

ATLASES & GAZETTEERS

1274 Atlas of the Federation of Rhodesia and Nyasaland. Salisbury, Department of the Surveyor-General, 1960-1964. 24 maps. 69 x 69cm. (24 topographic and thematic sheets, mostly at 1:2,500,000)

1275 U.S. Board on Geographic Names. **Rhodesia and Nyasaland: official standard names approved by the USBGN**. Washington, DC, 1956. 214pp. (Pp. 1-101, Northern Rhodesia; pp. 102-178, Southern Rhodesia; pp. 179-214, Nyasaland. Includes c.17,000 names. Later eds. pub. in separate vols. for **Malawi**, *see* **1311**, **Zambia**, *see* **1366**, **Southern Rhodesia**, *see* **1430**)

See also **1264**

EARTH SCIENCES

1276 Bond, G. et al. **Lexique stratigraphique international, 4, Afrique, fasc. 9: Fédération Nyassaland, Rhodésie du nord, Rhodésie du sud**. Paris, CNRS, 1956. 78pp. map.

BIOLOGICAL SCIENCES

1277 Coates Palgrave, Olive H. & Keith. **Trees of Central Africa.** Salisbury, National Publications Trust, 1957. xxviii, 466pp. + 110 col. plates. (Covers Malawi, Zambia, Zimbabwe. Semi-popular work with emphasis on illus.)

1278 **Flora Zambesiaca**, ed. Arthur Wallis Exell et al. London, Crown Agents & Flora Zambesiaca Managing Committee for Governments of Portugal, Federation of Rhodesia & Nyasaland [etc.] & the U.K., 1960- . 32 pts. covering 27,000 spp. pub. by 2006. Scheduled for completion in 14 vols. issued in c.50 pts. (One of the major African floras, a joint project by Natural History Museum, London, Royal Botanic Gardens, Kew and Botanical Institute, University of Coimbra. Covers Malawi, Zambia, Zimbabwe; Botswana, Namibia, Mozambique; also the Caprivi strip of Angola. Also available at: http://www.kew.org/floras/fz/intro.html which allows a single search across all vols. for particular taxa)
- - Schelpe, Edmund A.C. *Flora Zambesiaca*, **Supplement: Pteridophyta**. London, Crown Agents, 1970. 254pp. illus. map.
- - *Flora Zambesiaca*, **Supplement: vegetation map of the** *Flora Zambesiaca* **area**, ed. Hiram Wild & Abíio Fernandes. Salisbury, M.O. Collins, 1968. 68pp. text; 2 maps sheets at 1:2.5m
- - *Flora Zambesiaca*: **collecting localities in the** *Flora Zambesiaca* **area**, ed. Gerald V. Pope. Kew, Royal Botanic Gardens, 1998. xiv, 178pp.

1279 Smithers, Reay H.N. **The mammals of Rhodesia, Zambia and Malawi: a handbook.** London, Collins, 1966. 159pp. illus.

See also **815, 816, 1052, 3005, 3023, 3024, 3031, 3038, 3046**

MALAWI

Official Web site of the Government of Malawi
http://www.malawi.gov.mw/

Government of Malawi home page http://www.sdnp.org.mw/~caphill/

HANDBOOKS

1280 Blantyre and the southern region of Malawi: an official guide, comp. Vera Garland. Blantyre, Central Africana, 1991. 164pp. illus. maps. (One of series covering the whole country, with **Mzuzu and the northern region of Malawi: an official guide**, comp. Margaret Roseveare & Lee Myers. Blantyre, 1991. 93pp., **Lilongwe and the central region of Malawi: an official guide**, comp. Alison Mathews et al. Blantyre, 1991. 103pp.)

1281 Facts on Malawi, ed. Anthony Livuza. Blantyre, Department of Information, 1999. 72pp. illus

1282 G.B. War Office. Military Operations Directorate. **Military report on Nyasaland**. London, 1939. (B. 532). v, 100pp. (Covers history, administration, topography, ethnography, communications. Detailed coverage of Blantyre, Lilongwe, Limbe, Zomba.)

1283 Historical dictionary of Malawi. 3rd ed., comp. Owen J.M. Kalinga & Cynthia A. Crosby. Lanham, MD, Scarecrow Press, 2001. (African historical dictionaries, 84). xliv, 487pp (Review, *Choice*, 39, 2002, 1032-1033). - - Orig. pub. comp. Cynthia A Crosby. Metuchen, NJ, 1980. (African historical dictionaries, 25). xxxvi, 169pp; - - 2nd ed. Metuchen, NJ, 1993. (African historical dictionaries, 54). xxxv, 202pp. (Reviews, *African affairs*, 94, 1995, 449-450; "haphazard collection of entries which are mostly incomplete, sometimes inaccurate, and virtually always lack meaning"; *Choice*, 31, 1994, 750; *IJAHS*, 27, 1994, 696-697. Rated "good", Balay, 1996)

1284 Malawi: a country study; comp. Harold D. Nelson et al. Washington, DC, U.S. Department of Defense, 1979. xiv, 353pp. illus. maps. (Reprint of **Area handbook for Malawi**. Washington, DC, 1975. Review, *IJAHS*, 16, 1983, 148-149)

1285 Pozdniakova, A.P. **Respublika Malavi: spravochnik**. Moscow, Akademiia nauk, Institut Afriki, 1989. 184pp. illus. maps.

1286 Read, Frank E. **Malawi, land of progress: a comprehensive survey**. Blantyre, Ramsay Parker for Department of Information, 1969. 132pp. illus. - - Orig. pub. as **Malawi, land of promise: ...** Blantyre, 1967. 124pp. illus.

1287 Schimmelfennig, Else. **Malawi**. Bonn, K. Schroeder for Deutsche Afrika-Gesellschaft, 1965. (Die Länder Afrikas, 30). 95pp. illus. maps. (Expanded rev. of the relevant sections of **1265**)

See also **1006**

YEARBOOKS

1288 **Indigo business directory: Malawi, 1998/99-** . London, Indigo Publications for Malawi Chamber of Commerce & Industry, 1998- . Latest issue in NWU is for 2002/03.

1289 **Industrial and trade directory, 1972-** . Blantyre, Associated Chambers of Commerce & Industry of Malawi, 1973- . Irreg. 6th ed. 1982/83; 7th ed. 1988/89. Latest issue in NWU is 9th ed. 1994/95

1290 G.B. Colonial Office. **[Annual reports]: Nyasaland, 1891-1962**. London, 1894-1964. (As **Report ... on the first three years administration of the Eastern portion of British Central Africa**, 1894, **Report ... on the trade and general condition of British Central African Protectorate**, 1895/96-1896/97, **Annual report on the British Central African Protectorate**, 1897/98 (not pub. 1898-1902), **Report on the trade and general conditions of the British Central African Protectorate**, 1902-03, **British Central Africa Protectorate report**, 1903/04-1906/07, **Nyasaland Protectorate report**, 1907/08-1908/09, **Nyasaland Report**, 1909/10-1918/19, (all as Command papers); **Colonial Office annual report** [title varies], 1919/20-62 (not pub. 1926, 1939-45). 1962 report issued by Commonwealth Relations Office.

1291 Malawi. Department of Information. **Malawi yearbook**. Blantyre, 1968-?1982. Annual. (Title varies: **Malawi** (1968-1969); **Malawi: an official handbook** (1970-72). Not published 1976-77, when replaced by much briefer (24pp.) **Malawi: the year in review**. Last issue traced is for 1982 in CUL, SOAS.

1292 **Malawi business directory**. Blantyre, Government Printer for Postmaster General, 1995- . Annual.

1293 Malawi directory. Blantyre, A.C. Braby (Blantyre), 1966- . Annual. Last vol. in NLSA is for 1974.

See also **1015, 2760**

STATISTICS

1294 Country profile: Malawi. London, Economist Intelligence Unit, 1986-Annual

1295 Germany. Statistisches Bundesamt. **Statistik des Auslandes: Länderberichte: Malawi** (later **Länderbericht: Malawi**). Wiesbaden/Stuttgart, Metzler-Poetschel, 1967- . Irreg. Issues for 1967, 1984, 1986, 1988, 1992.

1296 IMF. **Malawi: selected issues and statistical appendix**. Washington, DC, 2004. (Country report, 04/390). 80pp. - - Earlier eds. (title varies), 1995 (Staff country report, 95/51); 2001 (Country report, 01/132); 2002 (Country report, 02/185). Full text of reports from 1997 also available online, *see* **334**.

1297 Malawi. National Statistical Office [etc.]. **Statistical yearbook/Malawi statistical yearbook**. Zomba, 1972- . Annual. Latest issue in NWU is for 2002. *Continues* Malawi. Ministry of Development Planning [etc.]. **Compendium of statistics**. Zomba, 1965-1970. 3 issues for 1965, 1966, 1970. - - Abbreviated version published as **Malawi in figures**. Zomba, 1981-. Annual.

1298 Malawi. National Statistical Office. **Monthly statistical bulletin**. Zomba, 1971- Latest issue in NWU is for 2004. *Continues* Malawi. Ministry of Finance [etc.]. **Quarterly digest of statistics**. Zomba, 1964-1970.

1299 Malawi. National Statistical Office. http://www.nso.malawi.net/. (Includes texts of latest *Monthly statistical bulletin, Statistical yearbook* and *Malawi in figures*; also of latest Census, and of **Malawi: an atlas of social statistics** (2002) *see* **1309**)

1300 Pryor, Frederic Leroy. **Income distribution and economic development in Malawi: some historical statistics**. Washington, DC, World Bank, 1988. (Discussion papers, 36). ix, 83pp.

1301 Southern Rhodesia. Central African Statistical Office. **Statistical handbook of Nyasaland**. Salisbury, 1950, 1952. Issues for 1949/1950, 1952.

DIRECTORIES OF ORGANIZATIONS

1302 Directory of non-governmental organisations in Malawi. Blantyre, Council for Non-Governmental Organisations in Malawi (CONGOMA), 1996. 80pp.

1303 Directory of science and technology institutions in Malawi. Lilongwe, National Research Council of Malawi, 2001. ii, 40pp.

1304 Doling, Tim. **Malawi: arts directory**. London, Visiting Arts, 1999. 48pp.

BIOGRAPHICAL SOURCES

1305 Biographies/profiles of the Malawi Cabinet and members of parliament, comp. & ed. M.J. Kaunjika. Blantyre, Information Depertment, 1996. (Portfolio with c. 170 single sheets, one for each biographee)

1306 M'Passou, Denis. **Who is who of Malawi**. Mulanje, Spot Pubs., 1995. 61pp.

ATLASES & GAZETTEERS

1307 Agnew, Swanzie & Stubbs, Michael. **Malawi in maps**. London, University of London Press, 1972. 144pp. (47 b. & w. maps and text)

1308 Malawi. Department of Survey. **Maps illustrating development projects 1970-1973**. Blantyre, 1970. 18pp. - - ..., **1978/79-1980/81**. Blantyre, 1978. 34p; - - ..., **1981/82-1983/84**. Blantyre, 1981. 37pp. - - ..., **1983/84-1985/86**. Blantyre, 1983. 37pp. (Series of atlases with col. maps at 1:2M showing wide variety of data)

1309 Malawi: an atlas of social statistics, comp. Todd Benson et al. Washington, DC, International Food Policy Research Institute/Blantyre, National Statistical Office, 2002. v, 94pp. col. maps. 34cm. Also available on National Statistical Office Web site http://www.nso.malawi.net/.

1310 National atlas of Malawi. Blantyre, Malawi Department of Surveys, 1985. vi, 79pp. loose-leaf in ring-binder. 45 x 48cm. (70 maps, including 20 general topographic maps most at 1:250,000, 41 thematic maps, most at 1:1M or 1:2M. Transparent overlay at 1:2M showing population distribution. Includes gazetteer)

1311 U.S. Board on Geographic Names. **Malawi: official standard names approved by the USBGN**. Washington, DC, 1970. (Gazetteer, 113). iii, 161pp. (Includes 10,200 names from 1:50,000 for central and southern areas, 1:250,000 for northern areas map series. A rev. of the section for Nyasaland in **Rhodesia and Nyasaland ...**, *see* **1275**)

EARTH SCIENCES

1312 Carter, George Stuart & Bennett, J.D. **The geology and mineral resources of Malawi**. 2nd ed. Zomba, Government Printer, 1973. (Bulletin of the Geological Survey Department, 6). viii, 62pp. illus. - - Orig. pub. comp. W.G.G. Cooper as **The geology and mineral resources of Nyasaland**. Zomba, 1946. 11pp; - - rev. ed. Zomba, 1957. 43pp.

1313 G.B. Directorate of Overseas Surveys. **Geological atlas of Malawi**. Zomba, Geological Survey of Malawi, 1970-1973. 10 sheets. 64cm x 94cm. (Scale 1:250,000)

1314 Lienau, Cay. **Malawi: Geographie eines unterentwickelten Landes**. Darmstadt, Wissenschaftliche Buchgesellschaft, 1981. (Wissenschaftliche Länderkunden, 20). xvi, 243pp. + 26pp. plates. illus. maps.

1315 Pike, John G. & Rimmington, G.T. **Malawi: a geographical study**. London, Oxford University Press, 1965. xv, 229pp. + 19pp. plates. illus.

BIOLOGICAL SCIENCES

Zoology

1316 Ansell, William F.H. & Dowsett, Robert J. **Mammals of Malawi: an annotated checklist and atlas**. Zennor, Trendrine Press, 1988. 170pp. + 53pp. plates. (Describes 180 spp. Reviews, *Mammal review*, 19, 1989, 174; *SAJZ*, 24, 1989, 366-367, "amount of information contained is amazing"). - - 'Addenda and corrigenda to **Mammals of Malawi**', *Nyala*, 15, 1991, 43-46

1317 Benson, Constantine W. **The birds of Malawi**. Limbe, D.W.K. Macpherson, 1977. 263pp. (Review, *Ibis*, 120, 1978, 379)

1318 Gifford, David. **A list of the butterflies of Malawi**. Blantyre, Society of Malawi, 1965. vi, 151pp. illus. map.

1319 Newman, Kenneth, et al. **Birds of Malawi: a supplement to** *Newman's birds of Southern Africa*. Halfway House, Southern Book Publishers, 1992. viii, 110pp. (Descriptions and illus. for 74 spp. occurring in Malawi and not covered by the parent work; checklist of 620 spp. with page refs. to the parent)

1320 Stewart, Margaret M. **Amphibians of Malawi**. Albany, NY, State University of New York Press, 1967. ix, 163pp. col. illus. map.

1321 Sweeney, R. Charles H. **Snakes of Nyasaland; with new added corrigenda and addenda**. Amsterdam, Asher, 1971. xi, 203pp. - - Orig. pub. Zomba, Nyasaland Society, 1961.

1322 Wilkey, Rupert. **A guide to the snakes of Malawi**. CD-ROM. (Covers 67 spp.) "In preparation" (*See* BL *Annual report*, 2002/03, p. 28)

Botany

1323 Binns, Blodwen. **Dictionary of plant names in Malawi**. Zomba, Government Printer for University of Malawi, 1972. ix, 184pp.

1324 Binns, Blodwen. **A first check list of the herbaceous flora of Malawi**. Zomba, Government Printer for University of Malawi, 1968. 113pp. map.

1325 Jackson, G. & Wiehe, P.O. **An annotated check list of Nyasaland grasses, indigenous and cultivated**. Zomba, Government Printer for Department of Agriculture, 1958. 75pp. illus.

1326 Makato, C.J.A. **A description of crop varieties grown in Malawi**. [Rev.ed.]. Lilongwe, Department of Agricultural Research, 1994. 68pp. - - Earlier eds. Lilongwe, 1991. 64pp; - - Lilongwe, 1986. 56pp.

1327 Moriarty, Audrey. **Wild flowers of Malawi**. Cape Town, Purnell, 1975. viii, 166pp. col. illus.

1328 Williamson, Jessie. **Useful plants of Malawi**. Rev. ed. Zomba, University of Malawi, 1972. 168pp. illus. - - Orig. pub. as **Useful plants of Nyasaland**. Zomba, Government Printer, 1956. 168pp. illus.

Trees

1329 Chapman, John D. & White, Frank. **The evergreen forests of Malawi.** Oxford, Commonwealth Forestry Institute, 1970. 190pp. + 45 plates. illus. (Largely phytogeographical in coverage)

1330 Hardcastle, P.D. **A preliminary silvicultural classification of Malawi.** Blantyre, Forestry Research Institute, 1977. (Forestry research record, 57). ii, 194pp. illus. maps.

1331 Pullinger, John S. & Kitchen, Alison. **Trees of Malawi, with some shrubs and climbers.** Blantyre, Blantyre Printers & Publishers, 1982. x, 229pp. col. illus. maps.

1332 Topham, P. **Check list of the forest trees and shrubs of the Nyasaland Protectorate.** 2nd ed. Zomba, Government Printer, 1958. 137pp. - - Orig. pub. as **Check-lists of the forest trees and shrubs of the British Empire. Vol. 2, Nyasaland Protectorate**, comp. Joseph Burtt-Davy & A.C. Hoyle. Oxford, Imperial Forestry Institute, 1936. 111pp.

1333 White, Frank et al. **Evergreen forest flora of Malawi.** Kew, Royal Botanic Gardens, 2001. x, 697pp. illus. (Originally conceived as the taxonomic companion volume to Chapman & White, 1970, *see* **1329**. Much delayed in compilation and after White died in 1994 the work was completed by Françoise Dowsett-Lemaire. Updates Topham, **1332**, for evergreen spp. Covers 712 indigenous spp. with illus. of some 400)

ZAMBIA

Zambia online: the national homepage of Zambia
http://www.zambia.co.zm/

Republic of Zambia, State House Web site http://www.statehouse.gov.zm/

HANDBOOKS

1334 Brelsford, William V. **The tribes of Zambia**. 2nd ed. Lusaka, Government Printer, 1965. xii, 157pp. illus. maps. - - Orig. pub. as **The tribes of Northern Rhodesia**. Lusaka, 1956. 128pp.

1335 Derricourt, Robin M. ed. **A classified index of archaeological and other sites in Zambia**. Livingstone, Republic of Zambia, National Monuments Commission, 1976. (Research pub. 3). x, 169pp. 29 x 39 cm

1336 Drescher, Axel. **Sambia: mit einem Anhang: Fakten, Zahlen, Übersichten**. Gotha, Klett-Perthes, 1998. 198pp.

1337 G.B. War Office. Military Operations Directorate. **Military report on Northern Rhodesia, 1939**. London, 1939. (B. 531). iv, 139pp. (Covers history, administration, ethnography and communications)

1338 Historical dictionary of Zambia. 2nd ed. comp. John J. Grotpeter. Lanham, MD, Scarecrow Press, 1998. (African historical dictionaries, 19). xxxv, 571pp. (Reviews, *ARD*, 84, 2000, 83-90; *Choice*, 36, 1998, 296; *IJAHS*, 33, 2000, 441-442). - - Orig. pub. Metuchen, NJ, 1979. xviii, 410pp. (Review, *JAH*, 23, 1982, 139-140. Rated "fair", Balay, 1996)

1339 Northern Rhodesia. Department of Information. **Northern Rhodesia handbook**. Rev. ed. Lusaka, 1953. 263pp. - - Orig. pub. Lusaka, 1950. 232pp. - - rev. ed. Lusaka, 1952. *Continues* **Northern Rhodesia handbook**. Lusaka, 1939. 144pp; - - **Northern Rhodesia official handbook**. Lusaka, 1947. 92pp. 1 folding map; - - 2nd ed. 1948. 98pp.

1340 Posthumus, Bram. **Zambia: mensen, politiek, economie, cultuur**. Amsterdam, Koninklijk Instituut voor de Tropen/The Hague, Novib, 1997. (Landenreeks). 78pp. illus. maps.

1341 Schmidt, Werner. **Zambia**. Bonn, K. Schroeder for Deutsche Afrika-Gesellschaft, 1965. (Die Länder Afrikas, 31). 176pp. illus. maps. (Expanded revision of the appropriate sections of **1265**)

1342 Solodovnikov, V.G. **Respublika Zambiia: spravochnik**. Moscow, Akademiia nauk, Institut Afriki, 1982. 277pp. illus. maps.

1343 Zambia. Central Statistical Office. **Country profile: Zambia**. Rev. ed. Lusaka, 1992. 64pp. - - Orig. pub. Lusaka, 1984. ix, 102pp; - - 2nd ed. Lusaka, 1986.

1344 Zambia. Information Services. **A handbook to the Republic of Zambia**. Lusaka, 1964. vi, 153pp. (Cover title: **Zambia today**. General topographical and historical information)

1345 Zambia: a country study. 3rd ed. comp. Irving Kaplan et al. Washington, DC, U.S. Department of Defense, 1979. 308pp. illus. maps. - - Orig. pub. as **Area handbook for Zambia**, comp. Harold D. Nelson et al. Washington, DC, 1969. xvi, 482pp. maps; - - 2nd ed. comp. Irving Kaplan et al. Washington, DC, 1974. lxxxvi, 484pp. maps.

See also **1006**

YEARBOOKS

1346 G.B. Colonial Office. **[Annual reports]: Northern Rhodesia, 1924/25-1962**. London, 1926-1964. (As **Colonial Office annual report**, 1924-62 (not pub. 1939-45). Pub. for 1924/25 and 1925/26, then annually, commencing 1926. One report pub. for 1961 and 1962).

1347 Zambia trade and investment directory, 1994/95- . Lusaka, Advantage Promotions, 1994- . ? Annual. NWU has issue for 1994/95 only.

See also **2760, 1267**

STATISTICS

1348 Country profile: Zambia. London, Economist Intelligence Unit, 1986- Annual

1349 Germany. Statistisches Bundesamt. **Statistik des Auslandes: Länderberichte: Sambia** (later **Länderbericht: Sambia**). Wiesbaden/

Stuttgart, Metzler-Poetschel, 1979- Irreg. Issues for 1979, 1983, 1985, 1987, 1991, 1995

1350 IMF. **Zambia: selected issues and statistical appendix**. Washington, DC, 2006. (Country report, 06/118). 72pp. - - Earlier eds. (title varies) 1994 (Staff country report, 94/6); 1996 (Staff country report, 96/98); 1997 (Staff country report, 97/118); 1999 (Staff country report, 99/43); 2004 (Country report, 04/150). Full text of reports from 97/101, 1997 also available online, *see* **334**.

1351 Southern Rhodesia. Central African Statistical Office. **Economic and statistical bulletin of Northern Rhodesia**. Salisbury, 1948-1954. *Continued by* **Monthly digest of statistics of the Federation of Rhodesia & Nyasaland** (*see* **1271**)

1352 Zambia. Central Statistical Office. **Monthly digest of statistics**. Lusaka, 1964- . Latest issues in NWU are for 2001

1353 Zambia. Central Statistical Office. **Monthly statistical bulletin**. Lusaka, ?1971- . SOAS has issues for 1971 to 1973

1354 Zambia. Central Statistical Office. **Quarterly digest of statistics**. Lusaka, 1994- . NWU has issues for 1994 to 1999

1355 Zambia. Central Statistical Office. **Statistical yearbook**. Lusaka, 1967-1971. Annual. 5 issues.

1356 Zambia. Central Statistical Office. **Zambia in figures**. Lusaka, 1980- . Annual. Latest issue in Stanford is for 2001.

DIRECTORIES OF ORGANIZATIONS

1357 A directory of non-governmental organizations in Zambia, 1993. Lusaka, Planning & Development Co-operation Division, 1993. xii, 273pp. (Lists 214 organizations A/Z, with a subject index under 19 headings)

1358 Doling, Tim. **Zambia: arts directory**. London, Visiting arts, 1999. 43pp.

1359 Zambia Catholic directory. Lusaka, Catholic Bookshop, 1991. 274pp.

BIOGRAPHICAL SOURCES

1360 Sampson, Richard. **They came to Northern Rhodesia: being a record of persons who had entered what is now the territory of Northern Rhodesia by 31ˢᵗ Dec. 1902.** Lusaka, Commission for the Preservation of Natural & Historical Monuments & Relics, 1956. xiv, 49pp. (Lists 874 names of those who had arrived before the large influx following the South African War. Very brief biographical information and a reference to sources)

1361 Who's who in Zambia, ed. Kelvin G. Mlenga. Ndola, Roan Consolidated Mines Ltd., 1979. 39pp. (Includes 168 entries). - - Earlier ed. **Who is who in Zambia 1967/68**. Lusaka, Kingstons (Zambia) Ltd., 1967. viii, 107pp.

ATLASES & GAZETTEERS

Atlases

1362 Atlas of the population of Zambia. Rev. ed. comp. G.H. Adika. Lusaka, National Council for Scientific Research, 1977. 15 col. maps. - - Orig. pub. comp. Mary E. Jackman & D. Hywel Davies, Lusaka. 1971. 9 maps. 56 x 65cm

1363 Davies, D. Hywel. **Zambia in maps**. London, University of London Press, 1971. 128pp. (Includes 55 thematic b. & w. maps with accompanying text. Reviews, *GJ*, 139, 1973, 181-182; *Zambia Geographical Association magazine*, 17, 1972, 40-43; 19, 1972, 37-40)

1364 Republic of Zambia Atlas. Lusaka, Survey Department/National Council for Scientific Research, 1966- . (Thematic atlas issued in sheets, mostly 45 x 54cm, some 74 x 90cm. Majority at 1:3M. Covers climate, soils, minerals, tribes and languages, education, medical facilities and agriculture. 31 maps on 49 sheets issued to date, latest in 1996, several in rev. eds.)

1365 Resource atlas for Zambia, comp. Veronica G. Chikuma et al. Lusaka, National Educational Company of Zambia, 1985. 96pp. illus. maps.

See also **1454**

Gazetteers

1366 U.S. Board on Geographic Names. **Gazetteer of Zambia**. 2nd ed. Washington, DC, 1983. 2 vols. (Includes 38,500 names). - - Orig. pub. as **Zambia: official standard names approved by the USBGN**. Washington, DC, 1972. iv, 585pp. (Rev. of section for Northern Rhodesia in **Rhodesia and Nyasaland ...** *see* **1275**)

1367 Zambia. Ministry of Lands and Mines. **Gazetteer of geographical names in the Republic of Zambia**. Lusaka, Government Printer, 1966. 319pp. (Includes c.35,000 entries arranged by province)

1368 Zambia. Ministry of Land and Natural Resources. **Gazetteer of geographical names in the Barotse Protectorate**. Lusaka, 1959. iii, 156pp. (Now the Western Province of Zambia)

EARTH SCIENCES

1369 Acharya, U.R. & Bhaskara Rao, N.S. **Meteorology of Zambia**. Lusaka, Zambia Meteorological Department, 1981. 3 vols. in 1. (Companion vol. to Peter Hutchinson. **The climate of Zambia.** Lusaka, Zambia Geographical Association, 1974. (Occasional study, 7). iv, 95pp.)

1370 Mendelsohn, Felix. **The geology of the Northern Rhodesian Copperbelt**. London, MacDonald, 1961. xvi, 523pp. illus. maps.

1371 Muchinda, M.R. **The agricultural climates of Zambia**. Lusaka, Zambia Meteorological Department 1985. xi, 183pp. illus. maps.

1372 Reeve, W.H. **The geology and mineral resources of Northern Rhodesia**. Lusaka, Geological Survey, 1962-1963. (Bulletin, 3). 2 vols. Vol. 1. ix, 213pp. illus; vol. 2. 27 maps.

1373 Schultz, Jürgen. **Land use in Zambia**. Munich, Weltforum Verlag, 1976. viii, 215pp. illus. maps. (Pt. 1, Traditional land use systems and their regions; pt. 2, Land use maps: 4 sheets at 1:750,000. Review, *GJ*, 143, 1977, 471-472, "the work is a mine of information")

1374 Schultz, Jürgen. **Zambia**. Darmstadt, Wissenschaftliche Buchgesellschaft, 1983. (Wissenschaftliche Länderkunden, 23). xviii, 332pp. illus. maps. (Physical and economic geography)

1375   Trapnell, C.G. & J.N. Clothier. **The soils, vegetation and traditional agriculture of Zambia**. Bristol, Redcliffe Press for Zambian Ministry of Agriculture, Food and Fisheries, 1996. 2 vols. (Re-issue of Trapnell's **The soils, vegetation and agriculture of North-eastern Rhodesia**. Lusaka, 1943 & **The soils, vegetation, and agricultural systems of Northwestern Rhodesia**. Lusaka, 1937. The original field notebooks of the surveys on which these were based have also been published as **Ecological survey of Zambia: the traverse records of C.G. Trapnell, 1932-43**, ed. Paul Smith. Kew, Royal Botanic Gardens, 2001. 3 vols. "For Zambia it is the primary source of basic ecological data", pref.)

BIOLOGICAL SCIENCES

Zoology

Birds & Mammals

1376   Ansell, William F.H. **The mammals of Zambia**. Chilanga, National Parks & Wildlife Service, 1978. v, 126pp. + 110pp. maps. (Covers 222 spp. with range maps and a table of distribution by biotic zones. Rev. ed. of his **Mammals of Northern Rhodesia: a revised checklist**. Lusaka, Governmemt Printer, 1960. xxxi, 155, 24pp; itself a rev. of D.G. Lancaster. **A check list of the mammals of Northern Rhodesia**. Lusaka, Government Printer, 1953. 56pp). - - 'Addenda & corrigenda, 1', *Black Lechwe*, n.s. 3, 1982, 17-25.

1377   Aspinwall, Dylan & Beel, Carl. **Field guide to Zambian birds not found in Southern Africa**. Lusaka, Zambian Ornithological Society, 1998. 106pp. 25 col. plates. (Accounts of 136 spp., 118 with col. illus. found in Zambia but not illus. in the Southern African field guides. Includes checklist of 739 spp. Reviews, *BABC*, 7, 2000, 78-79; *Ibis*, 141, 1999, 507-508)

1378   Benson, Constantine W. et al. **The birds of Zambia**. 2nd ed. London, Collins, 1973. 414, 20pp. - - Orig. pub. London, 1971. 414, 20pp. (Review, *Puku*, 7, 1973, 197-198). - - Dowsett, Robert J. et al. 'Further additions to the avifauna of Zambia', *Bulletin of the British Ornithologists' Club*, 119, 1999, 94-103 (Adds 24 new spp. recorded 1978 to 1995)

1379   White, Charles M.N. & Winterbottom, John Mial. **A check list of the birds of Northern Rhodesia**. Lusaka, 1949. viii, 168pp. map.

Reptiles, Amphibians & Fishes

1380 Broadley, Donald G. 'The reptiles and amphibians of Zambia', *Puku*, 6, 1971, 1-143. - - 'Additions and corrections', *ibid.* 7, 1973, 93-95

1381 Broadley, Donald G. **Snakes of Zambia: an atlas and field guide.** Frankfurt-am-Main, Chimaira, 2003. 280pp. col. illus. (Review, *African journal of herpetology*, 52, 2003, 135-138)

1382 Jackson, Peter B.N. **The fishes of Northern Rhodesia: a checklist of indigenous species.** Lusaka, Government Printer, 1961. xv, 140pp. illus. map. - - Bell-Cross, Graham. 'Additions and amendments to the checklist of the fishes of Zambia', *Puku*, 3, 1965, 29-43

Invertebrates

1383 Heath, Alan, et al. **The butterflies of Zambia.** Nairobi, African Butterfly Research Institute & Lepidopterists' Society of Africa, 2002. xvii, 137pp. + 1 CD-ROM

Botany

1384 Fanshawe, D.B. **The vegetation of Zambia.** Lusaka, Ministry of Rural Development, 1969. (Forest research bulletin, 7). iv, 67pp. illus.

1385 Phiri, P.S.M. **A checklist of Zambian vascular plants.** Pretoria, SABONET, 2005. (SABONET report, 32). xii, 169pp. illus.

1386 Storrs, A.E.G. **Know your trees: some of the common trees found in Zambia.** Ndola, Zambian Forest Department, 1980. xxi, 380pp. illus.

1387 White, Frank. **Forest flora of Northern Rhodesia.** Oxford, Oxford University Press, 1962. xxvi, 455pp. 72 text figs. map. (Detailed description of trees and shrubs, listing some 1,400 spp.)

See also **1065**

ZIMBABWE

Zimbabwe Government online http://www.gta.gov.zw/

HANDBOOKS

1388 Bossema, Wim. **Zimbabwe: mensen, politiek, economie, cultuur**. Amsterdam, Koninklijk Instituut voor de Tropen/The Hague, Novib, 1999. (Landenreeks). 78pp. illus. maps.

1389 **A concise encyclopedia of Zimbabwe**, ed. Denis Berens et al. Gweru, Mambo Press, 1988. viii, 444pp. (Mostly short entries, including biographies; longer articles on churches, education, international relations, law, literature, publishing, sports and trade unions. "Quick and concise answers for the person in a hurry", pref.).

1390 Demkina, L.A. et al. **Respublika Zimbabve**. Moscow, Akademiia nauk, Institut Afriki, 1985. 215pp.

1391 **Encyclopaedia Rhodesia**, general ed. Mark Akers. Salisbury, College Press, 1973. 445pp. 10 maps. (Short entries with particular emphasis on flora and fauna. Numerous line-drawings. Appendices with statistics, chronology, lists of office-holders, texts of treaties)

1392 Hachipola, Simooya Jerome. **A survey of the minority languages of Zimbabwe**. Harare, University of Zimbabwe, 1998. xxii, 126pp.

1393 **Historical dictionary of Zimbabwe**. 3rd ed., comp. Steven C. Rubert & R. Kent Rasmussen. Lanham, MD, Scarecrow Press, 2001. (African historical dictionaries, 86). xxxv, 451pp. (Reviews, *Choice*, 39, 2002, 120, "highly recommended"; *IJAHS*, 35, 2002, 191-192; *JAH*, 44, 2003, 193-194. - - Orig. pub. as **Historical dictionary of Zimbabwe/Rhodesia**, comp. R. Kent Rasmussen. Metuchen, NJ, 1979. (African historical dictionaries, 18). xxxiv, 445pp. (Reviews, *Africana J.*, 12, 1981, 169-170, "strongly recommended"; *JAH*, 23, 1982, 139, "systematic and generally reliable work of reference"; *IJAHS*, 15, 1982, 371-372); - - 2nd ed. comp. Steven C. Rubert, & R. Kent Rasmussen, Metuchen, NJ, 1990. (African historical dictionaries, 46). xxxviii, 502pp. (Review, *ARBA*, 23, 1992, 40, "this work now stands as the best reference on Zimbabwean history as well as a challenge for most other volumes in the series to meet". Rated "excellent", Balay, 1996)

1394 House, John, et al. **Zimbabwe: a handbook**. Harare, Mercury Press, 1983. 164pp. illus. (Popular approach, but solid detail).

1395 Owomoyela, Oyekan. **Culture and customs of Zimbabwe**. Westport, CT, Greenwood Press, 2002. (Culture and customs of Africa). xiv, 163pp. illus. map. (Covers history, religion, literature, art and architecture, social customs)

1396 Schmidt, Werner. **Rhodesien**. Bonn, K. Schroeder for Deutsche Afrika-Gesellschaft, 1970. (Die Länder Afrikas, 40). 231pp. illus. maps. (Expanded revision of the appropriate sections of **1265**)

1397 Tabex encyclopedia Zimbabwe. 2nd ed., ed. Katherine Sayce. Harare, Quest Publishing, 1989. xv, 448pp. illus. maps. (44 col. plates. Sponsored by Tabex, a local tobacco company. A/Z listing with subject index of some 20 broad headings. Emphasis on botanical and zoological entries. Extremely detailed and critical review in *Moto magazine* (Harare) 66, 1988, 22-24, emphasizes the lack of evenness of topic selection and level of entry. Very selective coverage of politicians of the colonial period "whose role was essentially negative", pref. - - Orig. pub. Harare, 1987. xv, 431pp. illus. maps.
- - **Svinga: a Zimbabwe encyclopedia**, comp. T. Mechin et al. Harare, Media Technology, 1990 is a CD-ROM "multimedia journal through Zimbabwe incorporating the **Tabex encyclopedia Zimbabwe"** (*Africana libraries newsletter*, 70, 1992, 11)

1398 Willson, Francis M.G. et al. **Source book of Parliamentary elections and referenda in Southern Rhodesia, 1898-1962**. Salisbury, University College of Rhodesia, Department of Government, 1963. (Source book series, 1). 255pp. (Provides chronological tables of parliamentary sessions, and detailed results of all general and by-elections)

1399 Zimbabwe: a country study. 2nd ed. comp. Harold D. Nelson et al. Washington, DC, U.S. Department of Defense, 1983. xxxiii, 360pp. - - Orig. pub. as **Area handbook for Southern Rhodesia**. Washington, DC, 1975. xiv, 394pp.

1400 Zimbabwe in brief: some basic facts about Zimbabwe. Salisbury, Ministry of Information, 1981. 55pp. - - Orig. pub. as. **Rhodesia in brief**. Salisbury, ?1974. 79pp. illus. maps. - - Earlier ed. Salisbury, 1965. 34pp.

See also **2704, 2746, 2748, 2754, 2755**

YEARBOOKS

1401 Bulawayo directory. Harare, Boldads, 1962- . 37th ed. 1998. *Continues*: Braby's Bulawayo directory.

1402 Official year book of the colony of Southern Rhodesia. Salisbury, Government Printer, 1924-1952. Irreg. 4 issues. (No. 1, 1924. xvi, 329pp; no. 2, 1930. xx, 862pp., "covering mainly the period 1924-1928"; no. 3, 1932. xiv, 804pp., "covering mainly the period 1926-1930"; no. 4, **Official year book of Southern Rhodesia**. 1952. xvi, 792pp., "with statistics mainly up to 1950". Nos. 2 and 3 compiled by Government Statistical Bureau (created 1928), no. 4 by Central African Statistical Bureau. A major source of detailed information, especially nos. 2 to 4. Includes gazetteer with 300/450 entries).

See also **2758, 2760**

STATISTICS

1403 Country profile: Zimbabwe. London, Economist Intelligence Unit, 1986- . Annual

1404 Germany. Statistisches Bundesamt. **Statistik des Auslandes: Länderberichte: Simbabwe** (later **Länderbericht: Simbabwe**). Wiesbaden/ Stuttgart, Metzler-Poetschel, 1985- . Irreg. Issues for 1985, 1987, 1990, 1995.

1405 IMF. **Zimbabwe: selected issues and statistical appendix**. Washington, DC, 2005. (Country report, 05/359). 116pp. - - Earlier eds. (title varies) 1999 (Staff country report, 99/49); 2002 (Country report, 02/126); 2003 (Country report, 03/225); 2004 (Country report, 04/296). Full text of reports also available online, *see* **334**.

1406 Roussos, Peter. **Zimbabwe, an introduction to the economics of transformation**. Harare, Baobab Books, 1988. xxi, 184pp. (Basically a collection of statistics)

1407 Southern Rhodesia. Central African Statistical Office [etc.]. **Economic and statistical bulletin of Southern Rhodesia 1933/34 [-1954]**. Salisbury, 1934-1955. Semi-monthly. 21 vols. *Continued by* **Monthly digest of statistics of the Federation of Rhodesia and Nyasaland** (*see* **1271**)

1408 Southern Rhodesia. Department of Statistics [etc.]. **Statistical yearbook of Southern Rhodesia: official annual of the social and economic conditions of the colony**. 2nd issue. Salisbury, 1947. xiv, 256pp. - - Orig. pub. Salisbury,

1938. xiv, 156pp. ("Decided that the **Year book** [i.e. **Official year book ...** *see* **1402**] should now be re-issued, but ... composed almost entirely of statistical tables", pref.).
- - **Statistical handbook of Southern Rhodesia**. 2nd issue, Salisbury, 1945. 33pp. (Compact abbreviated version of the **Statistical yearbook**). - - Orig. pub. Salisbury, 1939. 29pp.

1409 Zimbabwe. Central Statistical Office. **Quarterly digest of statistics**. Harare, 1983- . Latest issues in NWU are for 2003. *Continues* Rhodesia/Zimbabwe. Central Statistical Office [etc.] **Monthly digest of statistics**, Salisbury/Harare, 1964-1983. Not issued March 1966-September 1968.

1410 Zimbabwe/Rhodesia. Central Statistical Office [etc.]. **Statistical yearbook of Rhodesia** [later **Zimbabwe**]. Salisbury/Harare, 1975- . Annual. n.s. 1985- . Latest issue in NWU is for 1997.

DIRECTORIES OF ORGANIZATIONS

1411 Directory of libraries in Zimbabwe. [Rev ed.] comp. S.R. Dube, Harare, Zimbabwe National Archives. 1997. iv, 30pp. - - Orig. pub. as **Directory of Rhodesian libraries**, comp. A. McHarg & S. Phillips. Salisbury, National Archives of Rhodesia, 1969. vii, 29pp. (123 entries). Later eds, 1975, 1981, 1987. (*See* **2828** for earlier listings of Rhodesian libraries)

1412 Directory of organizations concerned with scientific research and technical services in Rhodesia. Salisbury, Scientific Council of Rhodesia, 1959-1979. Irreg. (eds. approximately every 3 years).

1413 Zimbabwe NGO directory. Harare, National Association on Non-Governmental Organizations, 2000. 201pp. - - Earlier ed. **Directory of non-governmental organizations in Zimbabwe, 1992**. Harare, 1992. 181pp. (Lists some 300 organizations)

See also **2806**

BIOGRAPHICAL SOURCES

1414 Hickman, Arthur Selwyn. **Men who made Rhodesia: a register of those who served in the British South Africa Company's Police**. Salisbury,

British South Africa Company, 1960. 462pp. illus. maps. (An historical survey of the Police, followed by a list of 879 names of those who served 1889-1892, arranged by date of enrolment with an index of names)

1415 Lloyd, Jessie M. **Rhodesia's pioneer women, 1859-1896**, rev. & enlarged by Constance Parry. Bulawayo, Rhodesia Pioneers' & Early Settlers' Society, [1974]. 105pp. - - Orig. pub. Salisbury, 1960. 65pp.

1416 Mitchell, Diana. **Makers of history: who's who 1981-82: nationalist leaders in Zimbabwe**. Salisbury, author, 1981. 170pp. - - **Supplement 1982/83**. Harare, 1983. 21pp. *Continues* Mitchell, Diana. **African nationalist leaders in Zimbabwe who's who 1980**. Salisbury, author, 1980. x, 106pp. - - Orig. pub. as **African nationalist leaders in Rhodesia who's who**, comp. Robert Cary & Diana Mitchell. Johannesburg, Africana Book Society/Bulawayo, Books of Rhodesia, 1977. 310 pp. (78 biographies)

1417 Profiles of Rhodesia's women. Salisbury, National Federation of Business & Professional Women of Rhodesia, 1976. 175pp. (Some 100 biographies, mostly of Europeans, with essays on local women's organizations)

1418 Prominent African personalities of Rhodesia. Salisbury, Cover Publicity Services, [1977?]. xi, 196pp. (Some 500 entries, many with portraits)

1419 Tabler, Edward C. **Pioneers of Rhodesia**. Cape Town, Struik, 1966. viii, 185pp. (Includes "adult male foreigners, including coloureds and a few Africans, who arrived in the defined area [Southern Rhodesia, the Caprivi Strip, Barotse Valley, Victoria Falls Region, the Tati Concession and part of Bechuanaland] 1836-1880", pref.)

1420 Who is who in Zimbabwe, 1993/94. Harare, Argosy Press, 1994. 88pp. (Large format work with some 600 entries, many accompanied by portraits)

1421 Willson, Francis M.G. et al. **Southern Rhodesia: holders of administrative and ministerial office, 1894-1964, and members of the Legislative Council, 1899-1923, and the Legislative Assembly, 1924-1964**. Salisbury, University College of Rhodesia, Department of Government, 1966. (Source book series, 3). 77, 10pp.

ATLASES & GAZETTEERS

Atlases

1422 Atlas of Zimbabwe. Harare, Department of the Surveyor-General, 1998. 32pp. col. maps. 29cm. (Majority of maps at 1:1M)

1423 Rhodesia: its natural resources and economic development. Salisbury, M.O. Collins, 1965. ii, 51pp. 43 x 38cm. (22 maps and text written by government officials. 4 topographical sheets at 1:1M, 18 thematic at 1:2,500,000 or 1:5M, covering climate, agriculture, natural resources and the economy. Gazetteer index to 1:1M maps)

1424 Road atlas of Zimbabwe. London, New Holland, 1995. (Globetrotter travel atlas). 64pp.

1425 Zimbabwe, Botswana and Namibia: a Lonely Planet atlas. Hawthorn, Lonely Planet, 1996. 61pp. (Tourist atlas with maps at 1:2M)

1426 Zimbabwe in maps: a census atlas. Harare, Central Statistical Office, Cartography Section, 1989. ii, 30pp. (Based upon 1982 Census)

Gazetteers

1427 Smith, R. Charer. **Avondale to Zimbabwe: a collection of cameos of Rhodesian towns and villages**. Borrowdale, author, 1978. 314pp. map. (Brief accounts of 130 towns and villages with geographical co-ordinates)

1428 Southern Rhodesia. Department of the Surveyor General. **Gazetteer of geographical place names in Southern Rhodesia**. Salisbury, 1963. 97pp.

1429 Southern Rhodesia. Division of Native Affairs. Information Services Branch. **Lore and legend of Southern Rhodesian place names**. Salisbury, 1960. 36pp.

1430 U.S. Board on Geographic Names. **Southern Rhodesia: official standard names approved by the USBGN**. Washington, DC, 1973. iv, 362pp. (Includes 22,500 names from 1:250,000 map series. Rev. of the appropriate section of **Rhodesia and Nyasaland ...** , *see* **1275**).

See also **2920**

EARTH SCIENCES

1431 Bartholomew, J.S. **Base metal and industrial mineral deposits of Zimbabwe**. Harare, Zimbabwe Geological Survey, 1990. (Mineral resources series, 22). 154pp. map. (Accompanies sheet map at 1:1M issued by Geological Survey, 1988)

1432 Chenje, Munyaradzi et al. **The state of Zimbabwe's environment, 1998**. Harare, Ministry of Mines, Environment & Tourism, 1998. viii, 509pp.

1433 Nyamapfene, Kingston W. **The soils of Zimbabwe**. Harare, Nehanda Publishers, 1991. 179pp. illus. maps.

1434 Stagman, J.G. et al. **An outline of the geology of Rhodesia**. Salisbury, Geological Survey, 1978. (Bulletin, 80). 126pp.+ 9pp. plates. illus. map. - - Orig. pub. as **An outline of the geology of Southern Rhodesia**, comp. W.H. Swift. Salisbury, 1961. (Bulletin, 50). 74pp.

1435 Staples, Raymond R. **An agricultural survey of Southern Rhodesia**. Salisbury, Government printer, 1961. 2 vols. illus. maps. Vol. 1, The agro-ecological survey; vol. 2, The agro-economic survey. (2 sheet-maps at 1:1M)

1436 Zimbabwe. Department of Meteorological Services. **Climate handbook of Zimbabwe**. Salisbury, 1981. 222pp. illus. maps.

BIOLOGICAL SCIENCES

Zoology

Birds & Mammals

1437 Irwin, Michael P. Stuart. **The birds of Zimbabwe**. 2nd ed. Harare, Quest Publications, 1987. 464pp. 25 plates. (Covers 635 spp., each illus.) - - Orig. pub. Harare, 1981. 464pp.

1438 Kenmuir, Dale & Williams, Russell. **Wild mammals: a field guide and introduction to the mammals of Rhodesia**. Salisbury, Longman Rhodesia, 1975. (Bundu series). vi, 136pp. + 32pp. col. plates.

1439 Smithers, Reay H.N. et al. **A check list of the birds of Southern Rhodesia, with data on ecology and breeding**. Cambridge, Rhodesian Ornithological Society, 1957. ix, 174pp. illus. maps.

1440 Smithers, Reay H.N. & Wilson, V.J. **Checklist and atlas of the mammals of Zimbabwe/Rhodesia**. Salisbury, National Museums & Monuments of Rhodesia, 1979. (Museum Memoir, 9). v, 193pp. maps.

See also **2975, 2986**

Reptiles, Amphibians & Fishes

1441 Bell-Cross, Graham & Minshull, John L. **Fishes of Zimbabwe**. Rev. ed. Harare, National Museums & Monuments of Zimbabwe, 1988. iv, 294pp. + 74 col. plates. (Review, *Copeia*, 1989, 809-810). - - Orig. pub. as **The fishes of Rhodesia**. Salisbury, 1976. viii, 262pp.

1442 Broadley, Donald G. 'A checklist of the reptiles of Zimbabwe with synoptic keys', *Arnoldia Zimbabwe*, 9(30) 1988, 369-430

1443 Broadley, Donald G. & Cock, E.V. **Snakes of Zimbabwe**. Rev. ed. Harare, Longman Zimbabwe, 1989. 152pp. illus. maps. Re-issue of **Snakes of Rhodesia**. Salisbury, Longman Rhodesia, 1975. 152pp.

1444 Lamberis, Angelo John L. **The frogs of Zimbabwe**. Turin, Museo Regionale di Scienze Naturale, 1989. 247pp. + 24 col. plates. maps. (Covers 66 spp. and sub-spp. Review, *Copeia*, 1991, 1150-1151)

Invertebrates

1445 Cooper, Richard. **Butterflies of Zimbabwe**. 2nd ed. Harare, Longman Zimbabwe, 1991. 138pp. + 22pp. col. plates.illus. (Describes 152 spp.). - - Orig. pub. Harare, 1973. 138pp.

1446 Pinhey, Elliot C.G. **Butterflies of Rhodesia: with a short introduction to the insect world**. Salisbury, Rhodesia Scientific Association, 1949. vi, 208pp.

Botany

1447 Chapano, Christopher. **A checklist of Zimbabwean grasses**. Pretoria, SABONET & National Herbarium & Botanic Garden, Harare, 2002. (SABONET report, 16). iv, 27pp. illus. maps.

1448 Coates Palgrave, Meg. **Key to the trees of Zimbabwe**. Harare, author, 1996. xii, 365pp. illus. (Field guide arranged under 6 primary habitats)

1449 Drummond, R.B. 'A list of trees, shrubs and woody climbers indigenous or naturalized in Rhodesia', *Kirkia*, 10, 1975, 229-285. map. (Checklist of 1,172 spp.)

1450 Flora of Zimbabwe http://www.zimbabweflora.co.zw/. ("This site is to make information about the flora of Zimbabwe more readily available. Currently, the main activity lies in building an online database of species. As of today, Sunday, 3 September 2006, there are images for 1,319 species", Web site opening screen)

1451 Mapaura, Anthony & Timberlake, Jonathan. **A checklist of Zimbabwean vascular plants**. Pretoria, SABONET & National Herbarium & Botanic Garden, Harare, 2004. (SABONET report, 33). 148pp. illus. maps.

See also **1064**

FRANCOPHONE CENTRAL AFRICA

YEARBOOKS

1452 L'Afrique des grands lacs: annuaire 1996/1997. Paris, Harmattan/Antwerp, Centre d'étude de la région des grands lacs d'Afrique, 1997- . (Comment on the political situation, directories of institutions, statistics)

DIRECTORIES OF ORGANIZATIONS

1453 Centre d'études africaines. CARDAN. **Bibliothèques et organismes de documentation: inventaire des bibliothèques et centres de documentation en Afrique centrale**, comp. F. Mbot. Paris, 1974. (*Bulletin d'information et de liaison*, 6(4) 1974). xxi, 154pp. (Covers 272 institutions in Cameroon, CAR, Chad, Congo, Gabon, Zaire)

EARTH SCIENCES

1454 Atlas climatique du bassin congolais. Brussels, Institut national pour l'étude agronomique du Congo (INEAC), 1971-1977. 4 vols. 32 x 33cm. (Vol. 4 entitled **... du bassin zaïrois**. Covers Zaire, Burundi, Rwanda, Congo, CAR, northern Angola, northern Zambia, western Tanzania. Maps with accompanying statistics and tables)

1455 Cahen, Lucien & Snelling, N.J. **The geochronology of Equatorial Africa**. Amsterdam, North-Holland, 1966. viii, 200pp. maps.

BIOLOGICAL SCIENCES

1456 Gautier-Hion, Annie et al. **Histoire naturelle des primates d'Afrique centrale**. Libreville, Ecofac, 1999. xi, 162pp. illus. + 1 CD. (Summary of current knowledge including information on recently identified spp. and subspp. CD contains 60 recordings of primate vocalizations. Covers Congo, Democratic Republic of Congo, CAR, Cameroon, Equatorial Guinea)

FORMER FRENCH EQUATORIAL AFRICA

HANDBOOKS

1457 **Afrique centrale: les républiques d'expression française**, ed. Gilbert Houlet. Paris, Hachette, 1962. (Les guides bleus). clxxxviii, 533pp. maps. (Introductory essays on topics such as geography, history and economics, followed by separate sections for Congo, Gabon, CAR, Chad and Cameroon)

1458 **L'Afrique équatoriale française**, comp. Edouard Trezénem. 3rd ed. Paris, Sociéte d'éditions géographiques, maritimes et coloniales, 1955. (Terres lointaines, 1[1]). 208pp. illus. maps. (Rev. ed. of the appropriate section of **La France équatoriale**. 2nd ed. Paris, Sociéte d'éditions géographiques, maritimes et coloniales 1950. 286pp. illus. maps. - - Orig. pub as **La France équatoriale, l'Afrique équatoriale française, le Cameroun**. Paris, 1947. (Terres lointaines, 1). ix, 250pp. illus. maps. (Includes pp. 3-122, L'Afrique équatoriale française by Edouard Trézenem. 3rd ed. of section for Cameroon published as **Le Cameroun** (1954, *see* **2224**)

1459 **Afrique équatoriale française: l'encyclopédie coloniale et maritime (encyclopédie de l'Union française)**. Paris, Encyclopédie coloniale et maritime, 1950. x, 590, viipp. 348 photos, 44 maps, 36 diagrs. ("Sous la direction d'Eugène Guernier". Detailed treatment of history, geography, politics and administration, communications, the economy and the arts. For the encyclopedia as a whole, *see* **54**)

1460 G.B. Admiralty. Naval Intelligence Division. **French Equatorial Africa and Cameroons**. London, 1942. (Geographical handbook series, B.R. 515). xi, 524pp. 59 illus. 2 maps in pocket. 113 maps & figs. in text. (Detailed topographical description, plus information on natural resources, peoples, administration, history (with separate section for the Cameroons), agriculture and trade. Descriptive gazetteer of some 70 settlements)

1461 Hänel, Karl. **Französisch-Äquatorial-Afrika**. Bonn, K. Schroeder for Deutsche Afrika-Gesellschaft, 1958. (Die Länder Afrikas, 1). 78pp. illus. maps.

See also **1253**

YEARBOOKS

1462 A.E.F. **Afrique équatoriale française**. Paris, 1922-1958. Annual. *Continues* **Annuaire du gouvernement générale de l'Afrique équatoriale française**. Paris, 1912-1922? (Annual report on the administration, with extensive statistics. Note also **Annuaire officiel illustré de la colonie du Congo, 1906/07**. Paris, R. Chapelot, 1906. 230pp. map. CCFR & G. Bruel, **Bibliographie de l'Afrique équatoriale française**. Paris, 1914, record this as a single vol. but LC. **Guide to official publications of French speaking central Africa**. Washington, DC, 1973, suggests that it was the first in this series)

1463 **Annuaire de la fédération des territoires de l'Afrique équatoriale française**. Paris, Compagnie française de propagande et publicité, 1951-1953. 2 issues : 1951. 374pp; 1953/54. 312pp. (Covers government and administration with a commercial directory and statistics)

1464 **Guid'Afrique centrale** Paris, Diloutremer, 1960- ?1970. Annual. (Title varies: **Guid'Afrique équatoriale 1960/61** [etc.]. 1960-1969. (Covers CAR, Chad, Congo, Gabon. From 1964 includes Cameroon, previously covered by **Guid'Cameroun**, *see* **2239**, from the same publisher. General information on topography, the economy, and administration, with directories of institutions and commercial enterprises. Last issue in NWU is for 1970)

1465 **Répertoire des entreprises/Business directory/Guía de empresas: Tchad, Centrafrique, Guinée équatoriale**. St. Peter Port, Guernsey, SEPIC Publications, ?1998- . Annual.

1466 Union douanière et économique de l'Afrique centrale (UDEAC). **Annuaire officiel**. Douala, 1972-1976. 5 issues. (Covers Cameroon, CAR, Chad, Congo, Gabon. For each country provides brief topographical, historical and demographic data, with details on communications, agriculture, industry, trade and finance. Amount of general information steadily declines: issue 2, 1973, 563pp; issue 5, 1976, 266pp)

STATISTICS

1467 A.E.F. Haut Commissariat. **Annuaire statistique de l'Afrique équatoriale française**. Brazzaville, 1950,1956. 2 issues for 1936/1950 (1950). 290pp; 1940/55 (1956). 207pp.

1468 L'A.E.F économique et sociale, 1947-1958. Paris, Alain for Haut Commissariat de la République en A.E.F., 1959. 112, xxiiipp. illus. maps. (Comp. with help of Fonds d'investissement pour le développement économique et social des territoires d'outre-mer)

1469 L'économie des pays de l'Afrique centrale. Paris, Ediafric-La documentation africaine, 1971. 279pp. (Special issue of *Bulletin de l'Afrique noire*. Covers Chad, CAR, Congo, Gabon. Largely statistical in content)

1470 Union douanière et économique de l'Afrique centrale (UDEAC). **Bulletin des statistiques générales**. Brazzaville, 1963-1965. Quarterly. Issues 1-12. *Continues* A.E.F. Service de la statistique générale [etc.]. **Bulletin mensuel de statistique**. Brazzaville, 1947-1959. Monthly. Issues 1-134. (Title varies: **Bulletin d'informations économiques et sociales** (1947-1949)

BIOGRAPHICAL SOURCES

1471 Personnalités publiques de l'Afrique centrale 1971. 2nd ed. Paris, Ediafric-La documentation africaine, 1972. 314pp. (Covers Cameroon, Chad, Congo, CAR, Gabon. Includes some 2,000 entries). - - Orig. pub. as **Personnalités publiques ... 1968.** Paris, 1969. 373pp. (Special issues of *Bulletin de l'Afrique noire*)

ATLASES & GAZETTEERS

1472 U.S. Board on Geographic Names. **Preliminary N.I.S gazetteer, Equatorial Africa: official standard names approved by the USBGN**. Washington, DC, 1952. iv, 636pp. (Pp. 1-447, French Equatorial Africa; pp. 449-574, French Cameroons; pp. 575-613, Spanish Guinea; pp. 615-636, São Tomé e Principe)

EARTH SCIENCES

1473 Atlas, agriculture et développement rural des savannes d'Afrique centrale: Cameroun, République centrafricaine, Tchad, ed. Jean-Yves Jamin et al. N'Djemena, Pôle régional de recherche appliquée au développement des savannes d'Afrique centrale (PRASAL)/Montpellier, CIRAD, 2003. 100pp. illus. col. maps. (Also on CD-ROM. Thematic atlas showing relief, vegetation, population, agriculture, etc. Series of maps of the whole PRASAL region, with 6 series of larger scale maps of selected sample areas)

1474 Franquin, Pierre. **Agroclimatologie du Centrafrique**. Paris, ORSTOM, 1988. 522p. illus. maps

1475 Gérard, George A. **Carte géologique de l'Afrique équatoriale française; notice explicative**. Paris, Imprimerie typographique d'édition for AEF. Direction des mines et de la géologie, 1958. 198pp. + atlas of 4 maps.

1476 Nicklès, M. **Lexique stratigraphique international, 4, Afrique, fasc. 6: Afrique équatoriale française**. Paris, CNRS, 1956. 60pp. map.

BIOLOGICAL SCIENCES

1477 Malbrant, René. **Faune du centre africain français (mammifères et oiseaux)**. Paris, Lechevalier, 1952. (Encyclopédie biologique, 15). 616pp. + 33 plates. illus. map. (Oiseaux, pp. 225-616). - - Orig. pub. as Malbrant, René & Maclatchy, Alain. **Faune de l'équateur africain française**. Paris, Lechevalier, 1949-1950. (Encyclopédie biologique, 35/36). 2 vols. illus. maps. Vol.1. Oiseaux; vol. 2, Mammifères.

1478 Rand, Austin L. et al. 'Birds from Gabon and Moyen Congo', *Fieldiana zoology*, 41(2) 1959, 221-411. map.

See also **1774-1777, 1782, 1785, 2136, 2143, 2147**

CENTRAL AFRICAN REPUBLIC

HANDBOOKS

1479 Atlas linguistique de Centrafrique (ALC). Paris, ACCT/Yaoundé, Centre régional de recherche et de documentation sur les traditions orales, etc., 1983-1984. (Atlas linguistique de l'Afrique centrale, ALAC). 2 vols. Vol. 1, 1983. Structures et méthodes, comp. M. Dieu; vol. 2, 1984. Situation linguistique en Afrique centrale, inventaire préliminaire, la république centrafricaine, comp. Pierre Sammy-Macfoy et al.

1480 France. Direction de la documentation. **La République centrafricaine**. Rev. ed. Paris, 1971. (*Notes et études documentaires*, 3833/3834, 10 Nov. 1971). 82pp. - - Orig. pub. Paris, 1960. (*Notes et études documentaires*, 2733, 19 Dec. 1960). 49pp.

1481 Historical dictionary of the Central African Republic. 3rd ed. comp. Pierre Kalck & Xavier Samuel Kalck. Lanham, MD, Scarecrow Press, 2005. (African historical dictionaries, 93). lxxiv, 233pp. (Review, *ARD*, 99, 2005, 51-54). - - Orig. pub. comp. Pierre Kalck. Metuchen, NJ, 1980. (African historical dictionaries, 27). xlii, 152pp. (Critical review in *JAH*, 23, 1982, 143); - - 2nd ed., comp. Pierre Kalck. Metuchen, NJ, 1992. (African historical dictionaries, 51). lvi, 188pp. (Rated "good", Balay, 1996)

1482 Kalck, Pierre. **La République centrafricaine**. Paris, Berger-Levrault, 1971. (Encyclopédie politique et constitutionnelle. Série Afrique). 51pp. map.

1483 La République centrafricaine. Paris, Service de presse du gouvernement de la RCA, 1961. 56pp. illus. maps.

YEARBOOKS

1484 Annuaire des entreprises industrielles, commerciales et des institutions non commerciales de la République centrafricaine. Bangui, Chambre de commerce, etc. ?1988- . Latest issue in NWU is 4th ed. 1995/1997.

STATISTICS

1485 Central African Republic/Ubangui-Shari. Direction de la statistique générale [etc.]. **Bulletin mensuel/Bulletin trimestrial de statistique.** Bangui, 1952- . Monthly/quarterly. Title varies: **Bulletin d'informations statistiques,** Issues 1-17. (1952-1956). Latest issue in NWU is for 2000.

1486 Central African Republic. Direction de la statistique générale [etc.]. **Annuaire statistique de la République centrafricaine 1952/62** [etc.]. Bangui, 1962- . Irreg. Issues for 1952/62 (1962), 1963/70 (1975), 1971/77 (1978). Latest issue in NWU is for 2001. *Continues* **Annuaire statistique de l'Oubangui-Shari 1940/1955.** Bangui, 1956. 206pp.

1487 Country profile: Central African Republic. London, Economist Intelligence Unit, 2003- . Annual. *Continues in part* **Country profile: Cameroon, CAR, Chad** . London, 1986-2002.

1488 France. Ministère de la coopération. **Centrafrique: octobre 1979: données statistiques sur les activités économiques, culturelles et sociales.** Paris, 1979. 127pp. illus.

1489 Germany. Statistisches Bundesamt. **Statistik des Auslandes: Länderberichte: Zentralafrikanische Republik** (later **Länderbericht: Zentralafrikanische Republik**). Wiesbaden/Stuttgart, Metzler-Poetschel, 1986- . Irreg. Issues for 1986, 1988.

1490 IMF. **Central African Republic: selected issues and statistical appendix.** Washington, DC, 2004. (Country report, 04/167). 52pp. - - Earlier issues (title varies) 1995 (Staff country report, 95/74); 2000 (Staff country report, 00/109). Full text of reports from 1997 also available online, *see* **334.**

ATLASES & GAZETTEERS

1491 Atlas de la République centrafricaine. Paris, Ministère de l'éducation nationale de la RCA & Institut géographique nationale, 1973. 20pp. 22 x 34cm. (Col. maps. No notes)

1492 Atlas de la République centrafricaine, comp. Pierre Vennetier. Paris, *Jeune Afrique,* 1984. 64pp. (19 thematic maps with text)

1493 Mangold, Max. **A Central African pronouncing gazetteer.** Saarbrücken, Universität des Saarlandes, Institut für Phonetik, 1985. (Africana Saraviensia linguistica, 10). 98pp. (Over 2,000 entries with official and phonetic spelling)

1494 U.S. Board on Geographic Names. **Central African Republic: official standard names approved by the USBGN.** Washington, DC, 1962. (Gazetteer, 64). iii, 220pp. (Includes 15,700 names from maps at 1:200,000. Rev. of the appropriate sections of **Equatorial Africa ...** *see* **1472**).

EARTH SCIENCES

1495 Boulvert, Yves. **Carte pédologique de la République centrafricaine à 1:1,000,000: notice explicative.** Paris, ORSTOM, 1983. 126pp. illus. maps.

1496 Mestraud, Jean-Louis & Bessoles, Bernard. **Géologie et ressources minérales de la République centrafricaine: état des connaissances à fin 1963.** Orléans, Bureau de recherches géologiques et minières (BRGM), 1982. (Mémoires, 60). 185pp. illus.

1497 Quantin, Paul. **Les sols de la République centrafricaine.** Paris, ORSTOM, 1965. (Mémoires, 16). 113pp. maps.

BIOLOGICAL SCIENCES

1498 Aké Assi, Laurent et al. **Contribution aux études ethnobotaniques et floristiques en République centrafricaine.** 4th ed. Paris, ACCT, 1985. (Médicine traditionnelle et pharmacopée). vii, 139pp. illus. maps. - - 3rd ed. **Contribution à l'identification et au recensement des plantes utilisées dans la médicine traditionnelle et la pharmacopée en République centrafricaine.** Paris, 1981. 139pp. illus. maps.

1499 Boulvert, Yves. **Catalogue de la flore de Centrafrique: écologie sommaire, distribution.** Bangui, Centre ORSTOM, 1977. 3 vols. in 4. 381pp. Mimeograph. (Vol. 1, Forêts denses et galeries forestières; vol. 2, Strate herbacée des savanes: A, Dicotyledons, B, Monocotyledons, Pteridophytes, Bryophytes; vol. 3, Strate ligneuse des savanes. Checklist including cultivated plants. Very much a working document)

1500 Carrol, Richard W. 'Birds of the Central African Republic', *Malimbus*, 10, 1988, 177-200. maps. (Lists 668 spp.). - - Dowsett, Robert J. et al. 'Additions and corrections to the avifauna of the Central African Republic', *Malimbus*, 21, 1999, 1-15 (Adds 44 spp. and deletes 54)

1501 Normand, Didier. **Identification des arbres et des bois des principales essences forestières de la République centrafricaine.** Nogent-sur-Marne, Centre Technique de Forestier Tropical, 1965. 78pp.

1502 Tisserant, Charles. **Catalogue de la flore de l'Oubangi-Chari.** Brazzaville, Institut des études centrafricaines, 1950. (Mémoires, 2). 166pp. map.

CHAD

HANDBOOKS

1503 Bourdette-Donon, Marcel. **Tchad 1998**. Paris, Harmattan, 1998. 159pp. maps. (Principally concerned with economic data)

1504 Chad: a country study. 2ⁿᵈ ed. comp. Thomas Collelo. Washington, DC, Library of Congress, Federal Research Division, 1990. xxiv, 254pp. illus. maps. Also available at: http://lcweb2.loc.gov/frd/cs/tdtoc.html. - - Orig. pub as **Area handbook for Chad**, comp. Harold D. Nelson et al. Washington, DC, U.S. Department of Defense, 1972. xiv, 261pp. maps.

1505 France. Direction de la documentation. **La République du Tchad**. Paris, 1967. (*Notes et études documentaires*, 3411). 63pp.- - Orig. pub. Paris, 1960. (*Notes et études documentaires*, 1696). 67pp.

1506 Fuchs, Peter. **Tschad**. Bonn, Schroeder for Deutsche Afrika-Gesellschaft, 1966. (Die Länder Afrikas, 33). 101pp. illus. maps.

1507 Gonidec, Pierre François. **La République du Tchad**. Paris, Berger-Levrault, 1971. (Encyclopédie politique et constitutionnelle. Série Afrique). 79pp.

1508 Historical dictionary of Chad. 3ʳᵈ ed. comp. Samuel Decalo. Lanham, MD, Scarecrow Press, 1997. (African historical dictionaries, 13). xlviii, 601pp. (Reviews, *ARD*, 84, 2000, 83-90; *Choice*, 35, 1998, 1686-1688, "writing is excellent, among the best in this series"; *IJAHS*, 31, 1998, 486; *JAH*, 40, 1999, 519). - - Orig. pub. Metuchen, NJ, 1977. xxiv, 413pp. (Reviews, *African affairs*, 78, 1979, 277-278; *ASA review of books*, 6, 1980, 199-209; *IJAHS* 21, 1988, 709); - - 2ⁿᵈ ed. Metuchen, NJ, 1987. xxxvi, 532pp (Detailed critical review, *IJAHS* 11, 1978, 376-379. Rated "good", Balay, 1996)

1509 Lanne, Bernard. **Répertoire de l'administration territoriale du Chad, 1900-1994**. Paris, Harmattan, 1995. 224pp. (Includes lists of administrative divisions and colonial officials)

1510 Malval, Jean & Tubiana, Marie-José. **Essai de chronologie tchadienne, 1707-1940**. Paris, CNRS, 1974. 156pp. (Concerned principally with French colonial activities. Review, *Africa*, 46, 1976, 108-109)

1511 Nanassoum, Goual. **300 dates de l'histoire du Tchad**. N'Djamena, Cefod-Editions, 1995. 67pp. map. (Historical chronology)

YEARBOOKS

1512 A.E.F. Gouvernement du Tchad. Service de l'information tchadien. **Annuaire du Tchad 1950/51**. Lille, 1950. ?No more pub. (Covers geography, history, archaeology and administration)

1513 Annuaire des sociétés industrielles, commerciales et agricoles du Tchad. N'Djaména, Chambre consulaire du Tchad, 1991- . Annual. Latest issue in LC is for 1997.

1514 Chad. Direction de l'information tchadien. **Annuaire officiel du Tchad**. Paris, Diloutremer, 1970-?1978. Annual. Last issue in BnF is for 1978.

STATISTICS

1515 Chad. Direction de la statistique [etc.]. **Bulletin de statistique**. N'Djamena, 1951- ?1989. Monthly/quarterly. Title varies: **Bulletin statistique** (1951-1957) ; **Bulletin mensuel de statistique** (1958-68). Not pub. August-November 1958, January-April, June-September 1959. NWU, SSL hold issues up to 1989.

1516 Chad. Direction de la statistique [etc.]. **Le Tchad en chiffres**. Fort Lamy, 1988- . Annual. *Continues* Chad. Sous-direction de la statistique [etc.]. **Annuaire statistique du Tchad**. N'Djamena, 1966-1976. Annual (irreg.) Not published 1971, 1973; Chad. Direction de la statistique. **Tchad: relance économique en chiffres**. N'Djamena, 1984-87. Annual

1517 Country profile: Chad. London, Economist Intelligence Unit, 2003- . Annual. *Continues in part* **Country profile: Cameroon, CAR, Chad**. London, 1986-2002

1518 France. Ministère de la coopération, Service des études et questions internationales. **Tchad: données statistiques sur les activités économiques, culturelles et sociales**. Paris, 1976. 179pp. illus. maps.

1519 Germany. Statistisches Bundesamt. **Statistik des Auslandes: Länderberichte: Tschad** (later **Länderbericht: Tschad**). Wiesbaden/ Stuttgart, Metzler-Poetschel, 1964- . Irreg. Issues for 1964, 1984, 1990.

1520 IMF. **Chad: statistical appendix**. Washington, DC, 2004. (Country report, 04/115). 46pp. - - Earlier eds. (title varies) 1995 (Staff country report, 95/31) ; 1997 (Staff country report, 97/66); 2002 (Country report, 02/28). Full text of reports from 97/101, 1997 also available online, *see* **334**.

See also **2120**

DIRECTORIES OF ORGANIZATIONS

1521 Chad. Centre nationale d'appui à la recherche. **Annuaire des chercheurs de la république du Tchad**. N'Djamena, 1992- . (1st issue lists 244 researchers under 30 subject fields)

1522 Chambre consulaire du Tchad. **Recensement des entreprises industrielles et commerciales du Tchad**. 2nd ed. Paris, Editeur Exclusif Sepic, 1989. 108pp. illus. maps

BIOGRAPHICAL SOURCES

1523 Lanne, Bernard. **Liste des chefs des unités administratives du Tchad (1900-1983);** précédée d'un aperçu sur l'organisation administrative territoriale. Paris, École des hautes études en sciences sociales, 1983. 194pp. (Tables of leaders with sources)

1524 Le Rouvreur, Albert et al. **Eléments pour un dictionnaire biographique du Tchad et du Niger (Téda et Daja)**. Paris, CNRS, 1978. (Contributions à la connaissance des élites africaines, fasc. 1). 48pp. (Author notes that he was inspired to produce this by the example of Richard Hill's **Biographical dictionary of the Anglo-Egyptian Sudan**, *see* **975**). *See also* **2446**.

ATLASES & GAZETTEERS

1525 **Atlas historique et géographique de Sarh (Tchad) de 1899 à 1970**, comp. Jacques Chauvet. Sarh, Centre d'études linguistiques, 1984. iv, 94pp. (Scale 1:36,000)

1526 Atlas pratique du Tchad, comp. Jean Cabot & Christian Bouquet. Fort Lamy, Institut national tchadien pour les sciences humaines/Paris, Institut géographique nationale, 1972. 78pp. 38 x 29cm. (34 thematic maps with accompanying text. Basic scale 1:5M. Includes archaeological and language maps. 4 town plans at 1:25,000 of Fort-Lamy/Ndjaména, Sarh, Moundou and Abéché)

1527 U.S. Board on Geographic Names. **Gazetteer of Chad**. 2nd ed. Washington, DC, 1989. xvi, 529pp. (Includes 20,000 names from maps at 1:250,000). - - Orig. pub. as **Chad: official standard names approved by the USBGN**. Washington, DC, 1962. (Gazetteer, 65). v, 232pp. (Includes 16,000 names from 1:200,000 series maps. Revision of appropriate section of **Equatorial Africa ...** *see* **1472**)

See also **2394**

EARTH SCIENCES

1528 Kusnir, Imrich et al. **Géologie, ressources minérales et ressources en eau du Tchad**. 2nd ed. N'Djaména, Centre national d'appui à la recherche, 1995. 115pp. illus. maps. - - Orig. pub. N'Djaména, 1993. 100pp.

1529 Pias, Jean. **Carte pédologique du Tchad**. Paris, ORSTOM, 1968-1970. 197pp. + 2 maps. 106 x 69cm. (Scale 1:5M)

1530 Schneider, Jean-Louis & Wolff, J.P. **Carte géologique et c̃artes hydrogéologiques à 1:1,500,000 de la république du Tchad: mémoire explicatif**. Orléans, Bureau de recherche géologiques et minières (BRGM), 1992. 2 vols. Vol. 1 (i), Introduction; (ii), Géologie annexes: cartes structurales, ressources minérales et énergétiques; index alphabétique; vol. 2. Hydrogéologie, annexes.

1531 Schneider, Jean-Louis. **Géologie, archéologie, hydrogéologie de la République du Tchad**. N.p., n.p., 2004. 2 vols. 446, 583pp. Vol. 1, Géologie, archéologie; vol. 2, Hydrogéologie.

See also **2128**

BIOLOGICAL SCIENCES

1532 Lebrun, Jean-Pierre et al. **Catalogue des plantes vasculaires du Tchad méridional**. Maisons-Alfort, IEMVT, 1972. (Étude botanique, 1). 289pp. maps.

(Covers north to 16° N. latitude). - - '1er supplément', comp. J.-P. Lebrun & A. Gaston, *Adansonia*, sér. 2, 15, 1976, 381-390; - - '2ième supplément', *Publications of the Cairo University Herbarium*, 7/8, 1977, 109-114

1533 Pias, Jean. **La végétation du Tchad: ses rapports avec les sols,** variations paléobotaniques au quaternaire: contribution à la connaissance du bassin tchadien. Paris, ORSTOM, 1970. (Travaux et documents, 6). 49pp. illus. maps.

See also **2139, 2144**

CONGO (CONGO-BRAZZAVILLE)

Site officielle d'information et de conseil sur le Congo-Brazzaville
http://www.congo-site.com/pub/fr/index.php

HANDBOOKS

1534 Area handbook for People's Republic of the Congo (Congo Brazzaville), comp. Gordon C. McDonald et al. Washington, DC, U.S. Department of Defense, 1971. xiii, 256pp. maps.

1535 Borisenkov, V.P. et al. **Narodnaia respublika Kongo: spravochnik**. Moscow, Akademiia nauk, Institut Afriki, 1977. 295pp.

1536 Dossier Congo. Paris, Rencontres africaines, Association de la maison de l'Afrique, 1986. 236pp.

1537 France. Direction de la documentation. **La République démocratique du Congo**. [Rev. ed.]. Paris, 1971. (*Notes et études documentaires*, 3765/3766, 20 Feb. 1971). 63p. - - Orig. pub. as **La République du Congo**. Paris, 1960. (*Notes et études documentaires*, 2732, 17 Dec. 1960). 38pp.

1538 Gabou, Alexis. **Chronologie politique congolaise**. Paris, Nouvelles perspectives éditions, 1999. 319pp.

1539 Historical dictionary of Congo. 3rd ed., comp. Samuel Decalo et al. Lanham, MD, Scarecrow Press, 1996. (African historical dictionaries, 69). xxxiv, 379pp. (Reviews, *Africa*, 69, 1999, 660; *Choice*, 34, 1997, 1134-1135). - - Orig. pub. as **Historical dictionary of the People's Republic of the Congo (Congo-Brazzaville)**, comp. Virginia Thompson & Richard Adloff. Metuchen, NJ, 1984. (African historical dictionaries, 2). viii, 139pp; - - 2nd ed. **Historical dictionary of the People's Republic of the Congo**. Metuchen, NJ, 1984. (African historical dictionaries, 2). xxi, 239pp. (Includes bibliography of only 10pp., very brief compared with most vols. in this series. Reviews, *African affairs*, 84, 1985, 619; *IJAHS*, 19, 1986, 167-168. Rated "excellent", Balay, 1996).

1540 Moukoko, Philippe. **Dictionnaire général du Congo-Brazzaville**: alphabétique, analytique et critique, avec des annexes et un tableau chronologique. Paris, Harmattan, 1999. 442pp. illus. maps. (Entries for people, organizations, places and events, with bibliographies. Index, 5 thematic maps, chronology of events from 1482)

1541 Nkouka-Menga, Jean-Marie. **Chronique politique congolaise: du Mani-Kongo à la guerre civile**. [Rev. ed.]. Paris, Harmattan, 1997. 381pp. + 8pp. plates. (Historical chronology). - - Orig. pub. Epinay sous Sénart, Éditions NEMAF, 1991. 90pp.

1542 **Situation linguistique en Afrique centrale: inventaire préliminaire: le Congo**. Paris, ACCT/Yaoundé, Centre de recherche et documentation sur les traditions orales, 1987. (Atlas linguistique de l'Afrique centrale, ALAC). 122pp. illus. maps. (Linguistic survey with extensive statistics)

STATISTICS

1543 Congo. Direction de la statistique [etc.]. **Annuaire statistique 1958/63** [etc.]. Brazzaville, 1966- . Irreg. Issues for 1966, 1969, 1974, 1982, 1988.

1544 Congo. Direction de la statistique [etc.]. **Bulletin mensuel de statistique**. (*formerly* **Bulletin mensuel rapide des statistiques**). Brazzaville, 1957-1962; n.s. 1963- . Monthly. Latest issues in NWU are for 1988.

1545 Congo. Ministère de l'économie et des finances chargé du plan et de la prospective. **La République du Congo en quelques chiffres**. Brazzaville, 1995- . Latest issue in NWU is for 1996.

1546 Country profile: Congo (Brazzaville). London, Economist Intelligence Unit, 1997- . Annual. *Continues in part* **Country profile: Congo, Gabon, Equatorial Guinea**. London, 1986-1992; **Country profile: Congo, São Tomé and Príncipe, Guinea-Bissau, Cape Verde**. London, 1994-1996.

1547 France. Ministère de la coopération. Sous-direction des études économiques et de la planification. **République populaire du Congo: dossier d'information économique**. Paris, 1975. 141pp. illus.

1548 Germany. Statistisches Bundesamt. **Statistik des Auslandes: Länderberichte: Kongo** (later **Länderbericht: Kongo**). Wiesbaden/Stuttgart, Metzler-Poetschel, 1986- . Irreg. Issues for 1986, 1988, 1993.

1549 IMF. **Republic of Congo: selected issues and statistical appendix**. Washington, DC, 2004. (Country report, 04/231). 96pp. - - Earlier eds. (title varies) 2001 (Country report, 01/03); 2003 (Country report, 03/104). Full text of reports also available online, *see* **334**.

DIRECTORIES OF ORGANIZATIONS

1550 **Répertoire culturel, le Congo**. Paris, ACCT, 1989. (Inventaire des activités, etc. des pays membres de l'ACCT). 237pp. illus.

BIOGRAPHICAL SOURCES

1551 Mamonsono, L.P. & Bemba, S. **Bio-bibliographie des écrivains congolais (belles lettres-littérature)**. Brazzaville, Éditions littéraires congolaises for Ministère de la culture et des arts, 1979. 32pp. (Covers 76 authors)

ATLASES & GAZETTEERS

1552 **Atlas de Brazzaville**; comp. Roland Devauges. Paris, ORSTOM, 1984. (Collection travaux et documents, 180). x, 100 maps + transparent overlay. ("Cartes réalisés par traîtement informatique des données urbaines", t.p. Maps at 1:20,000, mostly computer printed dots to show extent of topic illustrated. Topics are largely demographic and include age, literacy, education, occupation, types of buildings and services available)

1553 **Atlas du Congo**, ed. Anne Lerebours Pigeonnière. 2nd ed. Paris, Editions *Jeune afrique*, 2001. 76pp. col. maps. - - Orig. pub. as **Atlas de la République populaire du Congo**, comp. Jean Vennetier. Paris, 1977. 64pp. col. maps. (18 thematic maps with text)

1554 U.S. Board on Geographic Names. **Gazetteer of the Congo**. 2nd ed. Washington, DC, 1996. xv, 381pp. - - Orig. pub. as **Republic of the Congo (Brazzaville): official standard names approved by the USBGN**. Washington, DC, 1962. (Gazetteer, 61). iii, 109pp. (Includes 7,700 names. Rev. of the appropriate sections of **Equatorial Africa ...** *see* **1472**)

EARTH SCIENCES

1555 **Atlas du Congo**. Paris, ORSTOM, 1969. 10 sheets. 15pp. text. 50 x 62cm. (Coverage is principally of climate and geology)

1556 Dadet, Paul. **Notice explicative de la carte géologique de la République du Congo Brazzaville au 1: 500,000**; zone comprise entre les paralleles 2° et 5° S. Paris, Bureau de recherches géologiques et minières (BRGM), 1969. (Mémoires, 70). 104pp. illus. maps.

1557 Moukala, Noel. **Hydrogéologie du Congo**. Orléans, Bureau de recherches géologiques et minières (BRGM), 1992. (Document, 210). 128pp. illus. maps.

1558 Vennetier, Pierre. **Géographie du Congo-Brazzaville**. Paris, Gauthier-Villars, 1966. 170pp. illus.

BIOLOGICAL SCIENCES

1559 Adjanohoun, Edouard J. et al. **Contribution aux études ethnobotaniques et floristiques en République populaire du Congo**. Paris, ACCT, 1988. (Médecine traditionnelle et pharmacopée). 605pp. illus. maps.

1560 Dowsett-Lemaire, F. & Dowsett, Robert J. 'Liste préliminaire des oiseaux du Congo', *Tauraco research report*, 2, 1989, 29-51. (Lists 424 spp.). - - 'Additions and corrections to the avifauna of Congo', *Malimbus*, 15, 1993, 68-80; - - 'Further additions to and deletions from the avifauna of Congo-Brazzaville', *ibid.*, 20, 1998, 15-32.

GABON

HANDBOOKS

1561 France. Direction de la documentation. **La République gabonaise**. [Rev. ed.]. comp. Jacques Binet. Paris, 1970. (*Notes et études documentaires*, 3703, 27 June 1970). 36pp. - - Orig. pub. Paris, 1961. (*Notes et études documentaires*, 2795, 10 July 1961). 56pp.

1562 Gabon. Direction de l'information. **L'essentiel sur le Gabon**. 2nd ed. Libreville, 1961. 54pp. illus. maps. - - Orig. pub. Libreville, 1960. 54pp.

1563 Le Gabon, 1960-1980. Libreville, *L'Union*, 1981. 150pp. illus. (Political, economic and social data and statistics)

1564 Historical dictionary of Gabon. 2nd ed. comp. David E. Gardinier. Metuchen, NJ, Scarecrow Press, 1994. (African historical dictionaries, 58). xxxvii, 466pp. (Review, *Choice*, 32, 1994, 260-261). - - Orig. pub. Metuchen, NJ, 1981. (African historical dictionaries, 30). xxv, 254pp. (Review, *JAH*, 24, 1983, 142-143, "a reference work which is authoritative, internally consistent and easy to use"). 3rd ed. announced for 2006 (publisher's Web site).

1565 Neuhoff, Hans Otto. **Gabun**. Bonn, K. Schroeder for Deutsche Afrika-Gesellschaft, 1967. (Die Länder Afrikas, 35). 176 p.

1566 Raponda-Walker, André. **Etymologie des noms propres gabonais**. Versailles, Les classiques africains, 1993. 207pp.

1567 Raponda-Walker, André. **Notes d'histoire du Gabon, suivi de toponymie de l'estuaire Libreville et toponymie du Fernan-Vaz Port-Gentil**. Libreville, Editions R. Walker, 1996. 368pp. illus. maps. (Rev. and expanded ed. of **Notes d'histoire du Gabon**. Montpellier, Impr. Charité, 1960. (Mémoires de l'Institut d'Études centrafricaines, Brazzaville, 9). 158pp. illus. maps. A miscellaneous collection of information including biographies of 19th century African chiefs, classified list of ethnic groups, and a chronology of Gabonese history, 1300-1929)

1568 Zelenskii, Iu. I. **Gabon: spravochnik**. Moscow, Akademiia nauk, Institut Afriki, 1977. 235pp

YEARBOOKS

1569 Annuaire des entreprises du Gabon. Libreville, Chambre de commerce, d'agriculture, d'industrie & des mines du Gabon, 197?-. ? Annual.

1570 Annuaire gabonaise. Libreville, Éditions Gabon communité, 1966- . Annual. ALA records issue for 1987. (Includes civil list, commercial directory).

1571 Annuaire national de la République gabonaise. Libreville, Information Afrique, 1980- . Latest issue in NWU is for 1988/89.

1572 Gabon. Ministère de l'information & du tourisme du Gabon. **Annuaire national**. Paris & Libreville, Éditions des quatre points cardinaux, 1966- . Annual (irreg.). Latest issues in BnF are for 1976. Title varies: **Annuaire national officiel de la république gabonaise**. (Directory of the administration with biographies of ministers and leading officials, general economic information and statistics)

STATISTICS

1573 Country profile: Gabon. London, Economist Intelligence Unit, 2004- . Annual. *Continues in part* **Country profile: Gabon, Equatorial Guinea**. London, 1986-2003.

1574 L'économie gabonaise. Paris, Ediafric-La documentation africaine, 1976, 1982. 2 issues: 1976, var. paging; 1982. 245pp. (Special issues of *Bulletin de l'Afrique noire*)

1575 France. Ministère de la coopération, Service des études économiques et questions internationales. **Gabon: données statistiques sur les activités économiques, culturelles et sociales**. Paris, 1976. 241pp. illus. maps.

1576 Gabon. Direction générale de la statistique [etc.] **Annuaire statistique du Gabon 1957/64** [etc.]. Libreville, 1969- . Irreg. Issues for 1957/64, 1964, 1968, 1970/75, 1976/80. Latest issue in NWU is 1993.

1577 Gabon. Direction générale de la statistique [etc.] **Bulletin mensuel de statistique**. Libreville, 1959- . Monthly. Latest issues in NWU are for 1994.

1578 Gabon. Direction générale de la statistique [etc.] **Le Gabon en chiffres**. Libreville, 1987- . Annual. BL has issue for 1992.

1579 Gabon. Direction générale de la statistique [etc.] **Situation économique, financière et sociale de la République gabonaise en 1963-** [etc.]. Libreville, 1963- Annual. BnF has issues for 1963-1966; 1968-1969.

1580 Germany. Statistisches Bundesamt. **Statistik des Auslandes: Länderberichte: Gabon** (later **Länderbericht: Gabon**). Wiesbaden/Stuttgart, Metzler-Poetschel, 1978- . Irreg. Issues for 1978, 1985, 1987, 1994.

1581 IMF. **Gabon : selected issues and statistical appendix**. Washington, DC, 2005. (Country report, 05/147). 97pp. - - Earlier eds. (title varies) 1997 (Staff country report, 97/54); 1999 (Staff country report, 99/12); 2000 (Staff country report, 00/155); 2004 (Country report, 04/29). Full text of reports from 97/101, 1997 also available online, *see* **334**.

DIRECTORIES OF ORGANIZATIONS

1582 Répertoire des industries et activités du Gabon. Libreville, SEEDG [etc.], 1984- Annual. Latest issue in NWU is for 1994.

BIOGRAPHICAL SOURCES

1583 Les élites gabonaises: qui est qui au Gabon. 3rd ed. Paris, Ediafric, 1988. 231pp. - - Orig. pub. Paris, 1977. xxi, 217pp ; - - 2nd ed. Paris, 1983. xvi, 209pp.

1584 Notices et portraits des députés de la neuvième legislature, 1997-2002. Libreville, Secrétariat general de l'Assemblé nationale, 2002. 160pp.

1585 Verdier, Isabelle. **Gabon: 100 hommes du pouvoir**. Paris, Indigo, 1996. 202pp.

ATLASES & GAZETTEERS

1586 Atlas de la formation territoriale du Gabon: frontières et unités administratives des origines à nos jours, comp. Marc-Louis Ropovia & Jules Djéki. Libreville, Centre de recherches et d'études géopolitiques (CERGEP), 1995. 63pp. (Cartography by Institut national de cartographie, France. Historical maps, 15th century to the present. Scales 1:6M and 1:8M)

1587 **Atlas du Gabon,** comp. Danielle Ben Yahmed et al. Paris, *Jeune Afrique,* 2004. 74pp. col. maps.

1588 **Géographie et cartographie du Gabon: atlas illustré**. Paris, Edicef for Ministère de l'éducation nationale du Gabon, 1983. 135pp. 27 x 35cm. (30 thematic chaps. Text, col. maps at 1:3M, photos and statistics)

1589 **Petit atlas du Gabon,** ed. Francis Lafont. [Paris, Alain, 1958]. 48pp. incl. col. maps. 28 x 31cm. (Compiled for Chambre de commerce, d'agriculture et d'industrie du Gabon. Covers geology, climate, population, ethnography, education, missions, agriculture, and natural resources)

1590 U.S. Board on Geographic Names. **Gabon: official standard names approved by the USBGN**. Washington, DC, 1962. (Gazetteer, 59). iv, 113pp. (Includes 8,000 names from 1:200,000 map series. Rev. of the appropriate sections of **Equatorial Africa ...** *see* **1472**).

EARTH SCIENCES

1591 Gabon. Ministère des mines[etc.]. **Carte géologique de la République gabonaise: notice explicative**. 2nd ed. Pretoria, Council for Geoscience, 2001. v, 195pp. - - Orig. pub. as **Carte géologique de la République gabonaise au 1: 1,000,000: notice explicative**, comp. H. Hudeley & Y. Belmonte. Paris, Bureau de recherches géologiques et minières (BRGM), 1970. 192pp. maps.

BIOLOGICAL SCIENCES

1592 Adjanohoun, Edouard J. et al. **Contribution aux études ethnobotaniques et floristiques au Gabon**. Paris, ACCT, 1984. (Médecine traditionnelle et pharmacopée). 294pp. illus.

1593 **Flore du Gabon,** ed. André Aubréville et al. Paris, Muséum national d'histoire naturelle, 1961- . Issued in fascs. (Detailed research flora. 37 fascs. pub. to 2006, covering some 40% of the vascular flora. *See* J. Floret. 'Flore du Gabon', *Boissiera*, 24, 1976, 575-580)

1594 Gilbert, P. et al. **Les poissons du Gabon (eaux douces et eaux saumâtres)**. Libreville, Institut pédagogique national, 1989. xii, 216pp. illus. maps.

1595 Maisonneuve, J.F. & Manfredini, M.L. **Les bois du Gabon**. Libreville, Institut pedagogique national, 1988. 155pp. illus.

1596 Péllégrin, François. **Les légumineuses du Gabon**; description avec clefs des 125 genres et des 450 espèces signalés jusqu'à ce jour au Gabon. Paris, Larose, 1948. (Mémoires de l' Institut d'études centrafricaine, Brazzaville, 1). 284pp. + 8 plates. (Covers 450 spp.)

1597 Raponda-Walker, André. **Les plantes utiles du Gabon: essai d'inventaire et de concordance des noms vernaculaires et scientifiques des plantes spontanées et introduites**; description des espèces, propriétés, utilisations, etc. Paris, Lechevalier, 1961. (Encyclopédie biologique, 56). xii, 614pp. Reprinted, Libreville, 1995.

1598 Reitsma, J.M. **Végétation forestière du Gabon/Forest vegetation of Gabon**. Ede, Stichting Tropenbos, 1988. 142pp. illus. maps. (Parallel text in English and French)

1599 Saint Aubin, Guy de. **La fôret du Gabon**. Nogent-sur-Marne, Centre technique de forestier tropical, 1963. (Publication, 21). 208pp. illus. maps. Reprinted, Montpellier, CIRAD, 1996. (Field manual of the most significant commercial trees)

FORMER BELGIAN AFRICA

CONGO, DEMOCRATIC REPUBLIC (CONGO-KINSHASA/ ZAIRE)

Many of the sources listed here will also cover the countries of Burundi and Rwanda , especially for the period before 1961

HANDBOOKS

1600 Atlas linguistique du Zaire; situation linguistique en Afrique centrale; inventaire préliminaire, le Zaire. Paris, ACCT/Yaoundé, Centre régional de recherche et de documentation sur les traditions orales, 1983. (Atlas linguistique de l'Afrique centrale, ALAC). 161pp. illus. maps. (Lengthy critique by Mangula Motingea, 'L'atlas linguistique du Zaire: un travail à refair!', *Annales Aequatoria*, 14, 1993, 539-545)

1601 Belgian Congo and U.S.A. directory, 1943. New York, Moretus Press, 1943. 206pp. ("Information presented for the citizens of the U.S. on possessions of our allies". Includes texts of key documents, general topographical and statistical information, civil and military lists, commercial directory, and extensive descriptive gazetteer with c. 2,500 entries)

1602 Berwouts, Kris. **Congo: mensen, politiek, economie, cultuur**. Amsterdam, Koninklijk Instituut voor de Tropen/The Hague, Novib, 2001. (Landenreeks). 78pp. illus. maps

1603 Bevel, Maurice Louis **Le dictionnaire colonial (encyclopédie): explication de plus de 8,000 noms et expressions se rapportant aux diverses activités coloniales, depuis l'époque héroïque jusqu'aux temps présents**. 3rd ed. Brussels, E. Guyot, 1955. 202pp. + 1st Suppl. 26pp. bound with and apparently issued as part of 3rd ed; - - 2nd Suppl. Brussels, 1957. 20pp; - - 3rd Suppl. Brussels, 1959. 20pp. (Author was a former Administrator in the Belgian Congo. Includes Ruanda-Urundi. Numerous brief entries, c.50 to a page, double column, for flora and fauna, diseases, crops, ethnic groups, and settlements. Includes one-line biographies. Folding map at 1:4M). - - Orig. pub. Brussels, 1950-1951. 2 vols. illus. maps ; - - 2nd ed. **Le dictionnaire colonial (encyclopédie): explication de plus de 7,000 noms ...** Brussels, 1952. 202pp.

1604 Le Congo belge. Brussels, Office de l'information et des relations publiques du Congo belge et du Ruanda-Urundi (INFORCONGO), 1958-1959. 2 vols. illus. maps. (Vol. 1, 1958. 535pp. Covers topography, peoples, history, administration and the economy; vol. 2, 1959. xx, 189pp. 12 folding maps. Extensive statistical data to illustrate the narrative of vol. 1)
- - English trans. **Belgian Congo**. Brussels, INFORCONGO, 1959-1960. 2 vols. 547pp, 187pp.

1605 Congo belge et Ruanda-Urundi, guide du voyageur. 4th ed. Brussels, Office de l'information et des relations publiques du Congo belge et du Ruanda-Urundi, 1958. xvi, 798pp. illus. maps. (Emphasis on communications and topography, but includes much more detailed information on history, geography, administration and ethnography than the normal tourist guide).
- - Orig. pub. as **Guide du voyageur au Congo belge et au Ruanda-Urundi**. Brussels, Office du Tourisme du Congo belge et du Ruanda-Urundi, 1949. xxxix, 757pp. illus. Maps ; - - 2nd ed. Brussels, 1951. xxxix, 828pp. illus. maps; - - 3rd ed. Brussels, 1954. xxxix, 796pp. illus. maps. (Extracts also pub. as **Renseignements pratiques et itinéraires; extraits de la 3ième éd. du** *Guide* ... Brussels, [1954]. 745pp.)
- - English trans. pub. as **Traveler's** [sic] **guide to the Belgian Congo and Ruanda-Urundi**. 2nd ed. Brussels, Tourist Bureau for the Belgian Congo & Ruanda-Urundi, 1956. 790pp. illus. maps. - - Orig. pub. Brussels, 1951. 757pp.

1606 Congo-nil: guide du Congo belge et du Ruanda-Urundi. 7th ed. Brussels, Van Assche for Société des chemins de fer vicinaux du Congo, et Touring Club du Congo belge, 1950. 871pp. (Wide-ranging guidebook that includes detailed information on the history of the region, communications, administration, peoples, art, language, and commercial activities). - - Orig. pub. Brussels, [1934]. 491pp. illus. maps; - - 2nd ed. Brussels, 1936. 545pp. illus. maps; - - 3rd ed. **Congo-nil: ouvrage de documentation**. Brussels, 1937. 693pp. illus. maps; - - 4th ed. ... **1938/39**. Brussels, 1938. 663pp. illus. maps; - - 5th ed. ... **1939/40**. Brussels, 1940. 687pp; - - 6th ed. ... **1948/49**. Brussels, 1949.

1607 Dictionnaire d'histoire de Belgique, les hommes, les institutions, les faits, le Congo belge et le Ruanda-Urundi, ed. Hervé Hasquin. 2nd ed. Namur, Didier Hatier, 2000. 718pp. illus. maps. - - Orig. pub. as **Dictionnaire d'histoire de Belgique**. Brussels, Didier Hatier, 1988. 524pp. (Lacks coverage of African colonies)

1608 Encyclopédie du Congo belge. Brussels, Bieleweld, [1950-1953]. 3 vols. iv, 722pp; iv, 668pp; iv, 862pp. illus. maps. (Includes Ruanda-Urundi. Thematic arrangement. Vol. 1 covers prehistory, history, peoples, geology, climate, soils, botany and agriculture; vol. 2, forestry, fauna, fisheries, livestock and minerals; vol. 3, public health, the economy, industry, administration, public finance, mining and tourism. Statistics include information up to 1948. Signed articles by over 50 specialist contributors, but no sources given. Numerous photos and line drawings, and over 70 maps. Detailed contents lists for each vol. and general index in vol. 3. A major work of information on the countries in the period immediately following World War II)

1609 Ethnographic survey of Africa: Belgian Congo/Congo/Zaire. London, IAI/Tervuren, Musée royal du Congo Belge (*later* de l'Afrique centrale), 1954-1960. (Monographies ethnographiques). 5 vols. illus. maps. (Sub-series of the **Ethnographic survey** (*see* **86**). Vol.1. 1954. Les tribus Ba-Kuba et les peuplades apparentées, by J. Vansina. ix, 64pp; vol. 2. 1957. Les Bira et les peuplades limitrophes, by H. Van Geluwe. xii, 165pp; vol. 3. 1953. Les Mamvu-Mangutu et Balese-Mvubu, by H. Van Geluwe. xv, 195pp; vol. 4. 1959. Les peuplades de l'entre Congo-Ubangui, by H. Burssens. xi, 219pp; vol. 5. 1960. Les Bali et les peuplades apparentées, by H. Van Geluwe. ix, 130pp). *See also* **1006, 1253**

1610 G.B. Admiralty. Naval Intelligence Division. **The Belgian Congo**, comp. H.S.L. Winterbotham et al. London, 1944. (Geographical handbook series, B.R. 522). xiii, 558pp. 105 illus, 91 maps and figs. Detailed coverage of topography, history, peoples and economic data, with a descriptive gazetteer of 145 settlements, and a list of tribes with map of their distribution)

1611 Goncharov, L.V. et al. **Respublika Zair: spravochnik**. Moscow, Akademiia nauk, Institut Afriki, 1984. 253pp. maps.

1612 Historical dictionary of Democratic Republic of the Congo (Zaire). [2nd ed.], comp. F. Scott Bobb. Lanham, MD, Scarecrow Press, 1999. (African historical dictionaries, 76). xxvi, 597pp. (Reviews, *ASR*, 43, 2000, 138; *JAH*, 42, 2001, 350; *IJAHS*, 33, 2000, 453). - - Orig. pub. as **Historical dictionary of Zaire**. Metuchen, NJ, 1988. (African historical dictionaries, 43). xxxiii, 349pp. (Review, *Africa*, 60, 1990, 465. Rated "fair", Balay, 1996)

1613 Hochegger, Hermann. **Dictionnaire des rites**. Bandundu, Centre d'études ethnologiques du Bandundu (CEEBA), 1984-1992. 20 vols. (Encyclopaedia arranged A/Z, which describes individual Zaïrois rites, those of daily life, religious ceremonies etc., with reference to relevant sections of the same publisher's **La langage des gestes rituels**. Bandundu, 1981-1982)

1614 Kauffmann, Herbert. **Belgisch-Kongo und Ruanda-Urundi**. Bonn, K. Schroeder for Deutsche Afrika-Gesellschaft, 1959. (Die Länder Afrikas, 18). 144pp. illus. maps.

1615 Meyer, R. de. **Introducing the Belgian Congo**. Brussels, Office de publicité, 1958. 137pp.

1616 Mukenge, Tshilemalema. **Culture and customs of the Congo**. Westport, CT, Greenwood Press, 2002. (Culture and customs of Africa). xx, 204pp. illus. map. (Covers history religion, literature, art and architecture, social customs)

1617 **Profils du Zaire**. Kinshasa, Bureau du Président, 1972. 464pp. illus.

1618 Vanderlinden, Jacques. **La république du Zaire**. Paris, Berger-Levrault, 1975. (Encyclopédie politique et constitutionnelle. Série Afrique). 77pp.

1619 Willame, J.C. **Les partis politiques congolais**. Brussels, Centre de recherche et d'information socio-politiques (CRISP), 1964. (Travaux africains: dossier documentaire). 156pp. (Alphabetical list of parties with details of their history, activities, and leading figures)

1620 **Zaire: a country study**. 4th ed. comp. Sandra W. Meditz & Tim Merrill. Washington, DC, Library of Congress, Federal Research Division, 1994. lvii, 394pp. illus. maps. Also available at: http://lcweb2.loc.gov/frd/cs/zrtoc.html - - Orig. pub. as **Area handbook for the Republic of the Congo (Léopoldville)**. Washington, DC, U.S. Department of Defense, 1962. xii, 657pp. maps; - - 2nd ed. **Area handbook for the Democratic Republic of the Congo (Congo-Kinshasa)**, comp. Gordon C. McDonald et al. Washington, DC, 1971. xviii, 587pp. maps; - - 3rd ed., comp. Irving Kaplan et al. Washington, DC, 1979. xxi, 332pp. illus. maps.

Chronologies

1621 Bambi, Jean-Guy. **Chronologie des principaux faits et événements au Congo**. 2nd ed. Kinshasa, Centre de Commerce International, 1980- . Vol.1, 1980. 1482-1979.

1622 Banyaku Luape Epotu, Eugène. **Chronologie, monographie et documentation sur l'histoire politique du Congo des années 60 aux années 90**. Kinshasa, Centre interdisciplinaire d'études et de documentation sociale, 2000, 1,010pp. (Includes detailed lists of officials. Lacks table of contents. "Indispensable source", *ABPR*, 28, 2002, 215)

1623 Hoskyns, Katherine. **The Congo; a chronology of events, January 1960-December 1961**. London, Royal Institute of International Affairs (RIIA), 1962. 54, 42pp. (For this period *see also* **République du Congo devant l'opinion mondiale; chronologie des événements et commentaires de presse pour Juillet 1960**. Brussels, Comité de coordination, ?1960. 95pp. ... **pour Août 1960**. Brussels, ?1960. 56pp; U.S. Department of State. Bureau of Intelligence & Research. **Chronology of significant events in the Congo, January 1959-December 21, 1961**. Washington, DC, 1961. 32pp.)

1624 Mwanyimi-Mbomba, Mandjumba. **Chronologie générale de l'histoire du Zaïre (des origines à 1988)**. 2nd ed. Kinshasa, Centre de recherches pédagogiques, 1989. 191pp. (Post independence section is divided by subject, then province). - - Orig. pub. Kinshasa, 1985. 111pp.

See also **2865**

YEARBOOKS

1625 **Annuaire colonial**. Ghent, Foire internationale, 1951-55. Annual.

1626 **Annuaire de l'industrie et du commerce de la république démocratique du Congo, 1969/70**. Kinshasa, Sadiapic-Congo, 1970. (Noted in CCFR)

1627 **Annuaire du Congo belge: administratif, commercial, industriel, agricole 1897 [-1958/59]**. Brussels, Bodden & Dechy, 1897-?1960. Annual (irreg.) 7th ed. 1913, 10th ed. 1921, 41st ed. 1951. (Includes civil list, list of towns and principal villages with directory of the administration, missions, professional organizations and commercial firms)

1628 Belgium. Ministère des Colonies [etc.] **Annuaire colonial belge**. Brussels, 1908-1960. Annual (irreg). (Includes civil list for the Congo and relevant Belgian ministries and a commercial directory). *Continues* **Annuaire de l'État indépendant du Congo**. Brussels, 1903-1906. Annual. 4 issues

1629 Belgium. Ministère des Colonies [etc.] **Annuaire officiel/Officieel jaarboek**. Brussels, 1908-1960. Annual (irreg.) 36 issues. (Not pub. 1915-1920, 1949. 1940/41 issued as 1 vol. Includes texts of documents, civil lists, information on commercial companies)

1630 Belgium. Ministère des Colonies [etc.] **Rapport sur l'administration du Congo belge**. Brussels, 1909-1960. Annual. Title varies: **Congo belge: rapport annuel** (1919-1960). 1939/44, 1945/46 issued as combined vols.

1631 Centre de recherche et d'information socio-politiques (CRISP). **Congo 1959** [etc.]. Brussels, 1959-1966. Annual. 8 issues. (Annual surveys of the Congo, basically concerned with political life, reproducing documents)

1632 Congo (Congo-Kinshasa). Agence nationale de publicité congolaise. **Annuaire de la République démocratique du Congo**. Kinshasa, 1965- . Annual. NWU & Stanford have issues for 1965, 1969. (Includes political, administrative and economic data and commercial directory)

See also **1015, 2760, 2762**

STATISTICS

1633 Diamuangana, Gamela Nginu et al. **Evolution et transformation des structures de l'économie zaïroise, 1970-1984**. Kinshasa, Presses de l'Université de Kinshasa, 1987. 227pp. illus. maps. (Largely statistical data)

1634 European Communities. Statistical Office. **Reports on ACP countries: Zaïre**. Luxembourg, Official Publications Office of the European Communities, 1988. 87pp.

1635 IMF. **Democratic Republic of the Congo: selected issues and statistical appendix**. Washington, DC, 2005. (Country report, 05/373). 97pp. - - Earlier eds. (title varies) 1996 (Staff country report, 96/28); 2001 (Country report, 01/123); 2003 (Country report, 03/175). Full text of reports from 1997 also available online, *see* **334**.

1636 Léonard, Charles. **Profils de l'économie du Zaïre: années 1955-1987**. Kinshasa, Département de l'économie nationale et de l'industrie, 1987. 243pp. illus.

Bulletins & yearbooks

1637 Belgium. Ministère de l'intérieur [etc.]. **Annuaire statistique de la Belgique et du Congo belge**. Brussels, 1911-1959. Annual. *Continues* **Annuaire statistique de la Belgique** (1870-1910) and includes the Belgian Congo.

1638 Belgium. Ministère des affaires africaines. Direction des études économiques. **La situation économique du Congo belge et du Ruanda-Urundi**. Brussels, 1950-1959. Annual. 10 issues. (Ruanda-Urundi covered from 1955. Detailed tabulated statistics of the economy)

1639 Belgian Congo. Direction de la statistique [etc.]. **Bulletin annuel des statistiques du Congo belge**. Léopoldville, 1947-1959. Annual. (Title varies: **Discours de statistiques du Congo belge** (1947-1956)

1640 Belgian Congo. Direction de la statistique [etc.] **Bulletin mensuel des statistiques générales du Congo belge et du Ruanda-Urundi** (from 1960 ... **de la République du Congo**). Léopoldville, 1955-1961. Monthly. *Continues* **Bulletin mensuel des statistiques du Congo belge et du Ruanda-Urundi**. Léopoldville, 1950-1954. Vols. 1-5. Monthly.

1641 Congo Democratic Republic/Zaire. Institut national de la statistique. **Annuaire statistique du Zäire**. Kinshasa, 1971- ?1988. Irreg. Issue 1, 1958/ 1969; issue 2, 1969/1978; issue 3, 1979, issue 5, 1979/1988.

1642 Congo Democratic Republic/Zaire. Institut national de la statistique. **Bulletin trimestriel des statistiques générales**. Kinshasa, 1962-   . Quarterly. Not issued 1977 to 1987. Last issue in NWU is for 1989.

1643 Congo Democratic Republic/Zaire. Institut national de la statistique. **L'économie du Zaïre**. Kinshasa, 1988-   ? Quarterly. NWU has 1988 issue only.

1644 Country profile: Democratic Republic of Congo. London, Economist Intelligence Unit, 1997- . *Continues in part* **Country profile: Zaire, Rwanda, Burundi**. London, 1986-1992; *continues* **Country profile: Zaire**. London, 1993-1996.

1645 Germany. Statistisches Bundesamt. **Statistik des Auslandes: Länderberichte: Zaire** (later **Länderbericht: Zaire**). Wiesbaden/Stuttgart, Metzler-Poetschel, 1962- . Irreg. Issues for 1962, 1970, 1978, 1985, 1987, 1990, 1994.

DIRECTORIES OF ORGANIZATIONS

1646 Annuaire du Fédération des entreprises du Congo. Kinshasa, 2000- . Annual. Latest issue in NWU is for 2003. *Continues* **Annuaire des entreprises du Zaïre**. Kinshasa, l'Association nationale des entreprises du Zaïre, 1984-1987. 3 vols.

1647 Recensement des sociétés industrielles et commerciales du Zaïre. Kinshasa, Société d'études et de publications internationales au Zaïre, 1987- ?Annual.   NWU has 4th ed. 1991/92

1648 Répertoire de développement, Zaïre 1985, ed. W. Fleischle-Jaudas. Kinshasa, Centre d'études pour l'action sociale, 1985. 428pp. (A list of some 3,500 organizations in Zaire)

BIOGRAPHICAL SOURCES

1649 Artigue, P. **Qui sont les leaders congolais?** 2nd ed. Brussels, Éditions Europe-Afrique, 1961. (Collection Carrefours africains). 375pp. - - Orig. pub. Brussels, 1960. 139pp. (2nd ed. includes over 800 biographies of living figures, compared with some 200 in 1st ed.)

1650 Biographie belge d'outre-mer/Biographie coloniale belge. Brussels, Institut royal coloniale belge (*later* Académie royale des sciences d'outre-mer), 1948- . Vols. 1-8 pub. to 1998. Vols. 1-6 pub. 1948-1968; vol. 7a, 1973; 7b, 1977; 7c, 1989; vol. 8, 1998. Vols. 6 onwards entitled **Biographie belge d'outre-mer**. (Over 2,500 substantial, well documented biographies of deceased figures who contributed to the history and development of the Belgian Congo. Includes non-Belgians, e.g. Livingstone, Stanley. Each vol. has a complete A/Z sequence, with addenda and corrigenda and cumulative index to earlier vols.) - - **Biographie historique du Congo**. Lubumbashi, Université de Lubumbashi. Centre d'études et de recherches documentaries sur l'Afrique centrale (CERDAC), 2000-2005. (Travaux et documents, 20-23). 4 vols. (Intended as a supplement to the above)

1651 Diana, Pasquale. **Lavoratori italiani nel Congo Belge: elenco biografico**. Rome, Istituto Italiano per l'Africa, 1961. (Collana di studi di storia e politica Africana, 4). 483pp. (Over 3,000 biographies for Italian nationals active at any period in the Belgian Congo. Modelled on **1650**).

1652 Encyclopaedia Africana dictionary of African biography. Vol. 2, Sierra Leone and Zaire. Algonac, MI, Reference Publications, 1979. 372pp. (Zaire, pp. 178-372, ed. John C. Yoder. Includes 102 biographies, most with portraits and bibliographies. For the encyclopaedia *see* **11**; for the dictionary of biography *see* **545**)

1653 Mabi, Malumba & Mutamba, Makombo. **Cadres et dirigeants au Zaïre, qui sont-ils? Dictionnaire biographique**. Kinshasa, Éditions du Centre de recherches pédagogiques, 1986. 541pp. (830 biographies, mostly of those involved in politics and administration since independence)

1654 Répertoire des membres du Bureau politique (1967-1979), de l'Exécutif national (1960-1979), du Comité exécutif national du MPR (1967-1972), comp. République du Zaïre, Mouvement populaire de la révolution, Bureau politique. Kinshasa, Institut Makanda Kabobi, 1979. 102pp.

See also **1619**

ATLASES & GAZETTEERS

1655 Atlas de Kinshasa, comp. Jean Flouriot et al. Kinshasa, Institut géographique du Zaire/Paris, Institut géographique national, 1974-1978. 2 vols. 41 x 62cm. Vol. 1, 1974. 94pp. 44 double page maps; vol. 2, 1978. 27pp. 22 maps. Review, *Cahiers d'outre-mer*, 32, 1979, 413-417)

1656 Atlas de la République du Zaïre, comp. Georges Laclavère. Paris, *Jeune Afrique*, 1978. 72pp. col. maps.

1657 Atlas des collectivités du Zaïre, ed. Léon de Saint Moulin. Kinshasa, Presses Universitaires du Zaïre, 1976. 65pp. (14 b. & w. maps showing administrative sub-divisions, together with population statistics for each)

1658 Atlas du Congo belge et du Ruanda-Urundi, comp. Gaston Derkinderen. Paris & Brussels, Elsevier, 1955. viii, 207pp. illus. (Popular work with profusely illus. text and 15 col. maps)

1659 Atlas du Congo, de l'Afrique et du monde. Kinshasa, Afrique Editions, 1998. 72pp. col. maps.

1660 Atlas du Katanga. Brussels, A. Bieleveld for Comité spécial du Katanga, 1929-1952. 6 vols. in 5. cxvii, 405pp. 36 x 46cm. (Orig. ed. Hubert Droogmans et al. Compiled by Service géographique et géologique. Issued as loose sheets in portfolios, with photos and text. Scales vary between 1:200,000 and 1:1M. A massively detailed work. *See* Maurice Robert, 'Les fascicules 1 et 2 de *l'Atlas du Katanga*', pp. 290-294 in **Comptes rendus du [12] Congrès international géographique, Paris, 1931**. Paris, Armand Colin, 1932; J. Monteyne, 'Les cartes et *l'Atlas du Katanga*', pp. 136-139 in **Comptes rendus du [14] Congrès international de géographie, Amsterdam, 1938**. Leiden, Brill, 1938)

1661 Atlas général de la République du Zaïre. Brussels, Académie royale des sciences d'outre-mer, 1976. (Issued as sheets with explanatory pamphlets in English, French and Flemish. A rev. ed. of **1662**).

1662 **Atlas général du Congo et du Ruanda-Urundi**. Brussels, Institut royal colonial belge (*later* Académie royale des sciences d'outre-mer), 1948-1963. 39 x 39cm. (Large-scale thematic work, many years in the planning. 34 separate plates with accompanying text in French and Flemish. Sections for history, geodesy, physical geography, biology, anthropology and culture, politics, administration and society, economics. Most maps at 1:5M. Index of c.5,000 names. On the planning *see* M.H. Buttgenbach, 'Un atlas général du Congo belge', *Bulletin de la Société belge d'études géographiques*, 5, 1935, 21-24. Reviews, *Geographical review*, 41, 1951, 483; 47, 1957, 575; *JAH*, 3, 1962, 167-168. For rev. version *see* **1661**)

1663 **Atlas géographique et historique du Congo belge et des térritoires sous mandat du Ruanda-Urundi**, comp. René de Rouck. 5th ed. Brussels, Éditions de Rouck, 1954. 14pp. 12 plates col. maps. 36 x 27cm. - - Earlier eds. Brussels, 1938, 1945, 1947, 1951. (Eds. largely unchanged, with 45 maps, 7 city plans, index of 5,972 names)

1664 **[Atlas provincial du Congo belge]**. Léopoldville, Institut géographique du Congo belge, 1956. Issued as 6 separate vols: **Province de l'Équateur: cartes des térritoires, éd. provisoire**, 22 maps; **Province du Kasai ...**, 22 maps; **Province du Katanga ...**, 24 maps; **Province du Kivu ...**, 19 maps; **Province du Léopoldville ...**, 25 maps; **Province Orientale ...**, 25 maps.

1665 U.S. Board on Geographic Names. **Preliminary N.I.S. gazetteer, Belgian Congo: official standard names approved by the USBGN**. Washington, DC, 1953. ii, 349pp. (Pp. 1-322, Belgian Congo; pp. 323-349, Ruanda-Urundi)

1666 U.S. Board on Geographic Names. **Republic of the Congo (Léopoldville): official standard names approved by the USBGN**. Washington, DC, 1964. (Gazetteer, 80). iv, 426pp. (Includes 30,400 names from maps at 1:1M. Revision of the appropriate sections of **1665**)

1667 **Le Zaire économique**. Kinshasa, Bureau du Président-fondateur, 1983. 151pp. col. maps. (Thematic atlas. Maps at 1:3M)

See also **1601**

EARTH SCIENCES

1668 Atlas de l'agriculture des régions du Bandundu, du Bas-Zaire et de Kinshasa. Heverlee, Université Catholique du Louvain, Centre de recherche en économie agricole des pays en voie de développement, 1991. 131pp.

1669 Buttgenbach, Henri J.F. **Les minéraux de Belgique et du Congo belge**. Paris, H. Vaillant-Carmanne/Liège, Dunod, 1947. xvi, 573pp. illus. map.

1670 Cahen, Lucien. **Géologie du Congo belge**. Liège, Vaillant-Carmanne, 1954. xiii, 577pp. illus.

1671 Cahen, Lucien et al. **Lexique stratigraphique international, 4, Afrique, fasc. 7: Congo belge**. Paris, CNRS, 1956. 122pp.

1672 Carte des sols et de la végétation du Congo belge et du Ruanda-Urundi. 2nd ed. Brussels, Institut national pour l'étude agronomique du Congo belge (INEAC), 1960-1970. (Issued in 26 parts, each with maps and text). - - Orig. pub. Brussels, 1954-1960. 75 maps. 29 x 24cm

1673 Robert, Maurice. **Le Congo physique**. 3rd ed. Liège, Vaillant-Carmanne, 1946. 449pp. illus. maps. - - **Complément 1948 à la 3ème édition**. Liège, 1948. 83pp. maps. - - Orig. pub. Brussels, Lamertin, 1923. 315pp; - - 2nd ed. Brussels, Strop, 1942. 369pp.

1674 Robert, Maurice. **Géologie et géographie du Katanga**; y compris l'étude des ressources et de la mise en valeur. Brussels, Hayez, 1956. 620pp. illus. maps (General discussion of exploration and colonization as well as topography, hydrology, geology and mineral resources, mining, agriculture and animal husbandry)

1675 Van den Abeele, Marcel & Vandenput, René. **Les principales cultures du Congo**. 3rd ed. Brussels, Direction de l'agriculture, des forêts et de l'élevage, 1956. 932pp. illus. maps. - - Orig. pub. as **Notes sur les principales cultures du Congo Belge**, comp René Vandenput. Brussels, Ministère des colonies, 1939. 155, xxpp. - - 2nd ed. **Les principales cultures du Congo**. Brussels, 1951. 605pp.

1676 Wiese, Bernd. **Zaire: Landesnatur, Bevölkerung, Wirtschaft**. Darmstadt, Wissenschaftliche Buchgesellschaft, 1980. (Wissenschaftliche Länderkunden, 15). xxvi, 360pp. illus. maps. (Physical and economic geography. Review, *GJ*, 148, 1982, 70)

BIOLOGICAL SCIENCES

Zoology

1677 Chapin, James P. 'Birds of the Belgian Congo, pts. 1-4', *Bulletin of the American Museum of Natural History*, 65, 1932; 75, 1939; 75A, 1953; 75B, 1954, 638-738. 4 vols. pp. 1-809. (Gazetteer, pp. 638-738)

1678 Laurent, Raymond F. **Contribution à l'herpétologie de la région des grands lacs de l'Afrique centrale**. Tervuren, Musée royal du Congo belge, 1956. (*Annales. Sciences zoologiques*, 48). 390pp. + 31 plates. Part I, Généralités; pt. II. Chéloniens; pt. III. Ophidiens.

1679 Lippens, Léon & Wille, Henri. **Les oiseaux du Zaire**. Tilt, Editions Lannoo, 1976. 509pp. 600 col. photos, 1,086 maps. Review, *Ibis*, 119, 1977, 554).
- - Louette, Michel. 'Additions and corrections to the avifauna of Zaire', *Bulletin of the British Ornithologists' Club*, 107, 1987, 137-143; 108, 1988, 43-50; - - Demey, R. et al. 'Additions and annotations to the avifauna of Congo-Kinshasa', *ibid.*, 120, 2000, 154-172; - - Herroelen, P. 'Further annotations ... to the avifauna of the Democratic Republic of Congo,' *ibid.*, 126, 2006, 19-37

1680 Poll, Max & Gosse, Jean-Pierre. 'Contribution à l'étude systématique de la faune ichthyologique du Congo central', *Annales du Musée royal de l'Afrique centrale. Sciences zoologiques*, 116, 1963, 43-110. illus. map.

1681 Schouteden, Henri. **Faune du Congo belge et du Ruanda-Urundi**. Tervuren, Musée royal du Congo belge, Tervuren, 1948-1960. 4 vols. (*Annales du Musée du Congo belge, sciences zoologiques*; 1, 29, 57, 89). Vol. 1, Mammifères, vols. 2-4, Oiseaux. (Condensed versions of his **Les mammifères du Congo belge ...**. Tervuren, 1944-1947. (*Annales C, zoologie*, sér. 2, vol. 3). 576pp. *and* **Les oiseaux du Congo belge ...**. Tervuren, 1948-55. (*Annales, C, zoologie*, sér. 4, vols. 2, 3). 4 vols. in 10)

1682 Witte, Gaston-François de. **Genera des serpents du Congo et du Ruanda-Urundi**. Tervuren, Musée royal de l'Afrique centrale, 1962. (*Annales. Sciences zoologiques*, 104). viii, 208pp. + 15pp. plates.

See also **815, 816**

Botany

1683 Flore d'Afrique centrale. Brussels/Meise, Jardin botanique national de Belgique, 1967- . Issued in fascs. Latest issues, 2005. *Continues* **Flore du Congo belge et du Ruanda-Urundi** (from 1960, **Flore du Congo, du Rwanda et du Burundi**), ed. Walter Robyns et al. Brussels, Institut national pour l'étude agronomique du Congo (INEAC), 1948-1963. Vols. 1-7, 8(1), 9-10. (Currently issued in two series of fascs. for Pteridophytes and Spermatophytes. Large scale descriptive flora, still incomplete after almost 60 years)
 - - Bamps, Paul. *Flore d'Afrique centrale* **(Zaire-Rwanda-Burundi), répertoire des lieux de récolte**. Meise, 1982. 224pp. - - Orig. pub. as *Flore du Congo, du Rwanda et du Burundi*: **index des lieux de récolte**. Meise, 1968.

1684 Lebacq, Lucien. **Atlas anatomique des bois du Congo belge**. Brussels, l'Institut national pour l'étude agronomique du Congo belge (INEAC), 1955-1963. 5 vols. illus. Maps and accompanying text.

1685 Lebrun, Jean-Pierre & Gilbert, G. **Une classification écologique des forêts du Congo**. Brussels, l'Institut national pour l'étude agronomique du Congo belge (INEAC), 1954. (Série scientifique, 63). 89pp. illus. maps.

1686 Pichi-Sermolli, R.E.G. 'A contribution to the knowledge of the Pteridophyta of Rwanda, Burundi and Kivu (Zaire), Parts I & II', *Bulletin du Jardin botanique nationale de Belgique*, 53, 1983, 177-284; 55, 1985, 123-206 (Detailed critical account of ferns)

1687 Pieters, A. **Essences forestières du Zaire**. Ghent, Universitet Ghent, Onderzoekscentrum voor Bousbow, Bosbedrijfsfoering en Bospolitiek, 1977. 349pp. illus. map. (Describes the 112 principal spp. of forestry trees)

RWANDA & BURUNDI

Note that many of the titles recorded under **Democratic Republic of Congo (Zaire)** above, will also treat these countries.

HANDBOOKS

1688 Belgium. Office de l'information et des rélations publiques du Congo belge et du Ruanda-Urundi (INFORCONGO). **Le Ruanda-Urundi**. Brussels, 1959. 377pp. illus. 18 col. maps (6 in pocket). (Sections for geography, history, administration, economics and social life). - - English trans. by Goldie Blankoff-Scarr. **Ruanda-Urundi**. Brussels, 1960. 4 pts.

1689 Hausner, Karl-Heinz & Jezic, Béatrice. **Rwanda-Burundi**. Bonn, K. Schroeder for Deutsche Afrika-Gesellschaft, 1968. (Die Länder Afrikas, 36). 121pp. (Rev. ed. of appropriate sections of **1614**)

1690 Verlinden, Peter. **Rwanda, Burundi: mensen, politiek, economie, cultuur**. Amsterdam, Koninklijk Instituut voor de Tropen/The Hague, Novib, 1996. (Landenreeks). 83pp. illus. maps.

See also **1006, 1136**

YEARBOOKS

1691 Belgium. Ministère des colonies [etc.]. **Rapport sur l'administration belge du Ruanda-Urundi**. Brussels, 1921-1960. Annual. (Title varies slightly. Reports for 1939/44, 1945/46 issued as combined vols. Post 1946 vols. also issued with separate title-page as 'Rapport soumis par le Gouvernement belge à l'Assemblée Générale des Nations Unies au sujet de l'administration du Ruanda-Urundi'). *Continues* **Rapport sur l'administration belge des térritoires occupés de l'est-africain allemand et spécialement du Ruanda et de l'Urundi, 1917/21**. Brussels, 1921.

STATISTICS

1692 Germany. Statistisches Bundesamt. **Statistik des Auslandes: Länderberichte: Ruanda-Urundi**. Wiesbaden, 1962.

ATLASES & GAZETTEERS

1693 Atlas du Ruanda-Urundi. Brussels, De Visscher, [1952]. iipp, 21 maps. 22 x 30cm. (Thematic maps at 1:1M, covering geology, climate, population, health, education, trade, communications)

BIOLOGICAL SCIENCES

1694 Lebrun, Jean-Pierre. 'La végétation et les territoires botaniques du Ruanda-Urundi', *Naturalistes belges*, 37, 1956, 230-256

See also **1050, 1061, 1065**

BURUNDI

HANDBOOKS

1695 Area handbook for Burundi, comp. Gordon C. McDonald et al. Washington, DC, U.S. Department of Defense, 1969. xiv, 203pp. maps.

1696 Atlas linguistique du Burundi; situation linguistique en Afrique centrale; inventaire préliminaire, le Burundi, ed. Nicolas Mayugi & Pascal Ndayishinguje. Paris, ACCT/Yaoundé, Centre régional de recherche et de documentation sur les traditions orales/Bujumbura, Département des langues et littératures africaines, Université du Burundi, 1985. (Atlas linguistique de l'Afrique centrale, ALAC). 83pp. illus. maps.

1697 France. Ministère de la coopération. **Burundi: guide d'information, janvier 1993**. Paris, 1993. (Collection guides d'information). 85pp.

1698 Historical dictionary of Burundi. 2nd ed., comp. Ellen K. Eggers. Lanham, MD, Scarecrow Press, 1997. (African historical dictionaries, 73). lxxvi, 199pp. (Review, *IJAHS*, 31, 1998, 390-191). - - Orig. pub. comp. Warren Weinstein. Metuchen, NJ, 1976. (African historical dictionaries, 8). xvii, 368pp. (Review, *Africana J.*, 10, 1979, 120-128. Rated "good", Balay, 1996). 3rd ed. announced for 2006, *see* publisher's Web site.

1699 Mpozagara, Gabriel. **La République du Burundi**. Paris, Berger-Levrault, 1971. (Encyclopédie politique et constitutionnelle. Série Afrique). 72pp.

1700 Mukuri, Melchior. **Dictionnaire chronologique du Burundi: de Mwezi Gisabo à la chute de la monarchie (ca. 1850-1966)**. Bujumbura, Université du Burundi, 2001. 406pp.

1701 Sokolova, R.B. **Respublika Burundi: spravochnik**. Moscow, Akademiia nauk, Institut Afriki, 1992. 140pp.

YEARBOOKS

1702 Annuaire de l'administration publique burundaise. Bujumbura, Ministère de la Fondation publique, 198?- . Annual. ALA records issue for 1991.

1703 Annuaire des sociétés industrielles, commerciales et agricoles du Burundi. Bujumbura, Chambre de commerce, d'industrie, d'agriculture et d'artisanat, 1991- . Annual. NWU holds 3rd ed. 1993

STATISTICS

1704 Burundi. Centre national de documentation statistique (CNDS). **Statistiques sociales au Burundi: bibliographie [provisoire]**. Bujumbura, 1992. 129pp. (Lists 444 sources based on holdings of CNDS, and references on IBISCUS)

1705 Burundi. Département de statistiques [etc.]. **Bulletin de statistique**. Bujumbura, 1966-1992. Quarterly/bi-monthly. Title varies: **Bulletin statistique trimestriel**.

1706 Burundi. Institut de statistique et d'études économiques du Burundi (ISTEEBU). **Annuaire statistique 1962/65** [etc.]. Bujumbura, 1966- . Annual Until 1987 issued by Département de statistiques [etc.]. LC holds issue for 1999.

1707 Country profile: Burundi. London, Economist Intelligence Unit, 2004- Annual. *Continues in part* **Country profile: Zaire, Rwanda, Burundi**. London, 1986-1992; **Country profile: Rwanda, Burundi**. London, 1993-2003.

1708 Germany. Statistisches Bundesamt. **Statistik des Auslandes: Länderberichte: Burundi** (later **Länderbericht: Burundi**). Wiesbaden/Stuttgart, Metzler-Poetschel, 1967- . Irreg. Issues for 1967, 1984, 1986, 1988, 1990. *See also* **1692**

1709 IMF. **Burundi: selected issues and statistical appendix**. Washington, DC, 2006. (Country report, 06/307). 118pp. - - Earlier eds. (title varies) 1996 (Staff country report, 96/43); 1999 (Staff country report, 99/8); 2000 (Staff country report, 00/58); 2002 (Country report, 02/241); 2004 (Country report, 04/38). Full text of reports from 1997 also available online, *see* **334**.

DIRECTORIES OF ORGANIZATIONS

1710 Annuaire des enterprises. Bujumbura, Chambre de commerce, d'industrie, d'agriculture et d'artisanat du Burundi, 1990- . Annual.

ATLASES & GAZETTEERS

1711 **Atlas du Burundi**, comp. Jean-Louis Acquier et al. Paris, Ministère de la coopération/Bordeaux, Université de Bordeaux II & Centre d'études de géographie tropicale/Bujumbura, Université de Burundi, 1979. viiipp. 30 col. plates. 69pp. 32 x 42cm (Text interleaved with un-numbered pp. of b. & w. maps, charts, illus., statistics. Thematic coverage at 1:750,000, 4 thematic maps of Bujumbura at 1:36,000, map of Gitega at 1:13,000. No index or gazetteer)

1712 U.S. Board on Geographic Names. **Burundi: official standard names approved by the USBGN**. Washington, DC, 1964. (Gazetteer, 84). ii, 44pp. (Revision of appropriate sections of **Belgian Congo ...** *see* **1665**).

BIOLOGICAL SCIENCES

1713 Schouteden, Henri. **La faune ornithologique du Burundi**. Tervuren, Musée royal de l'Afrique centrale, 1966. (Documentation zoologique, 11). viii, 81pp.

RWANDA

Official Web site of the Republic of Rwanda. http://www.gov.rw/

HANDBOOKS

1714 Area handbook of Rwanda, comp. Richard F. Nyrop et al. Washington, DC, U.S. Department of Defense, 1969. xiv, 212pp. maps. Reissued 1982 as **Rwanda: a country study**.

1715 Corduwener, Jeroen. **Rwanda: mensen, politiek, economie, cultuur, milieu**. Amsterdam, Koninklijk Instituut voor de Tropen/The Hague, Novib, 2004. (Landenreeks). 74pp. illus. maps. (Rev. of the appropriate sections of **1690** above)

1716 Historical dictionary of Rwanda, comp. Learthen Dorsey. Metuchen, NJ, Scarecrow Press, 1994. (African historical dictionaries, 60). xvi, 437pp. (Reviews, *Africa*, 70, 2000, 304-305; *Choice*, 32, 1995, 1705)

1717 Vanderlinden, Jacques. **La République rwandaise**. Paris, Berger-Levrault, 1970. (Encyclopédie politique et constitutionnelle. Série Afrique). 63pp.

YEARBOOKS

1718 Annuaire des sociétés [entreprises] industrielles, commerciales et agricoles du Rwanda. Kigali, Chambre de commerce et d'industrie du Rwanda, 1993- . ?Annual. Latest issue in NWU is for 1997

STATISTICS

1719 Country profile: Rwanda. London, Economist Intelligence Unit, 2004-Annual. *Continues in part* **Country profile: Zaire, Rwanda, Burundi**. London, 1986-1992; **Country profile: Rwanda, Burundi**. London, 1993-2003.

1720 Germany. Statistisches Bundesamt. **Statistik des Auslandes: Länderberichte: Ruanda** (later **Länderbericht: Ruanda**). Wiesbaden/ Stuttgart, Metzler-Poetschel, 1985- . Irreg. Issues for 1985, 1987, 1992. *See also* **1692**

1721 IMF. **Rwanda: selected issues and statistical appendix**. Washington, DC, 2004. (Country report, 04/383). 108pp. - - Earlier eds. (title varies) 1996 (Staff country report, 96/140); 1998 (Staff country report, 98/115); 2001 (Country report, 01/30); 2002 (Country report, 02/187). Full text of reports from 1997 also available online, *see* **334**

1722 Rwanda. Direction de la statistique [etc.]. **Bulletin de statistique**. Kigali, 1964- . Quarterly. - - **Bulletin de statistique: supplément annuel**. Kigali, 1964- Annual. Wider coverage of topics than the **Bulletin**. ALA notes issue for 1991.

ATLASES & GAZETTEERS

1723 **Atlas du Rwanda**, ed. Christian Prioul & Pierre Sirven. Paris, Ministère de la coopération/Kigali, Université du Rwanda, 1981. ix, 67pp. 45 x 32cm. (32 col. maps, most at 1:800,000, with accompanying text and transparent overlay showing political divisions. Covers physical features, vegetation, population. 4 historical maps (pre 1896, 1896-1916, 1916-1962, Roman Catholic Church, 1900-1976).

1724 **Atlas rural du Rwanda**. Kigali, Ministère des travaux publics et de l'équipement, [1982]. 66pp. (26 col. maps with text covering administration, peoples, public services, mining and agriculture)

1725 U.S. Board on Geographic Names. **Rwanda: official standard names approved by the USBGN**. Washington, DC, 1964. (Gazetteer, 85). iii, 44pp. (Includes 3,000 names from 1:500,000 map series. Revision of the appropriate sections of **Belgian Congo ...** *see* **1665**)

EARTH SCIENCES

1726 Baudin, Bernard. **Minéralisations du Rwanda**. 2nd ed. Kigali, Université nationale de Rwanda, 1982-1983. 2 vols., viii, 293; 231pp. illus. maps. (Includes 'inventaire des minéraux du Rwanda'). - - Orig. pub. Kigali, 1979.

BIOLOGICAL SCIENCES

1727 Fischer, Eberhard & Hinkel, Harald. **La nature et l'environnement du Rwanda**: aperçu sur la flore et la faune rwandaise. Mainz, Johannes

Gutenberg Universität/Butare, Institut de recherche scientifique et technologique, 1992. 452pp. illus. maps. (Parallel French/German text. Arranged by biomes. Emphasis on plants and the herpetofauna)

Zoology

1728 De Vos, Luc & Snoeks, Jos. 'An annotated checklist of the fishes of Rwanda', *Journal of East African natural history*, 90, 2001, 41-68. illus. map. (82 spp.)

1729 Hinkel, Harald & Fischer, Eberhard. **Reptiles et amphibiens du Rwanda et leurs environnement**. Mainz, Johannes Gutenberg Universität, 1988. 52, 17pp. + 20pp. plates. illus. maps.

1730 Monfort, Nicole. **Les mammifères du Rwanda**. Kigali, Rotary Club de Kigali, 1985. 142pp. (Text in French and Kinyarwanda)

1731 Schoudeten, Henri. **La faune ornithologique du Rwanda**. Tervuren, Musée royal de l'Afrique centrale, 1966. (Documentation zoologique, 10). viii, 130pp.

Botany

1732 Delepierre, G. **Systématique des plantes cultivées au Rwanda**. Butare, Institut des sciences agronomiques du Rwanda, 1986. 175pp. illus.

1733 Raynal, Jean et al. **Contribution aux études floristiques au Rwanda**. 4th ed. Paris, ACCT, 1985. (Médicine traditonelle et pharmacopée). 286pp. illus. maps.

1734 Troupin, Georges. **Flore du Rwanda: Spermatophytes**. Butare, Institut national de la recherche scientifique/Tervuren, Musée royal de l'Afrique centrale, 1978-87. (*Annales. Sciences économiques*, 9, 13, 15, 16). 4 vols. (Lists seed plants with keys and illus. of representative members of each family)

1735 Troupin, Georges. **Flore des plantes ligneuses du Rwanda**. Butare, Institut national de la recherche scientifique/Tervuren, Musée royal de l'Afrique centrale, 1982. (*Annales. Sciences économiques*, 12). xii, 747pp. illus. (Covers some 700 spp. with copious illus.)

WEST AFRICA

General

Anglophone West Africa
Gambia   Nigeria
Ghana   Sierra Leone

Liberia
St. Helena (incl. Ascension, Tristan da Cunha)

Francophone West Africa (incl. Sahara, Sahel)
Benin   Mali
Burkina Faso   Mauritania
Cameroon   Niger
Côte d'Ivoire   Senegal
Guinea   Togo

Lusophone West Africa
Cape Verde   São Tomé e Principe
Guinea Bissau

Former Spanish Africa
Equatorial Guinea   Western Sahara

HANDBOOKS

1736 Atlas historique de la boucle du Niger; synthèse des colloques de Bamako et Niamey, 1975-1976-1977, comp. Yveline Poncet, et al. Paris, Association pour la recherche scientifique en Afrique noire, 1981. 23pp. 22 maps in portfolio. (L'empire du Ghana, l'empire du Mali, l'empire du Songhay. Maps at 1:500,000. *See* Y. Poncet, 'La cartographie historique dans le boucle du Niger', pp. 309-315 in **Actes du 2me Colloque internationale de Bamako**, 1976. Paris, Fondation SCOA, 1977)

1737 Centre des hautes études administratives sur l'Afrique et l'Asie modernes (CHEAM). **Carte des religions de l'Afrique de l'ouest: notice et catalogue**. Paris, La documentation française, 1966. 135pp.

1738 Ethnographic survey of Africa: Western Africa: English series. London, IAI, 1950-1960. 15 vols. Sub-series of **Ethnographic survey** (*see* **86**). Vol. 1. 1950. The Akan and Ga-Adangme peoples of the Gold Coast, by M.

Manoukian. 112pp; vol.2. 1950. The peoples of Sierra Leone Protectorate, by M. McCulloch. 102pp; vol. 3. 1950. The Ibo and Ibibio-speaking peoples of south-eastern Nigeria, by D. Forde & G.I. Jones. 80pp; vol.4. 1951. The Yoruba-speaking peoples of south-western Nigeria, by D. Forde. 102pp; vol. 5. 1951. Tribes of the northern territories of the Gold Coast, by M. Manoukian. 102pp; vol. 6. 1952. The Ewe-speaking people of Togoland and the Gold Coast, by M. Manoukian. 63pp; vol. 7. 1953. The peoples of the plateau area of Northern Nigeria, by H.D. Gunn. 111pp; vol.8. 1953. The Tiv of central Nigeria, by L. & P. Bohannan. 100pp; vol. 9. 1954. Peoples of the central Cameroons by M. McCulloch & M. Littlewood. 174pp; vol. 10. 1955. Peoples of the Niger-Benue confluence, by D. Forde et al. 160pp; vol. 11. 1956. Coastal Bantu of the Cameroons, by E. Ardener. 116pp; vol. 12. 1956. Pagan peoples of the central area of Northern Nigeria, by H.D. Gunn. 146pp; vol. 13. 1957. The Benin kingdom and the Edo-speaking peoples of south-western Nigeria, by R.E. Bradbury. 212pp; vol. 14. 1957. The Wolof of Senegambia, together with notes on the Lebu and the Serer, by D.P. Gamble. 110pp; vol. 15. 1960. Peoples of the middle Niger region of Northern Nigeria, by H.D.Gunn & F.P. Conant. 136pp.
- - **French series: Monographies ethnologiques africaines**. Paris, Presses universitaires de France for International African Institute, 1954-1963. 10 vols. Vol. 1. 1954. Les Bambara, by V. Paques. xiii, 131pp; vol. 2. 1954. Les Songhay, by J. Rouch. 100pp; vol. 3. 1955. Les Coniagui et les Bassari (Guinée française), by M. de Lestrange. 86pp; vol. 4. 1957. Les Dogon, by M. Palkau-Marti. xii, 122pp; vol. 5. 1957. Les Sénoufo (y compris les Minainka), by B. Holas. 183pp; vol. 6. 1958. Le groupe dit Pahouin, by P. Alexandre. vi, 152pp; vol. 7. 1959. Les Kongo Nord-Occidentaux by M. Soret. viii, 144pp; vol. 8. 1959. Les populations du Tchad by A. M.-D. Lebeuf. viii, 130pp; vol. 9. 1962. Les populations païennes du Nord Cameroun, by B. Lembezat. 252pp; vol. 10. 1963. Les populations du Nord-Togo, by J.-C. Froelich et al. 195pp.

1739 McConnell, Grant D. & Gendron, Jean-Denis, eds. **Atlas international de la vitalité linguistique. Vol. 3, L'Afrique occidental**. Quebec, Université Laval, Centre internationale de recherche en aménagement linguistique, 1995. 137pp. (Provides analysis by region, country and context of use, e.g. at school, in religion, in the media)

1740 Mauny, Raymond. **Tableau géographique de l'Ouest africain au moyen âge d'après les sources écrites, la tradition et l'archéologie**. Dakar, IFAN, 1961. (Mémoires, 61). 587pp. illus. maps. Reprinted, Amsterdam, Swets & Zeitlinger, 1975. (Detailed analysis of sources with sections on economic and human geography for 622-1434 A.D. Review, *JAH*, 5, 1964, 319-321, "likely to remain a standard work of reference for many years")

1741 Westermann, Diedrich & Bryan, Margaret A. **Languages of West Africa**. Rev. ed. Folkestone, Dawsons for IAI, 1970. 277pp. (Classified listing with estimates of numbers of speakers and their topographical distribution. Rev. ed. includes suppl. bibliography). - - Orig. pub. London, Oxford University Press for IAI, 1952. (Handbook of African languages, pt. 2). 215pp. map. (For the **Handbook**, *see* **158**. Reviews, *Africa*, 23, 1953, 163-16; *African affairs*, 53, 1954, 75-77)

YEARBOOKS

1742 **New African yearbook: West and Central Africa**. London, I.C. Magazines Ltd., 1983,1985. Issues for 1983/84, 1985/86. (Issued as vol. [2] of **New African yearbook**, 5th and 6th eds. (*see* **290**).

1743 **West Africa annual**. Lagos, John West Publications, 1962- . Irreg. 18th ed. 2005. (Ed. by L.K. Jakande (issues 1-10), B.A. Salau (issue 11-). Covers Anglophone, Francophone and Lusophone countries. Basic information on each country with history, topography, economy)

1744 **West African directory 1962 [-1967/68]**. London, Thomas Skinner, 1962-1967. Annual. 6 issues. (Covers Anglophone, Francophone and Lusophone countries. General information on topography, the economy and public and social services, with a commercial directory)

STATISTICS

1745 **West Africa: Cameroon, Côte d'Ivoire, Gabon, Ghana, Nigeria, Senegal: economic structure and analysis**. London, Economist Intelligence Unit, 1990. 195pp. maps. (Collection of statistics)

DIRECTORIES OF ORGANIZATIONS

1746 Banjo, A. Olugboyega. **Social science libraries in West Africa: a directory**. Lagos, Nigerian Institute of International Affairs (NIIA), 1987. 63pp.

1747 Bannerman, Valentia. **Directory of university libraries and professional librarians in the West African sub-region**. Winneba, Standing Conference of African University Libraries, Western Area, 2002. 411pp. (Anglophone and Francophone countries. Based on questionnaire. ASC4, 95)

1748 Directory of museums in West Africa. Dakar, West African Museums Programme (WAMP), 2002. 222pp. (Covers 145 institutions with contact details. ASC4, 96)

BIOGRAPHICAL SOURCES

1749 Fung, Karen. 'Index to "portraits" in *West Africa*, 1948-1966', *African studies bulletin*, 9, 1966, 103-120. ("Portraits" were short biographies)

1750 G.B. Commonwealth War Graves Commission. **The register of the names of those who fell in the First World War, and are buried or commemorated in Zaire, Algeria, Tunisia, Senegal, the Gambia, Madeira, Cape Verde, St. Helena and Ascension Island and Sierra Leone**. Rev. ed. Maidenhead, 1992. 46pp. - - Orig. pub. Maidenhead, 1931.

1751 G.B. Commonwealth War Graves Commission. **The register of the names of those who fell in the 1939-1945 War in West Africa (excluding Ghana and Nigeria)**. Maidenhead, 1982. xi, 38pp.

1752 Kirk-Greene, Anthony H.M., ed. **West Africa "portraits": a biographical dictionary of West African personalities, 1947-1977**. London, Cass, 1987. (Some 300 biographical sketches reprinted from the journal *West Africa*)

ATLASES & GAZETTEERS

Atlases

1753 Economic atlas of West Africa: maps, facts, figures and notes, comp. Dele Adébárá. Ibadan, Adébárá Publishing, 1978. 160pp. (Thematic b. & w. maps accompanied by statistics. Section on West Africa in general followed by country sections, covering both Anglophone and Francophone areas)

1754 International atlas of West Africa. Dakar, IFAN for OAU Scientific, Technical & Research Commission, 1968-1978. 3 vols. 44 sheets. 53 x 76cm. (Thematic atlas issued loose-leaf, with a portfolio. Scale 1:5M. Legend in English and French. Initial proposals made at a Dakar conference in 1945, working parties established in 1955/56, detailed schedule announced in 1963, and first 8 sheets published in 1968. Covers Benin, Burkina Faso, Gambia, Ghana, Mali, Mauritania, Niger, Nigeria, Senegal, Togo. A very detailed source. *See* R.C.B. Duru, 'National atlas of Nigeria and international atlas of West Africa', *African notes*, 2, 1964, 8-14; T. Monod, 'L'atlas général international de l'Ouest africain', pp. 223-237 in **Relatorio geral de 2a Conferência internacional dos Africanistas ocidentais, Bissau, 1947**. Vol.1. Lisbon, Ministério das Colónias, Junta de Investigações colonias, 1950; T. Monod, 'Atlas ocidental africano', pp. 59-70 in **Relatorio geral de 6 Conferência international dos Africanistas ocidentais, S. Tome, 1956. Vol. 1**. S. Tomé, 1957; R. Roy & D. Zidouemba, 'L'Atlas international de l'Ouest africain', *Bulletin de l'IFAN*, sér. B, 46, 1986/87, 207-210)

1755 Senior secondary atlas. London, Collins-Longman, 1983. 155pp. col. maps. 20 x 27cm. (Prepared for Nigerian schools. Includes 13 maps of West Africa in general, 37 maps of Nigeria, 49 of other West African countries, 64 of the rest of Africa, 64 of the rest of the world)

Gazetteers

1756 Kaké, Baba Ibrahim. **Glossaire critique des expressions géographiques concernant le pay des noirs, d'après les sources de langue arabe du milieu du VIIIe à la fin du XIIIe siècle**. Paris, *Présence Africaine*, 1965. 157pp. (Largely concerned with West Africa)

1757 Teixeira da Mota, A. **Topónimos de origem portuguesa na costa occidental de África: desde o Cabo Bojador as Cabo de Santa Caterina**. Bissau, Centro de Estudos da Guiné Portuguesa, 1950. (Publicaçoes, 14). 411pp. 5 maps. ('Contribuiçao do Centro de Estudos da Guiné Portuguesa para o Colloquium Internacional de Estudos Luso-Brasileiros'. Based upon 117 original and 26 secondary sources dating from the 14th to the 20th century. Lists 442 names with co-ordinates and citations to the sources for topographical features from Western Sahara round the coast to Fernando Po)

1758 U.S. Board on Geographic Names. **West Africa; official standard names approved by the USBGN**. Washington, DC, 1954. 2 vols. 1,645pp. Vol. 1, pp. 1-49, British Cameroons; pp. 51-103, Gambia; pp. 105-224, Gold Coast; pp. 225-583, Nigeria; pp. 585-636, Portuguese Guinea; pp. 637-688, Sierra Leone; pp. 689-741, Spanish Sahara; pp. 743-764, Togo; pp. 765-792, Togoland; vol. 2, pp. 795-1,645, French West Africa.

Pilots

1759 France. Service hydrographique [etc.]. **Instructions nautiques, C4: Afrique (côte ouest) de Râs Spârtel à Cape Palmas, Îles du large**. Brest, 2005. 400pp. - - **Instructions nautiques, C5: Afrique (côte ouest) de Cape Palmas à Cape Agulhas**. Brest, 2001. 482pp. *Continues* France. Service hydrographique [etc.] **Les Instructions nautiques: Afrique, côte ouest**.

Brest, 1980-1981. 2 vols. (Vol. 1, Au Nord de Cape Palmas; vol. 2, De Cape Palmas à Cape Agulhas). - - Earlier eds. (title varies) 1867, 1871, 1883, 1900, 1915.

1760 Germany. Deutsches Hydrographisches Institut. **Handbuch der Westküste Afrikas**. 3rd ed. Hamburg, 1973. looseleaf. - - Orig. pub. comp. Kriegsmarine Oberkommando. Berlin, Mittler, 1937-1940. 2 vols; - - 2nd ed. Hamburg, Deutsches Hydrographisches Institut, 1960-1964. 2 vols.

1761 G.B. Admiralty. Hydrographic Office [etc.]. **Africa Pilot. Vol. 1, Comprising the Arquipelago da Madeira, Islas Canarias, Arquipelago de Cabo Verde, the West coast of Africa from Cabo Espartel to Bakasi Peninsula**. 13th ed. Taunton, 1982. 364pp. - - Orig. pub. as **The African pilot; or sailing directions for the Western coast of Africa. Vol. 1. From Cape Spartel to the River Cameroon**. London, 1856. Other eds. (Sub title varies) 1880, 1885, 1890, 1899, 1907, 1920, 1930, 1939, 1963.
- - **Africa pilot. Vol. 2. Comprising the west coast of Africa from Bakasi Peninsula to Cape Agulhas; islands in the Bight of Biafra; Ascension Island; Saint Helena Island; Tristan da Cunha Group and Gough Island.** 14th ed. Taunton, 2004. xvii, 324pp. illus. maps. + 1 CD-ROM. - - Orig. pub. as **The African pilot; or sailing directions for the Western coast of Africa. Vol. 2. From the River Cameroon to the Cape of Good Hope**. London, 1868. Other eds. (Sub title varies) 1875, 1884, 1893, 1901, 1910, 1922, 1930, 1939, 1963, 1977, 1982.

1762 U.S. Defense Mapping Agency [etc.]. **Sailing directions (enroute) for the west coast of Europe and northwest Africa**. 6th ed. Bethesda, MD, 1994. (Covers harbours and coasts from Western Sahara to Liberia). - - Orig. pub. Washington, DC, 1976. (Publication, 143). 511pp. illus. maps. loose-leaf for updating. Later ed., 1991.

EARTH SCIENCES

1763 Irvine, Frederick R. & Ahn, Peter M. **West African agriculture**. 3rd ed. London, Oxford University Press, 1970. 2 vols. illus. Vol. 1. West African soils, by P.M. Ahn. xii, 332pp. illus. maps; vol. 2. West African crops, by F.R. Irvine. xvi, 272pp. illus. - - Orig. pub. as **A textbook of West African agriculture: soils and crops**, by F.R. Irvine. London, 1934. xii, 348pp; - - 2nd ed. London, 1953. 367pp.

1764 Morgan, William Basil & Pugh, John Charles. **West Africa**. London, Methuen, 1969. xviii, 788pp. illus. maps. (Principally human geography, "intended in some sense to provide a complement" (pref.) to Ronald J.

Harrison-Church. **West Africa: a study of the environment and man's use of it**. 8th ed. London, Longmans, 1980. (Geographies for advanced study). xxxi, 526pp. illus. maps. Previous eds. 1957, 1960, 1961, 1963, 1966, 1968, 1974)

1765 Papadakis, J. **Crop ecologic survey in West Africa: Liberia, Ivory Coast, Ghana, Togo, Dahomey, Nigeria**. Rome, FAO, 1966. 2 vols. Vol.1, Text; vol. 2, Atlas.

Climate & meteorology

1766 G.B. Meteorological Office. **Weather on the west coast of tropical Africa from 20°N to 20°S, including the Atlantic Ocean to 25°W**. London, HMSO, 1949. (MO, 492). 281pp. maps.

1767 Hayward, Derek F. & Oguntoyinbo, Julius S. **Climatology of West Africa**. London, Hutchinson, 1987. 288pp. illus. maps.

1768 Ojo, Oyedira. **The climates of West Africa**. London & Ibadan, Heinemann Educational, 1977. xvii, 219pp. illus. maps. (Claims to be the first work on regional climatology in Africa)

Geology & minerals

1769 Chnukov, E.-F. & Suzyumov, A. **Étude de la géologie marine de l'Afrique de l'ouest et du centre**. Paris, UNESCO, 1989. xii, 155pp.

1770 Fabre, Jean, ed. **Afrique de l'ouest: introduction géologique et termes stratigraphiques/West Africa: geological introduction and stratigraphic terms**. Oxford, Pergamon Press, 1983. (Lexique stratigraphique internationale, n.s. 1). 396pp. illus. maps. (Describes West Africa in general, the Sahara, Niger, Chad, Nigeria, Mali, Benin, Ghana and Senegal. Pp.175-365, 'lexique stratigraphique' of specific geologic formations, A/Z by locality with an index by geological period. The lexique updates the vols. at **1771**)

1771 Faure, Hugues et al. **Lexique stratigraphique international, 4, Afrique, fasc. 3: Sahara, Afrique occidentale française et portugaises**. Paris, CNRS, 1956. 77pp. map; - - Pollett, J.D. & Bates, D.A. **Lexique stratigraphique international, 4, Afrique, fasc. 3: Afrique occidentale anglaise: Sierra Leone et Gambie, Côte d'Or et Togo, Nigérie et Cameroun**. Paris, CNRS, 1956. 67pp.

1772 Wright, John B. et al. **Geology and mineral resources of West Africa**. London, Allen & Unwin, 1985. xiii, 187pp. illus. maps. (Undergraduate textbook with clear accounts of the rock formations and numerous maps)

BIOLOGICAL SCIENCES

Zoology

Birds

1773 Bannerman, David Armitage. **The birds of tropical West Africa, with special reference to those of the Gambia, Sierra Leone, the Gold Coast and Nigeria**. London, Crown Agents for the Colonies, 1930-1956. 8 vols. (Magisterial survey with enormous detail; one of the classic works of African ornithology in colonial times). - - **The birds of West and Equatorial Africa**. Edinburgh, Oliver & Boyd, 1953. 2 vols. xiii, 1,526pp. (Summary version of his **Birds of tropical West Africa**)

1774 Borrow, Nik & Demey, Ron. **The birds of Western Africa: an identification guide**. London, Christopher Helm, 2002. 832pp. 147 col. plates. (Describes and illus. 1,269 spp. recorded from the region. Covers 23 countries: Benin, Burkina Faso, Cameroon, CAR, Cape Verde, Chad, Congo, Côte d'Ivoire, Equatorial Guinea, Gabon, Gambia, Ghana, Guinea, Guinea-Bissau, Liberia, Mali, Mauritania, Niger, Nigeria, São Tomé e Principe, Senegal, Sierra Leone, Togo; i.e. includes some normally regarded as falling into Central Africa. For taxonomy, sequence and scientific names follows **Birds of Africa**, vols. 1-6, *see* **711**, modified by Dowsett & Forbes-Watson, *see* **708**. Reviews, *BABC*, 10, 2003, 38-39; *Ibis*, 144, 2002, 535; *Malimbus*, 24, 2002, 145-147, "indispensable"). - - **Field guide to the birds of Western Africa**. London, Christopher Helm, 2004. 496pp. 150 col. plates. maps. (Abbreviated version of the 2002 vol. Same plates with some new images, and updated maps. Covers 1,285 spp. Review, *Malimbus*, 27, 2005, 120-121)

1775 Mackworth-Praed, Cyril W. & Grant, Claude H.B. **African handbook of birds: Series III, Birds of West Central and Western Africa**. London, Longmans, 1970-73. 2 vols. xxii, 671p; vi, 818, 47pp. illus. (*See* **713** for the whole work)

1776 Serle, William & Morel, Gérard. **A field guide to the birds of West Africa**. London, Collins, 1977. 351pp. + 48 plates. illus. (Includes CAR, Chad, Congo and Gabon in addition to the traditional West African countries. Covers 521 spp. in detail and 205 in notes. Checklist of 1,097 spp. includes names but no further details of an additional 371 spp. Where scientific names used differ from **1773**, the Bannerman usage is given in brackets. Review, *Ibis*, 119, 1977, 556-557)

1777 Van Perlo, Ber. **Collins illustrated checklist: birds of Western and Central Africa**. London Harper Collins, 2002. 384pp. 109 col. plates. (Includes coverage of countries as in Borrow, **1774**, plus Democratic Republic of Congo. Covers 1,500+ spp. Review, *Malimbus*, 25, 2003, 69-71 which prefers illus. to those in Borrow)

Mammals

1778 Grubb, P. et al. **Mammals of Ghana, Sierra Leone and the Gambia**. St. Ives, Trendrine Press, 1998. vi, 265pp. maps.

1779 Rosevear, Donovan R. **The bats of West Africa**. London, British Museum (Natural History), 1965. xvii, 418pp. illus. (Covers 97 spp. occurring north to 18° S. Review, *Journal of mammalogy*, 49, 1968, 350-351)

1780 Rosevear, Donovan R. **The carnivores of West Africa**. London, British Museum (Natural History), 1974. xii, 548pp. illus. (Review, *Journal of mammalogy*, 58, 1977, 120-121)

1781 Rosevear, Donovan R. **The rodents of West Africa**. London, British Museum (Natural History), 1969. xii, 604pp. illus. (Review, *Journal of mammalogy*, 51, 1970, 209)

Reptiles & Amphibians

1782 Chippaux, Jean-Philippe. **Les serpents d'Afrique occidentale et centrale**. [Rev. ed.]. Paris, IRD, 2001. 292pp. illus. maps. - - Orig. pub. Paris, 1999. 278pp.

1783 Rödel, Mark-Oliver. **Herpetofauna of West Africa: vol. 1, Amphibians of the West African savanna**. Frankfurt-am-Main, Chimaira, 2000. 332pp. 400 illus. + 1 CD sound disc with frog calls. (Extensive revision of **Amphibien der Westafrikanischen Savanne**. Frankfurt-am-Main, 1996. 283pp.)

1784 Schiøtz, Arne. **The treefrogs (Rhacophoridae) of West Africa**. Copenhagen, Munksgaard, 1967. (Spolia Zoologica Musei Hauniensis, 25). 346pp. illus. map.

Fishes

1785 CLOSFECA: checklist of the sea fishes of the eastern central Atlantic & West African coast: a classified taxonomic checklist of species

recorded on the Calypso Ichthyological Database for sea area 050 Morocco to Namibia, ed. Gerald Jennings. London, Calypso, 1999. 122pp. Also on CD-ROM.

1786 Lévêque, Christian, et al. **Faune des poissons d'eaux douces et saumâtres d'Afrique de l'ouest (PEDALO)**. Rev. Didier Paugy. Paris, IRD & Muséum national d'histoire naturelle/Tervuren, Musée royal de l'Afrique centrale, 2003. (Faune et flores tropicales, 40). 2 vols. 457pp., 815pp. + 1 CD ROM. - - Orig. pub. Tervuren, Musée royal de l'Afrique centrale/Paris, ORSTOM, 1990-1992. (Faune tropicale, 28). 2 vols. 902pp. illus. (Lists 558 spp. Review, *Copeia*, 1994, 254-255)

1787 Seret, Bernard. **Poissons de mer de l'ouest africain tropical**. 3rd ed. Paris, ORSTOM, 1990. (Initiations-documentations techniques, 49). viii, 450p. illus. - - Orig. pub. Paris, 1981. iv, 416pp; - - 2nd ed. Paris, 1986. viii, 450pp.

Invertebrates

1788 Larsen, Torben B. **Butterflies of West Africa**. Stenstrup, Apollo Books, 2005. 2 vols. illus. maps. (Describes c.1,500 spp. Col. illus. of c.3,800 taxa)

Botany

1789 Aké Assi, Laurent. **Plants used in traditional medicine in West Africa**. Basle, Swiss Centre of Scientific Research in Ivory Coast & Roche, 1991. 151pp. + 52 col. plates.

1790 Akobundu, I. Okezie & Agyakwa, C.W. **A handbook of West African weeds**. Ibadan, International Institute of Tropical Agriculture, 1987. 521pp.

1791 Alston, Arthur H.G. **The ferns and fern allies of West tropical Africa**. London, London, Crown Agents, 1959. 89pp. (To complement **1795**)

1792 Ayensu, Edward S. **Medicinal plants of West Africa**. Algonac, MI, Reference Publications, 1976. 330pp. (Describes 187 spp.)

1793 Burkill, Humphrey M. **The useful plants of West tropical Africa**. Kew, Royal Botanic Gardens, 1985-2002. 6 vols. Vol. 1. 1988. Families A-D. xi, 686pp; vol. 2. 1994. Families E-I. xii, 636pp; vol. 3. 1995. Families J-L. xi, 857pp; vol. 4. 1997. Families M-R. xi, 969pp; vol. 5. 2000. Families S-Z, addenda, corrigenda, cryptogamata. xi, 686pp; vol. 6. 2002. Complete index to vols. 1-5. vii, 1,263pp. (Major rev. of J.M. Dalziel. **The useful plants of West tropical

Africa. Kew, 1937. "This revision is a supplement to the 2nd ed. of **The flora of West tropical Africa**, ed. Keay & Hepper", pref, *see* **1795**)

1794 Busson, F.F. **Plantes alimentaires de l'ouest africain: étude botanique, biologique et chimique**. Marseilles, Ministère de la coopération, 1965. xiv, 565pp. illus.

1795 **Flora of West tropical Africa:** the British West African colonies, British Cameroons, the French and Portuguese colonies south of the Tropic of Cancer to Lake Chad, and Fernando Po, comp. John Hutchinson & John MacEwan Dalziel. 2nd ed. rev. Ronald W.J. Keay & F.N. Hepper. London, Crown Agents, 1953-1972. 3 vols. 462 text figs. (Prepared at the Herbarium, Royal Botanic Gardens, Kew. The standard work for the region to which most other botanical sources for the region are referenced). - - Orig. pub. London, 1927-36. 2 vols. (Covers larger region than 2nd ed. extending north to the Tropic of Cancer, thus including much of the Sahara)
- - Hall, John B. **Gazetteer of plant collecting localities in Ghana cited in** *Flora of west Tropical Africa*. Accra, Ghana Universities Press, 1980. 122pp. maps.

1796 Oliver-Bever, Bep. **Medicinal plants in tropical West Africa**. Cambridge, Cambridge University Press, 1986. 375pp. (Orig. pub. *Journal of ethnopharmacology*, 5 (1) 1982, 1-72; 7(1) 1983, 1-93; 9(1),1983, 1-83)

1797 Olorode, Omotoye. **Taxonomy of West African flowering plants**. London, Longman, 1984. 158pp. illus.

1798 Steentoft, Margaret. **Flowering plants in West Africa**. Cambridge, Cambridge University Press, 1988. vii, 344pp. illus. (Major study of 38 families)

Trees

1799 Arbonnier, Michel. **Trees, shrubs and lianas of West African dry zones**. 2nd rev. ed. Paris, CIRAD, 2004. 573pp. col. illus. col. maps. (Covers some 360 species). - - Orig. pub. as **Arbres, arbustes et lianes des zones sèches d'Afrique de l'ouest**. Paris, 2000. 542pp. - - 2nd ed. Paris, 2003. 573pp.

1800 Poorter, Lourens et al. **Biodiversity of West African forests: an ecological atlas of woody plant species**. Wallingford, CAB International Publishing, 2004. 521pp. illus. col. maps. (The atlas section contains ecological profiles of 280 rare plant species and 56 large timber species)

ANGLOPHONE WEST AFRICA

THE GAMBIA

Republic of the Gambia official Web site http://www.gambia.gm/

HANDBOOKS

1801 Armand-Prévost, Michel. **La République de Gambie**. Paris, Berger-Levrault, 1973. (Encyclopédie politique et constitutionnelle. Série Afrique). 67pp.

1802 Bakarr, S.A. **The Gambia yesterday, 1447-1979: (an ideal compilation - every use)**. Banjul, Gambia Press Union, 1980. 106pp. (Historical chronology)

1803 Dinkiralu, Ada et al. **Historic sites of the Gambia: an official guide to the monuments and sites of the Gambia**. Banjul, National Council for Arts & Culture, 1998. 100pp. illus. maps.

1804 Gamble, David P. **Abbreviations and acronyms used in the Gambia; revised to 2004**. Rev. ed. Brisbane, CA, author, 2004. ii, 85pp. - - Orig. pub. San Francisco, CA, San Francisco State University, Department of Anthropology, 1981. ii, 28pp; - - Rev. ed. San Francisco, 1990. ii, 28pp. - - Rev. ed. Brisbane, CA, author, 2000. iii, 56pp.

1805 Gamble, David P. **The south bank of the Gambia: places, people and population**. Brisbane, CA, author, 1996- . (Gambian studies, 30, 32) 2 vols. to date; - - **The north bank of the Gambia : places, people, and population**. Brisbane, CA, author, 1999. (Gambian studies, 36, 37, 38). 3 vols.

1806 Historical dictionary of the Gambia. 3rd ed. comp. Arnold Hughes & Harry A. Gailey. Lanham, MD, Scarecrow Press, 1999. (African historical dictionaries, 79). xxii, 231pp. (Reviews, *ARD*, 84, 2000, 83-90; *IJAHS*, 33, 2000, 448; *JAH*, 42, 2001, 542-543). - - Orig. pub. comp. Harry A. Gailey. Metuchen, NJ, 1975. (African historical dictionaries, 4). viii, 172pp; - - 2nd ed. Metuchen, NJ, 1987. xxii, 176pp. (Weighted towards the 19th century. Critical reviews in *Africa*, 59, 1989, 540-541; *IJAHS*, 21, 1988, 720-721. Rated "fair", Balay, 1996)

1807 Schramm, Josef. **Gambia**, Bonn, K. Schroeder for Deutsche Afrika-Gesellschaft, 1965. (Die Länder Afrikas, 32). 52pp. illus. maps. (Rev. version of the appropriate section of K.H. Pfeffer, **Sierra Leone und Gambia**. Bonn, 1958. (Gambia, pp. 65-80)

1808 Smirnov, E.G. **Respublika Gambiia: spravochnik**. Moscow, Akademiia nauk, Institut Afriki, 1996. 102pp.

See also **2461, 2463**

YEARBOOKS

1809 The Gambia trade guide and business directory. Serrekunda, Toplink Communications & Ministry of Trade, Industry & Employment, 1996/97- . Annual. LC has issue for 2002. Issue for 1996 entitled **Gambia business directory**. *Continues* **Gambia trade directory**. Banjul, Gambia Ministry of Finance & Trade, 1983-1991. 3 vols.

1810 The Gambia year book, 1971/72 . Bathurst, Adara Bros., 1971- . ?No more pub.

1811 G.B. Colonial Office. **[Annual reports]: Gambia, 1848-1964/65**. London, etc., 1849-1966. As **Reports: the past and present state of H.M. colonial possessions**, 1848-1885, (not issued 1874), **Report on the Blue Book for the Gambia**, 1886-1889, **Annual report on the Gambia**, 1890-1919, (all as Command papers); **Colonial Office annual report**, 1920-63 (not issued 1939-45). 1950/51 to 1962/63 issued every 2 years. Report for 1964/18.2.1965 issued by the Government of Gambia.

STATISTICS

1812 Country profile: the Gambia. London, Economist Intelligence Unit, 2003- . Annual. *Continues* in part **Country profile: Senegal, Gambia, Guinea-Bissau, Cape Verde**. London, 1987-1991; **Country profile: The Gambia, Guinea-Bissau, Cape Verde**, 1992; **Country profile: The Gambia, Mauritania**. London, 1993-2002.

1813 Gambia. Central Statistics Department. **Statistical abstract of the Gambia**. Banjul, 1990- . Annual. Last issue noted by ALA is for 1993.

1814 Gambia. Statistics Office. **Statistical summary 1964 [-1967/68]**. Bathurst, 1965-1969. Irreg. (Issued as Sessional Papers of the Gambia House of Representatives: issues for 1964 (paper 7 of 1965); 1965 (paper 6 of 1966); 1966/67 (paper 9 of 1967); 1967/68 (paper 5 of 1969).

1815 Germany. Statistisches Bundesamt. **Statistik des Auslandes: Länderberichte: Gambia** (later **Länderbericht: Gambia**) Wiesbaden/ Stuttgart, Metzler-Poetschel, 1985- . Irreg. Issues for 1985, 1987, 1992.

1816 IMF. **The Gambia: statistical appendix**. Washington, DC, 2006. (Country report, 06/10). 56pp. - - Earlier eds. (title varies) 1997 (Staff country report, 97/116); 2004 (Country report, 04/142). Full text of reports from 97/101, 1997 also available online, *see* **334**.

BIOGRAPHICAL SOURCES

1817 **Who's who in the Gambia**. Banjul, National Library Book Production & Material Resources Unit, 1978. (Recorded in LC catalogue)

ATLASES & GAZETTEERS

1818 **The Gambia social studies atlas**. 2nd ed. London, Macmillan Education, 1995. 41pp. col. maps. - - Orig. pub. London, 1989. 41pp.

1819 Gamble, David P. **The Gambia: place names on maps and in travellers' accounts up to 1825**. Brisbane, CA, [1999]. (Gambian studies 35A, 35B). 2 vols. (Vol. 2 includes maps). - - **The Gambia: place names given by travellers and residents in the 19th and 20th centuries**. Brisbane, CA, author, 1999. (Gambian studies, 35C). 78pp. *See also* **1805**.

1820 U.S. Board on Geographic Names. **Gambia: official standard names approved by the USBGN**. Washington, DC, 1968. (Gazetteer, 107). ii, 35pp. (Includes 2,400 names from 1:50,000 map series. Revision of appropriate section of **West Africa,** *see* **1758**)

BIOLOGICAL SCIENCES

1821 Edberg, Etienne. **A naturalist's guide to the Gambia**. St. Anne, Alderney, J.G. Sanders, 1982. 96pp. illus. maps. - - Orig. pub. in Swedish as **Guide till naturen i Gambia**, 1979.

Zoology

1822 Barlow, Clive et al. **A field guide to the birds of the Gambia and Senegal**. London, Pica Press, 1997. 352pp. 48 col. plates. Rev. reprint. London, 2005. (Covers some 570 spp. Nomenclature basically follows

Dowsett & Forbes-Watson, *see* **708**, and **Birds of Africa**, *see* **711**, with cross references from alternative names used in Serle & Morel, *see* **1776**. Review, *Ibis*, 140, 1998, 702). - - Barlow, Clive, et al. **Bird song of the Gambia and Senegal: an aid to identification**. Swindon, Mandarin Productions, 2002. 3 CDs. (Calls of 265 spp. Linked to the field guide. Review, *BABC*, 10, 2003, 144-145)

1823 Gore, Michael E.J. **Birds of the Gambia: an annotated checklist**. 2nd ed. Tring, British Ornithologists' Union, 1990. (Checklist, 3). 148pp. 59 illus. (Lists 507 spp. Review, *Ibis*, 133, 1992, 428-429). - - Orig. pub. London, 1981. 130pp. illus. (Review, *Ibis*, 123, 1981, 558)

1824 Jensen, Jørn Vestergaard & Kirkeby, Jens. **The birds of the Gambia: an annotated checklist and guide to localities in the Gambia**. Århus, Aros Nature Guides, 1980. 284pp. (Covers 489 spp.)

See also **2491**, **2492**

Botany

1825 Götz, Erich. **Timber trees of the Gambia**, Hamburg, Stiftung Walderhalterung in Afrika & Bundesforschungsgemeinschaft für Forts- und Holz Wirtschaft, 1983. 104pp. illus.

1826 Hallam, G.M. **Medical uses of flowering plants in the Gambia**. Yundum, Department of Forestry, 1979. 208pp.

1827 Jones, Michael. **A checklist of Gambian plants**. Banjul, The Gambia College, 1991. ii, 46pp. (Systematic list of 966 spp.)

GHANA

Official Web site of the Republic of Ghana http://www.ghana.gov.gh/

HANDBOOKS

1828 Aboagbye, Festus B. **The Ghana army: a concise guide to its centennial regimental history, 1897-1999**. Accra, Sedco Publishing, 1999. 441pp. (Review, *ABPR*, 27, 2001, 98)

1829 Dako, Kari. **Ghanaianisms: a glossary**. Accra, Ghana Universities Press, 2003. 234pp. ("Vocabulary items peculiar to English in Ghana... found in print ... at least three times within the last eight years", pref.)

1830 Dijksterhuis, Heerko. **Ghana: mensen, politiek, economie, cultuur**. Amsterdam, Koninklijk Instituut voor de Tropen/The Hague, Novib, 2005. (Landenreeks). 74pp. illus. maps. - - Orig. pub. comp. Jos Moerkamp. Amsterdam, 1997. 78pp. illus. maps.

1831 Ghana: a brief guide. [Rev. ed.]. Accra, Information Services Department, 1994. 96pp. illus. (Brief details, arranged by region, covering history, agriculture and recent political developments). - - Earlier ed. pub. as **A brief guide to Ghana**. Accra, Ministry of Information & Broadcasting, 1958. 60pp. - - Rev. ed. Accra, 1960. 60pp; - - Accra, 1961. 71pp; - - [rev. ed.] **Ghana: a brief guide**. Accra, 1989. 30pp. - - [rev. ed.] Accra, 1991. 96pp.

1832 Ghana: a country study. 3rd ed. comp. Laverle Berry. Washington, DC, Library of Congress, Federal Research Division, 1995. xxix, 382pp. illus. maps. Also available at: http://lcweb2.loc.gov/frd/cs/ghtoc.html. - - Orig. pub as **Special warfare area handbook for Ghana**, comp. D.M. Bouton et al. Washington, DC, U.S. Department of Defense, 1962. xii, 533pp; - - 2nd ed. pub. as **Area handbook for Ghana**, comp. Irving Kaplan et al. Washington, DC, 1971. xiv, 449pp.

1833 Ghana: an official handbook. Accra, Ministry of Information [etc.]. 1961- . Irreg. Issues traced for 1961, 1969, 1971, 1972/73, 1974, 1975, 1976, 1977, 1991. Title varies: **Ghana 1974, a review of 1973** (1974); **Ghana 1975: an official handbook** (1975). (Substantial compilation, e.g. 1976 ed. 472pp., of social, economic, topographic and administrative information)

1834 A guide to the Parliament of Ghana. Accra, Parliament of Ghana, 2004. 123pp.

1835 Historical dictionary of Ghana. 3rd ed., comp. David Owusu-Ansah & Daniel Miles McFarland. Lanham, MD, Scarecrow Press, 2005. (African historical dictionaries, 97). 416pp. - - Orig. pub. comp. Daniel Miles McFarland. Metuchen, NJ, 1985. (African historical dictionaries, 39). lxxx, 296pp. (Reviews, *IJAHS*, 19, 1986, 558-559; *JAH*, 27, 1986, 410-411. Rated "good", Balay, 1996); - - 2nd ed. Metuchen, NJ, 1995. (African historical dictionaries, 63). lxxxviii, 383pp.

1836 Kropp Dakubu, Mary Esther, ed. **The languages of Ghana**. London, Kegan Paul for IAI, 1988. 181pp. ("To provide an easily accessible handbook of current knowledge about the languages of Ghana, their geographical distribution, their relationships", pref. Reviews, *Africa*, 60, 1990, 161-162, "must be judged on the whole as a success"; *JALL*, 11, 1989, 98-103).

1837 Pfeffer, Karl Heinz. **Ghana**. 2nd ed. Bonn, K. Schroeder for Deutsche Afrika-Gesellschaft, 19. (Die Länder Afrikas, 5). 152pp. illus. map. - - Orig. pub. Bonn, 1958. 104pp.

1838 Salm, Steven J. & Falola, Toyin. **Culture and customs of Ghana**. Westport, CT, Greenwood Press, 2002. (Culture and customs of Africa). xx, 224pp. illus. map. (Covers history, religion, literature, art and architecture, social customs)

1839 Vinokurov, IU.N. **Gana: spravochnik**. Moscow, Akademiia nauk, Institut Afriki, 2001. 199pp. illus.

YEARBOOKS

1840 Business directory of Ghana, 1986/87. Accra, Transcap Business Services, 1986- ? No more pub. Stanford has issue for 1986/87 only.

1841 Ghana. Ministry of Commerce and Industry. **Ghana handbook of commerce and industry**. Accra, 1957-?1967. Irreg. (1957 called 1st issue, but basically a continuation of **1847**. Issue for 1967, xix, 321pp.)

1842 Ghana 1966. Accra, Anowuo Educational Publications, 1967. 152, 7pp. ("An objective summary ... on current affairs", cover. Daily chronology of events)

1843 Ghana business directory. Accra, Ghana National Chamber of Commerce & Industry, 1991- . Irreg. Issue 1, 1991/92 (1992); issue 2, 2000.

1844 Ghana business directory. Accra, Surf Publications, 2002- . Annual. Stanford has issue for 2004.

1845 Ghana trade directory. London, Diplomatic Press & Publishing (Diprepu), 1959-1967. Irreg. 5 issues. for 1959, 1960, 1961/62, 1964, 1967. Title varies: **Directory of Ghana** (1959); **Directory of the Republic of Ghana** (1960-1961/62); **Trade directory of the Republic of Ghana** (1964). (Includes civil list, statistics, commercial directory, and in the issues for 1960 and 1961/62 a who's who section of about 200 names per issue)

1846 Ghana year book. Accra, *Daily Graphic*, 1953-?1978. Annual. Title varies: **Gold Coast year book** (1953-1956). Stanford has issue for 1978. (General survey of history and topography, civil list, statistics, commercial directory. Biographical section with c. 125 entries).

1847 Gold Coast. Ministry of Commerce, Industry & Mines. **Gold Coast: handbook of trade and commerce**. Accra, 1951-?1955. Irreg. (General economic information and statistics, with commercial directory. *See* **1841**)

1848 G.B. Colonial Office. **[Annual reports]: Gold Coast, 1846-1954**. London, 1847-1956. As **Reports: the past and present state of H.M. colonial possessions**, 1846-1886 (not issued 1862-66, 1872-74, 1880, 1883, 1887), **Report on the Blue Book for the Gold Coast,** 1888, (not issued 1889-91), **Annual report on the Gold Coast**, 1892-1919 (all as Command papers); **Colonial Office annual report**, 1920-54, (not issued 1939-45). No full report for 1857, 1861. Report for 1885 includes Lagos. Report for 1886 includes districts.

STATISTICS

1849 Country profile: Ghana. London, Economist Intelligence Unit, 1986- . Annual.

1850 Ewusi, Kodwo. **Statistical tables on the economy of Ghana, 1950-1985**. Accra, University of Ghana, Institute of Statistical, Social and Economic Research, 1986. xi, 235pp. tables.

1851 Ghana. Central Bureau of Statistics. **Quarterly digest of statistics**. Accra, 1981- . Not pub. 1973-1980. SOAS holds issues for 2001. *Continues* Gold Coast. Central Bureau of Statistics. **Monthly statistical bulletin of the Gold Coast**. Accra, 1948-1951. Issues 1-36; **Economic and statistical bulletin**. Accra, 1952-1953. vols. 1(1)-2(1); Gold Coast/Ghana. Central Bureau of Statistics. **Digest of statistics**. Accra, 1953-1972.

1852 Ghana. Central Bureau of Statistics. **Statistical yearbook**. Accra, 1961-1973. Annual. 7 issues. Issues for 1961 to 1964, 1965/66, 1967/68, 1969/70. Abridged version issued as **Statistical handbook**. Accra, 1966-1970. Annual. 4 issues.

1853 Germany. Statistisches Bundesamt. **Statistik des Auslandes: Länderberichte: Ghana** (later **Länderbericht: Ghana**) Wiesbaden/Stuttgart, Metzler-Poetschel, 1961- . Irreg. Issues for 1961, 1967, 1987, 1992.

1854 Hay, Geoffrey Barry & Hymer, Stephen. **The political economy of colonialism in Ghana: a collection of documents and statistics, 1900-1960**. Cambridge, Cambridge University Press, 1972. 431pp. (Statistics drawn mostly from the Blue books and covering population, wages, trade, finance, communications, and education)

1855 IMF. **Ghana: statistical appendix**. Washington, DC, 2005. (Country report, 05/286). 73pp. - - Earlier issues (title varies) 1995 (Staff country report, 95/77); 1996 (Staff country report, 96/69); 1998 (Staff country report, 98/02); 2000 (Staff country report, 00/01). Full text of reports from 97/101, 1997 also available online, *see* **334**.

DIRECTORIES OF ORGANIZATIONS

1856 **Directory of tertiary institutions in Ghana**. Accra, Inter-Universe Publishers, 2001. 364pp.

1857 **eBizguides Ghana**. Dublin, eBiz Guides, 2004. 252pp. (Business directory)

1858 **Ghana directory of industrial establishments, 1988**. Accra, Statistical Service, 1989. 306pp. *Continues* **Directory of industrial enterprises and establishments**, Ghana. Accra, Central Bureau of Statistics, 1963-1969.

BIOGRAPHICAL SOURCES

1859 **Encyclopedia Africana dictionary of African Biography. Vol. 1, Ethiopia and Ghana**. Algonac, MI, Reference Publications, 1977. 367pp. (Ghana section, pp. 167-342, ed. Ivor Wilks, with contributions from 39 scholars. Includes 138 biographies of Africans and Europeans, many with portraits, and list of sources. Concise guide to Ghana names and terms, pp. 330-338. Reviews, *IJAHS*, 11, 1978, 546-550; *ASA review of books*, 6, 1980, 285-

287 which is critical of "outdated and erroneous information". For encyclopedia, *see* **11**; for dictionary of biography, *see* **545**)

1860 Ephson, Isaac Sergius. **Gallery of Gold Coast celebrities, 1632-1958**. Accra, Ilem Publishing Co., 1973. 3 vols. in 1. Vol. 1 is a reprint of 1969 ed. (Covers 116 individuals, most with portraits). - - Orig. pub.Accra, 1969. Vol. 1. No more pub.

1861 Furley, J.T. 'Provisional list of some Portuguese governors of the Captaincy da Mina', *Transactions of the Gold Coast & Togo Historical Society*, 2, 1956, 53-62. (*See also* his 'Notes on some Portuguese Governors of the Captaincy da Mina', *ibid.*, 3, 1958, 194-214)

1862 Ghana who's who 1972/73: a fully-comprehensive annual biographical dictionary of prominent men and women in the country, including an encyclopaedia of useful information [etc], ed. Charles Bartels. Accra, Bartels, 1973. 454pp. ?No more pub. (Includes much miscellaneous data, such as membership of all assemblies since 1954)

1863 Sampson, Magnus John. **Makers of modern Ghana**. Accra, Anowuo Educational Publications, 1969- . Vol. 1, 1969. 190pp. illus. ?No more pub. (Twenty one biographies and portraits for the period 1742 to 1930. Vol. 2 was to have covered 1930s to 1960s) - - Orig. pub as **Gold Coast men of affairs, past and present**. London, A.H. Stockwell, 1937. Reprinted, London, Dawsons, 1969. 224pp. + 25pp. plates

See also **1845**, **1846**

ATLASES & GAZETTEERS

Atlases

1864 Atlas of population characteristics. Accra, Survey of Ghana & Census Office, 1964. (1960 Population Census of Ghana). ii, 29pp. 42cm. (26 maps, 2 col., with transparent overlay showing administrative areas. Scale 1:2M. Shows current and former distribution, education, occupations)

1865 Atlas of the Gold Coast. 5th ed. Accra, Gold Coast Survey Department, 1949. 9pp. 21 col. maps. (Thematic atlas at basic scale of 1:1.5M. Includes administrative areas, tribes, topography, geology, minerals, climate, forestry, agriculture and communications. 2nd to 5th eds. have town plans of Kumasi, 1:12,500, Takoradi, 1:18,000 and Accra, 1:25,000). - - Orig. pub. Accra, Gold Coast Survey Department, [1927-1928]. 26 pp. incl. 24 col.

maps. 43 x 30cm; - - 2nd ed. Accra, 1935. 3pp. 20 col. maps. 36 x 29cm. (Review, *Empire survey review*, 3, 1936, 497-498); - - 3rd ed. Accra, 1939. 5pp. 21 col. maps); - - 4th ed. Accra, 1945. 5pp. 21 col. maps. (Review, *Empire survey review*, 8, 1946, 273-274)

1866 Ghana national atlas; director E.A. Boateng. Accra, Ghana Council for Scientific & Industrial Research, National Atlas Project, 1973- . 60 x 45cm. Running title: **National atlas of Ghana**. (A potentially major source in the making with 200 sheets planned at 1:1.5M in 5 sections: topography, economics, population, transport, trade, but only 28 completed by 2006, mostly covering agriculture and population. Virtually no accompanying text, or details on basis of compilation. The Institute for Scientific and Technological Information (INSTI) Thematic Mapping Division is currently responsible for the project and reported in 2004 that 40+ 'map manuscripts' covering such themes as population density, health services, transport, crops and education had been completed and were awaiting publication. However there is no such specific information currently (Aug. 2006) on the Division's Web site: http://www.csir.org.gh/index1.php?linkid=120 &sublinkid=114)

1867 Ghana population atlas: the distribution and density of population in the Gold Coast and Togoland under U.K. Trusteeship, comp. Thomas E. Hilton. Edinburgh, Nelson for University College of Ghana, 1960. 40pp. 30 x 41cm. (16 maps, 3 col., at 1:1.5M/1:3M. Maps of population density, distribution and change based on 1931 and 1948 censuses)

1868 Modified atlas of the Gold Coast. Accra, Gold Coast Survey Department, 1947. 8pp. incl. 6 col. maps. 28 x 30cm (Maps at 1:3M)

1869 Portfolio of Ghana maps. Accra, Survey of Ghana, 1967-1969. 13 loose sheets in titled folder. (Sheet. 1, Administrative; 2, Physical; 3, Vegetation zones; 4, Great soil groups; 5, Geological; 6, Agricultural products; 7, Mineral deposits; 8, Annual rainfall; 9, Isogonic chart; 10, Accra plan, 1:25,000; 11, Kumasi plan, 1:4,000; 12, Sekondi Takoradi plan, 1:4,000; 13, Volta River Project. Thematic maps at 1:2M)

Gazetteers

1870 Berry, J. **The place names of Ghana (problems of standardization)**. [London, SOAS, 1958.]. 2 vols. (iii, 19, 11; 28, 4, 25, 7pp.)

1871 Ghana. Census Office. **1960 population census of Ghana. Vol. 1. The gazetteer;** alphabetical list of localities with number of population and houses. Accra, 1962. xxxiii, 405pp.

1872 Ghana. Census Office. **1970 population census of Ghana. Vol. 1. The gazetteer.** Accra, 1971. 662pp.

1873 Ghana. Statistical Service. **1984 population census of Ghana: the gazetteer; alphabetical list of localities with statistics, etc.** Accra, 1989. 2 vols. xliii, 893pp.

1874 U.S. Board of Geographic Names. **Ghana: official standard names approved by the USBGN.** Washington, DC, 1967. (Gazetteer, 102). iii, 282pp. (Includes 20,000 names from 1:250,000 map series. Revision of appropriate sections of **West Africa,** *see* **1758**)

EARTH SCIENCES

1875 Clerk, George Carver. **Crops and their diseases in Ghana.** Tema, Ghana Publishing Corporation, 1974. 144pp. + 12pp. plates. illus.

1876 Gnielinski, Stefan von. **Ghana: tropisches Entwicklungsland an der Oberguineaküste.** Darmstadt, Wissenschaftliche Buchgesellschaft, 1986. (Wissenschaftliche Länderkunden, 27). xviii, 278pp. illus. maps.

1877 Hirdes, Wolfgang, et al. **Explanatory notes for the geological map of southwest Ghana 1:100,000.** Stuttgart, E. Schweizerbart'sche Verlagsbuchhandlung, 1993-1999. (Geologisches Jahrbuch. Reihe B, Regionale Geologie des Auslandes, 83, 93). 2 vols. [Pt.1]. 1993. 139pp; [pt. 2]. 1999. 149pp. (Maps pub. Accra, Geological Survey Department, 1991)

1878 Kesse, Gottfried Opong. **The mineral and rock resources of Ghana.** Rotterdam, Balkema, 1985. xiv, 610pp. illus. maps.

1879 Usshar, A.K.L. **Climatic maps of Ghana for agriculture.** Legon, Ghana Meteorological Services, 1969. 36pp. (29 maps at 1:1.5M showing rainfall, temperature, solar radiation, winds)

1880 Wills, J. Brian. **Agriculture and land use in Ghana.** London, Oxford University Press for Ghana Ministry of Food & Agriculture, 1962. xviii, 503pp. illus. maps. (Review, *GJ*, 129, 1963, 96, "chapters on soils are invaluable")

BIOLOGICAL SCIENCES

Zoology

1881 Dankwa, Hederick R. et al. **Freshwater fishes of Ghana: identification, distribution, ecological and economic importance**. Tervuren, Musée royal de l'Afrique centrale, 1999. (*Annales, sciences zoologiques*, 283). 53pp. illus. map.

1882 Grimes, L.G. **The birds of Ghana**. London, British Ornithologists' Union, 1987. (Checklist, 9). 276pp. (Annotated checklist of 721 spp. with gazetteer of localities. Review, *Tauraco*, 1, 1989, 217-219). - - Dowsett, Robert J. 'A supporting gazetteer for the *Birds of Ghana*', *Malimbus*, 27, 2005, 116-119. (Adds cartographical co-ordinates for some 50 additional localities)

1883 Irvine, Frederick R. **Fishes and fisheries of the Gold Coast; with illustrations & an account of the fishing industry by A.P. Brown & classification & keys for the identification of the fishes by ... J.R. Norman & E. Trewavas**. London, Crown Agents for Government of the Gold Coast, 1947. xv, 352pp. illus.

Botany

1884 Abbiw, Daniel K. **Useful plants of Ghana: West African uses of wild and cultivated plants**. London, Intermediate Technology Publications & Royal Botanic Gardens, Kew, 1990. xii, 337pp. illus.

1885 Dokosi, Oscar Blueman. **Herbs of Ghana**. Accra, Ghana Universities Press for Council for Scientific & Industrial Research, 1998. xviii, 746pp. illus. (Arranged by scientific name with notes on local names, local, African and world distribution and uses. Review, *ABPR*, 28, 2002, 11)

1886 Hall, John B. **Gazetteer of plant collecting localities in Ghana cited in *Flora of west tropical Africa***. Accra, Ghana Universities Press, 1980. 122pp.

1887 Hawthorne, William D. **Field guide to the forest trees of Ghana**. Chatham, Natural Resources Institute for Overseas Development Administration, 1990. (Ghana forestry series, 1). vi, 276pp. 8 pp. plates. (Covers some 100 spp.)

1888 Irvine, Frederick R. **Woody plants of Ghana: with special reference to their uses**. Oxford, Oxford University Press, 1961. xcv, 868pp. 142 text figs. (No keys. Includes 35 lists of various categories of use. Rev. of appropriate sections of his **Plants of the Gold Coast**. Oxford, 1930. lxxix, 521pp.)

1889 Mshana, N.R. et al. **Traditional medicine and pharmacopoeia: contribution to the revision of ethnobotanical and floristic studies in Ghana.** Accra, OAU, Scientific, Technical & Research Commission, 2000. 920pp. illus. (Based upon an extensive survey of the existing literature. Describes some 600 spp., most with illus., habitat and medicinal uses)

NIGERIA

Nigeria direct: official information gateway of the Republic of Nigeria
http://www.nigeria.gov.ng/

Bibliographies of reference sources

1890 Asomugha, Chukwenedu N.C. **A brief guide to Nigerian reference books**. Onitsha, ABIC Publishers, 1978. v, 47pp. (Lists 85 titles)

HANDBOOKS

1891 Afunku, Ade et al. **A guide to Nigerian states**. Lagos, J. West, 1977. 160pp.

1892 The Chinua Achebe encyclopedia, ed. M. Keith Booker. Westport, CT, Greenwood Press, 2003. xxi, 318pp. (Includes summaries of his writings, an historical overview of Nigeria, and a bibliography of his interviews and works about him. Reviews, *Africa*, 75, 2005, 607-608; *Choice*, 42, 2004, 60-61)

1893 Facts about Nigeria. Lagos, Ministry of Information, 1961. 9 parts. (A series of self contained pamphlets covering topics such as topography, commerce, industry, and public utilities)

1894 The *Guardian* Nigerian handbook, 1982/83, ed. Michael Simmons & Ad'Obe Obe. London, Collins, 1982. viii, 183pp. (Covers politics, the economy, social life, and includes commercial directory)

1895 Historical dictionary of Nigeria. 2nd ed., comp. Anthony Oyewole & John Lucas. Lanham, MD, Scarecrow Press, 2000. (African historical dictionaries, 40). xxx, 599pp. (Reviews, *African affairs*, 100, 2001, 668-670; *ARD*, 84, 2000, 83-90; *Choice*, 38, 2001, 1250; *IJAHS*, 34, 2002, 231-232). - - Orig. pub. comp. Anthony Oyewole. Metuchen, NJ, 1987. xvii, 391pp. (Review *JAH*, 30, 1989, 340-341. Rated "good", Balay, 1996)

1896 Kauffman, Herbert. **Nigeria**. 2nd ed. Bonn, K. Schroeder for Deutsche Afrika-Gesellschaft, 1962. (Die Länder Afrikas, 2). 304pp. - - Orig. pub. Bonn, 1958. 83pp.

1897 Kochakova, N.B. et al. **Nigeriia: spravochnik**. Moscow, Akademiia nauk, Institut Afriki, 1993. 347pp. maps. - - Orig. pub. as **Sovremennaia Nigeriia: spravochnik**, ed. N.S. Asoian et al. Moscow, 1974. 411pp.

1898 Nigeria: a complete factfinder. Ibadan, Tee-Rex, 1995- . Irreg. Issue for 2002, 112pp. called Vol. 4 and claims to cumulate information in previous three eds. (Short essays, tables, charts)

1899 Nigeria: a country study. 5th ed. comp. Helen Chapin Metz et al. Washington, DC, U.S. Department of Defense, 1992. xxxiii, 394pp. illus. maps. Also available at: http://lcweb2.loc.gov/frd/cs/ngtoc.html; - - Orig. pub. as **Area handbook for Nigeria**. Washington, DC, 1961. viii, 579pp; - - 2nd ed. comp. John A. Cookson et al. Washington, DC, 1964. xvii, 579pp; - - 3rd ed. comp. Harold D. Nelson et al. Washington, DC, 1972. xvi, 485pp; - - 4th ed. Washington, DC, 1982. xxviii, 358pp.

1900 Nigeria: country profile. Washington, DC, Library of Congress. Federal Research Division, 2006. 23pp. Also available at: http://lcweb2.loc.gov /frd/cs/profiles/Nigeria.pdf.

1901 Nigeria: giant in the tropics. Lagos, Gabumo Publishing, 1993. 2 vols. Vol. 1. A compendium, ed. I.A. Adalemo & J.M. Baba. 496pp; vol. 2. State surveys, ed. R.K. Udo & A.B. Mamman. 598pp. (Major collection of data, but lacks a detailed contents list. Vol. 1 includes a list of ethnic groups, surveys of natural resources and history, 10 page thematic atlas at 1:3M. Vol. 2 has economic, social and political data, and an atlas, pp. 503-598 of thematic maps for each state).

1902 Nigeria: handbook on information and culture. Lagos, Federal Ministry of Information and Culture, 1994. 240pp. illus. map.

1903 Nigeria: the first 25 years, ed. Uma Eleazu et al. Lagos, Infodata & Heinemann Educational Books (Nigeria), 1988. xviii, 582pp. (To provide need for "an authorative handbook of information on Nigeria", pref. Pt. 1 provides a survey of political, legal and administrative developments since independence; pts. 2 and 3 cover the economy; pt. 4 gives a state by state survey, giving for each an account of history, topography, economic and social developments, tourist attractions. Statistical appendix, pp. 545-569)

1904 Nigerian political leadership handbook and who's who: a compendium on the dynamics of socio-economic development; ed.-in-chief Law C. Fejokwu. Lagos, Polcom Ltd., 1992. 924pp. (Includes lists of the 12 Nigerian states of 1967, the 19 of 1976, the 21 of 1987 and the 30 of 1991. Biographies of major leaders, articles on political parties. Major section gives statistical, political and biographical data for each state)

1905 Omonijo, Mobolade, ed. **Political factbook and who's who in Nigeria**. Ikeja, Winngam Communications, 1999. ix, 236pp. (A brief political history and statistics, who's who of political figures and handbook of important events. No index)

1906 Orizu, Nwafor. **Insight into Nigeria: the Shehu Shagari era; a reference book focusing on the statistical data of Nigerian States ...** . Ibadan, Evans Bros. (Nigerian Publications), 1983. xv, 324pp. (Author was formerly President of the Senate. Individual chapters for each of the 19 states and the federal government. Written in a discursive style but with a wide range of data)

1907 Oyenchi, N. Nik. **Nigeria's book of firsts: a handbook on pioneer Nigerian citizens, institutions and events**. Owerri, Nigeriana Publications, 1989. vii, 277pp. (Some 1,000 entries under 19 thematic headings such as politics, religion)

1908 Oyobolo, Eddie P. **Current affairs handbook**. Lagos, Ezekiel O. Fiyebo, 1993. iii, 87pp. (Miscellaneous collection of demographic, economic and political information. Includes biographies)

1909 Van der Aa, Gerbert. **Nigeria: mensen, politiek, economie, cultuur**. [Rev. ed.]. Amsterdam, Koninklijk Instituut voor de Tropen/The Hague, Novib, 2002. (Landenreeks). 74pp. illus. maps. - - Orig. pub. comp. Jos Moerkamp. Amsterdam, etc., 1994. 75pp.

Chronologies *See also* 1931

1910 Akpasubi, Jackson. **Chronology of Nigerian history, 1799-1995**. Lagos, Shalom Books, 1995. 107pp. illus. maps.

1911 Onuarah, Gina. **Twenty-one years of independence: a calendar of major political and economic events in Nigeria, 1960-1981**. Ibadan, Nigerian Institute of Social and Economic Research (NISER), 1981. iv, 121pp. (Historical chronology)

Ethnography

1912 Babalola, Adeboye & Alaba, Olugboyega. **A dictionary of Yoruba personal names**. Lagos, West Africa Book Publishers Ltd., 2003. 857pp. (Gives the meanings of over 20,000 names. Result of a twenty year project which was initially intended to cover place names as well)

1913 Falola, Toyin. **Culture and customs of Nigeria**. Westport, CT, Greenwood Press, 2001. (Culture and customs of Africa). xviii, 202pp. illus. map. (Covers history, religion, literature, art & architecture, social customs.

Review, H-Africa, http://www.h-net.org/~africa/reviews/ "first-rate reference book")

1914 Gordon, April A. **Nigeria's diverse peoples: a reference sourcebook**. Santa Barbara, CA, ABC-Clio, 2003. (Ethnic diversity within nations). xxv, 290pp. (11 sections on politics, history, social and ethnic issues, each with a brief chronology, and list of 'significant people, places & events')

1915 Imoagene, Oshomha. **Know your country series: handbooks of Nigeria's major culture areas**. Ibadan, New Era Publishers, 1990. 6 vols. Vol. 1. The Hausa and Fulani of northern Nigeria. x, 125pp; vol. 2. The Yoruba of southwestern Nigeria. xiii, 120pp; vol. 3. The Ibo of east-central Nigeria. xiii, 151pp; vol. 4. The Edo and their neighbours of mid-western Nigeria. xiii, 139pp; vol. 5. Peoples of the Niger-Benue confluence and plateau areas. xiii, 153pp; vol. 6. Peoples of the Cross-River Valley and the Eastern Delta. xiii, 183pp.

1916 Nitecki, Andre. **Nigerian tribes: preliminary list of headings for use in libraries**. Legon, University of Ghana, Department of Library Studies, 1972. vi, 106pp.

1917 Wente-Lukas, Renate. **Handbook of ethnic units in Nigeria**, comp. "with the assistance of Adam Jones". Wiesbaden, Franz Steiner, 1985. (Studien zur Kulturkunde Frobenius Institut, Universität der Frankfurt, 74). 466pp. (Alphabetical list of all known ethnic groups, some 550, with variant names, details of sub-groups, present and previous geographical locations, population estimates and language affiliations. Bibliography pp. 365-401. Reviews, *Africa*, 57, 1987, 391-396; *JALL*, 9, 1987, 61-63)

Language

1918 Asomugha, Chukwendu N.C. **Nigerian slangs: dictionary of slangs and unconventional English used in Nigeria**. Onitsha, Abic publishers, 1981. v, 82pp. - - Orig. pub. as **A pocket dictionary of selected Nigerian student slangs**. Onitsha, 1978. 28pp.

1919 Crozier, David Henry & Blench, R.M. **An index of Nigerian languages**. Abuja, Language Development Centre, Nigerian Educational Research & Development Council/Ilorin, Dept. of Linguistics & Nigerian Languages, University of Ilorin/Dallas, Summer Institute of Linguistics, 1992. iv, 137pp. map. - - Orig. pub. comp. Keir Hansford, et al. Accra, Summer Institute of Linguistics, 1976. 204ppp.

1920 Igboanusi, Herbert. **A dictionary of Nigerian English usage**. Ibadan, Enicrownfir Publishers, 2002. 307pp. (Very critical review, *ABPR* 29, 2003, 240-241)

1921 Jowitt, David. **Nigerian English usage: an introduction**. Ikeja, Longman Nigeria, 1991. xiii, 277pp.

1922 Williamson, Kay. **Orthographies of Nigerian languages**. Lagos, National Language Centre, Federal Ministry of Education, 1983. 2 vols.

YEARBOOKS

1923 G.B. Colonial Office. **[Annual reports]: Nigeria, 1914-57**. London, 1916-1961. As **Annual report on Nigeria**, 1914-19, (as Command papers); **Colonial Office annual report**, 1920-55, (not pub. 1939-45), no report pub. for 1956, **Annual report for Federal Nigeria, 1957**.

1924 National directory of Nigeria. London, Unimex, 1959- . Annual (irreg.) 3rd ed. 1963.

1925 Nigeria. Department of Commerce & Industries. **Handbook of commerce and industry in Nigeria**. Lagos, 1952-?1962. Irreg. 5 issues traced for 1952, 1954, 1957, 1960, 1962. (Despite title includes much general social and topographic information).

1926 Nigeria finance year-book. Lagos, Goldstar, 1993- . Annual. LC has issue 5, 1998/99. (Four sections: Banking; Insurance; Capital market; Non-banking financial services.)

1927 Nigeria [official] handbook. Lagos, Federal Ministry of Information, 1970-?1994. Annual (irreg.) Issues traced for 1970-74, 1975/76, 1977, 1978/79, 1982, 1991, 1993/94, 1995 (12th ed.) (Wide ranging general information including statistics, lists of members of government). *Continues* **Nigeria handbook**. London, Crown Agents for Government of Nigeria, 1953-1954. Annual. 2 issues. 1953, 339pp; 1954, 354pp. (Review, *African affairs*, 53, 1954, 258-259)

1928 Nigeria handbook [and review]. Lagos, Patike Communications Ltd., 1985- ?Annual. NWU holds issues for 1988/89, 1990, 1992, 1994-1996, 1999-2000. (Magazine format with essays, commercial directory, and who's who of 100/120 entries).

1929 Nigeria Jahrbuch: Politische und ökonomische Entwicklungen in der Bundesrepublik Nigeria. Göttingen, Duehrkohp & Radicke, 2001- . Annual.

1930 Nigeria year book. Lagos/Apapa, *Daily Times*, 1952-?1992. Annual. Latest ed. in NWU, SOAS is 38th, 1992. (Includes civil list, commercial directory, statistics, state by state surveys. Amount of data steadily increases: 1952 issue, 128pp; 1989 issue, 392pp.)

1931 Recall: a chronology of Nigerian events. Ibadan, Hope Publications, 2000- . Annual. Latest issue in NWU is for 2002. (Daily chronicle for preceding year)

1932 *Times* **trade and industrial directory**. Apapa, *Daily Times* Press, 1979-1984. Latest issue in NWU, SOAS is 6th ed. 1984/85 .

1933 Trade directory of the Federation/Federal Republic of Nigeria. London, Diplomatic Press & Publishing Co. (Diprepu Co.) Ltd., 1960-1965. Irreg. 4 issues for 1960, 1962, 1963/64, 1965/66. Title varies: **Directory of the Federation of Nigeria** (1960). (Includes civil list, statistics, commercial directory and in issues 1 to 3, "Biographical section" , c.200 entries)

STATISTICS

1934 Adamu, Samuel O. **The Nigerian statistical system: retrospect and prospect**. Ibadan, Ibadan University Press, 1978. xiv, 221pp. (Author was member of Nigerian Department of Statistics. Describes activities as of 1975. Lists statistical publications current in 1975 in Appendix 3, pp. 178-210)

1935 Country profile: Nigeria. London, Economist Intelligence Unit, 1986-Annual.

1936 European Communities. Eurostat. **Reports on ACP countries: Nigeria**. Luxembourg, Office for Official Publications of the European Communities, 1989. 101pp.

1937 Facts and figures about Nigeria. Lagos, Federal Office of Statistics, 1994- . 1995 ed. 36pp.

1938 Germany. Statistisches Bundesamt. **Statistik des Auslandes: Länderberichte: Nigeria** (later **Länderbericht: Nigeria**) Wiesbaden/ Stuttgart, Metzler-Poetschel, 1961- . Irreg. Issues for 1961, 1967, 1977, 1985, 1987, 1992.

1939 IMF. **Nigeria: selected issues and statistical appendix**. Washington, DC, 2005. (Country report, 05/303). 109pp. - - Earlier eds. (title varies) 1995 (Staff country report, 95/143); 1997 (Staff country report, 97/11); 1998 (Staff country report, 98/78); 2000 (Country report, 00/06); 2001 (Country report, 01/132); 2003 (Country report, 03/60); 2004 (Country report, 04/242). Full text of reports from 97/101, 1997 also available online, *see* **334**.

1940 Moses, S.C. 'Nigerian State statistical yearbooks', *African research & documentation*, 8/9, 1975, 57-59.

1941 Nigeria. Department of Statistics [etc.]. **Annual abstract of statistics**. Lagos, 1960- . Annual. Latest issue in NWU is 1998.

1942 Nigeria. Department of Statistics [etc.]. **Digest of statistics**. Lagos, 1951- . vols. 1-29, 1951-1984 (Quarterly); 1985- 2 p.a. (irreg). NWU has 1989, 1994 (Dec); 1996 (Dec); 1998 (Dec).

1943 Nigeria. Federal Office of Statistics. **Economic indicators**. Lagos, vols.1-13 (6); 1965-1977. No more pub.

1944 Nigeria. Federal Office of Statistics. **Nigeria statistical yearbook, 1996-** [etc.]. Abuja, 2000- LC has vol. for 1996 (2000).

See also **1906**

DIRECTORIES OF ORGANIZATIONS

1945 Directory of Nigerian associations (non-governmental organizations). Lagos, Komtran Konsultants, 1999- . ?Annual.

1946 Handbook of Nigerian artist(e)s. Lagos, Arts Illustrated Weekly, 1996. 66pp.

1947 National education, training and research directory (NETRED), ed. Adeleke Salami. Akure, International Network of Directories & Astate Associate Limited, 2002. 643 pp. (Wide range of information on institutions, Federal and State Education Departments, statistics, policy statements, etc.)

1948 Nigerian college and university guide, comp. Chukwendu N.C. Asomugha. Onitsha, ABIC Publishers, 1981. xii, 379pp.

1949 Nigerian social science resource database, comp. Jimi Adesina. Ibadan, Institut français de recherche en Afrique (IFRA), 2001. 225pp. (Lists c.1,300 researchers and some 120 institutions under 16 subject headings)

Finance & commerce

1950 Directory of companies incorporated in Nigeria. Abuja, Corporate Affairs Commission, 1996. var. paging. (Lists companies incorporated 1912-1995). - - Earlier ed. **Directory of incorporated (registered) companies in Nigeria (1912-1974)**. Lagos, ICIC, 1974. xl, 88, 448pp.

1951 Directory of establishments; [name of state]**; listing of establishments**. Abuja, Federal Office of Statistics, 1997- . Pub in 25 vols., one for each state. (Covers business, commerce and industry)

1952 eBizguides Nigeria. Dublin, eBiz guides, 2005. 308pp. (Business directory)

1953 The major 5,000 companies in Nigeria. Lagos, Goldstar Publications, 1998. 124, 655pp. - - Orig. pub. as **Nigeria's major 500 companies**. Lagos, 1991/92 to 1992/93. 2 issues.

1954 Major companies of Nigeria. London, Graham & Trotman, 1979- . ?Annual. Last issue in NWU is for 1983.

1955 Nigeria business directory. Lagos, Lagos Chamber of Commerce & Industry, 1984- . Latest copy in NWU is for 1997/98.

1956 Redasel's companies of Nigeria (RECON): corporate information on 2000 major companies in Nigeria. 2nd ed. Lagos, Research and Data Services Ltd, 1996. 328pp. - - Orig. pub. Lagos, 1988. 464pp.

Libraries, archives & the book trade

1957 Directory of law libraries in Nigeria. 2nd ed. 'incorporating a practical classification scheme for Nigerian law libraries', comp. A. Adefidiya. Lagos, Government Printer, 1970. 110pp. - - Orig. pub. Lagos, 1966.

1958 Directory of Nigerian book development, ed. Chukwuemeka Ike. Awka, Nigeria, Nigerian Book Foundation & Fourth Dimension Publishing, 1998. 228pp. (Sections for authors, publishing, printing, book distribution, libraries; "a remarkable and pioneering publication", *ABPR* 25, 1999, 8-9)

1959 A directory of Nigerian libraries and documentation centres, comp. M.A. Omoniwa & M.O. Salaam. Zaria, Ahmadu Bello University. Kashim Ibrahim Library, 1983. v, 132pp. (51 academic, 31 special, 25 public, 17 judicial)

BIOGRAPHICAL SOURCES

Bibliographies

1960 National Library of Nigeria. **A bibliography of biographies and memoirs on Nigeria**. Lagos, 1968. (National Library publications, 9). 11pp.

General

1961 2000 foremost Nigerians, ed. Olugbemi Fatula et al. Ibadan, Caltop Publications (Nigeria)/Ile-Ife, UNIFECS, Obafemi Awolowo University, 2000- Vol. 1, 2000. 339pp. (200 profiles; many entries based on secondary sources, especially newspapers); vol. 2, 2000. (100 outstanding Nigerians of the African International Biographical Order (AIBO)

1962 A national who's who, 1995/96- , ed. Okpala L.G. Ngor. Lagos, GPN Publishing, 1995- .

1963 The new who's who in Nigeria. Lagos, Nigerian International Biographical Centre, 1999. vi, 802pp. (Some 4,000 detailed entries based both on questionnaires and on interviews by travelling researchers)

1964 Nigerian Broadcasting Corporation. **Eminent Nigerians of the nineteenth century**. Cambridge, Cambridge University Press, 1960. 97pp. (Studies originally broadcast by the Nigerian Broadcasting Corporation)

1965 Orimoloye, Stephen Ademola. **Biographia Nigeriana: a biographical dictionary of eminent Nigerians**. Boston, MA, G.K. Hall, 1977. 368pp. (1,007 entries for living and recently deceased figures, based on questionnaires)

1966 People in the news, 1900-1999: a survey of Nigerians of the 20th century. Ikeja, Independent Communications Network Ltd, 2000. xi, 498pp.

1967 Ugowe, C.C. **Eminent Nigerians of the twentieth century**. Lagos, Hugo Books, 2000. xiii, 331pp.illus.

1968 Who's who in Nigeria, comp. "Amicus" pseud. (i.e. A.T. Odusanya). Ibadan, Advent Press, 1949. 59pp.

1969 Who's who in Nigeria. 3rd ed., ed. H.U. Ukegbu. Lagos, Biographical Centre of Nigeria Ltd., 1985. 23, 144pp. (Some 300 entries arranged in categories, e.g. politicians, businessmen, traditional rulers, religious leaders. No index) - - Orig. pub. as **Nigeria who's who, 1981-82**. Lagos, 1981. 95pp.

1970 Who's who in Nigeria, comp. Nyaknno Osso. Lagos, Newswatch, 1990-1991. 2 issues. (Each issue contains over 800pp. and 2,500 entries; one of the largest compilations of its kind for Nigeria before the pub. of **1963**. Review, *ABPR* 17, 1991, 294, "splendid resource")

1971 Who's who in Nigeria, 2ⁿᵈ ed. comp. Bankole Makinde. Ikeja, Lagos State, Newswatch, 2001. 1,387pp. (?Successor to **1970**)

1972 Who's who in Nigeria: a biographical dictionary. [4ᵗʰ ed.]. ed. James O. Ojiako, editor. Apapa, *Daily Times*, 1983. 558pp. - - Orig. pub. Lagos, 1956. 278pp. (Contains some 1,500 entries); - - 2ⁿᵈ ed. Apapa, *Daily Times*, 1971. 232pp. (Contains some 750 entries); - - 3ʳᵈ ed. **Who's who in Nigeria, 1978: biographies of some eminent Nigerian citizens**, ed. James O. Ojiako. Apapa, 1978. 173pp. (Contains about 500 entries, much fuller than those in previous editions)

See also **1904, 1905, 1928, 1933**

Special categories

1973 G.B. Commonwealth War Graves Commission. **The register of the names of those who fell in the First World War, and are buried or commemorated in Nigeria and Cameroon, West Africa**. Maidenhead, 1993. 67pp. - - Orig. pub. Maidenhead, 1931.

1974 Iroanwusi, Sam. **Nigeria's heads of state and government**. Lagos, author, 1997. xii, 180pp.

1975 Nigeria who is who in the Legislature (The House of Representatives), 1979-1983. Lagos, Nigerian Federal Department of Information, Research Section, 1983. 227pp. (Lists 445 members with brief biographies of nearly 300 arranged by state)

1976 Nigerian artists: a who's who and bibliography, comp. Bernice M. Kelly, ed. Janet L. Stanley. Oxford, Hans Zell, 1993. 622pp. col. illus. (Covers more than 350 artists active between 1920 and 1990 giving date of birth, address, details of exhibitions, awards, commissions. Based on collections at the National Museum of African Art, Smithsonian Institution Libraries. Includes bibliography of modern Nigerian art. Review, *Choice*, 31, 1993, 587)

1977 The Nigerian Legislature: who is who in the Senate, 1979-1983. [Lagos, Nigerian Federal Department of Information], 1983. 144pp. (93 short biographies with portraits)

1978 Osuji, Chuks. **His Royal Highness: a historical data and reference book on traditional rulers in Anambra, Cross River, Imo and River States**. Owerri, Opinion Research and Communications Consultants, 1984. viii, [158pp]. (Separate sections for each State. Lists c. 900 contemporary rulers, but fewer than 150 have full biographical entries, usually with a portrait)

1979 **Who's who of Nigerian women**, ed. Clara Osinulu & Oluremi Jegede. Lagos, Nigerian Association of University Women, 1985. 281pp. (257 entries. Index by profession)

ATLASES & GAZETTEERS

Atlases

1980 **Atlas du Nigeria**, ed. Danielle Ben Yahmed. Paris, Editions *Jeune Afrique* aux Éditions du Jaguar, 2003. 158pp. col. maps. (The first atlas in the *Jeune Afrique* series to be pub. covering a country of Anglophone Africa)

1981 **An atlas for the Northern States of Nigeria**, comp. I.A. Ikuponiyi. Zaria, Northern Nigerian Publishing Co., 1971. 25pp. col. maps.

1982 **National atlas of the Federal Republic of Nigeria**. Lagos, Nigeria Federal Surveys, 1978. vi, 136pp. 45 x 58cm. (Col. thematic maps compiled 1968-1977. Basic scale 1:3M. 12 town plans at 1:50,000. Includes gazetteer. Preceded by a series of 1:3M sheets published 1949-56 without text and known as the "Atlas series")

1983 **Nigeria in maps**, comp. Kenneth M. Barbour et al. London, Hodder & Stoughton, 1982. vii, 148pp. (60 thematic maps with accompanying text. Reviews, *GJ*, 149, 1983, 390-391; *Survey review*, 27, 1983, 142-143)

1984 **Nigeria in maps: eastern states**, ed. G.E.K. Ofomata. Benin City, Ethiope, 1975. 146pp. (18 contributors discuss 51 themes with accompanying maps. "First in a series which will eventually cover the whole country", pref. ?No more pub.)

1985 **Oxford atlas for Nigeria**. Rev. ed. London & Ibadan, Oxford University Press, 1978. 66, 12pp. (Comp. by the Cartographic Department of the Clarendon Press, with the advice of F.C.A. McBain. Pp. ii-vii, 1-21 cover Nigeria and West Africa). - - Orig. pub. London & Ibadan, 1968. 66, 12pp.

See also **1901**

Gazetteers

1986 Nigeria. Director of Federal Surveys. **Gazetteer of place-names**. 3rd ed. Lagos, 1973. ii, 836pp. - - Orig. pub. as **Gazetteer of place-names: Federal Republic of Nigeria**. Lagos, 1965. 2 vols. Vol. 1. Northern Nigeria. 172pp; vol. 2. Western Nigeria & Municipality of Lagos, Eastern Nigeria. 176pp.

1987 Nigeria. Director of Surveys. **Colony and Protectorate of Nigeria: gazetteer of place names on map of Nigeria 1:500,000**. Zaria, Gaskiya Corporation, 1949. 167pp. (Arranged in 5 sections: towns, villages and hamlets; rivers and creeks; lakes; mountains and hills; forest and game reserves)

1988 Nigeria. National Population Bureau. Demographic Division. **National gazetteer of place names**. Lagos, 1985. 20 vols. (One vol. for each state as in 1985: Anambra, Bauchi, Bendel, Benue, Borno, Cross River, Federal Capital Territory Abuja, Gongola, Imo, Kaduna, Kano, Kwara, Lagos, Niger, Ogu, Ondo, Oyo, Plateau, Rivers, Sokoto)

1989 Rothmaler, Eva. **Ortsnamen in Borno (Nordnigeria)**. Cologne, Köppe, 2003. xi, 247pp. illus. maps.

1990 U.S. Board on Geographic Names. **Nigeria: official standard names approved by the USBGN.** Washington, DC, 1971. (Gazetteer, 117). iv, 641pp. (Includes 42,000 names from 1:250,000 map series. Revision of appropriate sections of **West Africa**, *see* **2492**)

EARTH SCIENCES

1991 Agboola, S.A. **An agricultural atlas of Nigeria**. London, Oxford University Press, 1979. xiv, 248pp. maps.

1992 Akintola, Jacob O. **Rainfall distribution in Nigeria, 1892-1983**. Ibadan, Impact Publishers, 1986. xxi, 380pp. illus. maps.

1993 Garnier, Benjamin John. **Weather conditions in Nigeria**. Montreal, McGill University, 1967. (Climatological research series, 2). 163pp. illus. maps. (Review, *GJ* , 133, 1967, 538-539)

1994 Kowal, J.M. & Knabe, D.T. **An agroclimatological atlas of the Northern States of Nigeria**. Zaria, Ahmadu Bello University, 1972. 111pp. 16 folding maps. 30 x 41cm.

1995 Land resources of central Nigeria: agricultural development possibilities. Vol. 7, An atlas of resource maps. Tolworth, Overseas Development Administration, Land Resources Development Centre, 1981. (Land resource study, 29). ivpp. 19 maps.

1996 Ofoegbu, Charles O. **Groundwater and mineral resources of Nigeria.** Brunswick, F. Vieweg, 1988. vi, 159pp. illus. maps.

1997 Ologe, K.O. **An atlas of structural landforms in Nigeria.** Zaria, Ahmadu Bello University, Department of Geography, 1985. (Occasional papers, 9). iv, 105pp.

1998 Oyenuga, Victor Adenuga. **Agriculture in Nigeria: an introduction.** Rome, FAO, 1967. xviii, 308pp. illus.

1999 Reyment, Richard A. **Aspects of the geology of Nigeria: the stratigraphy of the Cretaceous and Cenozoic deposits.** Ibadan, Ibadan University Press, 1965. viii, 145pp. illus.

2000 Udo, Reuben K. **Geographical regions of Nigeria.** London, Heinemann, 1970. xii, 212pp. illus. maps. (The Coastlands, the Middle Belt and the Nigerian Sudan)

BIOLOGICAL SCIENCES

Zoology

2001 Boorman, John & Roche, Patrick. **The Nigerian butterflies.** Ibadan, Ibadan University Press, 1957-1973. 6pts. ("An atlas of plates with notes".)

2002 Elgood, John Hamel et al. **The birds of Nigeria: an annotated checklist.** 2nd ed. Tring, British Ornithologists' Union, 1995. (Checklist, 4). 305pp. illus. (Covers 883 spp. Review, *BABC*, 2, 1995, 57-58). - - Orig. pub. Tring, 1982. 246pp. (Review, *Ibis*, 124, 1982, 542)

2003 Happold, David C.D. **The mammals of Nigeria.** Oxford, Clarendon Press, 1987. xvii, 402pp. (Covers 247 spp. Reviews, *Journal of mammalogy*, 72, 1991, 427-428; *Mammal review*, 19, 1989, 91-92; *SAJZ*, 26, 1991, 206)

2004 Medler, John T. **Insects of Nigeria: checklist and bibliography.** Ann Arbor, MI, American Entomological Institute, 1980. (Memoirs, 30). vii, 919pp. (Bibliog. pp. 489-639)

2005 Nigeria. Federal Ministry of Agriculture & Natural Resources/G.B. Overseas Development Administration. **A guide to insect pests of Nigerian crops: identification, biology and control.** Chatham, Land Resources Institute, 1996. xi, 253pp. illus.

2006 Rosevear, Donovan R. **Checklist and atlas of Nigerian mammals, with a foreword on vegetation.** Lagos, Government Printer, 1953. 131, 103pp. maps. (Review, *Journal of mammalogy*, 35, 1954, 266-270)

2007 Schiøtz, Arne. 'The amphibians of Nigeria', *Videnskabelige Meddelelser fra Dansk naturhistorisk Forening*, 125, 1963, 1-101

Botany

2008 Flora of Nigeria, ed. Dennis P. Stanfield & Joyce Lowe. Ibadan, Ibadan University Press, 1970-1989. Issued in fascs. Fascs. 1-2, 1970-1974; Fasc. 1, 2nd ed. 1989. No more pub.
- - Ghazanfar, S.A. **Flora of Nigeria: Caryophyllales.** St. Louis, MO, Missouri Botanical Gardens, 1991. 39pp. illus. (An independent undertaking to continue the **Flora**. No more pub.)

2009 Gill, L.S. **Ethnomedical uses of plants in Nigeria.** Benin City, Uniben Press, 1992. ix, 276pp.

2010 Keay, Ronald W.J. **Outline of Nigerian vegetation.** 3rd ed. Lagos, Government Printer, 1959. 46pp. illus. (Col. map at 1:3M). - - Orig. pub. Lagos, 1949. 52pp.; - - [2nd ed]. Lagos, 1953. 55pp.

2011 Keay, Ronald W.J. et al. **Trees of Nigeria.** Oxford, Clarendon Press, 1989. viii, 476pp. illus. - - Orig. pub. as **Nigerian trees.** Lagos, Government Printer, 1960-64. 2 vols. (1989 volume is "rev. and abbreviated". Includes keys, but omits much of the detailed morphological description of the earlier ed. Cross references to **Flora of west tropical Africa**, *see* **1795**)

2012 Lowe, Joyce. **The flora of Nigeria: grasses.** 2nd ed. Ibadan, Ibadan University Press, 1989. xxii, 326pp. (Review, *ARD*, 55, 1991, 55). - - Orig. pub. as **Grasses**, comp. Dennis P. Stanfield. Ibadan, 1970. (The flora of Nigeria). 2 vols. ix, 118pp; viii, 58pp.

SIERRA LEONE

The Republic of Sierra Leone State House http://www.statehouse-sl.org/

HANDBOOKS

2013 Area handbook for Sierra Leone, comp. Irving Kaplan et al. Washington, DC, U.S. Department of Defense, 1976. xiv, 400pp.

2014 Background to Sierra Leone. Freetown, Office of the President 1980. 240pp. (Illus. handbook prepared for 17th Summit Conference of the OAU)

2015 The handbook of Sierra Leone. Freetown, Ministry of Information & Broadcasting, 1980. 47pp. illus.

2016 Historical dictionary of Sierra Leone. New ed. comp. C. Magbaily Fyle. Lanham, MD, Scarecrow Press, 2006. (African historical dictionaries, 99). lii, 288pp. maps. - - Orig. pub. comp. Cyril P. Foray. Metuchen, NJ, 1977. (African historical dictionaries, 12). lvi, 279pp. (Reviews, *African affairs*, 78, 1979, 124-125; *Africana J.*, 10, 1979, 120-128; *ASA review of books*, 4, 1978, 109-110, makes detailed corrections and suggestions for topics that might be included in a new edition. Rated "fair", Balay, 1996)

2017 Pfeffer, Karl Heinz. **Sierra Leone**. 2nd ed. Bonn, K. Schroeder for Deutsche Afrika-Gesellschaft, 1967. (Die Länder Afrikas, 11). 110pp. - - Orig. pub as part of **Sierra Leone und Gambia**. Bonn, 1958. (Sierra Leone, pp. 9-64).

2018 Smirnov, E.G. **Respublika Sierra-Leone: spravochnik**. Moscow, Akademiia nauk, Institut Afriki, 1988. 178pp. maps.

YEARBOOKS

2019 G.B. Colonial Office. **[Annual reports]: Sierra Leone, 1846-1958**. London, 1847-1960. As **Reports: the past and present state of HM Colonial possessions**, 1846-1882 (not pub. 1849, 1865, 1874, 1877-79, 1883-86), **Report on the Blue Book**, 1887-1889, **Annual report on Sierra Leone**, 1890-1919 (all as Command papers); **Colonial Office annual report**, 1920-1958 (not pub. 1939-45). Corrigendum added to report for 1956. 1881-82 pub. as one report. No full report for 1858-59, 1862, 1864, 1866, 1869, 1872, 1875.

2020 Sierra Leone. Central Statistics Office. **Directory of business and industry for Western Area and multiunit firms**. Rev. ed. Freetown, 1970. 109pp. - - Orig. pub. Freetown, 1968. 67pp. - - **Directory of business and industry: Northern, Southern and Eastern provinces**. Freetown, 1968. 47pp.

2021 Sierra Leone business directory, 1985/86. Washington, DC, Sierra Leone Business Advisory Service & Aurora Associates Inc., 1986- . ?No more pub. Stanford has vol. for 1985/86 only.

2022 Sierra Leone business directory, 1995/96- Freetown, Sierra Leone Chamber of Commerce Industry and Agriculture, 1995- . ?Annual. NWU and ICS have vol. for 1995/96 only.

2023 Sierra Leone business directory and tourist guide. 2nd ed. Freetown, Sierra Leone Business Publishing Company, 1969. 60pp.

2024 Sierra Leone directory of commerce, industry and tourism. Freetown, Ministry of Information & Broadcasting, 1985- . ?Annual. Stanford has vol. for 1985 only.

2025 Sierra Leone year book. Freetown, "Daily Mail", 1956-?1978 Annual (irreg.). Not pub. 1967, 1973-77. (Includes civil list, basic economic statistics, and 'who's who' (50/75 entries)

STATISTICS

2026 Bank of Sierra Leone. **Sierra Leone in figures**. Freetown, ?1983- . Annual. Stanford has copies for 1983, 1986,1988/93,1990/95

2027 Country profile: Sierra Leone. London, Economist Intelligence Unit, 2003- . Annual. *Continues in part* **Country profile: Sierra Leone, Liberia**. London, 1986-1992; **Country profile: Guinea, Sierra Leone, Liberia**. London, 1993-2002.

2028 Germany. Statistisches Bundesamt. **Statistik des Auslandes: Länderberichte: Sierra Leone** (later **Länderbericht: Sierra Leone**) Wiesbaden/Stuttgart, Metzler-Poetschel, 1962- . Irreg. Issues for 1962, 1984, 1986, 1989, 1994.

2029 IMF. **Sierra Leone: selected issues and statistical appendix**. Washington, DC, 2004. (Country report 04/420). 70pp. - - Earlier ed. (title varies) 1996 (Staff country reports, 96/11). Full text of reports from 1997 also available online, *see* **334**.

2030 Makannah, Toma J. **Handbook of the population of Sierra Leone**. Freetown, Toma Enterprises, 1995. 405pp. (Demographic statistics)

2031 Sierra Leone. Central Statistics Office. **Annual statistical digest**. Freetown, 1962- . Annual. (irreg.) 16th ed. 1989. Title varies: **Annual digest of statistics** (1962-1984). Latest issue in NWU is 2001.

2032 Sierra Leone. Central Statistics Office. **Statistical bulletin**. Freetown, 1963- . Title varies: **Quarterly statistical bulletin** (1963-1966). Latest issue in NWU is for 1971.

2033 Statistics Sierra Leone. http://www.statistics-sierra-leone.org/. (Link not working Sept. 2006)

BIOGRAPHICAL SOURCES

2034 Encyclopedia Africana Dictionary of African Biography. Vol. 2, Sierra Leone and Zaire. Algonac, MI, Reference Publications, 1979. 372pp. (Sierra Leone section pp. 35-178, ed. by U. Flett. 137 biographies of Africans and Europeans, many with portraits and lists of sources; also 'concise guide to Sierra Leone names and terms' and 4 maps. For encyclopedia, *see* **11**; for dictionary of biography, *see* **545**)

2035 Sierra Leone Society. **Eminent Sierra Leoneans (in the nineteenth century)**. Freetown, Department of Information, 1961. 85pp. (Mostly articles that originally appeared in *Sierra Leone studies*)

2036 Sierra Leonean heroes: fifty great men and women who helped to build our nation. [London, Commonwealth Printers, 1988]. 111pp.

2037 Who's who in Sierra Leone. [Freetown, Lyns Publicity, 1981]. 108pp. - - Orig. pub. ed. M.R. Johnson. Freetown, 1980. 56pp. (Some 180 entries)

See also **2025**

ATLASES & GAZETTEERS

2038 Atlas of Sierra Leone. 2nd ed. Freetown, Survey & Lands Department, 1966. iv, 16pp. col. maps. 40 x 27cm. (Includes 16 col. thematic maps. at 1:1M/1:3M, plans of Freetown, Bonthe, Magburaka and Bo at 1:15,000. Index gazetteer). - - Orig. pub. Freetown, 1953. 6pp. text. 16pp. maps.

2039 **Sierra Leone in maps** comp. John Innis Clarke. 2nd ed. London, University of London Press, 1969. 120pp. (Includes 51 b. and w. maps, mostly at 1:30M with facing text. Comp. by 14 past and present members of the staff at Fourah Bay College, with maps drawn in the Geography Department of the College. Review, *GJ*, 132, 1966, 583; *Nigerian geographical journal*, 9, 1966, 168-169). - - Orig. pub. London, 1966. 120pp.

2040 U.S. Board on Geographic Names. **Sierra Leone: official standard names approved by the USBGN.** Washington, DC, 1966. (Gazetteer, 101). ii, 125pp. (Includes 8,800 names from 1:250,000 map series. Revision of appropriate sections of **West Africa**, *see* **1758**)

EARTH SCIENCES

2041 Jabati, S.A. **Agriculture in Sierra Leone**. New York, Vantage, 1978. xxvi, 349pp.

2042 McFarlane, A. et al. **The geology and mineral resources of northern Sierra Leone**, rev. H. Colley. London, HMSO, 1981. (Institute of Geological Sciences, Overseas memoir, 7). 103pp. illus. maps.

BIOLOGICAL SCIENCES

2043 Cole, N.H. Ayodele. **The vegetation of Sierra Leone: incorporating a field guide to common plants**. Freetown, Njala University College Press, 1968. xii, 198pp. (Pt 1, History of agriculture and forestry; pt. 2, Plant communities; pt. 3, pp.140-185, Field guide)

2044 Gledhill, David. **Check list of the flowering plants of Sierra Leone**. Freetown, University of Sierra Leone, Department of Botany, 1962. 38pp. (Derived from **Flora of West tropical Africa** *see* **1795**)

2045 Savill, Peter S. & Fox, J.E.D. **Trees of Sierra Leone**. Freetown, Forestry Division, 1971. 316pp. illus. maps.

2046 Turay, B.M.S. **Medicinal plants of Sierra Leone: a compendium**. Edmonton, University of Alberta, Centre for the Cross-Cultural Study of Health & Healing, 1997. 125pp.

LIBERIA

HANDBOOKS

2047 Background to Liberia. Monrovia, Ministry of Information, Cultural Affairs & Tourism, [1979]. 160pp. illus.

2048 Facts about Liberia. Rev. ed. Monrovia. Ministry of Information, Cultural Affairs & Tourism, 1973. vi, 110pp. ("To supply basic information on contemporary Liberia for the benefit of the general public", pref. Brief data arranged under some 60 headings). - - Earlier eds. Monrovia, 1963. 41pp; - - Monrovia, 1971. 80pp.

2049 Handbook and directory of Liberia. Monrovia, Chamber of Commerce, 1963. 132pp.

2050 Handbook of Liberia. New York, Minden Press, 1940. 64pp. illus. map. (Recorded in Stanford catalogue)

2051 Historical dictionary of Liberia. 2nd ed., comp. D. Elwood Dunn, et al. Lanham, MD, Scarecrow Press, 2001. (African historical dictionaries, 83). xxxv, 436pp. (Reviews, *Africa today*, 50, 2003, 123-126; *African affairs*, 100, 2001, 668-670; *Choice*, 39, 2001, 92; *JAH*, 42, 2001, 544; *IJAHS*, 35, 2002, 205-207). - - Orig. pub. comp. D. Elwood Dunn & Sven E. Holsoe. Metuchen, NJ, 1985. (African historical dictionaries, 38). xx, 274pp. (All entries include refs. to sources. Reviews, *IJAHS*, 19, 1986, 573-575; *JAH* 28, 1987, 468-469, "far more scholarly than most ... Scarecrow volumes". Rated "excellent", Balay, 1996)

2052 Holsoe, Sven E. **A standardization of Liberian ethnic nomenclature**. Philadelphia, PA, Institute for Liberian Studies, 1979. ii, 28pp. (List agreed upon by a group of American scholars meeting at the Peabody Museum. Includes lists of alternative names)

2053 Liberia: a country study. 3rd ed., comp. Harold D. Nelson et al. Washington, DC, U.S. Department of Defense, 1984, 340pp. illus. maps. - - Orig. pub. as **U.S. Army area handbook for Liberia**, comp. Thomas D. Roberts et al. Washington, DC, 1964. xiii, 419pp; - - 2nd ed. pub. as **Area handbook for Liberia**. Washington, DC, 1972. xlviii, 388pp.

2054 Liberia: basic data and information, 1968. Monrovia, Liberia Trading & Development Bank, 1968. 107pp. illus.

2055 Olukoju, Ayodeji Oladimeji. **Culture and customs of Liberia**. Westport, CT, Greenwood Press, 2006. (Culture and customs of Africa). 176pp. illus. map. (Covers history, religion, literature, art and architecture, social customs)

2056 Petruk, B.G. **Respublika Liberiia: spravochnik**. Moscow, Akademiia nauk, Institut Afriki, 1990. 159pp. maps.

2057 Querengaesser, F.A. **Liberia**. Bonn, K. Schroeder for Deutsche Afrika-Gesellschaft, 1965. (Die Länder Afrikas, 24). 163pp. illus. maps.

2058 Tixier, Gilbert. **La République du Libéria**. Paris, Berger-Levrault, 1970. (Encyclopédie politique et constitutionnelle; Série Afrique). 49pp.

See also **2070**

YEARBOOKS

2059 **Directory with who's who in Liberia, 1970/71**, ed. J. Adighibe. Monrovia, A. & A. Enterprises, 1971. 340pp. ?No more pub. Cover title: **A. & A. directory and who's who**.

2060 **Liberian trade directory**. Monrovia, Liberia. Ministry of Commerce, Industry & Transportation, ?1974- . Irreg. Issues for 1974, 1975/76, 1979/80.

2061 **The Liberian yearbook**, ed. Henry B. Cole. London/Monrovia, *Liberian review*, 1956, 1962. 2 issues.. ("Not officially pub. ... but the contributions are confirmed by government officials as being accurate", pref. Includes historical background, details on contemporary politics, commerce and industry. Numerous statistics. Particularly detailed and well set out example of its kind)

STATISTICS

2062 **Country profile: Liberia**. London, Economist Intelligence Unit, 2003-Annual. *Continues in part* **Country profile: Sierra Leone, Liberia**. London, 1986-1992; **Country profile: Guinea, Sierra Leone, Liberia**. London, 1993-2002.

2063 Germany. Statistisches Bundesamt. **Statistik des Auslandes: Länderberichte: Liberia**. Wiesbaden/Stuttgart, Metzler-Poetschel, 1961- . Irreg. Issues for 1961, 1973, 1985, 1987, 1989.

2064 IMF. **Liberia: statistical appendix**. Washington, DC, 2006. (IMF country report, 06/167). 20pp. - - Earlier eds. (title varies) 2000 (Country report, 00/50); 2002 (Country report, 02/148); 2003 (Country report, 03/275); 2005 (Country report, 05/167). Full text of reports also available online, see **334**.

2065 Liberia. Bureau of Statistics. **Economic survey of Liberia**. Monrovia, 1967- . Annual. Pt. 1, General survey of the economy; pt. 2, Statistical abstract. Last issue in NWU is for 1983.

2066 Liberia. Bureau of Statistics. **Statistical bulletin of Liberia**. Monrovia, 1970- . Title varies: **Quarterly statistical bulletin of Liberia** (1970-1985). 2 issues p.a. Last issue in NWU is for 1989

BIOGRAPHICAL SOURCES

2067 Schick, Tom W. **Emigrants to Liberia, 1820 to 1843; an alphabetical listing**. Newark, DE, University of Delaware, Department of Anthropology, 1971. (Liberian studies research working paper, 2). vi, 111pp. - - Brown, Robert T. **Immigrants to Liberia, 1843-1865: an alphabetical listing**. Philadelphia, PA, Institute for Liberian Studies, 1980. (Liberian studies research working paper, 7). iv, 65pp; - - Murdza, Peter J. Jr. **Immigrants to Liberia, 1865 to 1904 : an alphabetical listing**. Newark, DE, Liberian Studies Association in America, 1975. (Liberian studies research working paper, 4). vi, 76pp. (Based on shipping lists, birth registers, etc.)

2068 Stewart, Roma Jones. **Liberia genealogical research**. Chicago, IL, Homeland Publications, 1991. 50pp.

See also **2059**

ATLASES & GAZETTEERS

2069 Liberia in maps, comp. Stefan von Gnielinski. London, University of London Press, 1972. 112pp. (50 b. & w. maps with text on facing page. Review, *GJ*, 139, 1973, 573-574)

2070 Republic of Liberia planning and development atlas. Monrovia, Liberia. Ministry of Planning & Economic Affairs & Deutsche Gesellschaft für Technische Zusammenarbeit, 1983. 74, 67pp. 58cm. (First section contains 37 maps at 1:1M with facing text, notes on utilization of the information, and three transparent overlays, 2 showing population density,

1 showing communications. Second section is a handbook of 67pp. with detailed information and statistics on a wide range of themes: natural resources, the economy, administration, agriculture, trade, etc; virtually an encyclopedia)

2071 U.S. Board on Geographic Names. **Liberia: official standard names approved by the USBGN.** 2nd ed. Washington, DC, 1976. 167pp. (Includes 10,600 names from maps at 1:250,000). - - Orig. pub. Washington, DC, 1968. (Gazetteer, 106). iii, 61pp. (Rev. of appropriate sections of **West Africa** *see* **1758**)

EARTH SCIENCES

2072 Richardson, Nathaniel R. **A brief outline of the mineral occurrences of Liberia.** Monrovia, Liberian Geological Survey, 1980. 42pp.

2073 Schulze, Willi. **Liberia: länderkundliche Dominanten und regionale Strukturen.** Darmstadt, Wissenschaftliche Buchgesellschaft, 1973. (Wissenschaftliche Länderkunden, 7). xxix, 329pp. illus. maps.

BIOLOGICAL SCIENCES

Zoology

2074 Fox, Richard M. **The butterflies of Liberia.** Philadelphia, American Entomological Society, 1965. (Memoirs, 19). 438pp. illus.

2075 Gatter, Wulf. **Birds of Liberia.** London, Pica Press, 1998. 320pp. 4 col. plates, 32pp. col. photos. (Atlas with range maps of 400 spp. Reviews, *BABC*, 5, 1998, 139-141; *Ibis*, 140, 1998, 704; *Malimbus*, 21, 1999, 66-67)

2076 Kuhn, H.J. 'A provisional checklist of the mammals of Liberia', *Senckenbergiana biologica*, 46, 1965, 321-340

Botany

2077 Harley, Winifred J. 'The ferns of Liberia', *Contributions from the Gray Herbarium of Harvard University*, n.s. 177, 1955, 1955, 58-101. illus. map.

2078 Kunkel, Günther W.H. **The trees of Liberia: field notes on the more important trees of the Liberian forests, and a field identification key.** Munich, BLV Bayerischer Landwirtschaftsverlag, 1965. (German Forestry Mission to Liberia, Report 3). 270pp. illus. maps.

2079 Voorhoeve, Alexander George. **Liberian high forest trees: a systematic botanical study of the 75 most important or frequent high forest trees with reference to numerous related species.** 2nd ed. Wageningen, Centre for Agricultural Publications & Documentation, 1979. (Agricultural research reports, 652). x, 416pp. illus. - - Orig. pub. Wageningen, 1965. x, 416pp.

St. HELENA (including ASCENSION & TRISTAN DA CUNHA)

St. Helena Government Web site http://www.sainthelena.gov.sh/

HANDBOOKS

2080 Kitching, Geoffrey Charles. **A handbook and gazetteer of the Island of St Helena including a short history of the island under the Crown 1834-1902**. St. Helena, author, [1937?]. 71pp. (Pub. a year earlier than the nominal starting point for AGRM2's coverage but included because of the scarcity of other sources. Author was Colonial Secretary of St. Helena at the time)

2081 Packer, John E. **The Ascension handbook: a concise guide to Ascension Island, South Atlantic**. 3rd ed. [?Georgetown], 1983. 54pp. illus. maps. - - 2nd ed. Georgetown, 1974. 54pp. - - Orig. pub. Georgetown, 1968. 68pp.

2082 The St. Helena guide. 2nd ed. Jamestown, Information Office, 1995. 29pp. illus.

YEARBOOKS

2083 G.B. Colonial Office. **[Annual reports]: St Helena, 1845-1973**. London, 1846-1976. As **Reports: the past and present state of HM colonial possessions**, 1845-1886 (not pub. 1852, 1874, 1883), **Report on the Blue Book, St Helena**, 1887-1889, **Annual report for St Helena**, 1890-1919 (all as Command papers); **Colonial Office annual report**, 1920-73 (not pub. 1939-46). From 1950-1951 pub. every 2 years, with 1970-73 covered in one report. No full report for 1861, 1863-68. Report for 1964 and 1965 issued by Commonwealth Office. From 1966 issued by Foreign and Commonwealth Office.

See also **2758**

STATISTICS

2084 St. Helena. Development & Economic Planning Department. **Statistical year book**. Jamestown, 1988- . Abridged version available as **St. Helena in figures**. Jamestown, ?1989- . Annual

2085 St. Helena. Economics & Statistics Unit. **Quarterly statistical review**. Jamestown, 1987- .

ATLASES & GAZETTEERS

2086 U.S. Board on Geographic Names. **South Atlantic: official names approved by the USBGN**. Washington, DC, 1957. (Gazetteer, 31). 53pp. (Includes St. Helena, 650 names, Ascension Island, Tristan da Cunha)

EARTH SCIENCES

2087 Duffey, Eric. 'The terrestrial ecology of Ascension Island', *Journal of applied ecology*, 1, 1964, 219-251

2088 Mitchell-Thomé, Raoul C. **Geology of the South Atlantic islands**. Berlin, Borntraeger, 1970. (Beiträge zur regionalen Geologie der Erde, 10). 367pp. maps. (Ascension, pp. 162-194; St. Helena, pp. 195-223; Tristan da Cunha, pp. 224-285)

BIOLOGICAL SCIENCES

2089 Ashmole, Philip & Ashmole, Myrtle. **St. Helena and Ascension Island: a natural history**. Oswestry, Anthony Nelson, 2000. 492pp. + 32pp. plates. illus. maps. (Includes sections covering geological and ecological history, colonisation by early animal and plant settlers, conservation, restoration and sustainable development and examines indigenous and introduced plants and animals)

2090 Brown, L.C. **The flora and fauna of St. Helena**. Tolworth, Overseas Development Administration, Land Resources Division, 1982. v, 88pp.

Zoology

2091 Andrew, T.G. et al. **Fishes of the Tristan da Cunha Group and Gough Islands, South Atlantic Ocean.** Grahamstown, J.L.B. Smith Institute of Ichthyology, 1995. (Ichthyological Bulletin 63). 43pp. illus. maps.

2092 Edwards, Alasdair J. **Fish and fisheries of Saint Helena Island**. Newcastle upon Tyne, University of Newcastle, Centre for Tropical Coastal Management Studies for Education Department, St. Helena, 1990. viii, 152pp. + 24 col. plates. illus. maps. (Includes detailed guide to 64 spp.)

2093 Edwards, Alasdair J. & Glass, Christopher W. 'The fishes of St. Helena Island, South Atlantic Ocean, 1: the shore fishes', *Journal of natural history*, 21, 1983, 617-686 (Lists 81 spp.); '2, the pelagic fishes', *ibid.*, 1367-1394 (Lists 53 spp.)

2094 McCulloch, Neil. **A guide to the birds of St. Helena and Ascension Island**. Sandy, Royal Society for the Protection of Birds (RSPB), 2004. 92pp. col. illus. (Describes and illustrates the 28 spp. "likely to be seen". Review, *BABC*, 12, 2005, 174-175)

2095 Musée royal de l'Afrique centrale. **La faune terrestre de l'Île de Sainte-Hélène**. Tervuren, 1970-1977. (Annales, sciences zoologiques, 181, 192, 215, 220). 4 vols.

2096 Rowlands, Beau. **Birds of St. Helena: an annotated checklist** . Tring, British Ornithologists' Union, 1998. (BOU Checklist, 16). 290pp. 50 col. photos. (Definitive work including a systematic list of all spp. reliably recorded on the island. Reviews, *BABC*, 6, 1999, 69-70; *Ibis*, 141, 1999, 162)

2097 Van Ryssen, W.J. **The birds of the Tristan da Cunha group and Gough Island**. Cape Town, University of Cape Town, Board of Extra-Mural Studies, 1976. 31pp.

Botany

2098 Clifton, Richard T.F. **St. Helena: a highly critical flora**: includes endemic and indigenous ferns, grasses, flowering plants. 2nd ed. Dover, The Geraniaceae Group, 1997. 198pp. - - Orig. pub. Dover, 1995. 96pp.

2099 Cronk, Quentin C.B. **The endemic flora of St. Helena**. Oswestry, Anthony Nelson, 2000. 119pp. + 25 col. plates. illus. (Descriptions and illus. of all endemic plants, discussing origins, history and present day conservation)

2100 Henry, P.W.T. **Forestry on St. Helena**. Tolworth, Directorate of Overseas Survey, 1974. (Land resource repoort, 2). 160pp.

2101 Wace, Nigel M. & Dickson, J.H. 'The terrestrial botany of the Tristan da Cunha Islands', *Philosophical transactions of the Royal Society*, series B, 249, 1965, 273-360 (Includes systematic list of native and introduced plants)

FRANCOPHONE WEST AFRICA

Including general works on the SAHARA and the SAHEL which frequently cover Mali and Mauritania and sometimes Niger

HANDBOOKS

2102 Afrique occidentale française: l'encyclopédie coloniale et maritime (Encyclopédie de l'empire français). Paris, Encyclopédie coloniale et maritime, 1949. 2 vols. Vol. 1. L'histoire et la géographie; la structure politique et administrative; économique. ix, 390, iiipp. 178 photos. 34 maps; vol. 2. Économique (contd.); l'équipement; tourisme et chasse; les arts et les lettres. Index. ii, 400, xpp. 244 photos. 24 maps. (Comp."sous la direction d'Eugène Guernier" with over 50 named contributors. Detailed scholarly coverage. For the encyclopaedia as a whole, *see* **54**).

2103 Afrique occidentale francaise [et le] Togo. [2nd ed]. Paris, Hachette, 1968. (Les guides bleus). ccxliv, 542pp. illus. maps. (Reprint of the 1958 edition with a 32pp. suppl. of updated information. Includes detailed essays on geography, economy, history etc. by scholars under the direction of Professor Théodore Monod of IFAN, followed by sections on each country). - - Orig. pub. Paris, 1958, ccxliv, 542pp.

2104 De Lavergne de Tressan, M. **Inventaire linguistique de l'Afrique occidentale française et du Togo.** Dakar, IFAN, 1953. (Mémoires de l'IFAN, 30). 241pp. 9 maps. Reprinted, Amsterdam, Swets & Zeitlinger, 1972. (Classification of languages with estimates of numbers of speakers and their location. Some account of neighbouring Anglophone and Lusophone areas. Reviews, *Africa*, 25, 1955, 190-191; *African affairs*, 53, 1954, 349-350).

2105 G.B. Admiralty. Naval Intelligence Division. **French West Africa.** London, 1943-1944. (Geographical handbook series, B.R. 512, B.R. 512ᵃ). 2 vols. 211 illus. 141 maps. (Vol. 1, The federation; vol. 2, The colonies including Togo. Detailed, wide-ranging coverage)

2106 Mauny, Raymond. **Glossaire des expressions et termes locaux employés dans l'Ouest africain.** Dakar, IFAN, 1952. 69pp. (In the vocabulary of the French community)

2107 Meillassoux, Claude. **Cartes historiques d'Afrique occidentale (Sénégal et Haut-Sénégal-Niger), 1802-1899, extraites du fonds des Archives nationales d'outre-mer.** Paris, Société des Africanistes, 1969. iiipp. 13 facsimile maps in portfolio.

2108 Person, Yves. **Cartes historiques de l'Afrique Manding (fin du 19e siècle)**. Paris, Centres de recherches africaines, 1990. 45 loose sheets in portfolio. (To accompany the author's **Samori: une revolution Dyula**. Dakar, IFAN, 1968-1975. 3 vols. Maps at scales from 1:200,000 up to 1:2.5M showing the Samorian Empire, covering modern Guinea and Côte d'Ivoire; also early French colonization in West Africa in the 1890s)

2109 Reichhold, Walter. **Französisch-Westafrika**. Bonn, K. Schroeder for Deutsche Afrika-Gesellschaft, 1958. (Die Länder Afrikas, 7). 80pp. (General survey to complement the vols. in the series for individual countries)

2110 Richard-Molard, Jacques. **Afrique occidentale française**. 3rd ed. Paris, Berger-Levrault, 1956. (L'Union française). xiv, 252pp. illus. maps. (Author was head of Section géographique at IFAN. General survey with sections for geography, peoples, history and the economy). - - Orig. pub. Paris, 1949. xiv, 239pp ; - - 2nd ed. Paris, 1952. xiv, 240pp.

2111 Spitz, Georges. **L'ouest africain français: A.O.F. et Togo**. Paris, Société d'éditions géographiques, maritimes et coloniales, 1947. (Terres lointaines, 2). 508pp. illus. maps. (Author was a colonial governor in West Africa. Pp. 17-422, A.O.F.; pp. 423-484, Togo. Detailed accounts of topography, peoples, history, administration, natural resources, agriculture, industry and commerce. Bibliography and 5 page list of maps)

YEARBOOKS

2112 **Annuaire des Républiques de l'Ouest africain**. Paris, Diloutremer, 1960-?1965. Annual. Incorporated into **Guid'Ouest africain**, *see* **2114** (Excludes Cameroon and Togo.)

2113 **Annuaire Noria. Guide économique Afrique occidentale française, Togo, Cameroun**. Paris, Larose, 1948-1962. Annual. Title varies: **Annuaire Noria de l'Afrique occidentale française** (1948-1950). Merged with **Annuaire Noria: Afrique noire: guide économique** (*see* **297**)

2114 **Guid'Ouest africain, 1947/48-** . Dakar, Agence Havas & Agence distribution de Presse/Paris, Diloutremer, 1948- ?1972/73. Annual/Every 2 yrs. Latest issue traced is for 1972/73 at Stanford. Title varies: **Guid'AOF ; l'AOF cercle par cercle** (1948-1958/59). (Excludes Cameroon for which *see* **Guid' Cameroun, 2239**. 400+ pp. per issue. Sections for each country. Political, historical and administrative information, lists of societies and commercial directory. Numerous maps and town plans)

STATISTICS

2115 A.O.F. Haut Commission. **Bulletin de la statistique générale de l'Afrique occidentale française**. Dakar, 1946-1956. 6 p.a. From 1956 merged with **2117**.

2116 A.O.F. Service de la statistique générale [etc.]. **Annuaire statistique de l'Afrique occidentale française, 1933/34** [etc.]. Dakar, 1936-1957. 6 issues. (Issue 1, 1936; 2, 1937; 3, 1939; 4, 1949-51; 5, 1955; 6, 1957)

2117 A.O.F. Service de la statistique générale [etc.]. **Bulletin mensuel de statistiques**. Dakar, 1949-1960. Title and name of issuing agency vary: **Bulletin économique mensuel** (August 1949-April 1954); **Bulletin statistique et économique mensuel** (May 1954-June 1960). Issues for July 1959-June 1960 pub. by Service fédéral de la statistique, Fédération du Mali. *Continued by* **Bulletin statistique et économique mensuel** issued by Service de la statistique, Sénégal , *see* **2472**.

2118 A.O.F. Service de la statistique générale [etc.]. **Bulletin statistique trimestriel/bimestriel**. St. Louis, 1953-1960. Quarterly/6 p.a. Vol. for 1959 issued by Service fédéral de la statistique générale, Fédération du Mali et République du Sénégal. Vol. for 1960 issued by Ministère du développement, Sénégal. After 1960 merged into **Bulletin statistique et économique mensuel** issued by Service de la Statistique, Sénégal, *see* **2472**.

2119 Banque centrale des états de l'Afrique de l'ouest. **Notes d'information et statistiques**. Dakar, 1956- . Monthly. Issues for 2003 recorded by CCFR. (Each issue highlights two or more member countries and includes detailed economic statistics)

2120 L'économie des pays du Sahel: Haute-Volta, Mali, Mauritanie, Niger, Sénégal, Tchad. Paris, Ediafric-La documentation africaine, 1976, 1978. 2 vols. (Pub. as special numbers of *Bulletin de l'Afrique noire*. Alternative title **Le dossier Sahel**)

DIRECTORIES OF ORGANIZATIONS

2121 Conseil de l'entente. Programme d'assistance aux entreprises africaines. **Répertoire des centres de documentation et bibliothèques: Bénin, Côte d'Ivoire, Haute-Volta, Niger, Togo**. Abidjan, 1980. 257pp.

BIOGRAPHICAL SOURCES

2122 Personnalités publiques de l'Afrique de l'ouest : Côte d'Ivoire, Haute-Volta, Mali, Mauritanie, Niger, Sénégal, Togo, 1971. 3rd ed. Paris, Ediafric-La documentation africaine, 1971. 428pp. - - Orig. pub. ... **1968.** Paris, 1969. 299pp. - -2nd ed. ... **1969.** Paris, 1970. 428pp. (Issued as special issues of *Bulletin de l'Afrique noire*. Each ed. contains some 2,500/3,000 brief biographies)

ATLASES & GAZETTEERS

2123 Atlas de l'Afrique du nord et saharienne: Maroc, Tunisie, Algérie, Libye, Mauritanie, Mali, Niger, Tchad. Evreux, Editions Atlas, 2000. 1 CD-ROM

2124 Cartes ethno-démographiques de l'Afrique occidentale, comp. Jacques Richard-Molard et al. Dakar, IFAN, 1952-1963. 30pp. text + 12 sheets. 97 x 65cm folded to 28 x 23 cm or smaller, in 4 folders + index map. (Each on 2 sheets. 1, Carte démographique d'Afrique occidentale; 2, Carte ethnique; Carte démographique; 3-4; Ethnographie; Demographie; 5, Carte des groupes ethniques de l'Afrique occidentale)

2125 Flutre, Louis-Fernand. **Pour une étude de la toponymie de l'AOF.** Dakar, IFAN, 1957. (Publications de la Section de Langues et Littéraires, 1). 188pp. (Discusses general problems of the region's toponymy, examines sources available and looks at the characteristics of place-names of European, Arab, Berber and African origin. Cites some 1,650 etymologies)

See also **1758**

EARTH SCIENCES

2126 Atlas agroclimatique des pays de la zone du CILSS. Niamey, Comité permanent inter-états de lutte contre la sécheresse dans le Sahel (CILSS), 1992. 11 vols. 30 cm. Vol. 1. Notice et commentaire, by Robert Morel; vols. 2-3. Pluviométrie, période 1950-1967; vols. 4-5. Pluviométrie, période 1951-1980; vols. 6-7, Pluviométrie, période 1968-1985; vol. 8. Températures, vent, humidité, evaporation; vol. 9. Cartes pluviométriques; vol. 10. Cartes climatiques; vol. 11. Cartes bilan hydrique des cultures.

2127 Barrère, Jean & Slansky, Maurice. **Notice explicative de la carte géologique au 2,000,000e de l'Afrique occidentale**. Paris, Bureau de

Recherches géologiques et minières (BRGM), 1965. (Mémoires, 29). viii, 120pp. (Map issued by the Bureau, 1960, on 9 sheets)

2128 Fabre, Jean, ed. **Géologie du Sahara occidental et central**. Tervuren, Musée royal de l'Afrique centrale, 2005. 572pp. illus. (Includes Chad, Côte d'Ivoire, Mali, Mauritania, Niger)

2129 Furon, Raymond. **Le Sahara: géologie, resources minerales**. 2nd ed. Paris, Payot, 1964. 313pp. illus. maps. - - Orig. pub. Paris, 1958. 300pp.

BIOLOGICAL SCIENCES

2130 Bousquet, Bernard. **Guide des parcs nationaux d'Afrique**: Afrique du Nord, Afrique de l'Ouest. Neuchâtel, Delachaux et Niestlé, 1992. 368pp. illus. maps. (Covers Francophone countries of the two regions)

2131 Durand, J.R. & Lévêque, Christian. **Flore et faune aquatiques de l'Afrique sahélo-soudanienne**. Paris, ORSTOM, 1980-1981.2 vols. xii, 873pp. illus. maps. (Vol. 1 covers plants, protozoa, molluscs etc.; vol. 2 covers insects, fish, amphibians, reptiles, birds and mammals)

Zoology

2132 Bigourdan, Jacques & Prunier, Roger. **Les mammifères sauvages de l'ouest africain et leur milieu**. Paris, Lechevalier, 1945. (Encyclopédie biologique). 367pp. 32 plates. 20 maps. - - Orig. pub. Paris, 1937.

2133 Le Berre, Michel. **Faune du Sahara**. Paris, Lechevalier, 1989-1990. (Terres africaines). 2 vols. Vol. 1, Poissons, amphibiens, reptiles; vol. 2, Mammifères. (Vol. 3 for birds never pub.)

2134 Villiers, André. **Les serpents de l'ouest africain**. 4th ed. Dakar, Université Cheikh Anta Diop, IFAN, 2005. (Initiations et études africaines, 2). 205pp. 307 illus. - - Orig. pub. Dakar, 1950. 148pp. (Review, *African affairs*, 50, 1951, 81-83); - - 2nd ed. Dakar, 1963. 190pp; - - 3rd ed. Dakar, 1975. 195pp.

2135 Villiers, André. **Tortues et crocodiles de l'Afrique noire francaise**. Dakar, IFAN, 1958. (Initiations africaines, 15). 354pp. illus

Botany

2136 Aubréville, André. **La flore forestière soudano-guinéenne (AOF – Cameroun - AEF)**. Paris, Société d'éditions géographiques, maritimes et coloniales for ORSTOM, 1950. 523pp. 115 plates. 40 maps. Reprinted, Nogent-sur-Marne, Centre technique de forestier tropical, 1975. (Covers forest, woodland and tree savanna zones of west and central Africa. Includes some distribution maps).

2137 Aubréville, André. **La forêt coloniale: les forêts de l'Afrique occidentale française**. Paris, Société d'éditions géographiques, maritimes et coloniales, 1938. 244pp. + 18 plates. illus. maps.

2138 Baumer, Michel. **Arbres, arbustes et arbrisseaux nourriciers en Afrique occidentale**. Dakar, Enda-Editions, 1995. (Série études et recherches, 168/170). 260pp.

2139 Chevalier, Auguste. **Flore vivante de L'Afrique occidentale Française. Vol. 1**. Paris, Muséum national d'histoire naturelle, 1938. xxxii, 360pp. illus. No more pub. (Covers Togo, Cameroun, Oubangui-Chari-Tchad, Sahara Francais).

2140 Geerling, Chris. **Guide de terrain des ligneux sahéliens et soudano-guinéens**. 2nd ed. Wageningen, Agricultural University, 1988. iv, 340pp. + 92 plates. illus. maps. - - Orig. pub. as **Ligneux sahéliens et soudano-guinéens**. Wageningen, 1982. iv, 340pp. (Illustrated guide to woody plants, with cross-refs. to **Flora of West tropical Africa**, *see* **1795**)

2141 Maydell, Hans-Jürgen von. **Trees and shrubs of the Sahel: their characteristics and uses**. Eschborn, Deutsches Gesellschaft für Technische Zusammenarbeit (GTZ), 1986. 525pp. illus. Updated Eng. trans. of **Arbres et arbustes du Sahel: leurs characteristiques et leurs utilization**. Eschborn, 1983. 531pp. - - Orig. pub. in German as **Baum- und Straucharten der Sahelzone, &c.** Eschborn, 1981. (Practical colour-guide to woody plants)

2142 Normand, Didier. **Manuel d'identification des bois commerciaux**. Nogent-sur-Marne, Centre technique forestier tropical, 1972. 2 vols. Vol. 1, Généralities; vol. 2, Afrique guinéo-congolaise. 335pp. illus.

2143 Ozenda, Paul. **Flore et végétation du Sahara**. 3rd ed. Paris, CNRS, 1991. 662pp. illus. Reprinted Paris, 2004. Corrected reissue of 2nd ed. with 40pp. suppl. (Covers from Atlantic to 20° E and from Maghreb south to 18/20°N, the approximate northern limit of **Flora of West tropical Africa** *see* **1795**). - - Orig. pub. as **Flore du Sahara septentrional et central**. Paris, 1958. 486pp; - - 2nd ed. **Flore du Sahara**. Paris, 1977. 622pp.

2144 Quézel, Pierre. **La végétation du Sahara, du Tchad à la Maurétanie**. Stuttgart, Gustav Fischer/Paris, Masson, 1965. (Geobotanica selecta, 2).

333pp. (Review, *GJ*, 133, 1967, 536, "monumental comprehensiveness").
- - Léonard, J. **Noms de plantes et de groupements végétaux cités dans Pierre Quézel, *La vegetation du Sahara* ...** Meise, Jardin Botanique National de Belge, 1980. 45pp.

2145 Roberty, Guy. **Petite flore de l'ouest-africain.** Paris, ORSTOM, 1954. 441pp. (Covers the more important spp. in Burkina Faso, Côte d'Ivoire, Guinea, Mali, Senegal)

2146 Schnell, Raymond. **Forêt dense: introduction à l'étude botanique de la région forestière d'Afrique occidentale, avec clefs de détermination pour les principales espèces arborescentes.** Paris, P. Lechevalier, 1951. vii, 331pp. illus.

2147 Tardieu-Blot, M.L. **Les ptéridophytes de l'Afrique intertropicale française.** Dakar, IFAN, 1953. (Mémoires, 28). 241pp. illus. (Covers Francophone West and Central Africa)

BENIN

Gouvernement de la République du Bénin http://www.gouv.bj/
(Available in English at http://www.gouv.bj/en/index.php)

HANDBOOKS

2148 Akindele, Adolphe & Aguessy, Cyrille. **Le Dahomey**. Paris, Société d'éditions géographiques, maritimes et coloniales, 1955. (Pays africain, 6). 126pp. illus. maps.

2149 Atlas sociolinguistique du Bénin. Abidjan, ACCT for Bénin Commission nationale de linguistique, 1983. (Atlas et études sociolinguistiques des états du Conseil de l'entente). 125pp.

2150 Ceccaldi, Pierrette. **Essai de nomenclature des populations, langues et dialectes de la République populaire du Bénin**. Paris, École des hautes études en sciences sociales, Centre d'études africaines, CARDAN, 1979. 2 vols. 328pp. (Reproduces card file of peoples and languages maintained at CARDAN, with details of relationships, references from alternative names, geographical locations, size of population/speakers, bibliographical sources)

2151 France. Direction de la documentation. **La République du Dahomey**. Paris, 1966. (*Notes et études documentaires*, 3307, 8 July 1966). 41pp.

2152 Gavrilov, N.I. et al. **Narodnaia Respublika Benin: spravochnik**. Moscow, Akademiia nauk, Institut Afriki, 1989. 190pp. illus.

2153 Glélé, Maurice A. **La République du Dahomey**. Paris, Berger-Levrault, 1969. (Encyclopédie politique et constitutionnelle. Série Afrique). 76pp.

2154 Historical dictionary of Benin. 3rd ed. comp. Samuel Decalo. Lanham, MD, Scarecrow Press, 1995. (African historical dictionaries, 61). xxxiii, 564pp. - - Orig. pub. as **Historical dictionary of Dahomey (People's Republic of Benin)**. Metuchen, NJ, 1976. (African historical dictionaries, 7). xii, 201pp. (Review, *Africana J.*, 10, 1979, 120-128); - - 2nd ed. Metuchen, NJ, 1987. (African historical dictionaries, 7). xxvii, 349pp. (Rated "good", Balay, 1996)

2155 Zimmer, Balduin. **Dahomey**. Bonn, K. Schroeder for Deutsche Afrika-Gesellschaft, 1969. (Die Länder Afrikas, 39). 94pp.

YEARBOOKS

2156 Annuaire des entreprises commerciales et industrielles du Bénin. Cotonou, Ministère du commerce et du tourisme, 1993- .

2157 Répertoire des opérateurs économiques. Cotonou, Chambre de commerce et d'industrie du Bénin, 2001- . Annual. Succeeds **Répertoire économique du Bénin.** Cotonou, 1996/97-2000.

STATISTICS

2158 Benin. Institut national de la statistique [etc.] **Annuaire statistique.** Cotonou, 1973- . Annual (irreg). Vol. 5-10, 1975-1992 ; vols, 11-17, 1997-2003 in NWU. *Continues* Dahomey. Institut national de la statistique et de l'analyse économique [etc.]. **Annuaire statistique.** Cotonou, 1967-1973. 4 vols

2159 Benin. Institut national de la statistique [etc.] **Bulletin de statistique.** Cotonou, 1966-84; n.s.1985- . Irreg. Latest issues in NWU are for 2002. *Continues* Dahomey. Service de la statistique générale. **Bulletin statistique du Dahomey.** Cotonou, 1953-1960. Monthly (irreg.); Dahomey. Direction des affaires économiques. **Bulletin économique et statistique.** Cotonou, 1960-1965. Irreg

2160 Benin. Institut national de la statistique [etc.]. **Revue statistique et économique de l'INSAE.** Cotonou, 2001- Quarterly.

2161 Le Bénin en chiffres. Cotonou, Université nationale du Bénin, Faculté des sciences agronomiques, Département économie et sociologie rurales, 1994- . ?Every 2 years. NWU has issue for 1994 only

2162 Country profile: Benin. London, Economist Intelligence Unit, 2003- . Annual. *Continues in part* **Country profile: Togo, Benin** . London, 1986-2003.

2163 Germany. Statistisches Bundesamt. **Statistik des Auslandes: Länderberichte: Benin** (later **Länderbericht: Benin**). Wiesbaden/Stuttgart, Metzler-Poetschel, 1984- . Irreg. Issues for 1984, 1986, 1988, 1990, 1994.

2164 IMF. **Benin: selected issues and statistical appendix**. Washington, DC, 2004. (Country report, 04/370). 99pp. - - Earlier eds. (title varies) 1995 (Staff country report, 95/55); 1998 (Staff country report, 98/88); 2002 (Country report 02/164). Full text of reports from 1997 also available online, *see* **334**.

DIRECTORIES OF ORGANIZATIONS

2165 **Dossier Bénin**. Paris, Rencontres africaines, 1987. 225pp.

2166 **Répertoire culturel, le Bénin**. Paris, ACCT, 1983. (Inventaire des activités, etc. des pays membres de l'ACCT). 80pp. illus.

2167 **Répertoire des chercheurs et scientifiques du Bénin**, comp. Centre béninois de la recherche scientifique et technique. Cotonou, Mission française de coopération et d'action culturelle, 1994. 201pp.

BIOGRAPHICAL SOURCES

2168 **Assemblée nationale du Bénin: première et deuxième législatures: 1991-1999**, comp. Friedrich-Naumann-Stiftung. Cotonou, Editions ONEPI/ *La Nation*, [c1995]. 193pp. illus.

2169 Institut de recherches appliquées du Dahomey (IRAD). **Dictionnaire bio-bibliographique du Dahomey**. Porto-Novo, 1969- . Vol. 1, 1969. 183pp. illus. ?No more pub.

ATLASES & GAZETTEERS

2170 **Atlas cartographique de la région sud du Bénin**. Cotonou, Société nationale de gestion immobilière (SONAGIM), 1985. 25pp. 32 x 46 cm. - - **Atlas cartographique de la région nord du Bénin**. Cotonou, Service d'études régionales d'habitat et d'aménagement urbain, 1992. 53pp. 43 cm.

2171 **Atlas cartographique des villes du Bénin**. Cotonou, Projet Plans d'urbanisme, 1983. 63pp. maps. 30 x 43cm

2172 **Atlas cartographique des villes secondaires du Bénin**. Cotonou, Société nationale de gestion immobilière (SONAGIM), 1987. n.p. 32 x 47 cm

2173 Atlas monographique des circonscriptions administratives du Bénin, comp. PLANURBA. Cotonou, Ministère de l'intérieur, de la sécurité et de l'administration territoriale (MISAT), Direction de l'administration territoriale et des collectivités (DATC), [1997]. 1 vol. (var. pagings)

2174 Beaudet, M. et al. 'Chronique ethnographique: origine des noms de villages', *Études dahoméennes*, 8, 1952, 57-88 (By administrative regions)

2175 U.S. Board on Geographic Names. **Dahomey: official standard names approved by the USBGN.** Washington, DC, 1965. (Gazetteer, 91). iv, 89pp. (Includes 6,250 names from 1:200,000 map series. Revision of appropriate sections of **West Africa**, *see* **1758**)

BIOLOGICAL SCIENCES

2176 Adjanohoun, Edouard J. **Contribution aux études ethnobotaniques et floristiques en République populaire du Bénin**. Paris, ACCT, 1989. (Médicine traditionelle et pharmacopée). v, 895pp. illus.

2177 De Souza, Simone. **Flore du Bénin**. Cotonou, Université Nationale du Bénin, 1987-88. 3 vols. Vol. 1. Catalogue des plantes du Bénin; vol. 2. Plantes du bord de mer et de mangrove; vol. 3. Noms des plantes dans les langues nationales béninoises. (A major new work, **Flore analytique du Bénin**, ed. A. Akoegninou et al. Leiden, Backhuys, 2006. 1,034pp. 715 illus. is announced by the publishers)

See also **2450**

BURKINA FASO

Site officiel du Premier Ministère du Burkina Faso
http://www.primature.gov.bf/

HANDBOOKS

2178 Breusers, Mark & Grumiau, Caroline. **Burkina Faso: mensen, politiek, economie, cultuur**. Amsterdam, Koninklijk Instituut voor de Tropen/The Hague, Novib, 2002. (Landenreeks). 74pp. illus. maps.

2179 Fischer, Wilhelm. **Ober-Volta**. Bonn, K. Schroeder for Deutsche Afrika-Gesellschaft, 1962. (Die Länder Afrikas, 26). 142pp. illus. map.

2180 France. Direction de la documentation. **La République de Haute-Volta**. Paris, 1960. (*Notes et études documentaires*, 2693, 19 Aug. 1960). 64pp.

2181 Historical dictionary of Burkina Faso (former Upper Volta). 2nd ed., comp. Daniel Miles McFarland & Lawrence A. Rupley. Lanham, MD, Scarecrow Press, 1998. (African historical dictionaries, 74). lxxvii, 279pp. (Review, *ARD*, 84, 2000, 83-90). - - Orig. pub. as **Historical dictionary of Upper Volta (Haute Volta)**, comp. Daniel Miles McFarland. Metuchen, NJ, 1978. (African historical dictionaries, 14). xxi, 217pp. (Review, *IJAHS*, 11, 1978, 560-561, "only reference work currently available in English". Rated "fair", Balay, 1996)

2182 Lippens, Philippe. **La République de Haute-Volta**. Paris, Berger-Levrault, 1972. (Encyclopédie politique et constitutionnelle. Série Afrique). 62pp.

2183 Sanou, Salaka. **La littérature burkinabé: l'histoire, les hommes, les œuvres**. Limoges, Presses universitaires de Limoges (PULIM), 2000. (Collection francophonie). 220pp. (Encyclopedic work with biographies of authors)

2184 Tiendrebeogo, Gérard. **Situation des langues parlées en Haute-Volta, perspectives de leur utilisation pour l'enseignement et l'alphabétisation**. Abidjan, ACCT & Institut de linguistique appliqué, 1983. (Atlas et études sociolinguistiques des états du Conseil de l'entente). iii, 74pp. (Lists peoples and languages with references to their associated groups, and notes on location and numbers of speakers)

YEARBOOKS

2185 Faso rama: répertoire politique, administratif et economique du Burkina Faso. Ouagadougou, Ministère de la communication et de la culture & Zama Publicité, 1997- . Annual. Latest issue in NWU is for 1998/99.

2186 Le guide de l'homme d'affaires voltaïque. Ouagadougou, Société internationale d'entretien, de gestion et d'organisation, 1978. 76pp.

2187 Répertoire national de Haute Volta. Paris, Marcomer, 1963- . ?No more pub. (1963 ed. includes lists of the administration, of major official and private organizations and biographical section with some 350 brief entries)

2188 Répertoire national des entreprises. Ouagadougou, Chambre de commerce, d'industrie et d'artisanat du Burkina Faso, ?1986- . Annual. ALA notes issue for 1992

STATISTICS

2189 Burkina Faso. Institut national de la statistique et de la démographie [etc.]. **Annuaire statistique du Burkina Faso**. Ouagadougou, 1984- . Annual. Latest issue in NWU is for 1999. *Continues* Haute Volta/Burkina Faso. Institut national de la statistique et de la démographie [etc.]. **Bulletin annuaire d'information statistique et économique** [etc.]. Ouagadougou, 1959-1983. Annual. Pub. as suppl. to **Bulletin mensuel, 2190** below, sometimes separately, sometimes in last monthly issue for the year. Title varies frequently: **Bulletin annuaire statistique et économique/Bulletin mensuel ... ; supplément/Bulletin annuaire de statistique**.

2190 Burkina Faso [Haute Volta]. Institut national de la statistique et de la démographie [etc.]. **Bulletin [mensuel] d'information statistique et économique**. Ouagadougou, 1960- . Monthly (irreg.). Title varies: **Bulletin mensuel de statistique** (1960-1964). Not pub. 1965-1968. n.s. vol. 9, 1969- . NWU has issues up to 1997.

2191 Country profile: Burkina Faso. London, Economist Intelligence Unit, 2003- . Annual. *Continues in part* **Country profile: Niger, Burkina [Faso]** London, 1986-1996; **Country profile: Burkina Faso, Niger**. London, 1997-2002.

2192 L'économie voltaïque. Paris, Ediafric-La documentation africaine, 1971. 198pp. (Special number of *Bulletin de l'Afrique noire*. Statistical tables)

2193 Germany. Statistisches Bundesamt. **Statistik des Auslandes: Länderberichte: Burkina Faso** (later **Länderbericht: Burkina Faso**). Wiesbaden/Stuttgart, Metzler-Poetschel, 1962- . Irreg. Issues for 1962, 1984, 1988, 1992

2194 IMF. **Burkina Faso: selected issues and statistical appendix**. Washington, DC, 2005. (Country report, 05/358). 95pp. - - Earlier eds. (title varies) 1996 (Staff country report, 96/5); 1997 (Staff country report, 97/14); 1999 (Staff country report, 99/57); 2002 (Country report, 02/93); 2003 (Country report, 03/198). Full text of reports from 97/101, 1997 also available online, *see* **334**.

ATLASES & GAZETTEERS

2195 Atlas de Haute Volta. Ouagadougou, Centre nationale de la recherche scientifique et technologie (*later* Centre voltaïque de la recherche), 1968-[1975]. 3 vols. ?No more pub. (Vol. 1. 1968. Carte provisoire des densités de populations, by Georges Savonnet. 16 maps at 1:1M; vol. 2. 1973. Cartes provisoires des principaux éléments climatiques, by Jean Renard. 11 maps; vol. 3. 1975. Essai d'evaluation de la végétation ligneuse, by Marin Terrible. 71pp. + 1 map at 1:1M. Vols 1 and 2 issued in portfolios)

2196 Atlas des villages de Haute Volta: cartes de localisation des villages par district de recensement: recensement général de la population, déc. 1975. Ouagadougou, Ministère du plan et de la coopération, Institut national de la statistique et de la demographie, 1982. 52 maps in portfolio. (Scale 1:200,000)

2197 Atlas du Burkina Faso.[5th ed.]. Paris, Éditions Jaguar, 2005. 115pp. - - Orig. pub. as **Atlas de la Haute-Volta**, comp. Yves Péron & Victoire Zalacain. Paris, *Jeune Afrique*, 1975. 48pp; - - 2nd ed. **Atlas du Burkina Faso**, comp. Ouétian Bougnounou. Paris, 1993. 54pp; - - 3rd ed. rev. Anne Lerebours Pigeonnière & S. Jomni. Paris, Éditions Jaguar, 1998. 62pp; - - 4th ed. rev. Anne Lerebours Pigeonnière & M.T. Ménage. Paris, 2001. 62pp. - - English trans. **Burkino Faso atlas**. 2nd ed. Paris, *Jeune Afrique*, 2001. 62pp. (Trans. of 4th French ed.). - - Orig. pub. Paris, 1998. 62pp. (Trans. of 3rd French ed.)

2198 U.S. Board on Geographic Names. **Upper Volta: official standard names approved by the USBGN**. Washington, DC, 1965. (Gazetteer, 87). iii, 168pp. (Includes 11,900 names from 1:200,000 map series. Rev. of appropriate sections of **West Africa**, *see* **1758**)

EARTH SCIENCES

2199 Hottin, Gabriel & Ouédraogo, O.F. **Notice explicative de la carte géologique à 1:1,000,000 de la république de Haute-Volta**. Paris, Bureau de recherches géologiques et minières (BGRM), 1975. 58pp.

2200 Marchal, Monique. **Les paysages agraires de Haute-Volta: analyse structurale par la méthode graphique**. Paris, ORSTOM, 1983. (Atlas des structures agraires au sud du Sahara, 18). 115pp. + 20 folded maps in pocket.

2201 Pallier, Ginette. **Géographie générale de la Haute-Volta**. Limoges, Université de Limoges, 1978. 241pp. maps.

2202 Sagatsky, Y. **La géologie et les ressources minières de la Haute Volta méridionale**. Ouagadougou, Direction des mines et de la géologie, 1954. (Bulletin, 13). 224pp.

2203 Sattran, Vladimir et al. **Géologie du Burkina Faso**. Prague, Czech Geological Survey, 2002. 136pp. + 8pp. plates. illus. maps.

2204 Sivakumar, M. V. K. & Gnomou, Faustin. **Agroclimatology of West Africa: Burkina Faso**. Patancheru, Andhra Pradesh, International Crops Research Institute for the Semi-Arid Tropics, 1987. v, 192pp. illus. maps. (Principally tabular data for rainfall, temperatures, water balance)

BIOLOGICAL SCIENCES

Zoology

2205 Blanc, Maurice & Daget, Jacques. 'Les eaux et les poissons de Haute-Volta', *Mémoires de l'IFAN*, 1957, 95-168. illus. maps.

2206 Román, Benigno. **Les poissons des haut-bassins de la Volta**. Tervuren, Musée royal de l'Afrique centrale, 1966. (*Annales, sciences zoologiques*, 150). 191pp. illus. map.

2207 Román, Benigno. **Serpents de Haute-Volta**. Ouagadougou, Centre national de recherche scientifique et technologique (CNRST), 1980. 129pp. illus. maps.

Botany

2208 Fontès, J. & Guinko, S. **Carte de la végétation et de l'occupation du sol du Burkina Faso: notice explicative**. Toulouse, Ministère de la coopération, 1995. 66pp. tables. maps.

2209 Lebrun, Jean-Pierre et al. **Catalogue des plantes vasculaires du Burkina Faso**. Maisons-Alfort, IEMVT, 1991. (Études et synthèses, 40). 341pp. (Covers 1,204 spp.)

2210 Terrible, Marin. **Atlas de Haute-Volta: essai de valuation de la végétation ligneuse**. Bobo-Dioulasso, Centre voltaïque de la recherche scientifique (CVRS), 1975. 71pp. (Includes loose map 'Arbres et arbustes' at 1:1M)

2211 Terrible, Marin. **Végétation de la Haute-Volta au millioniène: carte et notes provisiores**. Ouagadougou, Bobo-Dioulasso, 1978. ii, 40pp. Map at 1:1M.

2212 Toutain, Bernard. **Inventaire floristique du Sahel de Haute-Volta, et du Nord du pays Gourmantche: écologie des plantes, noms vernaculaires, intérêt fourrager; avec un guide de reconnaissance des plantules de quelques espèces sahéliennes**. Maisons-Alfort, IEMVT, 1978. 122pp. illus.

CAMEROON

See also sections relating to **Former German Africa** in the section for **Africa in general** above, and note that many French language reference sources treat Cameroon as a part of Central Africa, and will be listed above under **Central Africa: Francophone**.

Site officiel des services du P.M.: portail du gouvernement
http://www.spm.gov.cm/ (English version available)

HANDBOOKS

2213   Area handbook for the United Republic of Cameroon, comp. Harold D. Nelson et al. Washington, DC, U.S. Department of Defense, 1974. xiv, 335pp. maps.

2214   Atlas administratif des langues nationales du Cameroun, comp. Roland J.L. Breton & Bikia G. Fohtung. Paris, ACCT/Yaoundé, Centre régional de recherche et de documentation sur les traditions orales etc., 1991. 143pp.

2215   Cameroon. Yaoundé, Cameroon. Ministry of Information & Tourism/Paris, Presse Africaine Associée, 1970. 189pp. (General popular survey in English)

2216   Cameroun, Togo: encyclopédie de l'afrique française (Encyclopédie coloniale et maritime). Paris, Éditions de l'Union française, 1951. iii, 572, ixpp. 420 photos. 48 maps. ("Sous la direction d'Eugène Guernier, avec la participation de René Briat ". Pp. 1-388, Cameroun; pp. 389-572, Togo, each following the same sequence of 'Le cadre naturel, historique et humain'; 'la structure politique et administrative'; 'le progrès social'; 'le progrès economique'; 'l'équipment; tourisme, chasse, folklore'; 'l'oeuvre des missions'. The usual detailed coverage provided by all vols. of this encyclopaedia, *see* **54**)

2117   L'encyclopédie de la République unie du Cameroun. Abidjan, etc., Nouvelles éditions africaines, 1981. 4 vols. illus. (Vol. 1, Le milieu et les hommes; vol. 2, L'histoire et l'état; vol. 3, L'économie; vol. 4, La vie de la nation. Numerous illustrations)

2218   Fonkoué, Jean. Essai de nomenclature des populations et de langues du Cameroun. Paris, École de hautes études en sciences sociales & Centre d'études africaines, CARDAN, 1981. 2 vols. viii, 243pp. maps.

(Reproduces card files maintained at CARDAN arranged by preferred name of ethnic group or language, with references from other forms, location and numbers)

2219   France. Direction de la documentation. **La République du Cameroun**. Paris, 1961. (*Notes et études documentaires*, 2741, 16 Jan 1961). 56pp.

2220   France. Ministère de la coopération. **Cameroun: guide d'information, novembre 1996**. Paris, 1996. (Collection guides d'information). 82pp.

2221   Gonidec, Pierre-François & Breton, J.-M. **La République unie du Cameroun**. 2nd ed. Paris, Berger-Levrault, 1976. (Encyclopédie politique et constitutionnelle. Série Afrique). 77pp. - - Orig. pub. Paris, 1969. 88pp.

2222   Historical dictionary of the Republic of Cameroon. 3rd ed, comp. Mark W. DeLancey & Mark Dike. Lanham, MD, Scarecrow Press, 2000. (African historical dictionaries, 81). xxvii, 359pp. (Reviews, *African affairs*, 100, 2001, 668-670; *IJAHS*, 34, 2001, 248-249). - - Orig. pub. as **Historical dictionary of Cameroon**, comp. Victor T. Le Vine & Roger P. Nye. Metuchen, NJ, 1974. (African historical dictionaries, 1). 210pp; - - 2nd ed. comp. Mark W. DeLancey & H. Mbella Mokeba. Metuchen, NJ, 1990. (African historical dictionaries, 48). xxii, 297pp. (Rated "good", Balay, 1996)

2223   Kuczynski, Robert René. **The Cameroons and Togoland: a demographic study**. London, Oxford University Press for the Royal Institute of International Affairs, 1939. 579pp. maps. (Comp. at the request of Lord Hailey and the African Research Survey, *see* **14**. Analyses all population statistics from initial colonization to the contemporary. Sections for the German, British and French Cameroons and Togo)

2224   Lembezat, Bertrand. **Le Cameroun**. 3rd ed. Paris, Éditions maritimes et coloniales, 1954. (Terres lointaines, 1²). 208pp. illus. map. Eds. 1 and 2 published as **La France équatoriale**, *see* **1458**.

2225   Loginova V.P. **Obedinennaia Respublika Kamerun: spravochnik**. Moscow, Akademiia nauk, Institut Afriki, 1982. 268pp.

2226   Mbaku, John Mukum. **Culture and customs of Cameroon**. Westport, CT, Greenwood Press, 2005. (Culture and customs of Africa). xxiv, 236pp. illus. maps. (Covers history, religion, literature, art and architecture, social customs)

2227   Schramm, Josef. **Kamerun**. 3rd ed. Bonn, K. Schroeder for Deutsche Afrika-Gesellschaft, 1970. (Die Länder Afrikas, 9). 174pp. - - Orig. pub. comp. C. Weiler. Bonn, K. Schroeder for Deutsche Afrika-Gesellschaft, 1958. 120pp; - - 2nd ed. Bonn, 1964. 132pp.

2228   Seignobos, Christian & Tourneux, Henry. **Le Nord-Cameroun à travers ses mots: dictionnaire de terms anciens et modernes: province de l'Extrême-Nord**. Paris, IRD & Karthala, 2002. 334pp. (Collection of definitions of local terms)

2229   Situation   linguistique   en   Afrique   centrale: inventaire préliminaire: le Cameroun, ed. Michel Dieu & Patrick Renaud. Paris, ACCT/Yaoundé, Centre régional de recherche et de documentation sur les traditions orales, etc., 1983. (Atlas linguistique de l'Afrique centrale, ALAC). 475pp. maps. (Language atlas with various scales and detailed survey of language use)

2230   Tadadjeu, Maurice & Sadembouo, Étienne. **Alphabet général des langues camerounaises**. Yaoundé, Université de Yaoundé, 1984. (Collection Propelca, 1). 34, 31pp.

2231   Taguem Fah, G.L. **Cameroun 2001: politique, langues, économie et santé**. Paris, Harmattan, 2001. 178pp.

See also **1457, 1458, 1460**

YEARBOOKS

2232   Annuaire   des   entreprises   industrielles   et   commerciales   du Cameroun. Douala, Chambre de commerce, d'industrie et des mines du Cameroun, 1988- Annual. Latest issue in NWU is 1994.

2233   Annuaire du Cameroun. Douala, Agence africaine de publicité, 1952. 336pp. ?No more pub. (Very detailed, large format, double column compendium of historical, topographical, administrative and economic information, including commercial directory)

2234   Annuaire national/National year book. Douala, Ministère de l'information, 1963-?1993. Annual (irreg.) Not pub 1969 or 1972. NWU says ceased 1988, ALA records issue for 1993. Stanford has issues for 1968/69, 1971, 1973, 1975, 1980/81, 1986. (Directory of the administration and of commercial organizations, with some historical background).

2235 **Annuaire touristique et diplomatique du Cameroun**. Yaoundé, Editions Stella, ?1980- . 1980 issue recorded in LC catalogue.

2236 **Cameroon year book**, Limbe, Gwellem Publications, 1973- . Annual. Issues traced for 1973, 1974/75, 1985/86. (1985/86 ed. 270pp. contains c. 250 lengthy biographies)

2237 France. **Rapport du gouvernement français ... sur l'administration du Cameroun placé sous la tutelle de la France, 1920/21** [etc.]. Paris, 1922-1957. Annual. (Not pub. 1938-46. Presented initially to the League of Nations, then post 1946 to the Trusteeship Council of the United Nations. Detailed and well illus. Includes Annexe statistique)

2238 G.B. Colonial Office. **[Annual reports]: Cameroons, c.1917/21-1959**. London, 1922-1961. (As **Reports to the Council of the League of Nations on the British sphere**, c.1917/21, (Cmd.1647); **Reports on the British sphere**, 1922, **Report on the administration of the British Cameroons ...to the Council of the League of Nations,** [title varies], 1923-38, (not issued 1939-46), **Report ... to the Trusteeship Council of the UN**, 1947; **Report to the General Assembly of the UN**, 1948-59, (in Colonial series).

2239 **Guid' Cameroun**. Paris, Diloutremer, 1959-1964. Irreg. 3 issues for 1959, 1961, 1964. (Coverage of Cameroon then moves to the same publisher's **Guid' Afrique équatoriale**, *see* **1464**. Lists of government departments and other institutions and a commercial directory)

See also **1466**

STATISTICS

2240 Cameroon. Direction de la statistique [etc.] **Annuaire statistique du Cameroun**. Yaoundé, 1983- . Annual. Latest issue in NWU is for 1997/98.

2241 Cameroon. Direction de la statistique [etc.] **Bulletin mensuel de statistique**. Yaoundé, 1968- ? Monthly. SSL holds issues to 1984. *Continues* French Cameroon. Service de la statistique générale. **Bulletin de la statistique générale**. Yaoundé, 1950-1962. Monthly. Vols. 1-12; **Résumé des statistiques du Cameroun oriental**. Yaoundé, 1963-1967. Monthly. Vols. 1-5

2242 Cameroon. Direction de la statistique [etc.]. **Note annuelle de statistique**. Yaoundé, 1973- Annual. Latest issues in NWU are for 1997/98. (Abridged version published as **Le Cameroun en chiffres**)

2243 Cameroon. Direction de la statistique [etc.]. **Note trimestrielle sur la situation économique du Cameroun**. Yaoundé, 1964-1973. Quarterly. Title varies: **Note trimestrielle de statistique**.

2244 **Country profile: Cameroon**. London, Economist Intelligence Unit, 2003- . Annual. *Continues in part* **Country profile: Cameroon, CAR, Chad**. London, 1986-2002.

2245 **L'économie camerounaise**. Paris, Ediafric-La documentation africaine, 1973-1984. 5 issues for 1973, 1977, 1979, 1981, 1984. (Largely statistical)

2246 France. Ministère de la cooperation. Service des études économiques et questions internationales. **Cameroun: données statistiques sur les activités économiques, culturelles et sociales**. Paris, 1976. 205pp

2247 France. Service coloniale des statistiques/Cameroun. Service de la statistique générale. **Annuaire statistique du Cameroun**. Paris/Yaoundé, 1921-1939. Annual. *Continued by* vols. for 1938/45 (1947). 177pp ; 1946/57 (1959).

2248 Germany. Statistisches Bundesamt. **Statistik des Auslandes: Länderberichte: Kamerun** (later **Länderbericht: Kamerun**). Wiesbaden/ Stuttgart, Metzler-Poetschel, 1961- . Irreg. Issues for 1961, 1968, 1977, 1982, 1985, 1987, 1992, 1993.

2249 IMF. **Cameroon: statistical appendix**. Washington, DC, 2005. (Country report, 05/165). 61pp. - - Earlier eds. (title varies) 1995 (Staff country report, 95/05); 1996 (Staff country report, 96/125) ; 1998 (Staff country report, 98/17); 2000 (Country report, 00/81) ; 2002 (Country report, 02/257). Full text of reports from 1997 also available online, *see* **334**.

2250 Morel, Yves. **Tables économiques du Cameroun**. 2nd ed. Douala, Collège Libermann, 1978. 240pp. (147 tables of statistics, covering human resources, trade, communications, finance etc.). - - Orig. pub. as **Tableaux de l'économie du Cameroun**. Douala, 1978. 232pp.

2251 West Cameroon. Department of Statistics. **Monthly digest of statistics: West Cameroon**. Buea, 1965-?1972. (During the existence of the Cameroon Federal Republic (1961-1972), separate statistical series were issued for West Cameroon the former Southern Cameroons of the British mandate)

2252   West Cameroon. Department of Statistics. **Statistics annual report of West Cameroon/Annuaire statistique du Cameroun occidental, 1965/66 [-1968/69]**. Buea, 1967-1969. 2 issues for 1965/66-1966/67 (1967), 1968/69 (1969). *Continues* **West Cameroon digest of statistics/Résumé des statistiques du Cameroun occidental**. Buea, 1962-1965. Annual. Issues for 1955/62-1964/65.

See also **1453**

BIOGRAPHICAL SOURCES

2253   Belinga, Thérèse Baratte-Eno. **Écrivains, cinéastes et artistes camerounais: bio-bibliographie**. Yaoundé, Ministère de l'information et de la culture, 1978. 217pp. (93 entries)

2254   **Cameroun: les hommes de pouvoir; le guide permanant**. Paris, Indigo, 2000- . Updated 2 p.a.

2255   **Les élites camerounaises: qui est qui au Cameroun**. 3rd ed. Paris, Ediafric-La documentation africaine, 1987. 209pp. - - Orig. pub. Paris, 1976. xxxi, 233pp; - - 2nd ed. Paris, Ediafric-La documentation africaine, 1980. xxx, 254pp. (Pub. as special issues of *Bulletin de l'Afrique noire*. Over 1,700 brief biographies in 2nd ed.)

2256   Verdier, Isabelle. **Cameroun: 100 hommes de pouvoir**. Paris, Indigo, 1997. 238pp.

See also **1471**, **2236**

ATLASES & GAZETTEERS

2257   **Atlas aérien du Cameroun: campagnes et villes**, ed. Alain Beauvilain et al. [Yaoundé, Université de Yaoundé, Département de géographie], 1983. 138pp. illus. maps. 21 x 30cm. (Vertical aerial photographs of 20 cities, with text. No scales given, but most are between 1:8,000 and 1:20,000. Review, *Bulletin de l'IFAN*, sér. B. 46, 1984/85, 196-197)

2258   **Atlas de la province extrême-nord Cameroun**, ed Christian Seignobos & Olivier Lyébi-Mandjek. Paris, IRD, 2000. 171pp. illus., maps chiefly col. 58 cm. + 1 CD-ROM. (Pub. jointly with the Institut national de cartographie, République du Cameroun)

2259   **Atlas de la République unie du Cameroun**, comp. Georges Laclavère. Paris, *Jeune Afrique*, 1979. 72pp. col. maps. (20 thematic maps with text). - - English. trans. **Atlas of the United Republic of Cameroon**. Paris, *Jeune Afrique*, 1980. 72pp.

2260 **Atlas du Cameroun**, comp. J.H. Calsat. Paris, Editions SELPA for Haut Commissaire de la République française au Cameroun, [1946-1948]. 20pp. text + 8 folding col. maps. 33 x 25cm. (Most maps at 1:3M)

2261 **Atlas du Cameroun**. Yaoundé, Institut de recherches scientifiques/Paris, Société nouvelle de cartographie & ORSTOM, 1956-?1975. Issued as separate plates, 72 x 94cm or 72 x 47cm with accompanying text, and a slip-case, 36 x 47cm. Plate 1, 1956. Géologie. 2 sheets, 10pp.; plate 2, ?Not pub; plates 3 & 4, n.d. Climatologie. 4pp; plate 5, n.d. Fleuves et rivières. 7pp; plate 6, 1957. Les sols. 6pp; plate 7, 1958. Phytogéographie. 6pp; plate 8, 1969. Éléments de géophysique. 3pp; plate 9, n.d. Faits d'intêret médical. 3pp; plate 10, ?Not pub; plates 11 & 12, 1971-73. Démographie. 3 sheets, 10pp; plate 13, 1973. Activités de production etc. 6pp; plate 14, 1972. Les industries, 2 sheets; plate 15, 1975. Énergie électrique etc; plate 16, 1975. Les exploitations forestières. 3pp. (Scales vary: majority at 1:2M. *See* F. Bonnet-Dupeyron, 'Projet d'un atlas du Cameroun', pp. 39-46 in **Proceedings of the 6th International West African Conference, São Tomé, 21-28 Aug. 1956**, 1956). - - **Atlas du Cameroun: notes de presentation de la première partie**, comp, F. Bonnet-Dupeyron. Yaoundé, Institut de Recherches scientifiques, [1960]. 5pp.)

2262 **Atlas régional de la République Cameroun**. Yaoundé/Paris, ORSTOM, 1965-1974. 8 vols. [1] Sud-ouest 2; [2] Mandara-Logone; [3] Sud-est; [4] Ouest 2; [5] Sud-ouest 1; [6] Ouest 1; [7] Est 1; [8] Est 2.

2263 **Atlas régional Sud-Cameroun**, ed. Christian Santoir & Athanase Bopda. Paris, ORSTOM/Yaoundé, Institut national de cartographie, 1995. 53pp. 21 leaves. maps. 57 x 61cm. (Rev. ed. of the appropriate vols. of item **2262**. *See* A. Bopda & C. Santoir, 'La réactualisation des atlas régionaux du Cameroun: l'atlas sud-ouest 2', *Bulletin du Comité français de cartographie*, 136/137, 1993, 100-106)

2264 **Répertoire géographique du Cameroun**. Yaoundé, ORSTOM de Yaoundé, 1965- . Issued in numbered fascs., 1-19, 1965-1970, thereafter un-numbered. (Each fasc. is a 'Dictionnaire des villages' of an administrative district. Based on 1:200,000 series. Each entry contains co-ordinates and brief descriptions: population totals, major ethnic groups, existence of churches, schools, etc.)

2265 U.S. Board on Geographic Names. **Cameroon: official standard names approved by the USBGN**. Washington, DC, 1962. (Gazetteer, 60). 255pp. (Includes 18,000 names from maps at 1:200,000. Rev. of sections for

French Cameroons in **Equatorial Africa**, *see* **1472** and for British Cameroons in **West Africa**, *see* **2492**).

EARTH SCIENCES

2266   **Atlas agro-économique de la région Centre-Sud Cameroun**, essai de traitement des données sous la forme graphique, comp. Liliane Alt. Montpellier, 1985. 236pp. 21 x 30cm.

2267   **Géographie du Cameroun**. Yaoundé, Institut de pédagogie appliquée à vocation rurale (IPAR) & UNICEF, 1972. 288pp. illus. maps.

2268   Régnoult, J.M. **Synthèse géologique du Cameroun**. Yaoundé, Direction des mines et de géologie, 1986. 119pp. illus. maps.

2269   Suchel, Jean-Bernard. **Les climats du Cameroun**. St. Etienne, Université de Saint-Etienne, 1988. 4 vols. (Vol. 4 is an atlas)

BIOLOGICAL SCIENCES

Zoology

Birds & Mammals

2270   Depierre, Daniel & Vivien, Jacques. **Mammifères sauvages du Cameroun**. Nancy, Depierre, 1992. 249pp. illus. maps. (Covers 126 spp.)

2271   Good, Albert Irwin. **The birds of French Cameroon**. Dakar, IFAN, Centre du Cameroun, 1952-53. (Mémoires. Série sciences naturelles, 2/3). 2 vols. Part 1, 1952. 203pp. [Non-Passeriformes]; part 2, 1953. 269pp. Passeriformes. (Main sequence includes accounts of 748 spp. Part 2 also contains, pp. 195-198, Addenda to pt. 1, and, pp. 204-237, 'Other birds likely to be found in Cameroon', listing 183 spp.)

2272   Louette, Michel. **The birds of Cameroon: an annotated checklist**. Brussels, Koninklijke Academie voor Wetenschappen, Letteren en Schone Kunsten van België, 1981. (*Verhandelingen, Klasse der Wetenschappen*, 163). 295pp. 66 maps. (Covers 848 spp. Review, *Ibis*, 124, 1982, 367). - - Languy, M. et al. 'New bird records from Cameroon', *Malimbus*, 27, 2003, 1-12. (Reviews changes since Dowsett, *see* **708**. Adds 54 and deletes 2 spp.)

2273   Vivien, Jacques. **Faune de Cameroun: guide des mammifères et poissons**. Paris, Ministère de la coopération, 1991. 271pp. illus. maps.

Reptiles & amphibians

2274   LeBreton, Matthew. **A working checklist of the herpetofauna of Cameroon; with localities for species occurring in southern Cameroon**. Amsterdam, Netherlands Committee for IUCN, 1999. iv, 160pp.

2275   Perret, Jean-Luc. 'Les amphibiens du Cameroun', *Zoologische Jahrbücher, Abteilung für Systematik, Ökologie und Geographie der Tierre*, 93, 1966, 289-464. illus.

2276   Stucki-Stern, Martin C. **Snake report 721: a comparative study of the herpetological fauna of the former West Cameroon, Africa; with a classification and synopsis of 95 different snakes and descriptions of some new sub-species**. Teuffenthal, Herpeto-Verlag, 1979. vii, 650pp. illus. maps.

Botany

2277   **Flore du Cameroun**, ed. André Aubréville et al. Paris, Muséum national d'histoire naturelle/Yaoundé, Ministère de l'enseignement supérieur et de la recherche scientifique, 1963- . Issued in fascs. (37 fascs. pub. to 2005, covering some 30% of the vascular flora)

2278   Letouzey, René. **Etude phytogéographique du Cameroun**. Paris, Lechevalier, 1968. (Encyclopédie biologique, 64). 511pp. illus. maps. (Includes a history of botanical research in Cameroon and a survey of the principal floristic regions)

2279   Thirakul, Souane. **Manual of dendrology: Cameroon**. Quebec, National Centre for Forestry Development, 1985. iv, 640pp. illus. (Loose-leaf atlas with descriptive text and illus. on facing pages. Covers the spp. of central and southern Cameroon)

CÔTE D'IVOIRE

HANDBOOKS

2280   **Aspects des départements et des sous-préfectures**. Abidjan, Ministère d'information, 1968. 159pp. (Account of the divisions' administrative structure, history, topography, demography and economics)

2281   **Atlas linguistique de Côte d'Ivoire: les langues de la région lagunaire**. Abidjan, Université d'Abidjan, Institut de linguistique appliquée, 1971. (Documents linguistiques, 19). 323pp; - - **Atlas des langues gur de Côte d'Ivoire**, comp. Emmanuel N.A. Mensah & Zakari Tchagbale. Paris, ACCT/Abidjan, Université d'Abidjan, Institut de linguistique appliquée, 1983. vi, 318pp; - - **Atlas des langues mandé, sud de Côte d'Ivoire**, comp. Nazam Halaoui et al. Paris, ACCT/Abidjan, Université d'Abidjan, Institut de linguistique appliquée, 1983. vii, 227pp. (Despite their titles these vols. comprise basically tabular and statistical data)

2282   Avice, Emmanuel. **La Côte d'Ivoire**. Paris, Société d'éditions géographiques, maritimes et coloniales, 1951. (Pays africains, 1). 96pp. illus. maps.

2283   Ceccaldi, Pierrette. **Essai de nomenclature des populations, langues et dialectes de Côte d'Ivoire**. Paris, École pratique des hautes études & Centre d'études africaines, CARDAN, 1974. 2 vols. v, 145; 135, 34pp. (Reproduces card file maintained at CARDAN of names with references from alternative forms, geographical location and population of each group and bibliographical sources)

2284   Centre des hautes études administratives sur l'Afrique et l'Asie modernes (CHEAM). **Carte des religions de l'Afrique noire, République de la Côte d'Ivoire**. Paris, 1957. 53pp.

2285   **Côte d'Ivoire: a country study**. 3rd ed. comp. Robert E. Handloff. Washington, DC, Library of Congress, Federal Research Division, 1991. xxxii, 262pp. illus. map. Also available at: http://lcweb2.loc.gov/frd/cs/citoc.html. - - Orig. pub. as **Area handbook for the Ivory Coast**, comp. Thomas D. Roberts et al. Washington, DC, U.S. Department of Defense, 1962. xii, 485pp; - - 2nd ed. Washington, DC, 1973. lx, 449pp. (2nd ed. is a reprint of the 1st with addition of a 50 pp. survey of events, January 1963-December 1972 and a supplementary bibliography)

2286 **Ivory Coast: facts and figures, 1966**. Abidjan, Ministère d'information, 1966. 131pp. (Covers geography, history, economic and social life)

2287 **Dictionnaire économique et politique de la Côte d'Ivoire**. Paris, Ediafric-La documentation africaine, 1973. vii, 201pp. (Special issue of *Bulletin de l'Afrique noire*. Includes entries for persons, institutions, products, and services)

2288 Duprey, Pierre. **La Côte d'Ivoire de A à Z**. Abidjan, Textu, 1970. 125pp. illus.

2289 **L'Encyclopédie générale de la Côte d'Ivoire**. Paris, Les nouvelles éditions africaines, 1978. 3 vols. 1,187pp. illus. Vol.1. Le milieu et l'histoire; vol. 2. L'État et l'économie; vol. 3. La vie de la nation.

2290 France. Direction de la documentation. **La République de Côte d'Ivoire**. [Rev. ed.]. Paris, 1973. (*Notes et études documentaires*, 3989/3990, 21 May 1973). 56pp. - - Orig. pub. Paris, 1965. (*Notes et études documentaires*, 3308, 12 July 1966). 51pp.

2291 France. Ministère de la coopération. **Côte d'Ivoire: guide d'information**. Paris, 1996. (Collection guide d'information). 108pp. (Brief account of history, geography, politics, government and economics)

2292 Frick, Esther & Bolli, Margaret. 'Inventaire préliminaire des langues et dialectes en Côte d'Ivoire', *Annales de l'Université de l'Abidjan. Série H, linguistique*, 1, 1971, 395-416

2293 **Le grand dictionnaire encyclopédique de la Côte d'Ivoire**, ed. Raymond Borremans. Abidjan, Nouvelles éditions africaines, 1986-2004. 6 vols. (Title on spine **Dictionnaire Borremans**. Borremans died in 1988 and the work was completed by others. Lavish, large scale production with numerous illus. many in col. and maps. Short entries for places, people, flora and fauna, including bibliographical references. *See* Isabelle Verdier. **Marché du livre en Afrique noire francophone ... l'exemple du dictionnaire encyclopédique de Côte d'Ivoire**. Paris, 1987)

2294 **Historical dictionary of Côte d'Ivoire (the Ivory Coast)**. 2nd ed. comp. Robert J. Mundt. Lanham, MD, Scarecrow Press, 1995. (African historical dictionaries, 41). xxxiv, 367pp. - - Orig. pub. as **Historical dictionary of the Ivory Coast (Cote d'Ivoire)**. Metuchen, NJ, 1987. xxvi, 246pp. (Concentrates on post 1945 period. Reviews, *IJAHS*, 22, 1989, 347-348; *JAH*, 30, 1989, 541. Rated "fair", Balay, 1996)

2295 Mourgeon, Jacques. **La République de Côte-d'Ivoire**. Paris, Berger-Levrault, 1969. (Encyclopédie politique et constitutionnelle. Série Afrique). 45pp.

2296 Raynaud-Matheis, Franziska. **Elfenbeinküste**. Bonn, Schroeder for Deutsche Afrika-Gesellschaft, 1962. (Die Länder Afrikas, 25). 164pp. illus. maps.

2297 Tokareva, Z.I. **Respublika Kot-d'Ivuar: spravochnik**. Moscow, Akademiia nauk, Institut Afriki, 1990. 283pp.

2298 Van't Rood, Rogier. **Ivoorkust: mensen, politiek, economie, cultuur**. Amsterdam, Koninklijk Instituut voor de Tropen/The Hague, Novib, 2002. (Landenreeks). 78pp. illus. maps

YEARBOOKS

2299 **Annuaire**. Abidjan, Chambre de commerce et d'industries de Côte d'Ivoire, 1996- ?Annual. (1996 issue. 351pp.)

2300 **Annuaire international de la Côte d'Ivoire**. Paris, Edition INF-Afrique, 1964-1980? Annual. Title varies: **Annuaire nationale** (1964-1975). (Includes civil list and professional and commercial directories)

2301 **Annuaire statistique, économique, financier et social**. Abidjan, International Business Centre, 1988- . Annual. Latest issue in NWU is for 1998/99.

2302 **Le commercial Côte d'Ivoire: industries, services, informations économiques**. Abidjan, 1997- . ?Annual.

STATISTICS

2303 Côte d'Ivoire. Chambre d'industrie. **Statistiques économiques ivoiriennes**, Abidjan, 1972-?1982.

2304 Côte d'Ivoire. Direction de la statistique [etc.]. **Bulletin statistique de la Côte d'Ivoire** [etc.]. Abidjan, 1948- . Monthly. (Title varies: **Bulletin statistique mensuel/Bulletin mensuel de statistique**). NWU holdings cease in 1984.

2305   Côte d'Ivoire. Direction de la statistique [etc.]. **La Côte d'Ivoire en chiffres: annuaire statistique**. Abidjan, 1975- . Annual/Every 2 years. (Title varies: **Mémento chiffre de la Côte d'Ivoire** (1982/83-). Latest issue in NWU is for 1996/97. ?succeeded by **2308** and **2309**

2306   Côte d'Ivoire. Direction de la statistique [etc.]. **Inventaire économique et social de la Côte d'Ivoire, 1947 à 1958**. Abidjan, 1960. 283pp. (Detailed statistical compilation)

2307   Côte d'Ivoire. Direction de la statistique [etc.]. **Situation économique de la Côte d'Ivoire**. Abidjan, 1960-72. ?Annual.

2308   Côte d'Ivoire. Institut national de la statistique. **Annuaire des statistiques démographiques et sociales**. No.1, 1992/1998- . Abidjan, 2001-

2309   Côte d'Ivoire. Institut national de la statistique. **Annuaire des statistiques économiques., 1990/97–** . Abidjan, 1999- . Annual. Latest issue in NWU is vol. 4 for 2002

2310   Côte d'Ivoire. Institut national de la statistique. **Bulletin trimestriel**. Abidjan, 1992- .

2311   **Country profile: Côte d'Ivoire**. London, Economist Intelligence Unit, 2003- . Annual. *Continues in par*t **Country profile: Côte d'Ivoire**. London, 1986-1992; **Country profile: Côte d'Ivoire, Mali**. London, 1993-2002.

2312   **Dossier national: Côte d'Ivoire**, comp. Koman Georges Adje. Louvain-le-Neuve, Centre international de formation et de recherche en population et développement (CIDEP), 1995. 69pp. (Contemporary statistics)

2313   **L'économie ivoirienne**. Paris, Ediafric-La documentation africaine, 1970- . Irreg. (Issues traced for 1970, 1971, 1973, 1975, 1976, 1977, 1979 (8th ed.). Largely statistical)

2314   France. Ministère de la coopération. Direction des programmes. Sous-direction des études économiques et de la planification. **Côte d'Ivoire: données statistiques sur les activités économiques, culturelles et sociales**. Paris, 1976. 228pp. illus.

2315   Germany. Statistisches Bundesamt. **Statistik des Auslandes: Länderberichte: Côte d'Ivoire** (later **Länderbericht: Côte d'Ivoire**). Wiesbaden/Stuttgart, Metzler-Poetschel, 1962- . Irreg. Issues for 1962, 1969, 1984, 1986, 1988, 1991.

2316 IMF. **Côte d'Ivoire: statistical appendix**. Washington, DC, 2004. (Country report, 04/157). 64pp. - - Earlier eds. (title varies) 1996 (Staff country report, 96/135); 1998 (Staff country report, 98/46); 1999 (Staff country report, 99/70) ; 2000 (Staff country report, 00/17). Full text of reports from 1997 also available online, *see* **334**.

DIRECTORIES OF ORGANIZATIONS

2317 Côte d'Ivoire. Institut national de la statistique. **Répertoire des entreprises de la banque de données financières 1997**. Abidjan, 1999. 367pp.

2318 **Répertoire des centres de documentation de la Côte d'Ivoire**. Abidjan, Institut africain pour le développement économique et social (INADES), 1997. 111pp. (Lists 103 institutions). - - Earlier ed. Abidjan, 1993. 104pp.

BIOGRAPHICAL SOURCES

2319 Bonneau, R. **Écrivains, cinéastes et artistes ivoiriens: aperçu bio-bibliographique**. Abidjan, Nouvelles éditions africaines, 1973. 176p. (Covers 71 living figures. Entries based upon interviews)

2320 **Les élites ivoiriennes: who's who in Ivory Coast**. 4th ed. Paris, Ediafric-La documentation africaine, 1988. - - Orig. pub. Paris, 1976. xv, 178pp ; - - 2nd ed. Paris, 1978. xxvi, 235pp; - - 3rd ed. Paris, 1982. 209pp. (Each issue contains between 1,500 and 1,800 brief biographies)

2321 Verdier, Isabelle. **Côte d'Ivoire, 100 hommes de pouvoir**. Paris, Indigo, 1996. 190pp.

ATLASES & GAZETTEERS

2322 **Afrique noire: Côte d'Ivoire, Niger, Zäire: l'Afrique en cartes**. Brussels, Société royale belge de géographie, 1989. (*Revue belge de géographie*, 113 (1) 1989, Fasc. 42, n.s.). 44pp. illus. maps.

2323 **Atlas de Côte d'Ivoire**. Bondy & Abidjan, ORSTOM & Ministère du plan de Côte d'Ivoire/Université d'Abidjan, 1971-1979. [141pp]. 57 x 42cm. (45 col. plates of thematic maps mostly at 1:2M, originally issued in 14 sections with accompanying text. Includes series of maps showing development of administrative sub-divisions, 1893-1976. *See* G. Lecomte, 'La parution de la seconde tranche de l'Atlas de Côte d'Ivoire', *Annales de l'Université d'Abidjan, sér. G*, 1964, 6, 275-281. Review, *Bulletin of the Society of University Cartographers*, 9(2) 1975, 41-43)

2324   Atlas de la Côte d'Ivoire. 2nd ed. comp. Pierre Vennetier & Georges Laclavère. Paris, *Jeune Afrique*, 1983. 72pp. (20 col. Thematic maps with text). - - Orig. pub. Paris, 1978. 72pp.

2325   Atlas du nord-est de la Côte d'Ivoire. Abidjan, Ministère de l'économie et des finances/Ministère du plan/Université nationale de Côte d'Ivoire Institut de géographie tropicale, 1988. 50pp. + 31 plates, 42 cm. Issued loose in slip case; - - **Atlas de l'ouest de la Côte d'Ivoire.** Abidjan, Université nationale de Côte d'Ivoire, Institut de géographie tropicale, 1996. 68pp. illus.

2326   Répertoire des localités de Côte d'Ivoire et population: tome provisoire. Abidjan, Comité national de recensement, Bureau du recensement général de la population, 1975- . ?No more pub. - - Earlier eds. **Répertoire des villages de la Côte d'Ivoire.** Abidjan, Service de la statistique et de la mécanographie, 1955. 2 vols. Vol. 1. Classement par circonscription administrative. 477pp; vol. 2. Classement alphabétique. 273pp; - - **Répertoire des localités de la Côte d'Ivoire et population, classement par circonscription administrative.** Abidjan, Direction de la statistique, 1965. 269pp.

2327   U.S. Board on Geographic Names. **Ivory Coast: official standard names approved by the USBGN.** Washington, DC, 1965. (Gazetteer, 89). iv, 250pp. (Includes 17,700 names from maps at 1:200,000. Rev. of appropriate sections of **West Africa**, *see* **1758**)

EARTH SCIENCES

2328   Avenard, Jean Michel, et al. **Le milieu naturel de la Côte d'Ivoire.** Paris, ORSTOM, 1971. (Mémoires, 50). 2 vols. Vol. 1. 391pp.; vol. 2. 20 maps (On 11 sheets at 1:500,000 and 1:1M, showing climate, soils, hydrology, vegetation)

2329   Dabin, B. **Carte pédologique de la Côte d'Ivoire au 1:2,000,000; notice explicative.** Abidjan, Secretariat d'état à l'agriculture, 1960. 30pp.

2330   Environnement et ressources aquatiques de Côte-d'Ivoire. Paris, ORSTOM, 1993-1994. Vol.1, 1993. Le milieu marin, comp. Pierre Le Loeuff et al. 588pp. illus. maps; vol. 2, 1994. Les milieux lagunaires, comp. Jean-René Durand et al. 546pp. illus.

2331 Papon, André et al. **Géologie et minéralisations du sud-ouest de la Côte d'Ivoire**. Paris, Bureau de Recherche géologiques et minières (BRGM), 1973. (Mémoires, 80). v, 285pp. illus.

2332 Péron, Christine. **Atlas des indices minéraux de la Côte d'Ivoire au 1:4,000,000**. Abidjan, Société pour le développement minier de la Côte d'Ivoire (SODEMI), 1975. iii, 46pp. 22 x 30cm. 47 maps.

2333 Sawadago, Abdoulaye. **L'agriculture en Côte d'Ivoire**. Paris, Presses Universitaires de France, 1977. 367pp. illus. (Sections for each crop).

2334 Tagini, Bernard. **Carte au 1:2,000,000 et catalogue des gêtes et principaux indices minéraux de la Côte d'Ivoire**. Abidjan, Société d'État pour le Développement minier de la Côte d'Ivoire (SODEMI), 1981. (Rapport, 469). 72pp. maps. (Includes detailed catalogue of minerals and their location)

2335 Tagini, Bernard. **Esquisse structurale de la Côte d'Ivoire: essai de géotectonique régionale**. Abidjan, Société d'État pour le Développement minier de la Côte d'Ivoire (SODEMI), 1972. (Direction des Mines et de la Géologie, Bulletin, 5). 302pp. illus. maps.

2336 Wiese, Bernd. **Elfenbeinküste: Erfolge und Probleme eines Entwicklungslandes in den westafrikanischen Tropen**. Darmstadt, Wissenschaftliche Buchgesellschaft, 1988. (Wissenschaftliche Länderkunden, 29). xx, 303pp. illus. maps. (Physical and economic geography)

BIOLOGICAL SCIENCES

Zoology

2337 Courtois, Bernard & Chippaux, Jean-Philippe. **Serpents venimeux en Côte d'Ivoire**. Abidjan, Institut Pasteur de Côte d'Ivoire, 1977. 77pp. + 8pp. plates.

2338 Daget, Jacques & Iltis, A. **Poissons de Côte d'Ivoire (eaux douces et saumâtres)**. Abidjan, IFAN, 1965. (Mémoires, 74). xi, 385pp. illus.

2339 Thiollay, Jean-Marc. 'The birds of Ivory Coast: status and distribution', *Malimbus*, 7, 1985, 1-59 (Lists 683 spp.). - - Demey, R. &

Fishpool, L.D.C. 'Additions and corrections to the avifauna ...', *ibid.*, 12, 1991, 61-86.

See also **1456**

Botany

2340   Aké Assi, Laurent. **Contribution à l'étude floristique de la Côte d'Ivoire et des territoires limitrophes**. Paris, Lechevalier, 1963. (Encyclopédie biologique, 61). 322pp.

2341   Aké Assi, Laurent. **Flore de la Côte-d'Ivoire: catalogue systématique, biogéographie et écologie**. Geneva, Conservatoire et jardin botaniques de Gèneve, 2001-2002. (*Boisseria*, 57, 58). 2 vols. 396, 401pp. (Lengthy review, *Taxon*, 51, 2003, 831-844)

2342   Aubréville, André. **La flore forestière de la Côte d'Ivoire**. 2nd ed. Nogent-sur-Marne, Centre technique de forestier tropical, 1959. 3 vols. Vol. 1,. 370pp.; vol. 2. 341pp.; vol. 3. 334pp. ("In practice an awkward work to use", Frodin, 2001, 495). - - Orig. pub. Paris, Larose, 1936.

2343   Bouquet, Armand & Debray, Maurice. **Plantes médicinales de la Côte d'Ivoire**. Paris, ORSTOM, 1974. (Travaux et documents, 32). 231pp. illus. (Essentially a rev. ed. of Joseph Kerharo & Auguste Bouquet. **Plantes médicinales et toxiques de la Côte d'Ivoire/Haute Volta**. Paris, ORSTOM, 1950. 295pp.)

2344   Normand, Didier. **Atlas des bois de la Côte d'Ivoire**. Nogent-sur-Marne, Centre technique forestier tropical, 1950-1960. (Publications, 1, 19, 17). 3 vols. 168 illus.

2345   Sattler, Dieter. **Bois de Côte d'Ivoire: précis de reconnaissance des arbres commercialisés**. Abidjan, Centre d'édition et de diffusion africaines (CEDA), 1997. 387pp.

GUINEA

Site officielle de la République de Guinée http://www.guinee.gov.gn/

HANDBOOKS

2346   Area handbook for Guinea. 2nd ed. comp. Harold D. Nelson et al. Washington, DC, U.S. Department of Defense, 1975. xii, 386pp. maps. - - Orig. pub. comp. George L. Harris et al. Washington, DC, 1961. xii, 534pp.

2347   Borisenkov, V. P. et al. **Gvineia : spravochnik**. Moscow, Akademiia nauk Institut Afriki, 1980. 270pp.

2348   Charles, Bernard. **La République de Guinée**. Paris, Berger-Levrault, 1921. (Encyclopédie politique et constitutionnelle. Série Afrique). 69pp.

2349   France. Direction de la documentation. **La République du Guinée**. Paris, 1965. (*Notes et études documentaires*, 3202, 21 June 1965). 42pp.

2350   Historical dictionary of Guinea. 4th ed. comp. Thomas E. O'Toole & Janice E. Baker. Lanham, MD, Scarecrow Press, 2005. (African historical dictionaries, 94). lxviii, 288pp. (Review, *ARD*, 99, 2005, 51-54). - - Orig. pub. as **Historical dictionary of Guinea (Republic of Guinea/Conakry)**, comp. Thomas E. O'Toole. Metuchen, NJ, 1978. (African historical dictionaries, 16). xxiv, 157pp. (Reviews, *ASA review of books*, 6, 1980, 199-209; *IJAHS*, 12, 1979, 728-729, "a model for this series"); - - 2nd ed. **Historical dictionary of Guinea (Republic of Guinea/Conakry)**. Metuchen, NJ, 1987. xxv, 204pp (Review, *IJAHS* 21, 1988, 722-724, Rated "good", Balay, 1996); - - 3rd ed. **Historical dictionary of Guinea**, comp. Thomas E. O'Toole & Ibrahima Bah-Lalya. Metuchen, NJ, 1995. xxxix, 279pp

2351   Houis, Maurice. **La Guinée française**. Paris, Société d'éditions géographiques, maritimes et coloniales, 1953. (Pays africain, 3). 94pp. illus. maps.

2352   Iffono, Aly Gilbert. **Lexique historique de la Guinée-Conakry**. Paris, Harmattan, 1992. 234pp. (Some 300 entries for persons, places, events, government agencies, political parties). - - Orig. pub. as **Lexique historique de la République de Guinée**. Paris, 1990.

2353   Mogenet, Luc. **Guide de la Guinée**. Conakry, Éditions imprimerie mission catholique, 1999. 215pp. illus. maps. (General section on the country as a whole, followed by six regional sections with historical, demographic and cultural information. A wealth of miscellaneous material, with 20pp. bibliography. "Very valuable work", *ABPR*, 26, 2001, 214)

2354   Voss, Joachim. **Guinea**. Bonn, Schroeder for Deutsche Afrika-Gesellschaft, 1968. (Die Länder Afrikas, 37). 252pp. map.

YEARBOOKS

2355   **Annuaire des sociétés industrielles, commerciales et agricoles de Guinée**. Conakry, Chambre de commerce, d'industrie et d'agriculture de Guinée (CCIAG), ?1990- . Annual. Latest issue in NWU is 6th ed. 1995.

STATISTICS

2356   **Country profile: Guinea**. London, Economist Intelligence Unit, 2003- . Annual. *Continues in part* **Country profile: Guinea, Mali, Mauritania**. London, 1986-1992; **Country profile: Guinea, Sierra Leone, Liberia**. London, 1993-2002.

2357   **Dossier national: Guinée**, comp. Thiemo Marouana Thiello. Louvain-le-Neuve, Centre international de formation et de recherche en population et développement (CIDEP), 1996. 60pp. (Contemporary statistics)

2358   Germany. Statistisches Bundesamt. **Statistik des Auslandes: Länderberichte: Guinea** (later **Länderbericht: Guinea**). Wiesbaden/Stuttgart, Metzler-Poetschel, 1961- . Irreg. Issues for 1961, 1967, 1985, 1987, 1989, 1994.

2359   Guinea. Service de la statistique générale. **Bulletin spéciale de statistique**. Conakry, 1962- . Quarterly. *Continues* Guinea. Service de la statistique générale. **Bulletin statistique de la Guinée**. Conakry, 1955-1962. Monthly (irreg.). Title varies: **Bulletin mensuel de la statistique** (1957-58).

2360   IMF. **Guinea: selected issues and statistical appendix**. Washington, DC, 2006. (Country report, 06/25). 93pp. - - Earlier eds. (title varies) 1994 (Staff country report, 94/05); 1998 (Staff country report, 98/56); 2000 (Staff country report, 00/13); 2001 (Staff country report, 01/31); 2003 (Country report, 03/251); 2004 (Country report, 04/100); 2004 (Country report, 04/374); Full text of reports from 1997 also available online, *see* **334**.

ATLASES & GAZETTEERS

2361   U.S. Board on Geographic Names. **Guinea: official standard names approved by the USBGN.** Washington, DC, 1965. (Gazetteer, 90). iv, 175pp. (Includes 12,400 names from maps at 1:200,000. Rev. of appropriate sections of **West Africa,** *see* **1758**)

BIOLOGICAL SCIENCES

2362   Barnett, A.A. & Prangley, M.L. 'Mammalogy in the Republic of Guinea: an overview of research from 1946 to 1996, a preliminary checklist and a summary of research recommendations for the future', *Mammal review,* 27, 1997, 115-164. maps. (Lists 256 spp.)

2363   Morel, Gérard & Morel, Marie-Yvonne. 'Liste des oiseaux de Guinée', *Malimbus,* 10, 1988, 143-176. (Lists 204 spp.)

2364   Roger, François & Keita, Sory. **Plantes de Guinée à l'usage des éleveurs et des vétérinaires.** Maisons-Alfort, CIRAD/IEMVT, 1994. 237pp. illus. (Describes 371 spp.)

2365   Schneider, Wolfgang. **Field guide to the commercial marine resources of the Gulf of Guinea.** Rome, FAO, 1990. (FAO species identification sheets for fishery purposes). xii, 268pp. + 16 plates.

MALI

Présidence de la République du Mali http://www.koulouba.pr.ml/

HANDBOOKS

2366   Beuchelt, Eno. **Mali**. Bonn, K. Schroeder for Deutsche Afrika-Gesellschaft, 1966. (Die Länder Afrikas, 34). 153pp. illus. maps.

2367   France. Direction de la documentation. **La république du Mali**. Paris, 1961. (*Notes et études documentaires*, 2739, 13 Jan 1961). 65pp.

2368   France. Ministère de la coopération. **Mali: guide d'information, décembre 1992**. Paris, 1992. (Collection guide d'information). 66pp. (Brief account of history, geography, politics, government and economics)

2369   **Historical dictionary of Mali**. 3rd ed. comp. Pascal James Imperato. Lanham, MD, Scarecrow Press, 1996. (African historical dictionaries, 11). lxxxxv, 363pp. (Reviews, *ARD*, 75, 1997, 50-56; *IJAHS*, 31, 1998, 418-420. - - Orig. pub. Metuchen, NJ, 1977. xxxi, 204pp (Reviews, *African affairs*, 78, 1979, 277-278; *Africana J.*, 10, 1979, 120-128); - - 2nd ed. Metuchen, NJ, 1986. xvii, 359pp. (Lengthy critical review in *IJAHS*, 20, 1987, 565-569. Rated "fair", Balay, 1996)

2370   Jouve, Edmond. **La République du Mali**. Paris, Berger-Levrault, 1974. (Encyclopédie politique et constitutionnelle. Série Afrique). 99pp.

2371   Konaré, Alpha Oumar & Konaré Ba, Adamé. **Grandes dates du Mali**. Bamako, Éditions-Impr. du Mali, 1983. 284pp. + 40pp. plates. (Historical chronology. Includes lists of dynasties, colonial administrators, government ministers)

2372   Mali. Division du patrimoine culturel. **Répertoire général des sites historiques et archéologiques du Mali**. Bamako, 1984. 73pp.

2373   **Mali: country profile**. Washington, DC, Library of Congress. Federal Research Division, 2005. 20pp. Also available at: http://lcweb2.loc.gov/frd/ cs/profiles/Mali.pdf

2374   Ndiaye, Bokar. **Groupes ethniques au Mali**. Bamako, Éditions Populaires, 1970. 479pp. (Detailed account of the origins, history, customs and beliefs of some 20 major groups)

2375   Niakaté, Moussa. **Calendrier historique du Soudan français (Mali): 1090 à 1960**. Bamako, 1991. 80pp. (Historical chronology)

2376   Spitz, Georges. **Le Soudan français**. Paris, Société d'éditions géographiques, maritimes et coloniales, 1955. (Pays africains, 5). 112pp. illus. maps.

2377   Van Westen, Gus. **Mali: mensen, politiek, economie, cultuur**. Amsterdam, Koninklijk Instituut voor de Tropen/The Hague, Novib, 1996. (Landenreeks). 75pp. illus. maps.

2378   Vitukhina, G.O. et al. **Respublika Mali: spravochnik**. Moscow, Akademiia nauk, Institut Afriki, 1989. 252pp. - - Orig. pub. comp. G.F. Radchenko, et al. Moscow, 1977. 232pp.

STATISTICS

2379   **Annuaire des opérateurs économiques du Mali**. Bamako, Chambre de commerce et d'industrie du Mali, 1990- . ? No more pub.

2380   **Country profile: Mali**. London, Economist Intelligence Unit, 2003- . Annual. *Continues in part* **Country profile: Guinea, Mali, Mauritania**. London, 1986-1992; **Country profile: Côte d'Ivoire, Mali**. London, 1993-2002.

2381   France. Ministère de la coopération, Service des études économiques et des questions internationales. **Mali: données statistiques sur les activités économiques, culturelles et sociales**. Paris, 1977. 164pp. illus.

2382   Germany. Statistisches Bundesamt. **Statistik des Auslandes: Länderberichte: Mali** (later **Länderbericht: Mali**). Wiesbaden/Stuttgart, Metzler-Poetschel, 1966- . Irreg. Issues for 1966, 1984, 1986, 1988, 1990.

2383   IMF. **Mali: statistical appendix**. Washington, DC, 2006. (Country report, 06/89). 54pp. - - Earlier eds. (title varies) 1995 (Staff country reports, 95/138); 1998 (Staff country report, 98/14); 1999 (Staff country report, 99/20); 2000 (Staff country report, 00/128); 2002 (Country report, 02/01); 2004 (Country report, 04/10). Full text of reports from 1997 also available online, *see* **334**.

2384   Imperato, Pascal James & Eleanor M. **Mali: a handbook of historical statistics**. Boston, MA, G.K. Hall, 1982. xxv, 339pp. (Detailed comparative statistics covering 1935 to 1975)

2385 Mali. Direction nationale de la statistique [etc.]. **Annuaire statistique du Mali** [etc.]. Bamako, 1960- . Annual. Latest issue in NWU is 2002. - - **Flash des informations statistiques (FIS)**. Bamako, 1989- . Annual. (Summarized statistics for the year and chronology of national events)

2386 Mali. Direction nationale de la statistique [etc]. **Bulletin mensuel de statistique**. Bamako, 1959- . Monthly. Latest issues in NWU are for 1996. *Continues* Soudan francais. Service statistique. **Bulletin statistique du Soudan français**. Koulouba, 1952-1956. Monthly/quarterly.

DIRECTORIES OF ORGANIZATIONS

2387 **Annuaire des entreprises**. Bamako, Chambre de commerce, d'industrie et d'artisanat, 1997- . ?Annual. ?*Continues* **Annuaire des entreprises du Mali**. Bamako, Chambre de commerce, d'agriculture et d'industrie de Bamako, 1972- . ?Annual

2388 **Répertoire d'unités d'information au Mali**. 2nd ed. Bamako, Réseau Sahelien d'information et de documentation scientifique et technique (RESADOC), 1988. 82pp. (Lists 75 institutions)

2389 **Répertoire des centres de documentation et d'information du Mali**. Bamako, Centre Djoliba, 1993. 93pp.

BIOGRAPHICAL SOURCES

2390 **L'Assemblée nationale (3ème république, 1ère législature) 1992-1997**. Bamako, Société malienne d'édition, 1996. 80pp. illus.

2391 Jones, Jim. **Preliminary list of people in the history of the French Sudan**. West Chester, PA, West Chester University, 1993. 126pp.

2392 Konaré Ba, Adamé. **Dictionnaire des femmes célèbres du Mali, des temps mythico-légendaires au 26 mars 1991**. Bamako, Editions Jamana, 1993. 520pp. illus. (338 biographical articles arranged thematically)

ATLASES & GAZETTEERS

2393 **Atlas du Mali**, ed. Anne Lerebours Pigeonnière. 2nd ed. Paris, *Jeune Afrique*, 2001. 80pp. (20 thematic maps with accompanying text). - - Orig. pub. ed. Mamadou Traoré & Yves Monnier. Paris, 1981. 64pp.

2394   Petit atlas ethno-démographique du Soudan entre Sénégal et Tchad, comp. Yves François M.A. Urvoy. Paris, Larose, 1942. (Mémoires de l'IFAN, 5). 52pp. Reprinted, Amsterdam, Swets & Zeitlinger, 1968.

2395   U.S. Board on Geographic Names. Mali: official standard names approved by the USBGN. Washington, DC, 1965. (Gazetteer, 93). v, 263pp. (Includes 17,800 names from maps mostly at 1:500,000, some at 1:200,000. Rev. of appropriate sections of West Africa, see 1758)

EARTH SCIENCES

2396   Barth, Hans Karl. Mali: eine geographische Landeskunde. Darmstadt, Wissenschaftliche Buchgesellschaft, 1986. (Wissenschaftliche Länderkunden, 25). xxi, 395pp. + 14pp. plates. illus. (Detailed study of all aspects of geography, natural resources and population. Numerous statistics)

2397   Bassot, Jean-Pierre, et al. Notice explicative de la carte géologique à 1:1,500,000 de la République du Mali. Bamako, Ministère du développement industriel et du tourisme, Direction nationale de la géologie et des mines, 1981. 137pp.

2398   Notice explicative de la carte géologique du Mali occidental au 1:200,000. Duisburg, Klöckner Industrie-Anlagen for Ministère de l'industrie, de l'hydraulique et de l'energie, Direction nationale de la géologie et des mines, 1989. 92pp.

2399   Sivakumar, M.V.K. et al. Agroclimatology of West Africa: Mali. Patancheru, Andhra Pradesh, International Crops Research Institute for the Semi-Arid Tropics, 1984. 294pp. illus. maps. (Principally tabular data for rainfall, temperatures, water balance)

BIOLOGICAL SCIENCES

Zoology

2400   Joger, U. & Lambert, M.R.K. 'Analysis of the herpetofauna of the Republic of Mali; 1, Annotated inventory', Journal of African zoology, 110, 1996, 21-51

2401   Lamarche, Bruno. Atlas de répartition des oiseaux du Mali et de Mauritanie. Nouakchott, Association des naturalistes sahariens et ouest-africains, 1993-1994. (*Études sahariennes et ouest-africaines*, 5, nos. 1, 2, 3, 4(1), 4(2); 6, nos. 1, 2, 3, 4). 9 pts. (Distribution maps)

2402   Malzy, P. 'La faune avienne du Mali (Bassin du Niger)', *L'oiseaux et la revue française d'ornithologie*, 32, 1962, 1-81. (Lists some 220 spp.)

Botany

2403   Adjanohoun, Edouard J. et al. **Contribution aux études ethnobotaniques et floristiques au Mali**. 4th ed. Paris, ACCT, 1985. (Médicine traditionnelle et pharmacopée). 250pp. illus. - - 2nd ed. Paris, 1980. 291pp; - - 3rd ed. Paris, 1991. 291pp.

2404   Boudet, Gabriel & Lebrun, Jean-Pierre. **Catalogue des plantes vasculaires du Mali**. Maisons Alfort, IEMVT, 1986. (Études et synthèses, 16). 480pp. (Lists 1,739 spp. No illus.)

2405   Malgras, Denis. **Arbres et arbustes guérisseurs des savanes maliennes**. Paris, ACCT, 1992. 478pp. + 20pp. plates. (Describes 160 trees and shrubs with medicinal uses)

2406   Thoyer, Annik. **Plantes médicinales du Mali**. 2nd ed. Paris, author, 1987. 189pp. illus. - - Orig. pub. Paris, 1979. 173pp.

MAURITANIA

République islamique du Mauritanie Web site
http://www.mauritania.mr/fr/ index.php# (Also available in Arabic and in
English although link to the latter not working, July 2006)

HANDBOOKS

2407 France. Direction de la documentation. **La République islamique de Mauritaine**. Paris, 1960. (*Notes et études documentaires*, 2687, 29 July 1960). 50pp.

2408 France. Ministère de la coopération. **Mauritanie: guide d'information**. Paris, 1996. (Collection guide d'information). 76pp. (Brief account of history, geography, politics, government and economics)

2409 **Historical dictionary of Mauritania**. 2nd ed. comp. Anthony G. Pazzanita. Lanham, MD, Scarecrow Press, 1996. (African historical dictionaries, 68). xxviii, 315pp. (Review, *IJAHS*, 32, 1999, 527-529). - - Orig. pub. comp. Alfred G. Gerteiny. Metuchen, NJ, 1988. (African historical dictionaries, 31). xv, 98pp. (Review, *JAH*, 39, 1988, 173-174. Rated "fair", Balay 1996)

2410 **Introduction à la Mauritanie**. Paris, CNRS for Centre de recherches et d'études sur les sociétés méditerranéennes & Centre d'études d'Afrique noire, 1979. 421pp. (Surveys of 'Le cadre historique', 'Les aspects socio-culturelles', 'Économie et politique', 'Les relations extérieures'. Chronology, pp. 413-421)

2411 **Mauritania: a country study**. 2nd ed. comp. Robert E. Handloff. Washington, DC, Library of Congress, Federal Research Division, 1990. xxv, 218pp. illus. maps. Also available at: http://lcweb2.loc.gov/frd/cs/ mrtoc.html. - - Orig. pub as **Area handbook for Mauritania**, comp. Brian D. Curran & Joann Schrock. Washington, DC, U.S. Department of Defense, 1972. 185pp.

2412 Piquemal-Pastré, Marcel. **La République islamique de Mauritanie**. Paris, Berger-Levrault, 1969. (Encyclopédie politique et constitutionnelle. Série Afrique). 49pp.

2413 Reichhold, Walter. **Islamische Republik Mauretania**. Bonn, K. Schroeder for Deutsche Afrika-Gesellschaft, 1964. (Die Länder Afrikas, 28). 96pp. illus. maps.

2414   Truevstev, K.M. **Islamskaia Respublika Mavritaniia: spravochnik**. Moscow, Akademiia nauk, Institut Afriki, 1987. 147pp. maps.

2415   Vernet, Robert & Naffé, Baouba Ould Mohamed. **Dictionnaire archéologique de la Mauritanie**. Nouakchott, CRIIA/LERHI/Université de Nouakchott, 2003. 164pp. (Arranged in sections: Généralités, Paléolithique etc. Very critical review in *Afrique & histoire*, 3, 2005, 277-279)

STATISTICS

2416   **Country profile: Mauritania**. London, Economist Intelligence Unit, 2003- . Annual. *Continues in part* **Country profile: Guinea, Mali, Mauritania**. London, 1986-1992; **Country profile: The Gambia, Mauritania**. London, 1993-2002.

2417   **L'économie mauritanienne**. Paris, Ediafric-La documentation africaine, 1977. Various paging. (Special issue of *Bulletin de l'Afrique noire*)

2418   Germany. Statistisches Bundesamt. **Statistik des Auslandes: Länderberichte: Mauretania** (later **Länderbericht: Mauretania**). Wiesbaden/Stuttgart, Metzler-Poetschel, 1983- . Irreg. Issues for 1983, 1985, 1987, 1991.

2419   IMF. **Islamic Republic of Mauritania: statistical appendix**. Washington, DC, 2006. (Country report, 06/271). 31pp. - - Earlier eds. (title varies) 1996 (Staff country reports, 96/45); 1997 (Country report, 97/79); 2000 (Country report, 00/90); 2003 (Country report, 03/216); 2003 (Country report, 03/315) ; 2006 (Country report, 06/248). Full text of reports from 97/101, 1997 also available online, *see* **334**.

2420   Mauritania. Direction de la statistique [etc.] **Annuaire statistique**. Nouakchott, 1968- . Annual. ALA notes issue for 1990.

2421   Mauritania. Direction de la statistique [etc.]. **Bulletin mensuel statistique**. Nouakchott, 1960- . Monthly/quarterly. Title varies: **Bulletin statistique et économique/Bulletin trimestriel statistique**. Last issue in NWU is for 1967

ATLASES & GAZETTEERS

2422   **Atlas de la République islamique de Mauritanie**, comp. Charles Toupet & Georges Laclavère. Paris, *Jeune Afrique*, 1977. 64pp. col. maps.

2423 **Atlas migrations et gestion du territoire, république Islamique de Mauritanie/Atlas al higrat wa al tasîr al iqlimi**. Nouakchott, Université de Nouakchott/Rouen, Université de Rouen, 1999. 38 loose sheets in portfolio + 64pp. pamphlet

2424 U.S. Board on Geographic Names. **Mauritania: official standard names approved by the USBGN.** Washington, DC, 1966. (Gazetteer, 100). vii, 149pp. (Includes 10,000 names from maps at 1:200,000 for south and west, 1:500,000 for rest of the country. Rev. of appropriate sections of **West Africa,** *see* **1758**)

EARTH SCIENCES

2425 Mauritania. Direction des mines et de la géologie. **Notice explicative de la carte géologique à 1:1,000,000 de la Mauritanie: monographies géologiques régionales**. Paris, Bureau de recherches géologiques et minières (BRGM), 1975. 255pp. illus.

BIOLOGICAL SCIENCES

2426 Barry, Jean-Paul & Celles, Jean-Claude. **Flore de Mauritanie**. Nice, Université de Nice-Sophia-Antipolis/Nouakchott, Institut supérieur scientifique de Nouakchott, 1991. 2 vols. xlviii, 550pp. illus. maps. Vol. 1, Angiospermes dicotylédones; vol. 2, Angiospermes monocotylédones, Ptéridophytes, Chlamydospermes. (Covers some 1,400 spp.)

2427 Jaouen, Xavier. **Arbres, arbustes et buissons de Mauritanie**. Nouakchott, Centre cultural français, 1988. 113pp. illus. maps.

2428 Lamarche, Bruno. **Liste commentée des oiseaux de Mauritaine**. Nouakchott/Paris, Association des naturalistes sahariens et ouest-africains, 1988. (*Études sahariennes et ouest-africaines*, 1(4) 1988). ix, 164pp. maps. - - Salewski, V. et al. 'New bird records from Mauritania', *Malimbus*, 27, 2005, 19-32

2429 Lebrun, Jean-Pierre. **Catalogue des plantes vasculaires de la Mauritanie et du Sahara occidental**. Geneva, Conservatoire et jardin botaniques de la ville de Genève, 1998. (*Boissiera*, 55). 322pp. illus. maps.(Lists 853 spp.)

NIGER

HANDBOOKS

2430   Beuchelt, E. **Niger**. Bonn, K. Schroeder for Deutsche Afrika-Gesellschaft, 1968. (Die Länder Afrikas, 38). 147pp. illus. maps.

2431   **Cartes ethno-démographiques du Niger au 1:1M, notice des cartes**, comp. Yveline Poncet. Niamey, Centre nigérien de recherches en sciences humaines, 1973. 51pp. (Études nigériennes, 32)

2432   France. Direction de la documentation. **La République du Niger**. [Rev. ed.] Paris, 1973. (*Notes et études documentaires*, 3994/3995, 12 June 1973). 54pp. - - Orig. pub. Paris, 1960. (*Notes et études documentaires*, 2638, 26 Feb. 1960). 50pp.

2433   **Historical dictionary of Niger**. 3rd ed., comp. Samuel Decalo. Lanham, MD, Scarecrow Press, 1997. (African historical dictionaries, 72). xxxi, 486pp. (Reviews, *Choice*, 35, 1998, 1170; *CJAS*, 32, 1998, 201-202; *IJAHS*, 32, 1999, 187-189). - - Orig. pub. Metuchen, NJ, 1979. (African historical dictionaries, 20). xvii, 358pp. (Review, *African affairs*, 80, 1981, 141, "certainly one of the most successful ones"); - - 2nd ed. Metuchen, NJ, 1989. xxvi, 408pp. (Rated "good", Balay, 1996)

2434   Kio Koudizé, Aboubacar. **Chronologie politique du Niger de 1900 à nos jours**. Niamey, Imprimerie nationale du Niger, 1991. 70pp. illus. map.

2435   Martin, François. **Niger du Président Diori, chronologie, 1960-1974**. Paris, Harmattan, 1991. 421pp. illus.

2436   Niskaia, L.O. **Respublika Niger: spravochnik**. Moscow, Akademiia nauk, Istitut Afriki, 1989. 226pp.

2437   Séré de Rivières, Edmond. **Le Niger**. Paris, Société d'éditions géographiques, maritimes et coloniales, 1952. (Pays africains, 2). 96pp. illus. maps.

STATISTICS

2438   **Country profile: Niger**. London, Economist Intelligence Unit, 2003- Annual. *Continues in part* **Country profile: Niger, Burkina [Faso]** London, 1986-1996; **Country profile: Burkina Faso, Niger**. London, 1997-2002.

2439 European Communities. Eurostat. **Reports on ACP countries: Niger**. Luxembourg, Office for Official Publications of the European Communities, 1988. 92pp.

2440 France. Ministère de la coopération. Service des études et questions internationales. **Niger: données statistiques sur les activités économiques, culturelles et sociales**. Paris, 1978. 155pp. - - Orig. pub. Paris, 1975. 162pp.

2441 Germany. Statistisches Bundesamt. **Statistik des Auslandes: Länderberichte: Niger** (later **Länderbericht: Niger**). Wiesbaden/Stuttgart, Metzler-Poetschel, 1966- . Irreg. Issues for 1966, 1985, 1987, 1992

2442 IMF. **Niger : statistical annex**. Washington, DC, 2004. (Country report, 04/191). 51pp. - - Earlier eds. (title varies) 1995 (Country report, 95/30); 1997 (Staff country reports, 97/93); 2001 (Country report, 01/21); 2002 (Country report, 02/34). Full text of reports from 97/101, 1997 also available online, *see* **334**.

2443 Niger. Direction de la statistique et des comptes nationaux [etc.]. **Annuaire statistique**. Niamey, 1962- . Annual. Latest issue in NWU is for 1996/97.

2444 Niger. Direction de la statistique et des comptes nationaux [etc.]. **Bulletin trimestriel de statistique**. Niamey, 1959- . Quarterly. Title varies: **Bulletin de statistique** (1960-). Latest issues in NWU are for 1994.

BIOGRAPHICAL SOURCES

2445 Chaibou, Maman. **Répertoire biographique des personnalités de la classe politique et des leaders d'opinion du Niger de 1945 à nos jours**. Niamey, Démocratie, 2000-2003. Vol.1. Les parlementaires; vol. 2. Les présidents de la République et chefs d'état, les vice-présidents du Conseil de government.

2446 Le Rouvreur, Albert. **Eléments pour un dictionnaire biographique du Tchad et du Niger (Téda et Daja)**. Paris, CNRS, 1978. (Contributions à la connaissance des élites africaines, fasc. 1). 48pp. *See also* **1524**

ATLASES & GAZETTEERS

2447 Les arrondissements du Niger: images socio-économiques. Niamey, Ministère des finances et du plan/Ministère de l'équipement de l'habitat et de l'aménagement du territoire, 1993. v, 50pp. (21 thematic maps at 1:5,500,000 with text on facing page. Includes administrative divisions, urban development, communications, land use, education, health)

2448 **Atlas du Niger**, comp. Edmond Bernus & Sidikou A. Hamidou. Paris, *Jeune Afrique*, 1980. 64pp. col. maps. (19 thematic maps with text)

2449 U.S. Board on Geographic Names. **Niger: official standard names approved by the USBGN**. Washington, DC, 1966. (Gazetteer, 99). iv, 207pp. (Includes 14,700 names from maps at 1:200,000, for the south, 1:500,000 for the rest of the country. Rev. of appropriate sections of **West Africa**, *see* **1758**)

EARTH SCIENCES

2450 Atlas of natural and agronomic resources of Niger and Benin, ed. L. Herrmann et al. Institute of Soil Science and Land Evaluation, Universität Hohenheim, Stuttgart http://www.uni-hohenheim.de/~atlas308/startpages /page2/english/content/title_en.htm. (Originally set up with data collected in Stuttgart as at end of 1999. The intention is for updating by researchers submitting their own data to be reviewed for inclusion)

2451 Greigert, Jacques & Pougnet, Robert. **Essai de description des formations géologiques de la république du Niger**. Paris, Bureau de recherches géologique et minières (BRGM), 1967. (Mémoires, 48). 239pp. illus. maps.

2452 Sivakumar, M. V. K. et al. **Agroclimatology of West Africa: Niger**. 2nd ed. Patancheru, Andhra Pradesh, International Crops Research Institute for the Semi-Arid Tropics/Niamey, Direction de la météorologie nationale du Niger, 1993. v, 108pp. illus. maps. (Principally tabular data for rainfall, temperatures, water balance)

BIOLOGICAL SCIENCES

2453 Adjanohoun, Edouard J. **Contribution aux études ethnobotaniques et floristiques au Niger**. 2nd ed. Paris, ACCT, 1985. (Médicine traditionelle et pharmacopée). 251pp. illus. - - Orig. pub. Paris, 1980. 250pp.

2454 Giraudoux, P. et al. 'Avifaune du Niger: état des connaissance en 1986', *Malimbus*, 10, 1988, 1-140. illus. maps. (Follows taxonomy of Serle & Morel, 1977 *see* **1776**)

2455   Peyre de Fabrègues, Bernard & Lebrun, Jean-Pierre. **Catalogue des plantes vasculaires du Niger**. Maisons-Alfort, IEMVT, 1976. (Étude botanique, 3). 433pp. - - 'Premier supplément', comp. E. Boudouresque et al. *Adansonia*, sér. 2, 18, 1978, 377-390; - - 'Second supplément', comp. J.-P. Lebrun et al, *Bulletin de la Société botanique de France*, 130, *Lettres botaniques*, 1983, 249-256. (Suppls. add a further 74 spp.)

SENEGAL

Gouvernement du Sénégal Web site http://www.gouv.sn/

HANDBOOKS

2456 **Area handbook for Senegal**. 2nd ed. comp. Harold D. Nelson et al. Washington, DC, U.S. Department of Defense, 1974. xiv, 410pp. illus. maps. - - Orig. pub. as **U.S. Army area handbook for Senegal**, comp. Irving Kaplan et al. Washington, DC, U.S. Army, 1963. xiv, 489pp.

2457 Ba, Oumar. **L'histoire du Senegal au jour le jour. T. 1, Période de la conquête coloniale 1855-1856**. Dakar, Imprimerie St. Paul, 1989. 75pp ?No more pub. (Historical chronology)

2458 **Chronologie politique, économique et sociale du Sénégal (des origines à l'euro)**. Paris, Centre français du commerce extérieur (CFCE), 1998. 101pp.

2459 Ernst, Harald. **Senegal**. Bonn, K. Schroeder for Deutsche Afrika-Gesellschaft, 1965. (Die Länder Afrikas, 29). 112pp. illus. map.

2460 France. Direction de la documentation. **La République du Sénégal**. Paris, 1961. (*Notes et études documentaires*, 2754, 22 Feb. 1961). 48pp.

2461 Hesseling, Gerti & Kraemer, Hens. **Senegal/Gambia: mensen, politiek, economie, cultuur**. Amsterdam, Koninklijk Instituut voor de Tropen/The Hague, Novib, 1996. (Landenreeks). 83pp. illus. maps.

2462 **Historical dictionary of Senegal**. 2nd ed., comp. Andrew F. Clark & Lucie Colvin Phillips. Metuchen, NJ, Scarecrow Press, 1994. (African historical dictionaries, 65). xii, 353pp. (Reviews, *Africa*, 66, 1996, 458-464; *IJAHS*, 29, 1966, 159-161). - - Orig. pub. comp. Lucie Gallistel Colvin. Metuchen, NJ, 1981. (African historical dictionaries, 23). xiv, 339p. (Reviews, *Africa*, 54, 1984, 113-115; *JAH*, 24, 1983, 426, "one of the better ones in the series". Rated "good", Balay, 1996)

2463 Martin, Victor & Becker, Charles. **Répertoire des sites proto-historiques du Sénégal et de la Gambie: inventaire des tumulus, mégalithes et emplacements de villages anciens; cartographie**. Kaolack, authors, 1974. 93pp. + 7 maps in pocket.

2464   Mbaye, Saliou. **Dictionnaire de sigles, acronymes et timbres en usage au Sénégal**. Dakar, author, 1990. 141pp.

2465   **Sénégal: faits et chiffres**. New ed. Dakar, Direction des services de presse du Ministère de l'information, 1965. 1 vol. various paging. - - Orig. pub. Dakar, 1962. 49pp. illus.

2466   Séré de Rivières, Edmond. **Le Sénégal-Dakar**. Paris, Société d'éditions géographiques, maritimes et coloniales, 1953. (Pays africains, 4). 127pp. illus. maps.

YEARBOOKS

2467   **Annuaire de l'Union des chambres de commerce d'industrie et d'agriculture du Sénégal**. Dakar, 1991- . Annual. Last issue in NWU is 1993.

STATISTICS

2468   **Country profile: Senegal**. London, Economist Intelligence Unit, 1992- Annual. *Continues in part* **Country profile: Senegal, Gambia, Guinea-Bissau, Cape Verde**. London, 1987-1991

2469   **L'économie sénégalaise**. Paris, Ediafric-La documentation africaine, 1970- . Irreg. Issues for 1970, 1973, 1975, 1977, 1983. (Special issues of *Bulletin de l'Afrique Noire*)

2470   Germany. Statistisches Bundesamt. **Statistik des Auslandes: Länderberichte: Senegal** (later **Länderbericht: Senegal**). Wiesbaden/ Stuttgart, Metzler-Poetschel, 1985- . Irreg. Issues for 1985, 1987, 1990, 1993.

2471   IMF. **Senegal : selected issues and statistical appendix**. Washington, DC, 2005. (Country report, 05/105). 101pp. - - Earlier eds. (title varies) 1995 (Staff country report, 95/71); 1997 (Staff country report, 97/94); 1999 (Staff country report, 99/05); 2003 (Country report, 03/168). Full text of reports from 97/101, 1997 also available online, *see* **334**.

2472   Senegal. Direction de la statistique [etc.]. **Bulletin bimestrial** [later **trimestriel**] **de statistiques**. Dakar, 1998- . *Continues* **Bulletin statistique et économique mensuel** [later **Bulletin mensuel statistique**]. St. Louis/Dakar, 1960-1987. Monthly; **Bulletin statistique.** Dakar, 1988-1997. 6 p.a. *Successor to* **Bulletin de la statistique générale** and **Bulletin statistique trimestriel/ bimestriel** previously issued by government of A.O.F., *see* **2117**.

2473   Senegal. Direction de la statistique [etc.]. **Situation économique du Sénégal**. Dakar, 1962- . Annual. ALA notes issue for 1993.

2474   Senegal. Ministère des Finances et des affaires économiques. **Le Sénégal en chiffres**. Dakar, 1976- . Irreg. Latest issue in NWU is 1982/83.

DIRECTORIES OF ORGANIZATIONS

2475   **Répertoire culturel, le Sénégal**, comp. Pape Massène Sene & Jacqueline Falq. Paris, ACCT, [?1983]. (Inventaire des activités, etc. des pays membres de l'ACCT). 375pp.

2476   **Répertoire des entreprises du Sénégal**. Dakar, Chambre de commerce, d'industrie et d'agriculture, 1994- . Latest issue in NWU is 2000.

2477   **Répertoire des organismes de documentation et d'information scientifiques et techniques**. 3rd ed. Dakar, Centre nationale de documentation scientifique et technique, 1984. - - Orig. pub. Dakar, 1978. 184pp; - - 2nd ed. Dakar, 1981. (*Note also* **Répertoire des bibliothèques et organismes de documentation au Sénégal**, comp. D.H. Zidouemba. Dakar, Université de Dakar, École des bibliothécaires, archivistes et documentalistes, 1973. vi, 131pp)

BIOGRAPHICAL SOURCES

2478   **Les élites sénégalaises**. Paris, Ediafric-La documentation africaine, 1984. xix, 169pp. (Special issue of *Bulletin de l'Afrique noire*. About 1,000 brief biographies, mostly of government officials)

2479   Ndiaye, Babacar & Ndiaye, Waly. **Présidents et ministres de la République du Sénégal**. Dakar, 2000. 378pp. (188 biographical entries)

2480   **Sénégal, 100 hommes de pouvoir**. Paris, Indigo, 1999-   . Annual. BnF has issue for 2001.

ATLASES & GAZETTEERS

Atlases

2481   Atlas du Sénégal, ed. Mamadou Moustapha Sall. 5th ed. Paris, Editions Jaguar, 2000. 84pp. maps. - - Orig. pub. ed. Paul Pelissier. Paris, *Jeune Afrique*, 1980. 72pp. col. maps. (19 thematic maps with text); - - 2nd ed. ed. Paul Pélissier & Georges Laclavère. Paris, 1983. 72pp.

2482   Atlas national du Sénégal, ed. Regine Nguyen van Chi-Bonnardel. Dakar, IFAN, 1977. 147pp. including 65 plates. 54 x 40cm. (Produced with help of Institut géographique nationale, Paris, and ORSTOM. Thematic maps, the majority at 1:1,500,000. Includes a series on history showing archaeological sites, ancient kingdoms, colonization etc. Text includes diagrams and photos)

2483   Atlas pour l'aménagement du territoire. Dakar, Ministère du plan et de la coopération. Dakar 1977. 159pp. illus. maps. (Thematic maps at 1:5M). - - Orig. pub as **Cartes pour servir à l'aménagement du térritoire**. Dakar, 1965. 40 maps. 28 x 39cm.

Gazetteers

2484   A.O.F. Statistique générale. **Répertoire des localités de l'Afrique occidentale française classées par ordre alphabétique dans chaque colonie: Sénégal**. [St. Louis], ?1956. 290pp. mimeograph

2485   Mangold, Max. A Senegalese pronouncing gazetteer. Saarbrücken, Universität des Saarlandes, Institut für Phonetik, 1984. (Africana Saraviensia Linguistica, 7). 75pp. (1,100 entries, with Wolof pronunciation for 300)

2486   Senegal. Ministère des finances et des affaires économiques. Direction de la statistique. **Répertoire des villages**. 2nd ed. Dakar, 1972. 233pp. (Lists villages firstly by their location in administrative divisions, with population figures, secondly A/Z.). - - Earlier eds. St. Louis, Service statistique, 1958. 159pp; - - Dakar, Ministère du plan et du développement. Service de la statistique, 1964.

2487   U.S. Board on Geographic Names. **Gazetteer of Senegal: names approved by the USBGN**. 2nd ed. Washington, DC, 1990. xiv, 333pp. - - Orig. pub. as **Senegal: official standard names approved by the USBGN**. Washington, DC, 1965. (Gazetteer, 88). iv, 194pp. (Includes 13,600 names from maps at 1:200,000. Rev. of appropriate sections of **West Africa**, *see* **1758**)

EARTH SCIENCES

2488   Adam, Jacques-George, et al. **Climat, sols, vegetation**. St. Louis, Centre de recherches et de documentation du Sénégal (CRDS), 1965. (*Études sénégalaises*, 9; Connaissance du Sénégal, 3). 215pp. + 15pp plates, maps.

BIOLOGICAL SCIENCES

Zoology

2489   Cadenat, Jean. **Poissons de mer du Sénégal**. Dakar, IFAN, 1950. (Initiations africaines, 3). 345pp. illus.

2490   Le Tallec, Jean. **La grande faune du Sénégal, les mammifères: silhouettes d'identification, notes d'écologie, guide pour les parcs nationaux**. Dakar, Nouvelles Éditions africaines, 1979. 111pp. illus. maps.

2491   Morel, Gérard J. **Liste commentée des oiseaux du Sénégal et de la Gambie**. Paris, ORSTOM, 1972. 140pp.

2492   Morel, Gérard J. & Morel, Marie-Yvonne. **Les oiseaux de Sénégambie: notices et cartes de distribution**. Paris, ORSTOM, 1990. 178pp. illus. maps. (Covers 626 spp. Review, *Ibis*, 133, 1992, 428-429)

See also **1822**

Botany

2493   Berhaut, Jean. **Flore du Sénégal**. 2nd ed. Dakar, Clairafrique, 1967. viii, 485pp. (Checklist with brief details and keys. New ed. adds coverage of 'les forêts humides de la Casamance'). - - Orig. pub. as **Flore du Sénégal: brousse et jardins (savanes de l'Afrique occidentale)**: clé pratique permettant l'analyse facile et rapide des plantes. Dakar, 1954. viii, 300pp.

2494   **Flore illustrée du Sénégal**, ed. Jean Berhaut & C. Vanden Berghe. Dakar, Ministère du développement rural, Direction des eaux et forêts, 1971- . 11 vols. planned. Vols. 1-6, 9 pub. to 1988, none since. (Detailed atlas-flora. Barhaut died in 1977, the only vol. pub. since comp. by Vanden Berghe)

2495   Kerharo, Joseph. **La pharmacopée sénégalaise traditionnelle: plantes médicinales et toxiques**; avec la collaboration pour la partie botanique de Jacques Georges Adam. Paris, Vigot, 1974. 1,011pp. illus.

2496 Lebrun, Jean-Pierre. **Énumeration des plantes vasculaires du Sénégal**. Maisons-Alfort, IEMVT, 1973. (Étude botanique, 2). 209pp. (Checklist linked to Berhaut, 1967 *see* **2493**)

2497 Trochain, Jean. **Contribution à l'étude de la végétation du Sénégal**. Paris, Larose for IFAN, 1940. (Mémoires de l'IFAN, 2). 434pp. + 30 plates. (Detailed survey region by region)

TOGO

See also sections for **Former German Africa**.

République togolaise Web site
http://www.republicoftogo.com/fr/home.asp

HANDBOOKS

2498 Banque centrale des états de l'Afrique de l'ouest. **Togo 1960; faits et chiffres**. Lomé, 1960. vi, 217pp. (Compact and very detailed compilation of data, compiled with the help of government departments. Covers economic and social life, with sections on history, topography and peoples. Numerous statistics and bibliography)

2499 **Encyclopédie nationale du Togo**. Paris, Afrique biblio club, 1979. 6 vols. Vol.1. Sites et hauts lieux; vol.2. Coutumes et traditions; vol. 3. L'art et l'artisanat; vol.4. Petit atlas du Togo; vol. 5. La cuisine togolaise; vol. 6. L'hôtellerie togolaise.

2500 France. Direction de la documentation. **Le Togo**. Paris, 1968. (*Notes et études documentaires* 3531, 31 Oct 1968). 26pp.

2501 **Historical dictionary of Togo**. 3rd ed. comp. Samuel Decalo. Lanham, MD, Scarecrow Press, 1996. (African historical dictionaries, 9). xxvi, 390pp. (Review, *IJAHS*, 32, 1999, 486-487). - - Orig. pub. Metuchen, NJ, 1976. xviii, 243pp. (Review, *Africana J.*, 10, 1979, 120-128); - - 2nd ed. Metuchen, NJ, 1987. xxvi, 331pp. (Review, *IJAHS*, 22, 1989, 340-341, "an abundance of interesting and pertinent information". Rated "good", Balay, 1996)

2502 Norborg, Åke. **A handbook of musical and other sound-producing instruments from Togo**. Stockholm, Almqvist & Wiksell, 2001. xiv, 253pp. (Includes descriptions, illus., bibliography and discography)

2503 Prouzet, Michel. **La République du Togo**. Paris, Berger-Levrault, 1976. (Encyclopédie politique et constitutionnelle. Série Afrique). 53pp.

2504 Schramm, Joseph. **Togo**. 2nd ed. Bonn, K. Schroeder for Deutsche Afrika-Gesellschaft, 1962. (Die Länder Afrikas, 19). 92pp. - - Orig. pub. Bonn, 1959. 86pp.

2505   Tokareva, Z.I. **Togolezskaia respublika: spravochnik**. Moscow, Akademiia nauk, Institut Afriki, 1981. 242pp.

See also **2216, 2223**

YEARBOOKS

2506   Annuaire du Togo. Paris, Diloutremer/Lomé, Service de l'information du Togo, 1962-?1964. Annual. NWU has copies for 1962-1964. (Historical, administrative and economic data)

2507   France. **Rapport du gouvernement français ... sur l'administration du Togo placé sous la tutelle de France**. Paris, 1921-1957. Annual. (Presented initially to the League of Nations, then, post 1946, to the Trusteeship Council of the United Nations. Particularly detailed series, many vols. of over 300pp. with extensive statistics and numerous maps).

2508   G.B. Colonial Office. **[Annual reports]: Togoland, 1920-1955**. London, 1922-1956. (As **Report to the Council of the League of Nations on the British Mandated sphere of Togoland**, 1920/21 (Cmd.1698); **Report of administration under mandate**, [title varies], 1922-38 (not pub. 1939-46), **Report ... to the Trusteeship Council of the UN**, 1947, **Report ... to the General Assembly of the UN**, 1948-55 (in Colonial series).

2509   Togo. Service de l'information. **Annuaire économique officiel de la république togolaise**. Lomé, 1983- . Annual. Latest issue in NWU is for 1987. (Covers history, administration, resources and includes commercial directory)

STATISTICS

2510   Country profile: Togo. London, Economist Intelligence Unit, 2004- . Annual. *Continues in part* **Country profile: Togo, Benin** . London, 1986-2003

2511   France. Ministère de la coopération. **Togo: données statistiques sur les activités économiques, culturelles et sociales**. Paris, 1976. 157pp.

2512   France. Service coloniale des statistiques. **Quelques renseignements statistiques pour la période 1939-1945 sur le Togo**. Paris, 1946. (*Bulletin mensuel de statistiques coloniales*. Suppl. série études, 12). 30pp.

2513   Germany. Statistisches Bundesamt. **Statistik des Auslandes: Länderberichte: Togo** (later **Länderbericht: Togo**). Wiesbaden/Stuttgart, Metzler-Poetschel, 1961- . Irreg. Issues for 1961, 1969, 1978, 1984, 1986, 1988, 1991.

2514   IMF. **Togo: statistical annex**. Washington, DC, 1996. (Staff country report, 96/12). vi, 60pp.

2515   Togo. Direction de la statistique [etc.]. **Annuaire statistique du Togo**. Lomé, 1966- . Annual/Biannual from 1975/76. ALA and NWU note issue for 1986/87 (pub. 1991). *Continues in part* Togo. Direction de la statistique [etc.]. **Inventaire économique du Togo**. Lomé, 1956-1966

2516   Togo. Direction de la statistique [etc.]. **Bulletin mensuel de statistique**. Lomé, 1952- . Monthly. Latest issues in NWU are for 1998.

2517   Togo. Direction de la statistique. **Indicateurs de l'économie togolaise**. Lomé, 1970- . NWU holds vols. 1 to 7, 1970-1975/79.

See also **2507, 2508**

DIRECTORIES OF ORGANIZATIONS

2518   **Guide des entreprises du Togo**. Lomé, Ministère de l'industrie, des sociétés d'état et de la zone franche, ?1996. 128pp. illus. maps.

2519   **Répertoire culturel: le Togo**. Paris, ACCT, ?1985. (Inventaire des activités, etc. des pays membres de l'ACCT). 111pp.

2520   Togo. Chambre de commerce, d'agriculture et d'industrie. **Répertoire des entreprises du Togo 95/96** [etc.]. Lomé, Société des bureaux, conceptions et réalisations publicitaires, 1996- . LC has 1997/98 ed. 232pp.

ATLASES & GAZETTEERS

2521   **Atlas de développement régional du Togo**, ed. T.C. Addra. Lomé, Direction générale du plan du développement & Direction de la cartographie nationale et du cadastre, [?1989]. 207pp. 43cm. (81 thematic maps for 5 regions, most at 1:500,000, and 8 covering the country as a whole)

2522   **Atlas du Togo**, comp. Yéme E. Gù-Konu & Georges Laclavère. Paris, *Jeune Afrique*, 1981. 64pp. (25 thematic maps with accompanying text)

2523 U.S. Board on Geographic Names. **Togo: official standard names approved by the USBGN.** Washington, DC, 1966. (Gazetteer, 98). iii, 100pp. (Includes some 7,000 names from maps at 1:200,000. Rev. of appropriate sections of **West Africa,** *see* **1758**)

See also **1067**

BIOLOGICAL SCIENCES

2524 Adjanohoun, Edouard J. et al. **Contribution aux études ethno-botaniques et floristiques au Togo.** Paris, ACCT, 1986. (Médecine traditionnelle et pharmacopée). 672pp. illus. maps.

2525 Brunel, J.F. et al. **Flore analytique du Togo: Phanérogames.** Berlin, Botanischen Garten und Botanischen Museum Berlin-Dahlem, 1984. (Englera, 4). 751pp. illus. - - Akpagana, K. & Guelly, K.A. 'Espèces d'angiospermes nouvelles pour la flore du Togo', *Acta botanica gallica,* 141, 1994, 781-787. (Adds 233 spp.)

2526 Cheke, Robert A. & Walsh, J. Frank. **The birds of Togo.** Tring, British Ornithologists' Union, 1996. (Checklist, 14). 220pp. 53 col plates. (Reviews, *BABC,* 4, 1997, 138-139; *Malimbus,* 19, 1997, 48)

2527 Scholz, Hildemar & Ursula. **Flore descriptive des cypéracées et graminées du Togo.** Vaduz, J. Cramer, 1983. (Phanerogamerum monographiae, 15). 360pp. illus. map.

LUSOPHONE WEST AFRICA

2528 Gonçalves, José Júlio. **A informação na Guiné, em Cabo Verde e em São Tomé e Príncipe (Achegas para o seu estudo)**. Lisbon, Instituto Superior de Ciências Sociaia e Politícas Ultramarinas, 1966. 232pp.

CAPE VERDE

Página Oficial do Governo http://www.governo.cv/

HANDBOOKS

2529 Corrêa, Antonio Augusto Mendes. **Ilhas de Cabo Verde**. Lisbon, Agência Geral do Ultramar, 1954. (Ultramar Português, II). 262pp. illus. 9 maps. (Detailed handbook covering topography, geology, climate, natural resources, peoples, culture, administration and the economy. Each chapter has an English summary)

2530 **Historical dictionary of the Republic of Cape Verde**. 3rd ed. comp. Richard Andrew Lobban & Marlene Lopes. Metuchen, NJ, Scarecrow Press, 1995. (African historical dictionaries, 62). lii, 336pp. (Review, *Choice*, 33, 1996, 762, "high quality, better than most in the series"). - - Orig. pub. as **Historical dictionary of the Republics of Guinea-Bissau and Cape Verde**, comp. Richard A. Lobban. Metuchen, NJ, 1979. (African historical dictionaries, 22). xv, 193pp. (Review, *African affairs*, 80, 1981, 418-419, "contains too many errors"); - - 2nd ed., comp. Richard A. Lobban & Marilyn Halter. Metuchen, NJ, 1988. (African historical dictionaries, 42). xix, 171pp. (Review, *IJAHS*, 24, 1991, 446, comments favourably on the revised eds. of the Cape Verde and Guinea Bissau volumes, and sees them as "valuable reference works ... because of the dearth of information available on these two countries". Rated "good", Balay, 1996)

2531 Portugal. Agência Geral do Ultramar. **Cabo Verde: pequena monografia**. [3rd ed.] Lisbon, 1970. 124pp. (Handbook covering history, geography, natural resources and administration. List of governors, 1587-1962). - - Orig. pub. Lisbon, 1961. 53pp; - - [2nd ed.] Lisbon, 1966. 80, 10pp.

2532 **República de Cabo Verde: 5 anos de independência, 1975-1980**. Lisbon, Comissão do V Aniversário da Independência Nacional, 1980. 94pp. (General handbook covering geography, history, politics and the economy)

STATISTICS

2533 Cape Verde. Direcção Geral de Estatística. **Boletim anual de estatística**. Praia, 1987- . Annual.

2534 Cape Verde. Instituto Nacional de Estatística. http://www.ine.cv/. (Provides a wide range of on-line demographic and economic statistics)

2535 Cape Verde. Serviço Nacional de Estatística [etc.]. **Anuário estatístico, Colónia de Cabo Verde**. Praia, 1933-1952. Irreg. Issues 1-20.

2536 Cape Verde. Serviço Nacional de Estatística [etc.]. **Boletim trimestral de estatística**. Praia, 1949- . Quarterly. Latest issue in NWU is for 1987.

2537 Carreira, António. **Demografia caboverdiana: subsídios para o seu estado, 1807-1983**. Praia, Instituto Caboverdiano do Livro, 1985. 86pp. map.

2538 **Country profile: Cape Verde**. London, Economist Intelligence Unit, 2004- . Annual. *Continues in part* **Country profile: Senegal, Gambia, Guinea-Bissau, Cape Verde**. London, 1987-1991; **Country profile: The Gambia, Guinea-Bissau, Cape Verde**. London, 1992; **Country profile: Congo, São Tomé and Príncipe, Guinea-Bissau, Cape Verde**. London, 1994-1996; **Country profile: São Tomé and Príncipe, Guinea-Bissau, Cape Verde**. London, 1997-2003.

2539 **Elementos para apreciação da evolução socio-económica em Cabo Verde (1980-1987)**. Praia, Ministério do Plano e da Cooperação, 1989. 60pp. (Largely statistical; comparative statistics for other West African countries)

2540 France. Ministère de la coopération. Service des études économiques et questions internationales. **Cap Vert, août 1978**. Paris, 1978. (Dossiers information économiques). 69, 35pp.

2541 Germany. Statistisches Bundesamt. **Statistik des Auslandes: Länderberichte: Kap Verde** (later **Länderbericht: Kap Verde**). Wiesbaden/ Stuttgart, Metzler-Poetschel, 1990.

2542 IMF. **Cape Verde: selected issues and statistical appendix**. Washington, DC, 2005. (Country report, 05/319). 78pp. - - Earlier eds. (title varies) 1995 (Staff country reports, 95/9); 1998 (Staff country report, 98/31); 2001 (Country report, 01/175); 2003 (Country report, 03/153). Full text of reports from 1997 also available online, *see* **334**.

ATLASES & GAZETTEERS

2543   Lereno, Álvaro. **Dicionário corográfico do Arquipélago de Cabo Verde**. Lisbon, Agência Geral do Ultramar, 1952. 568pp. (Alphabetical list of place names, linking each to its administrative district, and including many alternative forms)

2544   U.S. Board on Geographic Names. **Portugal and the Cape Verde Islands: official standard names approved by the USBGN**. Washington, DC, 1961. (Gazetteer, 50). v, 321pp. (Pp. 309-321, Cape Verde Islands. Includes c.1,000 names from maps at 1:150,000)

EARTH SCIENCES

2545   Mitchell-Thomé, Raoul C. **Geology of the Middle Atlantic islands**. Berlin, Borntraeger, 1976. 382pp. maps. (Includes Cape Verde)

2546   Mitchell-Thomé, Raoul C. 'Outline of the geology of the Cape Verde Archipelago', *Geologische Rundschau*, 61, 1972, 1087-1109. maps.

2547   Teixeira, António José da Silva & Barbosa, Luís Augusto Grandvaux. **A agricultura do arquipélago de Cabo Verde: cartas agrícolas, problemas agrários**. Lisbon, Junta de Investigações do Ultramar, 1958. (Mémorias, 2ª série, 2). 178pp. + 78 plates. (Includes 10 col. agroclimatic maps)

BIOLOGICAL SCIENCES

Zoology

2548   Bannerman, David Armitage & Bannerman, W. Mary. **Birds of the Atlantic Islands, vol. 4: History of the birds of the Cape Verde Islands**. Edinburgh, Oliver & Boyd, 1968. xxxi, 458pp. 17 col. plates. (Review *Ibis*, 111, 1969, 259)

2549   Clarke, Tony. **Field guide to the birds of the Atlantic islands**. London, Christopher Helm, 2005. 320pp. (Includes coverage of the Cape Verde Islands, as well as the Canaries, Azores and Madeira)

2550   **Conspectus da entomofauna Cabo-Verdiana, Pt. 1**. Lisbon, Junta de Investigações do Ultramar, 1961-1968. Pt. 1, comp. Alberto Coutinho Saraiva,

1961. (Estudos, ensaios e documentos, 83). 189pp. map; pt. 2, comp. Maria Leonor Veiga. 1968. 200ff. illus. (Photocopy)

2551 De Naurois, René. **As aves do arquipélago de Cabo Verde/Les oiseaux de l'Archipel du Cap Vert**. Lisbon, Instituto de Investigação Cientifíca Tropical, 1994. xvii, 188pp. illus. (Review, *Malimbus*, 18, 1996, 61-62)

2552 Hazevoet, Cornelis J. **Birds of the Cape Verde Islands**. Tring, British Ornithologists' Union, 1995. (Checklist, 13). 180pp. 48 col. plates. (Covers 164 spp. Critical review, *Malimbus*, 18, 1996, 61-62)

2553 Reiner, Francisco. **Catálogo dos peixes do Arquipélago de Cabo Verde**. Lisbon, Instituto Português de Investigaçao Marítima, 1996. 339pp. illus. map.

2554 Ribeiro, Henrique et al. **Os mosquitos de Cabo Verde (*Diptera: culcidae*): sistemática, distribução, bioecologica e importância médica**. Lisbon, Junta de Investigações do Ultramar, 1980. (Estudos, ensaios e documentos, 135). 141pp.

2555 Rolan, Emilio et al. **Malacological fauna from the Cape Verde archipelago. Vol.1**. Hackenheim, Conchbooks, 2005- . Vol. 1, 2005. 440pp. illus.

Botany

2556 Brochmann, Christian. **The endemic vascular plants of the Cape Verde Islands, West Africa**. Oslo, Botanical Garden & Museum, University of Oslo, 1997. (Sommerfeltia, 24). 356pp. illus. maps.

2557 Diniz, Maria Adélia et al. **Flora das culturas agrícolas de Cabo Verde**. Lisbon, Instituto de Investigação Científica Tropica (IICT), 2002. 223pp. illus.

2558 **Flora de Cabo Verde**, ed. J. Paiva. Lisbon & Praia, Centro de Documentação e Informação do Instituto de Investigação Científica Tropica (IICT), 1995- . Issued in fascs. 106 fascs pub. to 2002, none since.

2559 **Flora of Macaronesia: checklist of vascular plants**. 4th ed. comp. Alfred Hansen & Per Sunding. Oslo, Botanical Garden & Museum, University of Oslo, 1993. (Sommerfeltia, 17). 295pp. illus. (Macaronesia comprises Azores, Canary Islands, Madeira, Cape Verde). - - Orig. pub. comp. Ove Eriksson et al. Umeå, Department of Biology, University of

Umeå, 1974. 66pp; - - 2nd ed. Oslo, 1979. 2 vols; - - 3rd ed. Oslo, 1985. (Sommerfeltia, 1). 167pp.

2560 Gomes, Samuel. 'Nomes vernáculos e vulgares de plantas de Cabo Verde', *Garcia de Orta, Sér. Botanica*, 12, 1994, 127-150. (Tables of common name/scientific name and vice versa. An expansion of 'Subsídos para um dicionário e glossário dos nomes vernáculos das plantas do arquipélago de Cabo Verde', comp. L.A.G. Badbosa, *Garcia de Orta*, 9(1) 1961, 37-94)

2561 Lobin, Wolfram et al. **The ferns and fern-allies (Pteridophyta) of the Cape Verde Islands, West-Africa.** Berlin, Cramer/Stuttgart, Borntraeger, 1998. (Nova Hedwigia, Beiheft, 115). iii, 115pp. illus.

2562 Sunding, Per. **Check list of the vascular plants of the Cape Verde Islands.** Oslo, Botanical Garden, University of Oslo, 1973. 36pp. - - 'Additions to the vascular flora ...', *Garcia de Orta, sér. Botanica*, 2, 1974, 5-30.

GUINEA-BISSAU

HANDBOOKS

2563 **Anuário da Guiné Portuguesa**, ed. F. Duarte. Lisbon, Governo da Colónia, 1946,1948. 2 issues. 1946. xxvii, 692pp; 1948. xxvii, 875pp. (One of the most detailed examples of its kind. Historical, topographical and economic data, civil list and commercial directory)

2564 Carreira, António & Quintino, Fernando Rogado. **Antroponímia da Guiné Portuguesa**. Lisbon, Junta de Investigações do Ultramar, 1964-66. (Memórias, 49, 52). 2 vols. (Personal names)

2565 Gomes Correia, João Cornélio. **Atlas dos instrumentos tradicionais da Guiné-Bissau**. Overasself, Fundação Bartolomeu Simões Pereira Neerlandês, [199-?]. 80pp. illus.

2566 **Historical dictionary of the Republic of Guinea-Bissau**. 3rd ed.. comp. Richard A. Lobban & Peter Karibe Mendy. Lanham, MD, Scarecrow Press, 1996. (African historical dictionaries, 22). xxiii, 412pp. (Review, *IJAHS*, 31, 1998, 230-232). - - Orig. pub. as **Historical dictionary of the Republics of Guinea-Bissau and Cape Verde**, comp. Richard A. Lobban. Metuchen, NJ, 1979. xv, 193pp. (*See* **2530**); - - 2nd ed. comp. Richard A. Lobban & Joshua Forrest. Metuchen, NJ, 1988. xx, 210pp.

2567 Portugal. Agência Geral do Ultramar. **Guiné: pequena monografia**. 2nd ed. Lisbon, 1967. 83pp. - - Orig. pub. Lisbon, 1961. 53pp

2568 Portugal. Agência Geral do Ultramar. **Síntese monográfica da Guiné**. Lisbon, 1972. 96pp. (Brief handbook covering history, administration, natural resources)

2569 Teixeira da Mota, A. **Guiné Portuguesa**. Lisbon, Agência Geral do Ultramar, 1954. (Monografias dos territórios do Ultramar). 2 vols. illus. maps. (Also covers São Tomé e Principe. Vol. 1, xxv, 394pp. Topography, vegetation, fauna, peoples and languages with English summary pp. 361-383; vol. 2, 297pp. History, administration, health, economy, education, production and trade, with English summary pp. 233-248)

2570 Tkachenko, A.A. **Respublika Gvineia-Bisau: spravochnik**. Moscow, Akademiia nauk, Institut Afriki, 1990. 150pp. map.

STATISTICS

2571 **Country profile: Guinea-Bissau.** London, Economist Intelligence Unit, 2004- Annual. *Continues in part* **Country profile: Senegal, Gambia, Guinea-Bissau, Cape Verde.** London, 1987-1991; **Country profile: The Gambia, Guinea-Bissau, Cape Verde,** 1992; **Country profile: Sâo Tomé and Príncipe, Guinea-Bissau, Cape Verde.** London, 1997-2003.

2572 Germany. Statistisches Bundesamt. **Statistik des Auslandes: Länderberichte: Guinea-Bissau** (later **Länderbericht: Guinea-Bissau**). Wiesbaden/Stuttgart, Metzler-Poetschel, 1986- . Irreg. Issues for 1986, 1990.

2573 Guinea-Bissau. Direcção Geral de Estatística [etc.]. **Anuário estatístico** [etc.]. Bissau, 1947- . SOAS has vols. for 1947-1951. [n.s.] 1974- Annual. Latest issue in NWU is for 1991.

2574 Guinea-Bissau. Direcção Geral de Estatística [etc.]. **Boletim trimestral de estatística** [etc.]. Bissau, 1938- . Quarterly. Last issues in NWU are for 1983.

2575 Guinea-Bissau. Instituto Nacional de Estatística e Censos. **Guiné-Bissau: estudo sobre perfil demográfico, socio-economico e sanitário dos países sahelianos.** Bissau, 2001. 188pp.

2576 IMF. **Guinea-Bissau: selected issues and statistical appendix.** Washington, DC, 2006. (Country report, 06/313). 64pp. - - Earlier eds. (title varies) 1997 (Staff country report, 97/37); 1999 (Staff country report, 99/123); 2001 (Country report, 01/23); 2002 (Country report, 02/152). Full text of reports from 97/101, 1997 also available online, *see* **334.**

ATLASES & GAZETTEERS

2577 **Atlas da Lusofonia. Vol. 1, Guiné-Bissau,** ed. Pedro Cardoso et al. Lisbon, Instituto Português da Conjuntura Estratégica & Instituto Geográfico do Exército, 2001. 79pp. illus. maps. + 1 CD-ROM. (Col. maps and illus. statistical tables, bibliographical references)

2578 **Primeira relação de nomes geográficos da Guiné Portuguesa.** Lisbon, Junta de Investigações do Ultramar, Centro de Geografia do Ultramar, 1948. 75pp.

2579   U.S. Board on Geographic Names. **Portuguese Guinea: official standard names approved by the USBGN.** Washington, DC, 1968. (Gazetteer, 105). iii, 122pp. (Includes 8,700 names from maps at 1:50,000. Rev. of appropriate sections of **West Africa**, *see* **1758**)

EARTH SCIENCES

2580   Costa, J. Carrington da. **Fisiografia e geologia da província da Guiné.** Porto, Moderna, 1946. 104pp. illus. maps.

2581   **Introdução à geografía económica da Guiné-Bissau.** Bissau, Comissariado de Estado de Coordenação Económica e Plano, 1980. 148pp. ("Basic resource for primary data on the country in late colonial period", R. Galli. **Guinea-Bissau.** Oxford, Clio, 1990, p.3)

2582   Quintino, Fernando Rogado. **Prática e utensilagem agrícolas na Guiné.** Lisboa, Junta de Investigações do Ultramar, 1971. 125pp. + 12pp. plates. illus. map.

2583   Teixeira, Antonio José da Silva. **Os solos da Guiné Portuguesa; carta geral, características, formação e utilização.** Lisbon, Junta de Investigações do Ultramar, 1962. (Estudos, ensaios e documentos, 100). 397pp. illus. maps.

2584   Teixeira, João Ernesto. 'Geologia da Guiné portuguesa', pp. 53-104 in **Curso de geologia do Ultramar. Vol. 1.** Lisbon, Junta de Investigações do Ultramar, 1968.

BIOLOGICAL SCIENCES

Zoology

2585   Frade, Fernando & Bacelar, Amélia. **Catálogo das aves da Guiné Portuguesa.** Lisbon, Junta de Investigações do Ultramar, 1955-1959. 2 vols. Vol. 1, Non Passeres (*Anais*, 10 (4,2), 1955). 194pp; vol. 2, Passeres (*Memorias*, 2ª série, 7; *Estudos de zoologia*, 1959). 116pp. (Describes 195 non-passerines and 149 passerines)

2586   Reiner, Francisco & Simões, P. **Mamíferos selvagens da Guiné-Bissau.** Lisbon, Centro Português de Estudos dos Mamíferos Marinhos, 1998. 429pp. illus. maps.

2587   Sanches, J. Gonçalves. **Catálogo dos peixes marinhos da República da Guiné-Bissau.** Lisbon, Instituto Nacional de Investigação das Pescas (INIP), 1991. (Publicações avulsas, 16). xxxix, 429pp. illus.

Botany

2588   Bancessi, Quintino. **Identificação e descrição de leguminosas e gramíneas da Guiné-Bissau.** Bissau, Instituto Nacional Estudios e Pesquisas, 1991. (Kacu Martel Série B, Ciências naturais e exactas, 1). 185pp. illus.

2589   **Flora da Guiné Portuguesa/Flora da Guiné-Bissau.** Lisbon, Jardim e Museu Agrícola do Ultramar. 1971-83. 7 fascs. No more pub.

2590   Gomes, Elsa Teixeira. **Plantas medicinais da Guiné-Bissau: manuel práctico.** Bissau, Acção para o Desenvolvimento, 2003. 74pp.

2591   Santo, J. Do Espírito. **Nomes vernáculos de algumas plantas da Guiné Portuguesa.** Lisbon, Junta de Investigaçoes do Ultramar, 1963. (Estudios, ensaios e documentos, 104). 113pp.

2592   Sousa, Ester da Conceicão Pereira de. 'Contribuições para o conhecimento da flora da Guiné Portuguesa', pts 1-8, *Anais de Junta de Investigaçoes do Ultramar [etc.]* , 1, 1946, 45-152; 3, (3,2), 1948, 7-85; 4 (3,1), 1949, 7-63; 5 (5), 1950, 7-64; 6(3) 1951, 7-62; 7(2), 1952, 7-78; 11(4, 2) 1956, 7-38; 12(3) 1957, 7-27; - - **Contribuições para o conhecimento da flora da Guiné Portuguesa,** 9. Lisbon, Junta de Investigaçoes do Ultramar, 1961. (Estudios, ensaios e documentos, 77). ix, 101pp; - - 10. Lisbon, Junta de Investigaçoes do Ultramar, 1963. x, 76pp. (Includes index to the whole series)

SÃO TOMÉ & PRÍNCIPE

São Tomé e Príncipe government. http://www.parlamento.st/

HANDBOOKS

2593   Alegre, F.C. **Mutété 1995: 525 anos de existência, 505 anos de gestação, 20 anos de inocência**. São Tomé, Cooperativa de Artes Gráficas, 1995. 185pp. (Historical chronology)

2594   **Enciclopédia fundamental de São Tomé e Príncipe**, ed. Carlos Espirito Santo. Lisbon, Cooperaçao, 2001. 603pp. illus. (Pub. under patronage of Instituto Camoes, Centro Cultural Portugûes em São Tomé e Príncipe)

2595   France. Ministère de coopération. **São Tomé et Príncipe: guide d'information**. Paris, 1995. (Collection guides d'information). 45pp.

2596   Portugal. Agência Geral do Ultramar. **São Tomé e Príncipe: a brief survey**. Lisbon, 1970. 137pp. illus. map.

2597   Portugal. Agência Geral do Ultramar. **São Tomé e Príncipe: pequena monografia**. Lisbon, 1964. 110pp. (Standard handbook, covering topography, natural resources, peoples, history, administration, the economy. Chronological list of governors, 1586-1963)

2598   Portugal. Agência Geral do Ultramar. **Síntese monográfica de São Tomé e Príncipe**. Lisbon, 1973. 91pp. illus.

2599   **São Tomé et Príncipe: breve memória descritiva e histórica e síntese estatística**. São Tomé, 1969. 161pp. map. (In Portuguese, French and English. Prepared for VI Congress of International Association of Asthmology, held in São Tomé, 1969)

2600   Unzueta y Yuste, Abelardo de. **Islas de Golfo de Guinea (Elobeyes, Corisco, Annobon, Príncipe y Santo Tomé)**. Madrid, Instituto de Estudios Políticos, 1945. 386pp. (Covers topography, resources, history, administration, ethnology)

See also **2569**

STATISTICS

2601 V centenário, 1470-1970. Vila Real de Santo Antonio, Emp. Litográfica do Sul, 1970. (*Boletim informativo, economia e estatística geral*). Número especial. 125pp.

2602 Country profile: São Tomé & Príncipe. London, Economist Intelligence Unit, 2004- . Annual. *Continues in part* **Country profile: Angola, São Tomé & Príncipe** London, 1986-1993; **Country profile: Congo, São Tomé & Príncipe, Guinea-Bissau, Cape Verde.** London, 1994-1996; **Country profile: São Tomé & Príncipe, Guinea-Bissau, Cape Verde.** London, 1997-2003.

2603 IMF. Democratic Republic of São Tomé and Príncipe: statistical appendix. Washington, DC, 2004. (Country reports, 04/107). 49pp. - - Earlier eds. (title varies) 1995 (Staff country reports, 95/65); 1996 (Staff country reports, 96/70); 1998 (Staff country reports, 98/93); 2002 (Country reports, 02/31). Full text of reports from 1997 also available online, *see* **334**.

2604 São Tomé e Príncipe. Direcção de Estatística. **Boletim semestral de estatística.** São Tomé, 1993- . ALA and NWU note issue for 1993 only.

2605 São Tomé e Príncipe. Direcção de Estatística. **São Tomé e Príncipe em números.** São Tomé, 1993- . Latest issue in LC is for 1998

2606 São Tomé e Príncipe. Repartição dos Serviços de Estatística. **Anuário estatistico.** São Tomé, 1973- . Annual.

2607 São Tomé e Príncipe. Repartição dos Serviços de Estatística. **Boletim trimestral de estatística.** São Tomé, 1939- . Monthly/quarterly. Text in French and Portuguese. Latest issue in NWU is for 1976

BIOGRAPHICAL SOURCES

2608 Quem é quem em São Tomé e Príncipe: who's who, comp. José Ramos de Assunção. Lisbon, Tiposet, 2001. 160pp.

ATLASES & GAZETTEERS

2609   Portugal. Junta de Investigações do Ultramar. Centro de Geografia do Ultramar. **Relação dos nomes geográficos de São Tomé e Príncipe.** Lisbon, 1968. 82pp. (Includes 38,000 names from the 1:250,000 map series)

2610   U.S. Board on Geographic Names. **Rio Muni, Fernando Po and São Tomé e Príncipe: official standard names approved by the USBGN.** Washington, DC, 1962. (Gazetteer, 63). iv, 95pp. (Pp. 83-95, São Tomé e Príncipe. Includes 800 names from map series at 1:150,000 for São Tomé, 1:75,000 for Principe. Rev. of appropriate sections of **Equatorial Africa**, *see* **1472**). *See also* **2645**

EARTH SCIENCES

2611   Bailim Pissarra, J. et al. **Mineralogia dos solos de São Tomé e Príncipe.** Lisbon, Junta de Investigações do Ultramar, 1965. (Estudios, ensaios e documentos, 118). 144pp. illus. (Includes English summary)

2612   Carvalho Cardoso, J. & Sacadura Garcia, J.A. **Carta dos solos de São Tomé e Príncipe.** Lisbon, Junta de Investigações do Ultramar, 1962. (Publicações, 39). 306pp. maps. (Based on detailed soil surveys carried out in 1956 and 1958. A general review of geomorphology, geology, climate and vegetation followed by a classification and description of soil types. Maps at 1:50,000)

2613   Tenreiro, Francisco José. **A ilha de São Tomé (estudo geográfico).** Lisbon, Junta de Investigações do Ultramar, 1961. (Mémorias, 24). 279pp. maps. (Covers physical geography, economic geography. "Indispensable source", C.S. Shaw, **São Tomé e Príncipe**. Santa Barbara, CA, ABC- Clio, 1994, p.6)

BIOLOGICAL SCIENCES

Zoology

2614   Christy, Patrice & Clarke, William V. **Guide des oiseaux de São Tomé et Príncipe.** Libreville, Ecofac, 1998. 144pp. 143 col. plates. (Field guide. Less descriptive detail than in de Naurois, **2615** below. Review, *Malimbus*, 21, 1999, 67-68)

2615   De Naurois, René. **Aves das ilhas do Golfo da Guiné/Les oiseaux des îles du Golfe de Guinée (São Tomé, Príncipe et Annobon)**. Lisbon, Instituto de Investigação Cientifica Tropical, 1994. xxi, 207pp. 24pp. col. plates. (Text in Portuguese & French. Reviews, *Ibis*, 138, 1996, 355; *Malimbus*, 18, 1996, 63-64)

2616   Jones, Peter & Tye, Alan. **The birds of São Tomé and Príncipe with Annobon, islands of the Gulf of Guinea: an annotated checklist**. Tring, British Ornithologists' Union, 2006. (BOU checklist, 22). 192pp. illus. maps.

Botany

2617   Exell, Arthur Wallis et al. **Catalogue of the vascular plants of São Tomé (with Príncipe and Annobon)**. London, British Museum (Natural History), 1944. xi, 428pp. illus. maps. (Based on field trips 1932, 1933). - - **Supplement**. London, 1956. v, 58pp.

2618   Figueiredo, Estrela. **Pteridófitos de S. Tomé e Príncipe**. Lisbon, Instituto de Investigação Cientifica Tropical (IICT), 2002. (Estudos, ensaios e documentos, 162). 209pp.

2619   **Flora de S. Tomé e Príncipe**, ed. Maria Cândida Liberato et al. Lisbon, Ministério da Cooperação; Junta de Investigaçoes Científicas do Ultramar; Jardim e Museu Agrícola do Ultramar, 1972-1982. 9 pts. Incomplete. ?No more pub.

2620   Roseiro, Luís Lopes. **Plantas úteis da flora de São Tomé e Príncipe: medicinais, industriais e ornamentais**. 2nd ed. Cruz Quebrada, Gráfica, 2004. 135pp. illus. - - Orig. pub. Lisbon, 1984. 100pp.

FORMER SPANISH AFRICA

HANDBOOKS

2621   Pélissier, René. **Les térritoires espagnols d'Afrique**. Paris, La documentation française, 1963. (*Notes et études documentaires*, 2951, 3 Jan 1963). 40pp. - - Spanish trans. **Los territorios espanoles de Africa**. Madrid, Consejo Superior de Investigaçiónes Científicas e Instituto de Estudios Africanos, 1964. 94pp. (For each colony gives basic data on geography, history, demography, the economy, trade and communications)

YEARBOOKS

2622   **Anuario de Canarias, Africa Occidental, Guinea Española**. Las Palmas, 1951- . Annual. Formerly **Anuario de Canarias**. Las Palmas, 1944-1950; scope enlarged in 1951 to include Spanish Sahara and Guinea. (For a detailed account of coverage of this work *see* Sandford Berman. *Spanish Guinea: an annotated bibliography*. MLS, Catholic University of America, 1961. pp. 123-124. Copy in SOAS)

STATISTICS

2623   Spain. Dirección General de Plazas y Provincias Africanas e Instituto de Estudios Africanos. **Resumen estadístico de Africa española 1947/52 [-1965/66]**. Madrid, 1954-1966. Irreg. Issues for 1947/52, 1953/55, 1956/58, 1959/60, 1961/62, 1963/64, 1965/66.

ATLASES & GAZETTEERS

2624   Spain. Dirección General de Marruecos y Colonías e Instituto de Estudios Africanos. **Atlas histórico y geográfico de Africa Española**. Madrid, 1955. 204pp. 47 col. maps. 43 x 31cm. (Atlas histórico, pp. 13-67, covers 23 topics, each with accompanying maps, including six historical maps covering peoples, prehistory, early and recent history, exploration and voyages. Atlas geográfico, pp. 69-165, contains physical and geological maps for Ifni, 1:200,000; Spanish Sahara, 1:3M; Spanish Guinea, 1:600,000; Fernando Po, 1:250,000; Annobon, 1:50,000. Text includes statistics and diagrams. Detailed index of place names)

EQUATORIAL GUINEA

HANDBOOKS

2625   Aulet, M.L. **Spanish territories of the Gulf of Guinea: a guide book to Fernando Poo/Territorios Españoles del Golfo de Guinea: guia de Fernando Poo**. Fernando Po, Import Colonial, 1951. 48, 46pp. 1 map. 1 plan. (English and Spanish text in 1 vol. Includes brief commercial directory, plans of Fernando Po and Santa Isabel)

2626   Baguena Corella, Luis. **Guinea**. Madrid, Consejo Superior de Investigaçiónes Científicas e Instituto de Estudios Africanos, 1950. (Manuales del Africa española, 1). 160pp. (Covers geography & geology, climate, natural resources, peoples, history and administration, communications)

2627   **Directorio nacional de empresas y establecimientos**. Malabo, Equatorial Guinea. Dirección General de Estadística, 1988?- Annual.

2628   **Equatorial Guinea: a country profile for U.S. businesses**. Washington, DC, Corporate Council on Africa, 2001. 54pp.

2629   **Historical dictionary of Equatorial Guinea**. 3rd ed. comp. Max Liniger-Goumaz. Lanham, MD, Scarecrow Press, 2000. (African historical dictionaries, 21). xlii, 567pp. (Reviews, *ARBA*, 32, 2001, 197, "almost impossible to find information efficiently"; *Choice*, 38, 2001, 1611, "highly recommended"; *JAH*, 42, 2001, 541-542). - - Orig. pub. Metuchen, NJ, 1979. xiv, 222pp; - - 2nd ed. Metuchen, NJ, 1988. xxx, 238pp. (Rated "good", Balay, 1996)

2630   Liniger-Goumaz, Max. **Connaître la Guinée équatoriale**. Paris, Éditions de peuples noirs, 1986. 235pp. maps.

2631   Liniger-Goumaz, Max. **La Guinée équatoriale: un pays méconnu**. Paris, Harmattan, 1979. 511pp. maps. (Historical dictionary. Very similar in overall structure and choice of entry terms to the 1st ed. of his **Historical dictionary ...**, *see* **2629**, but somewhat fuller in content)

2632   Norborg, Åke. **A handbook of musical and other sound-producing instruments from Equatorial Guinea and Gabon**. Stockholm, Musikmuseet, 1989. 469pp. (Includes descriptions, illus., bibliography and discography)

2633 Unzueta y Yuste, Abelardo de. **Guinea continental española.** Madrid, Instituto de Estudios Políticos, 1944. 394pp. illus. maps. (Encyclopaedic survey of history, politics, topography and ethnology)

See also **2600**

STATISTICS

2634 Country profile: Equatorial Guinea. London, Economist Intelligence Unit, 2004- Annual. Continues in part **Country profile: Gabon, Equatorial Guinea.** London, 1986-2003.

2635 Equatorial Guinea. Dirección General de Estadística. **Boletín estadístico anual.** Malabo, 1981- . Annual (irreg.) Summary version pub. as **Resena estadística de la República de Guinea Ecuatorial.** Malabo, 1981- .

2636 Equatorial Guinea. Dirección General de Estadística. **Guinea en cifras.** Malabo, 1987- . Latest issue in LC is for 1992

2637 Equatorial Guinea. Secretaría de Estado para el Plan de Desarrollo Económico y Cooperación, Dirección Técnica de Estadística. **Reseña estadística de la República de Guinea Ecuatorial.** Malabo, 1981. 117pp.

2638 Germany. Statistisches Bundesamt. **Statistik des Auslandes: Länderberichte: Äquatorialguinea (later Länderbericht: Äquatorial-guinea).** Wiesbaden/Stuttgart, Metzler-Poetschel, 1984- . Irreg. Issues for 1984, 1986

2639 IMF. **Republic of Equatorial Guinea: selected issues and statistical appendix.** Washington, DC, 2006. (Country report, 06/237). 120pp. - - Earlier eds. (title varies) 1998 (Staff country reports, 98/33); 2003 (Country report, 03/386); 2005 (Country report, 05/151). Full text of reports from 1997 also available online, see **334.**

2640 Liniger-Goumaz, Max. **Estadísticas de la Guinea Ecuatorial Nguemista: datos para explicar un desastre político.** Geneva, Éditions du Temps, 1986. 104pp. (In Spanish, English and French)

2641 Spain. Dirección General de Plazas y Provincias Africanos e Instituto de Estudios Africanos. **Resúmenes estadísticos del Gobierno General de los territorios epañoles del Golfo de Guinea.** Madrid, 1941-?1960. Irreg. Title varies: **Negoçiado de estadística: resumenes del año/Anuario estadístico de los territorios ...** Issues for 1941, 1942/43, 1944/45, 1946/47, 1948/49, 1950/51, 1952/53, 1954/55, 1956/57, 1958/59, 1959/60.

BIOGRAPHICAL SOURCES

2642   Liniger-Goumaz, Max. **Who's who de la Dictature de Guinée equatoriale; les Nguemistes, 1979-1993**. Geneva, Éditions du Temps, 1994. 351pp. (General social and political information, and biographies of political personalities. Review, *IJAHS*, 28, 1995, 703-704)

ATLASES & GAZETTEERS

2643   **Atlas de la Guinée équatoriale**, comp. Anne Lerebours Pigeonnière et al. Paris, *Jeune Afrique*, 2001. 64pp. col. maps.
- - Also pub. in Spanish as **Atlas de Guinea Ecuatorial**. Paris, 2001. 64pp.

2644   Baguena Corella, Luis. **Toponimia de la Guinea Continental Española**. Madrid, Instituto de Estudios Africanos, Consejo Superior de Investigaciónes Científica, 1947. 497pp. (Lists 3,477 names and features with notes on their etymology)

2645   U.S. Board on Geographic Names. **Rio Muni, Fernando Po and São Tomé e Príncipe: official standard names approved by the USBGN.** Washington, DC, 1962. (Gazetteer, 63). iv, 95pp. (Pp. 1-82, Rio Muni and Fernando Po. 5,700 names from 1:100,000 map series. Rev. of appropriate sections of **Equatorial Africa**, *see* **1472**). Appropriate sections later re-issued as **Spanish Guinea: official standard names**. Washington, DC, 1962. iv, 95pp.)
See also **2610**

See also **612**

EARTH SCIENCES

2646   Alia Medina, Manuel. **Datos geomorfológicos de la Guinea continental española**. Madrid, Instituto de Estudios Africanos, 1951. 63pp. + 9 plates.

2647   Capuz Bonilla, Rafael. **Guia meteorológica de las provincias de Guinea**. Madrid, Instituto de Estudios Africanos, 1961. 65pp. illus.

2648   Martínez-Torres, L.M. **Mapa geológico de Guinea Ecuatorial continental:** explicación del mapa geológico, 1:400,000, y evolución geodinámica de Guinea Ecuatorial. Bilbao, Asociación Africanista Manuel Iradier, 1996. 24pp. illus.

2649 Nosti Nava, Jaime. **La agricultura en Guinea española; vol. 1, La planta**. Madrid, Instituto de Estudios Africanos, 1955. 376pp.

2650 Nosti Nava, Jaime. **Climatología de los territorios españoles del Golfo de Guinea**. Madrid, Dirección General de Marruecos y Colonias, 1942. 67pp. + 13 plates. illus. maps.

2651 Nosti Nava, Jaime. **Notas geográficas, fisicas et económicas sobre los territorios españoles del Golfo de Guinea**. Madrid, Instituto de Estudios Africanos, 1947. 116pp. 4 maps. - - Orig. pub. Madrid, Dirección de Agricultura de los Territorios Españoles del Golfo de Guinea, 1942. 116pp.

2652 Terán, Manuel de. **Sintesis geográfica de Fernando Póo**. Madrid, Instituto de Estudios Africanos, 1962. 116pp. illus. maps.

BIOLOGICAL SCIENCES

2653 Aedo, Carlos et al. **Bases documentales para la flora de Guinea Ecuatorial; plantas vasculares y hongos**. Madrid, Consejo Superior de Investigaciónes Científicas, Real Jardín Botanico, 1999. 414pp. (Lists over 55,000 records of plants, with no taxonomic notes. Gazetteer of collecting sites)

2654 Basilio, Aurelio. **Aves de la Isla de Fernando Po**. Madrid, Coculsa, 1963. 202pp. illus.

2655 Basilio, Aurelio. **La vida animal en la Guinea española: descripción y vida de los animales en la selva tropical Africana**. 2nd ed. Madrid, Instituto de Estudios Africanos, 1962. 190pp. illus. - - Orig. pub. Madrid, 1952. 146pp.

2656 Gomez Marín, Encarnación & Cristóbal, Laureano Merino. **Plantas medicinales de Guinea Ecuatorial**. Malabo, Centro Cultural Hispano-Guineano, 1989. 258pp. illus.

2657 Guinea López, Emilio. **Ensayo geobotánico de la Guinea continental Espanola**. Madrid, Dirección de Agricultura de los Territorios Espanoles del Golfo de Guinea, 1946. 388pp. illus. (Section 4, pp. 219-388, enumerates the known vascular plants of Rio Muni, now Mbini)

2658   Pérez del Val, Jaime. **Las aves de Bioko, Guinea Ecuatorial: guía de campo**. Leon, Edilisa, 1997. 239pp. 25 col. plates. (Former Fernando Po. Includes 196 spp., with col. illus.). - - 'Species relegated from and added to the avifauna of Bioko Island (Equatorial Guinea)', *Malimbus*, 19, 1997, 19-31; - - 'Addenda & corrigenda', *ibid*. 22, 2000, 31-34.

2659   Román, Benigno. **Peces de Rio Muni, Guinea Ecuatorial (Aguas dulces y salobres)**. Barcelona, Fundación "La Salle" de Ciencias Naturales, 1971. 295pp. illus. maps.

See also **1456, 2615- 2617**

WESTERN SAHARA
(SAHARAWI ARAB DEMOCRATIC REPUBLIC)

For recent discussions of the political situation of Western Sahara, *see* Zoubir, Yahia H. & Benabdallah-Gambier, Karim. 'Morocco, Western Sahara and the future of the Maghrib', *Journal of North African studies*, 9, 2004, 49-77; Jensen, Erik. **Western Sahara: anatomy of a stalemate**. Boulder, CO, Lynne Rienner, 2005.

Western Sahara online (Web site of the Saharawi Arab Democratic Republic) http://www.wsahara.net/
Note also Mincom. Alaycom, Web site of the Kingdom of Morocco, Ministry of Communications http://www.mincom.gov.ma/

HANDBOOKS

2660   Carnero Ruiz, Ismael. **Vocabulario geografico-Saharico**. Madrid, Consejo Superior de Investigaciónes Científicas e Instituto de Estudios Africanos, 1955. 287pp. maps. (Descriptive dictionary of Ifni and Spanish Sahara. Includes entries for historical events, ethnic groups, and places)

2661   Gaudio, Attilio. **Le dossier du Sahara occidental**. Paris, Nouvelles éditions latines, 1978. 462pp. + 16pp. plates.

2662   **Historical dictionary of Western Sahara**. 3rd ed., comp. Anthony G. Pazzanita & Tony Hodges. Lanham, MD, Scarecrow Press, 2006. (African historical dictionaries, 96). lxv, 523pp. - - Orig. pub. comp. Tony Hodges. Metuchen, NJ, 1982. (African historical dictionaries, 35). xxxix, 439pp. (Review, *Africana J.* 12, 1981, 364-365, "superb". Rated "excellent", Balay, 1996); - - 2nd ed. comp. Anthony G. Pazzanita. Metuchen, NJ, Scarecrow Press, 1994. (African historical dictionaries, 55). lxxii, 560pp. (Reviews, *Africa*, 66, 1996, 623-624; *Choice*, 32, 1995, 1088; *IJAHS*, 29, 1966, 187-188)

2663   **La República Arabe Saharaui Democrática: pasado y presente: geografía, historia, sociedad**. n.p., Ministerio de Información y Cultura de la República Arabe Saharawi Democrática, 1985. 76pp.

STATISTICS

2664   Spain. Consejo Superior de Investigaçiónes Científica. **Resumen estadistíco del Sahara español 1969**. Madrid, 1970. 31pp. ?No more pub. *See* L.F.Sipe, **Western Sahara: a comprehensive bibliography**, New York, 1984, p.114.

2665 Spain. Instituto Nacional de Estadística. **Anuario estadístico de España**. Madrid, 1858- . Annual. (Vols. for 1959-1968 include Spanish Sahara under section 'Provincias africanos'; 1969-75 has separate section for 'Provincia africana del Sahara español/Sahara español')

2666 Spanish West Africa. Gobierno del Africa Occidental Española, Secretaría General. **Sahara español, anuario estadístico 1946 [-1950]**. Sidi Ifni, 1949-1953. Annual. 5 vols.

ATLASES & GAZETTEERS

2667 U.S. Board on Geographic Names. **Spanish Sahara: official standard names approved by the USBGN.** Washington, DC, 1969. v, 52pp. (Includes c.3,000 names from maps at 1:500,000. Rev. of appropriate sections of **West Africa**, *see* **1758**)

EARTH SCIENCES

2668 Flores Morales, Angel. **El Sahara Español: ensayo de geografia fisica, humana y económica**. Madrid, Alta Comisaría de España en Marruecos, 1946. 167pp. illus. maps. (Covers climate, resources, peoples, flora and fauna)

2669 Font Tullot, Inocencio. **El clima del Sahara (con especial referencia a la zona española)**. Madrid, Instituto de Estudios Africanos, 1955. 112pp. illus. maps. (Incorporates material previously pub. in his **El clima del Africa Occidental española**. Madrid, Servicio Meteorológico Nacional, 1949. viii, 88pp. illus. maps)

2670 Hernández-Pacheco, Eduardo, ed. **El Sahara español**. Madrid, Instituto de Estudios Africanos, 1962. (Empresas politícas, 4). 178pp. Pt. 1, Características geográficas y geológicas y rasgos de su flora y fauna, by E. Hernández-Pacheco; pt. 2, La Presencia humana y la obra española, by José María Cordero Torres. (Summary and updated version of **2668** & **2671**)

2671 Hernández-Pacheco, Eduardo et al. **El Sahara español: estudio geológico, geográfico y botánico**. Madrid, Instituto de Estudios Africanos, 1949. 808, cxxxivpp. illus. maps. (Large scale data compilation, a companion to Flores Morales, **2668**. Includes checklist of plants)

2672 Ratschiller, Ludwig Karl. **Lithostratigraphy of the northern Spanish Sahara**. Trieste, Università degli studi di Trieste, Facoltà di Scienze

Matematiche, Fisiche e Naturali, Istituto di Geologia, 1971. (Memorie del Museo Tridentino di Scienze Naturali, 18, Fasc.1). 78pp. + 22pp. plates.

BIOLOGICAL SCIENCES

2673 Geniez, Phillipe. **The amphibians and reptiles of the Western Sahara: an atlas and field guide**. Frankfurt-am-Main, Chimaira, 2003. 229pp. illus. maps. (Detailed coverage of 50 spp. Review, *African journal of herpetology*, 54, 2005, 103-104)

2674 Guinea López, Emilio. 'Catálogo razonado de las plantas del Sahara español', *Anales del Jardín Botánico de Madrid*, 8, 1948, 357-442.

See also **2671**

SOUTHERN AFRICA

South Africa

Namibia

Botswana
Lesotho
Swaziland

Indian Ocean Islands (Francophone Southern
    Africa)
    Comoro Islands   Mayotte
    Madagascar   Réunion
    Mauritius   Seychelles

Lusophone Southern Africa
    Angola
    Mozambique

Most sources which are principally concerned with the region represented by modern political **South Africa** are also at least partly concerned with one or more neighbouring countries, especially Namibia, Botswana, Lesotho and Swaziland, and Mozambique. No attempt has been made therefore to distinguish between sources relating to **Southern Africa** in general and those relating only to **South Africa** and all have been placed under the latter heading.

SOUTH AFRICA

South African Government online http://www.gov.za/

Bibliographies of reference sources

2675 Musiker, Reuben & Musiker, Naomi. **Guide to South African reference books**. 6th ed. London, Mansell, 1997. vii, 240pp. (Includes 1,139 entries, some duplicated under different headings. Review, *Choice*, 35, 1998, 1343). - - Orig. pub. Cape Town, University of Cape Town, School of Librarianship, 1955. ix, 43pp; - - 2nd ed. Cape Town, 1958. vii, 43pp; - - 3rd ed. Grahamstown, Rhodes University, 1963. ix, 161pp; - - 4th ed. Cape Town, Balkema, 1965. x, 110pp; - - 5th ed. Cape Town, Balkema, 1971. 138pp. - - **Cumulative suppl. to 5th ed. covering 1970-76**. Johannesburg, University of the Witwatersrand Library, 1977. iv, 112pp. (Thanks to the dedication of Musiker over more than fifty years, South Africa is better served with guidance than any other region of Sub-Saharan Africa. Older eds. of Musiker's titles, including those listed below, remain valuable for their coverage of contemporary material, not always repeated in later eds.)

2676 Musiker, Reuben. **South Africa**. Oxford, Clio Press, 1979. (World bibliographical series, 7). 220pp. ("This work succeeds the author's **Guide to South African reference books** [5th ed.] *see* **2675,** and all its suppls.", pref. Some 1,200 items)

2677 Musiker, Reuben. **South African reference books and bibliographies of 1979-80**. Johannesburg, University of the Witwatersrand Library, 1981. ix, 58pp. - - **...** **of 1979-83**. Johannesburg, 1983. vi, 100pp. (Detailed critical review including comment on Musiker's other works above in *ARD*, 36, 1984, 39-41)

HANDBOOKS

Bibliographies

2678 Inskip, Catherine A. **List of guide books and handbooks dating from 1800 to the present day dealing with South Africa and the Western Province**. Cape Town, University of Cape Town, School of Librarianship, 1949. 31pp. (Includes some directories and almanacks but concentrates on travel guides and emigration handbooks. No annotations)

General

2679 **Ensiklopedie van die wêreld**. Stellenbosch, C.F. Albertyn, 1971-1978. 11 vols. illus. - - **Suppls**. [1-5]. Stellenbosch, 1983. 376pp; 1987. 389pp; 1989. 354pp. 1991. 368pp; 1993. 455pp. (Based on the Dutch **Winkler Prins**. World coverage, but particularly detailed articles on Southern African topics)

2680 **Holcroft's South African calendar: facts, figures, dates**. 2nd ed. Pretoria, 1976. 126pp. illus. (Quick reference source with brief entries on fauna and flora, climate, education, government, population and sport). - - Orig. pub. Pretoria, Vergne, 1975. 128pp.

2681 Horrell, Muriel et al. **South Africa: basic facts and figures**. Johannesburg, South African Institute of Race Relations, 1973. vii, 115pp.

2682 Joyce, Peter. **South African family encyclopedia**. Cape Town, Struik, 1989. 431pp. illus. (For the general reader. Review article, E.G. Jones, 'A new South African encyclopedia', *Mousaion*, ser. 3, 10, 1992, 105-111)

2683 Luirink, Bart. **Zuid-Afrika: mensen, politiek, economie, cultuur**. Amsterdam, Koninklijk Instituut voor de Tropen/The Hague, Novib, 2003. (Landenreeks). 78pp. illus. maps

2684 Overseas reference book of the Union of South Africa; including South-West Africa, Basutoland, Bechuanaland Protectorate and Swaziland, ed. Julian Mockford. London, Todd, 1945. 567pp. illus. maps. (Editor was Public Relations Officer at South Africa House, London. General articles, followed by detailed chapters on industry, agriculture, population, trade and commerce. 'City and town guide' gives details of some 230. Civil list and lists of major commercial institutions, the press, societies and libraries. Detailed atlas section of 55 b. & w. maps. A valuable compilation of data from official sources on the region at the end of World War II)

2685 Pocket guide to South Africa. Yeoville, STE Publishers for Government Communication & Information System (GCIS), 2003- . Annual.

2686 Pokrovskii, A.S. et al. **IUzhno-Afrikanskaia Respublika: ekono-micheskii spravochnik** Moscow, Akademiia nauk, Institut Afriki, 1982. 279pp. illus.

2687 *Reader's digest* **illustrated encyclopedia of essential knowledge**. Cape Town, *Reader's digest* Association, 1996. 608pp. illus. maps. (Arranged under 23 sections each with an A/Z sequence. South African emphasis is particularly strong in sections on literature, history, politics and topography: elsewhere coverage is more general with some South African examples)

2688 Rosenthal, Eric, ed. **Encyclopedia of Southern Africa**. 7th ed. Cape Town, Juta, 1978. ix, 577pp. illus. (Some 5,000 brief entries, including biographies, together with some 20 longer articles which have their own contents lists. Covers Republic of South Africa and Namibia; Botswana, Lesotho and Swaziland; Malawi, Zambia and Zimbabwe, and Angola. Mozambique covered in 1st to 6th eds.). - - Orig. pub. London, Warne, 1961. viii, 600pp; - - 2nd ed. London, 1964. viii, 604pp; - - 3rd ed. London, 1965. viii, 628pp; - - 4th ed. London, 1967. viii, 638pp; - - 5th ed. London, 1970. xii, 653pp; - - 6th ed. London, 1973. xii, 662pp. (Review, *African affairs*, 72, 1973, 346-347, sees articles as "much too short to have value")

2689 Rosenthal, Eric. **South Africa in a nutshell: facts and figures for the visitor to the Union, June, 1948**. Pretoria, South African Tourist Corporation (SATOUR), 1948. 127pp. illus. map.

2690 Rosenthal, Eric. **Total book of South African records**. 2nd ed. Johannesburg, Total South Africa, 1982. 160pp. illus. (Includes a wide range of records relating to the natural world, sport, & the administration, also lists of honours & awards). - - Orig. pub. as **Total's book of Southern African records**. Johannesburg, Total South Africa, 1975. 160pp. illus.

2691 Schirmer, P. **Concise illustrated South African encyclopedia**. Johannesburg, Central News Agency, 1980. 211pp. illus. (Popular work with some 1,500 entries and over 400 illus.)

2692 Schmidt, Werner. **Südafrika: Republik Südafrika, Südwestafrika, Betschuanenland, Basutuland, Swaziland**. 2nd ed. Bonn, K. Schroeder for Deutsche Afrika-Gesellschaft, 1963. (Die Länder Afrikas, 4). 256pp. - - Orig. pub. as **Südafrikanische Union**. Bonn, 1958. 105pp. (1st ed. includes coverage of South-West Africa, Botswana, Lesotho and Swaziland in 4pp; 2nd ed. expands this coverage to 50pp)

2693 South Africa: a country study. 3rd ed. comp. Rita M. Byrnes et al. Washington, DC, Library of Congress, Federal Research Division, 1997. lxv, 532pp. illus. maps. Also available at: http://lcweb2.loc.gov/frd/cs/zatoc.html. - - Orig. pub. as **Area handbook for the Republic of South Africa**, comp. Irving Kaplan et al. Washington, DC, U.S. Department of Defense, 1971. xvi, 845pp. illus. maps; - - 2nd ed. **South Africa: a country study**. Washington, DC, 1981. 464pp. illus. maps.

2694 South Africa at a glance: history, politics, economy, trade, tourism, statistics, 1995- . Craighall, Editors Inc., 1996-   . Annual. Latest issue in Stanford is for 2003/04.

2695 Standard encyclopedia of Southern Africa, ed.-in-chief Dirk J. Potgieter. Cape Town, NASOU, 1970-1976. 12 vols. illus. maps. (Vols. 1 to 11, main text, A/Z; vol. 12, supplement & general index. Major work by some 1,400 contributors, many of them civil servants drawing on non-public information. Over 5,000 illus., many from newspaper libraries. "Emphasis on the Republic of South Africa ... and its immediate neighbours" but also lengthy treatment for Angola, Zaire, Kenya, Uganda and Tanzania. Over 10,000 articles ranging from short entries for biographies, flora and fauna to lengthy surveys, e.g. Anglo-Boer War, 19pp. Articles on documentary and institutional sources, e.g. 'Almanacs and yearbooks', 'Academies'. *See* **2757, 2837, 2968**)

2696 Turner, Barry. **Southern Africa profiled: essential facts on society, business and politics in Southern Africa**. London, Macmillan Reference, 2000. xvi, 306pp. illus. maps.

Regional

2697 Musiker, Naomi & Reuben. **Historical dictionary of Greater Johannesburg**. Lanham, MD, Scarecrow Press, 1999. lii, 480pp. (Reviews, *ARD*, 84, 2000, 78-79; *Choice*, 37, 2000, 1278; *JAH*, 42, 2001, 509-510). - - **A concise dictionary of Greater Johannesburg**. Cape Town, Francolin, 2000. 393pp. (Revised and slightly abridged version of the 1999 work)

2698 Natal official guide. Cape Town, R.Beerman/Durban, Selected Publications, 1959. 397pp. illus. (Introductory sections on history, topography and public services followed by descriptive sections for each major town and city)

2699 Official guide to the Province of the Cape of Good Hope. Cape Town, Beerman, 1953. 261pp. illus. (Arranged by regions, with entries for major towns and topics under each region)

2700 Orange Free State official guide. Cape Town, R. Beerman, 1956. 401pp. (General section, followed by descriptive gazetteer of individual towns. Over 400 illus.)

2701 Transvaal official guide: Union Golden Jubilee Souvenir ed. Cape Town, Beerman, 1960. 448pp. illus. maps. - - Earlier ed. Cape Town, 1955. 480pp.

Special subjects

Education

2702 The education atlas of South Africa, 2000, comp. Monica Bot et al. Houghton, Education Foundation, 2000. iv, 134pp. col. maps. (Updates **The education atlas of South Africa**, comp. Dulcie Krige et al. Durban, Indicator Press, University of Natal, 1994. 200pp. Education provision at magisterial district level. Maps show levels of education, language distribution, etc. with statistics from 1991 census. Review, *SAGJ*, 78, 1996, 50-51)

Ethnography

2703 Afolayun, Fuso. **Culture and customs of South Africa**. Westport, CT, Greenwood Press, 2004. (Culture & customs of Africa). xxiv, 301pp. illus.

Map. (Sections for land & people, history & political economy, religion, literature, media, art & architecture, social customs & lifestyle etc.)

2704 Ethnographic survey of Africa: Southern Africa. London, International African Institute, 1953-1954. 4 vols. illus. maps. Sub-series of **Ethnographic survey** (*see* **86**). Vol. 1. 1952. The Swazi, by H. Kuper. 89pp; vol. 2. 1953. The southern Sotho, by V.G.J. Sheddick. 86pp; vol. 3. 1953. The Tswana, by I. Schapera. 77pp; vol. 4. 1954. The Shona and Ndebele of Southern Rhodesia, by H. Kuper et al. 131pp.

History

2705 Joyce, Peter. **South Africa in the 20th century: chronicles of an era**. Cape Town, Struik, 2000. 248pp. illus. (Historical chronology)

2706 Mahida, Ebrahim Mahomed. **History of Muslims in South Africa: a chronology**. Durban, Arabic Study Circle, 1993. 154pp. (1652 to 1990. No index)

2707 Oberholster, Jacobus Johannes. **The historical monuments of South Africa**. Stellenbosch, Rembrandt van Rijn Foundation for Culture & Historical Monuments Council, 1972. 354pp. illus. (Descriptions and illus. of 367 designated national monuments)

2708 Richardson, Deirdre. **Historic sites of South Africa**. Cape Town, Struik, 2001. 272pp. (Arranged by province. No index)

2709 Saunders, Christopher C. & Southey, Nicholas. **A dictionary of South African history**. Cape Town, David Philip, 1998. xxix, 198pp. (Review article by C. Kros, *SAHJ*, 40, 1999, 257-266). Repub. with added bibliography as **Historical dictionary of South Africa**. 2nd ed. Lanham, MD, Scarecrow Press, 2000. (African historical dictionaries, 78). xlv, 375pp. (Reviews, *ARBA*, 32, 2001, 198-199, "major work of reference and scholarship"; *ASQ*, 8(1) 2004, http://www.africa.ufl.edu/asq/v8/v8i1a10.htm; *ASR*, 44(3) 2001, 95-96; *CJAS*, 35, 2001, 622-624; *IJAHS*, 34, 2001, 207-208; *JAH*, 42, 2001, 350-351) - - Orig. pub. comp C.C. Saunders. Metuchen, NJ, 1983. (African historical dictionaries, 37). xxviii, 241pp. (Reviews, *Africana J.*, 14, 1983, 359-360; *IJAHS*, 17, 1984, 709-710; *JAH*, 27, 1986, 408-409 "well above the standard of many others in this series". Rated "excellent", Balay, 1996)

2710 Saunders, Christopher C. ed. **An illustrated dictionary of South African history**. Sandton, Ibis Books, 1994. 283pp. (480 entries contributed by 25 historians, for persons, events and themes. Very enthusiastic review, *SAHJ*, 32, 1995, 312-313)

2711 Wiechen, Peter van. **Vademecum van de Oost- en West-Indische Compagnie: historisch-geografisch overzicht van de Nederlandse aanwezigheid in Afrika, Amerika, Azië en West-Australië vanaf 1602 tot heden**. Utrecht, Bestebreurtje, 2002. 381pp. illus. maps. (Includes data on persons and activities of the Dutch at the Cape)

Atlases

2712 Bergh, Johannes Stephanus & Visagie, Jan Christian. **The Eastern Cape Frontier Zone, 1660-1980: a cartographic guide for historical research**. Durban, Butterworths, 1985. 83pp. maps. (Atlas portraying 23 themes)

2713 Bergh, Johannes Stephanus. **Geskiedenisatlas van Suid-Afrika: die vier noordelike Provinsies**. Pretoria, Van Schaik, 1999. 375pp. maps. (Historical maps, essays, photographs and bibliographies for Northern Province, North-West, Mpumalanga and Gauteng)

2714 Böeseken, Anna J. et al. **Geskiedenis atlas vir Suid-Afrika**. 2nd ed. Cape Town, NASOU, 1953. xii, 92pp. maps. (World atlas. 80 b. & w. maps of which 32 cover South Africa). - - Orig. pub. Cape Town, 1948. x, 92pp.

2715 Bredekamp, Henry C. & Van den Berg, Owen. **A new history atlas for South Africa**. London, Edward Arnold, 1986. 99pp. maps.

2716 Christopher, Anthony John. **The atlas of changing South Africa**. New York, Routledge, 2001. vii, 260pp. 175 maps. (Also available as an e-book. Review, H-Africa, http://www.h-net.org/reviews. Conover-Porter Award, 2004.). - - Orig. pub. as **Atlas of apartheid,** New York, Routledge, 1994. xi, 212pp. (Reviews, *African affairs*, 93, 1994, 616-618; *GJ*, 161, 1995, 211-212; *SAHJ*, 32, 1995, 288-289)

2717 Ploeger, Jan & Smith, Anna H. **Pictorial atlas of the history of the Union of South Africa**. Pretoria, J. L. van Schaik, 1949. 196pp. maps.

Wars

2718 Austin, Ronald J. **The Australian illustrated encyclopedia of the Zulu and Boer wars**. Rosebud, Victoria, Slouch Hat Publications, 1999. 326pp. illus. maps. (Zulu War of 1879)

2719 Baker, Anthony. **Battles and battlefields of the Anglo-Boer War, 1899-1902**. Milton Keynes, author, 1999. vi, 260pp. (52 b. & w. maps with data superimposed, accompanied by 1 to 2 pages of text. Review, *ARD*, 80, 1999, 83-84). - - Orig. pub. Milton Keynes, Military Press, 1999, vi, 260pp.

2720 Cloete, P.G. **The Anglo-Boer War: a chronology**. Pretoria, Van der Welt, 2000. 351pp. (Daily summary. Review, *SAHJ*, 45, 2001, 291-294)

2721 Evans, Martin Marix. **Encyclopedia of the Boer War, 1899-1902**. Santa Barbara, CA, ABC-Clio, 2000. xxvii, 414pp. (Brief overview and chronology followed by A/Z entries on persons, battles, regions etc. Appendices include British forces, Boer forces, concentration & refugee camps. Reprints a number of contemporary documents. Reviews, *ASR*, 46(2), 2003, 125-127; *Historia*, 46, 2002, 552; *JAH*, 42, 2001, 351-352)

2722 Hall, Darrell. **The Hall handbook of the Anglo-Boer War**. Pietermaritzburg, University of Natal Press, 1999. ix, 272pp. illus. maps. (Review, *ASR*, 46 (2), 2003, 125-127)

2723 Johnson Barker, Brian. **A concise dictionary of the Boer War**. Cape Town, Francolin, 1999. 143pp. (Brief entries for commanders, battles, fighting groups, gallantry awards etc.)

2724 Jones, Anthony David. **The Boer army 1899-1902: a military handbook**. Milton Keynes, Military Press, 2000. ii, 90pp. (Review, *ARD*, 85, 2001, 89-90)

2725 Jones, Huw M. & Jones, Muirig G.M. **A gazetteer of the Second Anglo-Boer War, 1899-1902**. Milton Keynes, Military Press, 1999. 286pp. ("Sorts out major activity ... by place name rather than campaign or time or person", pref. Includes maps, indexes of persons and units. *See* Huw M. Jones, 'Compiling a gazetteer of the Second Anglo-Boer War', *ARD*, 84, 2000, 47-59. Reviews, *African affairs*, 99, 2000, 141-142; *ARD*, 80, 1999, 64)

2726 Laband, John. **The atlas of the later Zulu Wars, 1883-1888**. Pietermaritzburg, University of Natal Press, 2001. x, 140pp. 25 col. maps. (Large format. Includes illus. and text. Review, *IJAHS*, 36, 2003, 180-182)

2727 Laband, John & Thompson, Paul Singer. **A field guide to the war in Zululand and the defence of Natal**. 2nd ed. Pietermaritzburg, University of Natal Press, 1983. - - Orig. pub. as **A field guide to the war in Zululand, 1879**. Pietermaritzburg, 1979. vii, 88pp

2728 Laband, John & Thompson, Paul Singer. **The illustrated guide to the Anglo-Zulu War**. 2nd ed. Pietermaritzburg, University of Natal Press, 2004. xii, 201pp. - - Orig. pub. Pietermaritzburg, 2000. xii, 201pp. (Review, *IJAHS*, 34, 2001, 716-717)

2729 Thompson, Paul Singer. **An historical atlas of the Zulu rebellion of 1906**. Pietermaritzburg, P.L. Thompson, 2001. v, 73pp. (In addition to maps of battles includes thematic maps of Natal & Zululand at the time. Review, *SAHJ*, 49, 2003, 303-304)

Language

2730 **A dictionary of English usage in Southern Africa**, comp. Douglas Ridley Beeton & Helen Dorner. Cape Town, Oxford University Press, 1975. xix, 196pp. (Includes glossary of local vocabulary and idiom, and a record of 'mistakes and problems' in local usage)

2731 **A dictionary of South African English**. 4th ed, ed. Jean Branford. Cape Town, Oxford University Press, 1991. xxxi, 412pp. (4,000 entries ranging from historical terms to modern slang, with definitions, etymology, and examples of use in context). - - Orig. pub as **A dictionary of South Africanisms in English**. Cape Town, 1978. 352pp; - - 2nd ed. Cape Town, 1980. xxxi, 361pp; - - 3rd ed. Cape Town, 1987. xxxi, 444pp.

2732 **A dictionary of South African English on historical principles**, ed. Penny Silva et al. Oxford, Oxford University Press in association with the Dictionary Unit for South African English (DSAE), 1996. xxi, 825pp. (Major source based on 25 years work, covering the vocabulary from the late 16th to the late 20th centuries. Contains 5,000 entries with some 47,000 citations. Includes words derived from the many languages which have influenced English in South Africa, namely Dutch, Afrikaans, and the Malayo-Indonesian, Indian, Khoisan, Nguni and Sotho languages. The Dictionary Unit was set up at Rhodes University in 1969, "to collect and record English as used in South Africa"; *see*: http://www.ru.ac.za/affiliates/dsae/. Review article 'Language and society: reflections on South African English' by Willie Henderson, *African affairs*, 96, 1997, 113-120 expresses reservations over some of the inclusions but sees work overall "of huge linguistic and cultural significance and academic value" (p.120). Review, *Choice*, 34, 1997, 1473. *See also* **Voorloper: an interim presentation of materials for a Dictionary of**

South African English .... Grahamstown, Institute for the Study of English in Africa, Rhodes University, 1976. xxv, 921pp; **Agterryer: an interim presentation of materials for a Dictionary of South African English** .... Grahamstown, Rhodes University, 1984)

2733 Grobler, Elda et al. **Language atlas of South Africa: language and literacy patterns**. Pretoria, Human Sciences Research Council, 1990. 74pp. (23 language maps with accompanying analysis). *See also* **Language atlas of South Africa: a theoretical introduction**, by Esmé du Preez. Pretoria, Human Sciences Research Council, 1987. x, 90pp.

2734 Pettman, Charles. **Africanderisms: a glossary of South African colloquial words and phrases, and of place and other names**. London, Longmans, 1913. xviii, 579pp. (Reprinted, Detroit, MI, Gale, 1969). - - Swart, C.P. **Africanderisms: a suppl. to the Rev. Charles Pettman's glossary**. M.A. thesis, University of South Africa, Pretoria, 1934; - - Jeffreys, M.D.W. 'Africanderisms [not in Pettman]' , *Africana notes and news*, 16, 1964, 43-95; 17, 1967, 216-220; 19, 1970, 29-41 (Includes quotations to illustrate use)

2735 **South African concise Oxford dictionary**, ed. Kathryn Kavanagh et al. Oxford, Oxford University Press in association with the Dictionary Unit for South African English (DSAE), 2002. 1,392pp. (Based on 10th ed. of **Concise Oxford dictionary**. Oxford, 1999, with some 1,500 extra terms in South African English. *See also* **The South African pocket Oxford dictionary**, ed. Jean Branford. Cape Town, Oxford University Press, 1987. xxv, 903pp., based on **The pocket Oxford dictionary of current English**. 7th ed., ed. R.E. Allen. London, 1984)

2736 Van der Merwe, Izak Johannes & Van Niekerk, Louisa O. **Language in South Africa: distribution and change**. Stellenbosch, University of Stellenbosch, Department of Geography, 1994. iv, 68pp. ("This atlas is a follow-up on the **Language atlas...**", pref., *see* **2733**. 32 maps comparing the distribution of English, Afrikaans, and 9 other African languages, languages of European immigrants and oriental languages as revealed by the 1980 and 1991 population censuses)

Law

2737 Claassen, Cornelis Johannes. **Dictionary of legal words and phrases**. Durban, Butterworths, 1975-1977. 2 vols. (Based on J.J.L. Sisson. **The South African judicial dictionary: being a dictionary of words and phrases as interpreted by the superior courts in the Union, Southern Rhodesia and South West Africa**. Durban, Butterworths, 1960. 876pp. *and* William H.S. Bell. **South African legal dictionary**. 3rd ed. Durban, 1951)

Literature

2738 Adey, David, et al. **Companion to South African English literature**. Johannesburg, Donker, 1986. 220pp. (Contains some 450 author entries, 39 articles on literary genres, and entries for major titles or topics. Includes authors born or resident in South Africa, Botswana, Lesotho and Swaziland, together with those who made the region a major theme in their work)

2739 Crwys-Williams, Jennifer. **The Penguin dictionary of South African quotations**. 2nd ed. London/Sandton, Penguin Books, 1999. xii, 516pp. - - Orig. pub. London/Johannesburg, 1994. xi, 489pp.

2740 Grové, Alewyn Petrus. **Letterkundige sakwoordeboek vir Afrikaans**. 5th ed. Goodwood, NASOU, 1988. 153pp. (Dictionary of literary terminology. Includes bio-bibliographies of selected Afrikaans authors). - - Orig. pub. Cape Town, NASOU, 1964. 104pp; - - 3rd ed. Cape Town, 1976. 121pp; - - 4th ed. Goodwood, 1982. 135pp.

2741 Nienaber, Petrus Johannes. **Hier is ons skrywers: biografiese sketse van Afrikaanse skrywers; Dl.1**. Johannesburg, Afrikaanse Pers Boekhandel, 1949. 475pp. No more pub. (Biographies of Afrikaans writers)

2742 Scanlon, Paul, ed. **South African writers**. Detroit, Gale, 2000. (Dictionary of literary biography, 225). xx, 526pp. (Lengthy entries by specialists for 37 authors, with lists of works by and about them. Some are new articles for authors already covered by entries in previous general volumes of the Dictionary: an index at the end of the vol. identifies these)

2743 Van Coller, H.P. **Perspektief en profiel n'Afrikaanse literatuur-geskiedenis**. Pretoria, Van Schaik, 1998-1999. 2 vols. xi, 735; xi, 819pp. (7 essays, e.g. on Afrikaans drama, followed by very detailed biographical articles on 63 Afrikaans writers). *See also* **2741**.

Music

2744 **South African music encyclopedia (SAME)**, ed.-in-chief, Jacques P. Malan. Cape Town, Oxford University Press for Human Sciences Research Council, 1979-1986. 4 vols. (Compilation commenced 1962 under the auspices of National Bureau for Educational & Social Research. Covers history of music in South Africa 1652-1960, both European and indigenous. A/Z entries for musicians and composers, musical instruments, histories of music in particular cities, theatres and concert halls. Detailed sources given. Lengthy introduction to vol. 1 discusses the problems of compilation and gaps in coverage. No general index. Reviews, *ABPR*, 14, 1988, 108-109; *African affairs*, 85, 1986, 621-622)

Politics

2745 Davies, Robert H., et al. **The struggle for South Africa: a reference guide to movements, organizations and institutions**. Rev. ed. London, Zed Books for Centre of African Studies, Eduardo Mondlane University, 1988. 2 vols. (Accounts of specific political, religious, social and economic organizations. Rev. ed. retains text of the original and adds an update chapter at the end of each vol. covering events 1983-1987. Review, *IJAHS*, 23, 1990, 688-690). - - Orig. pub. London, 1984. 2 vols.

2746 Kalley, Jacqueline et al. **Southern African political history: a chronology of key political events from independence to mid 1997**. Westport, CT, Greenwood Press, 1999. 904pp. (Covers the SADC area: Angola, Botswana, Lesotho, Malawi, Mauritius, Mozambique, Namibia, South Africa, Swaziland, Tanzania, Zambia, Zimbabwe. For South Africa, covers from 1961. Review, *African affairs*, 98, 1999, 430.)

2747 Kotzé, Hennie & Greyling, Anneke. **Political organisations in South Africa, A-Z**. 2ⁿᵈ ed. Cape Town, Tafelberg, 1994. 332pp. illus. maps. ("Published in conjunction with the Centre for South African Politics at the University of Stellenbosch". Lists c.150 organizations A/Z with information on membership, policies and activities. Some general entries for e.g. churches, business organizations, sport. Biographical section of 50 'political opinion leaders'). - - Orig. pub. Cape Town, 1991. vi, 255pp. illus. maps.

2748 Lodge, Tom et al. **Compendium of elections in Southern Africa**. Johannesburg, Electoral Institute of Southern Africa (EISA), 2002. ix, 547pp. (Covers Democratic Republic of Congo; Malawi, Zambia, Zimbabwe; Tanzania, Zanzibar; South Africa, Namibia, Botswana, Lesotho, Swaziland; Angola, Mozambique; Mauritius, Seychelles. For each has historical, social and economic background, details on the political system and electoral process and where appropriate, details of recent, i.e. post independence elections, S.A. excluded. Appendix with text of 'Norms and standards for election management in the SADC region' recommended in 2000. Review, *Journal of African elections*, 2(2) 2003, 116-118. The Electoral Institute of Southern Africa also publishes a series of handbooks of electoral laws and regulations, e.g. for Mozambique, 1999, Zimbabwe, 2002)

2749 *Mail & Guardian* **A-Z of South African politics, 1999: the essential handbook**, ed. Phillip van Niekerk & Barbara Ludman. London, Penguin, 1999. viii, 327pp. (Single A/Z sequence of entries for parties, government departments and personalities. Previous eds. pub. as *Weekly Mail & Guardian* **A-Z** ... London, 1994, 1995, with a structured arrangement under personalities, organizations & institutions, etc.)

2750 Murphy, Malcolm. 'Executive officers at the Cape of Good Hope', *Quarterly bulletin of the National Library of South Africa*, 59 (1) 2005, 34-44. (Lists Governors and Acting Governors of the Dutch, British and self governing administrations of the Cape, and of other provinces affiliated with the Cape from 1652 to 1910 with specific dates of office. "Have long been aware of the many errors in published lists", p.34)

2751 Riley, Eileen. **Major political events in South Africa, 1948-1990**. New York, Facts on File, 1991. 250pp. maps. (Detailed account year by year, accompanied by some 30 brief biographies. Review, *Choice*, 29, 1991, 420)

2752 Schoeman, Elna. **South Africa's foreign relations in transition 1985-1992: a chronology**. Johannesburg, South African Institute of International Affairs, 1993. iii, 666pp.

2753 South African Council of Churches. **Glossary of current South African political terms**. Johannesburg, 1993. 65pp.

2754 **Südafrika Handbuch: Südafrika, Namibia und Zimbabwe: politisches Lexikon**. Wuppertal, Jugenddienst, 1982. (Handbücher für die entwicklungspolitische Aktion und Bildungsarbeit, 4). 436pp. illus. maps. (Comp. by Aktionskomitee Afrika. Pt. 1 is the lexikon with A/Z entries for current political leaders, parties and other groups and regions of Southern Africa. Pt. 2 has general articles on broad themes, pt. 3 is bibliographical)

2755 Williams, Gwyneth & Hackland, Brian. **Dictionary of contemporary politics of Southern Africa**. London, Routledge/New York, Macmillan, 1988. 339pp. (Covers South Africa; Botswana, Lesotho and Swaziland; Angola and Mozambique; Namibia; Malawi, Zambia and Zimbabwe; Tanzania. Entries for political figures, organizations, and terms)

Religion

2756 South Africa. Central Statistical Services. **Population census 1991: religion by development region, statistical region and district**. Pretoria, 1992. xxi, 706pp.

YEARBOOKS

Bibliographies

2757 Bosman, F.C.L. 'Almanacs and year-books', **Standard encyclopedia of Southern Africa**, 1, 1970, 307-311. (Usefully selective list of major titles, arranged by date of publication)

2758 Coates, Peter R. 'Southern African almanacs and directories', *Quarterly bulletin of the National Library of South Africa*, 59, 2005, 80-92 (Lists some 350 directories which commenced publication before 1980. Brings together many attempts by members of staff of the SAL/NLSA over the years to list such materials. Covers South Africa, the provinces, Lesotho, Mozambique, Namibia, St. Helena, Swaziland, Zimbabwe. Lists actual titles of vols. in the hand not attempting to link them to earlier or later versions). - - Hughes, Nigel. 'Supplementary information', *ibid.* 59, 2005, 141-142

2759 Els, Johan A. **A guide to directories, year books and buyers' guides in the Republic of South Africa**. Pretoria, Bureau of Market Research, University of South Africa, 1983. (Research reports, 104). 88pp. - - Orig. pub. ed. C.I. De Kock. Pretoria, 1978. (Research reports, 63). 60pp.

See also **2678**.

General

2760 **Braby's commercial directory of south, east & central Africa 1924/25** [etc.]. Durban, A.C. Braby, 1924- . Annual. Title varies: **Braby's commercial directory of south and central/ ... of southern Africa**. (Regional coverage varies, but basically includes modern South Africa and Namibia, Botswana, Lesotho and Swaziland, Angola and Mozambique, Malawi, Zambia and Zimbabwe, Réunion, Mauritius and Seychelles. In the late 1940s also included some coverage of Kenya, Uganda, Tanzania and Belgian Congo. 1926 ed. 996pp; 1949 ed. 2,718pp; 1985 ed. 3 vols. Braby's also publish a series of derived and expanded local directories for South African provinces and major cities; *see below* for some major provincial directories).

2761 **Business directory of South Africa**. Cape Town etc., Dennis Edwards, 1888- . Annual. Title varies; **The general directory of South Africa/United South Africa** (1888-1918). (Regional coverage varies over the years, but basically includes substantial coverage of South Africa, South-West Africa/Namibia, Botswana, Lesotho and Swaziland, and Mozambique, with more summary coverage for central and eastern African countries. Up to the change of name in 1919 much non-commercial information was included: lists of civil, military, naval, religious, legal and medical personnel, a press directory, lists of graduates from Cape Town University etc. After 1919, emphasis is on a commercial directory)

2762 Directory of southern Africa. Cape Town, *Cape Times* [etc.], 1933- . Annual. Title varies: **Cape Times South African directory** [etc.; **Cape Times directory of Southern Africa**. 38th ed. 1971, xliii, 36, 1434pp. 1987 ed. 4 vols. (Regional coverage varies but basically includes the modern South Africa and Namibia, Botswana, Lesotho and Swaziland, Mozambique, Malawi, Zambia and Zimbabwe. Earlier vols. also covered the Belgian Congo. Contains civil list, detailed commercial directory by country and province. A competitor to **Braby** *see* **2760**)

2763 Kompass South Africa, 1994 [etc.]. Zurich, Kompass, 1993- . Annual. Issues for 1995 to 1997 pub. Sandton, South African Foreign Trade Organization. Also available on CD-ROM (2005-)

2764 The national business directory of South Africa. Cape Town, National Publishing Co., 1928- . Annual. Title varies: **The 1955** [etc.] **national trade index and directory of southern Africa** (1955-68); **The business blue-books national trade-index of South Africa and Rhodesia** (1969-)

2765 Official South African municipal year book. Cape Town/Pretoria, South African Association of Municipal Employees, 1909- . Annual. (Gives brief description, administrative structure, lists of officials and statistics for municipalities of each province. Included South-West Africa/Namibia up to Namibia's independence. Early issues also include Rhodesia)

2766 Official SADC trade, industry and investment review, 1996- . Harare, Southern African Marketing for SADC Secretariat, 1997- Annual. Text of latest annual review also available at http://www.sadcreview.com/. *Continues* **The SADC industrial review 1991/2: the annual guide to business, industry and commerce in the SADC region**. Harare, Roblaw Publishers for SADC Secretariat, 1991-?1993.

2767 Promadata: promotion, marketing and advertising data. Johannesburg, Clarion Communications Media, 1981-?1986. Annual. Last issue in NLSA is for 1986. (Incorporates **Advertising and press annual of southern Africa**. Cape Town, 1956-1980, with a narrower S.A. focus.)

2768 SADC commercial directory. Pinetown, Braby's, 1998- . Annual. NLSA has vol. 4, 2006/07.

2769 SADC trade directory. Gaborone, B & T Directories, 1992- . Annual. Latest issue in NLSA is for 1997.

2770 South Africa. **Official year book of the Union of South Africa**. Pretoria, Board of Census and Statistics, 1917-1960. Annual (irreg.) 30 vols. Issues for 1917-1919, 1921-1925, 1926/27-1934/35, 1937-1941, 1946, 1948-1950, 1952/53, 1954-55, 1956-57, 1960. Title varies: from issue 3 (1919) **... and of Basutoland, Bechuanaland Protectorate and Swaziland**. Issues 1-7 (1917-1924) also issued in Dutch; from issue 8 (1925) onwards also issued in Afrikaans. (Each issue contains comparative statistics since 1910; issues 1 to 8 include an indication of this on the volume's spine (e.g. issue 5, 1922, has 1910-21) which has led some sources to catalogue the series as commencing publication in 1910. Very detailed information on every aspect, with excellent detailed table of contents. Many issues contain special articles whose existence can be traced from the indexes to later volumes. Coverage was eventually continued by **South Africa: official yearbook of the Republic of South Africa** (*see* **2771**) for general factual data, and **South African statistics** (*see* **2799**) for statistical tables)

2771 South Africa. Government Communication & Information Service (GCIS). **South Africa yearbook**. Pretoria, 1994- . Annual. 12th ed. 2004/05. ix, 682pp. *Continues* Department of Foreign Affairs and Information. **South Africa: official yearbook of the Republic of South Africa**. Pretoria, 1974-1993. Annual. (A continuation of the general reference data formerly contained in **Official yearbook of the Union of South Africa** (1917-1960, *see* **2770**). From 1991/92 (1991) appeared in a much shortened version of c.200 rather than 800pp).

2772 South Africa survey. Johannesburg, South African Institute of Race Relations, 1984- . Annual. Title varies: **Race relations survey**, 1984-1994/95. (Change of name for 1995/96 ed. "reflects the fact that the survey covers a great deal more than racial issues", pref. Covers politics, economics, social life, with statistics)

2773 South African Jewish year book: directory of Jewish organisations and who's who in South African Jewry. Johannesburg, South African Jewish Historical Society, [1929-62]. Issues for 1929, 1951, 1953/54 to 1961/62. Continued as part of **South African Jewry** *see* **2866**

2774 South and East African year book and guide. London, Sampson Low, Marston & Co. for Union Castle Mail Steamship Co., 1893-1940, 1947-1949. Title varies: **Brown's South Africa** (1893); **Guide to South Africa** (1894-1910/11); **Guide to South and East Africa** (1911/12-1918). (Initially ed. A.S. & G.G. Brown and covered South Africa. From 1911/12 added information on eastern Africa, reflecting extension of Union Castle's sailings, and from 1913 had separate East Africa section, including British East Africa, Uganda, German East Africa, Nyasaland, Portuguese East Africa, Zambesia. From 1921 includes 64pp. atlas, also coverage of Mauritius. A major long-running source of primarily topographic, social and economic information. *Continued by* **Year book and guide to East Africa** (1950-65) *see* **1015** and **Year book and guide to Southern Africa** (1950-71) *see* **2777**).

2775 **State of South Africa: economic, financial and statistical yearbook for the Republic of South Africa**. Johannesburg, Da Gama Publications, 1957-1978. Annual. Title varies: **State of the Union of South Africa: economic, financial and statistical yearbook for the Union of South Africa** (1957-1962). Sub-title varies. (Covers government and administration, population, education, natural resources, industry, agricultural and trade)

2776 **State of the nation: South Africa 1997/98-** . Cape Town, Human Sciences Research Council, 1998- . Irreg. Issues for 1997/98 (1998). 265pp; 2003/04 (2003). xv, 400pp; 2004/05 (2005). 604pp; 2005/06 (2005).

2777 **Year book and guide to Southern Africa**. London, Sampson Low for Union-Castle Mail Steamship Co., 1950-1971. Not published 1968, 1970. Title varies: **Guide to Southern Africa** (1969, 1971). (A continuation for Southern Africa of **Brown's South Africa** later **South & East Africa yearbook and guide**, *see* **2774**. Includes modern South Africa and Namibia; Botswana, Lesotho and Swaziland; Malawi, Zambia and Zimbabwe)

See also **1014**

Regional *A short selection of major long-lived titles*

2778 **[Braby's] Cape directory**. Cape Town, 1912- . Annual. Title varies **Donaldson & Braby's Cape Province directory** [etc.] (1912-1925); **Donaldson's Cape Province directory** (1925-55); **Braby's Cape Province directory** (1956-1994). Latest issue in NLSA is 2000. (At various times included coverage of Eastern Griqualand, Tembuland, Bechuanaland, South-West Africa)

2779 **[Braby's] KwaZulu Natal directory/Kwazulu directory, 1901/02** [etc.]. Pinetown [etc.], Braby (*formerly* Johannesburg, Donaldson & Hill), 1901- . Annual (irreg.). Title varies: **Donaldson & Hill's Natal directory** (1901-1907); **Braby's Natal directory** [etc.] (1908-1993). *Incorporates* **Natal almanac & yearly register/Natal directory/Davis's Natal Directory**. Pietermaritzberg, 1863-1917. (Lists of administration, residents and commercial directory).

2780 Braby's [Orange] Free State/ Northern Cape directory. Bloemfontein, Braby (*formerly* Johannesburg, Donaldson & Hill). 1899- . Annual (irreg.) Title varies: **Donaldson & Hill's Orange Free State/Orange River Colony directory** (1899-1905); **Braby's Orange River Colony directory**, n.s. issues 1-4 (1907-1910); **Braby's Orange Free State and Northern Cape directory**, issue 5 (1911-1994)

2781 [Braby's] Transvaal directory. Pinetown, Braby, (*formerly* Johannesburg, Donaldson & Hill, etc.,) 1898- . Annual (irreg.). Title varies: **Donaldson & Hill's Transvaal & Rhodesia directory** (1898-1905). **Donaldson & Braby's Transvaal and Rhodesia directory** (1910-1914); **Braby's Transvaal [& Rhodesia] directory** (1918-1991).

2782 *Cape Times* **peninsula directory**. Cape Town, *Cape Times*/ Juta,1897-1996. Annual. Title varies: **Juta's directory of Cape Town** (1897-1927); **Juta's directory of the Cape peninsula** (1928-32); *Cape Times* **Cape peninsula directory** (1933-1963/64)

STATISTICS

Bibliographies

2783 A guide to statistical sources in the Republic of South Africa. [4th ed.], comp. Henrietta Botha. Pretoria, University of South Africa, Bureau of Market Research, 1987. (Research report, 142). vii, 140, 35pp. (Lists some 600 sources). - - Orig. pub. comp. Gerrit Geertsma & J.R. Klerck. Pretoria, 1962. 2 vols; - - 2nd ed. comp. M.H. Naudé. Pretoria, 1972. (Research report, 30). 214pp; - - Rev ed. comp. E.M. Steenkamp. Pretoria, 1979. (Research report, 70). 177pp.

2784 Horner, D. et al. **A short list of South African statistical sources**, Cape Town, University of Cape Town, School of Economics, Division of Research, 1980. 23pp. (Features 31 major official sources, with a note on many more 'other sources')

2785 South Africa. Central Statistical Services (CSS). **STATIBIB: list of CSS publications as from 1978**. Pretoria, 1995- . Irreg. (*Continues* **2787**)

2786 South Africa. Central Statistical Services. **User's guide**. Pretoria, 1987- Quarterly.

2787 South Africa. Department of Cultural Affairs, Division of Library Services. **Bibliography of South African government publications: Department of Statistics, 1910-1968**. Pretoria, 1969. v, 123pp. - - **Suppl., 1969-1977**. Pretoria, 1978. 2pp. + microfiche.

General

2788 Development Bank of Southern Africa. **South Africa's nine provinces: a human development profile**, comp. Janine Erasmus. Halfway House, 1994. 129pp. illus. maps. (Demographic statistics)

2789 Mohr, Philip. **Economic indicators**. Rev. ed. Pretoria, University of South Africa, 2000. xii, 234pp. - - Orig. pub. Pretoria, 1998. xi, 237pp.

2790 Mouton, A.J. **Self-governing territories: statistical abstracts 1990**. Halfway House, Development Bank of Southern Africa, 1992. iv, 132pp.

2791 Shrand, David. **The financial and statistical digest of South Africa**. Cape Town, Juta, 1955. vii, 147pp.

2792 South Africa. Statistics South Africa. **Stats in brief 2004: ten years of democratic governance**, comp. Pali Lehohla. Pretoria, 2004. 144pp. + CD-ROM

2793 South Africa. Statistics South Africa, StatsOnline: the digital face of Stats S.A. http://www.statssa.gov.za/. (Extensive range of statistical data)

2794 **Southern Africa data**. Pretoria, Africa Institute of South Africa, 1969-1973. (Statistics issued as loose-leaf sheets in 11 topic groups: population, health, education, labour, field and animal husbandry, forestry and fishing, mining, water and electricity, transport, postal services, housing, judicial)

2795 **Union statistics for fifty years**. Pretoria, South Africa. Bureau of Census and Statistics, 1960. [vi, 448pp]. (A major compilation of comparative statistical data for 1910-1960)

2796 Zubori, Tufuku, et al. **The demography of South Africa**. New York, M.E. Sharpe/Pretoria, Statistics South Africa, 2005. 310pp. (Based on a project coordinated by the University of Pennsylvania with various African institutions to produce a series of studies together forming 'A general demography of Africa'. Uses the data from the 1996 census, the first to be held post apartheid, to provide statistical analysis of racial stratification in South Africa. Numerous statistical tables. Review, *Choice*, 43, 2006, 992)

Bulletins & yearbooks

2797 Country profile: South Africa. London, Economist Intelligence Unit, 1986- Annual

2798 Germany. Statistisches Bundesamt. **Statistik des Auslandes: Länderberichte: South Africa** (later **Länderbericht: South Africa**). Wiesbaden/Stuttgart, Metzler-Poetschel, 1985- . Irreg. Issues for 1985, 1987, 1991, 1994.

2799 South Africa. Central Statistical Services [etc.] **South African statistics**. Pretoria, 1964- . Annual, 1964-1966, then every 2 years. Latest issue in NWU is for 2003. Title varies: **Statistical yearbook** (1964-1966). (A continuation of the statistical section of the **Official yearbook of the Union of South Africa** (*see* **2770**). First issue, 1964, has lengthy section of comparative statistics for the period 1945-1963, not repeated in later issues).

2800 South Africa. Central Statistical Services. **Provincial statistics. Part 10, Republic of South Africa**. Pretoria, 1994- . Annual.

2801 South Africa. Central Statistical Services [etc.]. **Bulletin of statistics**. Pretoria, 1967- . Quarterly. Latest issue in NWU is for 1997. *Continues* South Africa. Office of Census and Statistics [etc.]. **Half-yearly abstract of Union statistics 1919/20**. Pretoria, 1919. 1 issue + suppl.; **Quarterly abstract of Union statistics**. Pretoria, 1920-1922. 12 issues; South Africa. Central Statistical Services [etc.]. **Monthly bulletin of [Union] statistics**. Pretoria, 1922-1967. Monthly/quarterly. (Title and frequency vary)

2802 Statistical abstracts on self-governing territories in South Africa. Sandton, Institute for Development Research, Development Branch of South Africa in collaboration with the governments of the territories, 1987- . ?Annual. ?No more pub.

DIRECTORIES OF ORGANIZATIONS

Abbreviations & acronyms

2803 De Coning, Chris. **Acronyms and abbreviations**. Pretoria, Human Sciences Research Council, 1998. 111pp.

2804 Lundie, Ruth. **A dictionary of acronyms**. Pietermaritzburg, Centre for Adult Education, 1990. 146pp.

General

2805 Bridge 1979 [etc.]: **an index of organizations at work in South Africa**. Grant Park, Human Awareness Programme/Pretoria, HAP Organisational Development Services, 1979- . Annual, 1979-1985; Every 2 years, 1987- . (Lists institutions A/Z and by province. Emphasis on NGOs in the fields of education, health and welfare, religion, legal aid and social assistance).

2806 Contac. Randburg, Thomson Publications, 1989-1996. 8 issues. Title varies: **Kontak**, 1989-1992. (Lists provincial and local government bodies, trade unions, industrial councils, the top 250 companies and political organisations in South Africa, also a variety of institutions including museums and universities in South Africa, Botswana, Lesotho, Swaziland, the homelands and Zimbabwe)

2807 Educational institutions in South Africa. Johannesburg, Erudita Publications, 1967, 1970. 2 issues.

2808 South Africa. Council for Scientific and Industrial Research (CSIR). **Directory of research organizations and facilities in South Africa**. Pretoria, 1991- . Annual. (?Continues **2810**)

2809 South Africa. Council for Scientific and Industrial Research (CSIR). **Directory of scientific and technical societies in South Africa**. Pretoria, 1967- . Annual. Not pub. 1976. *Continues in part* CSIR. **Directory of scientific resources in South Africa**. Pretoria, 1961-1966.

2810 South Africa. Council for Scientific and Industrial Research (CSIR). **Directory of scientific research organizations in South Africa**. Pretoria, 1967-1985. Annual. *Continues in part* CSIR. **Directory of scientific resources in South Africa**. Pretoria, 1961-1966. *Successor to* CSIR. **Directory of scientific research organizations**. Pretoria, 1950.

2811 South Africa. Council for Scientific and Industrial Research (CSIR). **Directory of scientific resources in South Africa**. Pretoria, 1961. looseleaf in continuation. (Updated until 1966, in 5 sections: research organizations; sources of scientific information in South African libraries; scientific societies; scientific & technical periodicals; list of acronyms. Succeeded by **2809** & **2810**)

2812 South Africa. Council for Scientific and Industrial Research (CSIR). **Directory of South African associations, 2000**. Pretoria, 2000. (Earlier eds. Pretoria, 1991, 1996)

2813 South Africa. Human Sciences Research Council. **South African directory of human sciences research institutions**, comp. Drienie Pienaar & Henda Van der Berg. Pretoria, 1993. 133pp. (Lists 165 organizations. Includes central, state and local governments, universities, etc.). - - Orig. pub. as **Directory of research organizations in the human sciences in South Africa**. Pretoria, 1969. 159pp; - - 2nd ed. Pretoria, 1972. vi, 227pp.

Arts

2814 **Art routes: a guide to South African art collections**, ed. Rayda Becker & Rochelle Keene. Johannesburg, Witwatersrand University Press, 2000. viii, 248pp. illus.

2815 Doling, Tim. **South Africa: arts directory**. London, Visiting Arts, 1998. 252pp. (One of the Visiting Arts Southern Africa Regional Arts Profiles of 11 vols., *see* index under Doling for others. Reviews, *ABPR*, 25, 1999, 355-356, "an extraordinarily useful and remarkably comprehensive set of reference tools", i.e. the series as a whole; *ARD*, 87, 2001, 110-111)

2816 **South African art information directory: the SAIID directory, 2003** [etc.] Cape Town, Global Art Information, 2002- . Annual. 2006 ed 480pp. ("A guide to art competitions, residencies and grants open to Southern Africans, regional and international arts networking for Southern African artists". Also available with updates at http://www.saaid.co.za/)

2817 **The South African handbook on arts and culture**. Rondebosch, Article 27 Arts & Culture Consultants/Cape Town, David Philip, 1998- . Annual. 2002/03 ed., comp. & ed. M. van Graan & Tammy Ballantyne. Cape Town, David Philip, 2002. xv, 460pp. (Directory of government departments, funding agencies worldwide, the press, competitions and awards. Chapters for craft, dance, film, literature, music, theatre, visual arts, heritage)

Development

2818 **People and projects in development: the directory of South African development organizations**. Gardenview, Dictum, 2002- Annual. (*Continues* **2819**. Lists organizations arranged under national government, provincial governments and international. 2004/05 ed. 2005. 1,136pp. Contact details with very brief notes on 'focus areas' for each institution)

2819 The Southern African development directory 1994/95 [- 2000/01], ed. David Barnard. Braamfontein, Human Sciences Research Council, S.A. Programme for Development Research (PRODDER), 1994-2000. Annual. (Lists development-related organizations in sequences for each of the 14 member countries of the Southern African Development Community (SADC), Angola, Botswana, Congo, Lesotho, Malawi, Mauritius, Mozambique, Namibia, Seychelles, South Africa, Swaziland, Tanzania, Zambia, Zimbabwe. Contact details, mission statements, note on areas of activity. 'Sectoral' (i.e. subject) index with 55 categories and institutional index). *Continues* **PRODDER's development directory 1992/93:** an assessment and comprehensive survey of Southern African development agencies and organizations. Braamfontein, PRODDER, 1993. ii, 614pp. *Continued by* **People and projects in development** *see* **2818**)

2820 The PRODDER directory. http://www.prodder.org.za/index.php. ("A free online NGO and Development Directory")

Finance & commerce

2821 McGregor's investor's handbook. Rustenberg, S.A., Purdey Publishing, 1980- . Annual. (1996 ed. 777pp.)

2822 McGregor's who owns whom: listed and unlisted companies. Rustenberg, S.A., Purdey Publishing, 1980- . Annual.

2823 U.S. and Canadian business in South Africa, 1989 : a directory of U.S. and Canadian corporations with business links to South Africa and Namibia, comp. Alison Cooper. Washington, DC, Investor Responsibility Research Center, 1989. xvi, 235pp

Libraries, museums & the book trade

2824 Fransen, Hans. **Guide to the museums of Southern Africa.** 2nd ed. Cape Town, South African Museums' Association, 1978. 231pp. (Arranged by country: South Africa, and Transkei; Namibia, Botswana, Lesotho, Swaziland; Malawi, Rhodesia, Zambia; Angola, Mozambique). - - Orig. pub. Cape Town, 1969. 147pp.

2825 Musiker, Reuben. **Companion to South African libraries.** Johannesburg, Donker, 1986. 256pp. illus. (Entries for libraries, associations, individuals, projects etc.)

2826 Publishers' Association of South Africa (PASA). **PASA Directory, 1996** [etc.]. Cape Town, 1997- . Annual. (2004. ed. 125 pp. lists some 170 publishers)

2827 Roussow, Fransie. **South African printers and publishers, 1795-1925: from** A South African bibliography to the year 1925. Cape Town, South African Library, 1987. ix, 253pp.

2828 State Library, Pretoria. **Directory of Southern African libraries, 1989.** Pretoria, 1990. xiii, 463pp. (1,377 entries for South Africa, the "homelands", Botswana, Lesotho, Swaziland; Malawi, Zambia, Zimbabwe). - - Earlier eds. **Directory of South African libraries: part 1, Scientific & research libraries.** Pretoria, 1965. 576pp. (336 entries for South Africa & SWA; Malawi, Rhodesia, Zambia); - - **Handbook of Southern African libraries.** Pretoria, 1970. cxiv, 939pp. (833 entries. Includes Rhodesia); - - **Directory of Southern African libraries, 1975.** Pretoria, 1976. ix, 301pp. (941 entries for South Africa, S.W. Africa; Botswana, Lesotho, Swaziland; Malawi, Zambia. Rhodesia omitted since it now had its own directory, see **1411**; - - **Directory of Southern African libraries, 1983.** Pretoria, 1984. xi, 553pp. (1,348 entries)

2829 State Library, Pretoria/National Library of South Africa. **Directory of South African publishers.** Pretoria, 1991- . Semiannual.

2830 Taitz, Laurie. **Directory of book publishing in South Africa, 1995.** Braamfontein, British Council & Publishers' Association of South Africa, 1995. xii, 146pp.

Religion

2831 Davids, Murshid. **Directory of Muslim institutions and mosques in South Africa.** Maraisburg, Society for the Promotion of Arabic Language (SPAL), 1996. 383pp. ?Annual. (1996 vol. lists 408 educational institutions, 455 mosques & 465 organizations arranged by subject)

Women

2832 **Women's organisations in South Africa: a directory,** comp. Programme for Development Research (PRODDER) at the Human Sciences Research Council et al. Johannesburg, PRODDER, 1995. 188pp.

BIOGRAPHICAL SOURCES

Bibliographies

2833 Johannesburg Public Library. **Alphabetical index to the biographical notices in** *South Africa*, **1892-1928**, comp. Eric Rosenthal. Johannesburg, 1963. 114pp.

2834 Olivier, Le Roux. **Versamelde Suid-Afrikaanse biografië: 'n bibliografie**. Cape Town, University of Cape Town, School of Librarianship, 1963. v, 71pp. (Guide to collected biography)

2835 Stern, M.J. **South African Jewish biography 1900-1966: a bibliography**. Cape Town, University of Cape Town Library, 1972. 28pp.

2836 Ushpol, Rowse. **A select bibliography of South African autobiographies**. Cape Town, University of Cape Town, School of Librarianship, 1958. iv, 48pp. (Lists 143 titles)

2837 Van Oordt, L.C. 'Biography, Dictionaries of', **Standard encyclopedia of Southern Africa**, 2, 1970, pp. 329-334 (Brief list of major titles arranged chronologically. Only sketchy bibliographical details)

General

2838 *Africa confidential* **who's who of Southern Africa**, ed. Patrick Smith. Oxford, Blackwell, 1998. vii, 235pp. (Some 400 entries for Angola, Mozambique, South Africa, Zambia and Zimbabwe. Includes lists of government office holders. Each entry contains factual career details, followed by 'commentary', i.e. more personalized details from the *Africa confidential* files. ASC4, 157)

2839 **Die Afrikaner-personenregister**. Johannesburg, Afrikaner se Koop Gids, 1942. 373pp. (Some 2,250 short biographies of Afrikaners, living and dead, with portraits)

2840 De Beer, Mona. **Who did what in South Africa**. Rev ed. Jeppestown, Donker, 1995. v, 154pp. (Some 1,400 entries for the living and the dead. Claims to include many figures who do not appear in the standard biographical dictionaries) - - Orig. pub. Craighall, Donker, 1988. 196pp.

2841 **Dictionary of South African biography (DSAB)**. Pretoria, Human Sciences Research Council [etc.], 1968-1987. Vol. 1. 1968; vol. 2. 1972; vol. 3.

1977, vol. 4. 1981, vol. 5. 1987. (A major work of co-operative scholarship. Founder and editor-in-chief until 1970, Willem Johannes De Kock; later eds. D.W. Krüger (1970-72), Coenrad Johannes Beyers (1973-1987). Each vol. has a self-contained A/Z sequence and an index to all entries in previous vols. Over 4,500 entries, signed and with detailed references. Most entries are at least a page, and some considerably longer, e.g. Smuts, 21pp. For a description of the extensive planning involved *see* W.J. De Kock, 'Launching the *Dictionary of South African biography'*, QBSAL, 17, 1962/63, 127-132. *See also* **Dictionary of South African biography: list of names of persons deceased prior to 31 December 1950, and proposed for inclusion in the main series**. Cape Town, National Council for Social Research, 1968. 350pp ("Published for the use of contributors to volume III and subsequent volumes")

- - **New dictionary of South African biography** Pretoria, Human Sciences Research Council/Vista University, 1995- . Vol. 1. 1995, ed. Elizabeth J. Verwey. viii, 310pp. (129 entries); vol. 2. 1999, ed. Nelly E. Sonderlin. x, 296pp. (125 entries). (A 'companion' to the *DSAB*. Coverage is much more inclusive ethnically than the original, articles are significantly shorter, and have added portraits. Each vol. includes cumulative indexes to all pub. vols. and also to the 5 vols. of the original *DSAB*. Reviews, *RREO*, 2003, B1, "a very impressive continuation ..., augmenting the strengths of the original work with an enlightened new standard"; *SAHJ*, 39, 1995, 279-280; *Journal for contemporary history*, 25, 2000, 111-113)

2842 **Encyclopaedia Africana dictionary of African biography. Vol. 3, South Africa, Botswana, Lesotho, Swaziland**, ed. K. Irvine. Algonac, MI, Reference Publications, 1995. 303pp. (228 biographies, of which 116 are of Africans. For the Encyclopedia *see* **11**, for the Dictionary of biography, *see* **545**. Reviews, *Africa*, 69, 1999, 475-476; *Choice*, 33, 1996, 1090-1092; *IJAHS*, 30, 1997, 627-628; *SAHJ*, 35, 1996, 236-237)

2843 **International who's who: Southern African trade business and industry**. 4th ed. Johannesburg, Who's Who South Africa (Pty) Ltd, 1994. xiv, 880pp. - - Earlier eds. Johannesburg, 1986. xv, [3], 554pp; - - Johannesburg, 1993. 1 vol. var. paging.

2844 Joyce, Peter. **A concise dictionary of South African biography**. Cape Town, Francolin, 1999. 288pp. (Brief entries, c. 8 to a page for some 1,500 persons living and dead)

2845 Nienaber, Petrus Johannes. **Afrikaanse biografiese woordeboek. Dl. 1**. Johannesburg, L. & S. Boek en Kunssentrum, 1947. 290pp. No more pub. (Just over 200 entries with references to sources, principally items in newspapers)

2846 Rosenthal, Eric. **South African dictionary of national biography**. London, Warne, 1966, xxxix, 430pp. (Some 2,000 brief entries for prominent personalities from 1460 to the present. Review, *African affairs*, 67, 1968, 82-83, "comprehensive, concise and accurate".)

2847 South African woman's who's who. Johannesburg, Biographies Ltd., 1938. 528pp.

2848 Uys, Ian. **South African military who's who, 1452-1992**. Germiston, Fortress, 1992. viii, 312pp. (Some 1,300 entries)

2849 Venter, E.A. **400 leiers in Suid-Afrika oor vier eeue: beskouinge oor vierhonderd leierfigure in Suid-Afrika sedert die grondlegging**. Potchefstroom, author, 1980. 511pp. illus. (Major figures of all periods)

2850 Who's who of Southern Africa. Johannesburg, Combined Publishers/ Ken Donaldson, 1959- . 97th ed. 2004. (The major continuing biographical source for the region. Includes some 1,500 biographies per issue, many with portraits. Sections for Central Africa also published separately as **Who's who of Rhodesia, Mauritius, Central and East Africa** (1960-) *see* **1273**. ASC4, 157-158. *Continues* **South African who's who 1907** [etc.]. Johannesburg, 1908-1958. Annual (irreg.). - - Orig. pub. as **Natal who's who: an illustrated biographical sketch book of Natalians**. Durban, Natal Who's Who Publishing Co., 1906-1907. Annual. 2 issues.

2851 Wie is wie in Suid-Afrika. Johannesburg, Vitae Uitgewers, 1958,1967. 2 issues. (Some text in English, some in Afrikaans. Includes SWA)

Special categories

Art

2852 Berman, Esmé. **Art and artists of South Africa: an illustrated biographical dictionary and historical survey of painters and graphic artists since 1875**. 3rd ed. Halfway House, Southern Books, 1993. xviii, 545pp. (Covers over 300 artists). - - Orig. pub. Cape Town, Balkema, 1970. xvi, 368pp; - - 2nd ed. Cape Town, 1983. 545pp

2853 Gordon-Brown, Alfred. **Pictorial Africana: a survey of old South African paintings, drawings and prints to the end of the 19th century, with a biographical dictionary of one thousand artists**. Cape Town, Balkema, 1975. x, 254pp. (Short biographies, and chronological list of lithographers and engravers. Essentially a rev. and much expanded version of his **Pictorial art in South Africa during three centuries to 1875, with notes on**

over four hundred artists. London, Sawyer, 1952. 172pp. illus. Addenda in *Africana notes and news*, 12, 1957, 229-269)

2854 Jeppe, Harold. **South African artists, 1900-1962**. Johannesburg, Afrikaanse Pers Boekhandel, 1963. 172pp. (Brief biographies). - - **Index**. comp. F.Y. Goldman. Johannesburg, Johannesburg Public Library, 1966. 6pp.

2855 Ogilvie, Grania. **The dictionary of South African painters and sculptors, including Namibia**. Johannesburg, Everard Read, 1988. xvii, 799pp. (Covers over 1,800 living artists)

2856 **Register of South African and South West African artists, 1900-1968**. Pretoria, South African Association of Arts, 1969. 83pp. (Brief biographies)

See also 1407.

Politics

2857 Gastrow, Shelagh. ed. **Who's who in South African politics**. 5th ed. Johannesburg, Ravan Press, 1995. xxxiii, 319pp. (Covers 102 persons, citing sources which are principally newspaper items and personal interviews. Includes list of all persons covered by eds. 1 to 5. Reviews, *African affairs*, 95, 1996, 298-299; *IJAHS*, 30, 1997, 630-632). - - Orig. pub. Johannesburg, Ravan Press, 1985. xiv, 347pp; - - 2nd ed. Johannesburg, 1987. 365pp; - - 3rd ed. Oxford, Hans Zell, 1990. vii, 368pp. (Reviews, *ARD*, 57, 1991, 33-34; *Choice*, 29, 1991, 72); - - 4th ed. London, Hans Zell, 1993. xxxviii, 333pp. (Review, *ARD*, 61, 1993, 27-28. Each of the earlier eds. includes between 100 and 130 entries)

2858 International Defence & Aid Fund (IDAF). **Prisoners of apartheid: a biographical list of political prisoners and banned persons in South Africa**. London, 1978. v, 180pp. (Brief biographies of 317 South African and 54 Namibian political prisoners, and of 175 banned persons)

2859 Karis, Thomas & Carter, Gwendoline M. eds. **From protest to challenge: a documentary history of African politics in South Africa, 1882-1964. Vol. 4. Political profiles**. Stanford, Hoover Institution, 1977. xv, 178pp. illus. (333 entries, including 48 whites, about half for living figures)

2860 **Parlementêre register/Parliamentary register, 1910-1984**. 3rd ed. Cape Town, Houses of Parliament, 1991. 236pp. (Listings of members of Parliament, and ministers' constituencies). - - Orig. pub. ... **1910-1961**. Cape Town, 1961. 153pp; - - 2nd ed. ... **1910-1982**. Cape Town, 1982. 331pp.

2861 The political directory of South Africa. Cape Town, Griffoulière, 1996. 314pp. (Lists of members of the government, parliament, provincial legislatures, and officials of political parties arranged in these categories. Biographical information varies from a few paragraphs to one line. Most entries have portraits. Index. Some sources, e.g. NLSA, suggest that this was to be an annual, but no other issues traced)

See also entries under HANDBOOKS: Politics above

Religio-cultural groups

2862 African who's who: an illustrated classified register and national biographical dictionary of the Africans in the Transvaal. 3rd ed. Johannesburg, Central News Agency, 1963. 373pp. - - Orig. pub. as **The African yearly register: being an illustrated national biographical dictionary (who's who) of black folks in Africa**. Johannesburg, R.L. Esson, 1930 - - 2nd ed. Johannesburg, 1932. xvii, 450pp; (All eds. comp. T.D. Mweli Skota. The first major biographical source for blacks only. 1st and 2nd eds. give coverage to all Africa although emphasis is very much on Southern Africa. 3rd ed. includes much miscellaneous information in addition to biographical entries, e.g. lists of black university graduates, lists of black schools and hospitals, notes on churches and clergy)

2863 The Black who's who of Southern Africa today. Johannesburg, African Business Publications, 1979, 1982. 2 issues. (1982. ed. Sheila Keeble 336pp. portraits. Introductory section on black organizations, universities, etc., followed by brief biographical entries)

2864 Deane, Dee Shirley. **Black South Africans: a whos who: 57 profiles of Natal's leading blacks**. Cape Town, Oxford University Press, 1978. xxiii, 210pp. illus. map. (Based largely on interviews. Review, *ABPR*, 5, 1979, 94)

2865 The South African Indian who's who & commercial directory 1936/37 [-1940]: a biographical sketch book with illustrations of South African Indians and an illustrated business directory, incorporating Southern and Northern Rhodesia, Nyasaland and Portuguese East Africa, ed. Dhanee Bramdaw. Pietermaritzburg, "Natal Witness", 1936-1939. 3 vols.

2866 South African Jewry: a survey of the Jewish community, its contribution to South Africa, directory of commercial institutions, and who's who of leading personalities, ed. Leon Feldberg. Johannesburg, Fieldhill Publishing Co., 1965-1976. 3 issues. Issues for 1965, 1967/68, 1976/77. (3rd ed, 1976/77. 1976. 529pp. "Incorporates **South African Jewish year book** [*see* **2773**], and **Who's who in South African Jewry**". pref.)

2867 Ubukhosi neenkokeli: a directory of Eastern Cape Black leaders, from c. 1700 to 1990, comp. David R. Owen. Grahamstown, Trustees of the Albany Museum, 1994. (New history series, 2). 94pp. (The Xhosa)

Genealogy & works on early settlers (including awards & honours, onomastics)

Bibliographies

2868 Cyndi's list of genealogical sources on the Internet: South Africa. Maintained by Cyndi Howells. http://www.cyndislist.com/soafrica.htm

2869 Lombard, Roelof T.J. **Handbook for genealogical research in South Africa**. 3rd ed. Pretoria, Human Sciences Research Council for Institute for Historical Research (IHR), 1990. (IHR Genealogy Publication, 6). 146pp. illus. (History of genealogy in South Africa, discussion of methodology, and descriptive guide to institutional sources. Select bibliography of works of collective biography & a very extensive list of individual family histories). - - Orig. pub. Pretoria, 1977. 146pp; - - 2nd ed. Pretoria, 1984. xii, 164pp.

See also **2909**

General

2870 Alexander, E.G. McGill et al. **South African orders, decorations and medals**. Cape Town, Human & Rousseau, 1986. 160pp. illus.

2871 De Villiers, Christoffel Coetzee. **Genealogies of old South African families**; completely rev. ed. augmented & rewritten by Cornelis Pama. 2nd ed. Cape Town, Balkema, 1981. 2 vols. - - Orig. pub. Cape Town, 1966. 3 vols. (A modern revision of C.C. De Villiers **Geslacht-Registers der oude Kaapsche familiën**. Cape Town, de Sandt de Villiers, 1893-94. 3 vols. De Villiers' work, seen through the press after his death by G. M. Theal, is the classic guide to South African genealogy that all later work has built upon. Suppl. by J. Hoge. **Bydraes tot die genealogie van ou Afrikaanse families: verbeterings en aanvullings op die Geslacht-register ... van C.C. de Villiers**. Rotterdam, Balkema, 1958. 224pp. Most genealogies in the original ed. end in 1806, while Pama's revision covers from 1652 to 1850, and includes some 1,500 families, mostly Dutch and German with some French and English. For a discussion of De Villiers' work and the reasons why a revision was thought necessary, see C. Pama, 'Genealogy in South Africa', QBSAL 10, 1955/56, 128-132. Explanations and origins of the Dutch and German names in De Villiers are given in J.D.A. Krige. **Oorsprong en beteknis van Nederlandse en Duitse familiename in die "Geslacht-**

register ...". Pretoria, van Schaik, 1934. 109pp. The whole of De Villiers/Pama is eventually to be incorporated into **SAG**, *see* **2886**).

2872 Hoge, J. 'Personalia of the Germans at the Cape, 1652-1806', *Archives yearbook for South African history*, 9, 1946, 1-495. (Identifies 4,000 names)

2873 Jones, E. Morse. **Roll of the British settlers in South Africa. Part 1: Up to 1826**. 2nd ed. Cape Town, Balkema, 1971. xi, 176pp. (Reprint of 1st ed. with 2pp. of additions and corrections. Produced under the auspices of the 1820 Settlers' Monument Committee. Short biographies of some 100, and minimal detail on an additional 500 settlers in three sequences according to whether they arrived prior to 1820, actually in 1820 or between 1821 and 1826). - - Orig. pub. Cape Town, Balkema, 1969. ix, 174pp.

2874 Kannemeyer, Agatha Johanna. **Hugenote-familieboek**. Cape Town, Unie-Volkspers, 1940. vi, 282pp. (Covers original French emigrants to the Cape with brief notes on their subsequent family history)

2875 Malherbe, Daniël Francois du Toit. **Stamregister van die Suid-Afrikaanse volk/Family register of the South African nation**. 3rd enl. ed. Stellenbosch, Tegniek, 1966. xxvii, 1,208pp. (Text in Afrikaans and English. Details of families not included in De Villiers, *see* **2871**, covering 1652 to 1961). - - Orig. pub. as **Driehonderd jaar nasiebou: stamouers van die Afrikanervolk**. Stellenbosch, Tegniek, 1959. xxv, 267pp; - - 2nd ed. Stellenbosch, 1959.

2876 Monick, S. **South African military awards, 1912-1987**. Johannesburg, South African National Museum of Military History, 1988. 58pp. illus.

2877 Nash, Marjorie Diane. **The settler handbook: a new list of the 1820 settlers**. Plumstead, Chameleon Press, 1987. 152pp. illus. map. (British settlers)

2878 Nienaber, Gabriël Stefanus. **Afrikaanse familiename: 'n Geselsie vir belangstellende leke oor die betekenis van ouer Afrikaanse vanne**. Cape Town, Balkema, 1955. 108pp. (The origins and development of Afrikaans family names)

2879 Pama, Cornelis. **British families in South Africa; their surnames and origins**. Cape Town, Human & Rousseau, 1992. 192pp. (Includes coats-of-arms)

2880 Pama, Cornelis. **Die groot Afrikaanse familienaamboek**. Cape Town, Human & Rousseau, 1983. 380pp. illus. (Lists some 3,000 family names with notes on their origin, and of the earliest known settlers bearing them. Numerous col. illus. of coats of arms)

2881 Pama, Cornelis. **Heraldry of South African families: coats of arms, crests, ancestry**. Cape Town, Balkema, 1972. x, 365pp. illus. (Describes more than 1,100 coats of arms, almost all illus.)

2882 Philip, Peter. **British residents at the Cape, 1795-1819: biographical records of 4,800 pioneers**. Cape Town, David Philip, 1981. xxiii, 484pp. (Covers the period before the first large scale British settlement beginning in 1820. Based on the Cape Archives, the works of G.M. Theal and printed sources. Only brief entries for those who also have entries in the *DSAB, see* **2841**. Review, *ABPR*, 8, 1982, 59-60)

2883 Raven-Hart, Rowland. **Before Van Riebeck: callers at South Africa from 1488-1652**. Cape Town, Struik, 1967. 216pp. (Some 100 biographies)

2884 Redelinghuys, Johannes Hermanus, ed. **Die Afrikaner-familienaamboek: sketse en besonderhede omtrent die voorgeslagte van bekende Afrikanerfamilies**. Cape Town, Publisitas, [1955]. 311pp.

2885 Rosenthal, Eric. **South African surnames**. Cape Town, Timmins, 1965. 262pp. (Gives origins and meanings of some 2,500 names of English, Afrikaans, Jewish and African origin)

2886 **Suid-Afrikaanse geslagregisters/South African genealogies (SAG)**; originally comp. Johannes Augustus Heese, ed. Roelof T.J. Lombard; now ed. Genealogical Society of South Africa (GISA). Pretoria, Human Sciences Research Council (vols. 1-2)/Stellenbosch, Genealogical Institute of South Africa (vol. 3-), 1986- . Vol. 12, So-Sz, pub. 2005. (When complete will be the single major source in its field, and will include all data currently in De Villiers/Pama, *see* **2871**, which is estimated to be some 13% of the entries envisaged. To contain complete family registers of all Afrikaans families from 1652 to about 1830; those of new progenitors of Afrikaans families up to 1867 and a number of English and coloured families. Vol. 1 includes some 75,000 names. For further information and an online list of all surnames included in SAG to date *see* Web site of the Genealogical Society of S.A. at http://www.ggsa.info/)

2887 Spencer, Shelagh O'B. **British settlers in Natal, 1824-1857: a biographical register**. Pietermaritzburg, University of Natal Press, 1981- . (7 vols. pub. to 2006, covering A-Guy. Complete work should contain some 2,600 names. Most entries are very detailed, except for those individuals already covered in the *DSAB, see* **2841**. Very full list of archival, manuscript and printed sources. Review of vol. 7, 2001, *SAHJ*, 45, 2001, 330-331)

2888 Tabler, Edward C. **Pioneers of Natal and south eastern Africa, 1552-1878**. Cape Town, Balkema, 1977. (South African biographical & historical studies, 21). 117pp. (Brief biographies of 244 individuals active in the area of modern Natal, Transvaal Low Veld, Swaziland and Southern Mozambique)

2889 Visagie, Jan Christian. **Voortrekkerstamouers, 1835-1845**. Pretoria, Universiteit van Suid-Afrika, 2000. xxii, 362pp. + 6 folded maps

2890 Zöllner, Linda & Heese, Johannes Augustus. **The Berlin missionaries in South Africa and their descendants**. Pretoria, Human Sciences Research Council, Institute for Historical Research (IHR), 1984. (Genealogy publications, 19). viii, 586pp. (Traces descendants of 130 German immigrants who came to South Africa as members of the Berlin Missionary Society, together with biographical details on another 65 who left no descendants)

ATLASES & GAZETTEERS

Chief Directorate: Surveys & Mapping, South Africa (CD:SM). http://w3sli.wcape.gov.za/

Atlases

2891 **Atlas of South Africa**: a selection of maps ... showing the distribution of crops, livestock etc. in 1946, comp. Anne Marie Talbot & William J. Talbot. Cape Town, University of Cape Town, Department of Geography, 1947. 48pp. maps. 25 x 41cm.

2892 **Atlas of the Union of South Africa**, comp. Anne Marie Talbot & William J. Talbot. Pretoria, Government Printer, 1960. [vii], lxiv, 177pp. 41 x 56cm. (Prepared in collaboration with the Trigonometrical Survey Office and under aegis of the National Council for Social Research. 592 b. & w. and 4 col. thematic maps, chiefly 1:8M, in seven sections: physical geography, climate, population, agriculture, industry, transport, trade. Text has descriptive data and very detailed statistical information. Includes coverage of Swaziland, Lesotho. Reviews, *GJ*, 129, 1963, 369-70, "material ... assembled, checked & mapped with meticulous care"; *SAGJ*, 42, 1960, 54-55)

2893 Atlas südliches Afrika. Rev. ed. Bonn, Südafrikanische Botschaft, 1993. 27pp. maps (some col.) 30 cm. (Includes statistical tables). - - Orig. pub. Bonn, Südafrikanische Botschaft, 1988. 23pp.

2894 Development atlas. Pretoria, South Africa. Department of Planning, 1966-1976. loose-leaf. Issued in sections 1. Physical background, 10 pp; 2. Social aspects, 30pp; 3. Water, 6pp; 4. Minerals and mines, 14pp; 5. Agriculture, 25pp; 6. Communications, 6pp; 8. Commerce, 6pp; 10. Economic aspects, 6pp. *Announced but ?not pub.* Sections 7. Industry; 9. Finance & 11. Possible development regions. (Most maps at 1:3,500,000)

2895 Economic atlas of South Africa, ed. Hendrik Lourens Zietsman & Izak Johannes Van der Merwe. Stellenbosch, University of Stellenbosch, Institute for Cartographic Analysis, 1981. (Publication, 8). 160pp. (Includes 132 partially col. maps. Based on data for 1970/71. Review, *SAGJ*, 63, 1981, 174-175 is critical of authors limiting themselves to official census data)

2896 Norwich, Oscar I. **Maps of Southern Africa**. Johannesburg, Donker & Jonathan Ball, 1993. 88pp. illus. col. plates. (Reproductions of maps in the author's collection from Waldseemüller, 1535 to W.Pepper, 1858)

2897 Population census atlas of South Africa, ed. Hendrik Lourens Zeitsman & Isak Johannes Van der Merwe. Stellenbosch, University of Stellenbosch, Institute for Cartographic Analysis, 1986. (Publication, 15). 212pp. illus. 34 x 30cm. (Review, *SAGJ*, 69, 1987, 172)

2898 *Reader's Digest* **illustrated atlas of Southern Africa**. 2nd ed. Cape Town, *Reader's Digest* Association, 1994. 232pp. 39cm. (Comp. in association with Directorate of Surveys & Mapping. 213 maps most at 1:500,000. Index gazetteer of 30,000 names). - - Orig. pub. Cape Town, 1984. 256pp.

2899 A socio-economic atlas of South Africa: a demographic, socio-economic and cultural profile of South Africa, comp. Nick Tait et al. Pretoria, Human Sciences Research Council, 1996. xiv, 257pp. (70 maps plus text and statistics on demography, employment, education, economics, languages, religions. Most data taken from 1991 census. Review, *SAGJ*, 78, 1996, 50-51)

2900 World Atlas for South Africans, ed. Peter Joyce. Johannesburg, Jonathan Ball, 2004, 160pp. (South African edition of **Collins Essential Atlas of the World** with a 32pp. encyclopedic section on South Africa)

See also **2684**, **2774**. For atlases on *Education, History* & *Language see* above under **Handbooks**.

Road atlases

2901 Road atlas of South Africa. 4th ed. London, New Holland, 2003. (Globetrotter travel atlas). 95pp. - - Orig. pub. London, 1994. 72pp; - - 2nd ed. London, 1997. 95pp; - - 3rd ed. London, New Holland, 2001. 95pp.

2902 Road atlas of South Africa: includes touring maps, regional maps, town plans, route maps and place name gazetteer. 2nd rev. ed. Braamfontein, Automobile Association of South Africa, 2004. 77pp. col. maps. *Continues in part* **Road atlas and touring guide of Southern Africa**. 4th ed. Johannesburg, Automobile Association of South Africa, 1974. 232pp. illus. maps. - - Orig. pub. Johannesburg, 1960. 192pp; - - 2nd ed. Johannesburg, 1963. 200pp; - - 3rd ed. Johannesburg, 1968. 200pp.

2903 Road atlas of Southern and East Africa. Cape Town, Mapstudio, 2001. 167pp. illus. maps.

2904 Touring atlas of South Africa and Botswana, Mozambique, Namibia, Zimbabwe. Cape Town, Sunbird Publications, 2000. 80pp. col. maps. (Also pub as **Larger ed** ... Cape Town, 2001. 80pp.)

2905 Touring atlas of Southern Africa, comp. Michael Brett & Alan Mountain. Cape Town, Struik, 1997. 192pp. illus. maps.

2906 Touring guide of Southern Africa: includes over the border maps, touring maps, regional maps, town plans, route maps and place name gazetteer, featuring Namibia, Botswana, Zimbabwe, Mozambique and Malawi. Braamfontein, Automobile Association of South Africa, 2000. 128pp.

Gazetteers (& place-name studies)

Bibliographies & manuals

2907 Jenkins, Elwyn R. et al. **Changing place names**. Durban, Indicator Press, 1996. 112pp. (Guide to changing geographical naming patterns and practices in post-apartheid South Africa. Lists authorities and guidelines)

2908 Raper, Peter E. et al. **Manual for the giving of place names**. Pretoria, Human Sciences Research Council, 1979. 24pp.

2909 Raper, Peter E. & Möller, Lucie Alida. **Onomastics source guide**. Pretoria, Human Sciences Research Council, 1970-1981. 2 vols. (A bibliography. Vol. 2 is a suppl. to vol. 1 covering literature pub. 1971-1978. Sources for both personal and place-names)

2910 Raper, Peter E. **Source guide for toponymy and topology**. Pretoria, Human Sciences Research Council, 1975. (Onomastic series, 5). xix, 478pp. (Detailed bibliography of books, articles, theses and newspaper items concerned with the study of places and place-names)

General

2911 Alphabetical classification of South African place names by magisterial areas, and magisterial areas listing South African place names, compiled from official maps and publications. Rev. ed. Killarney, Stability Print, 2004. 162pp. - - Earlier eds. Durban, Punched Card Services, 1949; Johannesburg, Stability Typing, 1970, 1974, 1984, 1990, 1992, 1997.

2912 Concise gazetteer of South Africa: edited in accordance with the recommendations of the UN Conferences on the Standardization of Geographical Names. Pretoria, Onomastic Research Centre, Human Sciences Research Council & Names Society of Southern Africa, 1994. 68pp. (Emphasises Afrikaans, English and Khoekhoen names. Topographical and administrative location. Glossary of generic words frequently found as terms in South African geographical names)

2913 Encyclopaedia of South African post offices and postal agencies (including their forerunners in the Cape, Natal, Orange Free State, and Transvaal, Basutoland, Bechuanaland, and Swaziland, etc.), comp. Ralph S. Putzel. Tokai, Putzel, 1986-1990. 4 vols.

2914 Leistner, Otto Albrecht & Morris, Jeffrey William. **Southern African place names**. Grahamstown, Cape Provincial Museums, 1976. (Annals, 12). 565pp. illus. (42,000 names for South Africa, Namibia, Botswana, Lesotho and Swaziland. Includes latitude and longitude and grid references)

2915 List of post offices in the Republic of South Africa, in South-West Africa and other countries of the African Postal Union. Rev. ed. Cape Town, South Africa Post-master General, 1970. 179pp. (For later coverage *see* **2913**). - - Earlier eds. **Post offices in the Union of South Africa and neighbouring territories**. Pretoria, 1949. 151pp; - - **Post offices in the Union of South Africa and neighbouring territories**. Pretoria, 1958. 192pp; - - **List of post offices in the Republic of South Africa and neighbouring territories**. Pretoria, 1964. 183pp.

2916 Merrett, Christopher E. **Index to the 1:50,000 maps series.** Pietermaritzburg, Natal Society Library, 1977. 2 vols. Vol. 1. Natal. 37pp.; vol. 2. Cape, Orange Free State, Transkei and Transvaal. 48pp. (Covers features of human settlement: villages, towns, mission stations, historic sites, game parks. References to sheet number and name, but no actual co-ordinates)

2917 Nienaber, Gabriel Stephanus & Raper, Peter E. **Hottentot (Khoekhoen) place names**; trans. P.S. Rabie. Durban, Butterworths for Human Sciences Research Council, 1983. (Southern African place names, 1). 243pp. illus. maps. (Based upon their Afrikaans work of 1977-82 (*see* **2918**)

2918 Nienaber, Gabriel Stephanus & Raper, Peter E. **Toponymica hottentotica.** Pretoria, Human Sciences Research Council, 1977-82. 3 vols. Series A, 2 vols. (Naamkundreeks 6, 7). vol. 1. 1977. A-G. xx, 502pp; vol. 2. 1979. H-Z. xviii, 503-1,126pp. Series B, 1 vol. (Naamkundreeks, 10). xviii, 822pp. (Supplementary entries, with a cumulated index of all names covered by the 3 vols.)

2919 Nienaber, Petrus Johannes. **Suid-Afrikaanse pleknaamwoordeboek. Vol. 1.** 2nd ed. Cape Town, Tafelberg, 1972. 418pp. No more pub. - - Orig. pub. Cape Town, Suid-Afrikaanse Boeksentrum, 1963. 428pp. (The origins of Hottentot, Bantu, Portuguese and French names)

2920 Official place names in the Republic of South Africa and in South West Africa approved to 1 April 1977. Pretoria, Department of Education, Arts & Science, Place Names Committee, 1978. 329pp. (Townships, post offices, agricultural holdings and railway stations. Includes some names from Botswana, Lesotho, Swaziland and Zimbabwe). - - Orig. pub. as **Official place names in the Union and S.W.Africa approved to end 1948.** Pretoria, 1951. 376pp; **+ Supplement, 1949-1952.** Pretoria, 1952. 54pp. *Supplemented by* **Official place names in the Republic of South Africa (approved 1977 to 1988).** Pretoria, 1991. vi, 37, vi, 37pp.

2921 Raper, Peter E. **New dictionary of South African place names.** 3rd ed. Johannesburg, Jonathan Ball, 2004. xviii, 421pp. (Covers Republic of South Africa; Namibia; Botswana, Lesotho and Swaziland. A descriptive gazetteer, with origins of names where known. Author was head of Onomastic Research Centre of the Human Sciences Research Council). - - Orig. pub. as **Dictionary of Southern African place names.** Johannesburg, Lowry, 1987. ix, 368pp; - - 2nd ed. Johannesburg, Jonathan Ball, 1989. x, 608pp.

2922 Smith, Anna H. **Johannesburg street names: a dictionary of street, suburb and other place-names, compiled to the end of 1968**. Cape Town, Juta, 1971. xiii, 629pp. (The most detailed work available for any single city)

2923 South Africa. Department of the Interior. Departmental Committee on the Form & Spelling of Geographical Proper Names. 'Provisional list of geographical proper names in the Union of South Africa and in South West Africa,' *Union of South Africa Government Gazette*, 113 (2359) 24 August 1938, 567-639. (In Afrikaans and English. Lists 9,000 names. The first official attempt to standardize place names. Detailed comments on the list and the problems it raised include: H.G. Fourcade, 'Geographical names', *South African survey journal*, 5, 1939, 164-169; Michel Aurousseau, 'Geographical names in South Africa', *GJ*, 94, 1939, 45-49. The South African Place Names Committee was appointed in 1940 to continue work on the list, and to be responsible for the approval of all proposed new or changed place names)

2924 U.S. Board on Geographic Names. **Gazetteer of South Africa: names approved by the USBGN**. 2nd ed. Washington, DC, 1992. 4 vols. 2,374pp. - - Orig. pub. as **Preliminary N.I.S. gazetteer South Africa: offical standard names approved by the USBGN**. Washington, DC, 1954. 2 vols. iii, 1081pp. Vol. 1. Union of South Africa, A-N; vol. 2. Union of South Africa, O-Z, Basutoland, Bechuanaland, South West Africa, Swaziland

See also **2684, 2734**.

Pilots

2925 France. Service hydrographique [etc.] **Instructions nautiques, L8: Afrique (côte est)**. Brest, 2000. 325pp. - - Earlier ed. **Instructions nautiques sur les côtes sud et est d'Afrique de la baie de la Table au cap Guardafui, etc**. Paris, 1900. x, 417pp. Other eds. (title varies) 1914, 1943, 1969.

2926 Germany. Deutsches Hydrographisches Institut. **Handbuch der Süd- und Ostküste Afrikas: von Kaap Hangklip bis Ras Hafun, Madagaskar und Inseln des mittleren indischen Ozeans**. 7th ed. Hamburg, 1987. Loose-leaf. - - Earlier eds. (title varies) 1912, 1931, 1966, 1982.

2927 G.B. Admiralty. Hydrographic Department [etc.]. **Africa pilot. Vol. 3. South and east coasts of Africa from Cape Agulhas to Ras Binnah, including the islands of Zanzibar and Pemba**. 13th ed. Taunton, 1980. (+ regular suppls.). - - Orig. pub. as **The African pilot. Vol. 3. The South and East coasts**. London, 1864. Later eds (title varies) 1865, 1878, 1889, 1897, 1905, 1915, 1929, 1939, 1967.

2928 South Africa. Navy. Hydrographic Office. **South African sailing directions**. New ed. Cape Town, 1994- . - - Earlier ed. **South African sailing directions**, ed. R.T. Tripp. Cape Town, 1975-1985. 4 vols. Vol.1. 1975. General information; vol. 2. 1979. The coasts of South West Africa and the Republic of South Africa from the Kunlene River to Cape Hangklip; vol. 3. 1985. The coasts of the Republic of South Africa from Table Bay to Great Kei River; vol. 4. 1982. The coasts of the Republic of South Africa and Transkei from East London to the Moçambique Channel.

2929 U.S. Defense Mapping Agency [etc.]. **Sailing directions (enroute) for the southwest coast of Africa**. 7th ed. Bethesda, MD, 1996. xi, 147pp. Earlier eds. 1981, 1983, 1986, 1990, 1993.

2930 U.S. Defense Mapping Agency [etc.]. **Sailing directions for southwest coast of Africa: Cape Palmas to Cape of Good Hope**. 5th ed. Washington, DC, 1969. looseleaf. - - Orig. pub. as **Africa pilot. Vol. 1. West coast of Africa from Cape Palmas to the Cape of Good Hope**. Washington, DC, 1916. Later eds. 1923, 1932, 1952. *Continues* U.S. Hydrographic Office. **West coast of Africa**. Washington, DC, 1873. 3 vols. Vol. 1, Cape Spartel to Sierra Leone; vol. 2, Sierra Leone to Cape Lopez; vol. 3, Cape Lopez to Cape of Good Hope. Later eds. (sub-title varies), 1893, 1908. (For **Vol. 2. South and East coasts of Africa from Cape of Good Hope to Ras Hafun**, *see* 2045)

EARTH SCIENCES

2931 Agricultural GeoReferenced Information System for South Africa (AGIS) http://www.agis.agric.za/agisweb/agis.html. ("Making South Africa's agricultural information available on the Internet". Includes 'dynamic maps', i.e. users can search at various scales and add layers of different information, entitled Orientation atlas, Natural resource atlas, Demography atlas, Foot & mouth Disease atlas, Agricultural infrastructure atlas)

2932 Allanson, Brian R. & Baird, Dan. **Estuaries of South Africa**. Cambridge, Cambridge University Press, 1999. xi, 340pp. (A companion to **2933**. Includes geomorphology, chemistry, vegetation, fauna and ecosystems in general)

2933 Allanson, Brian R. et al. **Inland waters of Southern Africa: an ecological perspective**. Dordrecht, Kluwer, 1990. (Monographiae biologicae, 64). xii, 418pp. Pt. 1. The subcontinent: geomorphology, climate, regional limnology; pt. 2. The rivers and their catchments, floodplains and wetlands; pt. 3. Natural and man-made lakes. (Review, *SAJZ*, 26, 1991, 145-147)

2934 Cole, Monica Mary. **South Africa**. 2nd ed. London, Methuen, 1966. xxx, 706pp. + 48pp. plates. illus. maps. - - Orig. pub. London, 1961. 696pp. (Classic work of physical and economic geography)

2935 Directory of environmental information and organisations in southern Africa. Vol. 1: SADC region, Botswana, Mozambique, Zambia, Zimbabwe, ed. Munyaradzi Chenje. Harare, Southern African Research & Documentation Centre (SARDC) & IUCN, 1996. xi, 163pp. 3 vols. announced. ?No more pub. (Includes region and country chapters with policy overviews followed by contact details. Review, *ARD*, 74, 1997, 93-94).

2936 Directory of southern African conservation areas: a report of the Committee for Nature Conservation Research, National Programme for Environmental Sciences, comp. T. Greyling & B.J. Huntley. Pretoria, Council for Scientific & Industrial Research (CSIR), 1984. (South African national scientific programmes, report 98). vi, 311pp.

2937 Environmental potential atlas for South Africa, ed. Willem Van Riet et al. Pretoria, J.L. Van Schaik for Department of Environmental Affairs & Tourism, Geographic Information Systems Laboratory CC & the University of Pretoria, 1997. v, 61pp. col. maps. 31 x 40 cm. (Maps at 1:6M and 1:15M. "All map information ... has been extracted from the 1997 version of the ENPAT NATIONAL digital atlas on CD-ROM")

2938 The enviropaedia: environmental encyclopaedia and networking directory of southern Africa. Simonstown etc., Eco-Logic Environmental, 2000- . Annual. 2004. 415pp. illus. Also available on CD-ROM from 2003.

2939 Klimm, Ernst et al. **Das südliche Afrika**. Darmstadt, Wissenschaftliche Buchgesellschaft, 1980-1994. (Wissenschaftliche Länder-kunden, 17,39). 2 vols. illus. maps. Vol. 1. South Africa, Swaziland, Lesotho; vol. 2. Namibia, Botswana. (Physical and economic geography. Review of vol. 1, *GJ*, 148, 1982, 69-70)

2940 Moyo, Sam et al. eds. **The Southern African environment: profiles of the SADC countries**. London, Earthscan, 1993. 354pp. illus. (Covers Angola, Botswana, Lesotho, Malawi, Mozambique, Namibia, Swaziland, Tanzania, Zambia and Zimbabwe. Review, *GJ*, 160, 194, 200, "more ... a work of reference than ... a discussion")

2941 Southern African environmental directory. Hout Bay, Woodbay, 1997- . Annual. Latest issue in NLSA is for 1998.

2942 State of the environment in Southern Africa: a report by the Southern African Research & Documentation Centre (SARDC) in collaboration with IUCN & SADC, comp. Andrea Booth et al. Harare, SARDC, 1994. xx, 352pp. illus. maps. (Reviews the climate, soils, woodlands, wildlife, freshwater and marine resources of the SADC countries and considers potential and actual threats)

2943 Wellington, John H. **Southern Africa: a geographical study**. Cambridge, Cambridge University Press, 1955. 2 vols. illus. maps. Vol.1. Physical geography. xxiv, 528pp; vol. 2. Economic and human geography. xviii, 282pp. (Review, *African affairs*, 55, 1956, 328-330, "standard authority … comprehensive, scholarly")

Climate & meteorology

2944 Diab, Roseanne D. **Wind atlas of South Africa**. Pretoria, Department of Mineral & Energy Affairs, 1995. v, 136pp. illus. maps. + 1 computer disk

2945 Schultze, Roland E. et al. **South African atlas of agrohydrology and climatology**. Pretoria, Water Research Commission, 1997. 276pp. illus. col. maps. (Mapping carried out by Department of Agricultural Engineering, University of Natal. Review, *SAGJ*, 81, 1999, 164, "standard work of reference for a wide range of related disciplines".)

2946 South Africa. Weather Bureau. **Climate of South Africa**. Pretoria, 1954-1990. 14 parts. *See* especially, **Part 8, General survey**, by B.R. Schulze. Pretoria, 1965. vii, 330pp. illus. maps.

2947 South Africa. Weather Bureau. **Climate of South Africa: climate statistics up to 1984**. Pretoria, 1986. xiv, 474pp.

2948 Tyson, P.D. & Preston-Whyte, R.A. **The weather and climate of Southern Africa**. 2nd ed. Oxford, Oxford University Press, 2000. xii, 396pp. illus. - - Orig. pub. as **The atmosphere and weather of Southern Africa**. Cape Town, Oxford University Press, 1988. 374pp. Review, *SAGJ*, 71, 1989, 64-65)

2949 U.S. Navy. Chief of Naval Operations. **Marine climatic atlas of the world. Vol. 4. South Atlantic Ocean**. Rev. ed. Washington, DC, U.S. Government Printing Office, 1978. xvii. 267 charts. 33 x 50cm. - - Orig. pub. Washington, DC, 1958.

Geology

2950 Dingle, Richard Vernon et al. **Mezozoic and tertiary geology of Southern Africa**. Rotterdam, Balkema, 1983. viii, 375pp. illus. (Covers South Africa, Namibia, Botswana, Lesotho and Mozambique)

2951 Du Toit, Alexander Logie. **The geology of South Africa.** 3rd ed. rev. Sidney H. Haughton. Edinburgh, Oliver & Boyd, 1954. xiv, 611pp. illus. maps. - - Orig. pub. Edinburgh, 1920. x, 465pp; - - 2nd ed. Edinburgh, 1939. xii, 539pp.

2952 Haughton, Sidney Henry. **Geological history of Southern Africa**. Cape Town, Geological Society of South Africa, 1969. 535pp. illus. maps.

2953 Moon, Bernard P. & Dardis, George F. **Geomorphology of Southern Africa**. Johannesburg, Southern Book Publishers, 1988. 320pp. illus. maps.

2954 Partridge, T.C. & Maud, Rodney R. eds. **The Cenozoic of Southern Africa**. Oxford, Oxford University Press, 2000. (Oxford monographs on geology and geophysics, 40). x, 406pp. (Arranged by theme rather than region or date. "Hope ... this volume ... will serve for many years to come as a work of reference for [all] with an interest in the geology ... of Africa during the last 65 million years", pref.)

2955 Truswell, John Francis. **The geological evolution of South Africa**. Cape Town, Purnell, 1977. 218pp. illus. maps. ("Introductory treatment": a rev. of his **An introduction to the historical geology of South Africa**. Cape Town, Purnell, 1977. 218pp)

2956 Van Eeden, O.R. **The geology of the Republic of South Africa: an explanation of the 1:1,000,000 map, 1970 edition**. Pretoria, Geological Survey of South Africa, 1972. (Special publication, 18). vi, 85pp. illus. maps.

2957 Visser, Dirk J.L. **The geology of the republics of South Africa, Transkei, Bophuthatswana, Venda and Ciskei and the kingdoms of Lesotho and Swaziland: explanation of the 1:1,000,000 geological map, 4th ed., 1984**. Pretoria, Geological Survey of South Africa, 1989. xiv, 491pp. (Companion to map sheets BRN 78582 and BRN 78599)

Minerals

2958 Anhaeusser, Carl R. & Maske, S. **Mineral deposits of Southern Africa**. Johannesburg, Geological Survey of South Africa, 1986. 2 vols. xxiii, 2,335pp. illus. maps. (Definitive descriptive account to its date)

2959 Cairncross, Bruce. **Field guide to rocks and minerals of Southern Africa**. Cape Town, Struik, 2004. 292pp. illus. (Covers South Africa, Namibia, Botswana, Lesotho, Swaziland, Zimbabwe and southern Mozambique. Includes more than 500 col. photos).

2960 Daltry, Vaughan D.C. **Mineralogy of South Africa: type-mineral species and type-mineral names**. Pretoria, Council for Geoscience, 1997. (Geological Survey handbook, 15). 114pp.

2961 Pelletier, René A. **Mineral resources of South-Central Africa**. Cape Town, Oxford University Press, 1964. 277pp. illus. 39 maps. (Systematic survey of South Africa, N. Rhodesia, Nyasaland, Congo Republic, Ruanda-Urundi, Angola, Mozambique, Kenya, Tanganyika, Uganda, looking at geographical features and mineral deposits. Review, *GJ*, 132, 1966, 414-415)

2962 Wilson, Michael G.C. & Anhaeusser, Carl R. **The mineral resources of South Africa**. 6th ed. Pretoria, Council for Geoscience, 1998. (Handbook of the Council for Geoscience (South Africa), 16). viii, 740pp. illus. maps. ("Commemorating a hundred years of geological research since the founding of the Geological Commission of the Cape of Good Hope in 1895, the Transvaal Geological Survey in 1897, and the Natal Geological Survey in 1899". General chapters followed by 66 sections for individual minerals. "Not a geological textbook but rather a concise yet comprehensive and practical guide to the country's array of mineral deposits", pref. Emphasizes economic aspects to complement Anhaeusser & Maske, **2958**). - - Orig. pub. as **Mineral resources of the Union of South Africa**. Pretoria, 1930. - - 2nd ed. Pretoria, 1936. xvi, 454pp; - - [3rd ed.] ... with a summary of the mineral resources of S.W. Africa. Pretoria, 1940. 544pp; - - 4th ed. Pretoria, 1959.xi, 622pp; - - 5th ed. **The mineral resources of South Africa**, ed C.B. Coetzee. Pretoria, Department of Mines, Geological Survey, 1976. viii, 462pp.

Soils

2963 South Africa. Soil & Irrigation Research Institute. Soil Classification Working Group. **Soil classification: a taxonomic system for South Africa: a report on a research project**. 2nd ed. Pretoria, Department of Agricultural Development, 1991. (Memoirs on the agricultural natural resources of South Africa, 15). xv, 257pp. illus. - - Orig. pub. as **Soil classification: a binomial system for South Africa**, comp. C.N. MacVicar et al. Pretoria, 1977. (Science bulletin, 390) x, 150pp. illus.

2964 Van der Merwe, C.R. **Soil groups and sub-groups of South Africa**. 2nd ed. Pretoria, South Africa Department of Technical Services, 1962.

(Science bulletin, 356). 355pp. illus. maps. - - Orig. pub. Pretoria, 1941. (Science bulletin, 231). 316pp. illus. maps.

BIOLOGICAL SCIENCES

2965 Branch, George M. et al. **Two oceans; a guide to the marine life of Southern Africa**. 2nd ed. Cape Town, Philip, 2005. 360pp. illus. (Field guide to over 1,400 spp.). - - Orig. pub. Cape Town, 1994. 360pp.

2966 Rutherford, Michael Charles & Westfall, Robert Howard. **Biomes of Southern Africa: an objective categorization**. 2nd ed. Pretoria, National Botanical Institute, 1994. (Memoirs, 63). vii, 94pp. illus. maps. (Identifies 7 biomes south of 22°S: Desert, Succulent Karoo, Nama-Karoo, Savanna, Grassland, Fybos, Forest). - - Orig. pub. Pretoria, 1986. (Memoirs, 54). 98pp. (Review, *SAGJ*, 70, 1988, 156)

2967 Werger, Marinus J.A. **Biogeography and ecology of Southern Africa**; with the assistance of A.C. van Bruggen for the zoological chapters. The Hague, Junk, 1978. 2 vols. 1,439pp. illus. map. (Vol. 1 covers geomorphology, climate, soils, and biomes; vol. 2 covers principally zoology. Review, *GJ*, 145, 1979, 466-468, "a scholarly work, compulsive for reference")

Zoology

2968 Potgieter, Dirk J. et al. **Animal life in Southern Africa**. Cape Town, Nasou, 1971. 469pp. illus. (Collection of appropriate articles originally published in **Standard encyclopedia of Southern Africa**, *see* **2695**)

Birds

Checklists

2969 Clancey, Philip Alexander. **South African Ornithological Society checklist of Southern African birds**. Rev. ed. Johannesburg, South African Ornithological Society, 1980. xiii, 325pp. (Review, *Ibis*, 124, 1982, 105-106). *Continued by* **Updating reports**; 1st, 1987. 43pp.; 2nd, 1991; 3rd, 1996. 2nd update includes as Annex 1. 'Orders and families of Southern African birds' arranged according to the new Sibley & Monroe system, *see* **708**. - - Orig. pub. as **Check list of the birds of South Africa**. Cape Town, University of Cape Town & South African Ornithological Society, 1969. x, 338pp.

2970 Drummond, Malcolm. **The official checklist of birds in Southern Africa: cross-referenced to** *Sasol birds of Southern Africa*. Cape Town,

Struik, 2004. 35pp. (*See* **2978**)

2971 Hockey, Phil A.R. **Birds of Southern Africa: checklist and alternative names**. 2nd ed. Cape Town, Struik, 1996. 80pp. (Cross referenced to Sasol guide, *see* **2978**, Newman, *see* **2977** and Roberts, *see* **2975**. Review, *BABC*, 3, 1996, 56). - - Orig. pub. Cape Town, 1994. 80pp.

2972 Percy Fitzpatrick Institute of African Ornithology. Roberts species list: common and scientific names from Roberts VI and VII (revised October 2005). http://www.fitzpatrick.uct.ac.za/pdf/roberts7.pdf. (List of spp. prepared for **Roberts' birds of Southern Africa**. 7th ed. 2005, *see* **2975**. For details of compilation *see* http://www.fitzpatrick.uct.ac.za/docs/ birdlist.html. "The 'official' list committee, most recently under the auspices of the Southern African Ornithological Society ... has fallen away. Assuming that the regional field guides come into line with the revised Roberts nomenclature, this list will *de facto* become the new list for the region")

Handbooks

2973 **The atlas of Southern African birds**: including Botswana, Lesotho, South Africa, Swaziland and Zimbabwe, comp. James A. Harrison et al. Cape Town, BirdLife, 1997. 2 vols. Vol. 1. Non-passerines. 785pp.; vol. 2. Passerines. 732pp. (Covers 932 spp. Reviews, *British birds*, 91, 1998, 189, "sets new standards in atlas production"; *Ibis*, 140, 1998, 546; *Ostrich*, 72, 2001, 62,100,108, "the final product does not do full justice to the ... work put into it". *See* **Guidelines for the bird atlas of Southern Africa: proceedings of a workshop...Cape Town, 23-24 August 1984**, ed. P.A.R. Hockey & A.A. Ferrar. Pretoria, 1985. iv, 55pp; James A. Harrison, 'The Southern African Bird Atlas project databank', *S.A. journal of science*, 88, 1992, 410-413)

2974 Ginn, Peter J. et al. **The complete book of Southern African birds**. Cape Town, Struik, 1989. 760pp. illus. maps. (Covers some 900 spp. with 1,000 col. photos. Reviews, *Auk*, 109, 1992, 208-209; *Ibis*, 133, 1991, 97-98)

2975 Roberts, Austin. **Roberts' birds of Southern Africa**. 7th ed. rev. Phil A.R. Hockey et al. Cape Town, Trustees of the John Voelcker Bird Book Fund, 2005. 1,296pp. illus. maps. (Latest major revision of one of the classic volumes of African ornithology which has been regularly up-dated and re-illus. over a period of 65 years. Covers S.A., Namibia, Botswana, Lesotho, Swaziland, Zimbabwe, Southern Mozambique. The 7th ed. has new text and illus. throughout, adopts a new taxonomic sequence based on Sibley & Monroe, *see* **708**, treats sub-spp. once more (omitted from 5th & 6th eds.), and includes refs. for the first time. Data on compilation, errata, etc. are on the Percy Fitzpatrick Institute of African Ornithology Web site at http://www.fitzpatrick.uct.ac.za/docs/roberts.html. 7th ed. no longer includes unique numbers for each sp. Most other works on the birds of Southern Africa quote 'Roberts numbers' as a cross-reference to earlier eds. of this work; note that these remained constant for eds. 1 to 4 but re-numbering took place for the 5th ed. - - Orig. pub. as Roberts, Austin. **The birds of South Africa**. London, Witherby, 1940. xxxii, 463pp. 56 col. plates. maps; - - 2nd ed., rev. G.R. McLachlan & R. Liversidge. Cape Town, South African Bird Book Fund, 1957. xxxviii, 504pp. 56 col. plates (re-issued, 1958, as **Roberts' birds of Southern Africa**); - - 3rd ed. pub. as **Roberts' birds of Southern Africa**. Cape Town, John Voelcker Bird Book Fund 1970. xxxii, 643pp. 56 plates; - - 4th ed. rev. Cape Town, 1978. xxxii, 660pp. 72 col. plates. (Reviews, *Ibis*, 121, 1979, 527; *Ostrich*, 49, 1979, 147-149); - - 5th ed. rev. G.L. Maclean. Cape Town, 1985. lii, 848pp. (Major revision which dropped descriptions of sub-spp. previously given. Review, *Ibis*, 128, 436-437) - - 6th ed. London, New Holland, 1993. 874pp. 74 col. plates. (Reviews, *Auk*, 111, 1994, 782-783; *Ibis*, 136, 1994, 504-505; *SAJZ*, 29, 1994, 197)

- - **Roberts multimedia birds of Southern Africa**. Version 3.0. Cape Town, Encarta for South African Birding, 2002. 2 CD-ROMs. (Covers 950 spp. with some 4,000 still photos, 650 videos and 850 recordings of bird sounds). - - Orig. pub. Cape Town, 1997. 1 CD-ROM

Field guides

2976 McLean, Gordon L. **The field companion to Roberts' birds of Southern Africa**. 2nd ed. Cape Town, Trustees of the John Voelcker Bird Book Fund, 2001. 184pp. illus. (Illus. by Kenneth Newman). - - Orig. pub. Cape Town ,1996. 179pp.

2977 Newman, Kenneth. **Newman's birds of Southern Africa**. 8th ed. Cape Town, Struik, 2002. 527pp. 217 plates. (Covers 900+ spp.). - - Orig. pub. Johannesburg, Macmillan South Africa, 1983. 461pp. illus. maps. (Review, *Ibis*, 127, 1985, 131-132); - - Updated [i.e. 2nd ed.] Johannesburg, Southern Book Publishers, 1988. 472pp. illus. maps; - - 1991 update [i.e. 3rd ed.]. Johannesburg, Southern Books/London, Harper Collins, 1991. 480pp. 209 plates; - - 1995 ed. [i.e. 4th ed.] Johannesburg, Southern Books, 1995. 512pp. 209 col. plates; - - 5th ed. "The Green edition". Johannesburg, 1996. 512pp; - - 6th ed. Cape Town, New Holland, 1998. 510pp; - - 7th ed. Cape Town, New Holland, 1999. 510pp. 2,000 col. illus. (Review *Ibis*, 143, 2001, 694)

- - **Newmans birds by colour**. Cape Town, Struik, 2000. 304pp. illus. (Illus. of more common birds arranged by colour rather than taxonomy)

2978 Sinclair, Ian (also known as Sinclair, J.C.) et al. **Sasol birds of Southern Africa**. 3rd ed. Cape Town, Struik/London, New Holland, 2002. 464pp. (Covers 900+ spp.). - - Orig. pub. Cape Town, 1993. 426pp. (Review, *Ibis*, 136,

1994, 249); - - 2nd ed. Cape Town, Struik/London, New Holland, 1997. 445pp. (The 1993 ed. is described in the intro. as "text based on **Ian Sinclair's guide to the birds of Southern Africa**, 1987". This was orig. pub. Cape Town, Struik, 1984. 368pp; - - 2nd ed. Cape Town, Struik, 1987. 368pp; - - 3rd ed. Cape Town, Struik, 1994. 368pp. Sasol is a South African chemical company. South Africa is unique among African countries in having two competing field guides, Newman & Sinclair, each regularly revised)

- - **Sasol - the larger illustrated guide to the birds of Southern Africa**. Cape Town, 1997. 448pp. (Larger format version of the 2nd ed. above). The plates alone have also been reproduced full-size as **Birds of Southern Africa - the Sasol plates collection**. Cape Town, Struik, 1995)

- - **Sasol e-birds of Southern Africa**. Version 2. Craighall, PDA Solutions, 2005. 1 PDA card (Requires a PDA running Microsoft Pocket PC 2003 or later. Includes text and pictures from the print ed. also sound recordings)

2979 Sinclair, Ian. **Photographic guide to birds of Southern Africa**. 4th ed. Cape Town, Struik, 2005. 144pp. illus. - - Orig. pub. as **Southern Africa birds: a photographic guide**. Cape Town, 1990. 144pp. - - rev. ed. Cape Town, 1999. 144pp; . - - 3rd ed. Cape Town, 2000. 144pp. illus.

2980 Sinclair, Ian & Davidson, Peter. **Sasol Southern Africa birds: a photographic guide**. Cape Town, Struik, 1995. 304pp. 2nd ed. announced by publisher for 2006.

Mammals

Checklists

2981 Ellerman, John Reeves et al. **Southern African mammals, 1758-1951: a reclassification**. London, British Museum (Natural History), 1953. 363pp. maps. (Employs a totally different classification from that used by Roberts, 1951 see **2985**. Review, *Journal of mammalogy*, 35, 1954, 460-461)

2982 Meester, Jurgens A.J. et al. **Classification of Southern African mammals**. Pretoria, Transvaal Museum, 1986. (Transvaal Museum monograph, 5). x, 359pp. illus. map. (Review, *Journal of mammalogy*, 70, 1989, 679-680; *SAJZ*, 23, 1988, 242-243)

2983 Swanepoel, Pierre et al. 'A checklist and numbering system of the extant mammals of the Southern African subregion', *Annals of the Transvaal Museum*, 32, 1980, 155-196

Handbooks

2984 Mills, Gus & Hes, Lex. **The complete book of Southern African mammals**. Cape Town, Struik, 1997. 356pp. 350 col. photos. (340 spp.)

2985 Roberts, Austin. **The mammals of South Africa**. 2nd ed. Johannesburg, Trustees of *The mammals of S.A.* Book Fund, 1954. xlviii, 700pp. plates. - - Orig. pub. Johannesburg, 1951. xlviii, 700pp. (Review, *Journal of mammalogy*, 34, 1953, 140-141)

2986 Smithers, Reay H.N. & Skinner, John D. **The mammals of the Southern African subregion**. 3rd ed. Cambridge, Cambridge University Press, 2006. 872pp. (300 line diagrams, 41 col. plates, 297 maps. Covers region south of the Cunene/Zambesi rivers, i.e. Namibia, Botswana, Lesotho, Swaziland, South Africa, Zimbabwe and southern Mozambique, and the coastal waters. Intended as a replacement for Roberts, *see* **2985**, with less emphasis on taxonomy and more on behaviour and distribution. For taxonomic arrangement 1st ed. followed Swanepoel, 1980, *see* **2983**, while 2nd & 3rd eds. follow Meester, 1986, *see* **2982**. Covers 338 spp. each with illus. and distribution map. - - Orig. pub. Pretoria, University of Pretoria, 1983. xxii, 736pp. illus. (Reviews, *Journal of mammalogy*, 65, 1984, 731-732; *Mammal review*, 15, 1984, 189; *Oryx*, 19, 1985, 122-123; *SAJZ*, 19, 1984, 317, "a major landmark"); - - 2nd ed. Pretoria, 1990. xxxii, 771pp. 38 col. plates. (Reviews, *Mammal review*, 22, 1992, 78; *Oryx*, 26, 1992, 122-123; *SAJZ*, 27, 1992, 94)

Field guides

2987 Maberley, Charles T. Astley. **Maberly's mammals of Southern Africa: a popular field guide**; a rev. by Richard Goss of Charles Astley Maberly's **The game animals of southern Africa**. Parklands, Jonathan Ball, 1990. 349pp. illus. maps. - - Orig. pub. Craighall, Delta Books, 1986. 347pp. illus.

2988 Smithers, Reay H.N. **Smithers' mammals of Southern Africa: a field guide**. New ed. rev. P. Epps. Cape Town, Struik, 2000. xvi, 364pp. - - Rev.ed. Cape Town, Airlife/Swan Hill Press, 1996. xvi, 364pp. - - Orig. pub. as **Land mammals of Southern Africa: a field guide**, comp. Reay H.N. Smithers & C. Abbott. Johannesburg, Macmillan S.A., 1986. xxiv, 229pp; - - 2nd ed. Halfway House, Southern Book Publishers, 1992. xxiv, 229pp. (Includes 197 spp. out of the 291 recorded in the region at the time)

2989 Stuart, Chris & Stuart, Tilde. **Field guide to the mammals of Southern Africa**. 3rd ed. Cape Town, Struik, 2001. 272pp. 500+ col. photos. maps. (Covers 337 spp.) - - Orig. pub. Cape Town/London, 1988. 272pp. illus. maps; - - 2nd ed. London, New Holland, 1995. 272pp.

Reptiles & amphibians

2990 Boycott, Richard C. **The Southern African tortoise book: a guide to Southern African tortoises, terrapins and turtles**. Rev. ed. Hilton, KwaZulu-Natal, O. Bourquin, 2000. x, 228pp. illus. - - Orig. pub. as **The South African tortoise book: ...** Johannesburg, Southern Book Publishers, 1988. 608pp. illus.

2991 Branch, Bill. **Field guide to the snakes and other reptiles of Southern Africa**. 3rd ed. London, New Holland, 1998. 399pp. 112 col. plates. 480 maps. (Covers 480 spp. Review, *Copeia*, 1999, 236-238). - - Orig. pub.as **Bill Branch's field guide ...** London, 1988. 328pp.

2992 FitzSimons, Vivian F.M. **FitzSimons' snakes of Southern Africa**, rev. & updated by Donald G. Broadley. Parklands, Jonathan Ball, 1990. 387pp. 81 col. plates. illus. 83 maps. (Covers 164 spp. and sub-spp.). - - Earlier ed. Johannesburg, Delta Books, 1983. 376pp. - - Orig. pub. as **Snakes of Southern Africa**, comp. V.F.M. FitzSimons. Cape Town, Purnell, 1962. 423pp.

2993 FitzSimons, Vivian F.M. **The lizards of South Africa**. Pretoria, Transvaal Museum, 1943. (Memoirs, 1). 528pp. 24 plates. 379 text figs. Reprint, Amsterdam, Swets & Zeitlinger, 1970.

2994 Marais, Johan. **A complete guide to the snakes of Southern Africa**. [2nd ed.]. Cape Town, Struik, 2004. 312pp. illus. (Review, *African journal of herpetology*, 53, 2004, 201-202). - - Orig. pub. Halfway House, Southern Book Publishers, 1992. ix, 208pp. illus.
- - **eSnakes of Southern Africa**. Craighall, PDA Solutions, 2005. 1 PDA card (Requires a PDA running Microsoft Pocket PC 2003 or later. Includes text and pictures from the print ed. Free software updates to be available)

2995 Minter, L.R. et al. **Atlas and red data book of the frogs of South Africa, Lesotho and Swaziland**. Washington, DC, Smithsonian Institution, 2004. xv, 360pp. + 32pp. plates. maps. (Review, *African journal of herpetology*, 53, 2004, 191-196)

2996 Passmore, Neville Ian & Carruthers, Vincent. **South African frogs: a complete guide**. Rev. ed. Johannesburg, Southern Books & University of the Witwatersrand Press, 1995. xiii, 322pp. illus. (Covers 97 spp. including distribution maps). - - Orig. pub. Johannesburg, 1979. 270pp. (Review, *Copeia*, 1980, 947-948. For a popular guide to frogs *see* Vincent A. Wager. **The frogs of South Africa**. Rev. ed. Cape Town, Delta Books, 1986. 183pp. (Review, *Copeia*, 1988, 271-272). - - Orig. pub. Cape Town, Purnell, 1965. 242pp)

2997 Poynton, John C. **The amphibia of Southern Africa: a faunal study**. Pietermaritzburg, Natal Museum, 1964. (Annals, 17). 334pp. illus. maps. (Covers 127 spp.)

See also **1255**

Fishes

2998 **Checklist of the fishes of the eastern tropical Atlantic (CLOFETA)**, ed. Jean-Claude Quéro et al. Paris, UNESCO & Societas Europea Ichtyologorum/ Lisbon, Junta Nacional de Investigaçao Cientifica e Tecnológica, 1990. 3 vols. xxxii, 1,492pp.

2999 **Common and scientific names of the fishes of Southern Africa**. Grahamstown, Rhodes University, J.L.B. Smith Institute of Ichthyology, 1975. (Special publication, 14). 2 vols. 213pp. Vol.1. Marine fishes, by Margaret M. Smith; vol. 2. Freshwater fishes, by Peter B.N. Jackson.

3000 Heemstra, Phillip C. & Heemstra, Elaine. **Coastal fishes of Southern Africa**. Grahamstown, NISC & South African Institute for Aquatic Biodiversity, 2004. xxiv, 488pp. illus. maps. (Review, *African zoology*, 40, 2005, 166)

3001 Skelton, Paul Harvey. **A complete guide to the freshwater fishes of Southern Africa**. New ed. Cape Town, Struik, 2001. xiv, 395pp. illus. - - Orig. pub. Johannesburg, Southern Book Publishers, 1993. xiii, 388pp. illus. (Covers 245 spp., all illus. Reviews, *Copeia*, 1996, 755-757; *SAJZ*, 29, 1994, 225)

3302 Smale, Malcolm J. et al. **Otolith atlas of Southern African marine fishes**. Grahamstown, J.L.B. Smith Institute of Ichthyology, 1995. (Ichthyological monographs, 1). 253pp. + 149 plates.

3003 Smith, Margaret M. & Heemstra, Phillip C. eds. **Smith's sea fishes**. 2nd ed. Cape Town, Struik, 2003. xxxi, 1,047pp. (Covers some 2,200 spp. in 270 families). - - Orig. pub. Johannesburg, Southern Book Publishers, 1986. xx, 1,047pp. (Reviews *Copeia*, 1987, 816-818; *SAJZ*, 22, 1987, 243). Rev. version of James L.B. Smith. **The sea fishes of Southern Africa**. Johannesburg, 1949. xvi, 550pp; - - [2nd ed.] Johannesburg, 1953. xvi, 564pp; - - 4th ed. Johannesburg, Central News Agency, 1961. xvi, 580pp; - - 5th ed. Johannesburg, 1965. xvi, 580pp. (Reissued, Johannesburg, 1977 as **Smith's sea fishes**)

3004 Van der Elst, Rudy. **A guide to the common sea fishes of Southern Africa**. 3rd ed. Cape Town, Struik, 1993. 398pp. illus. maps. (Describes 284 spp.). - - Orig. pub. Cape Town, 1981. 367pp; - - 2nd ed. Cape Town, 1988. 398pp.

Invertebrates

Butterflies & moths

3005 Henning, Graham Alan et al. **Living butterflies of Southern Africa: biology, ecology and conservation**. Hatfield, Umdaus, 1997- . To be complete in 5 vols. Vol. 1. 1997. Hesperiidae, Papilionidae and Pieridae of South Africa. 397pp. (Vol. 5 will cover spp. unique to Namibia, Botswana, Zimbabwe and Mozambique)

3006 Janse, Aantonius J.T. **The moths of South Africa**. Durban, E.P. & Commercial Printing, 1932-1964. 7 vols. in 12. illus.

3007 Migdoll, Ivor. **Field guide to the butterflies of Southern Africa**. 2nd ed. Cape Town, Struik, 1994. 256pp. illus. (Photographic field guide covering some 1,230 common spp.). - - Orig. pub. Cape Town, 1987. 256pp. illus.

3008 Pennington's butterflies of Southern Africa. 2nd ed. rev. Graham Alan Henning et al. Cape Town, Struik, 1994. 800pp. col. illus. (Review, *National University of Lesotho, journal of research*, 4, 1994, 158-159). - - Orig. pub. comp. Kenneth Misson Pennington, ed. Charles D.C. Dickson. Johannesburg, Donker, 1978. 670pp.

3009 Pinhey, Elliot C.G. **Moths of Southern Africa: descriptions and colour illustrations of 1,183 species**. Cape Town, Tafelberg, 1975. 273pp. + 32pp.

3010 Williams, Mark. **Butterflies of Southern Africa: a field guide**. Johannesburg, Southern Book Publishers, 1994. 302 pp. + 32pp. col. plates. (Photographic field guide to the most common 233 spp.)

Others

3011 Connolly, Matthew. **A monographic survey of South African non-marine mollusca**. Cape Town, South African Museum, 1938. (Annals, 33). iii, 660pp. + 19pp. plates. illus.

3012 Guide to the freshwater invertebrates of Southern Africa. Pretoria, Water Research Commission, 1999- . 10 vols. 8 vols. pub. to 2003. Vols. 2-4, Crustacea; vol. 5. Non Arthropods; vol. 6. Arachidna, Mollusca, Araneae; vols. 7 & 8. Insecta, I & II; vol. 9. Insecta III, Diptera. Vols. 1. Introduction &

10. Insecta, IV, Coleoptera, announced for pub. 2006. (Covers South Africa, Namibia, Botswana, Lesotho, Swaziland; Angola, Mozambique, Malawi, Zambia, Zimbabwe)

3013 Jupp, Peter G. **Mosquitoes of Southern Africa**. Hartbeespoort, Ekogilde, 1996. 156pp. illus. (Covers 175+ spp.)

3014 Picker, Mike et al. **Field guide to insects of South Africa**. Updated ed. Cape Town, Struik/London, New Holland, 2004. 440pp. (Covers c. 1,200 spp. each with a col. photo and a distribution map). - - Orig. pub. Cape Town, 2002. 440pp. (Review, *African zoology*, 38, 2003, 189-190)

3015 Pinhey, Elliot C.G. **The dragonflies of Southern Africa**. Pretoria, Transvaal Museum, 1951. (Memoir, 5). xv, 385pp. illus.

3016 Scholtz, Clarke H. & Holm, Erik. **Insects of Southern Africa**. Durban/Stoneham, MD, Butterworth, 1985. 502p. 150 col. illus. (Covers 600 families)

3017 Tarboton, Warwick & Tarboton, Michelle. **A fieldguide to the dragonflies of South Africa**. Modimolle, authors, 2002. 95pp. col. illus.

Botany

3018 Acocks, John P.H. **Veld types of South Africa**. 3rd ed. Pretoria, Botanical Research Institute, 1988. (Memoirs, 57). 146pp. illus. maps. (With col. vegetation map at 1:1,500,000. Describes 70 different veld types, each with a photograph). - - Orig. pub. Pretoria, 1953. (Memoirs, 28). 192pp. - - 2nd ed. Pretoria, Botanical Survey of South Africa, 1975. (Memoirs, 40). 128pp.

3019 Cowling, Richard M. et al., eds. **Vegetation of Southern Africa**. Cambridge, Cambridge University Press, 1997. xxxiv, 615pp. illus. maps. (Covers evolution of the region's landscape, including soils and climate, analysis of each vegetation type and underlying ecological themes, such as fire and conservation)

3020 Low, A.B. & Rebelo, Anthony Gomes. **Vegetation of South Africa, Lesotho and Swaziland: a companion to the vegetation map**. Pretoria, Department of Environmental Affairs & Tourism, 1996. 85pp. maps.

3021 PRECIS (PRetoria Computerized Information System) is maintained at the National Herbarium, Pretoria. ("Precis project mission is to develop, maintain and expand an electronic database system on Southern African plants". This database is increasingly used as the basis for compiling floristic works. 'It is hoped to make PRECIS partially accessible on this Web site http://www.nbi.ac.za/information/databases.htm in the near future', July 2006)

3022 South African National Biodiversity Institute (SANBI), Kirstenbosch http://www.nbi.ac.za/ (Established on 1 September 2004 as the successor to the National Botanical Institute. It maintains projects and databases such as APCD, PRECIS and POSA, *see* **3021, 3024, 3025**, and was responsible for managing SABONET, a GEF (Global Environment Facility) project implemented by the United Nations Development Programme (UNDP) as "a capacity-building network of southern African herbaria and botanic gardens with the objective of developing local botanical expertise". The SABONET project, 1996 to 2005, produced a number of guides, many listed below. SANBI's Interactive Flora Site at http://www.flora.sanbi.org/ currently has three datasets, all in the process of development, 'Interactive Flora of Southern and Southern Tropical Africa', *see* **3031**; 'Trees of Southern Africa', *see* **3046** and 'Interactive Mesembs')

3023 Southern African Network for Taxonomy (SAFRINET) http://www.natmus.cul.na/safrinet/ ("strives to make taxonomic information in a user-friendly format available throughout the region". Members are Angola, Botswana, Democratic Republic of Congo, Lesotho, Malawi, Mauritius, Mozambique, Namibia, Seychelles, South Africa, Swaziland, Tanzania, Zambia, Zimbabwe. *See* SAFRINET. **Manifesto and portfolio for technical co-operation**, ed. T. Jones & C. Eardley. Pretoria, 1999. 59pp.)

Checklists

3024 Plants of Southern Africa: an annotated checklist, comp. Gerrit Germishuizen & Nicole Laura Meyer. Pretoria, National Botanical Institute, 2003. (*Strelizia*, 14). 1,231pp. (Compiled from PRECIS, *see* **3021**. Update of **Plants of Southern Africa: names and distribution**, comp. Trevor Henry Arnold & Bente Carole De Wet. Pretoria, 1993. (*Memoirs*, 62). lv, 825pp. itself a rev. of **List of species of Southern African plants**, comp. G.E. Gibbs Russell et al. Pretoria, 1984-87. (*Memoirs*, 48, 51, 56).

- - African plant checklist and database project, APCD. (Ongoing project to combine the datasets of **Plants of Southern Africa** and Lebrun & Stork **Tropical African flowering plants**, *see* **775**. There will be a hardcopy publication of the completed work, and there is already an online version which will continue to be updated at http://www.nbi.ac.za/frames/infofram.htm)

3025 Plants of Southern Africa (POSA): an online checklist. Pretoria, South Africa National Biodiversity Institute (SANBI). http://www.nbi.ac.za/frames /infofram.htm. (Permits search by family, genus and species)

3026 Riley, Herbert P. **Families of flowering plants of southern Africa**. Lexington, KE, University of Kentucky Press, 1963. xviii, 269pp. (Introductory taxonomic survey)

3027 Smith, Christo Albertyn et al. **Common names of South African plants**. Pretoria, Botanical Research Institute, 1966. (Botanical Survey memoir, 35). vi, 642pp.

Floras

3028 Dyer, Robert A. **The genera of Southern African flowering plants**. 3ʳᵈ ed. Pretoria, Department of Agricultural Technical Services, Botanical Research Institute, 1975-77. 3 vols. viii, 1,040pp. Vol. 1. Dicotyledons; vol. 2. Gymnosperms and monocotyledons; vol. 3. Key to families and index. (Concise descriptive generic flora). - - Orig. pub. ed. E.P. Phillips. Cape Town, Botanical Survey of South Africa, 1926; - - 2ⁿᵈ ed. Cape Town, 1951.)
- - **Flora of Southern Africa: key to families and index to** The genera of Southern African flowering plants. Pretoria, Botanical Research Institute, 1977. 60pp.

3029 Flora of Southern Africa: which deals with the territories of South Africa, Lesotho, Swaziland, Namibia and Botswana, ed. Robert A. Dyer et al. Pretoria, National Botanical Institute, 1963- . 33 vols. proposed, 28 pub. to 2006. (The standard large-scale descriptive flora of the region. Sub-title varies: ... the territories of the Republic of South Africa, Basutoland, Swaziland and South West Africa; ... the territories of South Africa, Transkei, Lesotho, Swaziland, Bophuthatswana, South West Africa/Namibia and Botswana, etc. Successor to **Flora capensis**. Dublin, Hodges/Ashford, etc. Reeve, 1859-1933. 7 vols. (Vols, 1 to 3, ed. W.H. Harvey & O.W. Sonder, 1859-1865, cover Cape Colony, Kaffraria and Natal only; vols. 4 to 7 ed. W.T. Thistleton-Dyer and A.W. Hill, 1896-1933, cover whole of Southern Africa north to the Limpopo river)

3030 Goldblatt, Peter & Manning, John. **Cape plants: a conspectus of the Cape flora of South Africa**. Pretoria, National Botanical Institute/St. Louis, MO, Missouri Botanical Gardens, 2000. (Strelitzia, 9). 743pp. illus. maps. (Includes gymnosperms, angiosperms, ferns and fern allies with keys to families and genera. Spp. entries include a diagnostic description, flowering time, habitat and distribution. Successor to **Plants of the Cape flora: a descriptive catalogue**, comp. Pauline Bond & Peter Goldblatt. Cape Town,

Purnell for National Botanic Gardens of South Africa, 1984. (*Journal of S.A. botany*, Suppl. 13). xi, 455pp. col. illus.)

3031 The Interactive Flora of Southern and Southern Tropical Africa, http://www.flora.sanbi.org/its_page?comID=2 (Data set being developed by SANBI, *see* **3022**, to cover the Southern African region including Namibia, Botswana, South Africa, Swaziland, Lesotho, Angola, Zambia, Zimbabwe, Malawi, Mozambique. "Aims to provide an interactive identification system for the seed plants of southern Africa at several levels of the taxonomic hierarchy thereby facilitating naming of plants in the region")

Field guides

3032 Manning, John. **Photographic guide to the wildflowers of South Africa**. Pretoria, Briza, 2003. 352pp. illus. maps. (Covers some 900 of the most common and conspicuous spp. in South Africa, Lesotho, Swaziland and Namibia)

3033 Retief, Elizabeth & Herman, Paul P.J. **Plants of the northern provinces of South Africa: keys and diagnostic characters**. Pretoria, National Botanical Institute, 1997. (*Strelitzia*, 6). vii, 681pp. (Covers North-West, Gauteng, Northern and Mpumalanga provinces)

3034 Rourke, John P., ed. **Wild flowers of South Africa**. 2nd ed. London, New Holland, 1996. 128pp. 406 col. photos. (Comp. National Botanic Gardens, Kirstenbosch. Description and illus. of c. 300 spp.). - - Orig. pub. London, 1995.

3035 **South African wild flower guide**. Pretoria, Botanical Society of South Africa, 1988- . 11 vols to 2005 (Each vol. covers a specific botanical region. Some vols. regularly rev. e.g. Namaqualand. 3rd ed. Pretoria, 2005. 336pp.)

Specific taxonomic groups

3036 Chippindall, Lucy K.A. 'A guide to the identification of grasses in South Africa', pp. 1-527 in **The grasses and pastures of South Africa**, comp. Dudley B.D. Meredith et al. Cape Town, Central News Agency, 1955. xvi, 777pp. illus. maps.

3037 Cook, Christopher D.K. **Aquatic and wetland plants of Southern Africa**. Leiden, Backhuys, 2004. 281pp. illus. (Descriptive flora with 482 spp.)

3038 Court, Doreen. **Succulent flora of Southern Africa: a comprehensive and authoritative guide to the indigenous succulents of South Africa, Botswana, SWA/Namibia, Angola, Zambia, Zimbabwe/Rhodesia and**

Mozambique. 2ⁿᵈ ed. Rotterdam, Balkema, 2000. xii, 300pp. illus. maps. (Covers 164 genera in 9 families). - - Orig. pub. Rotterdam, 1981. xvi, 224pp.

3039 Grasses of Southern Africa: an identification manual with keys, descriptions, distributions, classification and automated identification and information retrieval from computerized data, comp. Garland Elizabeth Gibbs Russell et al., ed. O.A. Leistner. Pretoria, National Botanic Gardens/Botanical Research Institute, 1990. (Botanical Survey memoirs, 58). ix, 437pp. illus. maps. (Review, *National University of Lesotho journal of research*, 4, 1994, 141-142)

3040 Leistner, Otto Albrecht. **Seed plants of Southern Africa: families and genera**. Rev. ed. Pretoria, SABONET, 2005. (SABONET report, 26). 498pp. (Taxonomic treatment of some 230 seed plant families and their 2,600 genera both indigenous and naturalised, with a key to families, and to genera in each family). - - Orig. pub. Pretoria, National Botanical Institute, 2000. (*Strelitzia*, 10). 775pp.

3041 Rebelo, Anthony Gomes. **Sasol proteas: a field guide to the proteas of Southern Africa**. Vlaeberg, Fernwood & National Botanical Institute, 1995. 224pp. illus. maps. (Covers 370 spp.)

3042 Van Oudtshoorn, Frederik Petrus, et al. **Guide to grasses of South Africa**. [Rev. ed.]. Pretoria, Briza, 1999. 351pp. illus. maps. - - Orig. pub. Pretoria, Briza, 1992. 301pp.

Trees

3043 Coates Palgrave, Keith. **Trees of Southern Africa**. 3ʳᵈ ed. rev. & updated by Meg Coates Palgrave. Cape Town, Struik, 2002. 1,212pp. illus. (Major revision of the standard handbook including name changes, reclassifications, new spp., simplified key based on leaf, rather than flower characteristics). - - Orig. pub. Cape Town, 1977. 959pp; - - 2ⁿᵈ ed. Cape Town, 1988. 959pp.

3044 The national list of trees, ed. Bernard de Winter & Johannes Vahrmeijer. 3ʳᵈ ed. Pretoria, National Botanical Institute & Dendrological Foundation & Society, 1987. 269pp. (Assigns individual numbers to all known tree spp. These numbers are used by standard reference works such as Coates Palgrave, **3043**, Palmer & Pitman, **3045** and by the online Trees of Southern Africa project, **3046**). - - Orig. pub. Pretoria, 1972; - - 2ⁿᵈ ed. Pretoria, 1978.

3045 Palmer, Eve & Pitman, Norah. **Trees of Southern Africa: covering all known indigenous species in the Republic of South Africa, South-West**

Africa, Botswana, Lesotho and Swaziland. Cape Town, Balkema, 1972-73. 3 vols. 2,288pp. + 24 plates. (Covers area south of Cunene and Limpopo rivers. Lists over 1,000 spp. in 91 families, with some 2,000 photos and 900 drawings). - - Orig. pub. as **Trees of South Africa**. Cape Town, 1961. 352pp.

3046 Trees of Southern Africa, http://www.flora.sanbi.org/ its_page?comID=1 (Dataset maintained by SANBI, *see* **3022**, covering "any tree, erect shrub, scrambling shrub or woody climber with a woody main stem reaching a height up to 2 metres and higher" which permits search by family, genus and spp. Includes scientific and common (English and Afrikaans) names, tree number, and habitat, distribution and conservation data. As of July 2006 records 105 plant families, 438 genera, 1,537 taxa and 672 synonyms. Under development and is to include illus. and maps)

3047 Von Breitenbach, Friedrich. **The indigenous trees of Southern Africa**. Pretoria, Department of Forestry, 1965. 5 vols. 345 figs. (Mimeographed. Includes keys to all taxa).

3048 Von Breitenbach, Friedrich. **National list of indigenous trees**. 3rd ed. Pretoria, Dendrological Foundation, 1995. x, 372pp. - - Orig. pub. Pretoria, 1986. x, 372pp. illus. maps; - - 2nd ed. Pretoria, 1990. x, 372pp. Companion to his **National list of introduced trees**. 2nd ed. Pretoria, Dendrological Foundation, 1989. iv, 146pp. illus. - - Orig. pub. Pretoria, 1984. iv, 146pp.

3049 Von Breitenbach, Friedrich & Von Breitenbach, Jutta von. **Tree atlas of Southern Africa**. Pretoria, Dendrological Foundation, 1992- . 24 vols. planned. col. illus. maps. Vol. 1. 1992. xiv, 223pp. ?No more pub. (Organized according to the **National list of indigenous trees,** *see* **3048**)

Field guides

3050 Palmer, Eve. **A field guide to the trees of Southern Africa**. Rev. ed. London, Collins, 1981. 393pp. + 32 col. plates. 700 line drawings. (Covers some 800 spp.). - - Orig. pub. London, 1977. 352pp.

3051 Van Wyk, Piet. **Southern African trees: a photographic guide**. London, New Holland/Cape Town, Struik, 1993. 144pp. 300 col. photos. (250 spp.)

3052 Van Wyk, Piet & Van Wyk, Braam. **Field guide to trees of Southern Africa**. Cape Town, Struik, 1997. 536pp. illus. maps. (Covers 900 species) - - **eTrees of Southern Africa**. Craighall, PDA Solutions, 2005. 1 PDA card (Requires a PDA running Microsoft Pocket PC 2003 or later. Includes text and pictures from the print ed. Free software updates to be available)

Plants used by or affecting man

3053 Arnold, Trevor Henry et al. **Medicinal and magical plants of Southern Africa: an annotated checklist**. Pretoria, National Botanical Institute, 2002. (*Strelitzia*, 13). iv, 203pp. (Plants used in traditional medicine in the region, based on published information as well as toxicological, ecological, floristic and specimen data sources. Includes information on 215 families, 1,240 genera and 3,689 taxa of ethnomedicinal plants)

3054 Glen, Hugh F. **Cultivated plants of Southern Africa: botanical names, common names, origins, literature**. Johannesburg, Jacana & National Botanical Institute, 2002. iii, 428pp. (Lists nearly 9,000 types of plants cultivated over the years, based on specimens in the National Herbaria)

3055 Hutchings, Anne et al. **Zulu medicinal plants: an inventory**. Pietermaritzburg, University of Natal Press, 1996. xii, 450pp.

3056 Index herbariorum: Southern African supplement, comp. Gideon F. Smith & Christopher Willis. 2nd ed. Pretoria, SABONET, 1999. (SABONET report, 8). 181pp. illus. - - Orig. pub. Pretoria, 1997. (Report, 2). 55pp.

3057 Van Wyk, Ben-Erik. **People's plants: a guide to useful plants of Southern Africa**. Pretoria, Briza, 2000. 351pp. illus. (Botanical descriptions and guides to medicinal use of c. 650 plants. Note also his **Medicinal plants of South Africa**. Pretoria, Briza, 1997. 304pp. illus. (Covers 132 of the best known spp.) and his **Poisonous plants of South Africa**. Pretoria, Briza, 2002. 288pp. illus. (Descriptions of 135 plants noting for each its potential toxicity and its significance in human or livestock poisoning. 450+ col. photos)

3058 Watt, John Mitchell & Breyer-Brandwijk, Maria Gerdina. **The medicinal and poisonous plants of Southern and Eastern Africa: being an account of their medicinal and other uses, chemical composition, pharmacological effects and toxicology in man and animals**. Edinburgh, E. & S. Livingstone, 1962. xii, 1,457pp. - - Orig. pub. as **The medicinal and poisonous plants of Southern Africa**. Edinburgh, 1932.

3059 Wells, M.J. **A catalogue of problem plants in Southern Africa incorporating the national weed list of Southern Africa**. Pretoria, Botanical Survey of South Africa, 1986. (Memoirs, 53). vi, 658pp.

NAMIBIA

See also sections for **Former German Africa**. Many works published after 1920 and listed above under **South Africa** will also cover this region.

Government of Namibia network http://www.grnnet.gov.na/

HANDBOOKS

3060 Afrikaans-Deutsche Kulturgemeinschaft (ADK). **ADK facts and figures**. Windhoek, ADK, 1978-80. 6 vols. (A series of booklets: 1, What we should know about South West Africa; 2 & 3, The political groups of South West Africa; 4, My country, South West Africa; 5 & 6, The leaders of South-West Africa)

3061 Bayer, Marcel. **Namibië: mensen, politiek, economie, cultuur**. Amsterdam, Koninklijk Instituut voor de Tropen/The Hague, Novib, 1998. (Landenreeks). 79pp. illus. maps.

3062 Dierks, Klaus. **Chronology of Namibian history from pre-colonial times to independent Namibia**. 2nd ed. Windhoek, Namibia Scientific Society, 2002. xii, 484pp. - - Orig. pub. Windhoek, 1999. 267pp. (Review, *ABPR*, 27, 2001, 14). - - Also pub. in German as **Chronologie der namibischen Geschichte**. Windhoek, 2003. xiii, 674pp.

3063 France. Ministère de la coopération. **Namibie: guide d'information, novembre 1994**. Paris, 1994. (Collection guides d'information). 76pp. (Historical, political and economic background)

3064 Historical dictionary of Namibia, comp. John J. Grotpeter. Lanham, MD, Scarecrow Press, 1994. (African historical dictionaries, 57). xxxi, 724pp. (Review, *Choice*, 32, 1995, 1572)

3065 Hopwood, Graham. **Guide to Namibian politics: including A to Z of political personalities**. Windhoek, Meinert for Institute for Public Policy Research & Namibia Institute for Democracy, 2004. 304pp. illus.

3066 Namibia 1990: an Africa Institute country survey, comp. Erich Leistner & Pieter Esterhuysen. Pretoria, Africa Institute of South Africa, 1991. 240p. maps. (Detailed collection of data, with emphasis on economic statistics. Appendices include brief biographies of members of the government and opposition parties)

3067 Namibia: the facts. [Rev. ed.]. London, International Defence & Aid Fund for Southern Africa (IDAF), 1989. 112pp. (Adopts a partisan view in the presentation of historical, political and economic information, e.g. chap. 3, 'Economic exploitation'). - - Orig. pub. London, 1980. 100pp.

3068 Norborg, Åke. **A handbook of musical and other sound-producing instruments from Namibia and Botswana**. Stockholm, Almqvist & Wiksell, 1987. xxii, 454pp. (Descriptions, drawings, bibliography & discography)

3069 Putz, Joe, et al. **Namibia handbook and political who's who**. 2nd 'post election' ed. Windhoek, Magus, 1990. 446pp. (Lists active and inactive parties, and other political groups, with their history, policies and manifestos, and biographies of their leaders. Detailed introduction claims that no political opinions are to be implied by inclusions or exclusions, and discusses the problems of compilation, e.g. all SWAPO data are from secondary sources. Covers events up to September 1989, with details on the new constitution, biographies of the anticipated Cabinet and National Assembly). - - Orig. pub. Windhoek, Magus, 1989. 448pp. (A development of the earlier **Political who's who of Namibia**, *see* **3093**).

3070 SWA handbook 1971/72. 6th ed. Windhoek, South West Africa Agency, 1972. 131pp . illus. map. (Text in English/German/Afrikaans. Includes civil list, statistics, historical chronology, and coverage of topography, natural resources and fauna). - - Earlier eds. **...1960**. Windhoek, 1960. 100pp; - - **...1964/65**. Windhoek, 1964. 102pp; - - **... 1967/68**. Windhoek, 1966. 110pp; - - **... 1968/69**. Windhoek, 1969.

3071 SWA/Namibia today, ed. Rianne Selle. Windhoek, Department of Governmental Affairs, 1988. 128pp. (Covers topography, peoples, history, administration, the economy, natural resources and tourism). - - Orig. pub. ed Ina Van Rooyen. Windhoek, SWA/Namibia Information Service, 1979. 120pp. illus. map.

3072 Tötemeyer, Gerhard, et al. eds. **Namibia regional resources manual, 1996/97**. Windhoek, Gamsberg Macmillan, 1998. 260pp. - - Orig. pub. Windhoek, Friedrich Ebert Stiftung, 1994. 168pp. Loose-leaf. (Directory of the executive, legislative and judiciary for the country as a whole and its 13 regions. Statistics and maps. 2nd ed has 5 additional maps for each of the 13 regions, and includes data from the 1991 Population Census)

3073 Tötemeyer, Gerhard, ed. **South West Africa/Namibia facts, attitudes, assessment and prospects**. Randburg, Fokus Suid, 1977. x, 321pp. ("Intended to provide... factual background against which subsequent events in the territory may be judged", pref. Includes basic facts on the economy, peoples and politics. Detailed chronology. Essays by local political and religious leaders looking to the future)

3074 Vogt, Andreas. **National monuments in Namibia: an inventory of proclaimed national monuments in the Republic of Namibia**. Windhoek, Gamsberg Macmillan, 2004. xxii, 252pp.

See also **2754, 2755**

YEARBOOKS

3075 **Braby's SWA/Namibia business directory**. Durban, A.C. Braby, 1969-1990. Annual. Title varies: **Braby's South West Africa directory** (1969-1979)

3076 **Namibia facts and figures**. Windhoek, Ministry of Information & Broadcasting, 1991- . Annual.

3077 **Namibia trade directory, 1991/92-** . Windhoek, Advantage Promotions, 1991- . Annual. Latest issue in NWU is for 2000. 248pp. (Also available at http://www.tradedirectory.com.na/)

3078 South Africa. **Report by the Government of the Union of South Africa on the administration of South West Africa**. Pretoria, etc. 1918-1946. Annual. Title varies: South-west protectorate/South-west Africa Territory/ Territory of South-West Africa. **Report of the administrator** (1918-1924); **Report of the government of the Union of South Africa on South-west Africa** (1925-1927); **Report presented by the government of the Union of South Africa to the council of the League of Nations concerning the administration of South-west Africa** (1928-1938). ?Vols. for 1940-1945 not pub?

3079 **South West Africa annual/jaarboek/jahrbuch**. Windhoek, South West Africa Publications, 1945-?1986. Annual (irreg). Several issues cover 2 or 3 years. 19 vols. in total. (A collection of individual contributions in each issue rather than a standardised presentation of data, but often contains useful statistical information). - - **Index 1945-1972**. Windhoek, 1973.

See also **1269, 2760-2762, 2778**

STATISTICS

3080 **Country profile: Namibia**. London, Economist Intelligence Unit, 2004- . Annual. *Continues* **Country profile: Namibia**. London, 1986-1992; *continues in part* **Country profile: Namibia, Swaziland**. London, 1994-2003.

3081 Germany. Statistisches Bundesamt. **Statistik des Auslandes: Länderberichte: Namibia** (later **Länderbericht: Namibia**). Wiesbaden/ Stuttgart, Metzler-Poetschel, 1986- . Irreg. Issues for 1986, 1988, 1992.

3082 IMF. **Namibia: selected issues and statistical appendix**. Washington DC, 2006. (Country reports, 06/153). 109pp. - - Earlier eds. (title varies) 1996 (Staff country report, 96/84); 1999 (Staff country report, 99/09); 2005 (Country report, 05/96). Full text of reports from 1997 also available online, *see* **334**.

3083 Namibia. Central Bureau of Statistics. **Statistical abstract**. Windhoek, 1992- . Annual. ALA notes issue for 1995.

3084 Namibia. Central Statistics Office. **Development of statistics in Namibia: a five year plan 1993/94–1997/98**. Windhoek, Central Statistics Office, 1993. vi, 153pp. (Identifies categories on which statistics should be collected. Includes papers given at a Producer/Users Statistics Workshop held Aug/Sept 1993. Builds on recommendations of **Perspectives on the development of a statistical system for Namibia**, comp. Helge Brunborg, et al. Windhoek, Namibian Economic Policy Research Unit, 1992. ix, 104, 43pp.)

3085 Namibia. Department of Finance & SWA/Namibia Information Service. **Economic review**. Windhoek, 1982-?1994. 2 p.a. Title varies: **Statistical/economic review** (1982-1990).

DIRECTORIES OF ORGANIZATIONS

3086 **Directory of Namibian libraries, publishers and booksellers 1992**, comp. Johan Loubser et al. Windhoek, Ministry of Education & Culture, 1992. 53pp.

3087 Doling, Tim. **Namibia arts directory**. London, Visiting Arts, 1999. 76pp.

3088 Hillebrecht, Werner. **Namibian dictionary of acronyms and abbreviations; 1,735 acronyms and abbreviations used in Namibia**. Windhoek, Namibian Information Workers' Association (NIWA), 1997. (Suppl. to *NIWA Info*, 7 (1/4), 1996/97). 19pp.

3089 Moorsom, Richard. **Namibian development services directory**. Windhoek, Namibian Economic Policy Research Unit for National Planning Commission, 1994. 1 vol. var. pagings. (Directory of over 500 organizations, with contact details, notes on aims)

3090   Putz, Joe. **Business guide to Namibia**. Windhoek, Investment Centre of the Ministry of Trade & Industry, 1996. 271pp.

3091   **Republic of Namibia: directory of government offices, ministries and agencies**. Windhoek, Ministry of Foreign Affairs, Information & Broadcasting, 2001. 57pp.

See also **2823**, **2824**, **2828**, **3496**

BIOGRAPHICAL SOURCES

3092   **Namibian parliamentary directory, 1996/97**. Windhoek, New Namibia Books, 1997. v, 93pp. (Biographical sketches of members of parliament with lists of members of the Constituent Assembly, the National Assembly, the National Council and the Women's Caucus)

3093   Putz, Joe et al. **Political who's who of Namibia**. Windhoek, Magus, 1987. 313pp. (Later rev. and pub. with much additional non-biographical information as **Namibia handbook and political who's who**, *see* **3069**).

3094   Tabler, Edward C. **Pioneers of South West Africa and Ngamiland, 1738-1880**. Cape Town, Balkema, 1973. ix, 142pp. (Biographical notes on 333 adult male foreigners who travelled and settled in the region)

See also **2858**

ATLASES & GAZETTEERS

Atlases

3095   **Atlas of Namibia: a portrait of the land and its people**, ed. John Mendelsohn et al. Cape Town, David Philip for Ministry of Environment & Tourism, 2002. 200pp. Re-issued as **Atlas of Namibia: a cartographic profile of modern Namibia**. Cape Town, 2003. (Intended for the general reader but contains substantial collections of data, which can also be accessed as 'Digital Atlas of Namibia' at http://www.dea.met.gov.na/. Sections on physical geography, climate, plants and animals, land and people)

3096   **Namibia in maps: a census atlas**. Windhoek, Central Bureau of Statistics, 2001. 60pp. (Cover title **Namibia population atlas**. Maps at 1:9M)

3097   **National atlas of South West Africa (Namibia)**, ed. Johannes Hendrik Van der Merwe. Cape Town, University of Stellenbosch Institute for

Cartographic Analysis & Department of Civil Affairs & Manpower, SWA/Namibia, 1983. 184pp. illus. (Sections for natural environment; settlement structure; population structure; economic structure; infrastructure; urban structure. 92 col. maps, topographic and thematic, with detailed accompanying text, 29 tables, 50 diagrams and photos)

3098 A profile of north-central Namibia, ed. John Mendelsohn et al. Windhoek, Gamsberg Macmillan for Ministry of Environment & Tourism, 2000. 79pp. (Atlas)

3099   Road atlas of Namibia. 2nd ed., comp. B. & A. Revilio. London, New Holland, 1999. (Globetrotter travel atlas). 48pp. (Legends in English, German & French). - - Orig. pub. London, 1995. 48pp.

Gazetteers

3100 Albertyn, Andries P.J. **Die ensiklopedie van name in Suidwes-Afrika.** Pretoria, Sigma, 1984. 136pp. illus. (Gazetteer with etymologies)

3101 U.S. Board on Geographic Names. **Gazetteer of Namibia: names approved by the USBGN.** Washington, DC, 1988. xvi, 218pp. (Rev. of appropriate section of **2924**. 1st ed. 8,700 entries)

3102 Von Schumann, Gunter & Rusch, Walter. **Index of names appearing on the 'Kriegskarte von Deutsch-Südwestafrika 1904'.** Windhoek, National Archives, 1987. (Archeia, 9). ii, 38pp. 1 map. (Lists, with grid references, some 4,000 names, including 200 trans. into English shown on the 8 sheets of the war maps, originally issued 1904, reprinted Basle, Antiquariat am Klosterberg, 1987. The most detailed source for the region's early place names)

EARTH SCIENCES

3103 Daltry, Vaughan D.C. **Type mineralogy of Namibia.** Windhoek, Geological Survey of Namibia, 1992. (Bulletin, 1). 142pp. illus. maps.

3104 **The mineral resources of Namibia.** Windhoek, Geological Survey of Namibia, 1992. 1 vol. var. pagings.

BIOLOGICAL SCIENCES

Zoology

Birds & Mammals

3105 Barnard, Phoebe, ed. **Biological diversity in Namibia: a country study**. Windhoek, Namibian National Biodiversity Task Force, 1998. 331pp. illus. maps.

3106 Comley, Peter & Meyer, Salome. **A field guide to the mammals of Namibia**. Kasane, Africa Window, 1997. 112pp. illus. (The standard large-scale account remains Guy C. Shortridge. **The mammals of South-West Africa**. London, Heinemann, 1934. 2 vols.)

3107 Hoesch, W. & Niethammer, G. **Die Vogelwelt Südwestafrikas**. Rev. ed. Windhoek, Meinert, 1955. 300pp. illus. - - Orig. pub. as 'Die Vogelwelt Deutsch-Südwest-Afrikas', *Journal für Ornithologie*, 88, 1940. Sonderheft. viii, 404pp.

3108 Sinclair, Ian & Jackie. **Photographic guide to birds of Namibia**. Cape Town, Struik, 1995. 144pp. illus

3109 Winterbottom, John Mial. **A preliminary checklist of the birds of South-West Africa**. Windhoek, S.W.A. Scientific Society, 1971. 268pp. (Lists 576 spp.) *See also* **3158**

Reptiles, Amphibians & Fishes

3110 Bianchi, Gabriella et al. **Field guide to the living marine resources of Namibia**. Rome, FAO, 1999. x, 265pp. + 11pp. plates. (Rev. of her **The living marine resources of Namibia**. Rome, FAO, 1993. (FAO species identification field guide for fishery purposes). viii, 250pp. + 8pp. col. plates). *See also* **1785**

3111 Griffin, Michael. **Annotated checklist and provisional conservation status of Namibian reptiles**. Windhoek, Namibian Scientific Society, 2003. 168pp. (Lists 239 spp. with notes on distribution)

3112 Mertens, Robert. **Die Amphibien und Reptilien Südwest-Afrikas**. Frankfurt-am-Main, W. Kramer, 1955. (Abhandlungen der Senckenbergischen Naturforschenden Gesellschaft, 490). 170pp. illus.

3113 Mertens, Robert. **Die Herpetofauna Südwest-Afrikas**. Frankfurt-am-Main, W. Kramer, 1971. (Abhandlungen der Senckenbergischen Naturforschenden Gesellschaft, 529). 110pp.

Botany

3114 Clarke, Nicholas V. & Klaassen, Esmerialda S. **Water plants of Namibia: an identification manual**. Windhoek, National Botanical Research Institute, 2001. 185pp. illus. maps.

3115 Craven, Patricia. **A checklist of Namibian plant species**. Pretoria, SABONET, 1999. (SABONET report, 7). 204 pp. (Produced with National Botanical Research Institute of Namibia)

3116 Curtis, Barbara & Mannheimer, Coleen. **Tree atlas of Namibia**. Windhoek, National Botanical Research Institute, 2005. 674pp. (Covers over 400 spp. with some 300 maps. Special Commendation, Noma Award for Publishing in Africa 2006, "outstanding and beautifully produced book...a great achievement and scientific tool"; also available on CD, and available online, as part of the Living Namibia-Namibian Biodiversity Database, http://www.biodiversity.org.na/treeatlas/taphome.php)

3117 Klaassen, Esmerialda S. & Craven, Patricia. **Checklist of grasses in Namibia**. Pretoria, SABONET, 2003. (SABONET report, 20). 130pp. illus. maps. (Produced with National Botanical Research Institute of Namibia)

3118 Koenen, Eberhard von. **Medicinal, poisonous and edible plants in Namibia**. 2nd ed. Windhoek, Klaus Hess, 2001. 335pp. illus. Updated trans. of **Heil-, Gift- und Essbare Pflanzen in Namibia**. Göttingen, Klaus Hess, 1996. (Covers some 600 plants)

3119 Merxmuller, H. ed. **Prodromus einer Flora von Südwestafrika**. Lehre, Cramer, 1966-1972. 35 fascicles in 5 vols. 2,188pp. (Fasc. 35 includes introduction, list of family names, map, keys and index. In preparation for 15 years. "Object lesson to flora-writers in careful planning, extensive preparation, thorough distillation and rapid publication", Frodin, 2001, 459). - - 'Nachträge', *Mitteilungen der Botanischen Staatssammlung München*, 12, 1976, 361-373

See also **1278**

BOTSWANA

Republic of Botswana: the Government of Botswana Web site
http://www.gov.bw/home.html

HANDBOOKS

3120 Botswana. Paris, Karthala, 1995. 216pp. (Introductory survey of history, politics, the economy. Includes chronology and glossary)

3121 Botswana: an official handbook. 5th ed., ed. Russ Molosiwa. Gaborone, Department of Information & Broadcasting. Publicity Section. 1999. 232pp. (Covers topography, peoples, government and administration, commerce and industry. Includes statistics). - - Earlier eds. **Botswana, '83**. Gaborone, 1983; - - **Botswana '86**, Gaborone, 1986. xii, 188pp; - - **Botswana '91**. Gaborone, 1991. 152pp.

3122 Denbow, James & **Thebe**, Phenyo C. **Culture and customs of Botswana**. Westport, CT, Greenwood Press, 2006. (Culture & customs of Africa). 268pp. illus. map. (Covers history, religion, literature, art & architecture, social customs)

3123 Facts on Botswana, ed. Keboeletse Nkarabang. Gaborone, Department of Information & Broadcasting, 1990. 91pp. illus. maps.

3124 The guide to Botswana, Lesotho and Swaziland: a comprehensive companion for visitors and investors. Saxonwold, Winchester Press, 1983. 1,212pp. illus. maps. (Pp. 7-441, Botswana, by A. Campbell; pp. 443-863, Lesotho, by David Ambrose; pp. 865-1,212, Swaziland, by D. Johnson. A massively detailed compilation of factual information on the countries, their peoples and the economy, with brief notes on sources)

3125 Historical dictionary of Botswana. 3rd ed., comp. Jeff Ramsay et al. Lanham, MD, Scarecrow Press, 1996. (African historical dictionaries, 70). xxi, 321pp. - - Orig. pub. as **Historical dictionary of the Republic of Botswana**, comp. Richard P. Stevens. Metuchen, NJ, 1975. (African historical dictionaries, 5). 189pp. (Review, *JAH*, 20, 1979, 146-147); - - 2nd ed. comp. Fred Morton et al. Metuchen, NJ, 1989. (African historical dictionaries, 44). xx, 244pp. (Reviews, *African affairs*, 90, 1991, 147, "invaluable reference text"; *ARD*, 57, 1991, 34; *JAH*, 32, 1991, 174-175, "enters the canon of the dozen or so essential works of reference on Botswana". Rated "excellent", Balay, 1996)

3126 **The human development initiative data book: a compendium of information on Botswana**, ed. Isaac Makube Mazonde et al. Gaborone, Government of Botswana/UNDP/UNICEF, 1996. 171pp.

See also **3068**

YEARBOOKS

3127 **B. & T. Botswana directory**. Gaborone, B. & T. Directories, 1977- . Annual. Title varies: **Botswana directory** (1977-1996)

3128 **BOCCIM business directory**. Gaborone, Botswana Confederation of Commerce Industry & Manpower (BOCCIM), 1995- . Every 2 years.

3129 **Botswana business guide**. Gaborone, Business School of Botswana, 2003- . Annual.

3130 G.B. Colonial Office. **[Annual reports]: Bechuanaland, 1887/88-1965**. London, 1889-1966. As **Annual report of the Administrator** 1887/88, 1888/89, **Annual report on British Bechuanaland**, 1889/90, **Report on Bechuanaland Protectorate**, 1890/92, 1892/93-1903/04 (not issued 1895/96, 1897/98-1901/02); **Annual report on British Bechuanaland 1904/05-1919/20**, (all as Command papers); **Colonial Office annual report**, 1920/21-65 (not issued 1939-45). 1902/03 & 1903/04 and 1961 & 1962 issued as one vol. 1947-62 issued by Commonwealth Relations Office; 1963-64 issued by Colonial Office; 1965 issued by Commonwealth Office.

See also **1267, 1269, 2760-2763, 2778**

STATISTICS

3131 Botswana. Central Statistics Office. http://www.cso.gov.bw/

3132 Botswana. Central Statistics Office. **Country profile**. Gaborone, 1980- . Annual. (A general survey, with statistics). *Continues* **Statistical abstract**. Gaborone, 1966-1979. Annual. - - Abridged version pub. as **Botswana in figures**. Gaborone, 1980- . Annual. Stanford has issue for 2003.

3133 Botswana. Central Statistics Office. **Statistical bulletin**. Gaborone, 1972- . Annual. Issues 1-4. *Continues* **Statistical newsletter**. Gaborone, 1971-1975. Quarterly. SSL has issue 26/27 for 2000/02

3134 **Country profile: Botswana**. London, Economist Intelligence Unit, 2004- . Annual. *Continues in part* **Country profile: Botswana, Lesotho,**

Swaziland. London, 1986-1992; **Country profile: Botswana, Lesotho.** London, 1993-2003

3135 Germany. Statistisches Bundesamt. **Statistik des Auslandes: Länderberichte: Botsuana** (later **Länderbericht: Botsuana**). Wiesbaden/ Stuttgart, Metzler-Poetschel, 1985- . Irreg. Issues for 1985, 1987, 1992.

3136 IMF. **Botswana: statistical appendix.** Washington, DC, 2006. (Country report, 06/65). 46pp. - - Earlier eds. (title varies) 1995 (Staff country report, 95/1); 1997 (Staff country report, 97/29); 1998 (Staff country report, 98/39); 1999 (Staff country report, 99/132); 2002 (Country report, 02/243); 2004 (Country report, 04/212). Full text of reports from 97/101, 1997 also available online, *see* **334.**

DIRECTORIES OF ORGANIZATIONS

3137 Amanze, James N. **Botswana handbook of churches: a handbook of churches, ecumenical organizations, theological institutions and other world religions in Botswana.** Gaborone, Pula Press, 1994. xi, 314pp. (Detailed descriptions of 200+ organizations)

3138 **Directory of non-governmental organizations in Botswana.** [Rev.ed.] comp. Pony M. Hopkins. Oslo, Norwegian Agency for International Development (NORAD), 1995. 181pp. (Covers some 80 NGOs). - - Earlier eds. Oslo, 1985. 160pp; - - Oslo, 1989. 161pp.

3139 Doling, Tim. **Botswana: arts directory.** London, Visiting Arts, 1999. 60pp.

3140 Seboni, Barolong. **Botswana cultural directory.** Gaborone, Morula, 1994. ii, 96pp.

See also **2806, 2819, 2820, 2824, 2828**

BIOGRAPHICAL SOURCES

See **1273, 1414**

ATLASES & GAZETTEERS

Atlases

3141 **Botswana national atlas**, ed. Francis Sefe & Felicity Leburu-Sianga. Gaborone, Department of Surveys & Mapping, 2001. viii, 404pp. + 1 CD-ROM. (Extensive text & col. illus. arranged in 29 thematic chapters, each with maps. Majority of maps are at 1:8M, a few at 1:4M)

3142 **The Botswana Society social studies atlas**, gen. ed. Q. Neil Parsons. Gaborone, Botswana Society with Government of Botswana & Esselte Map Service, Stockholm, 1988. 49pp. (Pp. 6-17, Botswana, including 24 thematic maps; pp. 18-22, Southern Africa; pp. 25-31, Africa)

Gazetteers

3143 Botswana. Central Statistics Office. **Guide to the villages of Botswana**. Gaborone, 1973. xiv, 221pp. (Based on 1971 census. Includes maps at varying scales. Details for each village on population, dwellings, communal establishments and access to government services)

3144 Botswana. Ministry of Local Government & Lands. Place Name Commission. **Second list of names and recommended spellings**. Rev. ed. Gaborone, 1981. 142pp. (Some 2,000 names arranged by district; 1st ed. has 1,043 names in a single sequence). - - Orig. pub. as **List of names and recommended or accepted spellings** [Gaborone, 1970]. 39pp

3145 Irish, J. 'Gazetteer of place names on maps of Botswana', *Cimbebasia: journal of the State Museum, Windhoek*, 10, 1988, 106-146

See also **1030, 2913- 2915, 2920, 2921, 2923, 2924**

EARTH SCIENCES

3146 Bhalotra, Y.P.R. **Climate of Botswana**. Gaborone, Botswana Meteorological Services, 1984-1987. 2 vols. (Vol. 1. Climatic controls; vol. 2. Elements of climate)

3147 Botswana. Central Statistics Office. **Botswana environment statistics**. Gaborone, 2000- .

3148 Botswana. Central Statistics Office. **Selected environmental indicators**. Gaborone, 2002. iv, 47pp.

3149   Carney, J.N. et al. **The geology of Botswana**. Lobatse, Geological Survey Department, 1994. (Bulletin, 37). iii, 113pp. maps. (Complements geological map of the Republic of Botswana, 1984, at 1:1M.)

3150   Massey, Nicholas W.D. **Resources inventory of Botswana: industrial rocks and minerals**. Lobatse, Geological Survey Department, 1973. (Mineral resources report, 3). vii, 39pp. illus. maps. (Companion vol., J.W. Baldock et al. **Resources inventory of Botswana: metallic minerals, mineral fuels and diamonds**. Lobatse, Geological Survey Department, 1977. (Mineral resources report, 4). ix, 69pp. illus. maps)

3151   Silitshena, Robson M.K. & McLeod, G. **Botswana: a physical, social, and economic geography**. 2nd ed. Gaborone, Longman Botswana, 1998. 316pp. illus. maps. - - Orig. pub. Gaborone, 1989. 268pp. illus. maps. (Review, *SAGJ*, 72, 1990, 29)

BIOLOGICAL SCIENCES

3152   Cole, Desmond T. **Setswana: animals and plants/Setswana: ditshedi le ditlhare**. Prelim. ed. Gaborone, Botswana Society, 1995. xii, 337pp. illus. map. (Names of animals in Tswana/English and English/Tswana; names of plants in Tswana/Scientific name/English)

Zoology

3153   Auerbach, Ronald Daniel. **The amphibians and reptiles of Botswana**. Gaborone, Mokwepa Consultants, 1987. iii, 295pp. illus. maps. (Review, *SAJZ*, 24, 1989, 373-374 is critical of errors and of physical production)

3154   Comley, Peter & Meyer, Salome. **The field guide to the mammals of Botswana**. Kasane, Africa Window, 1994. 96pp. illus. maps. (Some 50 spp.)

3155   Newman, Kenneth. **Newman's birds of Botswana**. Johannesburg, Southern Books, 1989. vi, 344pp. col. illus. (Compiled with the Botswana Bird Club. Covers 550 + spp.). - - **Birds of Botswana**. Johannesburg, Southern Books, 1998. 68pp. col. illus. maps. (Pocket field guide based on the 1989 work)

3156   Penry, Huw et al. **Bird atlas of Botswana**. Pietermaritzburg, University of Natal Press, 1994, viii, 319pp. (Covers 495 spp. Review, *SAJZ*, 30, 1995, 59-60)

3157   Pinhey, Elliot C.G. 'Check-list of the butterflies of Botswana', *Botswana notes and records*, 1, 1968, 85-92; 3, 1971, 148-152; 6, 1974, 197-214; 8, 1976, 269-288 (Lists 205 spp. with b. & w. illus.)

3158   Smithers, Reay H.N. **A check list of the birds of the Bechuanaland Protectorate and the Caprivi Strip**. Salisbury, 1964. ix, 188pp. illus. maps.

3159   Smithers, Reay H.N. **A checklist and atlas of the mammals of Botswana**. Salisbury, National Museum of Rhodesia, 1968. iv, 169pp. illus. maps.

3160   Smithers, Reay H.N. **The mammals of Botswana**. Salisbury, National Museums & Monuments of Rhodesia, 1971. (Memoir, 4). 340pp. illus.

Botany

3161   Hedberg, Inga & Staugard, Frants. **Traditional medicinal plants**. Gaborone, Ipeleng, 1989. (Traditional medicine in Botswana, 3). 324pp. illus.

3162   Miller, O.B. 'The woody plants of the Bechuanaland Protectorate', *Journal of South African botany*, 18, 1952, 1-100. map. - - 'Corrigenda', *ibid*. 19, 1953, 177-182.

3163   Setshogo, Moffat P. **Preliminary checklist of the plants of Botswana**. Pretoria, SABONET, 2005. (SABONET report, 37). viii, 161pp.

3164   Setshogo, Moffat P. & Venter, Fanie. **Trees of Botswana: names and distribution**. Pretoria, SABONET, 2003. (SABONET report, 18). 152pp.

See also **1278**

LESOTHO

Lesotho Government online http://www.lesotho.gov.ls/

HANDBOOKS

3165   Ambrose, David. **The guide to Lesotho**. 2nd ed. Johannesburg & Maseru, Winchester Press, 1976. 370pp. illus. map. ("Expanded and completely revised", pref. Aimed at the 'tourist/visitor and resident' but with more detailed historical, topographical and social information than many such works). - - Orig. pub. Johannesburg & Maseru, 1974. 290pp.

3166   **Historical dictionary of Lesotho**. New ed., comp. Scott Rosenberg et al. Lanham, MD, Scarecrow Press, 2004. (African historical dictionaries, 90). xliii, 452pp. (Reviews, *ARD*, 99, 2005, 51-54; *Choice*, 41, 2004, 2029). - - Orig. pub. comp. Gordon Haliburton. Metuchen, NJ, 1977. (African historical dictionaries, 10). xxxv, 223pp. (Reviews, *Africana J.*, 10, 1979, 120-128; *JAH*, 20, 1979, 146-147. Rated "good", Balay, 1996)

YEARBOOKS

3167   Basutoland Red Cross Society. **Year book and diary**. Maseru, 1958-1962. 4 issues for 1958, 1959,1960, 1962. (S. Willett & David Ambrose. **A comprehensive bibliography of Botswana**. Oxford, Clio, 1980, p. 3, give useful details of the significant contents of individual issues: "of the four years, the 1959 **Yearbook** is the most comprehensive". Issues for 1959 and 1960 contain genealogical tables of chiefs)

3168   G.B. Colonial Office. **[Annual reports]: Basutoland, 1883-1964**. London, 1886-1965. As **Report of Resident Commissioner**, 1883/86, 1886/87-1889/90, **Annual report on Basutoland**, 1890/91-1919/20, (all as Command papers); **Colonial Office annual report,** 1920/21- 1964 (not issued 1939-45). Combined report pub. for 1934/35 as well as separate ones for 1934 and 1935; 1961 & 1962 issued as one vol. 1947-60 issued by Commonwealth Relations Office; 1961-63 issued by Colonial Office; 1964 issued by Govt. of Basutoland.

3169   Lesotho. Ministry of Information. **Annual report**. Maseru, 1966-1973. Irreg. Issues for 1966, 1967, 1968, 1971, 1972/73.

3170   **Lesotho business directory**. Maseru, A.C. Braby Lesotho, 1970-Annual. Latest issue in NWU is for 2004.

3171 **Lesotho government yearbook and diary**. Durban, Izwi Lama-Afrika Abumbene for Government of Lesotho, 1987-1990. 4 issues.

3172 **Lesotho [1996] official yearbook**. Maseru, Ministry of Information & Broadcasting, 1996- . (Review of 1996 issue by David Ambrose, *National University of Lesotho journal of research*, 7, 1997, 74-76 which also contains the information given above on **3169** to **3171**. NWU only holds issue for 1996)

See also **1269, 2760-2762**

STATISTICS

3173 **Country profile: Lesotho**. London, Economist Intelligence Unit, 2004- Annual. *Continues in part* **Country profile: Botswana, Lesotho, Swaziland**. 1986-1993; **Country profile: Botswana, Lesotho**. London, 1993-2003.

3174 Germany. Statistisches Bundesamt. **Statistik des Auslandes: Länderberichte: Lesotho** (later **Länderbericht: Lesotho**). Wiesbaden/Stuttgart, Metzler-Poetschel, 1987- . Irreg. Issues for 1987, 1992.

3175 IMF. **Kingdom of Lesotho: selected issues and statistical appendix**. Washington, DC, 2005. (Country report, 05/438). 75pp. - - Earlier eds. (title varies) 1995 (Staff country report, 95/88); 1998 (Staff country report, 98/29); 2001 (Country report, 01/80); 2002 (Country report, 02/97); 2004 (Country report, 04/23). Full text of reports from 1997 also available online, *see* **334**.

3176 Lesotho. Bureau of Statistics. **Half yearly statistical bulletin**. Maseru, 1978- . *Continues* **Quarterly statistical bulletin**. Roma, 1976-77.

3177 Lesotho. Bureau of Statistics. **Lesotho statistical yearbook/Statistical yearbook of the Kingdom of Lesotho**. Maseru, 1987- . Annual. No issues for 1989-1991. *Continues* **Annual statistical bulletin/review**. Maseru, 1964-1986. No issues for 1974 (which is covered in vol. for 1975). Latest issue in SOAS, Stanford is for 1996. Abridged version pub. as **Kingdom of Lesotho in figures** (1987- . Annual). Latest issue in Stanford is 1993.

3178 Makatjane, Tiiseto. **Sources of population statistics in Lesotho**. Roma, Demography Unit, Department of Statistics, National University of Lesotho, 1985. (Working papers in demography, 3). iii, 29 leaves.

DIRECTORIES OF ORGANIZATIONS

3179 Doling, Tim. **Lesotho arts directory**. London, Visiting Arts, 1999. 56pp.

3180 **Lesotho NGO profile: a presentation of the large number of non-governmental organisations in Lesotho**. 2nd ed. Maseru, Lesotho Council of Non-Governmental Organisations, 1998. Unpaged. - - Orig. pub. Maseru, 1993. 380pp.

See also **2806, 2819, 2820, 2824, 2828**

ATLASES & GAZETTEERS

3181 **1996 Lesotho population census atlas**. Maseru, Bureau of Statistics, 2000. 100pp. (Also called vol. 4 of 1996 population census)

3182 **Atlas for Lesotho**. Rev. ed. Johannesburg, Collins/Cape Town, Longman Southern Africa, 1983. 75pp. Comp. by David Ambrose & J.W.B. Perry. (World atlas with 3pp. maps of Lesotho). - - Earlier eds. Johannesburg, 1970, 1978.

3183 **Lesotho atlas of sustainable development**, comp. D.M. Bohra. Santa Clara, CA/Barmer, Rajasthan, author, 2003. xxvii, 480pp. illus. maps. (213 thematic maps, many simply bar or pie-charts superimposed on a generalised outline map. Covers a very wide range of socio-economic topics)

3184 **Population maps of Lesotho: 1986 census**, comp. D.M. Bohra. Roma, Department of Geography, National University of Lesotho, 1989. viii, 94pp.

3185 Webb, Ronald S. **Gazetteer for Basutoland: the first draft of a list of names, with special reference to the 1:250,000 maps G.S.G.S. no. 2567 of June 1911 (***Basutoland from a reconnaisance survey made in 1904-09***, by Capt. M.C. Dobson, R.F.A.)**. Paarl, Cape Province, the author, 1950. iii, 346, 66, 11pp. (Pt. 1 includes 5,600 place names derived from the Dobson map and other sources; pts. 2 and 3, 1,000 names from the border and adjacent areas. Copies of this work with manuscript additions by the author are available in various libraries: a copy with especially detailed annotations is in the Natural History Museum Library, London)

See also **2913-2915, 2920, 2921, 2923, 2924**

EARTH SCIENCES

3186   Bawden, Michael G. & Carroll, Douglas, M. **The land resources of Lesotho**. Tolworth, Directorate of Overseas Survey, Land Resources Division, 1968. (Land resource study, 3). viii, 89pp. maps.

3187   Carroll, Douglas M. & Bascomb, C.L. **Notes on the soils of Lesotho**. Tolworth, Directorate of Overseas Survey, Land Resources Division, 1967. (Technical bulletin, 1). vi, 75pp. col. maps. (Review, *GJ*, 134, 1968, 577)

3188   Schmitz, Gerald & Rooyani, F. **Lesotho geology, geomorphology, soils**. [Roma], National University of Lesotho, 1987. 204pp. illus. maps.

3189   Wilken, Gene C. **Agroclimatology of Lesotho**. Maseru, Ministry of Agriculture, 1978. (Colorado State University Lesotho Agricultural Sector Analysis Project, 1). 31pp.

BIOLOGICAL SCIENCES

Zoology

3190   Ambrose, David. **Birds, including annotated species checklist**. 2nd ed. Maseru, University of Lesotho, Institute of Education, 2005. (Lesotho annotated bibliography, 167). 242pp. - - Orig. pub. Maseru, 1998.

3191   Bates, M.F. & Haacke, W.D. 'The frogs of Lesotho', *Navorsinge van die Nasionale Museum Bloemfontein*, 19(1) 2003, 101-158

3192   Bonde, Kurt. **Birds of Lesotho: a guide to distribution past and present**. Pietermaritzburg, University of Natal Press, 1993. xii, 108pp. (Covers 272 spp.). - - Ambrose, David. 'New species for the Lesotho bird list', *Mirafra*, 16, 1999, 32-36 (Adds 17 new spp.)

3193   Kopij, Grzegorz. **Catalogus faunae invertebratae Lesotho**. Roma, National University of Lesotho, Department of Biology, 2000. 209pp. illus. maps.

3194   Lynch, C.D. 'The mammals of Lesotho', *Navorsinge van die Nasionale Museum Bloemfontein*, 10(4) 1994, 177-241

Botany

3195 Guillarmod, Amy Jacot. **Flora of Lesotho (Basutoland***). Lehre, Cramer, 1971. (Flora et vegetation mundi, 3). v, 474pp.

3196 Kobisi, Khotso & Kose, Lerato E. **A checklist of Lesotho grasses**. Pretoria, SABONET & National University of Lesotho, 1993. (SABONET report, 17). 22pp. illus. maps.

3197 Kobisi, Khotso. **Preliminary checklist of the plants of Lesotho**. Pretoria, SABONET, 2005. (SABONET report, 34). 84pp. illus. maps.

3198 Schmitz, Martine. **Wild flowers of Lesotho**. Roma, Essa, 1982. 252pp. illus. map. (Col. illus of 200+ spp.)

SWAZILAND

Swaziland Government online information portal
http://www.gov.bw/ home.html

HANDBOOKS

3199 **Historical dictionary of Swaziland**. 2nd ed.. comp. Alan R. Booth. Lanham, MD, Scarecrow Press, 2000. (African historical dictionaries, 80). xxxi, 403pp. (Reviews, *ARBA*, 32, 2001, 196, "in many ways this work probably stands as the best single vol. of the more than 80 ... published"; *Africa today*, 50, 2003, 97-99; *IJAHS*, 34, 2001, 432). - - Orig. pub. comp. John J. Grotpeter. Metuchen, NJ, 1975. (African historical dictionaries, 3). xiv, 251pp. (Review, *JAH*, 20, 1979, 146-147. Rated "good", Balay, 1996)

3200 Swaziland. Government Information Services. **A handbook to the Kingdom of Swaziland**. Mbabane, 1968. 126pp. illus. (A general overview of the country, with statistics, compiled to mark independence)

YEARBOOKS

3201 G.B. Colonial Office. **[Annual reports]: Swaziland, 1906/07-1966**. London, 1908-1969. As **Annual report on Swaziland**, 1906/07-1919/20 (as Command papers), **Colonial Office annual report**, 1920-66 (not pub. 1939-45). Reports subsequent to 1920/21, commencing with 1921, pub. for calendar year. 1947-62 issued by Commonwealth Relations Office; 1963 issued by Colonial Office; 1964-65 issued by Commonwealth Office; 1966 issued by Foreign and Commonwealth Office.

3202 **Swaziland, a review of commerce and industry**. Manzini, B. & T. Directories, ?1980- . Vol. for 1999.

3203 **Swaziland annual and trade index 1966/67**. Johannesburg, Norton, Glyn, 1966. ?No more pub. (Magazine format with brief statistics)

3204 **Swaziland business year book**. Mbabane, Christina Forsyth Thompson, 1992- . Annual. Latest issue in NWU is 14th ed. 2005.

3205 **Swaziland investment and business guide**. Washington, DC, International Business Publications, 2003- . Annual.

See also **1269, 2760-2762**

STATISTICS

3206 **Country profile: Swaziland**. London, Economist Intelligence Unit, 2004- . Annual. *Continues in part* **Country profile: Botswana, Lesotho, Swaziland.** London, Economist Intelligence Unit, 1986-1993; **Country profile: Namibia, Swaziland**. London, 1994-2003.

3207 **Country profile, Swaziland 1983**. Mbabane, Central Statistical Office/ Nairobi, UNICEF, Eastern Africa Regional Office, 1983. 48pp. illus. maps.

3208 Germany. Statistisches Bundesamt. **Statistik des Auslandes: Länderberichte: Swasiland** (later **Länderbericht: Swasiland**). Wiesbaden/ Stuttgart, Metzler-Poetschel, 1987- . Irreg. Issues for 1987, 1993.

3209 IMF. **The Kingdom of Swaziland: a statistical appendix**. Washington, DC, 2006. (Country report, 06/109). 70pp. - - Earlier eds. (Title varies) 1996 (Staff country report, 96/4); 1999 (Staff country report, 99/13); 2000 (Staff country report, 00/113); 2003 (Country report, 03/22). Full text of reports from 1997 also available online, *see* **334**.

3210 Swaziland. Central Statistical Office [etc.]. **Annual statistical bulletin**. Mbabane, 1966- . No issue for 1969. Latest issue in NWU is for 2000.

3211 Swaziland. Central Statistical Office [etc.]. **Quarterly statistical bulletin**. Mbabane, 1966-1977. Title varies: **Statistical news & economic indicators**, issues 1-33, 1966-74; **Quarterly digest of statistics**, issues 34-40, 1974-1977.

DIRECTORIES OF ORGANIZATIONS

3212 **Directory of non-governmental organizations in Swaziland**. 3rd ed., comp. Vincent Sithole. Mbabane, Coordinating Assembly of Non-Governmental Organizations (CANGO), 2000. 97pp. (88 entries)

3213 Doling, Tim. **Swaziland arts directory**. London, Visiting Arts, 1999. 48pp.

3214 **Swaziland Christian handbook 1994**, ed. Marjorie Froise. Welkom, Christian Info, 1994. x, 115pp. (Directory of sects and churches)

See also **2806**, **2819**, **2820**, **2824**, **2828**

BIOGRAPHICAL SOURCES

3215   Jones, Huw M. **A biographical register of Swaziland to 1902**. Pietermaritzburg, University of Natal Press, 1993. xxxv, 691pp. + 16pp. plates. maps. (Includes over 1,500 entries for persons active between 1750 and 1902. Reviews, *African affairs*, 94, 1995, 290-291; *ARD*, 71, 1996, 49-50)

3216   Ndwandwe, S.S. **Profiles of parliamentarians in the Kingdom of Swaziland: who is who in Parliament**. Mbabane, Swaziland Printing & Publishing Co., [?1968]. 44pp.

3217   Steinhauer, D.R. **Awards and honours in Swaziland: some suggestions for a national biographical dictionary**. Kwaluseni, Library, University College of Swaziland, 1978. vi, 71pp.

See also **2888**

ATLASES & GAZETTEERS

3218   **Atlas of Swaziland**, ed. Andrew S. Goudie & D. Price Williams. Lobamba, Swaziland National Trust Commission, 1983. (Occasional paper, 4). viii, 90pp. (40 b. & w. thematic maps with accompanying text)

For Gazetteers *See* **2913-2915, 2920, 2921, 2923, 2924**

EARTH SCIENCES

3219   **The geology of Swaziland: an explanation of the 1:125,000 geological map**, comp. Donald R. Hunter. Mbabane, Geological Survey & Mines Department, 1961. 104pp. (Pub. to support the Survey's geological map at 1:125,000, 1960)

3220   Murdoch, G. et al. **A land system atlas of Swaziland**. Christchurch, Directorate of Military Survey, 1971. 49pp. illus. maps. (Comp. by University of Oxford Department of Agricultural Science. Maps of natural resources)

BIOLOGICAL SCIENCES

Zoology

3221   Monadjem, Ara. **Mammals of Swaziland**. Mbabane, Conservation Trust of Swaziland & Big Game Parks, 1998. 154pp. (Handbook describing 127 spp. with distribution maps. Review, *African zoology*, 36, 2001, 113-114)

3222 Parker, Vincent. **Swaziland bird atlas, 1985-1991**. Mbabane, Websters, 1994. xvii, 274pp. (Covers 489 spp. Review, *BABC*, 4, 1997, 47-48)

Botany

3223 Braun, K.P. et al. **Swaziland flora checklist**. Pretoria, SABONET/ Malkerns, Swaziland, Swaziland National Herbarium, 2004. (SABONET report, 27). x, 113pp. maps. (Lists 2,715 native and 110 naturalized spp. No annotations. Update of Ellen S. Kemp. **A flora checklist for Swaziland**. Lobamba, Swaziland National Trust Commission, 1983. (Occasional papers, 2). 111pp.)

3224 Compton, Robert H. **An annotated checklist of the flora of Swaziland**. Kirstenbosch, Trustees of the National Botanic Gardens, 1966. (*Journal of South African botany*, Suppl. 6). iii, 191pp. (Includes notes on range and habitat, and a lexicon of vernacular names)

3225 Compton, Robert H. **The flora of Swaziland**. Kirstenbosch, Trustees of the National Botanic Gardens, 1976. (*Journal of South African botany*, Suppl. 11). 684pp. (Includes keys to genera and spp., Swazi names, history of botanical exploration). - - Kemp, Ellen S. **Additions and name changes for the** *Flora of Swaziland*. Lobamba, Swaziland National Trust Commission, 1981. 74pp.

3226 Kemp, Ellen S. **Trees of Swaziland**. Lobamba, Swaziland National Trust Commission, 1983. (Occasional papers, 3). vi, 59pp. (Lists 464 spp.)

3227 Roux, Jacobus Petrus. **Swaziland ferns and fern allies**. Pretoria, SABONET, 2003. (SABONET report, 19). 241pp. illus. maps.

INDIAN OCEAN ISLANDS
(*FRANCOPHONE SOUTHERN AFRICA*)

HANDBOOKS

3228   **La France de l'océan indien: Madagascar, les Comores, la Réunion, la Côte française des Somalis, l'Inde française**, comp. Raymond Decary et al. Paris, Société d'éditions géographiques, maritimes et coloniales, 1952. (Terres lointaines, 2). 314pp. illus. maps. (Pp. 1-225, Madagascar & Antarctic dependencies by Raymond Decary; pp. 227-242, Comoros by Pierre Coudert; pp. 243-276, Réunion by Hildebert Isnard; pp. 277-297, French Somaliland by Robert Lemoyne. Covers topography, peoples, history, administration and the economic structure)

3229   Hänel, Karl. **Madagaskar, Komoren, Reunion**. Bonn, K. Schroeder for Deutsche Afrika-Gesellschaft, 1958. (Die Länder Afrikas, 3). 121pp. (Pp. 5-100, Madagascar; pp. 101-105, Comoros; pp. 106-112, Réunion)

3230   **Indian Ocean: five island countries; area handbook series**. 3rd ed. comp. Helen Chapin Metz. Washington, DC, Library of Congress, Federal Research Division, 1995. xxvii, 407pp. (The sections for each country are also available online from the Library's Web site, *see* entries under individual countries below. - - Orig. pub. as **Area handbook for the Indian Ocean territories**, comp. Theodore L. Stoddard. Washington, DC, U.S. Department of Defense, 1971. xvi, 160pp. maps; - - 2nd ed. **Indian Ocean: five island countries;** comp. Frederica M. Burge. Washington, DC, 1983. xxvii, 346pp. illus. maps. (Pp. 1-126, Madagascar; pp. 127-166, Mauritius; pp. 167-194, Comoros; pp. 195-224, Seychelles)

3231   **Madagascar, Comores, Réunion, Île Maurice**, ed. Claude Janicot. Paris, Hachette, 1955. (Les guides bleus). 429pp. illus. map. (Detailed historical and topographical background in addition to itineraries. 'Aperçu géographique' by Charles Robequain; 'Aperçu historique' by Gilbert Saron & Roland Julienne; 'Aperçu ethnographique et folklorique' by Renaud Paulian; 'Aperçu linguistique' by Flavien Ranaivo)

3232   **Madagascar et Réunion: l'encyclopédie coloniale et maritime**, ed. Marcel de Coppet. Paris, l'Encyclopédie de l'empire français, 1947. 2 vols. illus. maps. (Vol. 1. xi, 372, iiipp. 164 photos. 37 diagrs. 34 maps. Madagascar ; vol. 2. iii, 368, xivpp. 184 photos. 23 diagrs. 28 maps. Pp. 1-232, Madagascar; pp. 233-264, Comoros; pp. 283-368, Réunion. Provides the usual detailed treatment associated with the volumes of this encyclopaedia, *see* **54**).

3233 Marquardt, Wilhelm. **Seychellen, Komoren und Maskarenen: Handbuch der Ost- afrikanischen Inselwelt**. Munich, Weltforum Verlag, 1976. (Afrika-Studien. Sonderreihe Information und Dokumentation, 5). 344pp. illus. maps. (Separate sections for the Seychelles, Comoros, Mauritius and dependencies, Rodrigues, Diego Garcia, and Réunion. Includes an historical chronology, bibliography and a wide range of statistical tables. Review, *GJ*, 143, 1977, 472)

3234 Walker, Iain. **The complete guide to the Southwest Indian Ocean Comores, Madagascar, Mauritius, Réunion, Seychelles**. Argelès-sur-Mer, France, Cornelius Books, 1993. 606pp.

YEARBOOKS

3235 **Annuaire Noria: Océan indien-Madagascar, La Réunion, Maurice 1960/61** [etc]. Limoges, Annuaires Noria, 1960-1961. 2 issues for 1960/61, 1961/62. Incorporated into **Annuaire Noria: Afrique noire** from 1963, *see* **297**. (Includes section for Comoro Islands. Brief data on each country, followed by commercial directory)

3236 **B. & T. Mauritius business directory**, incorporating Rodrigues & Réunion. Curepipe, B. & T. Directories, 1979- . Annual. Title varies: **Business directory of Mauritius, Réunion, and Seychelles** (1979-1983); **Mauritius and Seychelles business directory** (1984-2003)

3237 **Guide annuaire illustré des îles de l'Océan indien, économique, commercial, touristique**, ed. Urbain Faurec & Jean Bichelberger. Antananarivo, 1939. 347pp. illus. No more pub. (Text in French and English. Covers Comoros, Madagascar, Mauritius, Réunion)

DIRECTORIES OF ORGANIZATIONS

3238 Directory: **institutions/organisations and individuals in the South West Indian Ocean Islands and other French speaking countries/areas bordering the Indian Ocean**. Rose Hill, Centre de documentation, de recherches et de formation indianocéaniques, 1988. 261pp. (Lists 114 institutions arranged by island: covers Comoros, Madagascar, Mauritius, Réunion & Seychelles)

3239 **Mauriceguide 1969-70** [etc.]: **a commercial, industrial and tourist French-English directory of Mauritius, Madagascar and Réunion and**

Seychelles, ed. Camille Alex Mouton. Port Louis, *The Standard*, 1969- . NWU holds issue for 1975/76. (Sub-title varies)

ATLASES & GAZETTEERS

Atlases

3240 **Indian Ocean atlas,** ed. Prithvish Nag. Calcutta, National Atlas & Thematic Mapping Organisation, Department of Science & Technology, 1998. vipp., 19 double page maps. (Scales 1:25M & 1:50M)

3241 U.S. Central Intelligence Agency. **Indian Ocean atlas**. Washington, DC, 1976. 80pp. (Popular format, with accompanying photos and text. Thematic maps and tables for the Ocean as a whole, specific section (pp. 36-50) for islands: Zanzibar, Comoros, Madagascar, Réunion, Mauritius and Seychelles)

3242 U.S. Defense Mapping Agency. Hydrographic/Topographic Center. **Atlas of pilot charts, Indian Ocean**. Washington, DC, 1979. 12pp. col. maps.

See also **701**

Gazetteers & pilots

3243 France. Service hydrographique et océanographique de la marine. **Océan indien sud: Madagascar, îles éparses, terres australes et antarctiques françaises**. Brest, 1984. 424pp. illus. maps. - - Earlier ed., 1917.

3244 G.B. Admiralty. Hydrographic Office. **Admiralty sailing directions: South Indian Ocean pilot**. Taunton, 2004. 325pp. illus. *Continues* **South Indian Ocean pilot: Comores, Madagascar, Seychelles Group, La Réunion, Mauritius, Chagos Archipelago & other islands lying westward of longitude 90° east**. 10th ed. Taunton, 2001. xiv, 309pp. - - Earlier eds. (title varies) 1911, 1923-24, 1934, 1946, 1958, 1971, 1990.

3245 U.S. Board on Geographic Names. **Madagascar, Réunion and the Comoro Islands: official standard names approved by the USBGN**. Washington, DC, 1955. (Gazetteer, 2). iii, 498pp. (Pp. 1-440, Madagascar, 20,000 names); pp. 441-478, Réunion, 1,400 names; pp. 479-498, Comoros, 700 names)

3246   U.S. Defense Mapping Agency. Hydrographic Center [etc.] **Sailing directions (enroute) for East Africa and the South Indian Ocean**. 8th ed. Bethesda, MD, 2004. 1 CD-ROM. - - Orig. pub. Washington, DC, 1978. Later eds. 1983, 1986, 1990, 1995

3247   U.S. Defense Mapping Agency. Hydrographic Center [etc.] **Sailing directions for the Southeast coast of Africa: Cape of Good Hope to Ras Hafun**. Rev ed. Washington, DC, 1975. looseleaf. - - Orig. pub. as **Africa pilot. Vol. 2. South and East coasts of Africa from Cape of Good Hope to Ras Hafun**. Washington, DC, 1916. Later eds. (title varies) 1924, 1936, 1951, 1968.

3248   U.S. Defense Mapping Agency. Hydrographic Center [etc.] **Sailing directions for the South Indian Ocean: Madagascar and islands west of longitude 90°**. 4th ed. Washington, DC, 1952. Looseleaf. - - Orig. pub. as. **South Indian Ocean pilot: islands westward of longitude 92° east including Madagascar and the Comoro Islands**. Washington, DC, 1917. Later eds. (title varies) 1927, 1945.

EARTH SCIENCES

3249   **Geological–geophysical atlas of the Indian Ocean**. Moscow, Akademiia nauk, 1975. 151pp. maps. (Text in Russian and English. Based upon the findings of the Intenational Indian Ocean Expedition of 1960 to 1964)

3250   Hastenrath, S. & Lamb, P.J. **Climatic atlas of the Indian Ocean**. Madison, WI, University of Wisconsin Press, 1979-1989. 3 vols. col. maps. 23 x 34 cm. Vol. 1. Surface climate and atmospheric circulation; vol. 2. The oceanic heat budget; vol. 3. Upper ocean structure. (Reviews, *GJ*, 157, 1991, 216; *SAGJ*, 62, 1980, 193-194)

3251   **Informations sur les ressources en environnement dans les îles de l'Océan Indien, Comores, Madagascar, Maurice, Réunion, Seychelles: répertoire personnes, ressources, institutions et organismes, projets ou activités, bibliographies**. 2nd ed. comp. Réseau d'experts développement environnement sud océan indien. Antananarivo, Centre d'information technique et économique, 2001. 339pp.

3252   U.S. National Oceanographic Data Center. **Atlas of bathy-thermograph data: Indian Ocean**. Washington, DC, 1966. 129pp.

3253   U.S. Navy. Chief of Naval Operations. **Marine climatic atlas of the world. Vol. 3. Indian Ocean**. Washington, DC, U.S. Government Printing Office, 1957. xviipp. 267 charts. 33x 50cm.

See also **3583**

BIOLOGICAL SCIENCES

3254   Blanchard, Frédéric. **La Réunion, Maurice, Rodrigues: guide des milieux naturels**. Paris, Eugen Ulmer, 2000. 384pp. illus. maps. (Guide to vegetation and habitats, flora and fauna)

3255   Robyns de Schneidauer, Thierry. **Guide-nature de l'océan indien; Madagascar, Comores, Seychelles, Maurice, Réunion**. Brussels, Institut royale des Sciences naturelles de Belgique, 1982. 264pp. illus. maps. (Describes the more common flora and fauna)

Zoology

Birds

3256   Huguet, P. & Chappuis, Claude. **Oiseaux de Madagascar, Mayotte, Comores, Seychelles, Réunion, Maurice**. Paris, Société d'Études ornithologiques de France, 2003. 114pp. + 4 CDs. (Sound recordings for 327 spp. out of the 344 in the region. Review, *BABC*, 11, 2004, 161-164)

3257   Sinclair, Ian & Langrand, Olivier. **Birds of the Indian Ocean islands: Madagascar, Mauritius, Réunion, Rodrigues, Seychelles and the Comoros**. Cape Town, Struik/London, New Holland, 1998. 184pp. 65 col. plates. 1999 reprint entitled **Chamberlain's birds of the Indian Ocean islands**. (Similar format to Sinclair's **Sasol birds of South Africa**, *see* **2978** . Covers 359 spp. all illus in col. Relies largely on Langrand, **3339,** for nomenclature. Reviews, *BABC*, 6, 1999, 67-69; *Ibis*, 141, 1999, 515-517)

3258   Sinclair, Ian et al. **A photographic guide to the birds of the Indian Ocean islands; Madagascar, Mauritius, Seychelles, Réunion and the Comoros**. Cape Town, Struik/London, New Holland, 2006. 128pp. (Covers "the most commonly encountered and striking bird species")

Reptiles, Amphibians & Fishes

3259   Debelius, Helmut. **Riff-Führer Indischer Ozean: Malediven, Sri Lanka, Thailand, Südafrika, Mauritius, Madagaskar, Ostafrika, Seychellen**. Hamburg, Jahr Verlag, 1999. 321pp. illus.

- - English ed. **Indian Ocean tropical fish guide: Maledives [sic], Sri Lanka, Mauritius, Madagascar, East Africa, Seychelles, Arabian Sea, Red Sea**. Neu Isenberg, Aquaprint, 1993. 321pp. illus. maps. (Includes 1,000+ col. photos)

3260　**Fishes of the Indian Ocean**. London, Calypso, 2000. (Fishes of the world: modular regional database: taxonomic classification, vol. 6). 1 computer disk. (Based on the Calypso Ichthyological Database)

3261　Fricke, Ronald. **Fishes of the Mascarene Islands (Réunion, Mauritius, Rodriguez): an annotated checklist, with descriptions of new species**. Koenigstein, Koeltz, 1999. (Theses zoologicae, 31). viii, 759pp. maps.

3262　Henkel, Friedrich-Wilhelm & Schmidt, Wolfgang. **Amphibians and reptiles of Madagascar, the Mascarenes, the Seychelles and the Comoros Islands**. Malabar, FL, Krieger, 1998. vii, 316pp. illus. 275 col. photos. (Review, *African journal of herpetology*, 50, 2001, 47-50). - - Orig. pub. as **Amphibien und Reptilien Madagaskars der Maskarenen, Seychellen und Komoren**. Frankfurt, Ulmer Verlag, 1995. 312pp.

3263　Jennings, Gerald H. **The fishes of the Indian Ocean: the 1998 classified taxonomic checklist: ... over 1,850 species currently recorded on the Calypso Ichthyological Database**. London, Calypso, 1997. 252pp. - - **Addendum no.1**. London, Calypso, 1998. 33pp.

Invertebrates

3264　Bons, Jacques. **Mollusques marins de l'Océan indien: Comores, Mascareignes, Seychelles**. Paris, ACCT, 1984. 108pp. illus.

3265　Desegaulx de Nolet, A. **Lépidoptères Rhopalocères, Arctiidae, Sphingidae de l'Océan Indien: Comores, Mascareignes, Seychelles**. Paris, ACCT, 1984. viii, 81pp. illus.

Botany

3266　Gurib-Fakim, Ameenah & Brendler, T. **Medicinal and aromatic plants of Indian Ocean islands: Madagascar, Comoros, Seychelles and Mascarenes**. Stuttgart, Medpharm, 2004. viii, 567pp. illus. maps.

COMOROS

HANDBOOKS

3267 **Comoros : a country study**. Available at http://lcweb2.loc.gov/frd/cs/kmtoc.html. Appropriate section of **Indian Ocean: five island countries; area handbook series**. 3rd ed. comp. Helen Chapin Metz. Washington, DC, Library of Congress, Federal Research Division, 1995. (*See* **3230**)

3268 France. Ministère de la coopération. **Comores: guide d'information**. Paris, 1992. (Collection guides d'information). 68pp.

3269 **Historical dictionary of the Comoro Islands**, comp. Martin Ottenheimer & Harriet Ottenheimer. Metuchen, NJ, Scarecrow Press, 1994 (African historical dictionaries, 59). xviii, 137pp. (Reviews, *Africa*, 65, 1995, 327; *ASR*, 40, 1997, 176-178; *Choice*, 32, 1994, 756, "thoroughly competent and authoritative"; *IJAHS*, 29, 1966, 138-139)

3270 **Répertoire culturel, les Comores**. Paris, ACCT, [?1983]. (Inventaire des activités, etc. des pays membres de l'ACCT). 63pp. illus. maps.

See also **3347**

STATISTICS

3271 **Bulletin statistique des Comores**. Moroni, Ministère des finances, du budget et du plan, Direction de la statistique, 1999- .

3272 **Country profile: Comoros**. London, Economist Intelligence Unit, 1993- Annual. *Continues in part* **Country profile: Madagascar, Comoros**. London, Economist Intelligence Unit, 1986-1992; **Country profile: Tanzania, Comoros**. London, 1993-2002.

3273 France. Institut national de la statistique et des études économiques (INSEE). **Études sur les comptes économiques des territoires des Comores**. Paris, 1959- . Irreg.

3274 Germany. Statistisches Bundesamt. **Statistik des Auslandes: Länderberichte: Komoren** (later **Länderbericht: Komoren**). Wiesbaden/Stuttgart, Metzler-Poetschel, 1985- . Irreg. Issues for 1985, 1993.

3275   IMF. **Union of the Comoros: statistical appendix**. Washington, DC, 2005. (Country report, 05/296). 43pp. - - Earlier eds. (title varies) 1997 (Staff country report, 97/115); 2000 (Staff country report, 00/108); 2004 (Country report, 04/83); 2004 (Country report, 04/233). Full text of reports from 97/101, 1997 also available online, *see* **334**.

ATLASES & GAZETTEERS

See **3245**

EARTH SCIENCES

3276   Battistini, René & Verin, Pierre. **Géographie des Comores**. Paris, ACCT, 1984. 144pp. col. illus. col. maps.

3277   Brouwers, M. et al. **Les terres cultivables des Comores: synthèse**. Comoros, Centre national plan finances méthodes, 1977. 49pp. + 12pp. plates. maps.

BIOLOGICAL SCIENCES

3278   Adjanohoun, Edouard J. et al. **Contribution aux études ethno-botaniques et floristiques aux Comores**. Paris, ACCT, 1982. (Médicine traditionnelle et pharmacopée). 216pp. illus.

3279   Louette, Michel et al. **La faune terrestre de l'archipel des Comores**. Tervuren, Musée royal de l'Afrique centrale, 2004. (*Annales. Science zoologiques*, 293). 456pp. illus. map. (Covers mammals, birds, reptiles, amphibians, freshwater fish, invertebrates. Review, *BABC*, 12, 2005, 175)

3280   Louette, Michel. **Les oiseaux des Comores**. Tervuren, Musée royal de l'Afrique centrale, 1988. (*Annales. Science zoologiques*, 255). 92pp. 20 plates. (Covers 99 spp. Reviews, *Auk*, 108, 1991, 222; *Ibis*, 131, 1989, 622)

3281   Matile, Loïc et al. **Faune entomologique de l'archipel des Comores**. Paris, Muséum national d'histoire naturelle, 1978. (Mémoires, n.s. Série A, Zoologie, 109). 388pp. illus.

See also **3350**

MADAGASCAR

Official Web site of the Malagasy Government/Site officiel du
Gouvernement Malgache http://www.madagascar.gov.mg/

HANDBOOKS

3282 Adelaar, Alexander & Himmelmann, Nikolaus P. **The Austronesian languages of Indonesia and Madagascar**. London, Routledge, 2005. xxii, 841pp. (Chaps. 1 to 5, General ; chap 16, Malagasay by Janie Rasoloson & Carl Rubino)

3283 Atlas historique du peuplement de Madagascar, comp. Fred Ramiandrasoa. Antananarivo, Université de Madagascar, 1975. 31pp. (11 maps with accompanying French and Malagasay text, keyed to 181 sources listed in bibliography. Covers from prehistory to early 20th century)

3284 Cadoux, Charles. **La République malgache**. Paris, Berger-Levrault, 1969. (Encyclopédie politique et constitutionnelle; Série Afrique). 126pp.

3285 Dictionnaire encyclopédique malgache/Firaketana ny Fiteny sy ny Zavatra Malagasay. Antananarivo, 1937-?1970. 9 vols. 272 fascs. (Initial ed. E. Kruger. Originally issued in fascs. as suppls. to the journal *Fiainana* and paged in vols. Vol. 1 (fascs 1-36). 1937-1939. A-Ana. 586pp; vol. 2 (fascs. 37-81). 1940-1944. And-Avy. 511pp.; vol. 3 (fascs. 82-115). 1945-1947. B-D. 615pp; vol. 4 (fascs. 116-157). 1947-1952. E-F. 744pp; vol. 5 (fascs. 158-182). 1952-1956. G-H. 362pp; vol. 6 (fascs, 183-205). 1956-1958. I. 368pp; vol. 7 (fascs. 206-244). 1958-1963. J-K. 408pp; vol. 8 (fascs. 245-271). 1963-1970. L-M. 420pp; vol. 9 (fasc. 272). 1970. Ma. 20pp. ?No more pub. Text in Malagasay. Includes short entries for words, much longer entries for places, people, flora and fauna, etc.)

3286 Ethnographic survey of Africa: Madagascar. Paris, Presses Universitaires de France for International African Institute, 1959. (Le peuple malgache: monographies ethnologiques). 1 vol. illus. maps. (Sub-series of the **Ethnographic survey**, *see* 86). Vol. 1. Les Malgaches du sud-est by Hubert Deschamps & Suzanne Vianès. 1959. 118pp.

3287 France. Direction de la documentation. **La république malgache**. Paris, 1960. (*Notes et études documentaires*, 2737, 23 Dec. 1960). 61pp. maps.

3288 France. Ministère de la coopération. **Madagascar: guide d'information**. Paris, 1996. (Collection guide d'information). 109pp. (Brief account of history, geography, politics, government and economics)

3289   Gavrilov, N.I. **Demokraticheskaia Respublika Madagaskar: spravochnik**. Moscow, Akademiia nauk, Institut Afriki, 1985. 227pp. illus.

3290   **Historical dictionary of Madagascar**. 2nd ed., comp. Philip M. Allen & Maureen Covell. Lanham, MD, Scarecrow Press, 2005 (African historical dictionaries, 98). lxxxiii, 420pp. maps. - - Orig. pub. comp. Maureen Covell. Lanham, MD, 1995. (African historical dictionaries, 50). xlvi, 356pp.

3291   **Madagascar: a country study**. Available at : http://lcweb2.loc.gov/ frd/cs/mgtoc.html. Appropriate section of **Indian Ocean: five island countries; area handbook series**. 3rd ed. comp. Helen Chapin Metz. Washington, DC, Library of Congress, Federal Research Division, 1995. (*See* **3230**). - - Earlier ed. **Area handbook for the Malagasay Republic**, comp. Harold D. Nelson et al. Washington, DC, U.S. Department of Defense, 1973. xvii, 287pp. maps.

3292   Rajema-Raolison, Régis. **Dictionnaire historique et géographique de Madagascar**. Fianarantsoa, Librairie Ambozontany, 1966. 383pp. illus. maps. (Includes biographical entries and numerous maps and charts)

3293   Rajoelina, Patrick & Ramelet, Alain. **Madagascar, la grande île**. Paris, Harmattan, 1989. 329pp. maps. (General handbook covering natural resources, history, topography, economic and social life)

3294   Ranaivoson, Dominique. **Iza moa? Bref dictionnaire historique de Madagascar**. Antananarivo, Tsipika, 2004. 189pp.

3295   Rozeboom, Annelie. **Madagaskar: mensen, politiek, economie, cultuur**. Amsterdam, Koninklijk Instituut voor de Tropen/The Hague, Novib, 2003. (Landenreeks). 78pp. illus. maps

3296   Valette, Jean. **D'une table de concordance des calendriers grégorien et malgache**. Antananarivo, Service des Archives de la République malgache, 1960. 1 vol. var. pagings.

YEARBOOKS

3297   **Annuaire de Madagascar**. Antananarivo, Madagascar Print & Press Co./Editions Madprint, 1959-?1985. Annual. Not pub. 1974-1978. Ceased 1985, LC catalogue. Title varies: **Annuaire du monde politique, diplomatique, administratif et de la presse** (1959-1973); **Annuaire du monde politique, administratif et diplomatique de Madagascar** (1978-1981). (Sub-title: Guide permanent de l'administration des pays de l'Océan Indien. From 1982 issued in three vols; vol. 1. Politique et administratif; vol. 2. Diplomatique et internationale; vol. 3. Économique et financier)

3298 **Annuaire de Madagascar. Répertoire diplomatique**. Antananarivo, Éditions *Revue de l'Océan Indien*, 1994- . *Continues in part*, **Annuaire de Madagascar**, vol. 2 , *see* **3297** above). Latest issue in NWU is 1994

3299 **Annuaire du monde politique, administratif et diplomatique de Madagascar**. Antananarivo, 1965/66, 1978. Recorded in CCFR

3300 **Annuaire Minas de Madagascar, 1994/95-** . Antananarivo, Minas, 1995- Latest issue in NWU is for 1996/97. (Text in French, English, German, and Italian. 1st issue lists some 3,000 organizations. Includes lists of government ministries. Arranged by topic)

3301 **Annuaire-guide de Madagascar et dépendances**. Antananarivo, 1934-1938. Biannual. (CCFR records issues for 1934/35, 1936/37 & 1938/39)

3302 Madagascar. Directeur de l'Information. **L'économie au service des investisseurs**. Antananarivo, 1961-1977. Annual. Title varies: **Repoblika Malagasay: annuaire national, 1961/62** [etc.]. (1961-1969); **Annuaire national de l'industrie et du commerce** (1970-1977); **L'économie malgache** (1972). From 1973 to 1976 called **L'économie** … with sub-title changing annually to reflect changing coverage. (Issue for 1973 covers Madagascar, Mauritius, Réunion, Seychelles, Comoros; issue for 1974 adds Djibouti. Principal contents are the civil list, information on the economy and a commercial directory)

STATISTICS

3303 **Dossier national: Madagascar**, comp. Jean-Albert Randrianoelina. Louvain-le-Neuve, Centre international de formation et de recherche en population et développement (CIDEP), 1996. 66pp. (Contemporary statistics)

3304 France. Ministère de la coopération, Direction des programmes, Sous-direction des études économiques et de la planification. **Madagascar: données statistiques sur les activités économiques, culturelles et sociales**. Paris, 1976. 151pp. illus.

3305 IMF. **Republic of Madagascar: selected issues and statistical appendix**. Washington, DC, 2005. (Country report, 05/321). 122pp. - - Earlier eds. (title varies) 1996 (Staff country report, 96/59); 1999 (Staff country report,

99/17); 2001 (Country report, 01/219); 2003 (Country report, 03/07). Full text of reports from 97/101, 1997 also available online, *see* **334**.

3306 Pryor, Frederic Leroy. **Income distribution and economic development in Madagascar: some historical statistics**. Washington, DC, World Bank, 1988. (Discussion papers, 37). ix, 76pp.

3307 Razafindrakoto, Marius. **95, Madagascar d'aujourd'hui: bilan exhaustif de l'économie malgache**. Antananarivo, author, 1996. 198pp. illus. maps. On title page: **Madagascar en chiffres**. Recorded in NWU catalogue.

Bulletins & yearbooks

3308 **Country profile: Madagascar**. London, Economist Intelligence Unit, 1993- . Annual. *Continues in part* **Country profile: Madagascar, Comoros**. London, 1986-1992.

3309 Germany. Statistisches Bundesamt. **Statistik des Auslandes: Länderberichte: Madagascar** (later **Länderbericht: Madagascar**). Wiesbaden/Stuttgart, Metzler-Poetschel, 1962- . Irreg. Issues for 1962, 1973, 1984, 1986, 1988, 1991.

3310 Madagascar. Direction générale de la Banque des données de l'état. **Madagascar in figures**. Antanarivo. ?-1992. NWU has issue for 1992.

3311 Madagascar. Service de statistique générale. **Annuaire statistique de Madagascar 1938/51** [etc.]. Antananarivo, 1953. 186pp. No more pub.

3312 Madagascar. Service de statistique générale. **Bulletin mensuel de statistique**. Antananarivo, 1949- . Monthly. Title varies: **Bulletin de statistique générale de Madagascar** (1949-1954). ALA notes issues for 1991.

DIRECTORIES OF ORGANIZATIONS

3313 **Répertoire des bibliothèques et organismes de documentation de Madagascar**. Antananarivo, Ministère de la recherche scientifique et technologique pour le développement, 1989. 96pp. (Lists 92 institutions A/Z with subject index). - - Earlier ed. Antananarivo 1985. 32pp. (86 entries)

3314 **Répertoire des organismes de documentation, des maisons d'éditions, des imprimeries et des librairies de Madagascar**. Antananarivo, Bibliothèque nationale, 1985. n.p. (772 entries)

BIOGRAPHICAL SOURCES

3315   Hecht-Ranaivoson, Dominique. **Madagascar, dictionnaire des personnalités historiques**. Saint-Maur-des-Fossés, Sépia/Antananarivo, Tsipika, 2005. 218pp. col. illus.

3316   Verdier, Isabelle. **Madagascar, 100 hommes de pouvoir**. Paris, Indigo, 1995. 211pp.

See also **3347**

ATLASES & GAZETTEERS

3317   Atlas de Madagascar. Antananarivo, Bureau pour le développement de la production agricole, Association des géographes de Madagascar, & Centre de l'Institut géographique nationale à Madagascar, 1969-1972. x, 140pp. text. 62 plates. 32 x 40cm. ("Préparé … sous la direction de Françoise et Paul Le Bourdiec & René Battistini". 62 thematic maps at 1:4M with transparent overlay showing administrative divisions. Town plans at 1:50,000 of Antananarivo, Majunga, Antsirabe, Tulgar. Substantial notes on sources. The section 'Histoire de la géographie' shows exploration routes and lists 138 travellers' journies and points touched by voyages. *See* Paul Le Bourdiec, 'L'Atlas de Madagascar', *Bulletin du Comité français de cartographie*, 41, 1969, 219-221. Review, *Africa*, 42, 1972, 261)

3318   G.B. Army. GHQ Middle East. Survey Directorate. **East Africa: index gazetteer showing place-names in 1:500,000 map series**. Cairo, 1946-1948. 3 vols. in 4. (Vol. 3, 1948. iii, 257pp. Madagascar, Portuguese East Africa, Northern Rhodesia, Nyasaland and Southern Rhodesia. Coverage is basically of Madagascar and Portuguese East Africa) *See also* **801, 1031**

3319   Mangold, Max. **A pronouncing dictionary of Malagasay place names**. Hamburg, Helmut Buske, 1982. (Forum phoneticum, 25). vi, 176pp.

3320   U.S. Board on Geographic Names. **Gazetteer of Madagascar: names approved by the USBGN**. 2nd ed. Washington, DC, 1989. xvii, 826pp. (35,000 entries. Revision of appropriate sections of **2458**)

See also **1030**

EARTH SCIENCES

3321 **Atlas climatologique de Madagascar**, comp. Jacques Ravet. Antananarivo, Service météorologique de Madagascar, 1948. 6pp. text. 95pp. maps. 29 x 22cm.

3322 **Atlas des structures agraires à Madagascar**. Paris, Mouton for Maison des sciences de l'homme, 1973- . Pt. 1. 1973; pt. 3. 1976. ?No more pub. (Comp. ORSTOM & École pratique des hautes etudes)

3323 Battistini, René & Richard-Vinard, G. eds. **Biogeography and ecology in Madagascar**. The Hague, Junk, 1972. (Monographiae biologicae, 21). xv, 765pp. illus. (Sections in English and French. Wide-ranging coverage of topography, geology, soils, climate, limnology, flora and fauna and man and the environment. Review, *GJ*, 140, 1974, 128-129).

3324 Battistini, René et al. **Géographie de Madagascar**. Paris, Edicef, 1986. 187pp. illus. maps.

3325 Behier, Jean. **Contribution à la minéralogie de Madagascar**. Antananarivo, Service géologique, 1954-1958. (Travaux du Bureau géologique, 61, 89). 2 vols. 176pp. illus.

3326 Besairie, Henri M.E. & Collignon, M. **Géologie de Madagascar**. Antananarivo, Service Géologique, 1971. (Annales géologiques de Madagascar, fasc. 35). 463pp. + 89 plates. *See also* H.M.E. Besairie. **Précis de géologie malgache**. Antananarivo, Service géologique, 1971. (Annales géologiques de Madagascar, fasc. 36). 143pp. illus.

3327 Besairie, Henri M.E. **Gites minéraux de Madagascar**. Antananarivo, Service géologique, 1966. (Annales géologiques de Madagascar, fasc. 34). 2 vols. (Vol.1, Text; vol. 2, plates – chiefly maps)

3328 Besairie, Henri M.E. & Collignon, M. **Lexique stratigraphique international, 4, Afrique, fasc 11: Madagascar**. Paris, CNRS, 1956. 95pp. map.

3329 Donque, Gérald. **Contribution géographique à l'étude du climat de Madagascar**. Antananarivo, Nouvelle imprimerie des arts graphics, 1975. vii, 478pp.

3330 Jenkins, Martin D. ed. **Madagascar: an environmental profile**. Gland, IUCN, 1987. 374pp. (Prepared under the U.N. Global Environment

Monitoring System (GEMS). Includes faunal lists for several classes of fauna, and individual accounts of the most threatened spp.). - - French trans. **Madagascar: profil de l'environnement**. Gland, 1990. xv, 439pp.

3331 Minelle, Jean. **L'agriculture à Madagascar: géographie, climatologie, écologie, conditions: l'exploitation des sols, botanique malgache, productions agricoles, etc.** Paris, M. Rivière, 1959. 379pp. + 20pp. plates.

3332 Sick, Wolf-Dieter. **Madagaskar: tropisches Entwicklungsland zwischen den Kontinenten.** Darmstadt, Wissenschaftliche Buchgesellschaft, 1979. (Wissenschaftliche Länderkunden, 16). xvii, 321pp. (Physical and economic geography. Review, *GJ*, 148, 1982, 70-71)

BIOLOGICAL SCIENCES

3333 Goodman, Stephen M. & Benstead, J.P. **The natural history of Madagascar**. Chicago, IL, University of Chicago Press, 2003. xix, 1,709pp. (Enormously detailed work, probably the most thorough single compilation of its kind for any African country, which includes all classes of flora and fauna, also a history of scientific explorations. Review, *Journal of mammalogy*, 85, 2004, 813-814, "resource of unparallelled usefulness")

Zoology

3334 **Faune de Madagascar**. Paris, Muséum d'histoire naturelle etc. for Government of Madagascar, 1956-. 102 vols. in 90 to 2006. (A voluminous series, following the model of **Faune de la France** and unmatched for any other African country. Currently being comp. and pub. by CIRAD, the IRD and the Muséum national d'histoire naturelle (MNHN). Each vol. is devoted to a particular class or family. All classes are treated including birds, mammals, fresh and salt-water fishes, reptiles etc. The 90 vols. pub. to 2006 cover vertebrates (8 vols.), insects (64 vols.), other arthropods (8 vols.), molluscs (2 vols.), marine invertebrates (7 vols.) and zoogeography (1 vol.). A list of all vols. pub. to date and of those forthcoming is available at http://www.mnhn.fr/publication/faunemad/indexan.html.
- - **Supplément**. Paris, Muséum d'histoire naturelle, 1990- . Irreg.

3335 Garbutt, Nick. **Mammals of Madagascar**. London, Pica Press, 1999. 320pp. 3 col. plates, 160 col. photos. (Covers 117 species and subspecies. Review, *BABC*, 7, 2000, 152). - - **Mammals of Madagascar: a complete guide**. Announced as a field guide based on the 1999 title, forthcoming 2007.

3336   Glaw, Frank & Vences, Miguel. **A field guide to the amphibians and reptiles of Madagascar (including mammals and freshwater fish).** 2nd ed. Cologne, M. Vences & F. Glaw Verlag, 1994. 480pp. 448 col. photos, 552 b. & w. photos. 450 maps. (Review, *SAJZ*, 30, 1995, 57-58, "a major biological milestone"). - - Orig. pub. Cologne, 1992. (3rd ed. announced for 2006. Note also their **The calls of the frogs of Madagascar**. 2005. 3 CDs + 44pp. booklet)

3337   Goodman, Stephen M. et al. **The birds of southeastern Madagascar**. Chicago, IL, Field Museum of Natural History, 1997. (*Fieldiana zoology*, n.s. 87). 132pp. (Covers 189 spp. Review, *BABC*, 7, 2000, 79)

3338   Guibé, Jean. **Les batraciens de Madagascar.** Bonn, Zoologisches Forschungsinstitut und Museum Alexander Koenig, 1978. (Bonner zoologische Monographien, 11). 144pp. + 82pp. plates.

3339   Langrand, Olivier. **Guide to the birds of Madagascar**. New Haven, Yale University Press, 1991. 456pp. 40 col. plates. (Describes 256 spp. Review, *Ibis*, 133, 1992, 430). - - Langrand, Olivier & Sinclair, Jackie C. 'Additions and suppls. to the Madagascar avifauna', *Ostrich*, 65, 1992, 302-310.

3340   Morris, Pete & Hawkins, Frank. **Birds of Madagascar: a photographic guide**. Robertsbridge, Pica Press, 1998. 316pp. illus. (Review, *BABC*, 6, 1999, 67-69)

Botany

3341   Boiteau, Pierre et al. **Dictionnaire des noms malgaches de végétaux**. Grenoble, C. Alzieu, 1999. 4 vols. illus.

3342   Boiteau, Pierre. **Précis de matière médicale malgache**. Paris, ACCT, 1986. (Médicine traditionnelle et pharmacopie). 141pp. - - Orig. pub. as **Précis de matière médicale malgache, avec formulaire**. Antananarivo, Librairie de Madagascar, 1979. 97pp.

3343   Cabanis, Yvon et al. **Végétaux et groupements végétaux de Madagascar et des Mascareignes**. Antananarivo, Bureau pour le développement de la production agricole, 1969-70. 4 vols. 1,342pp. illus.

3344   Clifton, Richard T.F. **Madagascar's grasses: taxonomy and descriptive checklist**. Dover, Geraniaceae Group, 2004. 213pp.

3345   Clifton, Richard T.F. **Madagascar's plants: checklist of the endemic (and indigenous) flowering plants**: from data supplied by Rosemary Davies at *Index Kewensis*, modified and upgraded from material at Dover. 2nd rev.

ed. Dover, Geraniaceae Group, 2003. 384 pp. - - Orig. pub. Dover, 2002. 278pp.

3346   Conspectus of the vascular plants of Madagascar. St. Louis, MO, Missouri, Botanical Garden, 1995- . http://www.mobot.org/MOBOT/Madagasc/ (Online file of images linked to specimen and taxonomic name records in the TROPICOS database)

3347   Dorr, Laurence J. **Plant collectors in Madagascar and the Comoro Islands: a biographical and bibliographical guide to individuals and groups who have collected herbarium material of algae, bryophytes, fungi, lichens, and vascular plants in Madagascar and the Comoro Islands.** Kew, Royal Botanic Gardens, 1997. xlvi, 524pp. illus. maps. + 1 CD-ROM)

3348   Dransfield, John & Beentje, Henk. **The palms of Madagascar.** Kew, Royal Botanic Gardens, 1996. xii, 475pp. illus. (Includes 47pp. col. plates. Covers 190 spp.)

3349   Du Puy, David J.et al. **The Leguminosae of Madagascar.** Kew, Royal Botanic Gardens, 2002. x, 737pp. + 29 col. plates.

3350   **Flore de Madagascar et des Comores**, ed. Henri Humbert et al. Antananarivo, Gouvernement de Madagascar/Paris, Muséum national d'histoire naturelle, 1936- . Issued in fascs. 189 fascs. pub. to 2006. Title varies: **Flore de Madagascar (plantes vasculaires)**, 1936 to 1945; **Flore de Madagascar et des Comores (plantes vasculaires)**, 1946 to 1971. ("c. two-thirds complete by 1998", Frodin, 2001. *See* Henri Humbert, 'La *Flore de Madagascar et des Comores*: résultats et perspectives', *Adansonia*, 2, 1966, 315-317)

3351   Humbert, Henri & Darne, G.C. **Notice de la carte Madagascar.** Pondicherry, Institut français de Pondichéry, 1965. (Travaux de la section scientifique et technique, Hors série no. 6). iv, 162pp. (Commentary accompanying maps SE 38-39, SF-SG 38 and SD 38-39 in the series Carte internationale du tapis végétal et des conditions écologiques à 1:1,000,000)

3352   Koechlin, Jean, et al. **Flore et végétation de Madagascar.** Lehre, Cramer, 1974. (Flora et vegetatio mundi, 5). xiii, 687pp. illus. maps. Reissued, Lehre, 1997.

3353   Rauh, Werner. **Succulent and xerophytic plants of Madagascar.** Mill Valley, CA, Strawberry Press, 1995-1998. 2 vols. 343, 385pp.

3354 Schatz, George E. **Generic tree flora of Madagascar**. Kew, Royal Botanic Gardens/St. Louis, MO, Missouri Botanical Garden, 2001. xii, 477pp. illus. (A rev. of the mimeographed work 'Essai d'introduction à l'étude de la flore forestière de Madagascar', by R. Capuron. Antananarivo, 1957. 125pp.). - - Also pub. in French as **Flore générique des arbres de Madagascar**. Kew, Royal Botanic Gardens/St. Louis, MO, Missouri Botanical Garden, 2001. xii, 507pp.

MAURITIUS

Portal of the Government of Mauritius
http://www.gov.mu/portal/site/Mainhomepage/

HANDBOOKS

3355   Chelin, Antoine. **Maurice, une île et son passé**. Ste. Clotilde, Bibliothèque indianocéanienne/Éditions du CRI, 1989. 537pp. - - Orig. pub. as **Une île et son passé: île Maurice, 1507-1947**. Port Louis, Mauritius Printing Co., 1973. 476pp; - - **Supplément**. Quatre Bornes, Robert, 1982. iv, 100pp. (Chronology of Mauritius history)

3356   **Directory of libraries, documentation centres and bookshops in Mauritius**, comp. Yves Chan Kam Lon. Port Louis, National Library, 2000. 153pp.

3357   Favoreu, Louis. **L'île Maurice**. Paris, Berger-Levrault, 1970. (Encyclopédie politique et constitutionnelle; Série Afrique). 119pp.

3358   France. Ministère de la coopération. **Maurice: guide d'information**. Paris, 1994. (Collection guide d'information). 63pp. (Brief account of history, geography, politics, government and economics)

3359   **Historical dictionary of Mauritius**. 2nd ed., comp. Sidney Selvon. Metuchen, NJ, Scarecrow Press, 1991. (African historical dictionaries, 49). xxxii, 253pp. (Rated "good", Balay, 1996). - - Orig. pub. comp. Lindsay Rivière. Metuchen, NJ, 1982. (African historical dictionaries, 34). xxiv, 172pp. (Review, *IJAHS* 17, 1984, 527-528. Both authors were eds. of the local daily *Le Mauricien*)

3360   **Mauritius: a country study**. Available at : http://lcweb2.loc.gov/frd/cs/mutoc.html. Appropriate section of   **Indian Ocean: five island countries; area handbook series**. 3rd ed. comp. Helen Chapin Metz. Washington, DC, Library of Congress, Federal Research Division, 1995. (*See* **3230**)

3361   **Mauritius guide, 1968/69-[1969/70]**. Port Louis, Mauritius Chamber of Commerce, 1968-1969. 2 vols.

3362   **The Mauritius handbook**.   Port Louis, Ministry of Information, 1989. 130pp. + 29pp. plates. maps.

YEARBOOKS

3363   **Annuaire Minas de l'île Maurice: commerce, industrie, service.** Port Louis, Minas Co., 1989- . Latest issue in LC is for 1997/98

3364   **The business year book: a** *Business Magazine* **publication, 1993-94.** Port Louis, Business Publications Ltd., 1994-   Annual. (Issue for 1999/2000. 2000. 124pp. The same publishers also issue **The directory of financial institutions.** Port Louis, 1997- . Annual, & **The top 100 companies.** Port Louis, 1993- . Annual)

3365   G.B. Colonial Office. **[Annual reports]: Mauritius, 1845-1967.** London, 1846-1970. As **Reports: the past and present state of HM colonial possessions,** 1845-1885, **Report on the Blue Book for Mauritius [etc],** 1886-88, **Annual reports for Mauritius and Rodrigues,** 1889-1908, **Annual report for Mauritius,** 1909-19, (all as Command papers); **Colonial Office annual report,** 1920-67 (not issued 1939-45). 1964-65 issued by Commonwealth Office, 1966-67, issued by Foreign and Commonwealth Office.

3366   G.B. Colonial Office. **[Annual reports]: Rodrigues Island, 1879-1967.** London, etc., 1881-1967.   As **Reports: the past and present state of HM colonial possessions,** 1879-1885 (not pub. 1882), **Report on the Blue Book of Mauritius, Seychelles and Rodrigues,** 1886-1888 (all as Command papers). Subsequently pub. with annual report on Mauritius (*see* 1693). From 1949-66 **Annual report on Rodrigues** was pub. in Mauritius (not issued 1955-58). Issue for 1959 includes information for 1958.

3367   **International Mauritius directory.** Port Louis, P.P.L. Eds., 1983- . Latest issue in NWU is 18th ed. 2000.

3368   **Mauritius almanac and commercial handbook, 1869 [- 1939/41].** Port Louis, 1869-1939. Annual. Title varies: **Mauritius almanac and colonial register** (1869-1888); **Mauritius almanac** (1889-1919). (A very substantial work of its kind, most issues running to 400/500pp., containing historical, administrative and statistical information in addition to an institutional and commercial directory. Early issues contain texts of new laws, and cumulate 'Index to laws of Mauritius'. Numerous special articles in individual issues)

3369   **Mauritius year book, 1994** [etc.]. Port Louis, Ministry of Information, 1993- . Latest issue in LC is for 1997/98

See also **3302**

STATISTICS

3370   **Country profile: Mauritius**. London, Economist Intelligence Unit, 2003- . Annual. *Continues in part* **Country profile: Mauritius, Seychelles**. London, 1986-2002.

3371   Dinan, Monique. **Mauritius in the making: across the censuses, 1846-2000**. Port Louis, Ministry of Arts & Culture, Nelson Mandela Centre for African Culture, 2002. iv, 120pp. illus. (Decade by decade essays, 74 statistical tables)

3372   Germany. Statistisches Bundesamt. **Statistik des Auslandes: Länderberichte: Mauritius** (later **Länderbericht: Mauritius**). Wiesbaden/ Stuttgart, Metzler-Poetschel, 1987- . Irreg. Issues for 1987, 1993.

3373   IMF. **Mauritius: selected issues and statistical appendix**. Washington, DC, 2006. (Country report, 06/224). 89pp. - - Earlier eds. (Title varies) 1996 (Staff country reports, 96/1); 1998 (Staff country reports, 98/75); 1999 (Staff country report, 99/125); 2001 (Country report, 01/225);   2002 (Country report, 02/144); 2003 (Country report, 03/320); 2005 (Country report, 05/280). Full text of reports from 97/101, 1997 also available online, *see* **334**.

3374   Mauritius. Central Statistics Office. http://ncb.intnet.mu/cso.htm. (Wide variety of online statistics, including text of **Mauritius in figures, 3378**)

3375   Mauritius. Central Statistics Office. **Abstract of statistical data on Rodrigues**. Port Louis, The Office, 1995. 5 vols

3376   Mauritius. Central Statistics Office. **Annual digest of statistics**. Rose Hill, 1984- . Latest issue in NWU is vol. 48, 2003. *Continues* **Yearbook of statistics**. Rose Hill, 1946-1959. 12 vols; **Quarterly digest of statistics**. Rose Hill, 1961-1966 (First issue covers 1938 to 1951); **Bi-annual digest of statistics**. Rose Hill, 1966-1982. - - Abridged version pub. as **Statistical summary**. Rose Hill, 1979- . Annual. Latest issue in NWU is for 1996.

3377   Mauritius. Central Statistics Office.   **Digest of statistics on Rodrigues**. Port Louis, 1999- .

3378   Mauritius. Central Statistics Office. **Mauritius in figures**.   Port Louis, 1997- Annual. Vol. for 2004. Also available at http://ncb.intnet.mu cso.htm

BIOGRAPHICAL SOURCES

3379 **Dictionary of Mauritius biography/Dictionnaire de biographie mauricienne**. Port Louis, Société de l'histoire de l'Île Maurice, 1941- . Fasc. 1- . (Fasc. 56, 2003). Eds. Adolphe Toussaint (1941-1948), L.N. Regnard (1952-1972), J.R. D'Unienville (1975-). Each fasc. contains an individual A/Z sequence with articles in English and French. 'Mutatanda et addenda' issued as Suppls. 1 to 7 in fascs. 12, 16, 20, 28, 32, 36, 40. Index to fascs. 1-40 (totalling 1,223pp.) with c.1,800 names, issued 1984. "The **Dictionary** is to include notices of all who, identified with Mauritius whether by birth, adoption or temporary connection, played a part worth recording in [its] history", intro. to Fasc. 1. Signed entries with bibliographies. Major work of patient scholarship)

3380 **Mauritius who's and what's, 1976: bio-data of personalities, official structures, private sector structures, company profiles**, ed. Camille Alex Mouton et al. Port Louis, Mauriceguide, 1976. xvii, 249pp.

See also **1273**

ATLASES & GAZETTEERS

3381 **Atlas de Maurice**. Talence, Université Michel de Montaigne-Bordeaux 3/Moka, Institut Mahatma Gandhi, 1997. [154pp.] illus. 29 maps. 46cm.

3382 **Dictionnaire toponymique de l'Île Maurice: origine des noms de lieux**. Vacoas, Mauritius, Société de l'histoire de l'Île Maurice, 1997- . 3 vols. to 2003.

3383 Mauritius. Ministry of Education. **The place names of Mauritius**, comp. Peter D. Hollingworth. Port Louis, H.F. Kelly, 1961. 22pp.

3384 U.S. Board on Geographic Names. **Indian Ocean: official standard names, approved by the USBGN**. Washington, DC, 1957. (Gazetteer, 32). 53pp. (Covers Mauritius and Seychelles, also Maldives, Cocos, Christmas Island, all in a single sequence. Includes a total of 4,000 names). *See also* **3458**

EARTH SCIENCES

3385 Le Borgne, Jean. **Climatologie du sud-ouest de l'océan indien: le cas de l'Île Maurice**. Paris, ORSTOM, 1987. (Collection travaux et documents, 204). 2 vols. 676pp.

3386   Padya, B.M. **Weather and climate in Mauritius**. Moka, Mahatma Gandhi Institute, 1989. 283pp. illus.

See also **3431**

BIOLOGICAL SCIENCES

Zoology

3387   Cornic, Alain. **Fishes of Mauritius**. Rose Hill, Éditions de l'Océan indien, 1987. 336pp. illus. (Text in French and English)

3388   Michel, Claude. **Poissons de l'Île Maurice**. Rose Hill, Éditions de l'Océan indien, 1996. 137pp. illus. (Covers 74 spp.)

3389   Rountree, F.R.G. et al. 'Catalogue of the birds of Mauritius', *Mauritius Institute bulletin*, 3 (3) 1952, 155-217

3390   Terashima, Hiroaki et al. **Field guide to coastal fishes of Mauritius**. Albion, Petite Rivière, Albion Fisheries Research Centre, Ministry of Fisheries, 2001. viii, 191pp. illus. maps.

See also **3436**

Botany

3391   Adjanohoun, Edouard J. et al. **Contribution aux études ethno-botaniques et floristiques à Maurice (Îles Maurice et Rodrigues)**. Paris, ACCT, 1983. (Médicine traditionnelle et pharmacopée). 214pp. illus.

3392   **Flore des Mascareignes: la Réunion, Maurice, Rodrigues**, ed. Jean Bosser et al. Reduit, Sugar Industry Research Institute/Paris, ORSTOM, 1976- (Comp. with help of Royal Botanic Gardens, Kew. Scheduled to cover 203 families. Pub. in fascs. each covering one or more families: 55 covered to 2005)

3393   Gurib-Fakim, Ameenah & Guého, Joseph. **Plantes médicinales de l'Île Rodrigues: ... étude comparative des données ethnobotaniques avec celles des autres îles du Sud Ouest de l'Océan indien**. Réduit, University of Mauritius & Mauritius Sugar Industry Research Institute, 1995-1997. 3 vols. (*See also* A. Gurib-Fakim. **Mauritius through its medicinal plants: towards a better understanding of medicinal plants of the Indian Ocean islands**. Vacoas, Editions le Printemps, 2002. 216pp. Describes some 190 plants)

3394   Lorence, David H. 'The pteridophytes of Mauritius Island (Indian Ocean): ecology and distribution', *Botanical journal of the Linnean Society*, 76, 1978, 207-247. map; - - 'The pteridophytes of Rodrigues Island', *ibid*, 72, 1976, 269-283.

3395   Rouillard, Guy & Guého, Joseph. **Les plantes et leur histoire à l'Île Maurice**. Port Louis, authors, 1999. 752pp.

See also **3436**

MAYOTTE

HANDBOOKS

3396 Collectivité territoriale de Mayotte. **Guide des services publics et institutions de l'état à Mayotte**. Dzaoudzi, Préfecture de Mayotte, 1994. 68pp.

3397 Liszkowski, Henri Daniel. **Répertoire des sites archéologiques de Mayotte**. Saint-Médard-en-Jalles, Société archéologique et historique de Mayotte, 1997. 63pp. illus.

See also **3415**

YEARBOOKS

3398 **Annuaire professionnel de Mayotte, 1995/96-**. Dzaoudzi, Zi Kawéni, Grand public, 1995- . ?Annual

3399 France. Institut d'émission des départements d'outre-mer. **Mayotte: rapport annuel, 1999** [etc.]. Paris, 2000- . Annual. *Continues* Institut d'émission d'outre-mer. **Rapport d'activité**. Paris, 1969-1989. Annual. (From 1973 published in 5 parts, with one for Mayotte)

STATISTICS

3400 France. Institut national de la statistique et des études économiques (INSEE). **Tableau économique de Mayotte, 1998/99** [etc.]. Paris, 2000- Annual.

3401 France. Représentation du gouvernement Mayotte. Direction des affaires économiques. **Statistiques**. Mamoutzou, 1978- ?. Title varies: **Statistiques Mayotte**, (1978-1984). NWU has issues for 1984-1985.

3402 **Mayotte, 1985-1992: réalités statistiques du développement**. Mayotte, Direction de la coordination, de l'action économique et du tourisme, [1993?]. 73pp. illus.

BIOLOGICAL SCIENCES

3403 Louette, Michel. **La faune terrestre de Mayotte**. Tervuren, Musée royal de l'Afrique centrale, 1999. (Annales. Science zoologiques, 284). 247pp. illus. maps. ("Cet ouvrage... est le résultat d'une collaboration [avec] le Centre national de documentation et de recherche scientifique..., Union des Comores")

3404 Pascal, Olivier & Labat, Jean-Noel. **Plantes et forêts de Mayotte** Paris, Muséum national d'histoire naturelle, 2002. (Patrimoines naturels, 53). 108pp. illus.

RÉUNION

Préfecture de la Réunion - Portail des Services de l'Etat à la Réunion
http://www.reunion.pref.gouv.fr/

HANDBOOKS

3405 **À la découverte de la Réunion: tout l'univers réunionnais de ses origines à nos jours**, ed. Michel Albany. St. Denis, Favory, 1980-1982. 10 vols. Vol. 1. Géologie et volcanisme; vol. 2. Histoire; vol. 3. Approche géographique; vols. 4 & 5. La flore; vol. 6. La faune; vol. 7. L'homme et la langue créoles; vol. 8. Rites et croyances; vol. 9. L'art de vivre; vol. 10. L'art de dire.

3406 **Atlas linguistique et ethnographique de la Réunion**, comp. Michel Carayol & Robert Chaudenson. Paris, CNRS, 1984-1995. (Atlas linguistique de France par régions, 21). 3 vols. 845pp. (Vol. 1, 1984, maps 1 to 307; vol. 2, 1989, maps 308 to 613; vol. 3, 1995, maps 614 to 845. *See* **Présentation de l'atlas ...** Paris, CNRS, 1985. 14pp)

3407 **Chronologie de La Réunion, de la découverte à la départementalisation**, comp. Edmond Maestri & Danielle Momdedeu-Maestri. St. Denis, Université de la Réunion/Paris, Sedes, 2001. 184pp. illus. - - **Chronologie de la Réunion de la départementalisation à la loi d'orientation (1946-2001)**. St. Denis, 2001. 192pp. illus.

3408 **Dictionnaire illustré de la Réunion**, ed. René Robert et al. Paris, Diffusion culturelle de France, 1991-1992. 7 vols. illus. maps.

3409 **Encyclopédie de la Réunion**, ed. Robert Chaudenson. St. Denis, Livres-Réunion, 1980-1984. 10 vols. Vol. 1. 1980. Histoire et vie quotidienne. 105pp; vol. 2. 1980. La géographie de la Réunion. 129pp; vol. 3. 1980. La vie rurale. 145pp; vol. 4. 1980. La vie économique. 151pp; vol. 5. 1981. Les modes de vie. 149pp; vol. 6. 1980. Cultures et traditions. 133pp; vol. 7. 1980. La littérature réunionnaise. 139pp; vol. 8. 1981. La faune et la flora. 141pp; vol. 9. Choix de diapositives (col. slides). Vol. 10. 1984. Supplément.

3410 **Guide historique de l'Île de la Réunion**, comp. Gabriel Gérard. 2nd ed. Néroe, J. Owen, 1978. 437pp. illus. - - Orig. pub. as **Guide illustré de l'Île de la Réunion**. Néroe, [1970]. 413pp.

See also **3302**

STATISTICS

3411   France. Institut national de la statistique et des études économiques (INSEE). Service régional de la Réunion. **L'économie de la Réunion: revue d'information économique et sociale.** Ste. Clotilde, 1964- . 6 p.a. Title varies: **Bulletin de statistiques mensuelles** (1964-1976) ; **L'économie de la Réunion: séries statistiques mensuelles** (1977-1979)

3412   France. Institut national de la statistique et des études économiques (INSEE). Service régional de la Réunion. **Grandes entreprises de la Réunion,** ed. Yves Cheung Chin Tun. Ste. Clotilde, 1991. 126pp. (Numéro special of *l'économie de la Réunion,* 50/51, 1990/91. Reproduces data from 1987 to 1989)

3413   France. Institut national de la statistique et des études économiques (INSEE). Service régional de la Réunion. **La Réunion et ses communes,** comp. Didier Roy. St. Denis, 1994. 123pp.

3414   France. Institut national de la statistique et des études économiques (INSEE). Service régional de la Réunion. **Tableau économique de la Réunion** (*formerly* **Panorama de l'économie de la Réunion**). Ste. Clotilde, 1981- . Annual. Issued as suppl. to **L'économie de la Réunion,** *see* **3411**. *Continues* **Annuaire statistique de la Réunion, 1952/55 [-1969/72].** Ste. Clotilde, 1956-1973. Annual (irreg.); **Mémento statistique.** St. Denis, 1974-1980. Annual.

DIRECTORIES OF ORGANIZATIONS

3415   Bibliothèque universitaire de la Réunion. **Lire et se documenter à la Réunion et à Mayotte, 2005; répertoire des bibliothèques, centres de documentation, librairies, espaces presse, points de vente multimédia, éditeurs et associations, périodiques.** 3rd ed.   St. Denis, 2005. 158pp. - - Earlier eds. **Répertoire des bibliothèques, des centres et des services de documentation de la Réunion.** St. Denis, 1985. 151pp. - - **Lire et se documenter à la Réunion.** St. Denis, 1998. 146pp. (Coverage of Mayotte added with 3rd ed.)

BIOGRAPHICAL SOURCES

3416   Bruné, Paulin. **Personae Réunion, dictionnaire biographique des personnalités de l'Île de La Réunion.** St. Denis, Nymphéas, 2000. 341, 324pp. illus.

3417   Le dictionnaire biographique de la Réunion (Le "DB"), comp. Sabine Deglise et al. St. Denis, Édition CLIP/ARS Terres Créoles, 1993- . Vol. 1. 1993. 212pp; vol. 2. 1995. 215pp; vol. 3. 1998. 214pp. (Each vol. contains 100 biographies of 2pp. each, many with portraits)

3418   L'Épopeé des cinq cents premiers Réunionnais: dictionnaire du peuplement (1663-1713), comp. Jules Bernard & Bernard Monge. St. Denis, Éditions Azalées, 1994. 216pp. (Biographies of 500 persons from the first 50 years of settlement, compiled largely from French archives and the memoirs of Governor Boucher, 1702-1709)

3419   Lucas, Raoul & Serviable, Mario. Les gouverneurs de la Réunion, ancienne Île Bourbon. Ste. Clotilde, Éditions du CRI, 1987. 187pp. (Biographies of governors from 1665 to 1947, arranged chronologically. Includes portraits, tables of notable events, and much miscellaneous historical information. Complete list of governors shows that some 17 lack biographical entries)

3420   Ricquebourg, Camille L.J. Dictionnaire généalogique des familles de l'Île Bourbon (la Réunion) 1665-1890. Rosny-sur-Seine, author, 1983. 3 vols. lxi, 2,881pp. - - Orig. pub. **as Dictionnaire généalogique des familles de l'île Bourbon, 1665-1767 pendant la régie de la Compagnie des Indes**. Aix-en-Provence, Institut d'histoire des pays d'Outre-mer, 1976. xxxi, 892pp. - - Aupiais, Damien. Les immigrants Bretons à Bourbon (la Réunion) de 1665 à 1810, d'après *Le dictionnaire généalogique* .... Unpub. thesis, Université de la Réunion., n.d. 132pp. (Noted in CCFR)

ATLASES & GAZETTEERS

3421   Atlas de la Réunion. St. Denis, Université de la Réunion & Institut national de la statistique et des études économiques (INSEE), 2003. 143pp. 21 x 30cm

3422   Atlas de la santé à La Réunion, environnement, mortalité, morbidité, offre de soins. Ste. Clotilde, Direction régionale des affaires sanitaires et sociales de La Réunion, 2005. 87pp. col. maps.

3423   Atlas des départements français d'outre-mer. I: La Réunion. Paris, Centre d'études de géographie tropicale du CNRS & Institut géographique national, 1975. viii, 118 pp. text. 37 plates col. maps. illus. 58 x 48cm. (Published with the co-operation of the Université de La Réunion. Thematic maps for geology, climate, vegetation, history, population, land use, industry and communications. Base map at scale of 1:150,000 with transparent overlay showing topography and administrative divisions. Text includes b. & w. reproductions of older maps and photos, also town plans, e.g. Le Port at 1:10,000. Reviews, *Cahiers d'outre-mer*, 29, 1976, 102-105; *GJ*, 144, 1978, 376-377)

3424   Petit atlas de Bourbon. n.p., [1962]. 27pp. 25 x 30cm.

3425   Petit atlas de géopolitique de la Réunion, comp. Paul François Martinez & Jean-Michel Naria. St. Denis, Université de la Réunion, Département de géographie, [1992]. 56pp. 21 x 30cm. (To accompany the authors' **Géopolitique de La Réunion: documents et commentaries**. St. Denis, 1992, 42pp)

3426   La Réunion: atlas thématique et regional, ed. Wilfrid Bertile. St. Denis, Editions Arts graphiques modernes, [1987]. 162pp. col. maps.

See also **3245**

EARTH SCIENCES

3427   Atlas climatique de la Réunion, ed. Olivier Soler. Ste. Clotilde, Meteo-France Direction interrégionale, Bureau d'étude climatologique (Réunion), 1997. 79pp. illus. maps.

3428   Atlas de l'environnement, Île de La Réunion, comp. Christian Léger & Thierry Sabathier. Paris, Ministère de l'aménagement du territoire et de l'environnement, 2002. Var. paging. 32 x 47cm

3429   Atlas des espaces naturels du littoral de l'Île de la Réunion. St. Denis, Direction départementale de l'équipement & Université de la Réunion, 1992. 2 vols. Vol. 1. Atlas. 138pp.; vol. 2. Document d'accompagnement. 81pp.

3430   Atlas hydrogéologique de la Réunion, ed. L. Stieltjes. St. Denis, Service géologique régionale de l'Océan indien, Bureau de recherche géologiques et minières (BRGM), 1986. 24pp. col. maps. 32 x 47cm.

3431   Montaggioni, Lucien & Nativel, Pierre. **La Réunion, Île Maurice: géologie et aperçus biologiques, plantes et animaux**. Paris, Masson, 1988. (Guides géologiques régionaux). 192pp. illus.

3432   Raunet, Michel. **Le milieu physique et les sols de l'Île de la Réunion: conséquences pour la mise en valeur agricole**. Montpellier, CIRAD, 1991. 438pp. illus. maps.

3433   Rivals, Pierre. **Histoire géologique de l'Île de la Réunion**. St. Denis, Azalées, 1989. 400pp. illus

3434   Robert, René. **Climat et hydrologie à la Réunion: étude typologique, étude régionale des pluies, de l'alimentation, et de l'écoulement**. St. Denis, Université de Réunion, 1986. viii, 438pp. illus. maps.

BIOLOGICAL SCIENCES

Zoology

3435   Barré, Nicolas & Barau, A. **Les oiseaux de la Réunion**. 2nd ed. Rev. Nicolas Barré & Christian Jouanin. Paris, Les Éditions du Pacifique, 1996. 208pp. col. plates. (Covers 155 spp. Reviews, *BABC*, 4, 1997, 137; *Ibis*, 140, 1998, 186-187). - - Orig. pub. St. Denis, Imprimerie Arts Graphiques Modernes, 1982. 196pp.

3436   Drivas, Jean & Jay, Maurice. **Coquillages de la Réunion et de l'Île Maurice**. Singapore, Éditions du Pacifique, 1988. 159pp. illus.

3437   Keith, Philippe et al. **Atlas des poissons et des crustacés d'eau douce de Réunion**. Paris, Muséum national d'histoire naturelle, 1999. (Patrimoines naturels, 39). 136pp. col. illus. col. maps.

3438   Probst, Jean-Michel. **Animaux de la Réunion: guide d'identification des oiseaux, mammifères, reptiles et amphibiens**. Ste. Marie, Azalées, 1997. 167pp. col. illus.

Botany

3439   Cadet, Louis J. Thérésien. **Fleurs et plantes de la Réunion et de l'Île Maurice**. [15th ed]. Papeete, Éditions du Pacifique, 2000. 130pp. - - Orig. pub. Papeete, 1981. 130pp.

3440   Cadet, Louis J. Thérésien. **La végétation de l'Île de la Réunion: étude phytographique et phytosociologique**. St. Denis, Cazal, 1980. 312pp. + 8pp. plates. illus.

3441   Detienne, P. & Jacquet, P. **Identification des bois de l'Île de la Réunion**. Nogent-sur-Marne, CIRAD, 1993. 84pp. illus.

3442 Lavergne, Roger & Véra, R. **Étude ethnobotanique des plantes utilisées dans la pharmacopée traditionelle à la Réunion**. Paris, ACCT, 1989. (Médicine traditionnelle et pharmacopée). 236pp. illus. maps.

3443 Lavergne, Roger, ed. **Fleurs de Bourbon**. St. Denis, Impr. Cazal, 1980-1990. 10 vols.

3444 Lavergne, Roger. **Tisaneurs et plantes médicinales indigènes de l'Île de la Réunion**. Livry-Gargan, Orphie, 1990. 521pp. illus. (Reprinted. Ste. Clotilde, 2001)

See also **3392**

SEYCHELLES

Virtual Seychelles: official Web site of the Republic of the Seychelles
http://www.virtualseychelles.sc/

HANDBOOKS & YEARBOOKS

3445   G.B. Colonial Office. **[Annual reports]: Seychelles, 1850-1968**.
London, 1851-1970. As **Reports: the past and present state of HM colonial
possessions**, 1850-1886 (not pub. 1851-54, 1857, 1862, 1864, 1867-69, 1872-73,
1875), from 1887 to 1898 pub. with annual report on Mauritius (*see* **3365**),
Annual report for Seychelles, 1898-1919 (all as Command papers); **Colonial
Office annual report,** 1920-68   (not pub. 1938-1945). From 1949-1950 pub.
biennially. 1963 & 1964 issued by the Commonwealth Office. 1965 & 1966-1967
& 1968 issued by Foreign and Commonwealth Office.

3446   Répertoire culturel: Seychelles. Paris, Paris, ACCT, [?1985]
(Inventaire des activités, etc. des pays membres de l'ACCT).   95pp. illus.
maps.

3447   Seychelles. Central Statistical Office. **Seychelles handbook**. Mahé,
1976.   iv,   159pp.   (Covers   topography,   population,   towns,   trade,
communications, and includes extensive statistical information)

3448   Seychelles: a country study. Available at : http://lcweb2.loc.gov/
frd/cs/sctoc.html. Appropriate section of **Indian Ocean: five island
countries; area handbook series**. 3rd ed. comp. Helen Chapin Metz.
Washington, DC, Library of Congress, Federal Research Division, 1995. (*See*
3230)

See also **3302**

STATISTICS

3449   Country profile: Seychelles. London, Economist Intelligence Unit,
2003- . Annual. *Continues in part* **Country profile: Mauritius, Seychelles**.
London, 1986-2002.

3450   France. Ministère de la coopération. Service des études économiques
et questions internationales. **Seychelles, mai 1978: dossier d'information
économique**. Paris, 1978. 79, 80pp.

3451 Germany. Statistisches Bundesamt. **Statistik des Auslandes: Länderberichte: Seschellen** (later **Länderbericht: Seschellen**). Wiesbaden/ Stuttgart, Metzler-Poetschel, 1984- . Irreg. Issues for 1984, 1986, 1989, 1993.

3452 Seychelles. Statistics Division [etc.]. **Quarterly statistical bulletin**. Victoria, 1975-1982.

3453 Seychelles. Statistics Division [etc.]. **Seychelles in figures**. Victoria, 1986- . Annual. Latest issue in LC is 2004 which is also available online at http://www.seychelles.net/misdstat/

3454 Seychelles. Statistics Division [etc.]. **Statistical abstract**. Victoria, 1977- Annual. Latest issue in NWU is 2002.

ATLASES & GAZETTEERS

3455 **Atlas for Seychelles**. New ed., comp. A. Low-Nam & D. Lebon. London, Macmillan Education for Ministry of Education & Culture, Seychelles, 1983. 41pp. - - Orig. pub. London, 1977. 33pp.

3456 Jorre de St. Jorre, Danielle & Lionnet, Guy. **Esquisse d'un dictionnaire toponymique des Seychelles**. Victoria, Coopération française, n.d. [?1997]. 175pp.

3457 **Petit atlas des îles Seychelles**, ed. Bernard Rémy & Mario Serviable. St. Denis, Éditions du Centre de recherche india-océanique, 1986. 57pp. 21 x 30cm

3458 U.S. Board on Geographic Names. **Indian Ocean: official standard names approved by the USBGN**. Washington, DC, 1957. (Gazetteer, 32). 53pp. (Includes Mauritius and Seychelles, with Maldives, Cocos and Christmas Island all in a single sequence of 4,000 names). *See also* **3384**

EARTH SCIENCES

3459 **Atlas de l'environnement côtier des îles granitiques de l'archipel des Seychelles**, comp. Virginie Cazes-Duvat. St. Denis, Université de la Réunion/Montpellier, CIRAD, 2001. 88pp.

3460 Baker, Brian Howard. **Geology and mineral resources of the Seychelles archipelago**. Nairobi, Geological Survey of Kenya, 1963. (Memoir, 3). vii, 140pp. illus. maps (some col.)

3461   Piggott, Charles John. **A soil survey of Seychelles**. Tolworth, Land Resources Division, Directorate of Overseas Surveys, 1968. (Technical bulletin, 2). 89pp. illus. maps.

3462   Stoddart, David Ross, ed. **Biogeography and ecology of the Seychelles islands**. The Hague, Junk, 1984. (Monographiae biologicae, 55). xii, 691pp.

BIOLOGICAL SCIENCES

Zoology

3463   Gardner, Andrew Somerville. **Herpetofauna of the Seychelles**. London, British Herpetological Society, 1986. (Bulletin, 16)

3464   Jarrett, Alan G. **Marine shells of the Seychelles**. Cambridge, Carole Green Publishing, 2000. xiv, 149pp. illus.

3465   Legrand, Henri. **Lépidoptères des îles Seychelles et d'Aldabra**. Paris, Editions du Muséum, 1965. (Mémoires du Muséum d'histoire naturelle. Série A: Zoologie. n.s. 37). 210pp. + 16pp. plates.

3466   Nussbaum, Ronald. **Amphibians of the Seychelles islands**. Ann Arbor, MI, University of Michigan, 1981. 59pp. illus.

3467   Penny, Malcolm. **The birds of Seychelles and the outlying islands**. London, Collins, 1984. 160pp. - - Orig. pub. London, 1974. 160pp. 12 plates. (Covers 73 spp. in detail. Includes Aldabra. Review, *Ibis*, 117, 1975, 541-542)

3468   Skerrett, Adrian & Bullock, Ian. **Field guide to the birds of the Seychelles**. London, Christopher Helm, 2001. 320pp. 53 col. plates. (Covers all 242 recorded spp. with special detail of the 66 breeding spp. Reviews, *Auk*, 119, 2002, 877; *BABC*, 8, 2001, 70; *Ibis*, 143, 2001, 697)

3469   Smith, James L.B. & Smith, Margaret Mary. **The fishes of Seychelles**. 2nd ed. Grahamstown, Rhodes University, J.L.B. Smith Department of Ichthyology, 1969. vi, 223pp. illus. - - Orig. pub. Grahamstown, 1963. viii, 215pp.

Botany

3470 Adjanohoun, Edouard J. et al. **Contribution aux études ethnobotaniques et floristiques aux Seychelles**. Paris, ACCT, 1983. (Médecine traditionnelle et pharmacopée). 170pp. illus.

3471 Friedmann, Francis. **Fleurs et arbres des Seychelles**. Paris, ORSTOM, 1986. 196pp. col. illus. map. (Lists 1,139 spp.)

3472 Friedmann, Francis. **Flore des Seychelles: Dicotylédones**. Paris, ORSTOM for Institut français de recherche scientifique pour le développement en coopération, 1994. 663pp. illus.

3473 Müller-Ebeling, Claudia. **Heilpflanzen der Seychellen: ein Beitrag zur kreolischen Volksheilkunde**. Berlin, Verlag für Wissenschaft und Bildung, 1989. 92pp. illus. (Medicinal plants)

3474 Robertson, Stuart Andrew. **Flowering plants of Seychelles (an annotated check list of Angiosperms and Gymnosperms)**. Kew, Royal Botanic Gardens, 1989. xvi, 327pp. (Checklist of 1,150 spp. with illus. of some 200)

LUSOPHONE SOUTHERN AFRICA

ANGOLA

Official Web site of the Republic of Angola
http://www.angola.org/ (Not accessible, September 2006)

HANDBOOKS

3475 **Angola: a country study**. 2nd ed. comp. Irving Kaplan et al. Washington, DC, 1979. xxiii, 286pp. Also available at: http://lcweb2.loc.gov/ frd/cs/aotoc.html . - - Orig. pub. as **Area handbook for Angola**, comp. Allison B. Herrick et al. Washington, DC, U.S. Department of Defense, 1967. xii, 439pp.

3476 **Angola: tempos novos**. Luanda, Edipress, 1992. 139pp. illus. (Text in Portuguese, English & French. Covers history, topography, economics and political and social life)

3477 Gersdorff, Ralph von. **Angola: Portugiesisch-Guinea, São Tomé und Príncipe, Kap Verde-Inseln, Spanisch-Guinea**. Bonn, Schroeder for Deutsche Afrika-Gesellschaft, 1960. (Die Länder Afrikas, 23). 165pp. (Principal emphasis on Angola: other territories have only 18pp. between them)

3478 Gonzaga, Norberto. **Angola: pequena monografia**. Lisbon, Agência Geral do Ultramar, 1968. 363pp. illus. maps. - - Orig. pub. Lisbon, 1965. 357pp. (One of a series of standard handbooks on Portuguese territories). - - Also pub. in English as **Angola: a brief survey**. Lisbon, 1967. 213pp. illus. - - Also pub. in French as **Angola, petite monographie**. Lisbon, 1968. 280pp.

3479 **Historical dictionary of Angola**. New ed., comp. W. Martin James. Lanham, MD, Scarecrow Press, 2004. (African historical dictionaries, 92). iv, 228pp. (Reviews, *ARD*, 99, 2005, 51-54; *Choice*, 42, 2004, 466, which makes point that it is very much a suppl. to, rather than a replacement for earlier eds.). - - Orig. pub. comp. Phyllis Martin. Metuchen, NJ, 1980. (African historical dictionaries, 26). xxi, 174pp. (Review, *Africana journal*, 9, 1980, 359); - - 2nd ed., comp. Susan Broadhead. Metuchen, NJ, 1992. (African historical dictionaries, 52). xlv, 296pp (Review, *African affairs*, 92, 1993, 315; *Garcia de Orta, Série Geografia*, 15(2) 1996, 136-140. Rated "excellent", Balay, 1996)

3480 Kuder, Manfred & Moehlig, Wilhelm J.G. **Angola: Naturraum, Wirtschaft, Bevölkerung, Kultur, Zeitgeschichte und Entwicklungs-**

perspektiven. Munich, Weltforum Verlag, 1994. (Afrika-Studien, 122). 382pp. maps.

3481 Posthumus, Bram. **Angola: mensen, politiek, economie, cultuur.** Amsterdam, Koninklijk Instituut voor de Tropen/The Hague, Novib, 2003. (Landenreeks). 74pp. illus. maps

3482 Simpkins, Gregory B. **Angola: a chronology of major political developments, February 1961-September 1996.** Alexandria, VA, Institute for Democratic Strategies, 1996. 40pp. illus. map. - - Orig. pub. as **Angola: a chronology of major political developments, February 1961-January 1988.** Washington, DC, Angola Peace Fund, 1988. 24pp.

See also **1253, 2695, 2755**

YEARBOOKS

3483 **Angola: informacão geral. Anuário, 1957/58-[?1962/63]**. Luanda, Edições ABC, 1957-?1963. Last issue in NWU is 1962/63.

3484 **Anuário Angola, 1998/99** [etc.]. Lisbon, Camâra de Comércio e Indústria Portugal-Angola, 1998- . Issue for 1999/2000 in Biblioteca Nacional, Lisbon

3485 **Anuário comercial e industrial de Angola, 1950/54** [etc.]. Luanda, Editorial Ultramar, 1955- . ?Annual.

3486 **Anuário de Angola: indíce económico, 1938/39-[?1940/41]**. Luanda, 1938-1940. Last issue in NWU is for 1940/41.

STATISTICS

3487 Angola. Direcção dos Serviços de Estatística [etc.]. **Anuário estatístico/ Annuaire statistique, 1933 [-1973]**. Luanda, 1935-1974. Annual. Text in Portuguese and French. Summary version published as **Angola: informações estatísticas** (1970-?1989). Irreg.

3488 Angola. Direcção dos Serviços de Estatística [etc.]. **Boletim mensal de estatística**. Luanda, 1945-1973. Monthly. *Continues* **Boletim trimestral de estatística**. Luanda, 1933-1934, 1942-1943. Quarterly.

3489   Angola. Instituto Nacional de Estatística. **Angola em números.** Luanda, 1990/91 - . RHL has issue for 1997

3490   Angola. Instituto Nacional de Estatística. **Perfil estatístico económico e social de Angola, 1988-1991.** Luanda, 1992. 155pp.

3491   Country profile: Angola. London, Economist Intelligence Unit, 1993- . Annual. *Continues in part* **Country profile: Angola, São Tomé & Príncipe.** London, 1986-1992.

3492   Germany. Statistisches Bundesamt. **Statistik des Auslandes: Länderberichte: Angola** (later **Länderbericht: Angola**). Wiesbaden/Stuttgart, Metzler-Poetschel, 1984- . Irreg. Issues for 1984, 1988, 1989, 1991, 1993.

3493   IMF. **Angola: selected issues and statistical appendix.** Washington, DC, 2005. (Country report, 05/125). 82pp. - - Earlier eds. (title varies) 1999 (Staff country report, 99/25); 2003 (Country report, 03/292). Full text also available online, *see* **334.**

3494   World Bank. **Angola: an introductory economic review.** Washington, DC, 1991. 393pp. (Extensive statistics)

DIRECTORIES OF ORGANIZATIONS

3495   Angola investment and business guide. Washington, International Business Publications, USA, 2003. 1 vol. var. pp.

3496   Angola; Namíbia: guia. Lisbon, Associação Industrial Portuguesa, 1993. 152, 23pp.

3497   Directório dos centros de documentação e informação da Républica Popular de Angola. Luanda, Ministério de Industria, Centro de Informação Industrial, 1988. 27pp. (Detailed information on 19 collections)

3498   Doling, Tim. **Angola : arts directory.** London, Visiting Arts, 1999. 60pp

3499   Guia industrial de Angola; Edição única comemorativa do 30° aniversário da Associação Industrial de Angola. Luanda, Associação Industrial de Angola, 1960. 740pp. illus

See also **2824**

BIOGRAPHICAL SOURCES

3500   Parreira, Adriano. **Dicionário de biografias angolanas (Seculos XV-XVII).** Luanda, Edicões Kulonga, 2003. (História de Angola, 1). 254 pp. (Noted on PORBASE)

ATLASES & GAZETTEERS

3501   **Angola (1,246,700 kms²) e os seus 15 distritos.** Lisbon, Edições Spal, 1967. 16pp. (Includes 15 b. & w. maps, one for each administrative district). - - Orig. pub. Lisbon, 195?. 25pp.

3502   **Atlas da Lusofonia. Vol. 2, Angola,** ed. Pedro Cardoso et al. Lisbon, Préfacio, 2004. 86pp. illus. maps. (Col. maps and illus. statistical tables, bibliographical references)

3503   **Atlas geográfico: República Popular de Angola.** Luanda, Angola. Ministério da Educação e Cultura & Esselte Map Service, Stockholm, 1982- . Vol. 1. 1982. 49pp. 33 x 45cm. ?No more pub. (Thematic maps, mostly at 1:6M. 21 maps cover Angola, 17 the rest of Africa and the world).

3504   Milheiros, Mário. **Índice histórico-corográfico de Angola.** Luanda, Instituto de Investigação Científica de Angola, 1972. 291pp. (Historical gazetteer, citing references to legislation under which administrative divisions were created. Some lengthy entries, e.g. Luanda, 3pp)

3505   Parreira, Adriano. **Dicionário glossográfico e toponímico da documentação sobre Angola séculos XV-XVII.** Lisbon, Editorial Estampa, 1990. (Imprensa Universitária, 79). 250pp. (A general glossary and a glossary of place-names with references to their occurrence in the literature)

3506   Tio Antonito (*pseud.* i.e. de António Coxito Granado). **Dicionário corográfico comercial de Angola.** 4th ed. Luanda Ed. Antonito, 1959. lxvi, 847pp. illus. maps. (Includes list of 1,200+ localities). - - Orig. pub. Luanda, A.C. Granado, 1946. 406pp; - - 2nd ed. Luanda, Tip. Mondego, 1949. 470pp; - - 3rd ed. Luanda, Ed. Antonito, 1955. 636pp.

3507   U.S. Board on Geographic Names. **Gazetteer of Angola.** 2nd ed. Washington, DC, 1986. 549pp. (25,500 names taken from maps at 1:1,500,000). - - Orig. pub. as **Angola. Official standard names approved by the USBGN.** Washington, DC, 1956. (Gazetteer, 20). iii, 234pp. (19,200 names from maps at 1:1,500,000) *See also* **1454.**

EARTH SCIENCES

3508   Angola. Serviço Meteorológico. **Algumas cartas climáticas de Angola na escala 1:10,000,000.** Luanda, [1970?]. 3, 52pp. (Atlas)

3509   Botelho da Costa, J.V. & Azevedo, A.L. **Solos de Angola: contribuição para o seu estudo.** Lisbon, Junta de Investigações do Ultramar, 1953. (Mémorias. Série de pedologia tropical, 1). xvi, 374pp. illus. maps.

3510   **Carta geral dos solos de Angola,** comp. Missão de Pedologia de Angola e Moçambique. Lisbon, Junta de Investigações do Ultramar, 1959-1962. (Memórias, 2ª série, 9, 27, 45, 57, 63, 65, 69, 71). 8 vols. (One vol. for each province, containing soil maps at 1:1M, with accompanying description of soil types, climate and vegetation)

3511   Diniz, A. Castanheira. **Caracteristicas mesológicas de Angola**: descrição e correlação dos aspectos fisiográficos, dos solos e da vegetação das zonas agricolas angolanas. Nova Lisboa, Missão de Inquéritos Agrícolas de Angola, 1973. (Série Estudos, Missão de Inquéritos Agrícolas de Angola, 2). ix, 482pp. (Includes summaries in French and English)

3512   Kuder, Manfred. **Angola: eine geographische, soziale und wirtschaftliche Landeskunde.** Darmstadt, Wissenschaftliche Buchgesellschaft, 1971. (Wissenschaftliche Länderkunden, 6). xx, 290pp. illus.

3513   Mouta, Fernando. **Lexique stratigraphique international, 4, Afrique, 7b: Angola.** Paris, CNRS, 1957. 55pp.

3514   Mouta, Fernando. **Notícia explicativa do esboço geológico de Angola (1:2,000,000).** Lisbon, Oficinas gráficas de Ramos, Afonso & Moita, 1954. 148pp. + 13 plates. illus. maps.

BIOLOGICAL SCIENCES

Zoology

3515   Crawford-Cabral, J. & Mesquita, Luis Mario. **Indice toponímico de colheitas zoólogicas em Angola (Mammalia, Aves, Reptilia, Amphibia).** Lisbon, Instituto de Investigaçao Cientifica, 1989. (Estudios e documentos, 151). 206pp.

3516   Da Silva, S. Newton. **A grande fauna selvagem de Angola**. Luanda, Direcção Provincial dos Serviços de Veterinária, 1970. 153pp. illus.

3517   Dean, William Richard J. **The birds of Angola**. Tring, British Ornithologists' Union, 2000. (BOU Checklist, 18). 433pp. 16pp. col. plates. (Lists 915 spp. Reviews, *BABC*, 8, 2001, 67; *Ibis*, 143, 2001, 332-333; *Malimbus*, 23, 2001, 119-120). - - Dean, W.J.R. 'New records and amendments', *Bulletin of the British Ornithologists' Club*, 122, 2002, 180-185.

3518   Gofas, Serge et al. **Conchas e moluscos de Angola**. Luanda, Universidade Agonstinho Neto, 1984. 144pp. illus. (Text in Portuguese and French)

3519   Hill, John Eric & Carter, T. Donald. **The mammals of Angola, Africa**. New York, American Museum of Natural History, 1941. (*Bulletin of the American Museum of Natural History*, 78). 212pp. 17 plates.

3520   Laurent, Raymond F. **Reptiles et amphibiens de l'Angola: troisième contribution**. Lisbon, Companhia de Diamantes de Angola, 1964. (Publicações culturais, 67). 165pp. illus.

3521   Pinto, António Augusto da Rosa et al. **Ornitologia de Angola**. Lisbon, Instituto de Investigação Científica Tropical (IICT), 1983- . Vol. 1. cxxxvi, 696pp. 48 col. plates. Non-passerines. (Covers 442 spp. Introduction also in English. Review, *Ibis*, 128, 1986, 438-439) ? No more pub.

3522   Poll, Max. **Contribution à la faune ichthyologique de l'Angola**. Lisbon, Companhia de Diamantes de Angola, 1967. (Publicações culturais, 75). 381pp. illus.

3523   Ribeiro, Henrique & Ramos, Helena da Cunha. **Guia ilustrado para a identifição dos mosquitos de Angola (*Diptera: Culcidae*)**. Lisbon, Sociedade Portuguesa de Entomologia, 1995. (Suppl. ao *Boletim*, 4). 287pp.

Botany

3524   Barbosa, Luis Augusto Grandvaux. **Carta fitogeográfica de Angola**. Luanda, Instituto de Investigação Científica de Angola, 1970. xii, 323pp. (Vegetation map and description of each phytographic zone. An update of John Gossweiler & F.A. Mendonça. **Carta fitogeográfica de Angola**: memória descritiva dos principais tipos de vegetação da colónia, etc. ... segundo a nomenclatura de Rübel. Lisbon, Governo Geral de Angola, 1939. 242pp. illus. Issued together with 'Carta fitogeográfica de Angola' 1939, at 1:2M)

3525   Conspectus florae angolensis, ed. Arthur Wallis Exell et al. Coimbra, Instituto Botânico de Coimbra etc. 1937-70, Vols. 1-4(1). *Then* ed. L. Fernando et al. Lisbon, Junta de Investigações do Ultramar, etc., 1977- . issued in fascs. (Complementary to **Flora Zambesiaca**, *see* **1278**. Vols. 1 to 4 prepared with the co-operation of British Museum (Natural History). Detailed flora, of which only 3 fascs. have appeared since the change in pub. pattern in 1977, the most recent in 1993, when the work was estimated to be some 55% complete. "Future remains uncertain", Frodin, 2001, p.512)

3526   Costa, Esperanca et al. **A checklist of Angola grasses/Checklist das Poaceae de Angola**. Pretoria, SABONET, 2004. (SABONET report, 28). vi, 25pp. illus. maps. (Produced by Luanda Herbarium, Universidade Agostinho Neto)

3527   Gossweiler, John. **Nomes indígenas de plantas de Angola**. Luanda, Agronomia Angolana, 1953. ix, 587pp. + 77pp. plates

3528   Santos, Romeu Mendes dos. **Plantas úteis de Angola; contribução iconográfica**. Luanda, Instituto de Investigação Cientifica de Angola, 1967-1989. 2 vols. 67, 78pp.

3529   Vieira, M. F. da Motta. **Apontamentos sobre as principais culturas praticadas em Angola: dicionário de culturas**. Luanda, Organizaões Lusáfrica (Angola), 1964. 239pp.

See also **1278**

MOZAMBIQUE

Governo de Moçambique http://www.govmoz.gov.mz/

HANDBOOKS

3530 Alberto, M. Simöes & Toscano, Francisco A. **O Oriente africano português: síntese cronológica da história de Moçambique.** Lourenço Marques, Minerva Central, 1942. 303pp.

3531 Boléo, José de Oliveira. **Moçambique.** Lisbon, Agência Geral do Ultramar, 1951. (Monografias dos territórios do Ultramar). 562pp. illus. maps. (Sections for geography, flora and fauna, ethnology, history, administration, economics and social life. Brief summaries of each chapter in English and French)

3532 Boléo, José de Oliveira. **Moçambique: pequena monografia.** 2nd ed. Lisbon, Agência Geral do Ultramar 1966. 204pp. - - Orig. pub. Lisbon, 1961. 166pp. illus. (Standard handbook format covering topography, history, natural resources, administration, etc. Basically a summary version of his 1951 work, see **3531**. 2nd ed. has chronological list of 'grands-capitains, gouverneurs, etc.' 1505-1964). - - Also pub. in English as **Mozambique: a brief survey**. Lisbon, 1967. 157pp. - - Also pub. in French as **Mozambique: petite monographie**. Lisbon, 1967. 204pp.

3533 Bossema, Wim. **Mozambique: mensen, politiek, economie, cultuur.** Amsterdam, Koninklijk Instituut voor de Tropen/The Hague, Novib, 1995. (Landenreeks). 74pp. illus. maps.

3534 Gavrilov, N.I. et al. **Narodnaia Respublika Mozambik.** Moscow, Akademiia nauk, Institut Afriki, 1986. 239pp. illus.

3535 Gersdorff, Ralph von. **Moçambique.** Bonn, Schroeder for Deutsche Afrika-Gesellschaft, 1958. (Die Länder Afrikas, 14). 136pp.

3536 **Historical dictionary of Mozambique.** [Rev. ed.] comp. Mario Azevedo et al. Lanham, MD, Scarecrow Press, 2003. (African historical dictionaries, 88). xx, 302pp. (Reviews, *ARBA*, 35, 2004, 212-213; *Choice*, 41, 2004, 1640, "most current & comprehensive [work] available in English") - - Orig. pub. Metuchen, NJ, 1991. (African historical dictionaries, 47). xxx, 250pp. (Reviews, *Choice*, 29, 1992, 1514; "writing is excellent"; *IJAHS*, 26, 1993, 215-217. Rated "poor", Balay, 1996)

3537   Hoile, David. **Mozambique, 1962-1993: a political chronology.** London, Mozambique Institute, 1994. viii, 234 pp.

3538   Mozambique. Instituto Nacional de Estatística. **Situação linguística de Moçambique: dados do II recenseamento geral da população e habitação de 1997,** ed. Gregório Firmino. Maputo, 2001. 108pp.

3539   **Mozambique: a country study,** comp. Harold D. Nelson et al. Washington, DC, U.S. Department of Defense, 1984. 342pp. illus. maps. - - Orig. pub. as **Area handbook for Mozambique,** comp. Allison B. Herrick et al. Washington, DC, 1969. xiv, 351pp. maps; - - 2nd ed. comp. Irving Kaplan et al. Washington, DC, 1977. xx, 240pp. maps. (1st ed. remains the most detailed, and useful for information on the country at the end of the colonial period)

3540   **Mozambique: the key-sectors of the economy,** comp. Michele Miech-Chatenay. Paris, Banque d'information et de documentation de l'Océan indien, 1986. (An *Indian Ocean newsletter* publication). 300pp. illus. maps. (Also pub. in French. Covers background topography and politics, economics and finance, trade, energy resources, transport, agriculture and fisheries. Numerous statistical tables. Index of companies)

3541   Rafael, Saul Dias. **Dicionário toponímico, histórico, geográfico e etnográfico de Moçambique.** Maputo, Arquivo Histórico de Moçambique, 2001. (Série instrumentos de pesquisa, 1). v, 692pp. (Arranged A/Z in two columns. The vast majority of entries are for geographical entities, which provide latitude, longitude and grid references to the 1:250,000 and 1:50,000 map series. Most entries are very short other than those for major cities, e.g. Lourenço Marques, 55 lines, and major features, e.g. Limpopo river, 28 lines. No entries for individuals or events)

See also **2748, 2755**

YEARBOOKS

3542   **Anuário de Moçambique,** comp. A. de Sousa Ribeiro. Lourenço Marques, Rep. Tecnica de Estatística, 1908, 1917, 1940. 3 issues. (Recorded by M. Costa. **Bibliografia geral de Moçambique,** Lisbon, 1946 and by Biblioteca Nacional, Lisbon as a separate pub. from **3543**)

3543   **Anuário de Moçambique.** Lourenço Marques, A.W. Bayly, 1914-1978/79 (?) Annual. 53 vols. Title varies: **Anuário de Lourenço Marques** (1914-1947); **Anuário da Colónia de Moçambique** (1948-1950/51); **Anuário da Província de Moçambique** (1951/52-1970/71); **Anuário do Estado de**

Moçambique (1971/72); **Anuário de Moçambique** (1973/74-1978/79?). 53rd ed. 1978/79. (Detailed commercial and administrative directory, which also includes considerable historical and topographical data. The Portuguese language companion to the **Mozambique directory/Delagoa directory** below. Sources disagree regarding the separate identities and dates of publication of the Mozambique directories. Details for items **3543** and **3548** largely follow Colin Darch. **Mozambique**. Oxford, Clio, 1980. Costa, M. **Bibliografia geral de Moçambique**. Lisbon, 1946 lists **3544** (not in Darch) as a separate item, while LC suggests it as the first issue of **3543**. S.J. Gowan, **Portuguese-speaking Africa, 1900-1979: vol. 2, Mozambique**. Braamfontein, 1982, appears to conflate **3543** and **3548** into a single publication.).

3544   Anuário de Moçambique, 1894. Lourenço Marques, 1895. (Comp. J. da Graça Correia e Lança. (Costa, M. **Bibliografia geral de Moçambique**, Lisbon, 1946, records this as a separate work; LC suggests it is the first issue of **Anuário de Lourenço Marques** (later **Anuário de Moçambique** above).

3545   Directório comercial, 1991/92- . Maputo, Câmara de Comércio de Moçambique, 1992- . ?Annual. (1992 issue. 175pp. General information, with English summary, statistics, directory of commercial firms)

3546   Directório comercial de Moçambique. Maputo, Directório commercial, 2000- . Annual. Issue 5, 2004.

3547   Guia económico de Moçambique: edição oficial, 1951/52 [etc.]. Lisbon, Tipografia Astoria/Lourenço Marques, Junta de Exploração, 1951- ? Annual. Issues 3, 1953/54, 5, 1956/57 in NWU. (Includes commercial directory and statistics)

3548   Mozambique directory. Lourenço Marques, A.W. Bayly, 1899-1952. Annual. 51 issues. Title varies: **Delagoa directory** (1899-?1942); **Lourenço Marques directory** (?1943-1947). (51st ed.1950/51(1952). xxii, 902pp. Extremely detailed survey for Mozambique as a whole, followed by sections for Lourenço Marques and each district: civil and military lists, commercial directory, statistics, historical, social and topographic information)

See also **1015, 1267, 2761, 2762, 2778**

STATISTICS

Bibliographies

3549 Darch, Colin. 'Notas sobre fontes estatísticas oficias referentes à economia colonial moçambicana: uma crítica geral', *Estudos Moçambicanos*, 4, 1983-85, 103-125 (Valuable comprehensive study)

3550 **Principais fontes de informação estatística sobre aspectos sociais, económicos e demográficos da população de Moçambique**. Maputo, Direcção Nacional de Estatística, 1991. 55pp. (Detailed bibliographical guide to sources)

General

3551 IMF. **Republic of Mozambique: selected issues and statistical appendix**. Washington, DC, 2005. (Country report, 05/311). 72pp. - - Earlier eds. (title varies) 1995 (Staff country report, 95/70); 2001 (Country report, 01/25); 2002 (Country report, 02/59); 2004 (Country report, 04/51). Full text of reports from 1997 also available online, *see* **334**.

3552 Mozambique. Direcção Nacional de Estatística. **Informação estatística, 1975-1984**. Maputo, 1985. 96pp. (The first major compilation of statistics to be published after independence)

3553 Mozambique. Instituto Nacional de Estatística. http://www.ine.gov.mz/

3554 Mozambique. Instituto Nacional de Estatística. **Caderno de informação rápida, Moçambique 1996**. Maputo, 1997. 49pp. illus., map.

3555 Mozambique. Instituto Nacional de Estatística. **Estatísticas básicas de Moçambique, 2002: quanto?** Maputo, 2002. 74pp.illus. - - Orig. pub. Maputo, 2001. 57pp. illus.

Bulletins & yearbooks

3556 **Country profile: Mozambique**. London, Economist Intelligence Unit, 1986- Annual

3557 Germany. Statistisches Bundesamt. **Statistik des Auslandes: Länderberichte: Mosambik** (later **Länderbericht: Mosambik**). Wiesbaden/Stuttgart, Metzler-Poetschel, 1985- . Irreg. Issues for 1985, 1987, 1989.

3558   Mozambique. Direcção dos Serviços de Estatística [etc.]. **Anuário estatístico/Annuaire statistique 1926/28** [etc.]. Lourenço Marques, 1929-1976. Annual. (Last issue covers statistics of 1973)

3559   Mozambique. Direcção dos Serviços de Estatística [etc.]. **Boletim económico e estatístico.** Lourenço Marques, 1925-1975. Monthly (irreg.) Title varies: **Boletim mensal de estatística** (1932-38); **Boletim trimestral de estatística** (1938-1947); not published 1947-1960; **Boletim mensal estatístico** (1960-67); **Boletim mensal da Direcção Provincial dos Serviços de Estatística Geral** (1967-1975). For further details *see* Darch **3549**.

3560   Mozambique. Direcção dos Serviços de Estatística [etc.]. **Boletim mensal da Direcção Provincial dos Serviços de Estatística Geral.** Lourenço Marques, 1925-1975. Monthly (irreg.) Title varies: **Boletim econômico e estatístico** (1925-1932); **Boletim mensal de estatística** (1932-38); **Boletim trimestral de estatística** (1938-1947); not published 1947-1960; **Boletim mensal estatístico** (1960-67). For further details *see* Darch **3549**.

3561   Mozambique. Direcção Nacional de Estatística. **Moçambique: informação estatística 1980/81-[1988/89]**. Maputo, 1982-1989. Annual (10 issues).

3562   Mozambique. Instituto Nacional de Estatística. **Anuário estatístico,** 1995 - . Maputo, 1996- . From 2nd ed. 1996, text in Portuguese & English. Latest ed. in NWU is for 2000. - - Summary version **Moçambique en numéros.** Maputo, 1993- .

DIRECTORIES OF ORGANIZATIONS

3563   **Directório Moçambique, 2001.** Lisbon, Câmara de Comércio Portugal-Moçambique, 2002. (Statistics, addresses of commercial firms). - - Orig. Pub. ... **1998/1999**. Lisbon, 1998. 110pp.

3564   Doling, Tim. **Moçambique: arts directory**. London, Visiting arts, 1999. 63pp.

3565   **eBizguides Mozambique,** ed. Pascal Belda. Dublin, eBizguides, 2004. 252pp. (Largely a business directory)

See also **2824**

BIOGRAPHICAL SOURCES

3566   Pinto, Frederico da Silva. **Roteiro histórico-biográfico da cidade de Lourenço Marques**. [Lourenço Marques, Moçambique Editora], 1965. (Colectânea biográfica). 206pp.

3567   Quem é quem na Assembleia da República de Moçambique: V Legislatura. 2nd ed. Maputo, Assembleia da República, AWEPA, 2004. 217 pp. (Brief entries and portraits for the 250 members of the National Assembly). - - Orig. pub. Maputo, 1996. v, 256pp.

3568   Quem é quem no Governo de Moçambique, comp. Obed Horácio Chimene. 2nd ed. Maputo, Bureau de Informação Pública, 2000. 102pp. illus. (Noted in LC catalogue). - - Orig. pub. comp. Arlindo Lopes. Maputo, 1994. 54pp. Also pub. as **Who's who in government**. Maputo, 1997. 51pp.

3569   Quem é quem no Parlamento de A a Z. La legislature démocrática, 1994-1999, comp. Paul Leandro. Maputo, Leia Commercial, 1996. 128pp.

3570   Verdier, Isabelle. **Mozambique: 100 men in power**. Paris, Indigo, 1996. 194pp.

See also **2273, 2888**

ATLASES & GAZETTEERS

Atlases

3571   Atlas de Moçambique. Lourenço Marques, Empresa Moderna, 1960. viii, 44pp. 28 x 38cm. (Reprinted 1962, with minor corrections. Comp. by the Direcção dos Serviços de Agrimensura. 10 topographical maps at 1:1M on folding sheets; 21 thematic maps at 1:6M covering physical features, climate, demography, industry and communications. Includes gazetteer)

3572   Atlas demográfico e de saúde de Moçambique, comp. Juan Schoemaker et al. Maputo, Instituto Nacional de Estatística, 1999. 47pp. col. maps.

3573   Atlas geográfico. 2nd rev ed. [Maputo], Mozambique Ministério da Educação e Cultura, 1986. 2 vols., col. maps. - - Orig. pub. [Maputo], 1980-1983. 2 vols. (Prepared by Esselte, Stockholm, basically for school use. Col. maps. Vol. 1 covers Mozambique (pp. 8-29, 46) and Africa; vol. 2, the world)

3574   Atlas sócio-demográfico de Moçambique. Maputo, Instituto Nacional de Estatística, 2000. 49pp. (Includes information on administrative divisions, and demographic data since 1980. *See* M. Cahen et al. 'Pour un atlas social et culturel du Mozambique', *Lusotopie*, 2002(1), 305-362)

3575   **Guia do atlas geográfico de Moçambique**. 2nd ed. comp. Alberto da Baca. Maputo, Instituto Nacional de Desenvolvimento da Eduçao INDE)/Editoro Escolar, 1992- . Vol. 1, 1992. 82pp.

3576   Pililao, F. **Moçambique: evolução da toponímia e da divisão territorial, 1974-1987**. Maputo, Universidade Eduardo Mondlane, [1989?]. 128pp. (Atlas showing changes of names and boundaries of administrative divisions)

Gazetteers

3577   Cabral, António Carlos Pereira. **Dicionário de nomes geográficos de Moçambique: sua origem**. Lourenço Marques, [Empresa Moderna], 1975. 180pp. (Lists official forms with references from earlier variants, and explanations of origins and meanings)

3578   Gonçalves, Maria Leonor. **Índice toponímico de Moçambique**. 2nd ed. Lisbon, Junta de Investigações do Ultramar, Centro de Botânica, 1971. 128pp. - - Orig. pub. in typescript, Lisbon, 1962. 90pp.

3579   Mozambique. Direcção dos Serviços Geográficos e Cadastrais. **Primeira relação de nomes geográficos da província de Moçambique**. Lourenço Marques, Imprensa Nacional, 1962. 209pp. (Gives district locations for each name but no geographical co-ordinates)

3580   U.S. Board on Geographic Names. **Mozambique: official standard names approved by the USBGN**.. Washington, DC, 1969. (Gazetteer, 109). iv, 505pp. (Includes 32,500 names from maps at 1:250,000)

See also **1030, 3318, 3541**

EARTH SCIENCES

3581   Afonso, Rui S. et al. **A evolução geológica de Moçambique**. Lisbon, Instituto de Investigação Científica Tropical (IICT), 1998. 95pp. illus. maps.

3582   Afonso, Rui S. & Marques, J.M. **Recursos minerais da República de Moçambique: contribução para o seu conhecimento**. Lisbon, Instituto de

Investigação Científica Tropical (IICT), Centro de Documentação e Informação, 1993. 149pp. illus. maps.

3583   Atlas hydrologique du Canal de Mozambique (Océan indien), comp. B. Piton, et al. Paris, ORSTOM, 1981. (Travaux et documents, 132). 41pp. maps.

3584   Kuder, Manfred. Moçambique: eine geographische, soziale und wirtschaftliche Landeskunde. Darmstadt, Wissenschaftliche Buchgesellschaft, 1975. (Wissenschaftliche Länderkunden, 10). 347pp. illus. maps. (Physical and economic geography)

3585   Nunes, Artur de Figueiredo. Lexique stratigraphique international, 4, Afrique, fasc. 10a: Moçambique. Paris, CNRS, 1956.

3586   Pinna, Patrice et al. Notice explicative de la carte géologique 1:1,000,000 de la république populaire du Mozambique. Orléans, Bureau de recherches géologiques et minières (BRGM), [1986]. viii, 261pp.

BIOLOGICAL SCIENCES

Zoology

3587   Clancey, Philip Alexander. The birds of southern Mozambique. 2nd ed. Cape Town, African Bird Book Publishing, 1996. 386pp. 49 col. plates. - - Orig. pub. as 'A handlist of the birds of southern Mozambique', *Memorias de l'Instituto de Investigação Científica de Moçambique*, ser. A, 10, 1969/70-1971, 145-302; 11, 1971, 1-167 (Also issued as a single publication with an index. Review, *Ibis*, 116, 1974, 375)

3588   Dias, J.A. Travasso Santos. Abecedário dos mamíferos selvagens de Moçambique. Lourenço Marques, Empresa Moderna, SARL, 1975. 239pp. col. illus.

3589   Fischer, W. Guia de campo das espécies comerciais marinhas e de águas salobras de Moçambique. Rome, FAO, 1990. xxii, 424pp. + 42pp. plates. (Prepared in collaboration with Instituto de Investigação Pesqueira de Moçambique). - - Orig. pub. comp. Gabriella Bianchi. Rome, 1986. xv, 184pp

3590   Frade, Fernando. 'Catálogo das aves de Moçambique', *Anais da Junta das Missões Geográficas e de Investigações do Ultramar*, 6, 1951, 7-294.

3591   Parker, Vincent. **The atlas of the birds of Sul do Save, Southern Mozambique**. Cape Town, University of Cape Town, Avian Demography Unit/Johannesburg, Endangered Wildlife Trust, 1999. xxiii, 276pp. 23 col. photos. 525 maps. (Describes the geographical distribution, abundance and seasonality of all bird spp. observed in Mozambique south of the Save River during the period 1980 to 1998. Supplements **Atlas of Southern African birds**, 1997, *see* **2973,** which does not cover southern Mozambique. Review, *Ibis*, 142, 2000, 509)

3592   Pinhey, Elliot C.G. 'Checklist of the Odonata of Moçambique', *Occasional papers of the National Museums & Monuments, Rhodesia.* Ser. B, *Natural sciences*, 6(8) 1981, 557-632

3593   Silva, Joao Augusto. **Animais selvagens: contribuição para o estudo da fauna de Moçambique**. Lourenço Marques, Imprensa Naçional de Moçambique, 1956. 266pp. illus.

3594   Smithers, Reay H.N. & Lobao Tello, José L.P. **Checklist and atlas of the mammals of Mozambique**. Salisbury, National Museums & Monuments of Rhodesia, 1976. (Museum Memoir, 8). viii, 184pp. illus. maps. (Review, *Journal of mammalogy*, 58, 1977, 696-697)

See also **1052**

Botany

3595   Da Silva, Mário Calane et al. **Catálogo provisório das plantas superiores de Moçambique/A preliminary checklist of the vascular plants of Mozambique**. Pretoria, SABONET, 2004. (SABONET report, 30). 184pp. illus.

3596   **Flora de Moçambique**, ed. Abíio Fernandes et al. Lisbon, Junta de Investigações Cientificas do Ultramar, Centro de Botanica, 1969- . Issued in fascs. 120 issued by 1993 covering some 55% of the vascular flora. None pub. since 1993. (Detailed and generously illus. flora. Intended to be a companion to **Flora Zambesiaca**, *see* **1278,** and adapts many accounts from that work)

3597   Gomes e Sousa, Antonio de Figuerido. **Dendrologia de Moçambique**. [Rev.ed.]. Lourenço Marques, Imprensa Nacional, 1966-67. (Instituto de Investigacão Agronómica de Moçambique, Memórias, 1). 2 parts. 817pp. 229 plates. - - Orig. pub. Lourenço Marques, 1948-60. (Incomplete: Parts 1, 2, 4, 5 only). - - **Dendrology of Mozambique: some common commercial timbers**. Lourenço Marques, 1951. 248pp. (English trans. by A. de P. Bartolomeu of vol. 1 of 1st ed.)

3598   Jansen, Paulos C.M. & Mendes, Orlando. **Plantas medicinais: seu uso tradicional em Moçambique**. Maputo, Ministério da Saude, Gabinete de Estudos de Medicina Tradicional, 1983- . Vol. 3. 1990. 302pp. illus. maps; vol. 4, 1991. 299pp. illus. maps.

3599   Koning, Jan de. **Checklist of vernacular plant names in Mozambique**. Wageningen, Wageningen Agricultural University, 1993. 274pp. maps. (Text in English and Portuguese: indexes of vernacular/scientific names and vice versa)

3600   Schelpe, Edmund A.C. & Diniz, Maria Adélia. **Flora de Moçambique: Pteridophyta**. Lisbon, Junta de Investigações Cientificas do Ultramar, 1979. 257pp. illus. (Produced as a companion to **3596**)

See also **1064, 1278**

Author-title index

This includes entries for **authors and editors**, personal and corporate, and for all **titles** thought likely to be sought. Title entries are frequently abbreviated. No attempt has been made to index national statistical bulletins and annuals. Series which have a volume for virtually every country are not indexed individually, but have only an entry for the series. References are to item numbers, unless otherwise indicated as page references in the prelim matter (e.g. p. xlix). Filing is word by word.

Aulet, M.L. 2625
Aupiais, Damien 3420
Aurousseau, Marcel 622, 2923
Austin, Ronald J. 2718
*The Australian illustrated encyclopedia ...
Zulu & Boer wars* 2718
*The Austronesian languages of Indonesia &
Madagascar* 3282
Automobile Association of South Africa
632
Avenard, Jean Michel 2328
Aves das ilhas do Golfo da Guiné 2615
Las aves de Bioko, Guinea Ecuatorial 2658
Aves de la Isla de Fernando Po 2654
As aves do arquipélago de Cabo Verde 2551
Avice, Emmanuel 2282
Avondale to Zimbabwe 1427
Awad, Rushdi Said 985
Awards & honours in Swaziland 3217
Ayensu, Edward S. 1792
Azevedo, A.L. 3509, 3536
Azevedo, Mario 3536

Ba, Oumar 2457
Baba, J.M. 1901
Babalola, Adeboye 1912
Bacelar, Amélia 2585
Background notes on Africa 48
Background to Liberia 2047
Background to Sierra Leone 2014
Badbosa, L.A.G. 2560
Bader, Christian 914
Baguena Corella, Luis 2626, 2644
Bah-Lalya, Ibrahima 2350
Bailim Pissarra, J. 2611
Baird, Dan 2932
Bakarr, S.A. 1802
Baker, Anthony 2719
Baker, Brian Howard 3460
Baker, Janice E. 2350
Baker, Philip 392
Baker, S.J.K. 599
Balancie, Jean-Marc 237
Balandier, Georges 10
Balay, Robert p. xlix
Baldock, J.W. 3150
Ball, Joyce 318
Bambi, Jean-Guy 1621
Bamps, Paul 1683
Bancessi, Quintino 2588
Banda, Felix 1262
Banham, Martin 214
Banjo, A. O. 1746
Bank of Sierra Leone 2026

Bannerman, David Armitage 1773, 2548
Bannerman, Valentia 1747
Bannerman, W. Mary 2548
Banque centrale des états de l'Afrique de
l'ouest 2119, 2498
The Bantu languages 167
Banyaku Luape Epotu, Eugène 1622
Barau, A. 3435
Barbosa, Luis Augusto Grandvaux 3524
Barbour, Kenneth M. 986, 1983
Barlow, Clive 1822
Barnard, Phoebe 3105
Barnes, John W. 1239
Barnett, A.A. 2362
Barré, Nicolas 3435
Barrère, Jean 2127
Barrett, David B. 260
Barry, Jean-Paul 2426
Bartels, Charles 1862
Barth, Hans Karl 2396
Bartholomew, J.S. 1431
Barton, Frank 3
Bascomb, C.L. 3187
*Base metal & industrial mineral deposits of
Zimbabwe* 1431
*Bases documentales para la flora de Guinea
Ecuatorial* 2653
*Les bases floristiques des ... divisions
chorologiques de l'Afrique* 761
Basesreeksen Kenya, Tanzania, Uganda 1020
Basilio, Aurelio 2654, 2655
Bassot, Jean-Pierre 2397
Basutoland Red Cross Society 3167
Bates, D.A. 1771
Bates, M.F. 3191
Batiste, Angel D. 319
Batoma, Atoma 618
Les batraciens de Madagascar 3338
The bats of West Africa 1779
Battistini, René 3276, 3317, 3323, 3324
Battles & battlefields of the Anglo-Boer War
2719
Baudin, Bernard 1726
Baumann, Herman 80, 81
Baumer, Michel 2138
Baumhögger, Goswin 1008
Bawden, Michael G. 3186
Baxter, P.T.W. 1006
Bayer, Marcel 3061
Bayly, Christopher A. 121
Beadle, Leonard Clayton 695
Bearman, P.J. 255
Beaudet, M. 2174
Beauvilain, Alain 2257
Bebawi, Faiz Faris 1000

Le Borgne, Jean 3385
Le Bourdiec, Françoise 3317
Le Bourdiec, Paul 3317
Le Rouvreur, Albert 1524, 2446
Le Tallec, Jean 2490
Le Vine, Victor T. 2222
Lea, David 141
Leandro, Paul 3569
The least developed countries report 351
Lebacq, Lucien 1684
Lebedev, A.N. 673, 674
Lebeuf, A. M.-D. 1738
Lebon, D. 3455
Lebon, John Harold G. 988
LeBreton, Matthew 2274
Lebrun, Jean-Pierre 761, 768, 769, 772, 775, 846, 1532, 1685, 1694, 2209, 2404, 2429, 2455, 2496
Leburu-Sianga, Felicity 3141
Leclercq, Claude 871
Lecomte, G. 2323
Leedal, G.P. 1195
Léger, Christian 3428
Legère, Karsten 1067
Legrand, Henri 3465
Legum, Colin 18, 23, 274
Légumes africaines indigenes 788
Legumes of Africa: a check-list 776
Les légumineuses du Gabon 1596
The Leguminosae of Madagascar 3349
Lehohla, Pali 2792
Leistner, Erich 3066
Leistner, Otto Albrecht 2914, 3039, 3040
Lekyo, C.M. 1095
Lemarchand, Phillipe 131
Lembezat, Bertrand 1738, 2224
Lemoyne, Robert 3228
Lentz, Harris M. 555
Léonard, Charles 1636
Léonard, J. 2144
Leonard, Thomas M. 37
Lépidoptères de l'Afrique noire française 746
Lépidoptères … de l'Océan Indien 3265
Lépidoptères des îles Seychelles 3465
Lerebours Pigeonnière, Anne 591, 1553, 2197, 2393, 2643
Lereno, Álvaro 2543
Leroux, Marcel 675
Les langues communautaires africaines 170
Lesotho. Bureau of Statistics 3176, 3177
    Ministry of Information 3169, 3173
Lesotho arts directory 3179
Lesotho atlas of sustainable development 3183
Lesotho business directory 3170
Lesotho geology, geomorphology, soils 3188

Lesotho government yearbook & diary 3171
Lesotho NGO profile 3180
Lesotho official yearbook 3172
Lesotho population census atlas 3181
Letouzey, René 762, 2278
Letterkundige sakwoordeboek vir Afrikaans 2740
Lévêque, Christian 740, 1786, 2131
Levin, L.S. 1007, 1264
Levinson, David 93
Lewis, Adrian 1121
Lewis, I.M. 794, 919
Lexicon de stratigraphie Africa 685
Lexicon of geological terms for the Sudan 990
Lexikon afrikanische Kunst und Kultur 69
Lexikon der Afrikanistik 162
Lexique de la colonisation française 57
Lexique historique de la Guinée-Conakry 2352
Lexique stratigraphique international 682 & *see* section **Earth sciences** under countries in text
Liberato, Maria Cândida 2619
Liberia. Bureau of Statistics 2065, 2066
Liberia : basic data 2054
Liberia genealogical research 2068
Liberia in maps 2069
Liberian high forest trees 2079
Liberian trade directory 2060
The Liberian yearbook 2061
Library of Congress 9, 30, 576
    Census Library Project 314, 315
    Federal Research division. *Area handbooks/Country studies series, see* section **Handbooks** under countries in text
    Country profiles series: Eritrea 850, *Ethiopia* 862, *Kenya* 1079, *Mali* 2373, *Nigeria* 1900, *Sudan* 955
Lienau, Cay 1314
Lieux et peuples d'Afrique 638
Limb, Peter p. 1
The limnology, climatology etc. of the E. African lakes 1028
Lind, Edna M. 1071, 1252
Lindblad, J. Thomas 336
Lindfors, Berndth 197
Liniger-Goumaz, Max 2629-2631, 2640, 2642
Lionnet, Guy 3456
Lippens, Léon 1679
Lippens, Philippe 2182
Lipschutz, Mark R. 547
Lipsky, George A. 861, 872

Subject index

Since the great majority of the works listed are either broad-ranging in their subject coverage by their very nature (encyclopaedias, handbooks, yearbooks) or are already largely defined by the category in which they are placed under each country (statistical sources, directories of organizations, biographical sources, atlases and gazetteers) an attempt to provide detailed subject entries would be both impossible and unhelpful. Equally there is the danger that making a specific entry for the subject of a specific title may suggest, quite wrongly, that this is the only item listed that is useful for that subject. Nevertheless, an attempt is made in this index to complement the subject arrangement of the main sequence. It should be noted that there are **no** entries for broad and pervasive topics such as Economics, History, Politics, since several hundred titles could be cited for each of these; but there are entries for topics such as Art, Ethnography, Language, Literature and Place names. Of the earth sciences, there are **no** entries for the pervasive Geography, Geology, (but entries for e.g. Agriculture, Climate, Soils); for the Biological sciences **no** entries for the pervasive Amphibia, Birds, Fishes, Mammals, Reptiles, Invertebrates (but entries for individual families and genera such as Rodents, Snakes, Butterflies). Entries have also been made in CAPITALS for each broad topographic region or country used as a main heading in the text, and for any alternative names of countries that have been used in the works actually cited.